PEOPLE AND ORGANISATIONS

Employee Development

ROSEMARY HARRISON

INSTITUTE OF PERSONNEL AND DEVELOPMENT

This book is for my father
John Park
Born 30 December 1907
Died 11 April 1995

© Rosemary Harrison 1997

First published in 1997

Reprinted 1998

Design by Curve

Typeset by Fakenham Photosetting Ltd, Fakenham, Norfolk

Printed in Great Britain by
The Cromwell Press, Wiltshire

British Library Cataloguing in Publication Data
A catalogue record of this book is available from the British
Library

ISBN 0-85292-657-X

The views expressed in this book are the author's own and
may not necessarily reflect those of the IPD.

INSTITUTE OF PERSONNEL
AND DEVELOPMENT

IPD House, Camp Road, London SW19 4UX
Tel: 0181 971 9000   Fax: 0181 263 3333
Registered office as above. Registered Charity No. 1038333
A company limited by guarantee. Registered in England No. 2931892

Employee Development

Rosemary Harrison, Durham University Business School (DUBS), is Chief Examiner: Employee Development, Institute of Personnel and Development, a Fellow of the IPD, and a leading academic and writer in the field. Before joining DUBS in 1989 she lectured in personnel management and organisational behaviour at the then Newcastle Polytechnic, where she was for many years course leader of the Institute of Personnel Management's professional qualification programme. She is currently working on a long-term research programme with a group of colleagues at the Universities of Leiden and Durham, focused on 'The corporate curriculum as a vehicle for knowledge productiv··· ··· ··· ··· ··· ··· ᵒf organisations' strategic capability'.

ℙ

Other titles in the series:

Core Personnel and Development
Mick Marchington and Adrian Wilkinson

Employee Relations
John Gennard and Graham Judge

Employee Resourcing
Stephen Taylor

Employee Reward
Michael Armstrong

Personnel Practice
Malcolm Martin and Tricia Jackson

The Institute of Personnel and Development is the leading publisher of books and reports for personnel and training professionals and students and for all those concerned with the effective management and development of people at work. For full details of all our titles please telephone the Publishing Department at IPD House on 0181 263 3387.

Contents

EDITORS' FOREWORD   VII

ACKNOWLEDGEMENTS   X

INTRODUCTION   XII

PART 1 HUMAN RESOURCE DEVELOPMENT AND THE
BUSINESS   1

1 The nebulous harmonies of human resource development   1
2 The strategic framework for human resource development   18
3 Human resource development goals, strategy and plans   33
4 Training and development in the smaller organisation   47

PART 2 THE WIDER CONTEXT   67

5 National training policy: a review of the system   67
6 National education policy: the primary, secondary and
   tertiary systems   87
7 International comparisons   102

PART 3 MANAGING THE HRD FUNCTION   129

8 The politics of human resource development   129
9 Training and development roles, standards and
   responsibilities   145
10 Organising, managing and developing capable
   practitioners   166
11 Managing finance and marketing the function   187
12 Establishing outcomes and assessing the investment   201

PART 4 THE PERFORMANCE MANAGEMENT AND
DEVELOPMENT SYSTEM   223

13 Learning needs of individuals   223
14 Learning needs in the job   252
15 Purpose, objectives and strategy for learning events   270

16 Design, delivery and evaluation of learning events   288
17 Learning needs related to special groups and
    contingencies   312

PART 5   THE LANDSCAPE OF CORPORATE
             LEARNING AND KNOWLEDGE
             PRODUCTIVITY   329
18 Developing careers for individual and organisational
    growth   329
19 Enhancing managerial and strategic capability   354
20 Managing the knowledge-productive organisation:
    themes of survival and advancement   383

APPENDICES   415

REFERENCES   435

INDEX   459

Editors' foreword

People hold the key to more productive and efficient organisations. The way in which people are managed and developed at work has major effects upon quality, customer service, organisational flexibility and costs. Personnel and development practitioners can play a major role in creating the framework for this to happen, but ultimately they are dependent upon line managers and other employees for its delivery. It is important that personnel and development specialists gain the commitment of others and pursue professional and ethical practices that will bring about competitive success. There is also a need to evaluate the contribution that personnel and development approaches and processes make for organisational success, and to consider ways of making these more effective. Such an approach is relevant for all types of practitioner – personnel and development generalists and specialists, line managers, consultants and academics.

This is one of a series of books under the title *People and Organisations*. The series provides essential guidance and points of reference for all those involved with people in organisations. It aims to provide the main body of knowledge and pointers to the required level of skills for personnel and development practitioners operating at a professional level in all types and sizes of organisation.

The series has been specially written to satisfy the professional standards defined by the Institute of Personnel and Development (IPD) in the United Kingdom and the Republic of Ireland. It includes a volume designed for those seeking the Certificate in Personnel Practice (CPP), which often provides an access route into the professional scheme. The series also responds to a special need in the United Kingdom for texts structured to cover the knowledge aspects of new and revised National and Scottish Vocational Qualifications (N/SVQs) in personnel and training development.

Three 'fields' of standards have to be satisfied in order to gain graduate membership of the IPD: (i) core management (ii) core personnel and development and (iii) any four from a range of more than 20 generalist and specialist electives. The three fields can be tackled in any order, or indeed all at the same time. A range of learning routes is available: full or part time educational course, flexible learning methods or direct experience. The standards may be assessed by educational and competence-based methods. The books in the series are suitable for supporting all methods of learning.

The series starts by addressing *core personnel and development* and four generalist electives: employee reward, employee resourcing, employee relations and employee development. Together, these cover the personnel and development knowledge requirements for graduateship of the IPD. These also cover the knowledge aspects of training and development and personnel N/SVQs at Level 4.

Core Personnel and Development by chief examiner Professor Mick Marchington and his colleague Adrian Wilkinson addresses the essential knowledge and understanding required of all personnel and development professionals, whether generalists or specialists. Practitioners need to be aware of the wide range of circumstances in which personnel and development processes take place and consequently the degree to which particular approaches and practices may be appropriate in specific circumstances. In addressing these matters the book covers the core personnel and development standards of the IPD, as well as providing an essential grounding for human resource management options within business and management studies degrees. The authors are both extremely well-known researchers in the field, working at one of the UK's leading management schools.

Employee Reward by chief examiner Michael Armstrong has been written specially to provide extensive subject coverage for practitioners required by both the IPD's new generalist standards for employee reward and the personnel N/SVQ Level 4 unit covering employee reward. It is the first book on employee reward to be produced specifically for the purposes of aiding practitioners to gain accredited UK qualifications.

Employee Relations, by chief examiner Professor John Gennard and associate examiner Graham Judge, explores the link between the corporate environment and the interests of buyers and sellers of labour. It also demonstrates how employers (whether or not they recognise unions) can handle the core issues of bargaining, group problem-solving, redundancy, participation, discipline and grievances, and examines how to evaluate the latest management trends.

Employee Development, by chief examiner Rosemary Harrison, is a major new text which extends the scope of her immensely popular earlier book of the same name to establish the role of human resource development (HRD) and its direction into the next century. After reviewing the historical roots of HRD, she considers its links with business imperatives, its national and international context, the management of the HRD function, and ways of aligning HRD with the organisation's performance management system. Finally, she provides a framework that sets HRD in the context of organisational learning, the key capabilities of an enterprise and the generation of the new knowledge it needs.

Employee Resourcing by Stephen Taylor has also been designed specifically to address the IPD and N/SVQ standards in the area. The author draws upon his wide academic and personnel background to produce a book that examines practical issues but takes into account material from an extensive literature review. He presents readers with a series of options, encouraging them to consider those that are most appropriate in the specific circumstances of their own workplace. This results in a book that is both very readable and extremely comprehensive in its coverage.

Although each of these books is carefully tailored to the IPD and N/SVQ standards, Malcolm Martin and Tricia Jackson's *Personnel Practice* is focused on the needs of those studying for the Certificate in Personnel Practice. This also gives a thorough grounding in the basics of personnel activities. The authors are experienced practitioners and lead tutors for one of the UK's main providers of IPD flexible learning programmes.

In drawing upon a team of distinguished and experienced writers and practitioners, the *People and Organisations* series aims to provide a range of up-to-date, practical texts indispensable to those pursuing IPD and N/SVQ qualifications in personnel and development. The books will also prove valuable to those who are taking other human resource management and employment relations courses, or who are simply seeking greater understanding in their work.

Mick Marchington   *Mike Oram*

Acknowledgements

I am grateful to all the individuals and organisations who allowed me to write about them or whose reported examples of practice have provided source material for activities and case studies in the text. In particular I would like to thank Alan Rutter, University of Northumbria Business School, who originally collaborated with me in producing for earlier texts the material appearing in Chapter 11 with attribution; and locally based organisations Cummins Engine Ltd, Darlington, Hydro Polymers, Aycliffe and Newlands School, Gosforth whose personnel, by giving generously of their time in supplying information and views, enabled me to produce the case-studies in Chapters 3, 12, 13 and 20.

It is essential to stress that all real-life material reported in the book relates only to situations current at the dates given in the text, and that comments on all such information are either my own or those of the individual authors. Unless otherwise indicated they must never be taken to represent official views of the organisations concerned. All organisations move on, the actors within them naturally have different perceptions and memories of events, and even case-studies that are up to date at the time of writing may be of historical interest only by the time the book gets into print. In the field of HRD all of this is particularly true. History, however, has its own value – which is the theme of Chapter 1.

Research over the past three years has enabled me to produce the new frameworks and concepts about HRD and the strategies of the organisation that appear in this book. I acknowledge with gratitude the support of the Foundation for Corporate Education in the Netherlands who granted funding for much of that research; of a consortium of 130 organisations in the North-East of England who, by sending delegates to a conference and regular HRD seminars at Durham University Business School between 1993 and 1995, also generated significant research funding; and of the University of Durham and my director and colleagues at the Business School for enabling me to take almost a year of sabbatical leave to undertake the initial stages. Nicki Fonda of the Prospect Centre, London, first suggested to me the idea of linking HRD with the strategic capability of the firm, and our joint work in the field fuelled my research interest. The interlinked concepts of the landscape of corporate learning and of knowledge productivity were initially suggested to me by Joseph Kessels, Professor in

Corporate Education, Social and Behavioural Sciences at the University of Leiden, to whom I owe the greatest debt in the inspiration and development of my own research and thinking.

I wish, finally to thank my editor, Anne Cordwent, for her helpfulness and good humour, and also my family, without whose support nothing would have been possible.

Introduction

Although many themes, case-studies and self-checks from my last (1992) IPM text reappear in this one, the book itself is not a reworking or further edition of those texts. It is, and has had to be, quite new.

Over the past five years the world of human resource development (HRD) has moved on. The research and literature is now wider-ranging, more strategically focused, better-integrated with parallel fields of human resource management (HRM), business strategy and organisational learning. Examination of practice in the field shows an inevitably more nebulous situation. None the less, progress at national level is marked, the push for a more business-driven thrust to HRD at organisational level is clear, and the genuine intent of a number of employers to provide employability security in the face of diminishing ability to offer employment security should not be disregarded.

Problems certainly remain in trying to achieve progress in HRD when employee resource strategy, and even business strategy itself, often remain incoherent. The push to decentralise, delayer and downsize sits uneasily with commitments to 'invest in our people' and 'empower the workforce'. The downside of the 'flexible firm' – cheap, vulnerable and easily manipulated workers – can put a question mark against the meaningfulness of HRD in the business. Finally, as in the late 1980s in the UK so now, accusations continue to be made about the complacency and lack of expertise of many who practise and manage training and development in organisations. Such views should not be taken lightly. Too often they may be true. Yet often, too, they are misplaced. One of the main aims of the first chapter as well as of Part 2 of this book is to expose some of the more disheartening myths in order to see more clearly the real nature of the challenges to HRD, and how they are being tackled.

The major change for HRD has been that of the stage it now occupies. In the increasing exposure of organisations, however small and in whatever sector, to national, international and even global influences and pressures, HRD can no longer afford to be only about 'training and development' – important though the task of training must remain in ensuring and updating competency and flexibility at every level of the organisation. HRD needs to be a primary area of policy-making and strategy. It has the potential to be a key business process and is essential to secure the purposive development of the human and organisational capacity whereby goals and strategy themselves can be changed and expand through time.

TERMINOLOGY IN THE BOOK

Definitions of key terms related to HRD are given at relevant points in the text. However, it may be worth noting here that the word 'training' is used throughout as a shorthand for planned instructional activities, and sometimes (the context will make clear when) for wider developmental activities and processes. 'Development' relates to all learning experiences whereby growth occurs; when used in conjunction with 'training' it is in order to distinguish wider learning experiences from narrowly focused, planned, job-related events. The phrase 'learning event' applies to any planned learning experience whereby people's behaviour and performance is to be developed and/or changed.

SCOPE AND FORMAT OF THE BOOK

The historical roots of HRD are as important to understand as its present-day operations, because they explain its potential and its inherent tensions. I have endeavoured to explore both – in relation to HRD's opportunities, barriers and strategic role (Part 1); in its wider context of international and national vision and policies (Part 2); by reference to its professional managerial task (Part 3); in its contribution related to the performance management system of the organisation and the developmental drive needed for the future of the business (Part 4); and in its place in what Joseph Kessels (1996: 172) has memorably described as 'the rich landscape (of corporate learning) where personnel and teams find their way and construct knowledge'.

Although the book is a core text for IPD students and therefore covers all the major areas of the IPD's Professional Standards in Employee Development, it has also been written with the needs of other students and practitioners in mind, and in the hope of stimulating debate among academics to whom its themes represent important areas of teaching and research. To clarify scope and stimulate interest, each chapter starts with an identification of its learning objectives, and concludes with a summary of the main ground covered. In order to help readers move through the learning cycle of observation and reflection, analysis, creativity, decision-making/problem-solving, and evaluation (Chapter 13), its chapters also contain self-checks, case-studies, practical guidelines and frameworks.

KEY FRAMEWORKS

Certain frameworks are of particular importance in relation to the choice and implementation of HRD strategy in the organisation. They are identified here:

- a framework for matching business needs with HR planning and the organisation's learning and development strategies (Chapter 3)

- a typology of training and development roles (Chapter 9)

- a six-point guide to the strategic management of training and development resources (Chapter 11)

- a framework to integrate the performance management and employee development systems of the organisation (Chapter 13)

- an eight-stage approach to the inception, design and delivery of learning events (Chapter 13)
- a framework to integrate human resource planning, the organisation's overall employee development programme and its career management system (Chapter 18)
- a framework linking strategic HRD with the key capabilities of the business (Chapter 20)
- a matrix for building HRD into the business (Chapter 20).

MAJOR THEMES

A number of themes fundamental to HRD in its organisational context underpin the book:

The scope of human resource development

Throughout the book there is a tendency to use the term 'human resource development' (HRD) rather than the term 'employee development'. The latter is necessary in the book's title in order to conform with the IPD's official terminology. The former has been generally preferred within the text in order to make a statement: it is that at both theoretical and practical levels the development of people must take into account the needs not only of those employed by the organisation but of many of those 'individuals or groups who have some relationship with an organisation but are not in an employer–employee relationship' (Walton, 1996). These external stakeholders are people and institutions who have a direct interest in the business and who influence as well as benefit from its successful operations – self-employed subcontractors, suppliers, distributors and clients. Responding to their learning needs is crucial in a world where no organisation now can be an island, and where there must be an increasing reliance on trust, collaboration and recognition of mutuality of interest. Inter-organisational learning networks, too, enable the development of strategically valuable knowledge and new ways of thinking and understanding that help to counterbalance an organisation's natural tendency – in a preoccupation with current business goals – to become myopic, thus endangering its longer-term growth.

The HRD process

Throughout the book the importance of process is stressed. It is the way in which the tasks of HRD are tackled as much as – and indeed often more than – the tasks themselves that will impede or ensure its success. It is the ability to work with others in order to achieve shared aims that is essential if HRD professionals are to achieve a strong influence in the business. It is the process of developing links across organisational boundaries that will encourage the flow of new information to and from the organisation and stimulate the development of new knowledge. The literature of strategic management is replete with examples of the importance of process (Pettigrew, 1982). The literature and practice of HRD should be no different.

The need for consistency, coherency and integration

One of the accusations most frequently levelled against HRD is to do with the perceived *ad hoc* and fragmented pattern of much of its implementation in the workplace. Often training, education and other developmental interventions appear to be little more than sporadic and unsustained reactions to crises, produced without due thought to their feasibility or to alignment with the organisation's wider policies and systems. There may be no serious attempt to evaluate their outcomes or to assess their future value to the business.

Consistency – 'fit' – and coherency – 'making sense' - must both be achieved with those systems, policies and goals that form the organisational context for HRD. This was one of the main concerns of the IPD in drawing up its professional qualifications standards in employee development.

The need for a good fit with the wider employee resource system is of first importance, since without supportive employee resource policies and systems for recruitment, reward, retention and, where necessary, disengagement of human resources HRD cannot fulfil its role. Coherency in relation to business strategy is also essential, although here the proactive role that can be played by HRD professionals as the beneficial outcomes of effective development of key human capability are realised must not be forgotten. It is also important to achieve internal consistency in the planning and delivery of learning events to ensure that their outcomes meet the organisational needs they were intended to tackle. However, as Chapter 16 explains, internal consistency will be of little account unless 'external consistency' is achieved also. That concept, formulated by Kessels (1993) as a result of his doctoral research, refers to the need to ensure increasingly shared expectations and orientations of the key parties involved in a learning event, so that a close fit is achieved between the event itself and the external environment in which its learning must take root.

Finally, a positive relationship between HRD policy and its implementation on the one hand and the underlying vision of the business and top management's values about people in the organisation is essential. Too often the gap between the espoused and the real is wide – a theme raised towards the end of the first chapter and recurring thereafter.

HRD as a strategic and business-led process in the organisation
Strategic HRD is development that operates within an overall strategic framework. *Business-led HRD* is development that is responsive to the business needs of an organisation. The need for HRD to be both strategic and business led is now central to its survival and success and drives much of the direction of the book.

HRD and strategic capability
I define strategic capability as:

a capability that is based on a profound understanding of the competitive environment, the resource base and potential of the organisation, and the values that engender commitment from stakeholders to corporate goals. It provides the strategic vision, the rich and sustained knowledge development, the integrity of common purpose and the durable, coherent direction and scope to the activities of the firm that are needed to secure long-term survival and advancement.

The significance to an organisation of strategic capability, and ways in which it can be enhanced by HRD, is emphasised at key points in the book and is an explicit focus of Chapters 1, 2, 19 and 20. At present, little attention seems to be given to the vital link that could and should exist between what an organisation does to train and develop its people, the learning and knowledge that flow from that activity, and the quality and relevance of its vision, goals, strategic assets and strategy-making process. I have tried to show the importance of this potential link and the practical ways in which it can be developed.

The relationship between HRD, organisational learning, knowledge productivity, and the survival and advancement of an enterprise

The terms 'survival' and 'advancement' in relation to the success of the business often appear in the book, although they are not formally defined until Chapter 20 when the issues they raise become the primary focus of attention. For ease of reference, those definitions are also given here:

- By an organisation that 'survives' I mean the kind of organisation that remains in business essentially by 'sticking to its knitting'. By continuous improvement and high quality of human resources, as well as by astute leadership and direction, it may do so increasingly well through time – as did IBM during its first 50 years.

- By an organisation that 'advances' I mean one that from time to time radically innovates, completely changes direction – in other words, can achieve discontinuous change – in order to remain profitable and in the forefront of advance.

Influenced especially by Kessels' work on knowledge productivity and the corporate curriculum (1996) and by outcomes from my own current research programme, I suggest in Chapter 20 a framework setting HRD in the context of organisational learning, the key capabilities of an organisation, and the generation of collective knowledge whereby an enterprise can survive and advance. It is a complex relationship, imperfectly understood and with much research yet to be undertaken. It takes the reader far beyond the literature of employee resourcing and development or any professional syllabus for HR practitioners – so IPD students may at this point breathe sighs of relief! However, it is a relationship that is so crucial and with – I believe – such implications for the future direction of HRD, both as an academic subject area and as part of the managerial and professional field, that it must lie at the heart of any textbook such as this.

The scholarly base of HRD

In the UK there is a need for a more rigorous scholarly base to HRD if its practice is to be reinvigorated and focused on what is best not only in the field but also in academic thinking and research. That base, as I seek to explain in Chapter 1, was eroded long ago in the UK but is now being renewed. The connection between HRD's historical roots and its present condition needs to be more widely understood and reviewed by today's students and professionals.

HRD is now becoming academically respectable in a significant number of UK educational institutions rather than, as has long been the case, only in a few. More partnerships are now being forged between academics and practitioners in the inter-related fields of organisational behaviour, human resource management and development, organisational learning and business strategy. Such signs offer hope that the knowledge-base of HRD is being regenerated in coherent and durable ways. That is essential if practitioners are to be stimulated and helped to improve the implementation of HRD strategy in the workplace, and to innovate in response to unfamiliar challenges. However, it will happen only if the partnerships proliferate, and if academic minds become sufficiently engaged in developing more master's degrees in HRD, in encouraging more doctoral students to research HRD issues, and in producing more scholarly conferences, papers and texts on HRD-related themes. Never has there been more need for academics and practitioners to share and develop mutually important new knowledge to add meaning and value to the field of HRD, thus benefiting those working in non-profit making as well as those in for-profit organisations.

The need for vision

It is a truism that vision must drive the strategies of any organisation. If 'mission' has become a politically incorrect term in the volatile lexicon of management, 'vision' has not. Much is therefore said throughout the book about the inter-relationship between vision, strategy and action in the workplace.

However, this final point goes further. It concerns the need of each HRD professional to hold a personal view about the development of people in the organisational context, and to find in the pursuit of HRD, with all its frustrations and disappointments, something exciting and worthwhile. Private passion should only with wisdom be brought to bear on rational thought and action, yet without it there is a danger that self-confidence and motivation will flag in a terrain that may sometimes come to seem barren. The book has been written with a determination to avoid the messianic tone, yet hopefully it will in more covert ways engage emotions as well as intellect. If it can stimulate personal vision and also be an aid to practice, then it will have fulfilled its best intent.

Part 1

HUMAN RESOURCE DEVELOPMENT AND THE BUSINESS

1 The nebulous harmonies of human resource development

LEARNING OBJECTIVES

After reading this chapter you will:

- be aware of the general historical roots of human resource development (HRD), both in the USA and the UK

- appreciate the role of HRD in the workplace, especially in the leaner organisations

- have acquired an initial insight into the challenges involved in an approach to HRD that seeks to respond both to organisational and to individual needs.

INTRODUCTION

This first chapter contains no case-studies, no reviews, no check-lists. Its simple purpose is to place the development of people in organisations in a historical context, and to explore some of the challenges inherent in attempts to make that development serve both organisational and individual interests. In this chapter and for most of the book thereafter I shall use the term 'human resource development' (HRD) rather than 'employee development' (ED), since it draws attention to the need for an organisation's developmental scope to encompass increasing numbers who work for the organisation although they are not its direct employees. (More will be said in explanation at the start of Chapter 2.) The scope of the chapter inevitably involves use of a wide variety of reference materials, and in consequence the references listed throughout are numerous. Be reassured – this will not be the norm!

A sense of history is vital to us all in seeking to understand our human condition. The same is true for the history of HRD's present role in organisations, and is an aid to our reflection on the kind of future role it might fulfil. A historical perspective is a path to wisdom, enabling us to develop an informed view and to argue persuasively about the kind of contribution the development of people should make to the good of society, of the organisation and of the individual.

Let us start with a quotation, written at the end of the First World War:

> The controlling purposes of education have not been sufficiently particularized. We have aimed at a vague culture, an ill-defined discipline, a nebulous harmonious development of the individual, an indefinite moral character-building, an unparticularized social efficiency, or, often enough, nothing more than escape from a life of work.
>
> (Bobbitt, 1918: 14)

The quotation was pointed out to me by Professor Joseph Kessels (1993), a leading academic and consultant in the field of corporate education in The Netherlands. For him, it conjured up thoughts of the failure of organisations to take full advantage of the opportunities learning can offer, and of the need for a long-term, coherent and balanced approach to the development of people in the workplace. For me, it was the phrases 'nebulous harmonious development' and 'escape from a life of work' that aroused attention. The seventeenth-century alchemist Thomas Vaughan spoke of how 'The liberated soul ascends, looking at the sunset towards the west wind, and hearing secret harmonies'. But Bobbitt referred to 'nebulous' harmonies, and certainly the two concepts do seem far apart: the organisation tying human effort to the bottom line, current or envisaged; the individual seeking transformation through the realisation of human potential.

'Harmony' seems to be the crucial word here. Since harmony can arise only through the resolution of tensions, it should not surprise us that that the history of HRD is one of continuing frustration in finding a powerful organisational role and in striking a satisfactory balance between the good of the organisation and that of the individual. In the 1990s there are at last claims that the tensions have been resolved as HRD becomes a key enabler of the 'learning organisation'. Yet that phrase remains both ambiguous and controversial. It can be argued that there are still few signs of the achievement of harmonious organisational and individual development in the workplace.

HRD: A HISTORY OF NEBULOUS HARMONIES

A significant number of organisations claim commitment to harmonious HRD: Jaguar, Rover, Ford, Nissan, 3 Ms, to name only a few. In one sense, this commitment is not new. In the 1960s Volvo's Kalmar Plant was established in Sweden using a startlingly innovative approach to the design of factories, production systems and jobs. Management's hope was that by offering people more challenge, more responsibility and a more attractive form of social organisation in the workplace employees would become self-fulfilled, fully developed, motivated at work and committed to the business. However, even that famous experiment has attracted much controversy as repeated attempts have been made to establish its true outcomes (see especially Adler and Cole, 1993).

The early twentieth century to the 1970s: classical management, human relations and organisational psychology

Although the Kalmar plant was the result of ideas produced pragmatically by a group of management and workers, as a concept it fitted well with the philosophy of HRD prevailing in the USA at the time. The philosophy was, however, grounded in a somewhat ambiguous rationale, and this is where history comes into the matter. In the 1950s and 1960s behavioural scientists like Macgregor (1960), Argyris (1957), Likert (1961) and Herzberg (1968) were imbued with a passionate determination to transform the experience of life at work in ways that would also bring benefits for the bottom line of the business. They were inspired by a belief that improving workers' social environment and their instrinsic motivation – motivation to do with the inner life of the individual – would bring with it high levels of morale and commitment and thereby lead to improved productivity. This would resolve what Gilley and Eggland (1989: 18–19) have called 'the tension between workers and management ... caused by the organisational structure and interpersonal relationships'. During the following two decades HRD emerged as a professional field in its own right.

The true roots of their work, however, go deeper, and locating them reveals an important source of HRD's ambiguity. They are not to be found in those great social developments of the nineteenth and early twentieth centuries that in the UK led logically to a focus on welfare work in organisations. They lie rather in the research and consultancy work of social scientists and managers like Mayo (1933) and Taylor (1947) in the USA. Inspired by the imperative of managerial efficiency, Taylor's 'scientific management' approach and Mayo's 'human relations' perspective were not as far apart as some commentators have subsequently made them appear. As Butler (1986) pointed out, there is only a negligible difference between Taylor's model of 'economic' and Mayo's model of 'social' man. The one is based on a 'hard' approach, the other on a 'soft', but this does not make Mayo's attitudes any the less unitary or paternalistic than those of Taylor. 'They were simply more kindly in their expression' (Butler, 1986: 119).

The work of Elton Mayo and his colleagues at Harvard expanded the territory of human relations research that was being explored in the UK at that time by the Tavistock Institute of Human Relations (see, for example, Trist and Bamforth, 1951). However, the Americans' interest was unequivocally managerial: how to produce forms of industrial organisation that would result in a harmonious, non-conflictual workplace where the goals of management and worker were shared. It was with the same interest in mind that later organisational psychologists in the USA developed the concept of the self-actualising worker, whose intellectual as well as physical and social well-being had to be improved if there was to be a radical impact on productivity levels. Such work soon became widely known in the UK, where it had a powerful influence on practitioners' views about the management and development of people at work. That influence continues to this day, but many fail to realise the ambiguities inherent in a concept of HRD that is rooted in an uneasy mix of scientific management and a genuine idealism about the 'perfectability-of-man' in the workplace (Butler, 1986: 119).

The 1980s: the impact of international competition

In the 1980s in the UK there was another trigger to HRD as a force in the business: the rapid growth of international competition that resulted in every aspect of employee performance coming under management's intense scrutiny. This trigger contributed to the growing popularity of the concept of human resource management (HRM) in the UK – a concept that emphasised employers' need to take a strategic approach to the management of their workforces and to maximise the asset value of employees.

The historical development of HRD at this point could be said to have crystallised around a strong organisational focus. HRD offered the possibility of a coherent spectrum of activities and processes which, when interacting with the full range of employee resource policies in an organisation and when aligned with business goals, could significantly enhance competitive capability.

Yet ambiguities remained. These derived mainly from the different ways in which HRM was – and continues to be – perceived by key players. One perception is that HRM focuses on making best use of employees and placing human resource planning at the heart of business planning (see Marchington and Wilkinson, 1996: Part 3). In this relatively soft vision of HRM the contribution of the individual to the business can be maximised by introducing quality circles, lean production and just-in-time manufacturing processes, single status, individually-focused financial reward systems, teamworking and customer care training. Taylor (1994a: 11) noted that the aim here is to develop commitment and loyalty in the workplace in order to achieve world-class excellence in the competitive environment, and that, as the Trades Union Congress (TUC) in Blackpool emphasised in their 1994 policy document, such a stance emphasises social partnership and involves long-term investment in training.

However, there is a harder approach to HRM, which the TUC labelled in 1994 as a piecemeal attempt to select items from the HRM menu in the hope that this would improve company performance. To the TUC such a controlling approach embodied an exploitative, individualised and manipulative employer–employee relationship.

The debate over the true nature of HRM has been extensive (Harrison, 1993a: Chapters 2 and 3). It has implications for every area of employee resource policy (Marchington and Wilkinson, 1996: 88–9), notably for processes to do with the development of people. We shall return to this point later in the chapter.

The 1990s: strategic management and the core capabilities of the firm

By the late 1980s both in the literature and in the field there was increasing interest in the unique capabilities of an organisation as sources of its competitive advantage, critical in explaining variations in its performance in its environment. This managerial view of the firm was part of a growing preoccupation with the strategic management process (Teece, Pisano and Shuen, 1994). It has led to a particular concern throughout the 1990s to clarify the role of HRM in the development of human capability. Part of that concern has been a further assessment of HRD's strategic role.

In 1991 the American writers Noel, James and Dennehy saw HRD positioned to become 'a significant player in the strategic change process'. How? 'HRD professionals must work with top management, focusing on the organization's strategic initiatives and seeking ways to leverage the development of employees to achieve these objectives, in creative and impactful approaches' (Noel, James and Dennehy, 1991: 19). The professional must identify the key strategic initiatives to which the organisation is committed and build developmental programmes around these. Delayering and downsizing, for example, may achieve a leaner organisation, but it will not be a more productive one unless managers have been trained and developed to understand the new organisational structure in which they will have to work, unless they can become effective managers of teams rather than of individuals, and unless they can 'delegate, eliminate unnecessary work and procedures, and create an environment of risk taking' (Noel *et al*, 1991: 17).

Throughout this period there have been exhortations from academics and consultants to link HRD to business strategy (Coopers and Lybrand Associates, 1985; Handy, 1987; Hendry and Pettigrew, 1986; Ulrich, 1987; Fonda, 1989; Storey and Sisson, 1990; Ready, Vicere and White, 1994). Storey (1992: 114) described how Lucas Aerospace focused HRD in this way by ensuring:

- its link with total strategy, comprising marketing, product engineering, manufacturing systems engineering and business systems
- top management commitment to it
- its role in developing and executing the competitive achievement plans that every business unit was required to have
- the installation of business and engineering systems in the strategic business units
- the underpinning of business task forces through training on an essentially project-requirement basis.

Yet despite this focus on strategic management and development of people as a key to competitive success, UK empirical data have consistently failed to provide evidence of significant alignment of HRD with business strategy or any other policy areas (Keep, 1989: 117–19; Storey, 1992: 16; Rainbird, 1994: 87; Keep and Mayhew, 1994; Skinner and Mabey, 1995). Meanwhile in the USA it has been asserted that 'in most organizations, training needs and programs have little to do with business objectives and initiatives. Moreover, despite widespread enthusiasm, little research into training's role in supporting strategic planning is available' (Catalanello and Redding, 1989: 51). The same authors reiterated the need for the training function to identify and implement training programs that explicitly support strategic plans, thereby establishing a competitive advantage rooted in employee competence. They saw two further strategic roles for the function:

- to provide training that equips important managers to plan strategically, to think strategically and to understand key strategic issues

- to become involved in the formulation of strategic plans either directly through personal participation or indirectly through senior management.

We shall explore the meaning of these roles further in Chapters 2 and 9, but in essence they are to do with what can be described as 'strategic capability'. In outline, this can be described as follows:

> Strategic capability must provide the strategic vision, the rich and sustained knowledge development, the integrity of common purpose and the durable, coherent direction and scope to the activities of the organisation that are needed to secure its long-term survival and advancement.

The implications for HRD of the need to develop this capability in the organisation will emerge at different points throughout the book and will be a central theme of its final two chapters, where a more detailed definition will be provided. Suffice it to point out here that unless HRD does make an impact on the quality and spread of strategic learning, knowledge and capability in the organisation it is failing to make one of its potentially most powerful contributions to the business.

The learning organisation: the search for innovation and transformation

Strategic capability is concerned particularly with the development of learning and knowledge that will lead to the production of new products and services essential to the long-term growth of the business. The idea of regarding HRD as a set of processes that can enhance the organisation's capacity to learn and to generate new knowledge has become a familiar theme in the literature of strategic management and organisational learning. It lies at the heart of the concept of the 'learning organisation' promoted by writers in many different countries over the past 20 years (for example, Argyris and Schon in the USA (1978; 1996), Swieringa and Wierdsma in the Netherlands (1992), Senge in the USA (1990), Nonaka in Japan (1991) and Pedler, Burgoyne and Boydell in the UK (1991)).

Although, as will be seen in our final chapter, concepts of learning organisations and the management and development of knowledge are more complex, more ambiguous and more difficult to translate into practice than consultancy-based literature envisages, a persisting practitioner focus on the need for 'learning organisations' could widen the strategic remit of HRD. In the USA Nadler (1980) interpreted HRD as the entire range of educational, training and development facilities available in an organisation that enhance the learning processes essential to an organisation's capacity to change. Such a definition envisages HRD as having a major contribution to make to the management and development of organisational learning that can improve and transform the base of knowledge in the firm. Since it is on the quality of that knowledge base that the capability to produce strategic assets for the firm depends, this definition – as we shall see in our final chapter – bestows on HRD a much enhanced strategic status.

It is important to be wary of making grandiose claims for HRD. The development of knowledge is a central responsibility of the strategic management of the business (Chakravarthy and Doz, 1992). Any role here for HRD must be facilitative. My own definition tries to capture its essential dimensions without exaggerating its strategic potential:

> Developing people as part of an overall human resource strategy means the skilful provision and organisation of learning experiences, primarily but not exclusively in the workplace, in order that business goals and organisational growth can be achieved.
>
> Such development must be aligned with the organisation's vision and longer-term goals in order that, through enhancing the skills, knowledge, learning and innovative capability of people at every level, the organisation as well as the individual can prosper.

That last point takes us back to harmonies. If people at work are to be committed to acquiring the knowledge and skills that will have benefits for the business, there must be some personal incentive for them to do so. The provision of developmental opportunities at work can enable them to explore their attitudes towards career and personal life and to acquire a portfolio of experiences that will promote their personal ends. It is in this sense that Hall (1986: 252) sees development as helping the individual to become 'truly one's own person – self-directed, self-aware'. We shall look closely at this issue in Chapter 18.

A more business-focused approach to the development of people does seem to promise less nebulous outcomes for the business and for the individual. The Finance Sector Lead Bodies Group, for example, reported in 1995 that 60 per cent of banks in the midst of radical downsizing in order to improve competitive capability were also improving their training and development opportunities in order to ensure that employees would have greater employability. Since the late 1980s job losses in banking have run into tens of thousands. 'Employability security' in such a context takes on a powerful meaning. It is a theme to which we shall return later in this chapter.

It is in such ways that some see the historical tensions of HRD being resolved, with harmony of a new and more realistic kind achieved between the needs of the individual and of the business. From the concept of the learning organisation comes the vision of a company with the structures, systems and processes that will produce the culture, skills and knowledge that enable the innovation essential for success in today's increasingly global markets.

MEETING THE CHALLENGES

The prevailing organisational paradigm

What, then, of those nebulous harmonies? A glance at history has shown us that, through time, some have become less nebulous. We see at least in the literature a clearer grasp of the kind of relationship between the learning of individuals and the performance and strategic capability of the organisation that can prove fruitful for both parties. We can also see the history of HRD as a movement through various levels of 'imperfection' to some kind of ideal organisational state. The crucial question at this point is: has a real transformation of life at work been achieved in any significant number of workplaces? Is it within sight?

Doubts are expressed. Howard Davies, deputy governor of the Bank of England, speaking on BBC Radio 4 on 29 September 1995, commented ruefully on the phenomenon of the downsized, delayered, re-engineered organisations of today where, nevertheless, no one is 'fired' or 'made redundant'. Instead 'they have found themselves consulting outplacement counsellors – people skilled in separation management'. Behind the anodyne phrases he quoted lies a harsh reality as, in his sector of business, job losses continued to soar. In this drive for company survival the individual frequently does not survive. For commentators like Howard Davies, the other side of building a lean organisation is the loss of the soul of the organisation that 'lives in those people who have committed their lives, or a good part of those lives, to it'. There is a moral imperative here, to do with mutuality of obligation.

Many researchers are sceptical in a different way about the idea of a new paradigm ('pattern' or 'example', Allen, 1990) of social organisation in the workplace. Bratton and Gold (1994) believed that the machine model of organisation still dominates Western industrial society, leaving little place for the consideration of attitudes, feelings and personal development. They claimed that, in many organisations, learning and training remain subservient to accounting procedures which call for tangible outcomes for investment – usually short term. 'Even where organisations espouse an HRD approach, all too often sufficient amounts of the machine ideal remain in place, and hidden from view, to present an effective and powerful barrier to organisational learning' (Bratton and Gold, 1994: 228). So, the tensions may remain. Learning may in fact be pursued by powerful parties as a means of social and work control, although that aim may be largely hidden because cloaked in accessible and socially attractive learning approaches – open learning, personal learning plans, teamwork, continuous development, empowerment and growth for all.

If this suspicion is justified – and we shall return to this issue in our final chapter – then we can expect to find that even where there are a formal commitment at the highest levels to becoming a 'learning organisation' and the structures and production systems to support that intention, none the less the old tensions are still to be found under the surface. In that event, HRD may only by accident offer the individual any real escape from – or more accurately through – the life of work into some enriched personal existence the potential of which can be fully realised even when employed life is at an end.

The purpose of employing organisations

So what? you might say. Business organisations are not educational establishments or nannies. Such is not their purpose. They are there to feed the economy; other benefits are pure by-products. That, of course, is arguable. What is the economy for, after all? Whose interests does it serve, if not those of society and therefore ultimately of the individual? And whose is the responsibility to ensure that those interests are truly served?

Be all that as it may, businesses certainly need their people to be motivated, if for no other reason than that it makes life less costly if employees give willingly of their efforts rather than having to be whipped along. Enthusiasm and commitment (argue firms like Ford, Rover and ICI) are likely to occur if in return firms offer something of real value to individuals: a career path in, or out of, the organisation; trained skills; sets of competences; and a cluster of marketable qualifications.

Even for those without concern for wider societal goals there is still a need to focus on HRD. John Storey (1994a) agreed that in Japanese companies the often-vaunted superior approaches to HRD may be an illusion: life there may after all be scientific management in a new guise, with the controls in the hands of the team rather than of external experts, but rigid controls none the less. But he was clear that unless there is a genuinely new pattern of social organisation in the workplace, then UK organisations will never be able to make the strategic leaps forward that will give them long-term profitability. Without it they will be unable to comprehend, let alone use and manage, the 'New Wave Manufacturing methods' that offer incalculable competitive capability. Observing that in Japan the introduction of new technology in the workplace invariably involves the creation of a new work environment, he claimed that 'The social organisation of production is of at least equal and arguably of greater importance than (advanced manufacturing technology) in the successful adoption and implementation of the New Wave Manufacturing methods' (Storey, 1994a: 13).

The lean organisation

At this point let us consider the so-called flexible, adaptable workforce that we are so often told it is a major task of training and development to help to build. So far I have discussed HRD in the context of a conventional picture of the organisation, its structures changing, to be sure, but the basic concept still one of a mainly full-time workforce performing predictable tasks and in respect of whom organisation-wide developmental policies can be formulated. This is misleading.

In September 1994 the Institute of Management and the employment services company Manpower published a joint survey showing that, for the third year running, respondents believed that the main factor affecting the following year's decisions on employment levels would be the need to cut costs. Full-time core staff were increasingly being displaced by 'flexible' employees, including contract workers. Few predicted a return to traditional patterns as the trend to contracting out continued. Most expected that, among remaining core staff, work patterns would continue to change, with increases in part-time working and work-sharing. Greater use of older workers and of flexible retirement had become top priorities, presumably in the face of the relentless ageing of the economy's workforce – a pattern set to continue well into the next century.

By 1997 many commentators, abroad as well as at home, believed that employment in the UK had been tranformed from a rigid and poorly performing aspect of the economy to a fully flexible labour market. Certainly Britain's job market performed notably better in the early to mid-1990s than most of the rest of Europe. By the start of 1997 unemployment had fallen to 6.7 per cent of the workforce without triggering a sharp rise in wages, and about 800,000 jobs had been created during the previous decade (Smith, 1997a). For some, evidence of lasting structural changes to employment lay in the high level of part-time and temporary working: between 1951 and 1991 full-time work had fallen by 6 per cent, part-time working having grown by 595 per cent (Bassett, 1996).

As will be seen in Chapter 7, there is much debate as to the true reasons for, and extent of, these patterns. What is not in dispute, however, is that 'flexibility' is once more the centre of that debate and that it has many implications for employee resource policy in organisations (see especially Marchington and Wilkinson, 1996: 24–31). In its consultative document *The Lean Organisation* (1996b) the Institute of Personnel and Development (IPD) saw the key issue as the need to achieve optimum balance between long-term and short-term interests within organisations. It emphasised the importance of alleviating the human problems involved in transitional phases of restructuring, downsizing and delayering. It also called for positive policies to help middle managers and other employees to cope with the various forms of flexible working resulting from leaner structures.

A role for HRD: employment security or employability security?
The IPD's document noted that 'A failure to provide the right training and staff development often leads to pressures that foster precisely those failings that lean production systems were designed to overcome': Through HRD processes, people exiting from as well as entering the changing organisation can acquire the new skills they need to cope with emergent demands. HRD must also focus on fostering changes in attitudes and styles of managers faced with new relationships and new identities, especially in those organisations where

flexibility is more about lowering overheads and wage rates than improving productivity. In such a situation full-time employees are threatened as their prospects of longer-term job security vanish. Feelings of blame and isolation increase as many struggle with unrealistic workloads and spans of control; they come to perceive permanent, full-time work itself to be vanishing in a world of short-term contracts, part-time work and casualised labour.

Far from reducing the importance of HRD's role, however, such a scenario increases it. In a submission to the House of Commons Committee of Enquiry into the future of the trade unions in October 1993, the Involvement and Participation Association observed that unions should lobby for training budgets when times were hard, aiming to create a better balance between job security and job flexibility, because the casualised labour force of the 1980s lacked power in the labour market and needed the unions to protect it.

This idea of 'employability security' points to a valuable task for HRD. Its outcomes can help to resolve tensions created by the need to downsize and delayer on the one hand and to retain the loyalty and commitment of the workforce on the other. This theme is examined in detail in Chapter 7, but some of the key issues can be outlined here.

- *First, it is essential to put 'flexibility' into perspective* and see it in the context of employment policy in a highly competitive global market. In 1994 Moody's, a leading credit-rating agency, warned that Japan's tradition of lifetime employment was increasingly being seen as threatening the competitiveness and hence the creditworthiness of some of its largest companies. It observed that as long ago as 1992 several leading manufacturers in Japan had tried to move away from the social contract. Another commentator (Dawkins, 1994) agreed that growing international (especially Asian) competition in both cost and quality, plus the legacy of excessive Japanese industrial investment in the late 1980s, had left many companies bloated compared with their closest competitors.

- *Second, flexibility can help to reduce unemployment.* In a 1996 report the Paris-based Organisation for Economic Co-operation and Development (OECD) praised Britain for being one of the few countries that, through its labour market flexibility, had successfully tackled the problem of high unemployment (Segall, 1996). The report noted that unemployment in Europe averaged 11.5 per cent, compared with less than 8 per cent in Britain, and the widening of earnings differentials characteristic of Britian was in this context seen as a positive factor, enticing workers into jobs and encouraging them to upgrade skills. On the other hand, Europeans had little incentive, once unemployed, to seek new work because of the high level of job protection legislation and benefits provided by the State, and the 'excessive' minimum wages and administrative extension of wage agreements.

- *Third, labour laws must be seen in perspective.* Tackling those laws will not be enough to achieve the productivity improvement needed in the face of increasing cross-border competition and labour-saving technologies. Much will also depend on Europe's ability to maximise market opportunities and stimulate those businesses that have the potential to grow fast and profitably. Becoming and staying lean appears to be essential to survival for today's competitive organisations. It is the ways of achieving that state that need to be debated. Furthermore, while there is continuing concern about whether UK labour laws adequately protect the most vulnerable workers, those laws are less harsh than hitherto. In 1994 the House of Lords in a landmark ruling struck down provisions of the Employment Protection Act 1978. Their ruling gives part-timers unfairly dismissed or made redundant the same right as full-timers to compensation or redundancy if they have worked for the same employer for two years. This compares very favourably to the previous five-year qualifying period for those working between 8 and 16 hours a week and the lack of any protection for those working less than eight hours. By 1997, while 75 per cent of full-time workers had full employment rights compared with 70 per cent in 1990, among part-timers the figures were 57 per cent compared with 30 per cent (Smith, 1997).

• *Fourth, the concept of job security is less meaningful in today's economic climate than the concept of employability security.* The 1995 Oxford Review of Economic Policy showed a worrying picture of the bottom end of the labour market, characterised by higher turnover among the young and less skilled and the overrepresentation of part-time jobs. However, although by 1997 nearly 30 per cent of working people were in part-time employment, the growth had been gradual, the sharpest increase occurring in the supposedly secure 1950s (Smith, 1997). Nor are such employees necessarily in insecure or short-term jobs: in reality the average length of job tenure has not changed dramatically since the 1960s, and temporary work tends to be cyclical, enabling employers to adjust to seasonal surges in business, rather than something that may be used to exploit labour. Schonfield (1995) cited the conclusion of the 1995 Incomes Data Services Report: although widespread experience of mass redundancy has brought a sense of insecurity for millions, some companies are rediscovering the value of stable, permanent employment and there is in any case more stability in the workplace than appearances suggest. Such analyses emphasise the need for organisations who want committed employees to enable them to acquire skills and experience valued in the external labour market. This will help to provide the only kind of security that is likely to become common currency: employability security.

• *Fifth, loyalty and commitment can be misleading concepts for those working in the 'lean organisation'.* In his book on corporate restructuring Charles Heckscher (1995) pointed to the contradictions inherent in arguments that employers in today's tough competitive climate must continuously strive to win the loyalty and commitment of their employees. Recalling a comment made by Jack Welch, chairman of General Electric, that companies cannot guarantee jobs, only customers can, he observed that commitment can legitimately be demanded only by those employers with something meaningful to offer in return. If companies today cannot afford to give the long-term guarantees of job security upon which hitherto they have depended in order to elicit loyalty and commitment from their employees, then some other kind of contract needs to be forged between the parties. Loyalty to the project rather than to the corporation is, he suggested, the answer here. Work organised as a succession of team-based projects – each lasting anything from one to perhaps five or six years – can offer a company its route to profitability and growth while at the same time ensuring for those involved the opportunity to build up a record of effective performance, of teamworking, and of skills related to project work and to the internal and external networking that it requires. In those organisations which have to survive in increasingly turbulent environments and can no longer offer long-term job security, open recognition of mutuality of interest seems more likely to generate high performance and adaptability than appeals to loyalty and commitment.

Such discussions demonstrate the importance of education and training for those both in and out of work. At a macro level the picture here is striking. In the UK, job losses are significantly concentrated among lower-skilled male workers whose partners do not work. This, together with measures such as the abolition of wages councils, helps to explain the growing divergence between the lot of the skilled and the less skilled workers in our society. In the USA, despite its much more dynamic rate of job creation than other Group of Seven leading industrial nations, income disparities between the better trained and educated and the less well trained have widened dramatically (Graham, 1994). There, it is the skilled who get the good jobs, the unskilled who remain the economy's underclass. At national as at organisational level, employability security is proving to have more significance than employment security. This is because its consequences touch everyone and can directly influence a situation where 'whole segments of the population have been virtually shut out of the job market' (Graham, 1994: 4).

The importance of national HRD policy in this respect was highlighted by Robert Reich, US labour secretary, at the Group of Seven Conference in Detroit in 1994. He pleaded that citizens of advanced economies should not be forced into choosing between, on the one hand, more jobs that pay less and less and, on the other hand, good jobs that carry, however, the risk of high levels of unemployment. What is needed, he said, is:

> to combine the kind of investments in education and training and apprenticeship that we find in Europe with the dynamic labour mobility and flexibility we find in the US, all encased within macro-economic policies which encourage growth and jobs.
>
> (Graham, 1994: 4)

I believe that the HRD process must become more focused on enhancing employability security if it is to resolve its historical tensions and serve the interests of individuals as well as those of the organisation. There should not be an inevitable conflict between the achievement of business goals and a contribution to the wider well-being of society. It is to avoid such conflict and to build more mutuality of interest that a number of organisations work with employees and their representatives to develop positive policies around disengagement as well as recruitment. Such policies can cover mentoring, coaching, personal development and career planning, achievement of national occupational qualifications, pre-redundancy and pre-retirement planning, strategic partnerships with outplacement consultants, and redeployment and retraining initiatives. Such activity should be integrated to produce a strategy for building up and retaining valuable skills and experience for the organisation while at the same time giving support to individuals at critical transition points in their working lives. In this context a planned approach to career development both in the internal and external labour market is essential, as we shall see in Chapter 18.

In 1994 Robbie Gilbert, the CBI's employee affairs director, emphasised to a conference at Warwick University School of Industrial and Business Studies (Taylor, 1994) three points which put into context the variety of issues examined in this section:

- Employers increasingly need a workforce that can deliver 'higher productivity, work more efficiently, give reliable and customer-oriented service, be innovative and accept the need for continuous personal development and improvement'. However, obtaining long-term commitment of employees in the current climate of employment insecurity is going to be difficult.

- Trust is crucial here: companies will have to be more candid about explaining to employees the demands facing them in their joint need to secure business growth.

- 'In future a measure of the good employer is not necessarily one who pays the highest rate but who keeps workers' skills, and hence their employability, up to date.'

The need for integrative policies

What can be concluded at the national level from the complex and often contradictory debate about flexible workforces, unemployment, productivity and increasingly global competition is that it is the *integration* of related economic and social policies that will matter most in combating unemployment and in increasing national competitive capability. Goodhart (1994b: 4) describes the consensus being achieved across the USA, the UK and continental Europe, backed by the OECD, on the need for 'a combination of greater labour market flexibility, easier enterprise formation, more effective active labour market measures and improvements in education and training' in tackling the world's unemployment problem. Integration, coherency and consistency are the keys.

The same kind of conclusion can be reached at the organisational level. Any company seeking to achieve competitive advantage must have a range of interlocking strategies across the business that will enable all efforts to be integrated in the drive for business success. HRD should be treated as a strategic process. As we shall see in the following chapters, for it to make its fullest impact and best serve both organisation and individual it must support, and be supported by, a durable and consistent range of wider employee resource policies and systems. They in their turn must be aligned with the goals of the business.

There must also be a sense of proportion, and HRD can do a service here by producing an awareness in the organisation of the need:

- to plan for the longer as well as the short-term – something that can come about only if HRD practitioners secure more influence over the key decision-makers and gain the commitment of top management to treat the development of people as a strategic process

- to focus more positively on the downside of the flexible firm – the fragmented and vulnerable labour forces that help to give organisations much added value but that too often can be left with little of value for themselves.

THE DIFFERENCE BETWEEN THE INTENDED, THE APPARENT AND THE REAL

Storey (1994) emphasised the need to explore worker responses to New Wave Manufacturing. That raises one last question in my own mind. In a sense I think that it is the most difficult, and it is one to which I have already briefly referred. It is indicated in the following statement: 'The appearance of what we do is different from the intention with which we do it, and the circumstances at the time may not be clear' (St Augustine's *Confessions*, Book 3:9).

I thought of that statement when reading Storey's words in another of his books (1992: 16). He reminded us there that in the HRM literature there is little hard information about actual practices in real contexts. Too many case-studies 'tend to exaggerate the degree of change. They bestow upon it a coherence and neatness which distorts reality. Moreover, they rarely give details of the real difficulties encountered' (Storey 1992: 17). He told of visits to companies heralded in the literature as having made radical innovations, 'only to discover that the "breakthrough" was viewed as a peripheral trial, was hardly recognizable to the participants on the ground, or had been abandoned altogether'. So the exciting appearance was very different from the mundane intent.

He found, too, that the real circumstances at the time were not clear. For example, Lucas is a traditional mainstream company which, in seeking turnround, deliberately chose a radical strategic response, 'part of which has clearly involved a drive to enhance the capabilities and commitment of its human resources through the use of training' (Storey, 1992: 115). The intention was clear, and there was compelling evidence to show that few similar companies could match the fundamental nature of HRD investment made by the company. Yet, when Storey did a bit of 'digging around' he found that the impact as viewed by the intended recipients of such provision was minimal. Their view of events was very different.

This contrast between intent and appearance, this need to know more about the circumstances involved in order to determine what is really happening, was highlighted when Storey quoted an example from the Rover 'Working with Pride' Programme, where a plant director from Power Train told him:

> I spent every Friday afternoon for six months with a dozen foremen at a time on WWP. One said 'It's a load of bollocks, Ken.' It's difficult for them when they have got used to kicking arses for the past ten years.
>
> (Storey, 1994: 221)

In October 1996 an article appeared in *People Management*, the IPD's professional journal, lauding human resource (HR) strategy at CoSteel, Sheerness, especially in relation to union derecognition. The company's personnel director claimed that HR strategy had led to significant business improvements over the years (Billot, 1996). In November came a rebuttal from the union side (Leahy, 1996), giving a quite different and harsher interpretation of HRM in the company. At one level, this can be dismissed as politics. At another, it offers a further example of the problems that surround attempts to clarify the reality of human resource management and development in the workplace.

So what is really happening to the development of people in organisations? There are not only big questions to research – there are big issues of methodology too: how to collect, analyse and interpret the data so as to capture the intention, the appearance and the reality, and to illuminate the circumstances prevailing at the time.

ESCAPE FROM OR TO THE LIFE OF WORK?

I end this chapter with a quotation that takes us back to its start. Gilley and Eggland (1989: 354) concluded their book by observing that in HRD the trend is to move away from 'nice to know' subjects towards supporting business goals. Then they wrote: 'However, in response to changing values in the work force, these will be reexamined ... There is a need for HRD programs relating to employees' lives outside the work environment.' They saw that HRD may have to deal in the future with the social needs of employees who want to know how to deal with complex situations involving high levels of personal stress and responsibility. As demographic trends result in ageing workforces HRD may have to help them acquire the coping skills to adjust to constantly changing home environments. In a similar way Goldstein and Goldstein (1990) pointed to the small population available in the USA for entry-level jobs, and the consequent need for organisations to develop training programmes for the hardcore unemployed. They perceived that declining educational standards among young entrants to employment could require many organisations to add basic skill and literacy training to their traditional range of job-related programmes.

So, to take us back full circle to where we started, the separation between life at work and life outside is becoming ever more difficult to define – and that casts yet another perspective on Bobbitt's quotation, presenting a fresh challenge to those with a controlling influence over the learning and development of people in organisations.

CONCLUSION

In order to achieve the learning objectives of this chapter we have outlined four stages in the twentieth-century history of HRD in the USA and the UK. We have identified key challenges facing HRD and have explored its value in enhancing employability security in today's lean organisations. The need for the alignment of HRD with wider employee resource policies and systems of the firm has been emphasised, as has the importance – and the difficulty – of finding out how far those policies are implemented and understood in the workplace.

We have concluded that many tensions still exist in reconciling individual and organisational goals and interests, and that HRD has a vital part to play in improving their integration.

USEFUL READING

For students, three texts offering useful overviews of the body of behavioural science theory to which this chapter refers are:

PUGH, D.S. (ed.) (1971) *Organization Theory: Selected readings.* Harmondsworth, Penguin.

VROOM, V.H. *and* DECI, E.L. (eds) (1970) *Management and Motivation: Selected readings.* Harmondsworth, Penguin.

WILSON, D.C. *and* ROSENFELD, R.H. (1990) *Managing Organizations: Text, readings and cases.* Part II. London, McGraw-Hill.

2 The strategic framework for human resource development

LEARNING OBJECTIVES

- To understand the meaning of 'strategic, business-led' human resource development (HRD).

- To understand the factors inhibiting or enhancing the ability of HRD to operate within the strategic framework of the business.

TERMINOLOGY

In this chapter I want to look at some of the ways in which HRD can operate within a strategic framework. As we shall see in Part 2, there has been a widespread failure in UK organisations to think strategically about skill needs and, down through the years, a failure at governmental level to develop a vision and strategy to ensure the skilled and educated human resources needed to drive the economy. It is vital to make HRD serve the ends of the business as well as promote the growth of individuals. It is increasingly important to think and act strategically instead of reacting in an *ad hoc* fashion to immediately pressing needs.

Business-led HRD is development that is responsive to the business needs of an organisation, improving capability to achieve business goals. The term 'business' in this context refers to any kind of employing organisation, public or private sector, or service, process or product-driven; and the term 'business goals' refers to the corporate goals of the organisation. Business-led HRD can also make possible a widening choice of business strategies as the full potential of people at various levels of the organisation becomes evident. Business-led HRD must be a dynamic function, moving in line with the cycle of business change. For a real-life case-study illustrating all these points, read the story of Halford, Britain's biggest retailer of car accessories and cycles, during a critical period of business change in the 1980s (Sparrow and Pettigrew, 1988).

Strategic HRD is development that arises from a powerful vision about people's abilities and potential and operates within the overall strategic framework of the business. Although this book is entitled *Employee Development* in order to conform with IPD Professional Standards terminology, it has already been explained that throughout the book the tendency will be to use the phrase 'human resource development' (HRD) instead. This is because that term better conveys that the scope of developmental policy should in fact extend beyond those directly employed by an organisation to those 'individuals or groups who have some relationship with an organisation but are not in an employer–employee relationship' (Walton, 1996). As we shall see in Chapter 10, this can include stakeholders such as self-employed subcontractors, casualised workers, suppliers, distributors and volunteers. In so far as their contribution to the organisation's goals will be enhanced by various developmental experiences, and in so far as learning from them can bring value to the organisation, they are a rightful focus of developmental activity.

Vision is the picture that people hold in their minds about what kind of business theirs should be. Vision should be powerful and coherent across the organisation, yet should also be challenging and have sufficient ambiguity to encourage creative thinking about how to make the business grow and prosper.

The *mission* is the articulation of vision in some concrete form which then becomes a guideline for strategy. The word *policy* is often synonymous with *mission*, although usually a firm's overall policy in each of its key areas of activity, including human resource management (HRM), is more detailed than its mission statement. Sometimes people refer to an organisation's mission when what they actually mean is its vision. Sometimes a *mission statement* simply represents top management's view, and may be largely disregarded by many in the organisation. Currently the concept of mission is less popular than hitherto. It is more important to have a clear and powerful vision than to have a mission statement. However, research indicates that where the mission statement has been arrived at by a consultative process and is agreed across the organisation as an incentive to action, it then has value.

Strategy is the route that has been chosen for a period of time and from a range of options in order to achieve business goals. It is a guide to action and therefore sets the scene within which policies – including those employee resource (ER) policies relating to the learning and development of people – can be agreed and implemented. Because strategy unfolds as a pattern of decisions and activity through time, the term 'strategic' can only be meaningfully applied to activities in which the organisation wishes to invest now for some future return. Strategy must be adaptive, since it may from time to time have to be amended or even abandoned as the organisation's environment or internal circumstances place new pressures on the business, or provide hitherto unforeseen opportunities.

Implementation concerns the execution of strategy. The capability to implement strategy is all-important, and too often much time is spent generating strategic options and choosing from them without due attention to the factors – especially the human factors – that may in reality make a particular option impossible to carry out.

> **The vision and strategy of my organisation**
>
> In the case of your own organisation, identify its vision and the extent to which that vision is powerful, meaningful and shared across the organisation. Then assess how far the vision is reflected in an appropriate and feasible business strategy.
>
> Think about the sources of information you will use for this, and how you will discover whether your conclusions are accurate. Remember the warning at the end of Chapter 1 about confusing the apparent with the real!

HRD AND THE STRATEGIC FRAMEWORK OF THE BUSINESS

There are four factors that will significantly determine the extent to which HRD can become of strategic value to an organisation: the measures of performance that dominate the business; the attitude and commitment of top management; the role and position of HRD professionals in the organisation; and their strategic expertise and articulacy.

Measures of performance

There are many ways in which stakeholders measure the performance of an organisation, each with its own implications for HRD. Three of the most frequently used, either singly or in some combination, are:

- *financial performance*, as measured by return on assets (ROA), return on sales (ROS) and return on equity (ROE). These measures are to do with current profitability and the state of the end-of-year balance sheet.

- *strategic performance*, as measured by market-based measures such as market share, growth, diversification and product development. These measures are to do with taking a longer-term perspective, about growth of and/or share in existing businesses and with the future positioning of the organisation.

- *organisational effectiveness*, as measured by stakeholder-based measures related to such aspects as quality of products and employees, levels of employee morale and the quality of life in the workplace, and fulfilment of external social responsibilities.

Broadly speaking, organisations that are dominated by short-term financial measures of performance are unlikely to make any significant investment in HRD beyond job-related training and short-term competency development. It is in organisations measuring performance by strategic and/or organisational effectiveness measures that one can expect to find attitudes more supportive of investing in HRD over the longer term.

However, the distinction between financial and strategic measures can be a fine one. The crucial issue for HRD is the extent to which shareholders are concerned primarily with performance affecting the immediate bottom line or with investment and activity that will through time add value to the business. Thus one of the currently most popular measures that bridges the apparent gap between the financial and strategic categories is Economic Value Added (EVA), a measure 'that connects all decisions with the maximisation of wealth for shareholders' (Stewart, 1996: 2.5). Hailed by Peter Drucker as a unique measure because its continuous increase will always bring good, it 'shines a light on all four ways wealth can be created in business' (Stewart, 1996: 2.5): cost-cutting, release of unproductive capital, reduction in cost of capital and investment in value-added activity. The questions raised by such a measure are simple but fundamental: what company-wide impact will this strategy or activity or innovation have, and what kind of value will it add? Such an approach to measuring value is fully consistent with a commitment to developing people for the long term. However, the commitment must be informed. HR practitioners must, in promoting their vision and strategy, both look back at the kind of value released or created by HRD in the organisation in the past and look forward to assess the value it is likely to achieve. More will be said about this in Chapter 12.

Attitude and commitment of key stakeholders

If top management and other powerful stakeholders are unaware of the role that HRD can play in adding value, then they will not invest in it, regardless of the type of performance they seek from the organisation. Without the commitment of top management, too, line managers and the rest of the workforce will not be supportive. Attitude and commitment of key stakeholders must be positive if HRD is to make a strategic contribution.

Role, status and expertise of HRD professionals

Therefore it is vital for those with major responsibility for HRD in the business to gain a formal role that enables them to influence management at all levels. However, there is a difficulty here. If top management is not committed to HRD, the function itself is unlikely to be given high status and position; but if it does not have high status and position, how can it influence top management? It is at this point that the individual expertise and impact of the HR spokesperson for HRD at the top levels of the business become critical. We shall return to this point later in the chapter.

In the UK, although there is quite widespread training and development in relation to culture change, decentralisation, workforce competences and formal strategy planning skills, there is little indication of strong internal coherency and consistency in these initiatives (Storey, 1994). Furthermore, HRD is often unsupported by wider personnel actions in the firm, employee resourcing activity showing few signs of being strategically planned or of being tightly aligned with business strategy (Keep and Mayhew, 1994). All of this indicates an ignorance within the profession of the need for internal consistency across ER policies, as well as a lack of strategic alliances between HRD practitioners and line managers.

If in any organisation there is a lack of expertise, awareness and articulacy among HRD professionals, insufficient collaboration between HRD and other personnel practitioners in the business, or failure to build a strategic partership between HRD and line managers in the business, then it will not be surprising if the strategic development of human resources is virtually non-existent. On the other hand, if there is a credible, high-status, expert and business-focused HRD presence in the organisation, then there is a real opportunity for HRD's strategic potential to be fulfilled. Now here is a case (see boxed text) to explore in general terms the theme of barriers and facilitators to HRD in an organisation.

Recruitment in a local authority

Identify the main HRD issues in the following case-study. What should management do to reduce this kind of staff turnover?

Ensdale County Council is operating in an increasingly difficult climate: it tries to provide high-quality customer-focused services and achieve a variety of government-imposed standards, while having to cut costs and face increasing pressures on its scarce resources. None the less it has an enthusiastic HR manager who, working with a small team of six (most with long service in the authority), has in the past year or so introduced a range of initiatives to 'change the face of HRM at Ensdale'. These include a reduced reliance on full-time staff and increased employment of part-time and temporary staff across the authority; contracting out a range of activities, including many training operations; the introduction of a 'performance management system'; and a drive for total quality management. The initiatives have not all proved durable, and many claim that they are piecemeal and too costly for the likely benefits. None the less the department persists in its efforts, and the manager has recently had an article published in *People Management* about a 'flexible working' programme it has just run.

A year ago a young graduate was recruited as personnel assistant – the last one had left after a year, and a lot of effort went into producing an attractive recruitment brochure and a demanding selection procedure that would make clear that this was a professional and forward-looking department.

Michael came from outside the region; he had just left a new university with a good BA Honours in Business Studies, and had a promising school and university record. Throughout the selection process he was impressed by the emphasis on the need for someone prepared to be fully committed to continuous improvement and quality, who would be given plenty of scope to use their initiative. He liked, too, the idea of working with the small HR team, although he did not actually meet any of them (except the HR manager) during the selection period.

The HR manager made it clear that Michael would be working with a supportive team where his learning needs would have a positive response. He agreed to enrol immediately on a part-time Institute of Personnel and Development course at a local college, in order to 'start the process of continuous professional development', as his manager expressed it.

After nearly a year Michael had become frustrated and disappointed. Despite the new performance management system, his own appraisal by the HR manager was perfunctory. There was little clarification of forthcoming targets or meaningful feedback on work done. The manager was as ever preoccupied with employee relations issues and – ironically – with organising appraisal skills training across the authority. There was no real opportunity for Michael to innovate, and he was constantly being given routine or awkward jobs that others in the 'team' preferred not to do. He found that the culture of the small department was surprisingly backward-looking, and it soon became clear to him why, over the past three years, turnover of new young recruits in the HR department had been high. The only thing he enjoyed was his IPD course, where he was doing well and getting to know an increasing number of local personnel practitioners. It was at an IPD branch meeting that he heard of a vacancy in the personnel department of a local manufacturing organisation. The pay and conditions were little different from those he was currently receiving, but the firm's reputation as an employer was impressive. He knew through his IPD classes a couple of people who worked there, and so was able to get first-hand information on the excellence of the firm's HRD policies and the coherency of its HRM strategy and systems. He applied for the job and was successful. Once he was there, his real professional career began. For Michael it proved in every way a very lucky break.

Feedback notes
- The authority is having to operate in an increasingly tough environment and achieve goals which, being to do with both cost reduction and improved quality, are not easy to reconcile. The vision held by the HR manager is not being carried through in any meaningful way, and training and development evidently have to operate within an ineffective strategic framework.

- Michael was a wasted asset. Unless there is a better alignment of HRM with business and individual needs, others like him will continue to leave, or will become infected by the negative culture of the HR department and become increasingly demotivated and unproductive. Either way, the authority will keep losing valuable human resources and HRD will contribute little to the needs of either the organisation or individuals.

It is clear that in such a case the five steps critical to establishing HRD within a strategic framework (shown in Table 1) have not been taken.

Table 1 Five steps to ensure that ED operates within the strategic framework of the business

1	Relate investment in the development of people to the vision, values and strategic goals of the organisation.
2	Have a clear and internally consistent employee resource strategy, within which goals for ED are established.
3	Formulate an ED strategy to meet those ED goals.
4	Agree on realistic, specific, measurable and well-costed ED plans that are consistent with the wider framework of ER and business strategy.
5	Establish mechanisms for monitoring, feedback and further relevant action.

STRATEGIC HRD

In examining HRD in the context of its strategic framework in the organisation, seven questions are helpful to consider:

1) Is strategic HRD happening?

2) What prevents its happening more widely?

3) When is it most likely to happen?

4) What are the signs that it is happening?

5) How should the process of linking HRD strategy to business goals begin?

6) How can the outcomes of strategic HRD be measured?

7) How and why should HRD be linked with strategic capability?

1 Is strategic HRD happening?

Two simple conceptual frameworks are helpful here. Figure 1 helps us to focus on the organisational and external context of HRD. It draws attention to the fact that HRD in a business is a means to an end, not an end in itself. Operating within the wider function of ER policy in the organisation, it can either support or work against the vision and strategic goals of the business. It is helpful, in fact, to think about HRM as a door. Open, it signifies the removal of human barriers to achieving those goals, and the encouragement and facilitation of required human performance. Closed, it signifies the reinforcement of those barriers, and a consequent likelihood of poor human performance and failure to realise potential. Figure 2 shows the main processes – including developmental – that operate within the 'wheel' of HRM policy and systems in the workplace.

Figure 1 HRM and the business

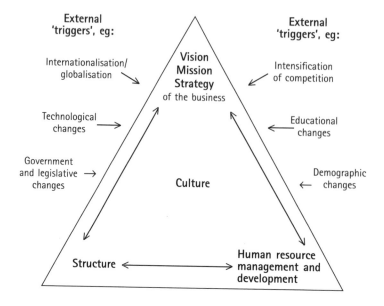

Figure 2 The wheel of HRM and the business

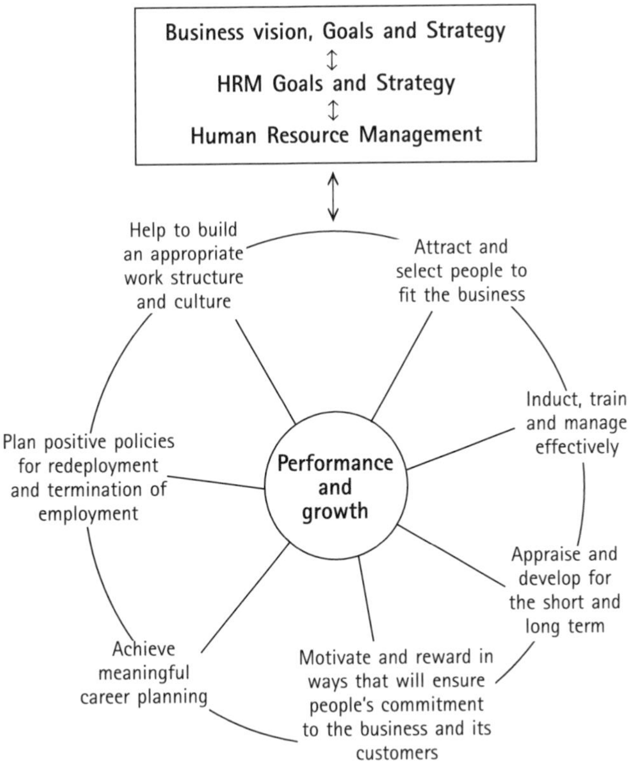

Based on Harrison, 1993a: 40

In the sense that it is conceived in Figures 1 and 2, strategic HRD is *not* really happening in the UK! Despite the hype that surrounds a number of organisations where the planned development of people *has* made a notable contribution to the achievement of business goals, we have already noted in Chapter 1 that research has failed to reveal any significant connection between HRD and business strategy across UK organisations at large.

2 What prevents its happening more widely?

There are many reasons, but the most widely prevalent are:

- the failure of personnel practices and systems to provide an adequate framework to support a strategic approach to HRD

- the lack of incentives for either individuals or organisations to invest in training, education and planned long-term development.

We have discussed the first point in the previous section (pages 21–23). The second involves a number of issues and needs clarification here.

For individuals in the UK (as will be seen in Part 2) there has been far less incentive to invest in training than in many competitor countries, notably Germany, where increased wages and career prospects are linked to training and qualifications, and young people are not distracted by high-pay temptations. If there is a significant labour market for young people without many educational qualifications, and if young people are offered attractive rates of pay, then they (and many others, in or out of work) will see little point in investing in vocational education and training, since it will not bring them better jobs, pay or career development. As we have seen in Chapter 1 (pages 11–12), this situation is showing some signs of changing, but there remains a major difference in incentives to invest between the UK and other European countries.

For organisations there are many factors that call into question the value of investing in HRD. Two predominate. In many organisations, business strategy is driven by short-term and mainly financial considerations. In many more, business strategy itself is incoherent or non-existent, so that it is difficult to conceive of a long-term investment in the future of the workforce when the future of the business overall is at the mercy of *ad hoc* decision-making.

In either situation there is little hope for strategic HRD. Instead, whoever is charged with responsibility for the 'training' function would do better to focus on performing operational tasks well than to pine for a strategic role. By ensuring that all training achieves agreed and measurable objectives, by working in partnership with line management, by benchmarking key activities and by being fully knowledgeable about the business and its competitive environment, HRD practitioners can build up the business credibility needed when the organisational situation changes. When it does, they will be poised to become strategic players.

3 When is it most likely to happen?
Organisations that do invest heavily not only in training but in a wide range of planned developmental initiatives include a significant number of little-known but highly committed medium-sized and small businesses in both the public and private sector, as well as the frequently quoted examples. So what are the pay-offs for them?

The reasons for investing in the development of people at work are never as simple as they seem, so any generalisation can mislead. However, there are five scenarios likely to highlight the need for an investment in longer-term, business-focused developmental activity. Each is common in today's world of globalised competition and of rapidly changing challenges to human capability, adaptability and inventiveness.

Costly capability gaps
These are caused by past reliance on *ad hoc* training and development activity. Where the results of failure to invest adequately in training in the past have led to severe problems that now threaten the viability of the organisation, it would be logical to expect not only an immediate but also a sustained investment in training (Prais *et al*, 1990). Lost opportunities in the market-place and longer lead times when developing new projects are typical results of miscalculation related to the development of people. On the other hand, the ability to react rapidly to changing external scenarios and obtain the benefits they offer can be enhanced by a more strategic approach to the

recruitment, retention and development of the right people, as is illustrated in an account of rapid change at the Benefits Agency (Bichard, 1996). Unfortunately, it may take a crisis on several fronts to produce an awareness of the need to invest in HRD – and this is where a constant search by HRD professionals for best practice outside the organisation can be a trigger for change.

Changes in the competitive environment of the firm's asset base

These can lead to new business goals to achieve long-term advancement. Such goals are invariably to do with a drive for quality, innovation and continuous improvement in commitment as well as in performance. A more strategic approach to HRD is essential to support such a drive.

Major workplace changes to achieve new business goals

A wide variety of HRM initiatives has been established in workplaces to support strategic and organisational change (Storey, 1992). Not all prove durable, but those which have particular implications for the training and development of people include:

- mission statements

- organisational delayering and devolved managerial decision-making

- culture change programmes

- harmonisation of terms and conditions of employment across the workforce

- a need for increased job flexibility, multi-skilling etc

- introduction of a drive for total quality

- performance appraisal across all sectors

- teamworking.

Major changes in the skills profile of the external labour market

Where an organisation can no longer recruit people with the abilities needed for adequate job performance, it will have to provide more than mere 'top-up' training for those recruits. There will have to be a focus on internalised training and development systems to ensure an effective workforce. This, in turn, will call for a more strategic approach to HRD across the organisation.

Major changes in the technical base of the business

These changes are of a kind that call for organisational restructuring, reskilling of large sectors of the workforce, and changed patterns of management and decision-making.

The strongest commitment to HRD in the organisation will arise from a shared awareness among stakeholders that HRD is a logical consequence of the kind of business goals that drive the organisation, and that it is central to the achievement of sustained competitive advantage. Regular monitoring of the performance and environment (internal and external) of the business will identify triggers calling for HRD to be placed within the strategic framework of the business, where it can act as a powerful lever to support corporate goals and long-term growth. It is a matter of focus and sustained direction of HRD that is the issue here: an increase in the cost of HRD to the business is by no means the invariable result of taking a more strategic stance.

4 What are the signs that it is happening?
When HRD is operating effectively within the strategic framework of the business it will be:

- *durable and meaningful* – integral to the long-term direction of the business

- *aligned* – tied closely to the organisation's mission and strategic goals

- *internally consistent* – supporting, and supported by, other ER policies

- *management-led* – with any specialist staff playing a supportive role

- *expert* – characterised by the skilful provision and management of learning that will improve current performance and lead to organisational growth.

Many companies are realising that if they are to remain competitive the whole workforce must be committed to achieving high quality and continuous improvement in a climate where change is the norm. This means moving away from hierarchical organisational structures with their inward-looking focus and their rigid job descriptions that erect barriers to co-operation and change. It also means investing carefully in initiatives related to training and continuous development of the workforce, without which there cannot be the human capability needed to ensure that business goals are achieved.

5 How should the process of linking HRD strategy to business goals begin?
To ensure that these conditions are achieved, HRD managers must 'work with top management, focusing on the organisation's strategic initiatives and seeking ways to leverage the development of employees to achieve these objectives, in creative and impactful approaches' (Noel, James and Dennehy, 1991: 19). Together they must identify the key strategic initiatives to which the organisation is committed and then agree on the HRD goals, strategy and plans that will best support them. For example, if a company is delayering and downsizing but also wants a responsive and adaptive workforce, then it will need training initiatives related to teambuilding and multi-skilling. It will also need the planned development of those who will have to manage that changed work system and workplace culture.

Here is a case-study: an example of an organisation where it has recently become essential to place HRD within a strategic framework if business success is to be achieved. The study is based on a real-life example.

Case-study: Wesdale Acute Hospitals NHS Trust

Wesdale Acute Hospitals NHS Trust is a major provider of health care, catering for the needs of around 300,000 people in its area. It has many stakeholders – patients, staff, the local Health Commission, Community Health Council, Community Healthcare and general practitioners. The Trust's philosophy is 'Partners in Quality – working together to deliver a sensitive, caring health service, changing to meet your individual needs – today and in the future'. Its current priorities are the building of a new District General Hospital (DGH) over the next five years and implementing an interim rationalisation plan related to that radical organisational change.

The Trust has four strategic goals, of which one is explicitly related to its people: 'valuing all those who work with and for us, and developing their capability and commitment through a wide range of individual and corporate training and development opportunities and programmes'. Triggered by the business goals and strategy put in place over recent years, the Trust must establish a strategic approach to training and development at three levels: corporate, business unit and operational.

At corporate level, the HR director to whom the HRD manager reports has a seat on the board and is responsible for HR policy. This, and a major HR agenda leading up to the opening of the new DGH, ensure that HRD goals and strategy are continually related to the goals of the Trust. As part of the Trust's Annual Plan, a training plan identifies a range of activities to be undertaken within the framework of overall corporate strategy and ensures evaluation of past activities as well as assessment of future investment needed.

At unit level, clinical directorates' business plans now include the training needed to support changes and developments in services. A multi-disciplinary Training and Development Group has been established, and oversees, the implementation of a corporate approach to the delivery of all initiatives. The Group identifies HRD responses to organisational requirements identified in the Annual Plan.

At operational level, the Trust was recognised two years ago as an 'Investor in People'. It has also been accredited to run a number of its own National Vocational Qualification (NVQ) programmes. This means that there is a business-led framework for HRD processes which, in the devolved management structure, are the primary responsibility of line management. Those processes include identification of training needs through annual appraisal, personal development plans for all staff, encouragement to achieve national occupational qualifications, monitoring of staff performance, and development and evaluation of training events. Together, they enable a 'bottom-up' as well as 'top-down' approach to be taken to developing HRD strategy in the Trust.

The Trust's HRD system derives initially from the strategic direction of the Trust. Ultimately, it feeds back into it, thereby aiming to improve the strategic as well as operational capability of the organisation.

Figure 3 Linking HRD to a Trust's strategic and business planning cycle

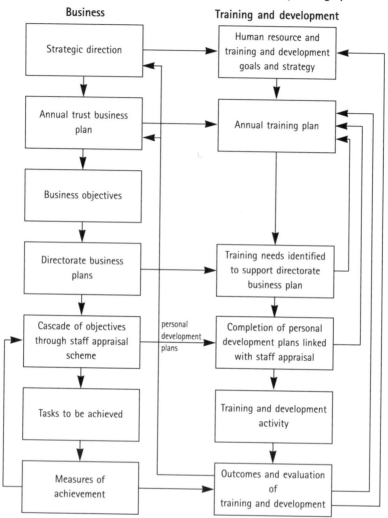

At this point, note in Figure 3 how HRD is becoming strategic in this NHS Trust:

- *All HRD activities are goal-driven* – they arise out of and feed back into HRD goals that in turn support the wider goals of the business.

- *HRD has true strategic status* – it is formally supported by corporate, unit level and operational management, and the function has a powerful voice at board level.

- *There is a formal HRD strategy* –and all HRD activities, including appraisal, training, continuous development, programmes to achieve multi-skilling, total quality and culture change, are being brought increasingly into line with that strategy.

- *There is increasing consistency with other human resource policies –* whether related to recruitment and selection, recognition and rewards, or redundancy and redeployment, all support and are supported by HRD policies.

6 How can the outcomes of strategic HRD be measured?

We shall look in detail at this issue in Chapter 12. Here we can note that at the stage when HRD strategy is being developed it is essential to agree on how its outcomes will be measured. The aim should be for simplicity and relevance in measurement, focusing on:

- agreement, within the framework of HRD strategy, on the HRD initiatives that will link to different business priorities – and on a budget for those

- milestones to mark each major stage in the implementation of those initiatives

- clear presentations to key parties as each milestone is reached, sharing progress and outcomes related to the initiatives

- amendment of initiatives in response to changes in the business or its strategy.

7 How and why should HRD be linked with strategic capability?

So far we have looked at how to develop HRD goals and strategy that explicitly support business goals, establishing a competitive advantage rooted in employee competence.

There is, however, a further aspect to HRD's strategic role, and this was mentioned in Chapter 1 (page 6). It is to help managers and others across the business to plan strategically, to think strategically, and to understand and take action on key strategic issues; in other words, to enhance their ability to produce and powerfully communicate a relevant vision of the organisation, to generate appropriate and challenging goals, and to choose and implement the strategies and assets that will best support them. This ability goes to the heart of what I call the 'strategic capability' of the organisation.

Strategic planning involves analysing trends and pressures, generating and assessing strategic options, and producing a business plan. However, strategic planning is only one component of strategic capability. What is also essential is strategic thinking – the kind needed (to quote Mintzberg, 1994: 109) 'to function beyond the boxes, to encourage the informal learning that produces new perspectives and new combinations'.

Informal learning can produce new business strategies. It can also produce modifications to planned strategies. But new or amended strategies will not emerge in this way unless senior managers know how to facilitate the process – and wish to do so. If those managers regard 'strategy' as only a formal planning task carried out at a fixed point in time by a particular group of people, then strategies derived from the informal learning of others in the business will not be developed and vital strategic learning will be wasted. Helping to produce widespread strategic capability in the organisation and stimulating an awareness that such capability is crucial to the future of the organisation are therefore an essential part of HRD's strategic role.

Are we talking here about a 'learning organisation'? Yes, if that rather hackneyed phrase means an organisation where there is continuous internal innovation and a capability to make and execute high-quality strategy. Such an organisation (as we shall see in Chapter 20) has the structure, systems and processes that enable organisational and business regeneration through changing times, and uses them skilfully. These themes of strategic capability, innovation and organisational learning will be amplified and explored in the final part of the book.

CONCLUSION

In order to achieve the learning objectives of this chapter, strategic HRD has been examined by reference to seven key questions. We have identified five scenarios likely to trigger a more strategic approach to HRD in the business, and noted five signs that a strategic approach to HRD is being achieved.

USEFUL READING

HARRISON, R. (1993) *Human Resource Management: Issues and strategies*. Wokingham, Addison Wesley.

MABEY, C. *and* SALAMAN, G. (1995) *Strategic Human Resource Management*. Oxford, Blackwell.

MARCHINGTON, M. *and* WILKINSON, A. (1996) *Core Personnel and Development*. London, Institute of Personnel and Development.

McGOLDRICK, A. (ed.) (1996) *Cases in Human Resource Management*. London, Pitman.

STOREY, J. (ed.) (1995) *Human Resource Management: A critical text*. London, Routledge.

WOODALL, D. *and* WINSTANLEY, D. (eds) (1992) *Case Studies in Personnel*. London, Institute of Personnel and Development.

3 Human resource development goals, strategy and plans

LEARNING OBJECTIVES

After reading this chapter you will:

- understand the importance of vision and values in developing a strategic approach to the development of people in an organisation

- understand the business-led approach to formulating HRD goals and strategy in larger organisations (HRD in medium-sized and small organisations – ie those employing up to around 500 people – will be discussed in Chapter 4)

- know how to approach the task of assessing the contribution of HRD strategy to the business.

VISION AND VALUES

Vision and values directly affect crucial decisions relating to investment and the deployment of the organisation's resources, including its people. HRD strategy of any kind relies on the presence, especially at the top of an organisation, of a vision of the business that sees a well-trained and continuously developing workforce as essential to its success. In Chapters 8 to 12 we shall explore ways in which HRD professionals can develop influence in their organisations and promote positive values about HRD at different organisational levels.

Having a written mission statement for HRD may or may not be relevant: it depends on the style of the company and the added value that such a statement might have. More important is a strong and compelling sense of shared purpose: HRD too needs its vision – but it must be consistent with the overall vision of the business, not exist in some separate dimension.

Case-study: My worst mistake

(*Source*: John Garnett, *The Independent on Sunday*, 8 March, 1992)

This point about the need for a convincing, business-led policy for developing people was emphasised in a revealing article by John Garnett, director of the Industrial Society from 1962 to 1986, who admitted that his worst mistake was trying to sell ideas in relation to his own objectives, rather than the objectives of the people to whom he was selling.

He described how his passionate vision about the value of developing people's abilities and potential blinded him during his time as personnel manager of the plastics division of ICI to the equally important need to relate what he did to the objectives of the business. It led to the loss of his job because, he explained:

> My work, in the view of the board, was irrelevant and more seriously, distracting. They were in the business of making profits in plastics, while I seemed to be in the business of developing people, which took their eyes off the main purpose.

Unless the purpose of HRD is seen to be about 'the business', then HRD will fail to convince the business of its value. This could lead to the function's demise. Typical attitudes that reflect a confused vision about HRD and do it no service must be confronted at this stage. Let us look at a few examples:

- *HRD is innately valuable.* Some will see the development of employees as a crucial task, and argue for a heavy investment in it while at the same time showing no real concern to put it in the context of specific business needs or to measure and evaluate its outcomes. Like John Garnett, they simply believe that developing potential is answering a central human need, and is of such innate value that it is bound to bring benefits to the organisation.

- *HRD is essential to keep up with the pack.* Others may argue that HRD must be worthwhile because 'the best companies do it'. Again, there will be no emphasis on clarity of purpose, responsiveness to specific needs, or measurement of outcomes. Best practice is a useful tool for standard-setting in HRD – but only when HRD itself is relevant to the business.

- *HRD is worthwhile in no matter what form.* Others may believe that investing in HRD is justified by a particular organisation's general employment philosophy, and that any developmental activities, providing that they are well designed and stimulate people's 'growth', are worthwhile.

If the prevalent vision of HRD in an organisation rests on these kinds of assumptions, then the outcome is predictable: HRD in practice will be unsystematic, non-strategic and unconvincing to sceptical managers because they do not see its business relevance.

THE WIDER FRAMEWORK OF HRM

A strong framework of HRM policy and systems is essential to the development and implementation of HRD strategy. Here is a case-study about the early stages of turnaround at Cummins Engine, Darlington. Much has been written about the company, and an extended version of this case-study appears elsewhere (Harrison, 1996a). We shall also learn about some of its current HRD practices in Chapter 12, but the purpose here is to show an organisation whose business strategy and HRM framework provided a strong underpinning for the strategic development of its people at a time when that development was crucial for the achievement of the company's long-term business goals.

Case-study: Cummins Engine Co. Ltd, Darlington, UK, 1979–90
(With acknowledgements to the company)

Cummins Engine Company Inc. is the world's largest independent manufacturer of diesel engines. Cummins Engine Co. Ltd. is the UK subsidiary of the company, and has three manufacturing locations, one of which is at Darlington, in the North-East of England. In 1979 the workforce at Darlington numbered around 3,000.

By 1984 the company worldwide was suffering from overcapacity and new competition in a stagnant market, especially from Japan. In the previous year the chairman, whose vision of the company was long-term – a company watchword was and remains 'We're in it for the long haul' – had announced a new strategy to achieve enhanced standards of excellence by investing heavily during the 1980s in order to achieve long-term growth in the 1990s and beyond. The strategy was to be driven by restructuring, high investment in new technology, research and engineering, immediate price-cutting and a compensatory 30 per cent cost-reduction target, to be achieved by mid-1986. At the Darlington works the prime needs were to drive down costs and, within 18 months, introduce sophisticated new technology at one of the sites. The need to negotiate changes with two major unions presented only one of the many challenges faced by the plant's management at that time.

HR strategy at Cummins Engine Co. Ltd, Darlington, 1984

In 1984 Darlington's HR strategy had to be closely aligned with the new UK-wide HR strategy, and had three components to achieve the overall goals of a flexible, efficient and high-quality workforce:

1) continuous reduction in unit labour costs

2) elimination of demarcation barriers, improved rewards for people, and complete harmonisation in terms of pay, terms and conditions of service

3) new forms of work organisation to improve the work flow processes.

This strategy involved three priorities for HRD policy to tackle:

• *To achieve a lean, high-quality and efficient workforce.* Reducing materials costs would make the most impact on the Cummins world-wide target of 30 per cent reduction in costs, since they accounted for 80 per cent of turnover, whereas labour costs accounted for only 20 per cent. The need therefore was to make the labour force more efficient rather than reduce it (although some downsizing was essential). All unit labour costs had therefore to be reduced, especially those related to production time, turnover and absenteeism, timekeeping, working methods and procedures, accidents, materials wastage, quality and inefficiencies due to demarcation.

• *To ensure the workforce had the skills needed to operate the new technology.* A new product, the 'B' series engine, was to be introduced at the Darlington site. Its smooth and fast installation was essential in order quickly to achieve full operational efficiency.

- *To develop a workforce with high added value.* With a target of growth in the 1990s it was essential to start straightaway to improve the skills base of the workforce and employees' ability to learn fast, and be flexible and adaptive. The aim was to reduce costs and add value to the human resource.

The next step, therefore, was to establish clear HRD goals within the framework of these priorities. The goals were:

- to help people achieve and apply the new competencies needed to operate more efficiently, and to adapt to the new culture needed to meet the challenges of change

- to encourage and enable people to work effectively in teams

- to develop managers, especially supervisors, who could manage teams effectively.

HRD strategy flowed from those three goals. Its components were:

- *building an enhanced quality of basic skills in the workplace.* Relevant training would be provided for those with the capability and wish to acquire the skills needed to operate the new technology. For those who were unable or did not wish to do so there were opportunities for early retirement; this also helped to reduce headcount in a relatively painless way.

- *training for all, geared to business needs.* Everyone was to have the opportunity to learn one new skill every year over the following few years. Each employee could achieve up to six skill module increments, and each module was worth 6.6 per cent of salary – a pay progression that supplemented annual pay negotiations.

- *teamworking.* The aim was to develop during the 1980s a new breed of supervisors who would operate quite differently from the way they had before and who, given initial training, would adapt quickly. This has proved to be one of the most challenging areas of HRD activity for the company. It is still involved in developing fully effective teamworking to support the extraordinary rate of increased productivity and advancement made at Darlington during the 1990s.

HRD goals and strategy at Cummins in the 1980s had three defining characteristics:

- They derived from a clear definition and measurements of 'productivity' in different sectors of the workforce and agreement with key parties on which needs would best be met by developing people, which by other kinds of HR policies.

- They were carefully aligned with overall HR strategy and corporate objectives; and they were consistent with wider HR activity, most crucially policies to achieve integrated pay systems and harmonisation of the entire workforce (Pottinger, 1989).

- The approach to HRD at Cummins was collaborative, business-led and pragmatic. Experienced HR practitioners with a fundamental grasp of the business and its environment worked with managers, unions and workforce in a long-term partnership. They operated on the basis of sound and comprehensive data and of learning from carefully monitored experience.

> **HRD vision and goals for your organisation**
>
> Taking your own organisation, or one with which you are familiar, identify the main internal and external challenges facing HRM in the business, and its priority areas.
>
> Draw up a handful of strategic goals for HRD in the organisation and assess how far – if at all – there is a formal or informal HRD strategy that currently supports them, identifying the main barriers or facilitators here. If you experience difficulty with this, you will find helpful insights in the next section to enable you to improve your performance, should you wish to have a subsequent attempt.

SETTING HRD GOALS AND STRATEGY

Today, it is the business-led approach that tends to be the dominating model in establishing the needs to be met by HRD in the organisation. At first sight this may seem to conflict with the principles of a 'learning organisation' with which, as we noted in Chapter 1, there is increasing practitioner interest. Those principles are to do with the natural emergence and resolution of learning needs as part of a continuous cycle of interactive individual and organisational development. The conflict is apparent rather than real, however. One reason is that, as yet, it is hard to find evidence of real-life learning organisations or of their unique characteristics. Another is that a commitment to fostering natural learning processes that can develop strategically relevant knowledge and adaptive, innovative people does not preclude a need also to ensure that learning gaps related to current and targeted business performance are monitored and matched by planned HRD activity.

In Part 5 of this book we shall look in particular detail at the ways in which organisations can operate in order to facilitate rich individual and organisational learning that will produce the knowledge needed for organisational survival and advance. Here, our concern is with ways in which key learning needs related to the proposed corporate and unit business plans can be regularly identified and fed into the planning cycle.

In addition to the business-led approach, there are at least two other approaches – the comprehensive and the problem-centred – that can also have a part to play in identifying learning and development needs in an organisation. These will be outlined later in this section and are described more fully in Appendix 1.

The business-led approach

> To link training with business drivers you have to stand back and take the overview, and ... you need the input of the managing director and the senior team of directors.
> (Ray Jennings, director of management development,
> Dowty Group PLC, 1991)

The business-led approach to developing HRD strategy focuses on those needs seen to arise from:

- the strategy for the business

- operational priorities

- key changes in the organisation's environment or its technical base.

These are what Jennings called the 'business drivers'. Other HRD needs to be taken into account include those revealed by information from performance appraisals and succession planning. The business-led approach is therefore both 'top down' and 'bottom up'.

With the business-led approach, the key decisions about HRD needs and strategy are initiated at board level. They are made at the stage when business strategy and other plans derived from it are being formulated, and should influence as well as be influenced by that strategy-making stage. These decisions are then communicated to business unit managers. Those managers must decide on the kind of HRD targets and plans they should set for their units in order to ensure adequate contribution to meeting corporate goals and effective performance of units within their local environments.

With the business-led approach, HRD information needed by the board has to be provided to it by whoever is responsible for HRD in the organisation. The onus is therefore upon that individual or group to provide accurate and timely information in a form that, when discussed in relation to business strategy, should lead to sound decisions about the direction HRD strategy should take and the goals it should serve. The HRD manager may perceive needs from his or her vantage point that no one at board level can as yet see. If that is the case, he or she must work hard to catch the board's attention and influence its judgement. Convincing the board – either directly or through an intermediary such as the personnel/HR director – is vital, since only the board can authorise HRD strategy and resource its implementation.

It is the business-led approach to HRD strategy, common now across many organisations, that makes the presence of a personnel/training professional at board level so important. Worryingly, research (Rainbird, 1994) indicates that even though in about two-thirds of UK organisations personnel practitioners do have such a presence, they tend to exercise little influence on the formulation of strategy. Their role, Rainbird found, is usually restricted to developing an HR plan to help implement that strategy. Furthermore, relatively few UK organisations have a written HRM strategy, even if most may have some kind of informally agreed direction to HRM in the business. An approach that leaves the crucial responsibility for analysing organisational HRD needs to a top level of management which may not have even an informal HRM strategy will pose particular problems for HRD in that organisation. Without a secure framework of employee resourcing to support HRD initiatives, those initiatives are unlikely to prove durable over time. Many are likely to fail at the initial stages of implementation.

The systematic training cycle

At this point it is relevant to distinguish between taking a systematic approach to HRD and taking a business-led approach to HRD strategy. The so-called 'systematic training cycle' was used to formulate the employer-led Lead Body Standards for Training and Development (to be examined in Chapter 9). The cycle involves a circular process of identifying and analysing a spectrum of training needs, planning and designing training, delivering training events, monitoring and evaluating their outcomes and effectiveness, and feeding the results of that evaluation into ongoing identification of needs. The cycle lies at the heart of the 'comprehensive approach' described below and in Appendix 1.

Although it has been speculated that HRD strategy-making will become an increasingly systematic activity as the Lead Body Standards achieve more visibility and influence (Marchington and Wilkinson, 1996: 182–4), it is perhaps more likely that the systematic approach will increasingly dominate the training-planning, design and evaluation process. Ensuring consistency throughout that process is after all the main purpose of that approach. In the matter of determining HRD goals for the business, as well as in the matter of passing final judgement on the success of HRD strategy, the ultimate power lies with top management. It does not lie with training managers or other HR professionals, no matter how senior. Whether or not that power is exercised in the rational, cool and detached way implicit in the systematic training cycle model, it is upon the exercise of that power that the direction of HRD strategy is likely to continue to depend.

In today's organisations, operating in increasingly turbulent and unpredictable environments, the reality tends to be that HRD must be seen to respond directly to business needs. A logical, systematic approach should of course be applied to analysing the nature of those needs in order to establish which require an HRD response, and to determine what kind of response that should be. If, however, there is failure to agree on whose logic and rationality should prevail in that analysis, and if the HRD spokesperson is unable to marshall his or her arguments with sufficient political skill and conviction, then systematisation of information will not be enough. At board level the language of functional reason rarely prevails when it is different from the established language and logic of the business. That base line is unlikely to alter.

The problem-centred and the comprehensive approaches
These approaches are described in more detail in Appendix 1. In outline, the *problem-centred approach* involves identifying those major current organisational problems with which HRD is best placed and most relevant to deal, and focusing the organisation's HRD investment mainly on responding to those problems. The *comprehensive approach*, on the other hand, involves obtaining from departmental or functional managers across the organisation – usually on an annual basis – their diagnosis of all needs facing their units, and agreeing with them on those to which HRD can offer an appropriate and efficient answer. The organisation's HRD investment is then focused on meeting those needs using some form of prioritisation.

The approaches may be used as alternatives or in conjunction within an organisation. For example, one may be used across most of the business, the other in just one or two areas of the business. Both approaches require HRD to be seen as business led, emphasising that it must be a means to an end (not an end in itself), cost effective, focused on business needs and driven by a collaborative process. Both approaches identify what HRD has been done in a business unit, what needs to be done, what can be done, and at what cost.

However, each has significant weaknesses. Reliance on the *problem-centred approach* may lead to failure to focus on development as distinct from simply training, and result in a short- rather than long-term perspective. Reliance on the *comprehensive approach* may lead to a narrowing preoccupation with individual departments' or business units' needs at the expense of the overall needs of the organisation. It is also a very time-consuming process, and therefore costly.

A practical framework linking individual learning, HR planning and the achievement of business needs

At corporate level the task is to link HRD strategy both to wider employee resourcing strategy and practice and to the anticipated and changing demands facing the business. This involves achieving an integration between HR planning, activity arising out of that planning, and organisational and individual learning strategies. We shall examine in detail in Chapter 13 how to identify and respond to individual learning needs in order to achieve individual and organisational growth, and in Chapter 18 how to achieve an integrative approach to career development. Here, we can establish an initial framework which relates HR planning to employee resourcing activity in the organisation, and takes a generalised look at the kind of learning strategies that are appropriate in each main area of HR planning. We shall amplify the framework in the later chapters.

You will find below an aid to improve your understanding of this interrelationship. Remember that at this stage we still have much ground to cover in relation to analysing and responding to the learning needs of individuals and groups. This is therefore only an initial opportunity to come to grips with the area of HRD planning activity in its wider planning context.

HR planning and generalised learning strategies in your organisation

You will find it helpful to read Hackett (1997: 34–52) before tackling this activity. You may also find the framework in Table 2 of use.

First, find out what overall HR plan exists in your organisation, and identify the main ways in which it is intended to support corporate goals and strategies.

Then take *one division or unit* of the organisation and identify the HR activity that has been and is taking place in order to implement that plan, and the general kinds of learning strategies that support that activity.

Analyse any inconsistencies you may find, either between intended and actual HR activity in the division/unit, or between HR activity and the learning strategies related to it. Then make any necessary recommendations to improve the implementation of the plan.

Table 2 A framework for matching business needs with employee resource planning activity and organisational learning strategies

HR planning	HR activity	Learning strategies
For staffing, to produce HR plan to enable corporate goals and strategies to be achieved.	Job analysis, job design. Audit of skills needed and analysis of external and internal skills supply. Plans to deploy personnel to build up a cohesive internal labour market.	Induction and basic skills training. Training in HR planning and related techniques for HR staff and line managers.
For performance management and development, to ensure continuous 'fit' between business needs and human performance.	Establishing desired performance levels. Plans to improve performance and to facilitate continuous development. Establishing reward systems. Assessment of potential. Planned approach to career development.	Coaching, mentoring and continuous feedback. Performance review and appraisal. Continuous learning and self-development. Promotions, job movement and access to continuing education and training opportunities. Training for HR staff and line managers in relevant HR skills and understanding related to performance management and development.
For change, to enable the organisation to respond to emergent challenges and needs.	New internal skills audit. Re-analysis of patterns of skill supply in external labour market. HR policies to achieve new balance of skills and capabilities needed to adapt to changed internal and external situation. Ensuring internal consistency of all HR policies and systems that will facilitate and support change.	Retraining of individuals, teams, management sector. Organisation development (OD) programmes to achieve cultural change and the development of new organisational and individual capabilities. Training in OD process and interventions and the facilitation of change for HR personnel.
For replacement and restaffing, to facilitate processes of transition and transformation.	Policies to ensure retention of strategic capability of the organisation at corporate, unit and individual levels. Integrative approach to disengagement and new recruitment.	Supportive disengagement strategies and timely phasing in of new internal and external recruits. Training for HR staff and line managers in awareness and competency related to disengagement and restaffing processes.

Developed from an original framework suggested in Schein, 1978: 201

PRODUCING HRD PLANS AT BUSINESS UNIT LEVEL

Once corporate goals and strategy for HRD have been established, plans covering each main area or sector of HRD activity can be drawn up.

Plans will usually operate on a rolling basis, and to ensure their effective implementation line managers and HRD professionals must collaborate closely in discussing and agreeing those plans. Direct and obvious indirect costs (such as lost opportunity time, lost production time, reduced quality and wastage during learning time, and so on) need to be identified, as must those benefits that will justify and hopefully outweigh the costs involved.

Objectives for HRD, and plans to achieve them, should be set at business unit, divisional, and departmental levels, and at individual operational levels. The aim should always be to produce clearly defined objectives, together with agreed methods of assessing the outcomes of HRD.

A company's annual report should contain a section within the business plan completed by every business unit about that unit's human resources and their performance and productivity levels. This should be matched with information about the unit's investment in HRD. Such an approach to business unit planning is a certain indicator that HRD is recognised throughout that company as crucial to business success.

It is particularly important that plans for individuals working in the business units are seen by those individuals to be relevant and rewarding. At this point there will often be tensions. Some will arise because manager and individual disagree over what training and further development are needed, and why. Some will arise because certain developmental objectives urged by the manager as essential in relation to business needs will not, if achieved, bring meaningful rewards for the individual; or because the parties disagree on priorities for objectives. All these tensions have to be resolved if HRD in business units is to respond to business needs while also having the commitment of individuals.

Five steps are usually involved in the process of producing HRD plans at unit level, as can be seen in Table 3.

Below is a case-study – significantly inspired by a model of training and development that was produced in Marks & Spencer plc in the early 1990s but that contains other elements also – to illustrate how HRD mission, strategy and plans can be aligned with the driving needs of the business. It shows how a business-led approach to determining HRD goals and strategy need not conflict with a commitment to foster also a learning culture in an organisation that needs not only to survive but also to innovate and advance.

Table 3 Five steps in producing HRD plans at unit level

1	Focus on corporate goals and the unit's business targets for the coming period, related to those goals.
2	Identify group and individual gaps in skills, knowledge and attitudes in the division or unit that it is essential to close in order to meet targets, and express these in terms of standards to be achieved.
3	Agree on HRD plans to meet the standards.
4	Set specific objectives for every component of plans.
5	Monitor HRD at regular milestones and adjust as necessary.

Case-study: Developing people in a quality-driven retail business

The competitive environment

The company is a national high-street retail store. It has always set an exceptionally high value on its workforce and the contribution they can make to the business. The issues it faces during the 1990s are typical of most such companies: continued expansion into international markets, more demanding customers, more innovative competition and changing composition of the business.

Challenges both outside and within the company that influence its overall employee resourcing policy are to do with:

• a more turbulent economic and competitive environment

• new technologies and computerisation demanding new skills and attitudes

• growing demands of new and existing employees, who are recruited because of their high calibre and potential

• the continuous pace of change

• a drive to achieve more with less but also to improve quality and customer service continuously.

HRD vision and mission

Recent review of various strategic options for the business involved an examination of existing training practice. The following weaknesses in that practice became evident:

• HRD was primarily about 'training'.

• Training took place off the job and away from people's place of work.

• It catered for generalised rather than specific needs.

• It was the responsibility of the specialist personnel function.

• It was remedial.

• It was not focused, nor was it targeted on business needs.

There is now a new vision of HRD in the company. It is that the most effective learning comes from experience, the primary place for this being the work environment; and that individuals and the company derive most benefit from a situation where people take responsibility for their own training and development.

A new mission, reflecting this vision, has been produced:

> HRD in this company will be business led, timely, and be driven by each individual and their line manager. Its purpose is to enable our people to become fully capable in their jobs and to be motivated to continuously improve their performance so that the goals of the business and of individuals can be achieved to their mutual benefit.

HRD policy

The new HRD policy is committed to ensuring that:

• every individual takes responsibility for his or her own continuous training and development, rather than leaving it in the hands of 'specialists'

- all managers actively support the development of their staff and that they will be appraised on this integral part of their job

- learning and work should be integrated, and so planned learning and developmental experiences will mainly take place in or adjacent to the workplace

- the development of people will be an activity that is fundamental to their ongoing work, and that HRD must lead to visible changes at work. Some of these changes will be immediate, others will become evident over the longer term.

HRD strategy and plans

The goals and strategy for HRD established at corporate level focus on key short-term and longer-term business needs. One major goal prioritises management development, since without fully capable managers the company cannot make and implement the strategic decisions that will bring it long-term profitability and growth. The company needs adaptable, flexible and innovative managers who can provide the vision and leadership that will ensure full motivation and understanding in the rest of the workforce. Its managers must learn quickly from experience and be outward looking, strategically minded and inquisitive to discover new trends, challenges and information that will be relevant to the company's future direction.

This goal has led to a strategy of focusing management training on technical skills and general management skills. Managers are developed through the jobs that they do, and there is a strong emphasis on discovering and fully realising their potential at key points in their career history. Policies and plans have been drawn up for those at junior management, middle management, senior management, executive and director levels. They detail learning objectives and outcomes to be achieved, the key features and time-scale of the learning system involved, those whose needs the plans are intended to meet, those who will be responsible for ensuring the effective delivery of the plans, and the monitoring and evaluation process.

ASSESSING THE CONTRIBUTION OF HRD TO THE BUSINESS

We shall be looking more closely at how to assess HRD's contribution to the business in Chapter 12. Here, however, it is important to note that there are four key questions to ask about the HRD function that seeks to make a strategic contribution to the organisation:

- Is there a good fit between the vision and strategy of HRD and wider ER and organisational vision and policy?

- Will the expected outcomes of HRD meet key business needs?

- Does the way the function is organised enhance its ability to implement and achieve its strategy?

- Are the HRD professionals expert in their roles and tasks?

In organisations whose values emphasise people as a major and long-term resource for the business, the need for an investment in HRD

Table 4 Eight key processes in producing and implementing business–led HRD strategy

1	Establish and maintain informed, proactive and collaborative relationships with the key parties in the organisation, especially at corporate and business unit levels.
2	Ensure understanding of key issues and commitment to action at the top level.
3	Walk and talk the job, in order to identify HRD needs and establish a proactive HRD presence in the business.
4	Carry out continuous data-gathering and planning with line management and other key parties.
5	Continuously align HRD policy and plans with business strategy through use of a wider ER strategy.
6	State desired outcomes and bottom-line contribution for HRD in the business.
7	Work with management to ensure ongoing monitoring and feedback of results, and relevant action arising from that feedback.
8	Keep fully informed about 'the business', acting on any changes in either corporate or ER strategy that have implications for the development of people.

strategy that will produce maximum growth of that human asset will probably be taken for granted. Where there is not such a culture, there is likely to be pressure from top management for HRD practitioners to 'assess the payback'. The greater that pressure, the more difficult the task, because in reality the HRD function is being required to justify its existence: its position in the business is clearly already under threat. It has to be acknowledged that in that kind of situation even the most systematic, rational and well-evidenced assessment may not be enough to defeat the opposition (see the case of Barratt in Harrison, 1992).

The assessment of HRD in the business is more a matter of process than of procedure. Expert HRD managers will ensure that the processes they use in all their work involve line managers from the earliest stages. To the extent that they are involved, and that HRD strategy and practice emerge from and build upon that involvement, HRD has a much improved chance of becoming accepted as a function that adds value in and to the business, rather than being one that is asked to prove its worth at every step.

Table 4 shows eight key processes involved in establishing business-led and strategic HRD in an organisation.

CONCLUSION

In order to achieve the learning objectives of this chapter we have examined the importance of establishing vision and values for both the organisation and for HRD policy, and have identified typical attitudes to HRD encountered across organisations. Having noted the importance for HRD of the wider employee resource system, approaches to analysing business needs to guide HRD goals and strategy have been explored. The business-led approach has been given priority, but the uses of two other approaches – comprehensive and problem-centred – have been indicated.

A planning framework has been proposed for matching business needs with organisational and individual learning strategies, and a five-step approach to producing HRD plans for the business has been provided.

Four key questions have been established to assess the contribution that HRD can make to the business – a topic to be explored in detail in Chapter 12. The importance of process in ensuring that HRD has a high value for the organisation has been noted, and eight processes have been identified as essential to the effective development and implementation of HRD strategy.

USEFUL READING

BURGOYNE, J. (1988) 'Management development for the individual and the organisation'. *Personnel Management*. Vol. 20, No. 6: pp. 40–44.

HACKETT, P. (1997) *Introduction to Training*. London, Institute of Personnel and Development.

HARRISON, R. (1992) 'Employee development at Barratt', in D. Woodall and D. Winstanley (eds), *Case Studies in Personnel*. London, Institute of Personnel and Development: 103–15.

MOORBY, E. (1991) *How to Succeed in Employee Development: Moving from vision to results*. Maidenhead, McGraw-Hill.

4 Training and development in the smaller organisation

LEARNING OBJECTIVES

After reading this chapter you will:

- understand the context for employee resourcing and development in the smaller organisation

- understand the main issues related to the practice and provision of training and development in the smaller organisation

- be able to identify where a more systematic and focused approach to training and development in the smaller organisation becomes appropriate.

SMALLER ENTERPRISES

Small to medium-sized enterprises (SMEs) are those independent organisations employing a workforce of up to about 500. Some argue that there is a case for also including in this category divisions and establishments of large groups that employ no more than 500 people, are in most respects autonomous, and operate in an insecure environment. SME definitions vary, but all involve dimensions of workforce size, ownership and annual turnover. The Department of Trade uses the following classification system:

- micro: up to nine people

- small: 10–99 people

- medium: 100–499 people.

Turnover can range from £500,000 for the smaller firms to around £33m. for medium-sized enterprises.

To obtain a perspective on the scale of small-firm employment and its impact on the economy, Becket (1996), generalising from a wide range of research findings, observed that:

- in 1993 there were 3.6m. active SMEs in the UK, of which 2.6m. were sole traders (including those self-employed) or partnerships without employees

- 96 per cent of all companies in Britain employ fewer than 20 people, and that 91 per cent have fewer than 10

- around one-third of all jobs are in firms with fewer than 20 employees, and half of all jobs are in firms with fewer than 100

- 3,000 of the UK's largest businesses account for 37 per cent of jobs and 43 per cent of total turnover, whereas 80 per cent of VAT revenue is collected from 1 per cent of businesses

- small companies account for 23 per cent of gross domestic product, and that in 1995 SMEs grew by 9 per cent, compared with 2 per cent for all GDP.

The nature and extent of SMEs' contribution to the economy has been much debated. According to the Institute of Directors, four out of five small firms now go under within six years. In the Fifteenth National Small Firms Policy and Research Conference held in November 1992, several of the contributors wanted support to be shifted away from encouraging start-ups towards helping mature SMEs. They thought it unlikely that stimulation of new businesses would promote more wealth or jobs: Britain had a far greater increase in self-employment in the 1980s than other developed countries, and created more new businesses than most of its international competitors, yet there is little evidence that this had any impact on total employment (Batchelor, 1992).

Whatever the arguments, the established smaller firm clearly has a role to play in promoting economic growth, in widening society's entrepreneurial base and exploiting new market opportunities and, in recession, in absorbing capable unemployed people – especially executives – who have suffered from the downsizing and delayering of larger organisations. In December 1992 the government announced the introduction of Business Link, a nationwide network of business advice centres to act as one-stop shops concentrating their activities on helping mature small firms.

MANAGING AND DEVELOPING PEOPLE IN THE SMALLER ORGANISATION

Most of the literature concerning HRM in the UK derives from its observation in larger organisations, but there is no evidence that the conclusions reached in that context will apply to managing people in smaller organisations (see Ritchie, 1993). Managerial issues, problems and feasible solutions in SMEs tend to be very different from those facing large firms. Keasey and Watson (1993: 195–200) explained some of the reasons:

- Costs – not least the cost of time spent dealing with paperwork – are a major preoccupation. Relatively high transaction costs typify the smaller firm, which has to deal with a complex set of regulatory requirements and negotiation, financing, monitory and bonding activities.

- Major uncertainties surround SMEs' continued viability and survival:

  - They have a limited customer and product base and are vulnerable in the market, especially when they operate in areas where competition is fierce or are struggling for a new market where there are many obstacles to entry.

- Capabilities of owner–managers vary widely and directly affect the firm's chances of survival. In the UK, given its poor record in management education, many will have little knowledge of basic management practice. Many, too, see no need to acquire any, priding themselves on 'gut feel' for the business they are in. (The term 'owner–manager' is used in this chapter as shorthand for those who run small firms as a single owner, a partnership, a franchisee, or similar.)

- Opportunities for growth may be passed over, the owner–manager often fearing that they will threaten his or her desire for independence and for doing a good job. Many small firm owner–managers do not have substantial growth as their goal: survival and stability constitute the focus of their financial strategy, and loss of control is seen as the greatest threat posed by growth.

- Face-to-face conflict is endemic in smaller firms because the owner–manager is so intimately involved in managing employee relations and carries a high burden of financial risk.

These factors, interacting in complex ways, exert unique pressures on areas of HRM such as recruitment, rewards, training and employee relations. They differentially affect the way each SME is structured, its decision-making processes, how much the owner–manager is paid and the extent of profit retention.

Management in the smaller organisation

Take any smaller organisation with which you are familiar; it may be a business or a charitable undertaking, a professional partnership or a franchise – there are many types from which to choose. Analyse the organisation by reference to the factors just listed and comment on the ways in which they appear to influence management style and systems in the organisation, and the kind of problems it typically experiences.

Employment relationships in the smaller firm are therefore not simple. Not all small-firm employees share the aspirations and outlook of the owner, so that the concept of employee protection through collective organisation can be highly relevant in some cases. Conditions in SMEs can be harsh and exploitative, far from the 'small is beautiful' image (Ritchie, 1993). None the less, the exercise of managerial control tends to be easier in the smaller than in the larger organisation, even if it is not necessarily more effective. Marlow and Patton identify common characteristics of small owner–manager firms that are relevant here (1992: 8, 9):

- SMEs are less likely to have a union presence, and owner–managers are unlikely to consider trade union issues relevant to their organisation. This gives the owner considerable power over the contractual relationship, work conditions and the management of performance.

- In the formative years especially, management style and tactics will exercise a dominating influence on the culture of the firm. Every employee will be directly exposed to the owner's managerial style and will know it well.

- Whatever their conditions of employment and work, employees will tend to identify strongly with the owner's strategies and business goals because their jobs and security are so directly tied up in them. Goal conflict, and the need for bargaining to resolve it, is however likely to develop once ownership spreads to more than one or two individuals, and once salaried managers are introduced.

- Recruitment and selection techniques will be biased towards identifying individuals who 'fit' the culture rather than those who possess formal professional managerial qualifications.

- SMEs are flexible and small enough to change their management practices and training initiatives as the organisation fluctuates in size. The necessity for and results of such change can also become quickly apparent.

In summary, management and development in the smaller as compared with the larger organisation operate in a context of more flexible labour, more individualised employment relationships, a clearer and shared perception of the primary goal and a greater awareness of the need for change.

HRM as a planned activity in SMEs

Given this general context, there are two ways of viewing HRM in smaller organisations. One is to see its practice as a conscious attempt to manage people in ways that will help the firm to achieve competitive edge. The other is to see it as no more than the essentially unplanned consequence both of lack of management skill to introduce formal HR systems and of the particular pattern of management–labour relations in the smaller firm (Marlow and Patton, 1992: 9).

There is in fact little evidence of a planned or strategic approach to HRM in SMEs in the UK. This is despite the fact that HRM practice and philosophy directly affect the predominantly informal and continuous processes of strategy-making and implementation in smaller organisations (Pettigrew, Arthur and Hendry, 1990). In 1990 Price Waterhouse looked at SMEs throughout Europe and concluded that although management and production skill shortages are critical barriers to growth, British SMEs are less likely to have employment management strategies or training schemes to overcome these barriers. It seems that HRM in smaller UK organisations is not widely held to 'matter' in any formal, strategic sense, even though the effective management and development of people is such a key determinant of their survival.

This apparent failure to take HRM seriously in smaller businesses is not, on reflection, surprising. Managers will always focus their attention on those factors that they see as most likely to bring success, and only rarely do management skills and the administration of the employment relationship come under scrutiny here. Financial factors are the most frequently quoted in studies of SME failure, and the widest-used measures of success relate to increased sales, employment growth and crude profit levels (Kelmar, 1990). HRM factors receive little attention, despite their self-evident importance: 'Effective and efficient use of human resources can make the relatively small differences which allow some firms to make step function increases in performance while others struggle to make marginal gains' (Marlow and Patton, 1992: 4).

Most owner–managers in the UK are also unlikely to have had any formalised management/HR education or training, and so are often unaware of HRM's true meaning and complexity. In a study of how best to implement Investors in People (IIP) programmes in smaller organisations, Harrison and Lord (1992: 6) observed that owner–managers 'are unlikely to be able to relate their fragmented and unfocused experience of managing people to the formal systems and procedures' involved in such programmes. Furthermore, they are preoccupied in the early growth years of the business and in transition and terminal stages with coping with urgent and demanding financial and market pressures, and so:

> are unlikely to have the time, knowledge or experience to make appropriate policies [or] to make the shift from task to people orientation. They have a strong need to appreciate the relevance of any initiative that may eat into their business time.

Understanding patterns of employee resourcing and development in SMEs

Hendry, Jones, Arthur and Pettigrew (1991) showed that to understand a smaller firm's employee resourcing practices it is necessary to:

* understand the history of the firm

* examine its survival and growth strategies

* identify its strategies to obtain skills, and the factors influencing those strategies

* examine its approach to training and development.

HR consultancy for the smaller organisation

You are a consultant advising a small enterprise on its business strategy (choose any kind of small organisation you wish for this exercise, but preferably one with which you are familiar since this will make the task more convincing). In discussion with the owner–manager you have quickly reached the point where you realise that you must convince him or her of the need for a more effective use of the enterprise's people. Your reasons are to do with business growth, complexity and change, and with the associated need to move into longer-term planning in order to advance in a competitive market. What should you do, and how, in order to help the owner–manager understand the issues and appreciate the need to develop some kind of planned approach towards the recruitment, retention and development of the kind of people the business now needs?

The check on page 51 is lengthier than usual, since it is intended to simulate a real-life experience in which you need to think through the kind of information that can give you a real understanding of a small firm's HR practices and needs. Rather than trying to use Hendry's four points directly, rely instead on your own common sense to guide your response.

Feedback notes
- Your aim is to raise the awareness of the small-firm owner–manager about the cost, value and potential of the human resource employed in the business. To do this you can use a series of apparently simple but revealing questions that focus consistently on cost and payback.

- Avoid any appearance of lecturing the owner–manager on 'the importance of personnel–HR management'. Speaking the language of the business is essential, but the real challenge will lie in applying it in a way that ensures that key HR issues emerge naturally as the dialogue unfolds. I once had to involve a small group of owner–managers on a business growth course in a discussion of this kind. Each came from an entirely different kind of business, and each had a quite different personal profile, history and approach to the management of his or her organisation. Their scepticism about 'HRM' was evident. At first they gave only short and fairly dismissive responses to questions. Soon, however, the probing nature of the questions made such responses impossible – they had to think things through. They became more actively involved and were soon engaged in heated discussion. Finally, all volunteered that they had not thought in this way about their people before – and that they had become aware of pressing issues that they had now to take seriously. The kinds of questions they were asked were quite straightforward. They included:

- What is the current turnover of the business, and how far has it increased or declined since last year? What is the target for next year?

- What are the main areas of cost – for example, what is your total salaries and wages bill?

- How much of your own time do you spend directly on people matters? What is that in terms of a proportion of your salary?

- What return do you get on your employee investment? Cost per unit of labour? Productivity per unit of labour? Do you know? If not, why not?

- If the business had to be closed down tomorrow, could you afford to do that – or would the cost of disengaging the workforce make that impossible? Could you 'sell' your workforce – would anyone else want to buy it?

- What kind of people do you have working for the business? Why? How did they come to be there? Should they be there?

- What kind of culture and structure does the firm have? Does it encourage and facilitate people's commitment and good performance? How do you know?

- What is the age, sex and occupational structure of the workforce? Do you know? Anything to be concerned about here?

- How are people 'inducted' into the organisation? Does the process familiarise them with the culture of the organisation as well as with their job?

- What do you do about training people, giving them feedback on performance and helping them to be as productive as possible? Are the processes effective? What is their cost-benefit?

- What do you do to retain people? Pay? Education and career development? Job design and organisation of work? Culture of the business? Anything planned at all? Do you keep the people you want, and for positive reasons?

- Have you got the people you need for the future? How do you know?

- What about management style, both of individuals and teams? Any concerns here? Any controls?

- What about discipline and grievances? Any consistent procedures? Are they fair and open? Do they work?

- What about communications? Do people get the information they need to do their work and to remain committed to the firm? Do they get it in a timely and clear fashion? Do they understand and accept it?

TRAINING PRACTICE AND PROVISION IN THE SMALLER ORGANISATION

Training practice

Training should be a key issue for any smaller firm once it has survived the initial start-up period. However, its scope and direction are strongly influenced by obvious factors such as the stance of the owner–manager, the impact of technology, the interface between training and development within and outside the smaller firm, and the type of firm it is. Four of the factors that, interacting together, form the most powerful context for training in the SME are its size, sector, the stage reached in its life cycle and its skill supply strategy (Hendry *et al*, 1991).

Size

There is an indirect rather than a direct relationship between the size of the firm and its training policy. Increasing size usually brings a more complex occupational structure into the firm, and it is that structure that has a direct impact on training needs and practice.

Larger firms tend to employ staff in all recognised skill categories, indicating a high proportion of clearly defined jobs, whereas about 70 per cent of micro firms (see page 47) do not employ any workers in most recognised skill categories (Cambridge University Small Business Research Centre, 1992: 53). Such firms are also less likely to need or to undertake formal training, and tend to have a low regard for the standards and quality of external training – often through ignorance. Larger firms tend to do more internal training because they see it as flexible and relevant to their needs. They also tend to recruit significantly from national labour markets, whereas smaller firms are more dependent on their local market (Pettigrew *et al*, 1990: 16).

Sector
Recruitment and training needs differ significantly through different sectors. For example, most SMEs (except micro firms) in manufacturing and service sectors have problems in recruiting the skills mix needed to maximise their competitive potential, even at times of high unemployment. Those needs are complex as they respond to technological change and try to survive in increasingly segmented markets (Cambridge University Small Business Research Centre, 1992: 53). There is thus an emphasis on internal training in firms in these sectors. Even here, however, easy conclusions cannot be drawn; service firms, for example, tend to recruit more trained staff (Cambridge University Small Business Research Centre, 1992: 54).

Looking at subsectorial differences, it is skills in the technological and science areas that have grown most, especially in manufacturing firms. This directly affects the recruitment and training strategies of such firms, although the relationship here is not simple because so much depends on the availability of skills within and outside the individual firm.

The stage reached in the firm's life cycle
Ritchie (1993: 112–15) distinguished between first, second and third order firms (in which he included co-operatives, some professional partnerships and franchises). He observed that there are many firms within this typology where specialised HR support hardly looks viable. In order to decide where it might fit it is therefore essential to understand how different all these firms can be and then identify those where a drive for HRM would be appropriate. That said, it seems safe to assume that HR needs in most SMEs will change as the firm itself moves from start-up, through growth, to either a period of stability or further growth, or to failure and close-down.

In start-up ventures the need is often – although not always – to have labour flexibility and loosely defined tasks. Recruitment takes place in that context, and training will tend to be informal and on the job, restricted to teaching or showing people how to reach required performance levels (Hendry *et al*, 1991: 84). During the period of initial growth, as in the start-up period, any except the most obviously necessary training will tend to receive little attention, since other pressures weigh more heavily and other issues more directly determine the chances of survival. In these two periods the factors most likely to influence the ways in which people are attracted, retained, rewarded or disposed of are the values and style of the entrepreneur and an interacting range of product market structure and industry structure factors. In so far as HRM is recognised as being important, most attention will be paid to recruitment, pay and termination.

As the firm becomes more mature, often undergoing change of

ownership, organisational structure and managerial style, the need to develop people for the future as well as ensuring good current performance will be more likely to become evident. At that point the opportunity emerges for training and development to make a strategic contribution to the business. However, there is a problem here. At the time, it may well in fact be impossible to establish what stage of development a firm is entering or leaving – such stages are easier to perceive in retrospect. Also, progress through stages of the life cycle is by no means necessarily a linear process. A deliberate choice may be taken not to grow the firm beyond a certain size or to 'go for growth'. An owner–manager may decide to close the firm down prematurely, or for no apparent reason let it be acquired at some stage. A poll commissioned in 1996 for *The Sunday Times* (Oldfield, 1996) indicated that as many as a quarter of owner–managers would like to sell their business. Most of the firms were not in financial difficulty; it was simply that, for various personal reasons, most owner–managers wanted to 'retire'. In the smaller firm the quirks of human behaviour are more visible than in the larger – but in both it has to be appreciated that economic rationality and a systematic approach can only go so far in influencing action related to the management and development of people.

Skill supply strategy

All firms have some kind of skill supply strategy, no matter how intuitive or disorganised. Hendry *et al* (1991) suggested at least seven internal patterns across various kinds of SME, and the determinants of external and of internal patterns can vary greatly from one firm to the next. In view of this diversity, it is clear that smaller firms will benefit from consciously planning how best to obtain and retain people with the required level of skills; and how and to what purpose those people should be trained and developed.

Keasey and Watson (1993: 211) observed that although in the early days the entrepreneur is likely to favour the internal market, new managerial skills and new levels of sophistication in existing skills are needed as growth occurs. They found that in responding to such pressures there appear to be three types of skill supply strategy:

- The owner may him- or herself develop new skills or implement new procedures.

- There may be internal promotion and development.

- New people may be recruited from outside.

Provision of training

The way in which training is organised and provided in the smaller organisation is, again, to do with a number of interacting factors such as:

- the value attached to training

- the extent and type of training done

- the pace of change affecting skills within the organisation

- the extent to which an enterprise has a significant proportion of key and/or genuinely unique jobs, leading to an emphasis on firm-specific skills

• an emphasis on personal qualities and recruitment from unconventional sources

• the cost of training (Cambridge University Small Business Research Centre, 1992: 54) compared to its likely immediate benefits, and the organisation's relationship with external providers.

It is important to clarify what is meant by 'training provision' in the smaller enterprise. It means that training activity is actually taking place, no matter how or by whom it is being provided. Abbott (1994) found in his research into 350 owner-managed firms employing a maximum of 25 people that a number of constraining factors, including lack of financial resources and time, made the provision of training extremely difficult. This did not, however, necessarily mean that training was either absent or low. He found that in some sectors where there appeared at first sight to be uniformly low levels of training, firms tended to make less use of public provision and rely more on informal training. Some owners, however, did not think that such a way of acquiring or developing skills was 'training' and so did not enter it as such in their official returns on training provision.

In assessing the provision of training in smaller organisations, some commentators tend to regard 'high' (planned, strategic) training as superior to 'low' (informal, fragmented) training. This is misleading. It is not that 'high' is better than 'low', but that these two forms of training are different. The critical issue is whether the training carried out, be it high or low, will most effectively raise the skill base of the labour force.

There is much informal training in SMEs, and it makes a vital contribution to the business (Jones and Goss, 1991: 25). The sector of the firm is important here: in a sector such as the free house, restaurant, and wine bar informal training is widely prevalent for various obvious reasons to do with the nature of the job, the small workforces and the wide geographical dispersion of the sites. Such training can be extremely effective and efficient.

There is another aspect of informal training: it is to do with the nature of the critical skills needed in smaller businesses and how they are acquired. 'Tacit' skills are crucial in small firms (Manwaring and Wood, 1985: 172–3). These are skills that are not taught or acquired by formal processes. They are largely instinctive, part of the individual's repertoire of natural talent or skills mastered so long ago that they have now become habitual and are practised without the need to think about them. They are typified in the way in which someone develops their unique 'knack' of tackling a job and always does it to a high standard of performance and quality. The worker may not be able to explain quite what the key is to this consistent success, but as others watch, copy and listen to him or her as he or she works, they too can begin to achieve similar outcomes.

We shall say more about tacit skills and their value in the final chapter of this book. Suffice it to stress here that for a small firm, as for larger organisations, tacit skills can represent vital strategic assets. This is because their derivation is obscure, they are hard to understand and therefore to copy, and they explain much of the high performance and excellent results that are achieved by the business. Where they are unique to the people of the particular organisation and are valuable in the market, they give competitive advantage. They illustrate powerfully that the informal development of people in the smaller firm (and often in the larger) is in no way inferior to formal training methods – it will in fact be superior where it helps to spread, yet also obscures the true nature of, tacit skills in the workforce. Once a skill becomes explicit, and systematically based training can be provided for it, then the skill becomes mobile and can be poached or copied by other organisations. Loss of valuable tacit skills represents a loss of strategic assets. Hendry and his colleagues found that there was a high proportion of genuinely unique jobs in many smaller firms, and noted the 'desire of SMEs to hang onto and keep hidden specific skills and competences developed within the firm' (Hendry *et al*, 1991: 84).

Here is a case-study to consolidate some of your learning thus far. It is fictional, but draws on many real-life small business scenarios. In it we can see two major issues: the need for the owner–manager to adopt a more planned and coherent approach to developing employees as the firm grows and enters a more complex stage of development, and the high investment this owner–manager has always made in training and development, little of which, however, is likely to be recorded on any official return about 'training' in the firm.

Case-study: Management, training and change in the small firm

Rob Jones, now 47, is the owner–manager of a small manufacturing firm which he founded eight years ago. It has secured a solid place in the market and is now expanding as demand for the product increases. Turnover has increased from £1m. in the early years to nearly £5m. in the current year.

Rob has a team of three key people who, with him, carry the responsibility for the management of the firm. All are around his age and were recruited at start-up. They are hard working and dedicated to the success of the firm, but are not yet agreed on future strategy. Rob and Mark, the production manager, see an international future as the ultimate goal to go for. On the other hand, Bill, the finance manager, is concerned about the implications of that and feels that an expansion within the national market, clearly targeted, would be desirable: it should generate sufficient profit and investment revenue without ultimately leading to the likelihood of merger or takeover. Tony (sales and marketing) is keen to expand the customer base, but has concerns about the fast-growing firm's ability to maintain its quality, delivery and sales standards. The team is shortly to go away for a three-day hotel break in order to hammer out their future goals and strategy – a technique used regularly, but in this case they have a particularly challenging task because of the growing complexity of the business and of the strategic choices it faces.

Rob set up the firm after working for some years as a marketing executive in a multi-national firm. In a major restructuring and delayering exercise, he was one of several to take a golden handshake. Having benefited from a good university education, he is a believer in the educational system and therefore invested some of his severance pay in a 'small business growth course' at a local university business school. He formed many useful academic and small-business contacts while on the course, and at its end he established his own firm, which has prospered.

Rob has always believed that management development in a small firm must mainly be achieved by natural learning processes: their relevancy, low cost and direct relationship to the work situation bring unique benefits. He also believes that the structure of the firm, like the jobs within it, will directly affect flexibility, quality and commitment. The flat, matrix structure he and his small team have carefully developed has so far produced the flexible labour force and adaptable culture that the firm has needed to ensure its survival and growth.

There are three watchwords in the firm: quality, service and best-in-class. Managers and team leaders attend external learning events regularly in order to keep up to date and to develop strong networks; Rob's business school and other external links are productive here.

Rob sees 'development' as getting and keeping a high-calibre management group and workforce team, and enhancing their capabilities for the future. Training means, for him, a combination of informal on-the-job learning and skills-based formal interventions. He uses a management consultant with whom the firm has worked since start-up to help him either provide or buy in the necessary expertise here. As issues of management succession, organisational restructuring and skills change bite deeper, Rob realises the need for a longer-term and planned approach to training and development, and is wondering quite how this can be achieved.

Rob has always spent a large proportion of his time on people-related activities – about 75 per cent, he estimates. Now, with the business entering the most complex and highly pressured stage of its existence, he has major decisions to make – not only about future direction and investment in the business, but about the management and development of an increasingly diversified workforce. He can see that the influx of people at different levels, not least the managerial level, bringing with them different histories and work experiences, has implications for skill and pay levels and for expectations, culture and behaviour in the workplace. He is unsure at this stage whether to continue to rely on consultants for advice in these areas, or whether to buy in some kind of HR person.

Triggers for a more systematic approach to training and development in SMEs

One of the issues in the above case-study is to do with triggers for a more systematic provision of training and development in smaller firms. Hendry et al (1991) found in their research that although the growth of formal business planning in the firm did not tend of itself to act as a trigger, often – like Rob – the managing director had a view of where the company should be in the future and would broadly support educational initiatives in line with that. It is in this way that a focus on development rather than just on immediate training can emerge. Harrison and Lord (1992: 10) found that training and development activities consumed a significant proportion of time in smaller firms. They became more managerially oriented with growth, many being 'related to new staff or potential "stars" who were identified to take the weight from the owner manager in terms of administrative help or staff training'.

Common triggers

Hendry *et al* (1991) identified a number of common triggers for a more formalised and systematic approach to training in the smaller enterprise. Their interactions tend to be complex and peculiar to the particular firm, but there is value in identifying them at this point:

- *The skill supply strategy of the firm.* Inability to achieve the kind of skill supply it needs often directs a firm's attention to the value of a longer-term, planned and systematic approach to training within the firm. The extent to which this trigger operates, and the way in which it does, will be influenced by several interacting factors: the competitive environment, the firm's existing or proposed technology, the type of external labour market from which it can draw its labour, typical pay rates and training costs in its sector, the vulnerability of its labour market to government intervention of various kinds, and the firm's size and stage of development.

- *Acquisition of new technology.* The introduction of new technology may in some firms lead to a drive for training or retraining, but in others it could lead to a drive for recruitment, or to a reorganisation of the workforce. Again, the specifics of the situation are the determinants of the kind of drive that is triggered.

- *Customer relations.* Attempts to improve quality systematically can lead to specific training programmes, but also increasingly generate an HRD environment – project teams, worker involvement and participation, improved work systems, re-education in the workplace etc. They also often result in the workforce raising wider developmental issues such as personal career advancement, demands for a job-grading structure and clearer pay progression.

- *Growth.* Growth, like the acquisition of new technology, affects different firms in different ways. With rapid growth, and especially with pressure of production, training may be influenced adversely or positively. Adverse effects will occur, for example, if management has a short-term perspective with no forward planning or vision. Too much will then be likely to happen at once for there to be the clarity of thought that will produce ordered training and longer-term development strategy. 'A strategic vision – backed by market projections but not necessarily embodied in a formal plan – is therefore an important underpinning' (Hendry *et al*, 1991: 69).

- *Management culture related to training.* Whoever owns or controls the SME is its key figure (or figures) whose values and perceptions have a crucial influence on all aspects of the business. Often they may be ignorant as to how training and development can contribute to performance and growth. On the other hand, if they are convinced of the need for a planned, systematic investment, then that conviction will become a major trigger.

- *Workforce expectations and desire for betterment.* Although these are strongly affected by management's stance towards training, employee attitudes can be ambivalent. It is their own background and qualifications that will be as important as those of top managers in setting the climate for training in the firm (Hendry *et al*, 1991: 70).

- *Systematisation of pay in relation to skill.* The introduction by a firm of a pay structure that defines skill requirements and specifies how these can be acquired through training and education is a powerful trigger for a more systematic and formal approach to training in that organisation.

- *A recognised structure of skills and vocational qualifications for the whole workforce.* Such a structure will have the same kind of effect as the pay structure just noted, and should help to ensure that the potential of everyone in the firm is realised, rather than some advancing more than others. Over time it should produce a positive and committed culture related to training and development in the firm.

- *The advent of a large cohort of new recruits.* The sudden recruitment of a relatively large cohort into a smaller firm can radically disrupt planned training and distort patterns of growth. For SMEs it is particularly important to provide a 'natural life-cycle of training which matches the cohort progression of employees' (Hendry *et al*, 1991: 82).

- *Costs of training.* Constrained resources – especially of finance – can significantly inhibit training in the smaller firm; another constraint is the difficulty of releasing people for off-the-job training. What will matter most is the cost of formalised training balanced against the extent to which it can give demonstrably short-term, bottom-line results to offset those costs (Cambridge University Small Business Research Centre, 1992: 54).

The local infrastructure of education and training

There is evidence (quoted in both Cambridge University Small Business Research Centre, 1992 and in Hendry *et al*, 1991: 84) to indicate that although government agencies are perceived much less favourably in terms of standards and quality than further education institutions, smaller firms give considerable support to external vocational education. Awareness of group training schemes and facilities, external funding, and cheap but good-quality external educational provision can all help to minimise formal training costs.

Most Government initiatives have been launched and delivered without real evaluation (Jennings, Richardson and Beaver, 1992: 10) and in consequence there is little certainty that external training provision will meet a firm's needs. National Vocational Qualifications (NVQs) and the work of the Management Charter Initiative (MCI), defining national standards related to management, are often judged to do little 'to meet the needs of flexibly structured, flat, often matrix managed small firms' (Harrison and Lord, 1992: 10). All in all, it is unsurprising that some conclude that:

> The current provision and delivery system fails to meet the needs of small business owner–managers, primarily because of the lack of contextualisation towards the special requirements of the sector. Equally the products and services on offer do not address core strategic issues of particular relevance to the current, difficult pressures which restrict business development.
>
> (Jennings *et al*, 1992: 26)

Training in the smaller organisation

From your reading on employee development (ED) in smaller organisations thus far, and from your own knowledge of SMEs in your locality, what appear to be the main barriers to providing a more coherent approach to training in an SME and the main factors likely to overcome them?

Feedback notes

The most common barriers to a more coherent approach to training and development in the smaller organisation are:

- *scepticism about value*. Often this comes from history – 'a bad training experience can be damaging to training provision' (Kirby, 1990) and repetition of such experiences reinforces the scepticism.

- *constrained resources*. There is often a perception of inability to pay, of lack of time, and of the likelihood of lost opportunity costs.

- *ignorance and complacency*. These usually come in the form of failure to recognise skills shortages and areas of lack of managerial capability.

- *lack of awareness of sources of external provision and expertise*. Harrison and Lord (1992), in their study of the impact of IIP on a sample of small firms, found that very few owner–managers or their customers had significant awareness of the standard. Those that did often confused it with other standards such as BS 5750 and feared becoming ensnarled in more bureaucratic procedures. The bulky IIP toolkit often created a set of negative expectations. On the positive side, 1996 statistics from Investors in People (UK) showed that 43 per cent of organisations that had attained the standard employed fewer than 50 staff, and there were signs of growing interest from small firms (Thatcher, 1996: 21).

- At the time of writing (mid–1997) NVQ users were working in organisations employing more than 500 people, and although a Small Firms Lead Body had produced a framework of occupational standards and qualifications for owner/managers, the SME unit of the Confederation of British Industry (CBI) found that employers still have insufficient knowledge of and a real concern about the accessibility of NVQs, excessive administration, bureaucracy and costs.

To reduce such barriers, various measures can be taken, sometimes by a key manager within the firm with a commitment to HRD and a perception that it has a valuable contribution to make, but often by an external party – not necessarily, but frequently, an experienced and effective consultant:

- *The firm can be helped to identify a particular area of need with a clear impact not only on the current bottom line but on future capability.* The provider should work closely with key parties in the firm to provide a cost-efficient learning experience targeted to achieve one or two clear objectives, and should agree at the start on measures to indicate the success of the initiative. Achieving that success, and using collaborative processes to do so, will provide a model for a more systematic and focused approach to training in the organisation. A progression of such carefully planned and targeted learning initiatives should slowly begin to change the culture to one that sees 'value' (rather than 'cost') in planned learning (rather than 'training') in the firm.

- *The use of benchmarking, internal as well as external best practice and increased involvement in external local learning networks* should also do much to reduce scepticism and promote interest and perception of relevance. Again, there has to be an agent of change here in order to encourage such moves. By mid-1997 the Department of Trade and Industry (DTI) was planning to establish a small-firms benchmarking service available through Training and Enterprise Councils (TECs) and Business Links.

- *Inability to pay may be an illusion,* since money can usually be found for activities believed to be of direct value for the firm. Where, however, a particular initiative is genuinely too costly, explore other ways of facilitating that learning – mentoring and work-shadowing, for example, instead of formal induction; project teams rather than expensive outdoor development programmes; regular team briefings rather than consultant-led 'teambuilding' courses. Since providing stimulating, cost-beneficial and efficient learning is one of the hallmarks of the good training professional or consultant, this again will generate a model of training for the future in that organisation.

- *Training costs can also be reduced by better knowledge of external provision.* A good consultant can help the smaller firm to become more aware of funding sources and of provision, in line with their needs and their purse. Ineffective consultants are, of course, key barriers to systematising training provision and many consultants lack experience and understanding of SMEs (Jennings *et al*, 1992: 26). Using the local network to find out about consultants and their track record is crucial because 'Small businesses ... find it hard to select the right training of the right quality in a market over supplied with consultants and private providers of training' (Wood, 1992: 8).

- *External and intra-organisational learning networks provide access to many sources of HRD aid for the firm and also stimulate interest and boost confidence.* Two national initiatives illustrate this point.

  1 *Skills challenge,* a government-backed scheme encouraging small

firms to work together to develop new ways of meeting their skill needs, was launched in 1995. In that year 180 firms won between them £5m. in recognition of their innovative training systems.

2   *Business Bridge,* a company mentoring scheme, was launched in 1996. It aimed to give small firms access to experience from top UK executives by getting executives from 30 large companies to work as mentors with teams of owner–managers from over 100 small firms. It is based on the European Union Plato programme, which has helped to raise participating firms' turnover and staff numbers by up to 24 per cent.

OUTCOMES OF TRAINING AND DEVELOPMENT IN THE SMALLER ENTERPRISE

There is little evidence in smaller organisations of training in training needs analysis or training plans (Harrison and Lord, 1992: 10). Failure to document either needs or plans can give the impression either that no training is being done, or that any that is taking place must be unplanned and therefore invalid. As noted earlier, such conclusions can easily be mistaken. In relation to the IIP initiative, for example, Harrison and Lord's research (1992: 12) 'demonstrated a considerable amount of "hidden" training and informal and undocumented human resource management practice which in many cases meet the objectives which the IIP initiative promulgates'.

Pettigrew *et al* (1990: 25) showed that the outcomes of HRM and training in SMEs can be evaluated:

• in terms of impact on current performance goals, as indicated by a range of measures (performance will be the dominating criterion at an early stage of the firm's life cycle)

• in terms of development, as indicated by impact on prospective medium-term outcomes associated with planned changes in products or services, or adjustments to environmental forces

• in terms of learning related to prospective long-term outcomes that are impossible to specify but can be assured only by the growth of strategic capabilities 'so that the firm can cope with crisis or make the big strategic leap forward which unexpected opportunities may present'.

It is important to achieve strategic awareness and thinking across the workforce in smaller organisations, and forms of development and work experience that can enhance those abilities are therefore of particular value.

Training and development pose particular challenges in the smaller firm, but an effective approach to those challenges can offer a better model of alignment of HRD with business needs and of consistency with other areas of HR practice than is to be found in many large-scale businesses. In the smaller firm, for the development of people to survive, let alone succeed, it has no choice but to become an integral part of the everyday operations and processes of the firm. For the

HRD practitioner to be effective – whether as internal or external consultant – he or she must have a comprehensive grasp of the business and its competitive environment, must speak in the language that stakeholders understand, and must be expert at managing the training and development infrastructure of the firm. Such skills are essential to the effectiveness of any HR professional or manager, yet are often found wanting in larger organisations.

Finally, many smaller organisations come close to being what can be recognised as 'learning organisations'. They are fast-reactive, well informed about their external and internal environments, and foster a climate of continuous learning leading to the development of knowledge that is used to innovate and advance. They operate like this not necessarily because there has been any conscious decision to do so, or even an awareness that this is what is happening, but simply because it is in this way that those organisations thrive and manage to attract and retain high-calibre people. (See, for an example of this, the story of HMH Sheetmetal Fabrications Ltd, Co. Durham, in Harrison, 1993b: 335–9).

CONCLUSION

In order to achieve the learning objectives of this chapter we have explored the reasons for differences in approaches to managing and developing people in smaller, as distinct from larger, organisations. Four issues enabling a better understanding of HRM practice in smaller organisations have been discussed.

Training practice and provision in smaller firms have been examined by reference to four aspects of their context and to a number of interacting factors that underpin the organisation and provision of training. Interrelated triggers tending to produce an increasingly systematic approach to training in smaller organisations have been identified.

It has been noted that for training and development to survive, let alone lead to positive outcomes for smaller organisations, those processes must be closely linked to business needs and be planned and managed by people who fully understand the small business world.

Attention has been given to the importance to the smaller firm of informal as well as formal processes of learning in order to develop and retain valued tacit as well as explicit knowledge and skills. Finally, it has been made clear that small firms achieving an effective balance between meeting immediate and longer-term performance and development needs provide models of a 'learning organisation' that can offer instructive lessons for bigger enterprises.

USEFUL READING

ABBOTT, B. (1994) 'Training strategies in small service sector firms: employer and employee perspectives'. *Human Resource Management Journal*. Vol. 4, 2: 70–87.

HARRISON, R. (1993) 'Strategic human resource management at HMH Sheetmetal Fabrications Ltd., 1993', in R. Harrison (ed.),

Human Resource Management: Issues and strategies. Wokingham, Addison Wesley: 335–9.

HENDRY, C., ARTHUR, M.B. *and* JONES, A.M. (1995) *Strategy through People: Adaptation and learning in the small-medium enterprise.* London, Routledge.

KEASEY, K. *and* WATSON, R. (1993*) Small Firm Management: Ownership, finance and performance.* Oxford, Blackwell.

MARLOW, S. and PATTON, D. (1992) 'Employment relations, human resource management strategies and the smaller firm' in *Proceedings of 15th National Small Firm's Policy and Research Conference.* November. Southampton, UKEMRA.

RITCHIE, J. (1993) 'Strategies for human resource management: challenges in smaller and entrepreneurial organisations' in R. Harrison (ed.), *Human Resource Management: Issues and strategies.* Wokingham, Addison Wesley: 111–35.

Part 2

THE WIDER CONTEXT

---

5 National training policy: a review of the system

LEARNING OBJECTIVES

After reading this chapter you will:

- understand the main trends in, and pressures upon, national training policy and strategy in the UK

- have carried out a critical analysis of the present system in order to identify its main strengths and weaknesses

- be able to assess the kind of national training framework most likely to be effective in the UK.

THE 1990s' VISION OF NATIONAL VOCATIONAL EDUCATION AND TRAINING

The current Government's vision of National Vocational Education and Training (NVET) is that 'everyone has the opportunity and incentive to continue learning throughout life, and that the economy has the skills it needs to meet and beat the best in the world' (Employment Department Group, 1991: 28). The vision involves an integration of three areas which will be examined in this and the following chapter. At the end of Chapter 6 they will be pulled together in an overview. The first area, carrying the shorthand title of 'national training policy' is primarily concerned with the education and training of those seeking or in employment. The second area focuses on National Vocational Qualifications (NVQs). The third area, covered in Chapter 6, is to do with key aspects of national educational policy at primary, secondary and tertiary levels.

NATIONAL TRAINING POLICY

Introduction: policy or politics?
The White Paper *Training for the Future* referred to the twofold purpose of NVET policy as being:

Economic and social – to have the right workers in the right place at the right time, with the right skill, and to provide better opportunities to individuals to develop their skills and use their abilities to the full.

(White Paper, 1972)

This duality of purpose poses a problem for national training policy: how best to achieve both economic and social ends? This raises another question: can both ends be achieved in tandem, or will the attempt lead to a constant repetition of that stop-start pattern of reactions that has characterised national training activity throughout most of this century? Such a pattern is mirrored in the attitude towards training in too many UK organisations: a function left to chance, not seen as a strategic contributor to business results.

Between 1964 and 1981 there was no evidence of any meaningful vision guiding national training policy (see Marchington and Wilkinson, 1996: 52–8). Movements into and away from a regulatory framework all coincided with fluctuations in wider economic and social problems and with changing governmental approaches to dealing with them.

However, from 1981 to 1989 during the 'Thatcher years' there was a clear attempt by government to provide a meaningful 'cradle to grave' vision for NVET together with a consistent long-term policy in relation to training for employment. The delivery of policy relied, and still relies, on a voluntary and market-led system introduced in 1989. We shall now examine this system, first by reference to policy and then by reference to the framework by which policy is delivered.

Policy

In 1991, as Table 5 shows, seven aims were established for national vocational training policy. These aims are continuously monitored and will be updated for the year 2000. Let us look at some of the practical questions they raise.

Table 5 The seven aims of national training policy listed in the White Paper *Education and Training for the 21st Century* (1991)

1	To ensure that high-quality further education or training becomes the norm for all 16- and 17-year-olds who can benefit from it.
2	To increase the all-round levels of attainment by young people.
3	To increase the proportion of young people acquiring higher levels of skill.
4	To ensure that people are more committed to develop their own skills throughout working life, and more willing to invest their own time, money and effort in doing so.
5	To help the long-term unemployed and those at other kinds of disadvantage to make their full contribution to the economy.
6	To ensure that trainers and teachers remain responsive to the needs of individuals and business, working closely with business and widening individual choice.
7	To encourage and increase employer commitment to training by having effective enterprise plans that complement work.

Are there adequate incentives for individuals to invest?

For individuals, there has been far less to encourage them to invest in training than in many competitor countries, notably Germany, where increases in wages and career prospects are linked to training and qualifications and where young people are not distracted by high-pay temptations. Of course, some UK firms do make links between qualifications and pay, but there is still a long way to go before this becomes a significant national trend. Tax relief could improve the individual's motivation to acquire vocational qualifications, and in 1992 there were tax concessions to encourage people to pursue vocational training courses. Training credits were by 1997 available for every 16- and 17-year-old leaving full-time education, enabling them to 'spend' up to £1,000 purchasing further vocational training or education of their choice. Such moves, together with career development loans, aim to produce 'market-led' training investment by helping individuals who want to make a new career move or upgrade their skills, and companies wanting to retrain the workforce or adapt to new technology. The Labour Party had by 1997 expressed commitment to the idea of individual learning accounts linked to an extension of tax breaks for vocational learning.

However, the question remains: how far do any such incentives make a significant difference to individuals' motivation to acquire skills and qualifications when the latter are still not tied to a universal reward system? In 1992 a London School of Economics (LSE) study concluded that training did not give sufficient financial reward for post-compulsory education and training, and that young people could be quite rational in not pursuing training because the rewards were too small. It also found that low-level vocational qualifications did not provide earnings equal to academic qualifications often thought of as equivalent (*Personnel Management*, 1992b). A 1994 survey by South and East Cheshire TEC revealed that a significant number of school-leavers who had stayed on in full-time education until the age of 18 obtained jobs little different from those they could have found at 16 (Goodhart and Wood, 1994). Indicators of individuals seeing little value in investing in their own vocational development also appeared in 1992–3 when only 10,000 career development loans were approved, compared with a target of 15,000 (Unemployment Unit and Youthaid, 1996), and when in 1994 the use of training credits by school-leavers going into Youth Training Schemes dropped, as it had been doing every year since introduction, this time to 12 per cent.

Are there adequate incentives for organisations to invest?

This is doubtful. Reasons include the following:

- *Short-termism dominates the financial base of most organisations and the structure of industry generally in the UK*. Large-scale domination of UK businesses by the financial sector and accountancy profession inhibits long-term strategic investment. This leads to the inevitable cycle of times of prosperity, characterised by high profits for shareholders, followed by times of recession, characterised by cutbacks often made in order to avoid overlarge cuts of profits, problems with shareholders, and danger of hostile takeovers just when maintenance of skills and build-up for recovery are needed.

Hostile takeovers are themselves inevitable when companies cannot grow steadily by re-investing retained profits at times of economic fluctuation and when they are pressurised by high interest rates and high dividend yields (Yates, 1990). It is the same vicious circle that explains much of the UK's failure to invest adequately in scientific research and development. Over the long term, as Yates commented, the economy is likely to move into a downwards spiral as its true sources of engendering wealth decline.

- *Fear of poaching.* This fear is valid as long as only the minority of organisations invest heavily in training. Surveys and reports still show that the majority do not have the capacity, or do not see the need, to offer long-term security of employment and a related internal career system. This being the case, many people, especially the upwardly mobile and those possessing valued skills, will move in and out of organisations searching for better terms, conditions and opportunities, and will be open to higher bids for their labour.

- *The real nature of the 'skills market' is not one of a highly mobile population of workers touting their skills to the highest bidder.* If the whole labour market were in fact 'free' in terms of movement of people and skills, then the voluntary approach would work and poaching would not matter, because there would always be a natural balance between supply and demand. In reality, however, most employees are not continuously mobile, and so national skill shortages continue to occur (Dore, 1987). As we shall see later in this chapter, although skill shortages were not widespread by 1997, there remain key areas where supply consistently fails to meet demand – notably in the manufacturing sector.

In 1995 the World Competitiveness Report published by the World Economic Forum stated that the UK's global competitiveness had slipped from 14th in 1994 to 18th. The issue was not only one of labour market efficiency but also of having the skills needed to develop the economy. How best to improve the situation – by a strengthened voluntary training system or by re-introducing some form of levy as a regulatory measure – is a matter for debate, and will be returned to in Chapter 6.

National training policy

What vision and assumptions underpin national training policy, and how far are they realistic?

Feedback notes
- The vision for NVET in the UK is of lifelong continuous learning to ensure that the economy has the skills it needs to meet and beat the best in the world. Implicit in the vision is a twofold purpose to do with meeting both economic and social needs. This duality of purpose poses problems for national training policy.

- National training policy ignores the fact that there are still inadequate incentives for individuals and organisations to invest in vocational education and training to the extent needed by the economy. For the individual, doing so does not, in most cases, lead directly to rewards in terms of jobs, pay or career development. For organisations, there are a number of reasons for continued failure to invest, especially:

* short-termism

* fear of poaching

* lack of a universally mobile skills market.

* For these challenges to be tackled effectively, national training policy needs a workable strategy and framework.

Strategy

National training strategy seeks to achieve an adequate investment in training by a voluntary partnership at local, sectoral and national levels between Government, business, training and education organisations, individuals and the broader community. This partnership exists within a market-led vocational training system whose costs are borne by those who operate in the market – ie mainly by employers and individuals. The six national strategic objectives shown in Table 6 have, since 1989, guided strategy and planning at local level.

The strategy arose from a determination to defeat the weaknesses that, up to 1989, had characterised the national training system:

* Training had consistently been tackled at national rather than local level.

* Central planning had failed to serve national or local interests.

* Programmes tended to be bureaucratic and inflexible.

* Training was often done, or promoted, for training's sake.

* Responsibility for training was laid at the door of government.

Table 6 **The six national training strategic objectives**

1	Employers must invest more effectively in the skills their businesses need
2	Young people must have the motivation to achieve their full potential and to develop the skills the economy needs.
3	Individuals must be persuaded that training pays and that they should take more responsibility for their own development.
4	People who are unemployed and those at a disadvantage in the job market must be helped to get back to work and to develop their abilities to the full.
5	The providers of education and training must offer high-quality and flexible provision which meets the needs of individuals and employers.
6	Enterprise must be encouraged throughout the economy, particularly through the continued growth of small business and self-employment.

Source: Employment Department Group, 1991: 33–6

Framework

The framework for implementing national training strategy operates at national, sectoral and local levels.

At national level

The Department for Education and Employment (DfEE) holds responsibility to the Secretary of State for Education, training and enterprise planning, and functions. Enterprise planning is also a responsibility of the Department of Trade and Industry (DTI) (which, *inter alia*, has a division responsible for industrial relations, including employment agencies).

High quality HR information is essential if national policy and local strategies and plans related to NVET are to be valid. A development framework set up in the early 1990s helps Training and Enterprise Councils (TECs – see below) to improve the quality of training by promoting and sponsoring research that will either help their locality or will have spin-offs relevant to local initiatives. Reponsibility for all statistics relating to employment and unemployment now rests with the Office of National Statistics (although training statistics have stayed with the DfEE).

A National Training Task Force was established in 1989 to assist the Secretary of State to develop the TEC network. This body has now been replaced by the business-led National Advisory Council on Education and Training Targets (NACETT, see page 81). In 1994 another business-led and government-supported body called Investors in People (IIP) UK was launched to boost national promotion of the IIP standard, which seeks to link training to the business needs of companies. A key task is to ensure uniformity in standards of IIP assessment.

The major task at national level is the development of national occupational standards and vocational standards linked to them. This aspect will be reviewed later in the chapter.

At sectoral level

By 1997 there were about 120 non-statutory Industry Training Organisations (ITOs). Independent and local-employer-led, their main role is to identify and monitor key skills needs and training requirements in their sectors and encourage investment in training. Most of them are also Lead Bodies responsible for developing and maintaining standards of competence as a basis for related NVQs. Their success was questionable from the start, and by 1997 it was clear that they would soon be merged with Lead Bodies and Occupational Standards Councils. Some perceived this move as a vehicle for putting more weight behind present Government policies on NVQs rather than as a serious step to focus on employers' and individuals' needs, but others welcomed the attempt to rationalise an overcomplex sectoral framework.

At local level: the TEC system

The TEC system is so fundamental to the whole delivery of NVET policy that it is described here in a separate section.

The TEC system

TECs, introduced in a White Paper in 1989, form the corner-stone of the NVET framework at local level in England and Wales. Their equivalent in Scotland and Northern Ireland are Local Education Councils (LECs). Hereafter we shall refer to 'TECs' as a shorthand for both, since although there are differences in the legal and administrative constitution of TECs and LECs, their public roles are essentially the same.[1] More information about their history and operation is given in Marchington and Wilkinson (1996: 52–4).

TECs are legally autonomous bodies which control the public funds allocated to them, can raise private funds, and are employer-driven in the sense of being dominated in their membership by senior executives from local private-sector organisations. The purpose of the TEC system is to interact with local organisations to regenerate the community and stimulate business growth, particularly through reskilling programmes.

To ensure that they approach their task in a strategic way, TECs have each to produce a detailed Business Plan with local strategic objectives linked in to the six national strategic priorities. These Business Plans have to be approved by the Secretary of State in order to obtain funding. Since 1994 TECs have also had to draw up detailed three-year corporate plans involving details of local partnerships that they are developing.

TECs operate under a rigorous contract specifying standards for their management and performance, and are responsible for national training programmes focused on four key areas:

1 Opportunities for young people
TECs have the task of implementing the Government's guarantee that every young person will have access to Youth Training – relevant education or training leading to recognised vocational qualifications and to a job. A key programme here is Modern Apprenticeship (see page 76).

2 Opportunities for the unemployed
The main programme here is Training for Work, aimed at helping unemployed adults and the disabled to gain qualifications relevant to employment. The major criteria of success are the number of people who achieve NVQs and how many are placed in meaningful jobs.

3 Promoting training for the employed
TECs can provide advice on training needs and how to meet and resource them; enhance access to information about training; encourage use of cost-effective and flexible methods; organise groups of employers with common training needs so that they can invest collectively in learning resources and facilities; design customised training programmes to prepare new recruits for jobs in skill-shortage occupations; and arrange assessment of organisations seeking IIP status (see Marchington and Wilkinson, 1996, Chapter 8). TEC funding can give significant help in establishing certain kinds of training initiatives in local organisations (see, for example, how Barratt, the construction firm, was successful in attracting £74,000 of

pump-priming funding for its new, business-led Sales Training Programme, in Harrison, 1992).

4 Business Growth

TECs work with other local organisations to help new enterprise and expanding businesses by assessing the kind of services they need, advising on how best to meet those needs, and disbursing funds for business growth and enterprise initiatives.

Existing business organisations like Chambers of Commerce and the Confederation of British Industry (CBI) often form the nucleus of a TEC, which is thereby able to build on existing local communications and training networks. Local educational institutions and professional bodies such as the Institute of Personnel and Development and the British Institute of Management can also give help to organisations and individuals. Wider local enterprise funding can be obtained through the Department of Trade and Industry and the European Commission.

Assessing the value of TECs

Why are TECs such an important part of the NVET delivery framework, and what benefits do they offer?

In responding to the above question you will find it helpful not only to revise the previous section but also to contact one or two of your local TECs or LECs to obtain information about their current business plans, their record of achievement, and their links with other local organisations.

Feedback notes

- TECs constitute a radical innovation in the UK training system. They are intended to ensure that NVET is driven by local needs, is based on an active partnership of local interests, and is geared to making a major impact on business growth in every TEC area.

- TECs represent a major source of expertise, funding and other support for local organisations. Since they are at the centre of a powerful local training and enterprise network they should be well placed to help organisations wishing or needing to invest, or increase their investment, in employee development.

- TECs' primary purpose is to influence local labour markets and unemployment. Marchington and Wilkinson (1996: 54) suggest this may mean that the task of training receives a lesser focus and certainly in 1994 the third *Financial Times* survey of TEC directors found that most of them expressed even stronger support than they had done in the previous year for the promotion of economic development as their top priority (Wood, 1994b). On the plus side, however, this concern should ensure that training never becomes an end in itself but is treated as a vehicle for reskilling and regenerating the local economy.

While the concept of getting local, employer-led bodies to head the drive for better investment in training is attractive, the problems come in making that happen. Let us look at some of the problem areas. They are to do with provision for the disadvantaged, remedying national skills shortages, the need for overhauling the TEC system and the challenge facing TECs as they seek to achieve a coherent strategic role.

Providing for the disadvantaged

Since the inception of the TEC system there have been growing concerns about the adequacy of its provision for the disadvantaged in society. This concern has focused particularly on labour market returners and part-time workers, now an invaluable component of the workforce, and most of them women (Equal Opportunities Commission, 1993); on the disabled; and on the most economically, socially and educationally disadvantaged of those young people not in full-time education. Many in these groups are felt by some commentators to be receiving 'training for training's sake' or training that does not help them find work.

The Government's announcement in 1994 that TECs were to move to a performance-related funding contract for training was welcomed in principle because the main focus now was to be on putting trainees into jobs, on their achievement of vocational qualifications, and on training those with special needs, such as the long-term unemployed and the disabled. The move was clearly essential in a situation where only 27 per cent of unemployed people gained jobs after completing a Training for Work (TFW) scheme.

However, there were fears that, in practice, the need to achieve their outcome-oriented targets would drive TECs to place even more young people into unsuitable training and to look carefully at those already on their programmes, as well as at those they would take on in future. The fear was heightened by the fact that TECs had to make a surplus from Government programmes in order to fund schemes of their own. In October 1995 a leaked report from the NEC National Council outlined 'a catalogue of errors and bureaucratic ineffeciencies in the implementation of the TFW programme' (Thatcher, 1995). In November a survey carried out by the Institute of Employment Studies (Littlefield, 1995b) confirmed that the cut of 17 per cent in funding for the TFW programme that had accompanied the move to performance-related funding had reduced the TECs' ability to provide the longer and higher-level skills training needed by the most acutely disadvantaged, and was causing discrimination against such people.

The director of NACRO (the National Association for the Care and Resettlement of Offenders), a large provider of training for disadvantaged people, including ex-offenders, summed up widely felt frustration when she labelled the new regime the ultimate blow to risk-taking and struggling with the most difficult people (Wood, 1995). In September 1996 the Government announced that it was giving TECs £25m. extra funding for 'discretionary projects', including schemes for the most disadvantaged; it remains to be seen how far such funding boosts will go towards improving what remains a major area of concern.

Remedying national skills shortages

The issue of national skills shortages is much debated. Bodies like the Trades Union Congress (TUC) repeatedly call for increased investment, especially to bridge the gap with international competitors on technical and supervisory qualifications. It is this concern that led the TUC to back the introduction of Modern Apprenticeships in 1993 (see below); to focus more on negotiating training with employers; and to support IIP and training leading to nationally recognised standards (*Personnel Management*, 1993).

In November 1993 the Government announced the Modern Apprenticeship scheme. At its core was an apprenticeship compact setting out what employer and trainee expected from one another and including targets for achieving NVQs Level 3 (the equivalent of A level) as opposed to Level 2, which Youth Training (YT) trainees were supposed to obtain. A substantial increase in funding supported this initiative, which was stressed as an economic rather than an unemployment measure. A 'universal credit' was also to be offered to all young people from 1995 who, at the age of 16, were going into part-time or full-time education and training. In introducing the scheme the Government was clearly conscious of the fact that the DfEE was spending around £700m annually on YT, but that the training offered by employers to the 210,000 YT trainees was highly variable, with YT itself still widely regarded simply as a way of keeping unemployment figures down.

Despite the usual fears about resourcing and employer and trainee scepticism – strongly expressed in a *Financial Times* survey of TEC directors in 1994 (Wood, 1994) – the scheme was vital in a situation where in 1993 Britain had only about 250,000 classifying themselves as undergoing an apprenticeship compared with about two million in Germany, and where the apprenticeship system was collapsing after the abolition of most of the Industry Training Boards during the 1980s. (Further discussion about such international differences follows in Chapter 7.) In this sense, TECs clearly have a vital role to play in tackling crucial skills shortages across the UK.

There is, however, a more cautionary view about the TECs' role in relation to tackling skills shortages. Commentators like Goodhart and Wood (1994) fully support the Modern Apprenticeship scheme but fear that even if enough young people can be persuaded to take up all of its places, the impact on national skills shortages can only be small. Of much more importance will be the support of employers in upgrading their employees' skills.

This cautionary view goes further. By mid-1994, despite a CBI survey finding that only 7 per cent of companies were complaining about output being held back by skills shortages, some manufacturing companies had grave concerns. These arose from the nature of those shortages that continued to exist, notably in the construction industry, one of the key sectors in national economic regeneration, and in other critical areas such as information technology and engineering. In this context the lack of interest in manufacturing apprenticeships among young people remains worrying, as have been the mixed messages sent out by the Government. On the one hand, there is heavy emphasis on the value of modern, company-based apprenticeships; on the other hand, there has been a major effort spent on boosting staying-on rates at school. By 1994 nearly 73 per cent of 16-year-olds were in full-time education – an all-time high achieved despite a decrease in the size of that age group.

With blue-collar unemployment significantly higher than white-collar unemployment, and with fewer young people available for apprenticeships, key skills shortages are likely to increase rather than decline over the longer term. Goodhart and Wood (1994: 21) observed that 'skill shortages will lead to an overheated labour market and choke the economic recovery' unless apprenticeships provide the necessary catalyst to improve the abilities of the UK. From this viewpoint, although TECs must persuade employers and trainees of the importance of the national apprenticeship programme, what is essential is that the Government makes clearer its central priority, and tailors policy accordingly.

Despite these concerns, the outlook for Modern Apprenticeships seems promising. In 1995 take-up had exceeded the national target of 2,000, with 2,115 starts achieved. By April 1996 more than 20,000 young people were in apprenticeship, with a quarter of places taken by women: an improvement on previously published figures of one in eight. The Government target by 1997 was 40,000 apprentices graduating each year.

A system in need of overhaul?

As we have already seen, a basic tension in the system is that TECs are accountable not to the local community but to central government for their key funding. From the start, too, they have had a massive workload related to developing NVQs – where they have to deal with 180 or so Lead Bodies instead of the 10 or 20 common in other countries – and to taking over and running national training programmes. The latter should be the foundation from which local leaders assess local needs and plan and implement action. In reality, however, TECs have struggled to run the schemes through years of constrained public spending and high unemployment rates.

In 1993, following its second survey of TEC directors, the *Financial Times* called for a radical overhaul of the tangled TEC system and better co-ordination at national level between those key bodies responsible for education, training and economic regeneration: the DfEE and the Department of Trade and Industry (DTI) (Wood, 1993a). It pointed to the muddle also existing at local level, where county councils, district councils, the Employment Service and TECs all worked to different priorities. Further confusion was caused by the Single Regeneration Budget which absorbed some of the funds TECs had previously been given for business support and which drew together enterprise and regeneration programmes from four government departments (Wood, 1994a). The introduction of Business Link, the government's attempt to produce a one-stop shop as a local umbrella for assistance and advice to business, added another layer of complexity.

Despite considerable progress, in particular by the merging of the former Departments of Employment and of Education in 1994 (to form the DfEE), by 1977 there was still a climate of confusion. It is therefore hardly surprising that critical views of the TECs repeatedly emerge as they struggle to achieve their targets. In one of the first large-scale surveys of business attitudes to TECs, the Industrial Relations Services (1994) found that although 87 per cent of companies were now using their services, only one-third of those did so about issues they held to be of central importance. Contact was mainly to do with national training programmes and vocational qualifications. More than a quarter found TECs and LECs inflexible, and one in five criticised the relevance of the help they received from them.

Interviewed in 1996, the TECs' Director of Policy and Strategy, Chris Humphries, claimed tangible successes for the councils: drop-outs from youth training down by 70 per cent and costs halved; a doubling of the number of adult unemployed gaining qualifications; and IIP covering more than 60 per cent of leading businesses (Gribben, 1996). There had also been a positive study in 1995 by PA Cambridge Economic Consultants, finding that for every £1 of TEC spending, firms heeding the development advice given by TECs generated £81 of extra turnover and £11.40 more in investment.

The TECs themselves are anxious to rationalise the system, and by mid-1996 10 had merged with Chambers of Commerce. A further 10 mergers were under discussion, and the TEC National Council was urging more amalgamation. In July 1996 the Council called for the abolition of the current muddle of bodies involved in NVET, substituting them with a new framework of employer-owned and -led bodies with enough funding to make them effective. There was also pressure to reduce the number of TECs from 82 to 45, and to have TEC board members elected and paid.

Achieving a coherent strategic role
There are three key challenges facing TECs as they struggle to fulfil a strategic role:

- The role itself has inbuilt tensions. TECs' accountability to government for the most substantial part of their funding complicates their task of ensuring greater local involvement. Likewise their need to focus substantially on running national training programmes does not always fit easily with their brief to foster local regeneration, especially in a climate of continuously stretched resources.

- The meaning of 'local' in the context of TECs' operations is ambiguous. TECs may be able to offer much to small and medium-sized organisations in their immediate locality. Large employers, however, face a confusing picture: they have to deal with as many TECs as they have sites in different regions, and with as many non-statutory training organisations as they have different sectoral groups. Allied to this is the fact that many TECs correspond with local authority rather than local economic boundaries, especially within large conurbations. This creates a number of tensions which can reduce TECs' ability to improve supply to meet local needs in their areas and to meet the training needs of local companies where labour is very mobile. There is also the danger that in their preoccupation with local needs they risk overlooking needs of national importance.

In November 1993 the CBI criticised the government for being too prescriptive in the detailed running of TECs while failing to give them strategic leadership, and highlighted a need for reform to enable them better to integrate and perform their enterprise and training roles (Wood, 1993). This call was taken up by the Manchester-based Centre for Local Economic Strategies (*People Management*, 1996a), who want regional education and training boards to replace the present system. This would mean education priorities and monitoring of progress decided by genuinely local bodies with a real measure of financial and operational independence. The bodies would be drawn from TECs, local authorities, trade unions, the Employment Service and the education sector.

• The IIP campaign is central to the success of TECs in their local training role but its impact on business results is still to be convincingly proved. Although the rate of IIP take-up continues to rise steadily in organisations, there are still very mixed employer reactions to its value, and many employees remain unimpressed by the training and development programmes they experience in the workplace (*Personnel Management*, 1994).

In 1995 an Institute for Employment Studies (IES) study of 1,700 employers in England and Wales revealed that two-thirds who had experienced improved business performance put the change down to IIP (*People Management*, 1995). This was corroborated by a Cranfield Management College survey, which also indicated that IIP-accredited employers were more forward-thinking on HR issues such as empowerment and employee communications (Littlefield, 1995a). In 1996 a survey carried out by IIP UK (*People Management*, 1996) showed that IIP was being used as a strategic catalyst for change within organisations, with 72 per cent of companies surveyed hoping to gain a real competitive edge thereby.

Despite these promising outcomes NACETT (see page 81) warned in July 1996 that the IIP campaign was still not achieving its full potential impact. In October that year a report by Coopers and Lybrand and IIP UK (1996) revealed that employees were sceptical about the value of the millions spent by their organisations on training and development, despite the espousal by chief executives of the need to 'invest in people'. About a third to a half judged their organisations ineffective in really making connections between business aims and individual workers. So, as the IES study concluded in 1994, the link between IIP and business results has still to be conclusively proven. The challenge facing IIP and the TECs in aligning employee development with business needs remains.

Nonetheless by mid-1996 the TECs had reason to feel clearer and more optimistic about their overall strategic role. The Government's paper on competitiveness had acknowledged their importance in becoming not only marketers and providers of training and business development initiatives but also their overall designers (Welch, 1996).

The Secretary of State, speaking at the TEC annual conference, also stressed the leading task they had in promoting and achieving national targets. With four central manifesto documents on the TECs role in economic development, education and training for young people, reskilling and the unemployed, and lifetime learning the TEC National Council made it clear at the conference that it was aiming for a major independent political voice in the future. Its new partnership with the TUC to promote work-based training, and TECs' increasingly strong links with local bodies, promised a greater capability to deliver at local level than ever before, and the chance to develop at last a more effective and integrated strategy.

Delivering national training policy

Can the TEC system deliver national training policy, and are TECs likely to survive?

Feedback notes

- The delivery of NVET policy rests significantly in the hands of TECs, and the debate over whether or not they are fulfilling a meaningful role in that respect continues. In February 1994 a study by the LSE urged overhaul of TECs that 'have become a quango: a business-led body mainly doing government's job for the unemployed' and likely to lose the commitment of business leaders. In September of the same year, however, official figures on the performance of all 82 TECs (although covering only YT, TFW and IIP) showed that TECs were delivering the best results thus far, with the number of qualifications higher and the cost of achieving them lower. In 1995 came the favourable study from PA Cambridge. None the less, in the same year 37 TECs made trading losses and one – South Thames – collapsed into bankruptcy, owing £5m.

- Despite this mixed record the TEC system appears likely to survive. In August 1994 the Labour Party said in a policy statement that 'the TECs have the potential to make a valuable contribution to local and regional economies' and that Labour would, as part of its policy on national training, review the role, functions and accountability of the councils in recognition of the frustration widely felt among TEC members (*Personnel Management Plus*, 1994).

NATIONAL VOCATIONAL STANDARDS AND QUALIFICATIONS

Another cornerstone of the national training framework, and one that also underpins all current national educational policy, is the National/Scottish Vocational Qualification system (hereafter referred to as the NVQ system). Comments on the Scottish system appear below, since it is significantly different from the system in England and Wales. Vocational qualifications are those that relate directly to a person's competence in employment. By 1986 less than one-third of the UK labour force held vocational qualifications, significantly less than in other competitor countries. Fundamental reform of the whole national vocational qualification system was an urgent national priority.

The NVQ system in England and Wales

The NVQ system offers Britain for the first time in its history a structure of occupational qualifications comprising agreed national standards of competence across every recognised occupational area.

An NVQ represents a statement of competence confirming that the individual can perform to a specified standard at one of five levels in a range of work-related activities, and has the related skills, knowledge and understanding that make that performance possible in a work setting. NVQs are awarded by various examining bodies whose courses incorporate standards laid down by the various industry Lead Bodies. The courses have been accredited by the National Council of Vocational Qualifications (NCVQ), and certificates carry both the NVQ stamp and that of the examining bodies. In September 1997 a new Qualifications and National Curriculum Authority was to come into operation, merging the current Schools Curriculum and Assessment Authority (reponsible for GCSEs and A levels) and the NCVQ.

Lead Body Standards have been developed by a lengthy consultative process. This has involved a functional analysis approach to the identification of standards, breaking a job down first into general functional areas of competence, each comprising abilities and skills, and then into more detailed elements of competence. Given that the NCVQ's membership is employer-dominated, it can fairly be claimed that it is employers and the professions, not some central government body insensitive to employers' needs, who 'drive' the NVQ movement and who give its products their seal of approval. A more detailed explanation of NVQs is given in Appendix 2.

In 1993 a business-led National Advisory Council on Education and Training Targets (NACETT) was established by the Government to speed up the introduction of NVQs and give them a stronger profile with employers. Its role is to monitor progress towards targets, publish an annual report, and advise the Government. In May 1995 revised national education and training targets for the year 2000 were published in the Government's second competitiveness White Paper. These stressed the need, in the interests of improving national competitive capability, for more people to reach existing targets; for core skills to have a special focus; and for new targets for the achievement of high-level qualifications (Appendix 3).

The Scottish system

Pickard (1996: 24) gave a valuable summary of the Scottish system, explaining that for a variety of historical, educational and geographical reasons it has proceeded more smoothly than the system in England and Wales. Ninety-five per cent of NVQs are awarded by one body, the Scottish Vocational Education Council (SCOTVEC), which also has the accrediting role held by the NCVQ in England and Wales. All standards and Scottish highers (the equivalent of A levels) are also awarded by a single body, the Scottish Examinations Board.

SCOTVEC awards are delivered and assessed in modules following changes in further educational qualifications in 1985. Modules can be taken by anyone, at any time, in school, in further and higher education, and in or out of work. Employers accept a series of modules rather than whole certificates as entry to certain jobs.

What have NVQs achieved thus far?

Areas of concern

Given the immensity of the task of overhauling the UK's vocational qualification system it is not surprising that reforms thus far have attracted criticisms as well as praise. NVQs are popular in certain industries which previously had few recognised qualifications, for example the retail industry, where their take-up has been extremely high. However, there is a fear that the NVQ system will deteriorate into a mass of standards set at very low levels which have no equivalent across the rest of Europe. Many employers also see NVQs as irrelevant to their in-house needs – a stand taken by British Home Stores in 1994 when it abandoned NVQs in favour of its own qualification (*Personnel Management*, 1994).

As Pickard's informative article (1996) made clear, progress in developing purpose-built NVQs has been slow in organisations. Take-up has been faster in educational institutions, but many still run traditional and NVQ routes in parallel, and there are complex problems to do with delivery. The system was meant to ensure progression from education into work and qualifications for those in work. However, the simulated settings offered by educational providers are seen by many employers as lacking in credibility, and the cost of providing an NVQ route in a college is so high – in terms of training needed to run the route, of time, of materials and of expertise – that, as resource constraints bite harder into the educational system generally, the feasibility of offering that route comes into question.

As Pickard observed (1996: 25), there is also a 'ferocious conflict between employers and educationalists' concerning the whole concept of competence gained in one setting being transferrable to another and of ability to do a series of tasks being a valid indicator of ability to do a whole job. With the advent of the new Qualifications and National Curriculum Authority, employers fear that the power of the educationalists will be significantly advanced and that the design of NVQs will be modelled rather on the educational needs of 16- to 19-year-olds than on the skills needs of adult workers in employment. The latter was the originally intended focus of the NVQ system, and it remains crucial to the competitive capability of UK businesses that it should be retained.

Key reports on the NVQ system

In 1996 one of the key reports on NVQs to date appeared – the Beaumont Report. It surveyed the first 100 NVQs/SVQs and found widespread employer support for the NVQ/SVQ concept and a general acceptance that the benefits of the system outweighed its costs. None the less, the report produced a formidable series of recommendations to tackle deficiencies to do particularly with a costly and imperfect delivery system, excessive bureaucracy and jargon, inconsistency in funding arrangements, and differences in the interpretation of standards by key parties across the system (Beaumont, 1996: 7).

A major blow to NVQs' credibility came in October 1996 when a study by the Centre for Economic Performance (a Government-backed body at the LSE) condemned the whole system, set up at a cost of more than £100m., as having achieved almost nothing. The study concluded (Clare, 1996a) that although the Government's intention had been to rationalise the structure of vocational qualifications, it had simply added to its complexity, displacing some traditional qualifications particularly in such areas as clerical and secretarial work, and hairdressing. The obscurity surrounding the qualification was emphasised. The authors expressed concern that although designed to be assessed primarily in the workplace, two-thirds of NVQs were taught in simulated environments at schools. They estimated that far fewer than the official estimate of one million people had an NVQ and that, of 794 NVQs available, 364 had not yet been awarded to anyone, and a further 43 had each been awarded to sole individuals: at that rate the Government target of 50 per cent of the workforce working towards an NVQ by 1996 would take 96 more years to achieve. There was also heavy criticism of the GNVQ system (see Chapter 6).

NCVQ rebutted the claims made in the report, saying that its conclusions had been based largely on statistics for 1994. Until and unless convincingly favourable statistics are produced, however, it will be hard to mitigate the damaging effect on employers of a highly critical and well-publicised report from the Government's own watchdog body.

Areas of progress
Despite these caveats, there is no doubt that NVQs have the potential to become the universal form of qualification for people in work. Of the three bodies awarding certification for occupational skills – the Business and Technology Education Council (BTEC), City and Guilds and the Royal Society of Arts (RSA) – only the latter is allowing traditional skills courses and NVQ routes to co-exist, and in that case it is likely that through time RSA certificates will become NVQ units. The spread of competence-based qualifications internationally is another factor favouring the rapid spread of NVQs.

By 1997 over 85 per cent of all occupations offered NVQs, within a national framework showing interrelationships between qualifications. Standards can thus be compared between different jobs on the same level, so that the individual can see how he or she could use his or her skills in different areas of work. Many corporate, medium-sized and smaller organisations in the UK are making acquisition of NVQs part of their strategic development of a workforce, and are consistently achieving outcomes of benefit not only to the individual and organisation but also to the national economy. The following case-study is an example of how NVQs can be used to attract, develop and reward employees.

Case-study: NVQs in a pub chain

Pub chain Scottish and Newcastle Retail has made NVQs available to all its 25,000 full- and part-time staff in order to attract and keep high-calibre people. Five different NVQs are offered at Level 1. This enables staff to train in a variety of skills. Employees should need only two or three months to complete the first NVQ, leaving the rest for completion within seven or eight more months. Staff who gain NVQs receive pay increases, on the basis that improved competency merits a financial reward. The company proposes to expand its range of NVQs into Levels 2 and 3 and is developing its own training materials accredited by City and Guilds.

(*Source*: *People Management*, 1995b)

The NVQ/SVQ system

Outline the NVQ/SVQ system and assess its benefits and weaknesses.

Feedback notes
- The main difficulties are to do with simplifying the complexity of the vocational qualification system, making it coherent and of high quality, and improving its accessibility and image. Employers remain ambivalent. Some reasons follow:

  - The system seems obscure and excessively bureaucratic to many, and is expensive, with accreditation fees in addition to extra training costs.

  - Some feel that NVQs are too broad, others too narrow.

  - There are concerns that standards will vary when assessment is done in-house; and that assessments carried out in educational institutions lack credibility and consistency because of the simulated nature of the NVQ-related courses.

  - Some employers fear that workers will demand more pay for attaining NVQs.

  - Although TECs, when advising on the IIP standard, place a major emphasis on a company training to NVQ standards, such training is not yet mandatory in order to achieve the IIP standard.

  - There is still little sign of parity of esteem between academic and vocational qualifications.

  - There is doubt about the extent to which the current separate qualification routes can meet the differing needs of young people, the unemployed and adults in work. There are fears that failure here will threaten both the competitive capability of organisations and the job prospects of the young.

  - There is widespread concern over the discrepancy between national standards and the reality of local delivery, which often falls short in terms of quality, consistency, cost and meaningfulness.

- The potential benefits explain why many actively support the NVQ system (see, for example, the story of Bassetlaw Hospital in Evans, 1993, and of NVQs in the accountancy profession in Evans, 1993a). These benefits are:

  - improved profitability and economic performance

  - development of a more adaptable workforce, updating and modifying skills through credit accumulation and transfer

  - increased co-operation between employers, training organisations and awarding bodies

  - increased individual motivation and awareness of standards, through the real value of the qualifications the employer helps them to achieve

  - easier recruitment of competent staff because employers know what an NVQ stands for

  - clear goals set for continued learning and staff development, providing the opportunity for improvement in corporate performance

  - improved ability to attract and retain staff.

CONCLUSION

In order to achieve the learning objectives of this chapter we have identified the national vision for vocational education and training in the UK. National training policy has been discussed by reference to the nature of that policy and the difficulties it has faced, given the inadequate reasons for many organisations and individuals to invest in vocational training. The aims of the 1989 national training strategy and its implementation framework have been identified. The TEC system, the cornerstone of that framework, has been explained, with particular reference to its four key areas of activity and to the four major problems it continues to face.

The NVQ system has been outlined. Important reports on it published during 1996 have been summarised, and the achievements thus far of that system have been balanced against the reasons for employers' continuing ambivalence.

USEFUL READING

BEAUMONT, G. (1996) 'Review of 100 NVQs and SVQs', a Report submitted to the Department for Education and Employment. 25, Albion Road, Chesterfield, S40 IBR (Freepost SF10305), Beaumont.

HILLIER, J. (1995) 'Questioning the value of NVQs'. *People Management*. Vol. 1, 3: 26–8.

MARCHINGTON, M. *and* WILKINSON, A. (1996) *Core Personnel and Development*. London, Institute of Personnel and Development.

The information in Chapter 5 will need to be regularly updated, and the following are recommended as particularly helpful reading:

* the IPD's publication, *People Management*. This contains reliable, accessible and up-to-date information.

* the quality press – and especially the Sunday 'heavies' and the *Financial Times* – for their regular articles and editorials on matters relating to the field of secondary and tertiary education, and national training.

* *The Times Educational Supplement* and *The Times Higher Educational Supplement* should also be consulted on a fairly regular basis by students.

Local TECs have much up-to-date information that is of value to practitioners and students, and the Employment Occupational Standards Council, 2 Savoy Court, The Strand, London, WC2R OEZ (Tel.: 0171-240 7474; Fax: 0171-240 6264) can advise on a wealth of publications related to NVQs and national occupational standards.

ENDNOTE

Differences in the education system and funding arrangements in Scotland from those in England and Wales mean that some of the more detailed points in the strategic guidelines given to TECs are not directly relevant to the Scottish LECs; also Scottish Enterprise, Highland and Island Enterprise, and their local enterprise companies have wider responsibilities than TECs in relation to the objective of encouraging enterprise and helping small businesses to grow. Responsibility for training in Wales was transferred from the Secretary of State for Employment to the Secretary of State for Wales in 1992.

6 National education policy: the primary, secondary and tertiary systems

LEARNING OBJECTIVES

After reading this chapter you will:

- understand the vision and policy for national education at primary, secondary and tertiary levels

- understand the key stages in the implementation of policy since the mid-1980s

- be able to assess the strengths and weaknesses of the current educational system and the relationship of that system to the wider National Vocational Education and Training (NVET) framework and policy.

NATIONAL EDUCATIONAL POLICY

If the NVET system whose vision was given at the start of Chapter 5 is to work, then national policy that guides educational provision at primary, secondary and tertiary level must ensure the intellectual and practical development that young people need. In this chapter there is no intention to give a comprehensive commentary on educational policy: what is offered is a guide to the main themes and challenges that are relevant in the context of the NVET system overall. The chapter concludes by reviewing the main achievements of NVET policy to date and identifying key challenges that remain.

Vision

The vision guiding national educational policy is of every child receiving foundation learning that is best suited to its abilities, aspirations and to the range of employment opportunities likely to be available on leaving full-time education.

Policy

This vision can be realised only if young people improve their basic educational level and are able to learn and apply new knowledge and skills in a rapidly changing world as well as in an academic context. National policy seeks to end what are seen to be obsolete divisions between academic and vocational learning and achieve a coherent cradle-to-grave framework. In such a system young people will receive relevant vocational preparation and qualifications at school, continuing this process until age 18, whether or not they leave school at 16; and adults both in or out of employment will be enabled and motivated to improve their formal vocational attainments in line with the economy's needs.

Strategy
This focuses on:

• progressively introducing the National Curriculum in schools and ultimately linking it to the national vocational qualification system

• improving vocational education in schools in order to clarify and expand choice, and to promote parity of esteem between academic and vocational qualifications

• creating a new post-16 vocational education and training sector.

PROGRESS AND CHALLENGES

The educational system is in a state of flux as it struggles for coherency in order to realise its vision. The easiest way to explain the main issues and challenges facing it is to take a historical approach, outlining the main stages in the Government's attempts to implement policy and the ways in which it has responded to ongoing problems and emergent needs.

Reforms in the primary and secondary education system 1985–96
Nationalising the curriculum
The 1980s were years when the need to improve the nation's skills in order to achieve competitive capability was accompanied by growing concern about declining standards in education. To the Government it was essential to break the control over the educational system that was exercised by local education authorities and educationalists, and centralise control over curriculum and standards. At the same time the aim was to decentralise sufficiently for education to become more exposed to market forces.

In 1985 the radical step was taken of replacing the General Certificate of Education (GCE) and the Certificate of Secondary Education (CSE) with a single General Certificate of Secondary Education (GCSE), whose aim was to offer the majority of 16-year-olds the chance to acquire an accreditation of their five years of secondary education. It was part of a national policy dedicated to developing coherent and universal technical and vocational, as well as academic, pathways in a system hitherto dominated by the latter.

In 1986, following the introduction of the Certificate in Pre-Vocational Education in 1984–5, came the Technical and Vocational Education Initiative. These initiatives typified costly and, in the main, unsuccessful attempts made in the 1980s to help children acquire vocational skills, knowledge and experience in their formative years.

It was the Education Reform Act 1988 that marked a radical break with the past. It was the most fundamental overhaul of the educational system since the Butler Education Act 1944 divided the State system into three types of secondary school: grammar, technical and vocational. Now, by 1994 all children in State schools would have to meet standard assessment targets of a National Curriculum covering both core and foundation subjects. Children were to be banded according to ability in each assessed area. Assessments were to be mainly based on subject areas and use a combination of continuous assignment and project work together with national examinations – a clear move towards the encouragement of competence and firm links with the National Vocational Qualifications (NVQ) system. Testing would occur at the ages of 5, 7, 11, 14 and 16. It was essential for the reforms to begin at the primary level so that there would be the educational standards in place throughout a child's school life that would ultimately ensure an adequately educated and skilled workforce for the economy.

The push of curriculum reform over the years has incorporated a strong attack on the child-centred 'discovery' approach to primary school learning that became increasingly prevalent from the late 1960s. With the drive for a common curriculum focused on the need to achieve outcomes has come a return to teacher-centred education, the belief being that it will bring with it an improvement in falling standards of attainment.

Re-organisation and the market
At the same time that the education of children was tackled, so too was the governance, funding and management of their schools. The Education Act 1988 gave schools the power in certain circumstances to opt out of local authority control. The intention was to break the control exercised by Local Education Authorities (LEAs), cut through the red tape and give greater freedom to schools showing that they could manage effectively. The aim was market-driven: to help to ensure a greater responsiveness to customer needs as expressed not by children and teachers, but by parents and employers. More changes followed in 1992 to strengthen and extend the system. In September 1995 the Government announced a further set of measures to improve primary education, to speed up the pace of opting out and to give grant-maintained schools (an arrangement whereby money goes straight from the Government to the schools, bypassing LEAs) more freedom to select their pupils as they saw fit. The main outcomes of this reform have been that:

- schools have the opportunity to opt out of local authority control and obtain their funding direct from the Government

- all schools, State and independent, have to publish examination results, National Curriculum test scores, truancy rates and leavers' destinations in a standard form; the details are summarised annually in local and national league tables

- every State school in England and Wales (27,000 in 1988) is monitored once every four years by teams of independent inspectors whose reports are published; school governing bodies must tell parents how they propose to act on the inspectors' findings

- all 16-year-olds have to stay in school until the end of the summer term instead of leaving at Easter without taking their final exams

- all parents have to receive an annual written report on their children's progress.

With the 1988 reforms, school governors and heads now held major managerial responsibilities like their counterparts in the tertiary system (see the following section). However, the Secretary of State still retained significant power, a new national agency for schools gradually taking over from LEAs wherever schools opted out. The Secretary of State was enabled to submit his or her own plans to close down surplus schools and refer these to a public enquiry, and to set up educational associations to take over failing schools.

Educational reform in Britain in the late 1980s

Assess the main changes introduced in the education reform acts of the late 1980s.

Feedback notes
- Whatever the intensity of the education debate, there is no doubt that before the 1988 legislation large numbers of children were not learning even basic skills, whether at primary or secondary level. Now, primary school teachers had to focus on separate, identifiable subjects and their content, not on vaguely defined 'projects'. Parents were to receive some identification of levels of achievement by children and schools. Diversity among schools could be achieved while at the same time every pupil would leave with at least the basics in terms of knowledge and skills. In the same spirit that drove the Training and Enterprise Council (TEC) system, providers (schools) were to be judged by measurable and publicised outcomes – in this case, examination results.

- However, although the changes decentralised the system by pushing it out towards the market, they also produced more centralisation by nationalising the curriculum and reducing the funding power of LEAs. This introduced further tensions into the system.

Tensions in the system
Tensions between the forces of centralisation and decentralisation emerge in a variety of controversial issues, some of which are indicated here.

The extent to which the National Curriculum and accompanying assessment processes dominate teaching time has produced heavily increased teaching and administrative workloads and raised concerns that the system with 'its inflated syllabuses and monopolistic approach to testing does not permit meaningful diversity' (O'Hear, 1993). The difficulty of achieving meaningful choice and educational quality in its widest sense has been exposed both in the plight of inner city schools, where truancy rates and socio-economic conditions make poor academic outcomes inevitable, and in well-publicised cases such as a governing board's decision in 1996 to sack the head of Cheltenham College. It was a school with non-selective entry, a long-established reputation for high-quality, all-round education for every child whatever their academic ability, but with league table results perceived by the governors to be unsatisfactory. With 500 parents in outcry at the governors' decision to get rid of a widely respected educationalist, the questions 'Whose choice?', 'What kind of quality?' and 'Who governs?' were inevitable.

Standards remain a battlefield. The failure of attempts to set criteria for awarding grades for the new GCSE examinations meant that the only benchmark was comparison with the old O level and CSE examinations; but the O level itself had no fixed standards, and syllabi and papers had in any case radically changed. In 1992 came further changes aimed at tightening standards, and the introduction of a more precise 10-level grading system where Level 10 was higher than an A grade. Confusingly, there was no precise equivalent of Grade C, then the O-level benchmark.

In November 1993 Sir Claus Moser's independent National Commission on Education (NCE) – a body that consistently through the years had published reports showing disturbingly wide gaps between educational standards and the attainment of children in England compared with their European counterparts' – produced another set of damning statistics (NCE, 1993). The percentage of 16-year-olds in Germany, France, Japan and England who achieved the equivalent of a GCSE pass in maths, science and the national language was 62, 66, 50 and 27 per cent respectively. In 1990 the percentage obtaining an upper secondary school qualification at 18 had been 68 in Germany, 48 in France, 80 in Japan, but only 29 in England. For too long, according to Moser, the system had concentrated on the needs of the academically able at the expense of the rest. This was compounded by widening educational gaps between richer and poorer and north and south, as well as by differences of gender and ethnic origin. The message was clear: every child and young person had to learn how to succeed at school, and for this to happen there had to be a 'new deal in the classroom'. There were radical proposals to achieve reform, focusing especially on the abolition of local authority control, reduction of class size, and further nationalisation of the curriculum through the umbrella of a single, all-embracing 'General Education Diploma'.

Dubbed a 'left-wing agenda' by some, the report received widespread backing. It preached a powerful message: in the knowledge society how can everybody join in fully, not only at work but also as a citizen, if they are educationally deprived? The message was particularly important because of its focus on knowledge as the new currency of the workplace. In the same year Peter Drucker, the American management guru, was highlighting the twin challenges facing education: the economic and the social. He emphasised the primacy of knowledge as the basic economic resource of a country and the key role of the 'knowledge worker' in society. He observed the need to ensure the dignity of the less intellectually gifted service workers who would also be essential in post-capitalist society (Drucker, 1993).

Also in 1993 Her Majesty's Inspectors concluded in their annual report that despite rising GCSE results true standards were still in decline, pupils failing to master the basic principles of their subjects. In 1996 the Government announced that A-level standards were to be overhauled in order to achieve a return to more rigorous standards set in the past.

Early in 1993 Sir Ron Dearing had been appointed head of the new School Curriculum and Assessment Authority, a body replacing separate councils in charge of educational curricula and examinations (a body which itself was to be replaced in 1997 by an overarching Qualifications and National Curriculum Authority). In January 1994, following the publication of a Report by Dearing, national curricular entitlements were shorn in order to ease the over-loaded teachers and give them more freedom and discretion. The bureaucratic complexity of the attainment and assessment system, however, remained – and, with this, much of the true cause of the overload.

In 1993 a new General National Vocational Qualification (GNVQ) was piloted across Britain, with a basic pass roughly equivalent to two grade-D A levels. It was a major attempt to achieve parity of esteem between the academic and vocational pathways. The hope was that it would attract students who enrolled for A levels because there was nothing more suitable, or who dropped out at 16, or who pursued other, less valuable, vocational courses. If successful, the GNVQ route would help to end the multiplicity of qualifications and establish the GNVQ itself as the market leader in the public mind. It would also offer a more consistent standard of assessment than most of its precursors.

In 1994 GCSE results were again at record level. However, well under half of England's 16-year-olds achieved at least five C grades, and in some inner cities there were high truancy rates and individual schools achieving hardly any passes at high grades. Ofsted (the official body monitoring educational standards in Britain) produced a 'damning' report on the state of science teaching in secondary schools that cast doubt on the meaningfulness of the record science pass rate of 46.6 per cent at GCSE level announced a week later (Clare, 1994). Both Ofsted and the Further Education Funding Council found that GNVQs, although they had rapidly become very popular, had serious shortcomings, including variable standards, weak links with industry and commerce, and some high drop-out rates. Expert commentators like Clare were convinced that the game had fundamentally changed and the coinage had become debased.

Early in 1995 the Royal Society of Arts (RSA) launched a Diploma of Achievement to provide a better grounding in core skills that had still not been adequately developed by the A-level system and that GNVQs had been attempting to improve. The Diploma took only four terms and could therefore be attempted in addition to three or four academic A levels. Its core skills were those particularly valued by employers.

By now, although a quarter of all 16-year-olds were currently working for a GNVQ, two-thirds of those enrolled for one failed to complete their course on time. In March 1996 came the publication of the Dearing Report into 16- to 19-year-old vocational qualifications. It was a body-blow to the system whose academic/vocational divide it found 'damaging to the national interest and to the optimal development of the wide range of talents among young peope' (Clare, 1996).

The British educational system

By 1996, what had become the main needs to tackle in the education system, and what were the main tensions?

Feedback notes

- The main needs and tensions have been outlined in the preceding section, and are well illustrated in the recommendations of the 1996 Dearing Report.

- The review set out a new national framework of qualifications to take the place of the existing 'jungle' of academic, applied and vocational examinations. The proposals were welcomed in general by Government and employers, even though they did not convince everyone that the divide between academic and vocational pathways would soon disappear. Key recommendations (Littlefield and Welch, 1996) were for:

- equal weighting for academic (A level), applied (GNVQ) and vocational (NVQ) pathways

- a new advanced national diploma for those with vocational and academic qualifications

- achievement across all pathways to be pegged to four national levels: entry, foundation, intermediate and advanced

- an AS level to credit one year of A-level study, allowing greater breadth of study

- key skills added to the curriculum

- the relaunch of Youth Training (YT) as national traineeships (a particularly welcome proposal for an unpopular scheme, and one that promised to offer a clearer route into GNVQs and modern apprenticeships)

- revision and relaunch of the National Record of Achievement to promote lifelong learning (a step heralded by Rover Group's education and careers manager, John Berkely, as capable of making 'perhaps the single greatest difference to promoting and sustaining the idea of lifelong learning' – the concept that lies at the heart of the NVET vision)

- encouragement for accreditation and awarding bodies to 'join forces' to provide a more coherent provision of awards.

There is no doubt that the impact of the Dearing Report will be considerable. In February 1997, for example, a range of initiatives were announced by the Government related to syllabus change, improving teaching quality, new performance targets and league tables, a reduction in examination boards and a wider diversity of qualifications. It remains to be seen what the long-term effects of these and other reforms will be. Dearing criticised a system whose complexity makes it well-nigh incomprehensible to those not closely involved with it, and in his recommendations tried to introduce clarity and to close the gaps between educational pathways. To his own critics, however, he was an educational mandarin who failed to appreciate that 'academic and vocational education are inevitably different' (*Daily Telegraph* editorial, 1996). The fear was that the strong centralising tendency of the report threatened the independence and quality of a traditionally decentralised examination system.

The tensions between centralisation and decentralisation that are evident in relation to nationalisation of the curriculum, to educational philosophy and control, and to standards remain. Many see the need for sufficient centralisation to achieve national standards of education in a system still failing to deliver, and for enough exposure to the market to prevent complacency and to achieve relevancy. Others echo the view of Lord Skidelsky, professor of political economy at Warwick University and a leading political thinker, who wrote in 1994 that the message of the system seems to be 'You can shop at any of our supermarkets but you must all buy the same goods' (Skidelsky, 1994: 34).

Reforms in the tertiary education system

Throughout the late 1980s and the 1990s the further and higher education sector was undergoing similar changes. There is a bewildering number of providers in this sector. The Government's intention was to create a unified framework for the provision of education and training for post-16-year-olds, applying to it the same principles of local autonomy, competition in an open market, and responsiveness to customer needs that underpin reforms of the national training system and the secondary education sector.

Restructuring and control

Under the Education Reform Act 1989 and the Further and Higher Education Act 1992 the first radical steps were taken:

• Universities, polytechnics and major colleges of higher education were all by 1994 to be brought together into a single structure for higher education, with power to award their own degrees, thus ending the binary line that had divided universities from other major higher education bodies for 25 years.

• New quality assurance measures were introduced, including external scrutiny by a quality audit unit developed in essence by the educational institutions.

• Remaining further education and sixth form colleges were given independent corporate status. They were to be funded by the Government through the Further and Higher Education Funding Councils on the basis of number of students enrolled and completing courses.

The long-term success of colleges is now dependent on managerial skills, as they carry out their dual role of providing quality services and acting as major employers. Teachers are also having to act as managers of teams. With this emphasis on professional management, industrial, business and professional interests have become increasingly dominant on governing bodies. Effective collaboration between these institutions and schools and local employers is particularly important in areas like sandwich courses, profiling and assessment of pupils and students, careers guidance, and the design of sandwich courses and work experience. It is also essential to ensure open access and non-discrimination.

In post-16 vocational education and training, as in the TEC system, there is now a part-centralised, part-decentralised framework controlled largely by employers and the professions, and needing to be sensitive to local training and education demands. TECs, local education providers at secondary and tertiary levels, and employers are required to work closely together in improving the quality, levels and relevance of vocational educational provision and attainment, and TECs must achieve stated targets in all these areas.

In the university system there is continuing tension between pressure of numbers – the UK by mid-1994 covering almost as many 18-year-olds as in Germany and the USA – and the determination to provide courses of sufficient quality that will not only develop in students the vocational skills they need but also the intellectual capability to manage their lives in a rapidly changing world. Many fear, too, that the system is not flexible enough to give access to the public throughout their lives rather than just for three years after leaving school.

In June 1994 the Confederation of British Industry (CBI) in 'Thinking Ahead' pointed to the importance of easy transfer between universities, taking career breaks, and following courses while working. In the same month the Higher Education Quality Council, a self-regulatory body of university vice chancellors backed by the Government, published 'Choosing to Change'. They advocated a new flexible system of academic credits or modules offering a common currency for accumulating credits towards a degree, regardless of whether credits came from conventional higher education or vocational training.

By then, about 85 per cent of UK universities had some system of credit accumulation, or plans to introduce it, so common standardisation should be possible. There were fears that attempts at such a system would result in sinking to a lowest common denominator. The CBI none the less welcomed the report.

The following study shows the kind of positive but also negative impact that a decade of radical change has had on the further education system. It is fictional but based on an amalgam of several factual cases.

Case-study: Notown College

Notown Technical College was located in a large north-west town where unemployment was relatively high but where during the 1980s there were important initiatives related to business growth and industrial development.

The college had served local needs well for many years with a traditional mix of technical and educational vocational courses. In 1992, in response to Government legislation and in order to develop a stronger hold over the local market-place, it was reorganised into a tertiary college. There was a new governing body, and a new principal and senior management team. A group of middle managers was recruited from industry with the intention of giving a sharper edge to performance. The main body of staff was recruited from the former technical college and from local schools.

Immediate tasks at the new Notown College included establishing a corporate image, producing a mission statement and formulating a five-year business plan. Internally it was vital to abolish the old division between teaching and non-teaching staff and to promote a flexible team-based culture, driven by goals of quality and service to the customer. HRM became a corporate function, headed at vice-principal level and incorporating staff development related to all employees. An initial exercise involved all staff in drawing up a mission statement which included five specific commitments as the basis for corporate planning. A functional organisational structure was introduced, emphasising accountability at middle management level. There was a concerted effort to improve industrial relations.

In parallel with corporate goals and team objectives put in place and communicated to all employees, a consultancy firm worked with management to introduce a major organisational change programme. Its focus was on culture change, with particular emphasis on teambuilding and team skills. This was helped by a benchmarking exercise with a local manufacturing firm which, during a long turn-round period in the late 1980s and heavily influenced by its Japanese strategic partner, had developed a reputation for excellence in those areas. Team meetings took place weekly and a development programme for team leaders was put in place to support this. Communication channels became of vital importance, and many new ideas were generated and put into practice.

The college's new governing body was keen to establish quickly a strong local image that would make its current and potential customers aware of the change. A marketing manager was appointed to carry out a sophisticated marketing campaign. The college's products were expanded and improved, and a new training consultancy division established. Accommodation was upgraded, and a new logo and colours were introduced. Collaboration with local schools, industry and commerce had always been good, but now became of critical importance to the business.

The college achieved a rapid increase in full-time enrolments of over 40 per cent, with enrolments overall up well over 20 per cent. Many of its secondary education courses attracted for the first time able boys and girls from independent as well as State schools – and not only those who were doing GCSE or A-level resits, but those who had chosen to take post-16 academic and technical courses first time round at the college. Particular attention had been paid in the five-year business plan to improving access for adult learners, and equal opportunities was built into both planning and operational processes and systems. Again, the benefits were evident in enrolment rates. All educational institutions were at this time seeing more demand than they could satisfy, and those which, like Notown College, had reorganised along more 'business-like' lines seemed poised to take best advantage of this.

However, during the first year there were already signs of problems that were to grow increasingly severe. They mirrored tensions now becoming widespread in the further education sector at large. Renegotiation of contracts with academic staff, the balancing of needs against resources, attempts to produce harmonisation of terms and conditions of service across the college: none of these challenges proved amenable to quick solutions as the old bureaucratic system struggled to come to terms with the profound changes necessary to ensure its transformation.

Over the next few years the college continued to make progress in the market-place, but by the mid-1990s the pace of success had diminished as 'customers' became more knowledgeable and as Government targets and local competition generated further pressures. Locally a number of educational institutions merged as they sought to achieve a crucial edge in a market crowded with education and training providers. There was a long and bitter battle with the unions and, on its resolution, further restructuring took place in order to achieve a leaner, more performance-oriented system that could reassert its lead in the locality.

In 1996 the young director of human resources, who herself had been recruited from the private sector two years before, moved back into that sector, frustrated at the failure of the college to achieve the culture necessary to achieve its strategic goals and at the resilience of the traditional divisions between occupational grades. Her post was not filled as the college's management debated the extent to which it was necessary to have HR represented at board level rather than being 'passed to the line' – a line, however, which itself was uncertainly defined in the new structure.

Current pressures

There continue to be major pressures on colleges and universities. They derive from the big expansion in numbers due in 1997, from a constant squeeze on funding, from what are widely perceived to be declining educational standards of young people entering the higher education system, and from the competitive market-place. By 1992 the number of full-time students in higher education had jumped from 208,000 to 436,000 and the proportion of school-leavers going to university was 31 per cent. Forty-one former polytechnics and colleges already had university status, and in the decade to 1992 full-time students at the new universities and colleges had doubled, while older universities had experienced a rise of 40 per cent (Authers, 1994). As the market was 'flooded' with new courses to 'woo students who had never thought about higher education' (Scott-Clark and Rayment, 1995) the same drift of standards being experienced in the primary and secondary sectors was feared to be developing. The lines between the roles of old and new universities became increasingly blurred and the rise in the number of places at the latter greatly exceeded those at the former. In 1993 the Government capped growth in numbers until 1998.

Pressures on universities also come from the Higher Education Funding Council, operating different assessment processes relating to the quality of research and teaching. To achieve excellence in both seems increasingly impossible as resource constraints and the burden of additional numbers of young people entering the system bring into conflict longer-term ends to do with research and teaching coherence and knowledge creation, and short-term ends to do with funding and status. In September 1994 the Committee of University Vice-Chancellors and Principals expressed grave concern that slippage of standards was spreading across the system. It was recommended that a national body be formed to rectify the situation.

NATIONAL EDUCATION AND TRAINING POLICY: CAN THEIR GOALS BE ACHIEVED?

At this point we can pull together the themes that have run through this and the preceding chapter.

NVET policy must somehow reconcile the educational and training needs of the individual, the employer and the economy in ways that will increase the competitiveness of organisations and of British industry as a whole. At the same time, development of individuals must be of a kind to enable them to lead meaningful, satisfying lives. The framework for such a twofold policy must be strong and lead to effective implementation.

Since 1986 there has been a clear intent to achieve a workable national framework for NVET. In that year the then Manpower Services Commission (MSC) assumed a central role, aiming for 'an integrated, national strategy for managing change in education and training across the entire age range – from school to the mature, even advanced, ages of adult working life' (Keep, 1986, quoting Bryan Nicholson, then MSC chairman). At the same time the Government was pursuing a policy of encouraging a switch away from the humanities and towards science and technology subjects. There was also speculation that, at last, there was going to be a formal merger between the Department of Employment and the MSC to create a single Ministry of Education and Training (Keep, 1986). In fact it was only in 1994 that the Department of Education and Science and the Department of Employment were merged to create the Department for Education and Employment, but that step marked a radical and welcome change in Government thinking. The merger of the Schools Curriculum and Assessment Authority (reponsible for GCSEs and A levels) and the NCVQ into a Qualifications and National Curriculum Authority, planned for September 1997, promised further progress in achieving an administratively more integrated national education and vocational training system.

Despite such progress, reaching agreement on how to reconcile the often conflicting needs of NVET policy can seem impossible, given the varied interests and philosophies of the stakeholders. Ron Johnson, chairman of the (then) Institute of Personnel Management's National Committee for Training and Development, said in June 1990:

> There [does] not appear to be a coherent national strategy on the acknowledged to be key areas of education, training and development. This state of affairs persists despite an avalanche of sensible and respectable research reports, strategic papers and polemics coming thick and fast in the last decade. What they all lack, however, is either thoughts on the implementation of policies or consensus on implementation in a real, practical sense
>
> Johnson, 1990: 30

In overall terms, his criticism no longer carries the conviction it did at the time. However, his fears about implementation do still carry weight.

What should drive national education and training provision?

What vision and policy drive the provision of national education and training? Should the present voluntarist and market-led approach continue, or be reversed by a compulsory system?

In order to respond to this question, you will find it helpful both to revise relevant parts of Chapters 5 and 6 and to do some additional reading, especially in professional personnel and training journals.

Feedback notes
- The vision of NVET is one of lifelong learning from cradle to grave for every citizen, the economy having a continuous supply of relevant skills to compete successfully in the global market-place. The policy seeks to achieve those economic and social ends through a largely self-regulated system which is decentralised and powerfully driven by local needs.

- During the late 1980s and the 1990s, the introduction of the TEC framework, changes in the method of funding secondary and tertiary education, a focus on targets, and well-publicised league tables achieved a significant change of direction and shift in the locus of control over the NVET system.

- Although there is still some support for measures to ensure compulsion to train, this is declining. The Labour Party by early 1997 had moved away from its initial commitment to a training levy on employers, and seemed attracted instead to individual learning accounts and to expanding the Investors in People (IIP) scheme. As Roy Harrison, IPD policy adviser on training and development, pointed out in *People Management* (1995: 40) a culture of levies and exemptions is not consistent with the spirit of the IIP standard.

- Harrison, like many others, believed that the voluntary system has offered much-needed immediate, practical, relevant and flexible help in meeting skills needs. It has also developed a real partnership of local bodies working together to achieve national education and training targets which 'give both a focus and a measure of progress for improvements to the UK's skill base'. He suggested that the most appropriate next steps woud be to focus strongly on the needs of businesses, core skills essential for organisations and individuals being incorporated in educational and vocational qualifications, and careers guidance playing a more central role in helping to achieve a more flexible national workforce.

- Many would like to see new employer-led education and training councils replace TECs at local level in order to build on the TECs' achievements while also developing a stronger power-base for the integration of education and economic regeneration. There is also a concern that the present system is not providing sufficiently for those with special educational and training needs. Holland (1995) advocated integration of provision for those of school age with the activity of disablement resettlement offices, employment rehabilitation and sheltered workshops.

• There remain strong tensions between the forces of centralisation and decentralisation across the NVET system. The State retains much financial and discretionary power, and there are always concerns that this power bends to party political pressures and short-termism. Greater autonomy is valuable to schools doing well in the league tables. However, less successful schools do not always benefit, and it is in such cases that the State's discretionary power can have value. Also, while local-led training bodies have achieved much, it is essential to maintain strong strategic direction at the centre if the co-ordination and coherency required to achieve the overall vision of NVET is to be achieved.

The NVET system is so exposed to the unpredictabilities of the market that short-termism and expediency remain major threats to the realisation of the vision that underlies Government intent. Balance and quality are in danger of being lost here, and the concerns are greatest in relation to the educational sector. When he wrote that 'the present government's proposals for education suggest that parents know the needs of their children better than teachers' Fr Dominic Milroy (1992), head of Ampleforth College, the Roman Catholic public school, was not only making a plea for educationalists to be recognised as professionals with a vital role to play in society as well as in the economy, he was also highlighting the danger of subordinating the individual's right to real quality of learning to the demands of an official curriculum and of educational reforms that could threaten creative partnership between government, teachers and trainers.

Lord Skidelsky (see page 94) did not carry his own concerns lightly. Convinced that there must be a system of genuine choice truly reflecting the variety of individual demands placed on it, he resigned from the School Examinations and Assessment Council in 1993, having concluded that 'In education, there is no halfway house between compulsion and freedom' (Skidelsky, 1994: 36).

Work-related skills, intellectual development, the advancement of learning and a contribution to the cultural life of society are all important tasks for the education system, but they do not fit easily together. The strains on that system grow as demand intensifies, yet it is also spread across increasingly diverse and resource-constrained provision. They increase, too, as employers expect not only intellectual, problem-solving and interpersonal skills in young recruits but also practical and knowledge-specific capability.

Without intellectual development, new knowledge cannot be generated and innovation cannot therefore occur. Without learning ability, new knowledge cannot be absorbed. Without skills development, new knowledge cannot be applied. The importance of knowledge creation and productivity has a particular relevance for employing organisations, as will be seen in the final chapter. At this point, however, it serves to illustrate three principles:

- There must be a powerful integrating vision driving NVET policy overall.

- There must be coherency, collaboration, and integration between the different bodies that provide education and training across the NVET system, especially at local levels.

- There must be a constant preoccupation to achieve a better balance between longer-term and immediate aims in order to ensure that NVET does serve economic and social ends.

Unless these principles are realised, the State's vision of NVET can never be achieved and the UK will continue to fall behind its main rivals in the search not only for competitive advantage but also for the well-being of its society.

CONCLUSION

In order to achieve the learning objectives of this chapter, the aims of national educational policy and strategy have been outlined. Progress and challenges in the implementation of strategy have been discussed by reference to reforms in the system over the past decade and to tensions between the forces of centralisation and decentralisation. Those tensions have been outlined in relation to nationalisation of the curriculum, to educational philosophy and control, and to educational standards. Finally, three principles have been noted as essential to drive policy if national NVET vision is to be realised.

USEFUL READING

NATIONAL COMMISSION ON EDUCATION. (1993) *Learning to Succeed – A radical look at education today and a strategy for the future.* London, Heinemann.

The information in Chapter 6 will need to be regularly updated, so the following are recommended as particularly helpful reading:

- The IPD's publication, *People Management*. This contains reliable, accessible and up-to-date information.

- The quality press – and especially the Sunday 'heavies' and the *Financial Times* – for their regular articles and editorials on matters relating to the field of secondary and tertiary education, and national training.

- *The Times Educational Supplement* and *The Times Higher Educational Supplement* should also be consulted on a fairly regular basis by students.

7 International comparisons

LEARNING OBJECTIVES

After reading this chapter you will:

- have a context for understanding the international – and especially the European – scenario relating to vocational education and training (VET)

- understand the key differences between national vocational education and training (NVET) systems in major competitor countries and the UK

- be able to assess what lessons such comparisons offer both for UK Government policy on VET and for human resource development (HRD) policy in individual organisations.

NVET: A FRAMEWORK FOR UNDERSTANDING

Many – especially students – have an aversion to studying international aspects of HRD. They see the field as so complex and rapidly changing that it is impossible to form a clear view about issues and trends. In fact there is nothing instrinsically different about finding a framework for understanding HRD in an international context from finding a national or organisational framework. What is needed is a set of concepts enabling everything to fall into a manageable perspective, helping us to place in the context of a relatively enduring basic scenario the flux of changing events.

We have seen in previous chapters that the development of people operates within a context of vision and strategies of the organisation and, ultimately, of the nation. The same is true when we seek to understand HRD on the international stage: the basic context is still one of vision, policies and strategies. In this chapter – longer than most because of the range of comparisons we need to make, but not, hopefully, more complex – a straightforward conceptual framework is presented. It involves three of a number of contexts that interact both with one another and in relationship to organisations: the socio-economic, the labour market and the educational.

The first section deals with the European framework for NVET. Next come some cross-country comparisons. Then there is a more detailed look at Germany and Japan, whose models of NVET are both distinct from one another and very different from that in the UK. Finally, lessons are drawn for the UK and for individual organisations.

VET POLICY IN EUROPE

The socio-economic context

The completion of the Single European Market (SEM) in 1993 had two aims (Hendry, 1994: 93):

- the removal of all artificial barriers to the stimulation of trade within the European Community (EC)

- the improvement, by means of their restructuring and internationalisation resulting from that stimulation, of European firms' competitive capability in the global market.

These two aims involve tensions between economic and social interests. The European Commission's vision of VET is one of many powerful contributors to the development of the EC, meeting a range of social and economic public policy objectives (Commission of the EC, 1989: 3). This vision may seem essentially the same as the vision for VET policy in the UK (page 87).However, the way in which policy is formulated and implemented across most of Europe is very different from the UK's non-regulatory approach.

At Community level the Directorate General for employment, industrial relations and social affairs holds responsibility within the Commission for training. Policy is executed by a Task Force on Human Resources, Education, Training and Youth. An advisory committee for vocational training and an education committee meet regularly with union and employer bodies to discuss training as part of the 'social dialogue'.

'Social dialogue' is an important term. It refers to a process involving the social partners in training policy in order to encourage employers to contribute to long-term profitability and economic performance rather than training only for immediate needs. This dialogue enables stakeholder interests, in the shape of organisations representing employers and unions, to agree on policy that is informed by practical knowledge and expertise, and increases the likelihood of successful implementation. Together, the Community's social partners have produced a series of joint Opinions endorsing the importance of education and training within the SEM (Rainbird, 1993: 185). Most member states (apart from the UK) mirror this Community-level approach by having some form of regulation of the VET system, and by incorporating employer and trade union interests into the policy-making process.

The labour market context

A labour market matrix

A country's labour market can be divided broadly into two segments (van der Klink and Mulder, 1995):

- *primary*. Entry to this segment requires professional qualifications and sometimes specific vocational training. People in the primary segment of the labour market usually enjoy favourable terms of employment and working conditions, relatively high job security, and good promotion prospects.

- *secondary.* In this segment most jobs involve routine manual work, and what training there is tends to be focused on improving productivity on the job, not on opening up career paths for individuals. There are few, if any, of the advantages enjoyed in the primary segment, since there are minimum training requirements, poor terms of employment and little job security.

The labour market itself has two aspects:

- *external* – people waiting for employment, including relatively large numbers of school-leavers, the unemployed and women returners

- *internal* – comprising the human resource base of the organisation, where employee resourcing policy can produce an integrated flow of people into, through and out of the organisation, with a particular focus on performance management, personnel development, career paths and an interlinking HRD policy.

Such a matrix helps to demonstrate the extent to which a country's labour market links its educational system to its business organisations. National policy must strive to achieve a productive balance between the two.

Europe's routes to competitive advantage

Although competing on efficiency and low costs are two possible routes to competitive advantage, their benefits can cancel each other out in net terms. It is the quality route, focusing on high added value, which promises to minimise the immediate costs of the SEM and to maximise its longer-term benefits. That route involves 'capital investment in new production techniques and products, an expanding knowledge base, and a more highly skilled workforce' (Hendry, 1994: 98). A high-skill strategy requires a strong and successful VET drive. Without this, a large proportion of the labour force will remain trapped in the secondary segment of the labour market and it will not be possible to sustain a drive for quality and innovation.

The UK, like Spain and Greece, is disadvantaged in a drive for long-term quality, being competitively strong only in some (perhaps one-third) of its industrial sectors. Germany, on the other hand, possesses competitive strength in most of its sectors, with 73 per cent of its employment in the primary segment of the labour market. Another source of disadvantage for the UK is that its large firms distribute significantly more of their profits to investors and significantly less to employees than do such firms elsewhere in Europe. This means that employees have less sense of ownership, and also that there is a lower level of investment in those areas that fuel innovation and growth – research and development and HRD – than is the case generally across the rest of Europe. This culture of short-termism and of shareholder domination of the business has already been discussed in Chapter 5. Here we see its typical consequences: a low level of average wage and of productivity, reflecting and reinforcing lack of adequate investment in education and training for skills and in employee rewards.

Hendry (1994) pointed out that in the UK's low-wage economy, which is also more internationalised than any other economy in the EC, workers are particularly vulnerable. Internationalised companies require strong social controls in order to avoid exploiting low-wage economies, but the UK has consistently resisted the Social Chapter's attempts to provide such controls.

It would be easy to conclude from the above comments that in a European Community where the quality route is the one being chosen by the majority of countries, the few who, like the UK, are low-wage economies with relatively unregulated labour markets are likely to lose. However, there is another viewpoint, and it needs examination since – along with the UK's long history of *laissez-faire* regarding NVET – it helps to put the UK's labour and VET policies in a rather different perspective.

Achieving a flexible labour market
It was always predicted that there would be job losses on a major scale in the first few years of the SEM's existence as administrative barriers came down, but the position was expected to correct itself after about six years. In reality, unemployment rates across most of the European Union (EU) are still high, averaging over 8 per cent in early 1997, and job creation has been low. However, economies like the USA and the UK which have deregulated labour markets and more labour flexibility have generated more service-sector jobs than has Continental Europe. Many of these jobs have been part-time, and many taken by women (Wolf, 1994). These countries have also achieved lower youth and female unemployment rates. The USA has the additional advantages of a thriving domestic economy and a mobile population, and so does not have the persistent divide between high and low unemployment regions characteristic of Europe.

The EU also suffers from poor export performance and slow growth of output. An important factor here is its heavy labour costs, to which three major contributors are protective labour legislation, relatively high taxation, and a flabby and highly bureaucratised public sector. The steady appreciation of European currencies against the US dollar has added to the EU's competitive disadvantage.

These failures to achieve the expected benefits of the SEM are putting increasing pressure on a hitherto highly differentiated labour market across Europe. Signs of convergence are becoming evident. Country differences rarely explain comparative competitive advantage, since weaknesses in one area of practice tend to cancel out gains in another, leaving the total package of labour costs, flexibility and skill levels similar across Europe (Goodhart, 1994). Now, as Balls and Goodhart have identified (1994), wage restraint is becoming a trend across Europe. There have been few signs of significant social dumping – a process that involves such measures as lowering wage costs, cutting social benefits, increasing hours of work and reducing restraints on employers. Reductions in direct wages and job cuts have occurred but by 1997 were proving to be the consequence less of a deliberate dumping policy or of the feared cheap labour/low-cost competition from Far East countries, but more a consequence of technical and organisational change.

Flexibility is the real issue here. Rising real wages and failures in training and education systems are leaving European countries ill equipped to compete with the USA and Japan in future high-tech products, in the same way as cheap imports from low-wage developing countries are undercutting the expensive products of European manufacturers of medium- and low-tech goods (Balls and Goodhart, 1994). As the shift towards more sophisticated technology grows in advanced economies and as fewer, better educated workers are employed in manufacturing, wage and labour flexibility become vital for Europe. Failure to adjust is in time bound to lead to high and persistent unemployment.

There is a growing perception that there must be more labour market deregulation in the EU. It needs to be sufficient to give the necessary wage and labour flexibility but not enough so as to threaten the level of job security needed to maintain workers' commitment. Some commentators feel that the labour market models of the UK and the USA are proving more relevant for the future than the tightly regulated Germanic model spreading across The Netherlands, Belgium and France. Certainly in the USA's highly deregulated labour market job creation has been strong, and the wages of the skilled have steadily climbed. In the decade up to 1997, Britain also achieved faster growth in productivity than its European partners.

That said, it must also be conceded that Britain has had much more ground to make up than most, and that its poor training record means that it lacks the large pool of skilled workers essential to competitiveness. Some companies are well aware of this. One provides a case-study in how to enhance both internal job security and the skills needed for growth in a deal offering mutual benefit to employer and workforce.

Case-study: The Blue Circle Social Partnership deal

In January 1997, Blue Circle, Britain's biggest cement producer, announced what has been hailed by some as a pioneering 'social partnership' deal with the Transport and General Union and the general workers' union (GMB). Its scope was over 2,000 drivers and process workers.

The essence of the deal was no compulsory redundancies for the following three to five years (depending on type of job) in return for modest pay rises. It went much wider than the previous biggest deal made by BMQ-owned Rover in return for working practices, because it not only involved closer co-operation but also productivity and training (Gribben, 1997).

The deal was attractive to the key parties. The company kept the freedom to request voluntary redundancies in future, and stood to gain considerably from the savings generated by changes in working practices while also gaining a tighter grip on wage inflation. For the unions, it offered stability in industrial relations, enhanced power within the company, and protection against the alternative possibilities of enforced job losses with the outsourcing of distribution and other services to non-union businesses. To the employees concerned, it promised enhanced employment and employability security at little personal cost.

The extent to which the Blue Circle deal did in fact break new ground is uncertain. For some it was merely a sophisticated example of the kind of agreement typical of the last Labour administration, offering no durable advantage to the company since, should there be an economic upturn, workers could still threaten to leave unless wages were increased. To others, however, it marked a significant recognition by a major company that improving the internal labour market was still important and possible, even if the horizons of the 'longer-term future' were now perforce somewhat short term.

(*Source*: The *Daily Telegraph*, 1997)

The plight of the unskilled underclass

The emphasis on training in the case-study is important. To be unskilled in today's global market-place is to belong to the most vulnerable of groups in the labour market. As we have noted in Chapter 1, in the USA as in Europe employment creation inevitably favours the more highly skilled workers. Furthermore, in 20 countries across Europe there is strong evidence to indicate that the labour market has an overall bias against less skilled or lower-paid workers (Wood, 1994). The plight of this 'underclass' is growing, particularly with the influx of the cheap unskilled labour that gives Third World countries their competitive edge. The underclass consistently forms between 10 per cent and 20 per cent of all earners, and there are fears that although its size may be decreasing as basic educational standards improve, those who are left within it are falling yet further behind (Marris, 1995).

In the UK and the USA the effects have been worse in this respect than elsewhere, even though in terms of per capita earnings unskilled workers have done better over the past decade than in mainland Europe (Marris, 1995). Whether, as in the UK, the unskilled tend to form the bulk of the unemployed or whether, as in the USA, they tend to form the bulk of the very poorly paid, they consistently fare worst in the competition for jobs and wages. Their lack of a good basic education compounds their vulnerable position.

There needs to be an investment in training that will give core workers sound basic education and the opportunity to invest and reinvest in workplace skills. Although in terms of good basic education Europe overall compares favourably with the USA, it compares unfavourably with Pacific Rim countries; and at higher educational level it also compares unfavourably with the USA, only 30 per cent of young Europeans moving into tertiary education, as opposed to nearly 70 per cent of young Americans.

In the UK there are at last signs that lessons have been understood. As we have seen in Chapters 5 and 6, NVET policy now aims to improve both the basic education system and vocational training. It also aims, through a national system of vocational qualifications and closer partnership with unions and employers, to remove occupational barriers in a hitherto rigidly divided labour market.

'Training as social engineering won't work'

Consider the following argument, and then provide a counter-view.

'Profit comes first, then training', said a *Daily Telegraph* editorial in 1996, continuing with the argument that in a period of steady growth and low inflation, such as was then being enjoyed, the provision of training by employers rises naturally without the need for government intervention, because successful companies spend money on training when they can afford it. Naturally they are wise to reduce investment in hard times, because training adds to costs, and in hard times rising costs are not affordable, leading usually to higher unemployment. Therefore the Government should focus its investment not on improving national vocational training schemes – which in any case have high drop-out rates and are ill equipped to meet the real needs of industry – but on improving the basic educational system – as in Japan and the USA – so that young people have the necessary standards of literacy and numeracy for skills development in-company when they enter the labour market.

Smith (1996a) believed that training as social engineering will not work: the role of training is to improve the labour market position of those who receive it, not to change the unemployment figures. He observed that Sweden spends four times as much on training as a share of national income than Britain, but it has a higher unemployment rate, which extensive national training programmes, especially for young people, have not dented. On the other hand Britain has grown faster than Europe in recent years despite a poor VET record. He concluded that investment in training can make a real difference to emerging economies, lifting them to a position where they can compete internationally, but that thereafter it has little impact on competitive capability.

(*Sources*: D. Smith, 1996a: 8; The *Daily Telegraph*, 1996: 19)

Feedback notes

- The claim that 'Training as social engineering won't work' is too simplistic. The strongest argument for a higher level of investment in VET in the UK lies not in a claim that it will reduce current unemployment or lead directly to job creation, but that it is essential to the economy's long-term and sustained growth, and to reduce the disparities between skilled and unskilled in competition for well-paid jobs.

- Without a larger pool of high-skilled, well-educated workers, an inability to raise the general level of competitiveness in the key sector of our economy – manufacturing – will continue to hold back our chances of strong economic growth. Although Germany, the Netherlands and Britain have similar numbers of world-class manufacturers, overall Britain comes bottom in practice and performance, because it has a long tail of poorer-performing companies (Hanson and Voss, 1994). This is exemplified in a McKinsey consultancy study of the world's component-making nations reported by Lorenz (1996). The study found that British companies emerged bottom of world productivity levels, even though on quality they lead the rest of Europe and the USA – primarily, it is thought, because of the standards set by Japanese-owned companies. Britain trails the majority of other countries in labour productivity (value-added per hour) and in value-added per worker. Its advantage in low labour costs is thus lost, so that 13 British companies studied in the early 1990s came last out of eight countries in average return on sales (Lorenz, 1996). Admittedly, some were just moving forward after start-up, take-over or restructuring, but the gap in productivity was still wide.

- Without a strong and flexible primary labour market segment and adequate investment in research and development, the economy cannot generate the innovation that will provide the means for future growth.

- Without better basic education and adequate vocational training, those who are unskilled will continue to form the bulk of the unemployed and underpaid in our society. They will also constitute a major barrier to the more flexible labour market essential to competitive advantage. National investment must therefore focus not only on educational reform but also on providing a strong national vocational training and qualification system, with free access for those in the secondary as well as primary segments of the labour market.

The internal labour market

As van der Klink and Mulder (1995) explained, if there is a rigid division of labour within a company then it is very difficult for manual workers to acquire the professional competencies that could gain them entrance to the primary sector of the labour market.

New technologies can of course provide the impetus to integrate hitherto rigidly separated categories of work. This integration is what management in many organisations is trying to achieve. However, for it to be possible, employees must be able to acquire the necessary competencies. If their educational background is weak and their grasp of practical skills poor, then retraining may be impossible. When that happens a company will be forced to maintain its division of labour, buying in the requisite skills but not resolving the fundamental weakness of a workforce that cannot respond rapidly and creatively to market changes because it is so segmented and inflexible.

Inescapably, therefore, the lack of an adequate VET system will lead to a labour market geared mainly to the manufacture of comparatively cheap mass products, because that is what it has the competencies to produce. In such an economy there will be a declining demand for skilled employees. This, in turn, reinforces lack of investment in a system of vocational training that could produce more who are capable of entering the primary rather than the secondary labour market segment. Caught in such a vicious cycle it is not surprising that

British companies have not been keen to invest in HRD (van der Klink and Mulder, 1995: 164).

Here is a case-study based on one that I set in 1996 as part of a specimen paper for IPD students taking the employee development professional qualifying examination. It is based on a real-life company. Answering the question will be a way of revising material covered thus far.

Sentex Engineering Company Ltd

What are the basic issues underlying training and development at Sentex?

Context

Sentex Engineering Company Ltd, formed in 1950, manufactures small, high-quality electronic machines for use in a specialised field. Six years ago the business was operating in a narrow and declining market in which its product was a high-quality mechanical specialist machine. However, after a management buy-out and the development and piloting of a prototype electronic machine, a more multi-faceted machine was produced. This rapidly captured the British market and moved successfully into the wider European market. Now, the firm has captured about 40 per cent of the world market within its specialised sector, but faces increasing competition as it seeks to expand its European market base. With the world population for the specialist product rising, the aim for Sentex is growth by acquisition and diversification.

Corporate strategy

The firm has a strong vision of trail-blazing, excellence and world-class products. The MD's style is open and discussion-based, but he believes that participation in strategy is best restricted to those at the top unless there is genuine difficulty or failure to agree. He has set one long-term corporate goal ,which relates to the need for continuing growth. Within that goal the directors annually draw up shorter-term objectives for their own functional areas and agree with their staff on how these can be achieved. Particular issues such as product reliability, quality and standards are targeted over an agreed time-scale.

Strategic strengths and weaknesses

The major strengths of the firm are its 300 employees, especially the management team and certain key individuals; excellent basic products; good tools and machines; strong capability in research and development (R&D) and engineering; a first-class network of licensees; and a secure financial base.

Main weaknesses arise from the fact that the firm has been very slow to make the transition from mechanical to sophisticated electronic manufacturing, and is still trying to master the complexities of operating in an international market.

Human resource management issues

The MD has not until now felt the need for an explicit HR strategy. Now, however, human resources are becoming a priority issue because the firm must have more flexibility of skills. Currently, the main skills shortages are in R&D, where there is also very high turnover. There are also regular shortages in production and services. In the component assembly area such problems are tackled by buying-in. The assembly operation is amateurish, and there is no mechanism for ideas for improvements coming from the shop floor. The new manager there takes the view that anyone who performs inadequately after basic training must leave, and that any but job-related training is an unaffordable cost to the business. Service staff are particularly difficult to obtain. They also take years to train in the variety of skills they need and have to be away from home for up to nine months of the year, making training difficult. Training has been limited to only a few of this staff's skill areas; for the rest, they have to pick things up as they go along.

The MD sees a bigger and more strategic investment in training as an urgent priority. However, with the company developing so fast, it is difficult to foresee exactly what training will be needed. Staff are continually firefighting, and usually they are so busy that time off for training cannot be found.

Feedback notes

There are many issues relating to the development of the workforce at Sentex. Chief among them relating to themes covered in this chapter are the following:

• Sentex has chosen a high-quality route to competitive advantage, and is operating in an increasingly competitive international market. It therefore needs to build a workforce that is flexible, without any rigid division of labour, and with well-educated employees who either already possess or who have the potential to acquire the competencies needed in a rapidly changing situation. This has obvious implications for recruitment, selection, pay, training and continuous and career development systems.

• Some of the trends noted under the heading 'Human resource management issues' are worrying in this respect. It is clear that there are tensions between the need for cost efficiency and high immediate productivity, and the need to develop skills and competencies for the future. Since that future is unpredictable, investing in an integrated, well-educated workforce will be essential, with strategic thinking and creative behaviour encouraged in every worker.

• On the other hand, there are favourable signs: an MD who is committed to a more strategic investment in training and development, a vision focusing on world-class excellence and long-term growth, and high-calibre employees. In such a situation an expert HR manager can make a strong case for a better balance of the short and the longer term in HRD strategy, and especially for interventions to improve the vocational attainments and competencies of the workforce. There must also be a drive for management development to ensure managerial style and skills better suited to achieving the high-quality, world-class goals essential to the success of the business over time.

The educational context

The socio-economic and labour market contexts described earlier in the chapter explain why the European Commission in its educational policy must do two crucial things:

• improve the level of basic education in certain States

- spread scarce skills more efficiently across the Community and increase the stock of those skills. Greater mobility will make the labour market more efficient, and so the Commission is working for common vocational standards, transferability of qualification, and student exchanges.

A country's educational system determines its levels of basic education and also the acquisition and potential to acquire work-based competencies. Basically, that system can be either full-time or dual (van der Klink and Mulder, 1995: 159).

In the *full-time system* students do most of their training at a State (or independent) institution of study – a school, college or university – and least in-company. In such a system the main emphasis will be on obtaining theoretical qualifications. Funding is likely to be split, the State helping to resource external provision and the employer carrying the main responsibility for funding training in employment. The UK system is of this kind.

The *dual system* is a partnership in which vocational training is largely provided on the job with less, but complementary, provision in institutions of study away from the company. In such a system there is bound to be a dominating emphasis on students' obtaining the practical competencies they need to practise their profession. Theoretical qualifications will be focused on acquiring knowledge that will underpin such competencies. Funding is likely to be shared between State and employers. The German system is of this kind.

Particular weaknesses in the UK's VET system, compared with those of key competitors, include:

- separation of VET roles in the system as between the State, employers and educational establishments

- lack of incentives for individuals or organisations to invest in VET

- far fewer numbers and proportions achieving craft-level qualifications and technical qualifications

- a 'low-wage/low-skill economy' (Hendry, 1994: 102) in which a high proportion of the workforce tends to be trapped by rigid division of labour and high demand for a low level of skills

- a narrow base of skills and knowledge, limiting employee flexibility.

Despite an improving situation related to basic education in Britain, the gap with most European countries remains wide.

SOME KEY INTERNATIONAL DIFFERENCES IN VET

At country level as well as across countries, NVET systems are influenced not only by socio-economic, labour-market and educational differences but also by differences to do with legal systems, history and tradition, and work-related values and other cultural dimensions. Reliable and meaningful comparative data are also difficult to obtain. That said, there are still insights to be achieved as we compare NVET in key competitor countries with our own loosely regulated, increasingly market-led system. Holden (1991: 114) has produced a comprehensive account of international differences. In this section the aim is simply to achieve a generalised overview.

Vocational qualification rates

In 1991 only 18 per cent of the UK workforce was qualified to craft level, whereas in Germany the figure was 56 per cent, in France 33 per cent, and in the Netherlands 38 per cent (Authers and Wood, 1993, using OECD figures). Reports from the independent National Institute for Economics and Social Research consistently show how far Britain is behind in terms of its education and training compared with competitor countries. By 1995 40 per cent of 13-year-olds in English schools were lagging two years behind their German equivalents and never caught up; only 30 per cent of Britain's workforce by then had vocational qualifications, compared with over 60 per cent in Germany (Clare, 1995).

This weakness in basic educational capability means that once such young people enter the labour market they are likely to have access only to the secondary segment and to remain trapped there. The need for dramatic improvement is the greater because of changes in jobs that will take place over the next 20 years. Higher-level professional, scientific, technical, managerial and administration jobs will continue to grow fast against a backdrop of an ageing workforce with large inflows of new young workers no longer possible, because of demographic downturn.

In the 1960s France had more acute problems of skills shortages and educational levels than the UK faced at the end of the 1980s. There was also, as in the UK, a widespread reluctance of employers to take a lead in the vocational training of young people. In the 1970s and 1980s the pace of technological and skills change in the French economy was great, yet France managed to equip her workforce to cope effectively with all the demands that faced it. The key to success was the use of Government-set targets of vocational attainment using full-time education to provide courses leading to the combined craft and general education CAP certificates. 'A coherent range of qualifications means that practically the whole ability range can gain nationally recognized qualifications which are frequently rewarded by higher pay' (Steedman, 1990). A set of vocational A levels was added in the late 1980s, based on the craft-level CAP (equivalent to City and Guilds craft certificate and several GCSE passes) but still able to lead to higher education. Subsequently, as will be seen below (page 115) there have been concerns about CAP, and new legislation in the early 1990s aimed to improve the quality and flexibility of apprenticeship in France. The similarities with curriculum and other VET reforms in the 1990s in the UK are obvious.

Vocational education and training

Although the school-leaving age across Europe varies from 14 to 16, there is already a major emphasis on extending full-time education and training to the age of 18 in Sweden, Belgium, Luxembourg, Greece and Ireland. There is a similar emphasis in France, but there both full-time vocational and apprenticeship training are important for the age group. In Germany and the Netherlands, part-time attendance at a school or college is compulsory up to age 18. In Denmark the emphasis is on young school-leavers moving into the apprenticeship system, as it is in Germany where, however, the term covers most jobs that 16-year-olds can be employed to do. In the UK in 1990 only 53 per cent of children were staying on in school or college, but by 1994 the figure had reached nearly 73 per cent. However, it is estimated that only 50 per cent of such UK students can be considered to be in vocational training, compared with 80 per cent in Germany (Smith, 1995).

In Greece, vocational education can start at 15. In France, technical subjects can start at 13 or 14, as they can in Belgium, Luxembourg, Ireland and the Netherlands. By 1986 only 15 per cent of young French people left full time education without completing a vocational course, and more than 70 per cent of 16- to 18-year-olds were staying on in full-time education, compared with just over 30 per cent in Britain (Steedman, 1990).

In the UK, vocational education starting at 14 is still struggling for effective integration with mainstream academic pathways (see Chapter 6) but attempts to develop a unified sector of VET for the 16- to 18-year-old age group are beginning to bear fruit. The proportion of those aged 16 and 17 in education and training combined rose to 78 per cent in 1990, and although much of that proportion was on Youth Training (YT) programmes where there were high rates of non-completion and of non-attainment of vocational qualifications, Training and Enterprise Councils' (TECs) funding for YT has subsequently been tied heavily to attainment of National Vocational Qualifications (NVQs) and to success in job search.

Occupational standards

In most EU countries (except the UK) youth wages are low until a significant level of vocational qualification has been achieved. In most competitor countries, too, occupational training is tied to the attainment of national standards, and it is widely assumed that young people without a degree will be vocationally qualified. In Germany the aim (achieved in 1984 by over 90 per cent of its young people) is that none without a satisfactorily completed apprenticeship should enter the labour market. It is also illegal in Germany, as it is not in the UK, to stop youth training before it has gone full term, or to stop the off-the-job element during the training period.

Over the past decade there has been concern in a number of European countries (for example, Greece, France, the Irish Republic and Portugal) to improve the legal framework governing apprenticeship. Some have introduced more flexibility at local level to vary course length and content to suit local needs (for example, The Netherlands and France). Even in Germany, the dual system that remains a model for the rest of Europe has attracted criticism relating to inflexibility, length, its overtheoretical nature and the lack of co-ordination between examining bodies, leading to inconsistent standards (Incomes Data Services, 1993: 64). Britain, then, is not alone in its struggle to improve occupational standards.

In Germany, employers and unions work with the authorities to determine the content of training and in the trade testing procedures in the apprenticeship system (Johnson, 1984a). In France high levels of unemployment and doubts about the usefulness of the state-provided CAP qualification, together with concerns that, as in Britain, many young people were failing to secure apprenticeships and so were entering the workplace without professional qualifications led to a resolve to move towards the German dual system. The apprenticeship system was in consequence overhauled in 1992 through a national collective agreement and legislation (Incomes Data Services, 1993: 37). It is now more flexible in relation to length of contracts, and course content is decided at branch level. There are interesting parallels, therefore, between recent French and British innovations in the apprenticeship system.

In the UK, as we saw in Chapter 5, there has been promising action taken in relation to rebuilding the apprenticeship system. However, progress towards a national vocational qualification system remains fraught with difficulty and controversy. By 1997 the assessment of standards was still being left to around 400 examining and industrial training bodies, all involved also in the design of courses (and often their delivery), incorporating standards laid down by the various industry Lead Bodies. Although the National Council of Vocational Qualifications accrediting all courses is due to be replaced during 1997 by an overarching Qualifications and National Curriculum Authority, there is still no independent national system of assessment of standards.

Continuous learning and development
In our major competitor countries there is a significantly higher committment to adult training, retraining and continuous development, both in and out of employment, than in the UK. The need for continuing education and training in order to ensure advancement and adaptation is widely accepted in those countries. In Germany and France, local chambers of commerce make available training for employed workers, and in most countries there are now arrangements to train the unemployed – often, too, to help those likely to become unemployed. Johnson (1984) pointed out that although provision of adult education and training in Europe has arisen for the most part in unplanned ways, the distinction between education and training is often not as marked as in the UK, and the distinction between vocational and non-vocational education and training is even less so.

Coverage of industrial training
Per head of the workforce Germany was by the mid-1980s training each year twice as many mechanics, electricians and construction workers, and even more office and distributive trade workers, as the UK (Prais and Wagner, 1981; Prais, 1985). In the UK, managers and supervisory training tend generally to receive the highest level of investment, followed by technical and professional training, and then by blue-collar worker training. There is, however, concern about our standards of managerial competency (see Chapter 19), and our clerical training is very poor in both quantity and quality compared with

France and Germany (Steedman, 1987). There are also relatively poor opportunities for women, although marked progress has been made in some sectors – notably the National Health Service. This uneven distribution of the training investment in the UK means that there is a serious shortage of skills in the middle and lower ranks of workforces, impeding the implementation of technological change and more flexible work patterns.

Training for manual workers in the UK has been almost entirely in the form of apprenticeships, with the cost, after the demise of the industrial training boards, borne by employers. As already noted (page 76), the Government has made a significant attempt to reverse the disastrous decline that occurred in manufacturing (as in other) apprenticeships between 1964 and 1986 by introducing the Modern Apprenticeship scheme in 1993, but there is still much ground to be made up before national skills shortages in key areas significantly diminish.

Organisational and national investment in VET
Inter-country comparisons of levels of investment in VET are particularly fallible because of the differences in the way data are collected and analysed, and because relatively little is known about in-company investment and its outcomes. Evaluation of the effectiveness of training, for example, is weak in most European countries (although, interestingly, stronger in the UK). It is therefore impossible to know much about the true value added by investment in training in those countries. The following are simply some of the most obvious differences between key countries. A fuller account can be found in Holden (1991) and in Incomes Data Services (1997).

Information from the Price Waterhouse/Cranfield HRM project indicates that across most countries of Western Europe the HRM 'wheel' (see Chapter 2, Figure 2, page 25) is not turning smoothly. Selection, integration, and the reward and development of people are not strategically oriented or integrated with each other. However, certain common trends in HRD emerged from the survey (Sparrow and Hiltrop, 1994: 312–14):

- an increasing investment in training

- high importance attributed to training

- increasing use of HRD as a recruitment strategy to attract people from the external labour market.

The high value they place on education and training means that most of our competitor countries acknowledge the need for substantial investment, shared between the key parties. German employers voluntarily bear the burden of most of the cost and effort involved, working closely with unions and the authorities to provide a high-quality and rigorously administered and controlled NVET system. In Japan the costs are shared by the education system and the employer, with only limited state-sponsored public-sector provision. In France collective agreements usually link pay to vocational and technical qualifications, and small means-tested allowances are available to pupils in secondary and tertiary education.

In the UK the cost of industrial training is borne in the main by employers, but there is a State-funded primary and secondary education system. Central funding of the tertiary system is diminishing, with an increased possibility of the costs of fees as well as maintenance being passed to the students. The Government is standardising the school curriculum to a high degree, and now exercises significant control over the funding of schools as it attempts to develop an education system offering more integrated and comprehensive academic and vocational pathways and more sensitivity to market needs.

In Sweden the State pays for the integrated upper secondary school; in Italy, France, Belgium, Luxembourg and the Netherlands the State pays for full-time training. In both France and Germany apprentices receive only a modest income, whereas in the UK, as noted in Chapter 5, starting wages at 16 years old can be high, and until recently (with the Modern Apprenticeship scheme) they have not been tied to vocational qualifications.

The French have a training tax, set at a minimum level of expenditure (1.1 per cent of total payroll) to be invested in training by qualified trainers. As was the case with the now defunct British levy-grant system, it is widely felt to lead to irrelevant training. It has not played any central part in the successful building up of a skilled, highly qualified workforce.

In the USA the ethos of individual initiative and of the innate value of education and training means that individuals invest highly in them, and companies give support where needed. They try to fit training around production in order to minimise lost output costs (Coopers and Lybrand, 1985). The system is less formalised than in Germany, the pressure on employers to provide training coming more from individuals. In 1983 a framework of locally based Private Industry Councils (PICs) was set up, responsible for local implementation of the Job Training Partnership Act, which involves distributing funds for training redundant and disadvantaged unemployed workers. PICs have met with mixed success, but none the less provided a major model for the British TEC system.

After the Second World War Japan, Germany and the Netherlands rebuilt their education systems, and students today in their schools lead the world in advanced maths, science and other technical subjects. The way that the money is spent matters more than the amount: Germany and Japan spend about 50 per cent less than the USA, yet consistently rank higher in terms of educational standards and attainments. Countries that value educators and education tend to keep students in school longer: in South Korea, for example, 55 per cent of students go on to college.

In Japan and Germany teaching is a highly paid and prestigious profession. In Germany teacher training is rigorous and operates at a high academic standard, every type of school requiring its own kind of training course. In the UK, by contrast, there is growing concern over a relatively poorly paid and low-status teaching profession, and over the effectiveness of teacher training. The secondary education system has not focused adequately on science and technology pathways, and this has led to a critical undersupply of teachers in those subject areas and to poor teaching standards.

The USA tends to invest more money on buildings and administration, relatively less going on teacher salaries. As in the UK, there is increasing concern at poor standards of teaching and attainment, especially in relation to maths and science instruction. However, participation of young people in the American university system is very much higher (at around 70 per cent) than in European countries overall.

NVET in the UK and competitor countries

Identify some of the key areas of difference between NVET in the UK and in leading competitor countries. In what kind of context should such differences be viewed?

Feedback notes
- Key differences exist in the six areas already discussed.

- International comparisons are fallible because of differences in the bases and interpretation of data, and because of a range of inter-country differences to do with socio-economic, labour market and educational factors, as well as with cultural dimensions. However, it is clear that in overall terms VET is taken much more seriously at all levels in most of the UK's competitor countries, with recognition of its significant relationship to business performance and to socio-economic well-being.

VET IN GERMANY: A CLOSER LOOK

The socio-economic and labour market context
Germany is one of the major industrial countries in the world in terms of overall economic performance and trade. By the mid 1990s, however, it was facing urgent problems to do with a slowing down of economic growth, rising unemployment and inflation, and the impact of unification. High labour costs mean that an increasing number of companies relocate plant in cheaper countries and this trend is putting pressure on patterns of investment in VET.

The whole VET system is rigorously regulated and is carried out by a social partnership. The unions have always played an active role in helping to decide on the structure and content of training provision and on manpower plans. Unlike unions in the UK, they represent all workers in an entire branch of industry, and are party-politically and denominationally neutral, as well as having the power to withdraw from firms the right to undertake initial training (Coopers and Lybrand, 1985). The social partnership of State, employers and unions has underpinned the stability of the whole economic system.

The employers' and employees' organisations and the Government in Germany jointly design the curriculum, the Government financing the educational component, which takes place at school. Businesses see it as their responsibility to train young people in order to develop a national pool of labour, and responsibility for financing the work component lies mainly with the employers. The federal Institute for Employment gives young people and adults subsidies and loans for vocational training if needed, and also promotes vocational further training and retraining in other skills. This helps the unemployed to adapt their skills to rapidly changing demands on the labour market.

Most companies seek to gain competitive advantage by the high-quality route rather than by low-cost mass production (van der Klink and Mulder, 1995: 167). This means that the external labour market must have a high percentage of skilled workers and few divisions of labour. Because the education system produces people with a broad education where there is a good integration of academic and vocationally-oriented study and work, the labour market overall has tended thus far to have the skill and attitudinal characteristics that the economy needs.

The internal labour market is characterised by a high degree of integration of planning, supervisory and manual tasks in organisations. This facilitates the drive for quality and innovation, and is made possible by the fact that employees have been educated to possess the competence and attitudes that allow them to control the quality of their own work. There are fewer separate jobs for operation and servicing equipment than in the UK, because employees are more knowledgeable about the production process (van der Klink and Mulder, 1995: 168). Since students in the dual system are trained to feel responsible, intensive supervisory control is also unnecessary, and the typical organisation of work enables full utilisation of the broad competencies of students graduating under the dual system (van der Klink and Mulder, 1995: 167).

Anyone seeking to become a manager in a German organisation must have a Meister qualification (see below), and this shared educational route to promotion means that managers and manual workers have the same technical expertise, making communications much less hierarchical than typically in UK organisations. There is far less division of labour in Germany than there is in the UK, and competency development focuses on producing all-round employees, rotating them between jobs to this end.

The education system
The German reverence for trade crafts is at the heart of its three-track high-school system, considered to be the best in the world. About one-third of children attend a *Gymnasium* (high school), from which most go on to university. The remaining two-thirds attend vocational and technical schools. The three-track system is flexible, allowing movement between schools at any time.

By law every young person should begin their working life with vocational training. To achieve this, there is a 'dual system' (see page 112) which combines school and in-company training so that, once they have completed their basic education, most young people go on to receive some form of vocational training. This training, made mandatory in the Vocational Education and Training Act 1969, offers a broadly conceived basic preparation for an occupation and the necessary technical abilities and knowledge to engage in a skilled form of occupational activity.

Thirty per cent of young Germans spend on average six years at an academic or technical university, or at a specialised institution of higher education, emerging with high-level academic or technical qualifications. For the other 70 per cent or so who leave school at 15 or 16 years old, apprenticeship programmes offered by approved employers are accepted as the normal entry route to employment. The training given must, by law, be parallelled for three years by education and training in a vocational school or, exceptionally, at an employer's centre.

Company training
'Apprenticeship' is a term with a far wider meaning than in the UK. Traineeships relate to all (about 400) officially recognised occupations. Apprenticeship training in firms must, by law, be under the supervision of an appropriately qualified person, usually a *Meister* (a master tradesman); this system helps to explain the exceptional quality of the skilled trades in Germany. Trainees have a legal contract with their employer, which varies between two and three-and-a-half-years, depending on industry and occupation. The training wage increases annually. The contract is registered with a supervising authority, usually a chamber of commerce, which administers qualifying examinations. Apprenticeship syllabi are set out in training regulations issued by the Federal Governments, and occupational examinations are held by the self-governing business organisations designated by the State. Those who do well in their skilled worker tests and examinations may proceed in further education and training towards technician level or *Meister* qualification.

Continuous education and development are seen as essential in order to cope with increasing and ever-changing work demands. Major companies have their own training centres, and smaller companies have joint training facilities used within the context of the dual system and for training of employees. In addition, Adult Education Centres, dating back to the end of the nineteenth century, are seen as part of an overall system of further education. They are usually operated communally or by local governments or registered associations, with the *Länder* (states) contributing funds.

Companies invest heavily in company training and management development, mainly using off-the-job training programmes for highly educated staff who will be apppointed to management positions. They spend a smaller amount on training skilled and semi-skilled employees, and increasingly they focus on training within the workplace since this is considered efficient for developing key competences, and is a route well suited to adult learners.

Training programmes for adults in employment tend to be organised half in company time, half in employees' time. Large firms like BMW run major adult development programmes in order to improve output and results, obtain individual commitment to innovation and achieve high-quality performance. In 1985 a broad qualification 'offensive' began in the former Federal Republic. The aim is to expand vocational further training in order to preserve and improve employment prospects, cut unemployment and reduce the shortage of skilled workers.

Here is a case-study showing what can be done by a UK organisation basing its approach to VET on the German dual-system model.

Case-study: Dual system of education and training at Hoechst UK

Hoescht is a Frankfurt-based chemical conglomerate with an excellent record of vocational training. In 1991 Hoechst UK introduced its own 'dual system' of education and training for British management trainees, basing it on the German management apprenticeship system.

Hoescht has always been very committed to youth training, but by 1991 the supply of Youth Training Scheme (YTS) youngsters had dried up, so the company decided to refocus on A-level entrants who wanted an alternative to university. Two courses were run in 1991, the first in Frankfurt with the first group of (five) British management trainees. Four of the group, who studied alongside German trainees, were due to finish the modular *Industrie Kaufmeister* course in 18 months, and the fifth in the average time of two years. All scored highly in their final examinations.

The second group of (12) trainees was based in the UK. There they combined practical experience at the three Hoechst sites in the UK with either a Business Technology and Education Certificate (BTEC) or a Diploma in Management course at Thames Valley College or Kingston Polytechnic (as it then was). Trainees also learnt German at the company's language laboratory and did business games. Placements in Frankfurt during their training were also possible.

(Source: Personnel Management, 1991: 9)

The Hoechst story has developed in many fascinating ways since 1991 (for a full account, see Sparrow and Hiltrop, 1994: 396–400), and the drive for a dual VET system has been an increasingly powerful lever in the company's quest for world-class status and maintenance of competitive edge in the international market.

Strains in the system
While the quality of the German VET system is incontrovertible, it is (as already noted – see page 114) not without its weaknesses. Overall it is bureaucratic and expensive, with hourly labour costs at double UK levels. During the 1980s productivity growth in German industry was among the slowest in Europe, and by 1996 Germany's unemployment figure had reached 8.7 per cent of the workforce in the former West Germany and 14.9 per cent in the East, compared with 8 per cent in the UK (Smith, 1996).

The German economy, under great additional pressures because of the costs of reunification, remains in downturn, and the social partnership is under strain. Unions continue to demand shorter hours, better conditions and higher pay, adding to labour costs without commensurate productivity gains. The difficulties being experienced in the motor manufacturing sector typify a worrying scenario: capped prices – because of the entry of Japan into the luxury car market – plus rising labour costs and falling sales that have dragged down profits. Meanwhile Germany suffers from skills shortages because, increasingly, 16-year-olds are opting for an academic rather than a manual education.

Universities are finding it impossible to accommodate the high numbers entering the tertiary system particularly as a result of reunification but also because, in recession, employers offer fewer trainee posts. As many as 40 per cent of students drop out after two or three years, and because of the economic downturn the German Länder were forced to cut education spending in 1992 for the first time since the 1960s (Genillard, 1993). These trends threaten prosperity. There is a major concern to reform the education system – and especially university education – to make it more oriented to market needs, and to spread cost and control more evenly between the State and the private sector. The parallels with UK experience are illuminating. Many in the UK fear that the success of the drive to increase participation rates in university education will lead to similar pressures to those now being experienced in Germany.

VET IN JAPAN: A CLOSER LOOK

The socio-economic and labour market context

Japan faces a difficult economic situation as it fights recession. The stock market has fallen and the cost of capital has risen, so cheap finance from banks and the stock market can no longer be relied on to underpin industrial growth, and major restructuring faces most Japanese companies. In July 1996 the Long-Term Credit Bank of Japan, one of the leading lenders, announced that it was to make large cuts in its equity stakeholdings in Japan's corporate sector. The move was thought likely by some commentators to lead to the unwinding of the cross-shareholdings that laid the foundations of Japan's post-war development. However, Japan has a proven capability in restructurings and has notable strengths to bring into play: its well-educated workforce, its deep financial reserves built up over time, its good technology and strong market position, and some high-quality senior management.

The steady appreciation of the yen against the US dollar is forcing Japanese manufacturers to relocate production overseas, while manufacturing costs at home suffer particularly from a rigidly structured internal labour market characterised in large companies by long-term job security for a significant proportion of workers. Although in 1995 unemployment was only 3 per cent, it is estimated that it could increase to 7 per cent by the turn of the century unless new jobs are created to replace those lost in the manufacturing sector.

As Nakamoto (1995) explained, such trends are being experienced across Europe as developing countries with cheap labour costs move into the global labour market. In this situation Japan's strategy is to focus on developing and retaining a higher value-added manufacturing base, taking advantage of new technologies.

The education system

The differences between the Japanese and UK education systems are profound; the Japanese system is different, too, from the German dual system. In Japan, there is little pre-vocational or vocational training in schools. The purpose of the education system is to lay a broad, non-specialised foundation of knowledge and attitudes to underpin future training, and to set high standards of educational attainment upon which employers can then build with organisation-specific training and development. Science and technology subjects start in elementary school, where 25 per cent of time goes to science and maths; the standard of teaching and attainment in these subject areas is exceptional, with a focus on problem-solving and application of knowledge and skills. Central control over the education system is very tight.

Full-time upper secondary education is almost universal, 96 per cent of young people staying at school up to the age of 18 or 19, or above. Most of that education is general and a decreasing proportion vocational. By 1989, 42 per cent of males and 34 per cent of females were entering higher education (Keep, 1989a).

Company training

In the bigger companies employers train and develop new recruits in their own training schools and on the job. After a brief period of initial training, all workers (and there is little distinction between blue- and white-collar workers in Japan) are then given as wide a range of experience as is feasible. As employees' years of service increase, so does their carefully organised experience, broad on-the-job training being supplemented with short in-service off-the-job training periods which, through the years, give a theoretical background to blue-collar workers' wide-ranging experience. Short courses provide a wide coverage of topics concerned with management problems, thus giving a widening perspective and understanding.

The culture is for employees to continue learning at work and also to continue education outside work and at their own expense. All big Japanese firms have their own education and training colleges, and some of them – Hitachi and Nippon Telegraph and Telephone (NTT) – are international showpieces. As is the case with German workers, continuous development together with a high level of basic education and encouragement to learn and use standard problem-solving techniques mean that the Japanese quickly gain an intellectual understanding of the structure of the machines and products and of the production process. They can thus deal remarkably well with any changes that occur, and can usually themselves suggest and determine with their supervisor how to improve efficiency.

Working practices like these are widespread, an estimated half of even the smallest companies with fewer than 50 employees adopting them for their essential skilled personnel (Koike, 1988). Even where there are fewer than 50 employees, it appears that only 20 per cent of such companies look on an approach based on 'poaching' as an ultimately positive measure rather than one to be adopted out of necessity (Koike, 1988).

Cultural pressures significantly drive training provision. Japanese firms work continuously to involve employees in the business, the larger companies employing a wide-ranging developmental strategy which includes job rotation and transfer, multi-task working, and participation in quality circles and zero defect groups. Larger firms link quality checks to training for subcontractors.

Strains in the system

Lifetime employment has never been available for more than about one fifth of workers in bigger Japanese companies. Smaller firms hire and fire more or less at will. 'Jobs for life' have, however, added to the high cost structure of Japanese industry. More labour flexibility is essential for the emergence of the new, highly competitive service industries evolving in information technology, environment protection and social welfare (Nakamoto, 1995). In 1994 Toyota announced the introduction of one-year contracts for white-collar workers, and this, in such an old, conservative company, signified a fundamental shift in practice in Japan. Toyota moved 20 per cent of its 4,000 white-collar workers to new project divisions where the business had greater need of their skills, so that rather than job loss the move resulted in more flexibility and adjustment to staff levels to match pressures in the external environment (Gurdon, 1994).

The education system has a rigidly structured, test-centred national curriculum that is coming under pressure now that Japan is fighting to retain international competitiveness in the technology race. In 1994 the president of NTT, the largest telecommunications operator, expressed concern about an education that was encouraging memorisation at the expense of creative thought and was 'geared to creating disciplined, quality labourers' (Terazono, 1994). Creativity is essential to generate patents, for example – and patents are increasingly important strategic assets. There is also a wider concern to achieve more independence of thought in Japan's system of government. Changes seem inevitable. However, as Terazono observed, as long as conformity characterises every aspect of Japanese life, the emergence of creativity will be difficult.

WHAT LESSONS CAN BE LEARNT FROM INTERNATIONAL COMPARISONS?

Lessons to be learnt from international comparisons

Looking at key differences between NVET in the UK and in leading competitor countries, and at the type and extent of competitive pressures in the international market-place, what are the main lessons that emerge for the UK, both at national and organisational levels?

Feedback notes

At national level the main needs are for:

- *an effective, competence-based qualification system.* The Government has sought to establish three routes into the world of work: a work-based route through NVQs, the General National Vocational Qualification (GNVQ) A-level route, and the 'academic' A-level route. Success is proving difficult, and there is a need to learn from practice across most other European countries. Both a practical and a theoretical grasp of tasks must be developed and tested – preferably by external examiners in order to ensure uniformity and consistency of skill standards – before a qualification is awarded.

- *adequate investment across different levels of training.* A formula has still to be found to ensure such adequacy, particularly in the field of craft and technician training.

- *testing to be more rigorously linked to the needs and characteristics of the workplace.* This should be not only in terms of standards reached but also in terms of reliability, punctuality and quality.

- *education and training for flexibility.* When future patterns of demand for skills are so unpredictable, flexibility of skills at an early age is vital, which can be achieved only by a good basic education, together with well-integrated academic and vocational pathways. This also gives young people a wider career choice. In Germany attempts are being made to establish a basic vocational training year in apprenticeships, and in France there is a twin focus on broadening general education and developing core transferable competencies in training programmes. In the UK 'the NVQ and SVQ system as it applies to young people fails to address the need to provide a broad basis of education and training for life for all our young people up to the age of 18' (Johnson, 1994: 33). Modern apprenticeships and current developments in the NVQ field may right the balance in due course, but as yet there is much progress to make.

- *continuous development of the workforce.* Johnson observed (1984) that on the Continent adult education and training are taken seriously by individuals, employers, trade unions and governments alike, adding that the vital ingredient is the commitment of top people. He conceded that all the best methods can be found in the UK, but doubted whether there is the will to use them to the full to help people cope with change and innovate.

- *stronger stakeholder involvement in VET policy and its implementation.* As was shown in Chapter 5, there needs to be a more effective framework to link stakeholders – workers as well as industrialists and Government – strongly in the formulation and implementation of national labour and training policy.

- *due focus on the long-term.* In the UK employers are expected to assume increasing responsibility for training, taking charge of delivering Government training for the unemployed through TECs/LECs and training for the employed by signing up to the IIP standard. The concern here is that, in a preoccupation with those demanding tasks, a short-term view will increasingly dominate national as well as local training. The dangers are a national workforce inadequately prepared for the future, and inequality across geographical locations in the treatment of individuals seeking training (Johnson, 1994: 32).

At organisational level, it is essential to reduce rigid divisions in the internal labour market and enhance basic education and occupational standards in order to achieve higher quality, flexibility and added value. There is also a need for improved management styles and competencies, especially in those operating at international level (Whitfield, 1995). Meeting such needs will achieve social as well as economic ends. It will give an improved capacity to secure competitive advantage and the innovation essential to growth. Finally, it will help those in lower-level jobs to improve their skills and so to be able to compete on more equal terms for entry to the primary segment of the internal as well as external labour market.

CONCLUSION

In order to achieve the learning objectives of this chapter we have first recalled the framework that can enable VET to be understood in a national context. VET in Europe has then been examined in a three-dimensional context. Within that context, four key issues related to the labour market have been discussed: routes to competitive advantage; the importance of achieving flexibility; the plight of the unskilled underclass; and the relative emphasis that different countries place on internal and external labour markets.

Six areas of difference have been identified across the UK and major competitor countries in relation to VET policy and practice, and the systems in Germany and Japan have been examined in detail. Seven lessons have been drawn for the UK from such comparisons.

USEFUL READING

RAINBIRD, H. (1993) 'Vocational education and training', in M. Gold (ed.), *The Social Dimension: Employment policy in the European community*. London, MacMillan. pp. 184–202.

HENDRY, C. (1994) 'The Single European Market and the HRM response', in P.A. Kirkbride (ed.), *Human Resource Management in Europe: Perspectives for the 1990s*. London, Routledge. pp. 93–113.

HENDRY, C. (1995) 'Skills and training in the European Union and beyond', in C. Hendry, *Human Resource Management: a Strategic Approach to Employment*. London, Butterworth-Heinemann. pp. 406–27.

INCOMES DATA SERVICES. (1997) *Recruitment, Training and Development*. London, Institute of Personnel and Development.

HOLDEN, L. (1991) 'European trends in training and development'. *International Journal of Human Resource Management*. Vol. 2, 2: 113–31.

VAN DER KLINK, M. *and* MULDER, M. (1995) 'Human resource development and staff flow policy in Europe', in A-W. Harzing and J. van Ruysseveldt (eds), *International Human Resource Management*. London, Sage. pp. 157–78.

The information in Chapter 7 will need to be regularly updated, and the following are recommended as particularly helpful reading:

• The IPD's publication, *People Management*. This contains reliable, accessible and up-to-date information.

• The quality press – and especially the Sunday 'heavies' and *The Financial Times* – for their regular articles and editorials on matters relating to VET in Britain and competitor countries, and to patterns of employment and movements in the economies of those countries.

Part 3

MANAGING THE HRD FUNCTION

8 The politics of human resource development

LEARNING OBJECTIVES

After reading this chapter you will:

- understand what is meant by 'the politics of human resource development (HRD)'

- know how to analyse the context of an organisation by reference to its primary culture, structure and power sources

- be able to diagnose the main political issues in a challenging training and development situation, and outline a strategy for dealing with them.

THE POLITICS OF HRD

Politics, or 'the art of achieving the possible', is what HRD is often about, and politics is one of the enduring facets of human and organisational existence. Perhaps it is for this reason that it has not been necessary to alter much of substance in this chapter since earlier versions appeared in my 1988 and 1992 IPM textbooks.

In Chapter 5 we saw how national vocational education and training (NVET) in the UK has for decades been the creature of political activity that, at Government level, has been preoccupied with other concerns. HRD at organisational level often mirrors that wider situation as it so often becomes subordinated to matters thought to be more pressing. The negative image is made worse in organisations where no strong case is made for HRD and there is scant attempt to convince powerful parties that it is worth a significant level of investment.

There are predictable reasons for this failure to make an impact. Specialist training functions are quite often headed by managers with little formal status in the organisation. Sometimes, too, training managers (regardless of position) operate in ways that fail to gain them credibility in the eyes of those whose support they need: line managers, unions, the workforce, the board. Or there may be a lack of supportive employee resource systems to ensure the effective implementation of theoretically valuable HRD initiatives. Whatever the reason, there is much evidence – as we have seen in Chapters 5 and 7 – to show that the verdict of the *Challenge to Complacency* report in 1985 still has considerable validity today: many employers do not perceive training to be central enough to their business for it to become a main component of corporate strategy (Coopers and Lybrand Associates, 1985).

If HRD is to make its optimum contribution to organisational goals, those responsible for the function at different levels must examine their own role, position, resources, skills and organisational context, and identify what it is possible and necessary to achieve. Then an appropriate strategy must be adopted. In this sense the management of HRD is like a military activity, with a set of goals, an overall strategy for achieving them and short-term tactics to meet different contingencies. Political skill is crucial to success, not just for the specialist but for all those in the organisation who have a major responsibility for the development of people. (For an illustration, see Harrison, 1992.)

Triggers for training and development
So how can support for training and development be obtained? In Chapter 2 we examined different scenarios likely to highlight the need for an investment in longer-term, business-focused developmental activity. In Chapter 4 we looked at the many potential triggers for a more focused approach to training provision in the smaller to medium-sized enterprise. Now we shall identify specific triggers for training in larger organisations (Pettigrew *et al*, 1988).

- *Business strategy.* As we have seen in Part 1, an organisation's business strategy will give rise to a range of needs with immediate and longer-term implications for the training and development of the workforce. Careful analysis of those needs, and agreement with management on plans to meet them, will be one of the most important ways of ensuring support for HRD.

- *Internal values and systems.* Once there is a commitment to HRD among powerful parties in the organisation who can then influence the rest of the organisation, HRD has its best opportunity to prove its strategic value.

- *Internal labour market needs.* A variety of needs can trigger training. Examples include the need for a multi-skilled workforce, for new skills related to technological innovation, for reduction in labour turnover by improved induction, training and development, or for HRD strategies that will attract and retain scarce personnel.

- *External labour market shortages.* Publicity is often given to the higher profile that training is bound to achieve in the face of demographic shifts in the labour market. However, it was noted in Chapter 5 that in the UK a typical response to this is to turn to recruitment and pay rather than to training. It is up to personnel and training practitioners to convince managers of the limitations that these approaches often impose compared with the long- as well as short-term benefits that effective training and development can offer.

• *External support agencies.* As seen in Chapters 4 and 5, there are many external agencies that can give valuable support to HRD initiatives within the organisation. Real, lasting support for HRD activities, however, comes with one thing only – success. Choosing the areas of priority where training and development will make the most noticeable impact on the organisation's effectiveness, then succeeding in those areas and ensuring awareness of that success, is all an essential part of the 'politics of HRD'.

But first, what about failure? We all make mistakes, and denying them outright is neither honest nor, usually, convincing. How does the skilled politician deal with failure?

Explaining failure

How do you deal with your failure in a particular task or area of work when it has to be discussed with your manager, or with a powerful colleague, or admitted to those working for you? Identify three or four of your typical methods of dealing, in such discussions, with your failures.

Feedback notes

You have probably mentioned at least one of the following. There are so many ways of coping with failure that this is by no means an exhaustive list – just a few of the most common methods:

• I admit the failure, and try to show that I have learnt from it and that it will not recur.

• I try to cover up, blaming other people, events, problems.

• I minimise the seriousness of the failure, and try to show that there were compensating successes.

• I attempt to convince others that it was not actually failure at all but part of a plan, and that the true benefits are shortly/in the longer term going to emerge. I deflect attention to the plan and its benefits so that it, rather than my failure, becomes the focus of discussion.

As can be seen by watching the behaviour of politicians, political success is, sadly, more often than not a matter of practising the last three tactics rather than the first. As has already been said, politics is after all the art of achieving the possible, and to be seen to fail too often and too badly is the one sure way of never achieving anything. However, it is important to remember that tactics must fit the individual and the situation. Sometimes the organisational climate is such that honest admission of failure, together with convincing evidence that it will not recur, is the most effective way of responding. Sometimes dealing with failure is not so easy.

It has to be realised that in many situations (and generally, too, the higher up the organisation you are) surviving failure is hard. Compelling reasons for overlooking it and continuing to attract the support and resources you need have to be found. Only the individual can decide how to operate in these harsher political systems – but honesty is, of course, central to the professional ethics of human resource (HR) practitioners, and compromising personal and professional values is not the hallmark of the respected HR manager or specialist. At the end of this chapter we shall tackle a case-study which will require you to look in some detail at this difficult area of dealing with failure. For the time being, let us note that:

> Politics is the art of the achieving the possible, and of surviving. Strategies for both achieving and surviving are essential.

THE POLITICAL CONTEXT OF HRD

So far we have discussed politics in a general way and have reached the conclusion that the essence of politics in training is to get support, to be seen to be successful, and to know how to survive failure. But we have also observed that politics are rooted in the particular situation. Success in politics is about understanding the context in which you have to operate, and adapting to it.

You will probably have met at least one manager who came to his or her present job with an excellent record of success, but who somehow failed to repeat that success. On analysis, some factor or factors in the two situations or 'contexts' will be different, and inability to identify and respond to that difference can be disastrous. So now we need to consider the particular context of training, its specific situation. We shall examine three key aspects of context: culture, structure and power.

There are, of course, many other factors that the manager must consider when drawing up plans for training and development. There are also many more complex and insightful ways of analysing the political reality of organisational life (cf Silverman, 1970; Pfeffer, 1981) and the different meanings that people attach to it (Morgan, 1986). However, in this chapter use is made only of the simplest possible approach compatible with developing a practical understanding of organisational politics. It is in the culture, structure and power system of the organisation that politics are embedded. If, therefore, we are unable to analyse these three aspects, we shall have no chance of success in handling the politics of HRD.

Organisational cultures and structures

First, cultures and structures. Try to give your own definitions of these terms. If you are familiar with organisation theory that should not be difficult but, if you are not, have a guess anyway. Think about phrases like 'the culture of our country' or 'the structure of the family', because they contain some clues.

> **Culture and structure**
>
> What, in general terms, is meant by the 'culture' of an organisation?
>
> What, in general terms, is meant by the 'structure' of an organisation?

Feedback notes

If you have responded with anything similar to the following, then you are clearly familiar with what we are going to discuss. If you have not, then hopefully your queries will be answered in the next few pages. You should also read Torrington, Hall, Haylor and Miles (1991: Chapters 8 and 9) for a fuller exposition of organisational structure and culture.

- The 'culture' of an organisation refers to the set of norms, practices, ideas and beliefs about 'how things ought to be done' in the organisation or in a particular part of it. Sometimes the word 'climate' is used instead; it carries the same kind of meaning.

- The 'structure' of an organisation refers to the network of roles and relationships whereby activities are allocated to different levels, parts and people of the organisation. It concerns the way the organisation is designed, or 'shaped'. We can envisage structure as the 'skeleton' of an organisation. In its more detailed sense structure also encompasses the systems and procedures that regulate and shape activity in the organisation.

The culture of the organisation is critical to the achievement of its mission and goals, as we saw in Chapter 2. Much has been written both in the consultancy and scholarly literature about organisational culture and its consequences (Hofstede, 1980, 1984; Peters and Waterman, 1982; Deal and Kennedy, 1982), but one comment is useful to note at this point:

> A corporation that can create a strong culture has employees who believe in its products, its customers and its processes. They sell it willingly because it is part of their own identity. (Payne, 1991: 27)

Organisational structure has long been a focus of research and an acknowledged primary influence on organisational behaviour and performance. Child (1984) wrote in clear and practical terms about how to analyse structure and select what is appropriate for the particular organisation. Mintzberg (1983) developed one of the widest-known models for the analysis of structure. Drucker (1988) provided a critique of the whole area.

Culture and structure do not exist in isolation from one another but are tightly inter-related. Roger Harrison developed in 1972 the first version of a widely used and much-adapted 'culture-structure' model. Commenting on it, Handy (1985) observed that every organisation has its own distinctive culture, which both gives rise to and in turn arises from (among other things) its particular structure. Many organisations, especially larger ones, contain more than one culture and structure, so that a differentiated system prevails. These writers identified at least four main types of culture to be found among and often within organisations, each associated with a particular structure.

Subsequently Handy has moved away from this straightforward set of concepts to raise complex questions about the kinds of structure that an increasing number of organisations may have to design, given the discontinuous types of change now facing them in their turbulent environments (as in Handy, 1989). None the less Harrison's original four-fold model and Handy's initial comments on it still provide a useful introductory guide to understanding our own organisations. The model (amended in one crucial respect) is summarised here.

The power culture and web structure

This is the culture of centralised power. It is most often found in small entrepreneurial firms, and at the top of large, bureaucratic organisations. Control is exercised by one person, or by a small set of people, from whom rays of power and influence spread out, connected by functional or specialist strings. The structure to which such a culture gives rise is therefore web-like.

Essentially such organisations, or parts of them, are political. Decisions are taken largely on the outcome of the balance of power rather than according to set procedures or on purely 'rational' grounds. People who succeed in this kind of organisation are those who want and can handle power, the politically skilled, risk-takers rather than people concerned with security. Such organisations, since all key decisions in them are made only by one or a few people, move fast and react quickly to threats: they 'think on their feet'. Success means getting the results desired by the point of central power; means tend to count for relatively little. Organisational life is highly competitive, and survival even at the centre is difficult. In the end, the quality of those at the centre is their key to success, and when a key figure goes or is displaced the balance of power in the system may change radically.

Those concerned with, or responsible for, HRD in such a system have to produce the kinds of success desired by the central power source, and to relate training objectives and plans to needs recognised as important by that source: by no means an easy task.

The role culture and pyramid structure

This is the culture of bureaucracy, sustained by the belief that an organisation should have its purpose and overall plan defined at the top, and then rest for its strength on a clearly defined hierarchy of functions or specialisms. Co-ordination of the descending levels of departments is carried out at the top by a narrow band of senior management, advised by specialist functions. Rules and procedures govern every role and position in this pyramid, or temple, or hierarchy. They also govern communications and the conduct of disputes. Precedents dominate decision-making, and the whole organisation tends to be security-oriented, with a tendency to rigidity rather than to innovation. Role cultures and structures are slow to see and accept the need to change. Change itself is usually a lengthy and difficult process, with job descriptions, rules, established working practices and routines all capable of pulling people back to the past rather than forward into the future. At the same time, the role structure is probably the most widely used way of organising large numbers of people around a common goal, not only in work organisations but in States and religions: one has only to think of mid-twentieth-century China, Germany, the Soviet Union or the Catholic Church to realise the enduring organisational power of the bureaucratic model, as well as the dangers inherent in its misuse.

The formal position allocated to whoever carries special responsibility for HRD in such a system will be the major initial source of power. The higher the position, the more the possibility of influencing events. However, even if formal position is fairly low or peripheral, all is not lost: knowing ways round and through the rules, the files and 'the system' can often enable the achievement of desired ends.

The greatest danger is that in this departmentalised and inward-looking world open-minded, objective and 'professional' vision can become 'departmentalised' too. How many managers have you met who have become absorbed in the goals and interests of their little empire, rather than striving for the benefit of the whole? But given the type of culture that prevails, is such behaviour surprising?

The human investment culture and network structure

Handy (1985) used the phrase 'task culture' to describe an organisation where people come together because there is a job or project to be done, irrespective of personal power or of formal position. Later he used the term 'shamrock' and other variants on this theme, but the emphasis remained on the team rather than the individual. The culture so described was one of teams brought together to work on projects as they come in, and which are then disbanded, with new teams formed as new projects arise. The structure could be pictured as a net, with some of the strands thicker and more permanent than the rest. Much of the power lies at the permanent knots of that net.

There are many organisations that have this form of matrix structure. In the strategic management literature, however, researchers like Miles and Snow (1995) have taken the concept further, claiming that the evolution of network organisations is forcing a new view of human resources and that a new, spherical structure typifies many businesses today. These are delayered systems that have to be highly flexible and responsive to market forces. They 'array themselves on an industry value chain according to their core competences' (Miles and Snow, 1995: 5) and use strategic alliances and outsourcing to this end. Firms with a spherical structure 'rotate competent, self-managing teams and other resources around a common knowledge base', and can be linked together in a multi-firm network, as the authors illustrated in their paper (Miles and Snow, 1995: 6). The keys to success for such a structure are knowledge as a key intangible asset and expert people who can operate with minimal supervision, interacting continuously and in complex ways with others inside and outside the business. Keywords are partnership, co-operation and collaboration, trust and mutual interindependence.

Success for the individual is achieved by expertise and networking, and by acquiring, retaining and transforming knowledge. Speed of reaction, flexibility, sensitivity and creativity are often more important than depth of expertise. Life may be challenging and stimulating, but few find it easy because it requires constant effort to keep up to date in expertise, to move through a maze of networks, to accept the need for continuing co-operation and trust in working with others, and to remain committed to the matter in hand no matter how stressful the pressures it generates. As Miles and Snow (1995: 11) observed, the work demands effective 'relationship management' skills and working with partners in a continuous self-development process. Management in such a structure is about building people's strengths and investing in their long-term development; acting as partner of individual employees and supporting the work of self-managing teams; and managing the changing knowledge base of the organisation. We shall return to the concepts behind this thinking in Chapters 19 and 20.

When resource-limitation begins in this kind of system, the norms of the culture become challenged. Often there is a shift towards either a power or a role culture, and sometimes this can lead to a permanent change and to a new structure. Specialist skills, not specialist functions, are the need in such structures, and over the past few years, as organisational shapes have gradually changed, many training managers have lost their roles, even their jobs, through lack of planning against such a contingency.

The person culture and galaxy structure

This is not so much a type of organisation (although some professional partnerships operate on this basis), but more a way of describing those clusters of individuals to be found in most organisations who see their job and the resources available to them mainly as a means of serving their own interests. Often these cultures exist where there is one person who has a unique contribution to make on the basis of specialist skills or knowledge, thus becoming the 'star' around whom everything and everyone tend to revolve.

Anyone trying to promote development of people in such a situation can find it a hard task. Often 'star' individuals not only need development themselves, but are also exercising a stifling effect on the development of others. Because they have unique and valued skills, they can usually get other jobs without too much difficulty, and the threat of moving on is one they will often use. Or they may have protected tenure, again adding to their power base. In either case, they will probably fail to acknowledge any expertise as greater or more compelling than their own. Appealing to that expertise may, however, prove to be one way of persuading them to develop others. Few can resist the flattering plea to help those less gifted than themselves by passing on the benefit of their wisdom and experience.

A different way of looking at person cultures is to see them as dominated by a belief in people's potential, and therefore characterised by a focus on the development of people and on delegating to individuals as much responsibility for decision-making and resources as is feasible. The skill of management in such a culture is to hold in continual balance this belief, with its concern for appreciating and responding to individual needs and aspirations and continuously developing abilities and potential, with the responsibility of ensuring that work targets and commitment to organisational goals are also achieved.

The structure and culture of my organisation

Take an organisation with which you are familiar, or a division of it, and analyse its primary structure and culture. The questionnaire originally designed by Harrison (1972) and subsequently amended by many, including Handy (1985), offers a straightforward and effective way of achieving practical insights into organisational culture and structure.

Start your analysis with a brief explanation of the 'organisation' and whether your chosen frame of reference is the whole organisation or a particular part of it. Explain, too, how far your organisation, or your chosen part of it, is considered to be 'successful', and any major problems and/or opportunities it faces in operating. Thereafter pay particular attention to the following points, illustrating your analysis with practical examples and explanations wherever possible:

- the kind of culture and structure you think top management intends and believes to exist, and the kind of culture and structure you feel actually exists

- how far the culture and structure promote or hinder the achievement of organisational goals at various levels

- the kind of people who 'get on' in the system, and the reasons for their success

- the kind of people who are unsuccessful in the system, and the reasons for their failure

- how far people's needs, aspirations and development are matters of real concern to the organisation

- the pressures and opportunities facing HRD because of the culture and structure of the organisation.

Feedback notes

There are no set answers to this exercise: the results are bound to be different for each person who attempts it. However, if you are a student tackling the analysis wholly or partly as a class exercise, your tutor could split the class up into groups so that in each group members can exchange information arising from their analyses. A plenary session thereafter can obtain from each group what are judged to be the most interesting outcomes from those discussions. The sorts of issue that can be examined include the following:

- Where people come from the same, or similar, organisations, are their perceptions of the culture and structure in which they work the same, or different? Why? For example, someone employed in a rigid bureaucracy may none the less work in an HR department organised as a task structure. Its management culture may favour teamwork, participative decision-making and achieving a dynamic, pro-active role for HR in the authority. In that case the individual's perception of 'the organisation' will be very different from that of a colleague working in a more bureaucratised area.

- What about personnel and training staff? Have they influential roles in their organisation? If not, why not? If they are influential, what explains this?

- How has political skill, or lack of it, affected the performance and credibility of personnel and training staff?

- How far is development of people in the different organisations a major responsibility of the personnel department; and/or of a training specialist or function; or primarily the responsibility of line management?

- What sorts of attitudes and policies are there about HRD in the various organisations, and how do these relate to the cultures and structures of those organisations?

To summarise thus far:

In this section we have been looking at different kinds of cultures and structures between and within organisations, and we have seen that one easy and useful way to classify them is by using a four-fold system.There are at least four main types of culture, each with its typical associated structure. It is essential for anyone seeking to promote the development of people in an organisation to identify the primary culture and structure to which they must relate, and to adapt their strategy accordingly.

Culture and structure are two of the three factors relating to the political context of HRD. The third factor is power.

Power in organisations

> Power is a property that exists in any organisation ... Politics is the way power is put into action.

> (Torrington and Weightman, 1985)

It is essential for anyone trying to promote the development of people in an organisation to understand the bases of organisational power and how to acquire and use it in order to achieve objectives.

There are innumerable studies of power in organisations. One of the most compelling is the social action analysis contained in Silverman's

---

Types of power in organisations

Here are six types of power commonly met in organisations. Please write what you think each means:

- physical power

- resource power

- position, or legal, power

- expert power

- personal power

- negative power.

complex but fascinating book (1970). French and Raven (1959), Pfeffer (1981) and Handy (1985) also offer absorbing discussions. With acknowledgement to such work, I list in the box on page 138 six types of power and ask you to explain what you think each means. If you cannot respond at this stage, don't worry: this is simply a way of opening up discussion.

Feedback notes
* *Physical power* means the power that derives from physical strength, appearance or presence. Often someone's mere presence in a workplace is enough to galvanise people into action.

* *Resource power* derives from control of resources valued by those you wish to influence. The resources can be anything: money, promotion, a bigger carpet in the office. What matters is that they are wanted, valued. Many of those who are responsible for developing others have few direct resources of their own, and so one of their first tasks must be to discover who holds the resources that they need, and how to obtain those resources.

* *Position power.* The importance of position as a source of power in a role culture, and the implications for those trying to develop people in such a system, have already been noted.

* *Expert power* in one's field is, as we have seen, highly valued in human investment cultures, although less reliable as a power source in a role culture (where the 'expert' can quite quickly be cut down to size by rules and procedures, time lags, and the many convoluted decision-making mechanisms).

* *Personal power* is seen at its most obvious in power cultures, where it is often used to reinforce all the other power sources of the person or group at the centre. However, it is an important quality for a training practitioner to possess if working in a task culture, where interactions are often difficult and sensitive to manage. When confronted with a person culture, some other holder of personal power may offer the only hope of influencing the 'stars' when they are causing problems in the system.

* *Negative power* is the power, possessed by us all, to withdraw our energy and effort and commitment. Sometimes the results are not as we had hoped. Unless we are in a job, or have a skill, that is vital and is difficult to replace, then withdrawal of effort even by a large number of people may have no real impact. However, HRD depends for its success on securing the full commitment and enthusiasm of everyone – from the manager who provides or withholds crucial information about the learning needs of staff, to the individual required to learn but not necessarily motivated to do so. Inability to understand and deal with the exercise of negative power is a major weakness in anyone responsible for developing learning in the organisation.

There are many power sources in an organisation. It is important to identify the type of power possessed by oneself and by others. Knowing how to use and relate to different types of power is an essential political skill.

So far in this chapter we have looked at three aspects of organisational life that relate centrally to the politics of HRD: the culture, structure and power system of the organisation. We have recognised that to be successful in HRD a high level of political skill may be required, and that the ability to analyse and understand organisational politics is an important element of that skill. Now here is a case to put some of these ideas to the test. Please read it carefully before tackling the questions. It can be used as a self-learning exercise or (if you are a student) as coursework or a class activity.

The management training problem

You are a training officer, aged 26, working for the past three years in the HR department of a large, private-sector service organisation in the Midlands. Previously you worked as a training officer in a local authority, where most of your work involved administration of a Youth Training Scheme (YTS). You have a degree in business studies, and in your present post you are responsible for the administration of various management and supervisory programmes and for organising short courses, mainly of a technical nature.

You have no formal personnel or training qualifications, although you would like to acquire some. There are several other personnel staff, one of whom is a training officer specialising in technical training.

Your boss, the HR director, is Roger Mason, IPD-qualified, and considered by top management to be effective. He has been with the organisation for 10 years, and before that had 15 years' experience in a variety of firms. He is not so highly regarded by the other staff in the organisation, who see the personnel function as a very bureaucratic department, too absorbed in paperwork and procedures. Currently Mason is heavily involved in drawing up an equal opportunities policy for the organisation. He has always tended to 'manage by exception', which translates in his case into 'start to worry only when things go wrong'. Staff are reluctant to ask him, or each other, for help, as they are afraid that this may be construed as a sign of incompetence on their part. Most stick rigidly to their job descriptions. You do not much like working in the department, but are hoping that once you have a little more experience you will get another post and move on. You intend to specialise in training.

Just after you joined the organisation, Mason told you to 'do something about educating our junior and middle managers'. He said top management felt that the performance of these groups, and of supervisors below them, was not always as good as it might be (although he gave you no specific evidence on this score). Furthermore, the younger people at least, many of whom were in technical functions, would be moving up in the next few years, and it was felt that they needed a greater awareness of what general management involved. He wanted some courses organising, although nothing too expensive.

Although you know little about management training, it nevertheless seemed to you that education should be an important part of employees' development. It broadened their minds and gave them new knowledge and ideas. You therefore suggested that about six managers at various levels and from different departments in the organisation should be sent on a two-year part-time Diploma of Management Studies (DMS) course at the local university each year.

Mason liked the idea, particularly as it did not involve his department in anything more than calling for nominees and organising their attendance. Subsequently 16 managers have gone on the DMS, at the rate of around five a year. All were chosen by Mason from nominations made by the superior officers of the staff concerned. He did not explain to you the criteria for nominations or selection. Mason has just been asked by top management for some information about the management programme to go into the Annual Report. Last week he came to you in a panic, asking you to provide the information for him in two weeks' time.

You have now talked to everyone who has been through a DMS or is still studying for it. It is popular with the staff from departments like management services and sales and marketing, all of whom tend to be in their twenties or thirties, with degrees or equivalent qualifications. They find the content intellectually stimulating, and some are able to apply newly learnt techniques to their jobs, although the majority find that there is no real support for or interest in this within their departments. However, the remark made by one of them to you typifies the general feelings of this group:

> I won't be here for ever, so I'll be able to use the learning in the next job I get. In the meantime, it's certainly made me more aware of the deficiencies of this place – especially how out of date my boss is! Pity you couldn't persuade *him* to do one of these courses!

The nine staff from this group who have gone through the DMS or who are currently studying for it have all done well in coursework and final examinations, and have particularly enjoyed the project work.

Unfortunately the seven staff from technical departments are neither so satisfied nor so successful. Their average age is mid-thirties to mid-forties, and all have technical qualifications, one a degree. Some of them have managerial responsibilities, others do not. All find the course hard, some because so much of the content is outside their experience completely and the others because, to quote one:

> We've been doing our jobs perfectly well up to now. Why are we being pushed onto these college courses? We're not going to get more pay or promotion, and there's nothing new in any of it except that organisational behaviour stuff – and that's just common sense, anyway – a lot of jargon, but that's all it really is.

One of the technical staff dropped out after two months, and although three others passed the examinations last year, one did not, and has to resit this year. Most feel that the DMS is pointless for them. It does not help them with their daily problems, and they resent the fact that while 'whizz kids from sales and marketing have got it made' they themselves cannot even get cover when they are away each week, and they already have such a mass of work to do that piling up 'all this homework business' is just an impossible burden.

You have had a preliminary chat with Mason about these reactions, and he is rather concerned, especially about the technical people and their managers, with whom he has never had particularly good relationships. He has asked you to see him tomorrow to discuss the situation, and to decide what should be reported about the programme. Your discussion will need to be handled with considerable political skill.

Why? What are the main 'political' issues? Outline how you propose to deal with the discussion, and what you hope and intend to get out of it.

Feedback notes

The training officer will have to explain the failures in the programme to his or her HR director not only in a way that will leave the training officer's credibility intact but in a way that will help the director in turn to present a positive rather than a negative picture in his Annual Report.

- *Clarify the outcomes sought from the discussion.* The training officer's major concern should be that, in future, needs for training are accurately assessed, training objectives and plans are agreed and understood, and training has the commitment of all the interested parties. The design of courses should motivate and help learners to gain results that are of value to the organisation and to the individual. He or she will also want to leave the meeting with the active support of the HR director. Aiming for these outcomes will give focus and direction to the discussion.

- *Put failure into context and look for successes.* The benefits from the programme so far (and there are quite a number) need to be identified, and failures put into context. The programme has, after all, run for three years, so some failures are inevitable. Furthermore, major activities such as this not infrequently uncover problems that were probably always there, and could have come to the surface at any time. For example, the gaps between older and younger staff, and between different specialists and generalists, involve essentially organisational issues which must be viewed in that wider context. What rewards does the organisation offer its older managers and supervisors for the effort required of them in going through a tough examination course, for example? How far does its salary and career structure support such initiatives? What explanation was offered to staff initially about their enrolment on the DMS? Why is there inadequate support for many of the staff when they try to put their new learning into practice? (For a discussion of such problems, see Fairbairn, 1991.)

- *Develop support for training.* Having looked at the successes of the programme, and emphasised the need for a wider perspective on some of the problems which have come to light during the three years, the training officer can then suggest that joint planning and design between training, managerial and supervisory staff would be a positive way forward. Other, more work-related, developmental initiatives may be relevant now, rather than just concentrating on educational courses, and the ideas of the staff and their managers will be essential here. Such work-based activities would also be relevant and motivating for older staff and those in technical positions. Involving their managers in discussions would also be a way of getting those managers more interested in the whole idea of developing their staff, and thus of reducing the problems of learning transfer that some staff experienced when they tried to apply learning from the DMS course to their jobs.

- *Consider culture, structure and power factors.* The situation described on pages 140–42 is very common in a large bureaucratic organisation with an HR culture that does not encourage a systematic or creative approach to HRD, or stress its relationship to business needs. Of course the training officer should have queried the need for the focus on managerial training and development in the first place: what was the evidence that there were deficiencies here? Or that training was the best response to those deficiencies? And of course he or she should have looked at other ways of responding to the HR director's instructions: what about training and development through work-based activities rather than, or as well as, an educational programme? There should have been careful monitoring of the selection and progress of staff on the DMS, together with evaluation at the end of each course, and, later, when staff got back into their jobs. And what about pre-course briefing and post-course de-briefing for the staff?

- *Be focused.* So there are many things the training officer should have done, but obviously inexperience and a junior position in the HR department help to explain the failure to do them. No doubt by now he or she is well aware of personal deficiencies. For the discussion, however, it is essential to avoid overmuch breast-beating, otherwise the training officer may be made a scapegoat by the HR director rather than achieving anything constructive. The aim instead should be to agree with the director on establishing positive links between training and line management staff, and on developing simple but effective procedures for the diagnosis of learning needs, and for selection and monitoring of staff on training and educational programmes. The training officer should also point to the value of trying to take a wider perspective on HRD in the organisation.

Since our interest here is related to political issues, don't worry if you missed some of the more specialised points that I have covered in the feedback notes – it is the general political stance that it is important to consider. To summarise:

- Be clear about the outcomes you seek from the discussion.

- Reflect on culture, structure and power factors.

- Put failure into context and identify successes.

- Get support for training and development initiatives.

Only one more factor needs emphasis in this chapter: the value of a clear vision about the place HRD should have in the particular organisation. This has been covered in Chapter 3, where we noted that lack of vision, whether at organisational, national or international levels, leads to lack of a convincing strategy.

CONCLUSION

In order to achieve the learning objectives of this chapter we have examined specific triggers for training and development in larger organisations, and explored the political context of HRD by reference to three factors: organisational culture and structure, and power. Six types of power have been identified, and a four-step guide to dealing with failure in HRD has been provided.

USEFUL READING

ANTHONY, P. (1994) *Managing Culture*. Buckingham, Open University Press.

JOHNSTON, R. (1996) 'Power and influence and the HRD function', in J. Stewart and J. McGoldrick (eds), *Human Resource Development: Perspectives, strategies and practice*. London, Pitman. pp. 180–95.

COOPERS AND LYBRAND ASSOCIATES. (1985) 'A challenge to complacency: changing attitudes to training'. *A Report to the Manpower Services Commission and the National Economic Development Office*. Sheffield, MSC.

DEAL, T.E. and KENNEDY, A.A. (1982) *Corporate Cultures: The rites and rituals of organizational life*. Reading, Mass. Addison Wesley.

DRUCKER, P. (1988) 'The coming of the new organisation'. *Harvard Business Review*. January/February: 45–53.

MILES, R. and SNOW, C. (1995) 'The new network firm: a spherical structure built on a human investment philosophy'. *Organizational Dynamics*. Vol. 23, 4: 5–18.

9 Training and development roles, standards and responsibilities

LEARNING OBJECTIVES

After reading this chapter you will:

- understand training and development occupational and professional standards and the contribution they can make to practice

- be able to identify the main training and development roles and responsibilities in an organisation, and the expertise and commitment they involve at different organisational levels

- be able to produce guidelines for improving the status and contribution of human resource development (HRD) in an organisation.

INTRODUCTION

What do we mean by 'role'? The dictionary definition is '*Role*: an actor's part ... person's or thing's characteristic or expected function' (Allen, 1990). This is a useful way of thinking about 'role' because of the emphasis on playing a part, on interacting in a particular way with others, as well as on functions to be performed. It also highlights the concept of dynamism: every actor differs in his or her interpretation of a given part, and makes of it something unique, as well as fulfilling its formal requirements. These related ideas of a given and a developed role are emphasised in much of the published research about training roles.

Let's now look at three perspectives on training and development roles, and the standards involved in performing in them:

- a typology of training and development roles

- the national occupational standards for training and development

- the Institute of Personnel and Development (IPD) professional standards.

A TYPOLOGY OF TRAINING AND DEVELOPMENT ROLES

The change in the conceptual and practical base of HRD over the past few years has been considerable. This becomes clear when we look at one of the best-established typologies of training roles and note its current limitations. For at least a decade after it was first developed in 1982, the classification produced by Pettigrew and his colleagues (1982) provided a meaningful description of the range of activity in which training staff were involved across different organisational settings. They identified the following roles:

- *The change agent.* This role is concerned with the definition of organisational problems and with helping others to resolve these through changing the organisational culture.

- *The provider.* 'The provider offers training services and systems which are primarily oriented to the maintenance and improvement of organisational performance rather than to changing the organisation in any major ways' (Pettigrew, Jones and Reason, 1982: 8). This is the operational delivery role which reinforces the organisational status quo.

- *The passive provider.* Again, a role concerned with the maintenance, not with the changing, of the organisation, but it differs from the 'provider' role because of the lack of expertise implied (especially of political skills) in putting across and developing even that role with conviction. It operates at a low level of activity and influence.

- *The training manager.* In this role the focus is on the managerial aspect of training, being primarily concerned with the planning, organisation, direction and control of training operations. The training manager may have responsibility for a group of training staff, or may simply be responsible for co-ordinating the provision of training courses and operations.

- *The role in transition.* A description of a role that is in the process of changing from that of 'provider' to that of 'change agent' and therefore includes elements of both kinds of activity.

The typology still holds true for many in the training field today. However, it does not adequately reflect – nor could it be expected to do so – the profoundly changed environment in which many others now work. Reid and Barrington (1997: 189) took the view that the 'change agent' role is a difficult and not always a legitimate role for training. None the less today it is this role that comes closest to describing the activities in which senior professionals in HRD are involved. Its significance has increased with the growing realisation of the need to develop people to cope with unstable environments. The management of change is a major theme in today's businesses, and HRD practitioners must able to advise on appropriate change strategies and on the learning experiences that can support them.

The change agent and the provider roles do not, however, adequately describe the current spectrum of HRD activity. We can recall here some of the forces noted in Chapters 1 and 2 that are changing its focus and direction:

- *Learning needs in organisations tend to be more complex*, related to a requirement for more highly skilled, more adaptive and more committed workforces operating in leaner, tougher and more 'flexible' organisations.

- *The 'personnel' department is increasingly repositioning itself as the 'human resource function'.* Whether or not the change in title represents any significant change in orientation or practice is not really the point. What is important is the language being used and what it is intended to convey: HRM as a strategic business function which in many organisations is being devolved to line management, with HR professionals in a partnership role – hopefully a more strategic one, but certainly one that is business-led.

- *There is a greater awareness of the importance of HRD in enhancing the competitive capability of organisations.* This is not to say that HRD has actually become a more strategic function – as we have seen in Chapter 2, there is no evidence of this on any wide scale. It is, however, the case that there is more appreciation in organisations of the need to take HRD seriously as a contributor to the business.

- *'Training' is no longer a universal shorthand* for the increasingly wide range of activity involved in managing learning in the workplace and developing a culture to support it. The widespread use of such terms as 'employee development/human resource development/development of people/learning facilitation' indicates the perceived need to represent that activity in a different way.

- *The relationship between HRD and organisational learning is a major focus of interest.* The links that can or should exist between various forms of planned training and development at individual, group and organisational levels and 'organisational learning' itself are much debated. However, they remain unclear. Certainly there is no inherent relationship between individual and collective learning, nor should there be an assumption that learning (in the active sense) automatically leads to the acquisition and development of knowledge. Yet it is organisational knowledge, rather than organisational learning, that provides the base for decision-making and the generation of strategic assets. The critical question is therefore how the HRD process can influence that knowledge base. We shall return to this theme throughout the book, and it becomes the central issue in the final chapter.

So the 1982 typology needs to be expanded. Sloman (1994: 224) claimed that the world of training could no longer be adequately managed as the orderly, sequential series of planned learning interventions envisaged by the systematic training model. He proposed a two-fold typology of roles for the training professional: the internal consultant and the strategic facilitator.

The internal consultant
This focuses on the practitioner as someone who provides a service for internal customers, and who must work alongside them in order to ensure that the service is relevant and of high quality. It makes us think of the need to be 'professional', to be clear about targets, costs, activities to be carried out, and ways of establishing what outcomes have been achieved (for practical techniques to help internal consultants improve their effectiveness, see Thomas and Elbeik, (1996), and, for a useful article on the skills such a role requires, see

Linklater and Atkins (1995). In reality it equates with the provider role, but Sloman's terminology emphasises the collaborative and customer-oriented nature of the role.

However, practitioners who are only consultants are in danger. They have, by definition, no core strategic role, and potentially they are in competition with external consultants. Competition may sharpen their efforts, but it also means that they and their operations can be outsourced. As we shall see in Chapter 10, although outsourcing should be viewed as a healthy challenge that can bring benefits to HR personnel as well as to their organisations, it is now seen as a major threat confronting training professionals in the USA and the UK. In a world of downsizing and concern for added value, the internal consultancy concept is capable of creative interpretation that should send out warning-signs to 'career trainers', especially any who are merely passive providers. It can be expected to gain wider currency in the climate of business-led training and development that must enhance competitive capability.

Case-study: Changing training roles at Barclays Bank, 1997

In 1997 Barclays Bank 'embarked on a fundamental shift in its approach to training' by identifying skilled managers to develop as trainers 'more akin to business consultants than simple deliverers of training packages'. Their role involves carrying out business output analyses on units and making recommendations on staff training needs, staffing levels and workloads. They must develop competency-based performance criteria within departments. They are themselves required to gain national occupational qualifications and are offered a range of professional and higher educational qualification opportunities also.

The move, typifying a direction being considered by many banks following the downsizing referred to in Chapter 1 and their increased exposure in the competitive market-place, is a response to the results of a company-wide survey showing employees wanting more opportunities to develop their skills. It is also seen by the company as a way of giving units and branches more flexible resources. The Bank's central training unit welcomed the innovation as one that enabled the unit to adopt a proactive position, working with the managers as a team of internal consultants to market themselves alongside external suppliers. Some commentators, however, queried whether such a move might ultimately point to the demise of internal career trainers.

(Source: Welch, 1997: 7)

The strategic facilitator

Sloman used this term to describe a role he saw as essential for training professionals today. It makes clear the need for them to express and ensure the implementation of 'a clear training strategy with clear targets, clear control and clear accountability' (Sloman, 1994: 26). It also encompasses the need to develop and manage an appropriate learning culture in the organisation. It is this kind of role with which Chapters 2 and 3 were concerned.

The skills required in this role involve those of strategic awareness, diagnostic capacity and influencing skills (Sloman, 1994: 27). It is a role that someone in the organisation must carry out. If it is not taken up by the training professional, it will fall to others. It may do that anyway. There is little evidence that training professionals have significant influence at board level; but within that boardroom there is a growing awareness of the importance of employee development to enhance competitive capability. As Sloman (1994: 27) observed: 'The training professional may prefer the delivery role. He or she may have the luxury of choice; the organisation doesn't ... There is a huge empire of trainers operating in isolation.'

Developing a typology of HRD roles

Having read the information in this section, produce a simple typology of HRD roles that encompasses the activities in which most of today's HRD practitioners are likely to be involved.

Feedback notes

This can only be a speculative exercise because, to be confident about a typology, research into organisational practice is essential. However, an initial and straightforward classification system can be produced by combining the Pettigrew and the Sloman frameworks as follows:

- the strategic facilitator
- the organisational change agent
- the internal consultant
- the manager of HRD
- the role in transition
- the passive provider.

NATIONAL OCCUPATIONAL TRAINING AND DEVELOPMENT STANDARDS

The employer-led Training and Development Lead Body (TDLB) was established in 1989 to set national occupational standards and provide the basis for vocational qualifications for all those with a training and development responsibility.

Following national consultation, a set of standards was published in 1992. However, the standards proved unacceptable. There were complaints about unfathomable language, inflexibility and overlap of standards, failure to match the reality of jobs, failure to focus sufficiently on the links between training and business and organisational development, and absence of reference to professional ethics or equal opportunities. There was also a major stumbling block posed by the mandatory nature of all units, and the impossibility of equating this with the wide range of HR tasks faced by professionals in the workplace. The standards were referred back for reworking.

In 1994 the Employment Occupational Standards Council (EOSC) was established, amalgamating the TDLB, the Personnel Standards Lead Body and the Trade Union Sector Development Body. In 1995 the EOSC published fully revised standards up to Level 4. Standards for Level 5 were produced in 1996. There are no standards at Levels 1 and 2.

Levels 3, 4 and 5 are described as follows (EOSC, 1996: 6–8):

• *Level 3: Training and Development* – for those who deliver training and development programmes and those who carry the responsibility for their design and evaluation.

• *Level 4: Human Resource Development* – for those who have management responsibility for training and development, and who are involved in identifying organisational training and development needs, and planning the implementation of training and development objectives. They will also be responsible for the improvement of a range of training and development programmes.

• *Level 4: Learning Development* – for those involved in the delivery of learning programmes and more concerned with the facilitation of a broader range of learning opportunities than the direct instructional training which characterises Level 3.

• *Level 5: Training and Development Strategy* – for those with a strategic responsibility in HRD who may either be employed at a senior level in an organisation or be a consultant at a strategic level. These standards encompass, *inter alia*, training and development within the wider context of an organisation and its human resource (HR) policies, developing organisational culture and values, and complying with professional and ethical requirements, as well as evaluating and developing own practice.

At each level, qualification now involves the completion of a number of core units plus a number of optional units instead of mandatory completion of all units.

If we return to our typology of roles, we can see in Table 7 how a simple matrix can now be assembled.

Table 7 A matrix of employee development roles, levels and functions

Role	Lead Body Level	Lead Body functional areas
Strategic facilitator	4,5	Learning development; training and development strategy
Change agent	4	HRD, organisational learning
Internal consultant	3, 4, 5	Training and development; HRD; learning development; training and development strategy
HRD manager	4, 5	HRD; training and development strategy
Passive provider	3	Training and development
Role in transition	4	HRD; learning development

The matrix is not entirely satisfactory. This is because the Lead Body standards are based on the concept of training and development as a set of functional tasks and skills operating at different organisational levels. HRD also involves learning and developmental processes that must cross functional boundaries; and many HRD practitioners have to carry more demanding responsibilities than their titles and organisational level alone reveal. In this matrix, for example, the role of strategic facilitator might have to be attempted by a middle-level 'internal consultant'. Likewise a senior HRD professional operating at strategic level needs also to be an HRD manager, sharing with other senior managers responsibility for developing organisational learning as well as planning and co-ordinating training and development operations across the business. In some organisations, too, even the larger ones, the person in overall charge of HRD in the business may

---

Occupational standards for training and development

In the information below you will find an outline explanation of the national occupational standards for training and development. List six uses for such standards in an organisation. Then assess how far the standards are likely to provide an adequate basis for effective employee development in the workplace.

Training and development are seen in the standards to have a dual purpose: to develop human potential to assist both organisations and individuals to achieve their objectives.

In producing the standards, the systematic training cycle was used to define five functional areas of competence related to the overall purpose. Appendix 4 gives a detailed explanation of the relationship between that cycle and the areas, but in outline those areas are:

A Identify training and development needs   (Identify)

B Plan and design training and development   (Plan and design)

C Deliver training and development   (Deliver)

D Review progress and assess achievement   (Evaluate)

and

E Continuously improve the effectiveness of training and development.

These functional areas are subdivided into 14 subareas (see Appendix 4), each of which contains a number of Units of Competence. These are, in turn, composed of two or more Elements of Competence which include associated performance criteria (the national standards). Range statements then describe the range of contexts and applications in which a competent person would be expected to achieve the element. An evidence specification is attached to each standard.

Some training and development activity requires competence in other occupational areas also, including roles such as training manager, training administrator and training centre manager. Standards for other Lead Bodies can be added to the training and development standards for such roles.

be located at Level 4 yet may be fulfilling elements of all roles (except passive provider) as they strive to achieve an effective contribution for HRD to that business.

The Lead Body would not, of course, recognise the role of passive provider, but it is useful none the less to include that role in the matrix. It describes not a given role but one that has developed around an incumbent. It draws attention to an area of weakness in HRD in a number of organisations. Now let us have a closer look at the standards.

Feedback notes

- Occupational standards in training and development can be used:

  - as a basis for job descriptions of training and development staff

  - as a guide to recruitment and selection of training and development staff

  - as an aid to organisational and individual development, career-planning and progression

  - as a benchmark to ensure best practice

  - to help evaluation of the effectiveness of training and development both at individual and at organisational level and as a basis for appraisal

  - to encourage greater flexibility and responsiveness to changing demands on organisations and individuals.

- The standards offer a common and universally recognised basis for training and development activity. Adherence to these standards would improve levels of competence in the field and enable managers and practitioners to examine critically what they do and how they do it. By specifying a core series of units, a common base of competence and knowledge can be achieved. By allowing optional units, flexibility and adaptability to individual work roles are facilitated.

- There are, however, limits to the value of the standards. While they should improve competence, they cannot ensure that HRD practitioners, whatever their level in the organisation, will make a fully effective contribution to the business.

The limitations just referred to derive from the functional basis of the standards, from the national approach they embody, and from the training-oriented language of the standards.

The functional basis of the standards
The functional analysis approach used to identify standards has resulted in training and development being defined in terms of a logical sequence of five functions, which change in scope but not in essence as they move through Levels 3 to 5. This framework contrasts sharply with the role analysis approach used in the first section of this chapter. Analysis of roles actually held by practitioners enables the different kinds of relationships between those practitioners and their

organisations to be captured and understood. Since the type of training and development tasks carried out by practitioners varies greatly according to work settings and cultures, these are not the main focus of attention in role analysis, whereas with functional analysis they are all that is considered.

The rational approach they embody

Functional analysis involves an atomistic approach to identifying standards. Sloman's (1994) criticism of the systematic training model which underpins the work of the Lead Bodies is relevant to recall from the previous section: the orderly and sequential tasks that it – and functional analysis – imply do not adequately represent the messy and complex world of practice. Each training or developmental intervention must fit well with wider HR policies and systems or it will not take root. A culture favourable to learning and development, as distinct from simply training, has to be established in the workplace. The practitioner also needs to exercise many interpersonal, intellectual and creative skills in attempting to build up status and credibility and achieve managerial commitment to HRD. Those skills cannot be developed prescriptively, although an attempt is made to describe their nature in, for example, the Level 5 standards relating to 'Managing relationships with colleagues and customers'.

The training-oriented language of the standards

Although the revised standards now make a distinction between training and development and between operational and strategic activity, the basic language is still that of training and of planned, systematic learning events. In reality, however, at the highest level the development role should involve helping to build and manage the knowledge base of the firm so that the organisation can become a learning system capable of generating new strategic assets and of ensuring people's full contribution to organisational transformation and growth. As we have already noted, facilitating the learning of individuals and groups does not of itself result in organisational learning or necessarily add anything permanent to the base of knowledge possessed by the organisation. Such complex matters to do with the management and development of the firm's knowledge base do not yield to functional analysis, yet they must be a central preoccupation of the HRD process in the many organisations that are operating in increasingly turbulent and unpredictable environments (see Chapter 20).

IPD PROFESSIONAL STANDARDS

The IPD – formed in 1994 from the merger between the Institute of Personnel Management (IPM) and the Institute of Training and Development (ITD) – has produced a set of professional standards relevant for practitioners regardless of their precise role or type of organisation. The IPD's purpose in this is to do with the establishment, monitoring and promotion of standards and ethics for its profession. Standards have therefore been defined across the whole spectrum of personnel and development, taking both generalist and specialist activity into account.

The format in which these professional standards are expressed is modular. Each module explains the rationale for the standards it covers, the learning outcomes that will demonstrate competence in the standards, the particular areas related to each outcome in which candidates must demonstrate their competence, and the areas where they must demonstrate knowledge and understanding. Indicative content follows. There is thus a clear basis for comparability between the IPD professional standards and national occupational standards. This has made it possible for the professional standards to be mapped against National Vocational Qualifications (NVQs) and Scottish Vocational Qualifications (SVQs) and to contribute to their acquisition 'resulting in a structure which provides a wide variety of routes through which to qualify as professionals' (IPD, 1996a: 3).

The employee development professional standards are contained in:

- *the Certificate in Training Practice* – devised to cover those skills required by proficient trainers whether specialists or line managers, and underpinning the Level 3 NVQ in training and development

- *the Core Personnel and Development (P&D) module* of the Professional Qualification Scheme

- *the generalist and specialist modules* relating to employee development – the modules which map Levels 4 and 5 of the national occupational standards.

The IPD's professional standards recognise vital non-functional professional and workplace dimensions in a more meaningful way than functional analysis can provide. These dimensions are to do with professionalism and ethics, the commitment of line management, and integration.

Professionalism and ethics
Issues of professionalism and ethics imbue standards in all modules instead of being expressed themselves as standards. They are therefore presented as an integral part of professional practice in every area.

Commitment of line management
Another theme running through the IPD standards is the need to obtain the commitment of line management colleagues by convincing them of the importance of professional activity in personnel and development. Without that commitment there cannot be full relevance and impact of HR policies and actions in the organisation.

Integration
In requiring all candidates to achieve the Core P&D standards, the IPD is emphasising the need for vertical integration across HR and business activity in the organisation. These standards focus on the links between personnel and development, broader business strategies and the organisational context. In so doing they aim to improve the understanding and competence of HR professionals in taking a wide-ranging and informed view of the business issues and the context to which HR policies and practice must always relate.

The professional qualification structure involves another kind of integration – the horizontal. Core P&D provides the spine for the key generalist modules on resourcing, development, relations and reward, thus addressing the issue of the need for internal consistency and coherency across all employee-resource-related areas. Each of those modules focuses on the generalist skill and competences that are crucial to effective practice in the workplace. Applying the same principle of horizontal 'fit' to the specific fields that derive from each main employee resource process, each generalist module has attached to it an evolving set of specialist modules. For employee development there are currently six, each consistent with the former ITD approach and with national occupational standards. Candidates can obtain professional status by choosing four specialist electives, or by going across various areas of HR activity in order to emerge with a more generalised grounding in personnel and development work.

The IPD is also an awarding body for vocational qualifications and for assessor/verifier awards in personnel and development. It has over 30 licensed external verifiers all with high levels of generic and occupational competence. One of its roles is to approve centres that wish to provide programmes for these qualifications. Since there are some 160 centres, with 15,000 candidates in 1997 undertaking competency-based programmes with the IPD's Awarding Body, the influence of the IPD over professional standards and the quality of NVQ provision and verification is expanding significantly.

Code of conduct

As Marchington and Wilkinson (1996: 60–86) described, the ethical issues and dilemmas faced by HR professionals tend to increase as they rise in the organisation. The need to be informed and to take a stance on the ethical dimensions of HRD may not always be in the forefront of the busy practitioner's mind. Ethical behaviour is, however, one of the hallmarks of the professional. The inclusion of ethics in both the occupational and the professional standards is therefore a vital contribution to HRD practice and progress. An extract from the IPD's Code of Professional Conduct and Professional Conduct Regulations (1996) is given in Appendix 5. The key standards are to do with:

- accuracy
- confidentiality
- counselling
- developing others
- equal opportunities
- fair dealing
- self-development.

However, codes are only a beginning. What is essential is to find ways of ensuring that ethics go to the heart of the business. HR professionals need to develop an awareness of the meaning and importance of ethics in the organisation, and this is no easy task. One important way in which HRD practitioners can contribute here is to ensure that culture-change programmes have an ethical core, encouraging, *inter alia*, relationships based on greater mutual respect. Valuable work here is being done by organisations like the Alliance and Leicester Building Society (Pickard, 1995a), but it has to be accepted that unless there is a strong HRD power-base in the organisation such initiatives will founder.

Comparing national occupational standards and the IPD professional standards

Looking at the functional map of national standards for training and development contained in Appendix 4 and the description of employee development standards contained at various points in the IPD's 1996 Professional Standards Guide (which all IPD students possess), identify two or three general ways in which the two sets of standards compare or contrast.

Feedback notes

- The concept of HRD embodied in both the occupational and the professional standards is that of an area of organisational activity which is business-led and strategic, and which must be integrated with wider HR policy as well as with business needs and strategy if it is to be effective.

- Both sets of standards should lead to a significant improvement in the overall competence of those carrying HRD responsibilities in organisations. Both sets, too, emphasise the wider professional and ethical context within which HRD managers and specialists should perform their roles.

- National standards have been developed across a narrower area and go into greater (even minute) detail in the performance criteria and range statements than the professional standards. They are used to define current competence in the workplace, and as the basis for N/SVQs.

- Professional standards have been developed across a broader area (including both personnel and training and development) than national standards, leaving more flexibility for application in the particular organisational context. They are used to define professional competence and also as bases for educational and developmental programmes. They therefore place more emphasis on knowledge and understanding.

- The professional standards are not derived from functional analysis – although there is recognition of the need for functional skills and knowledge – but from agreement with stakeholders on outcomes to be achieved in each major area of training and development. The role and work of HRD is thereby acknowledged to be more than a mere aggregation of functional parts.

- The professional standards also emphasise context: the context of the workplace and its practices; of the business and its needs; of the competitive national and international environment; and of the professional standards and ethics that should influence the values, behaviour and work of practitioners in whatever organisation they are currently located.

• In these ways the professional standards can be argued to relate more closely to the real world of training and development, reflecting more meaningfully the scope, responsibilities and complexity of the HRD process in organisations.

FACTORS INFLUENCING TRAINING AND DEVELOPMENT ROLES IN THE ORGANISATION

When actors play a part, it is the interplay of their given role and the way they develop it together with their own personality that explains the uniqueness of their performance. Relating this concept to training, we can say that *formal and informal factors influence the parts, or roles, that people play, and so also influence training and development roles in a particular organisational context.*

Factors influencing training and development roles

Please describe, by reference to our typology of roles (see page 145), the role held by whoever carries the main formal responsibility for employee development in your own organisation, or in some organisation with which you are familiar. (It may, for example, be a personnel director or manager, or a training manager, or a designated line manager.) Identify the main influences on that person's role and the way in which it has developed.

Feedback notes
What follows not only gives feedback on the work you have just completed, but also expands on and concludes our discussion of factors influencing training responsibilities and roles. The comments are therefore quite lengthy, but they include some of the most important influences.

• *The environment of the organisation.* This refers to the outer world of the organisation and the opportunities and constraints, and threats and challenges that it presents. Training policy in an organisation that is fighting for survival in an increasingly competitive market will have no choice but to be business-led; key roles will be the change agent and the strategic facilitator, the provider remaining relevant but usually only at the operational levels. On the other hand, in a stable organisation facing few internal or external changes, training may largely be a matter of continuing to carry out long-established routines with little questioning of their relevance either to the organisation or to the individual; in that event, the most likely roles are the passive provider and the training manager. However, in many hitherto bureaucratised private- and public-sector organisations (eg the National Health Service, higher education and local authorities) HRD has become a function of critical importance in order to cope with the demands of a turbulent environment. In such organisations, where management costs are also being cut, 'passive providers' are having to become effective internal consultants or perish.

The external political environment is an important influence on training and development roles, too. In the 1960s the advent of industrial training boards and the increase in training operations to which they gave rise often led to more position power for the training function and an increase in training manager roles. Such effects can be short-lived: the abolition of most boards in the early 1980s was followed in many cases by a rapid decline in the power of training departments and of training as a function.

Training and Enterprise Councils (TECs), as we saw in Chapter 5, offer funding, learning resources and networks which can help to further the cause of HRD in the organisation (see Mackinnon, 1995). One important external initiative is the Investors in People (IIP) standard, also discussed in Chapter 5. It can do much to promote a strategic, business-led role for HRD, although caution should be exercised in deciding to sign up to the standard, since the IIP process is valuable only if it is timely, suits the organisation's situation and developmental needs at the time, and will be supporting business strategy that itself is relevant and coherent (see Marchington and Wilkinson, 1996: 173–8 for a critique).

- *Business goals and strategy.* As we have seen, especially in Chapters 2 and 3, the direction and type of business goals and strategy fundamentally determine HRD policy and plans, and therefore also the HRD roles and responsibilities appropriate to the particular organisation.

- *Organisational structure and culture.* The corporate philosophy about people, the values and styles of leadership and management, and the social system in the workplace will act either as enablers or inhibitors of HRD policies and strategies. The primary culture of an organisation is closely related to its structure, since it is structure that determines formal roles, responsibilities and tasks, as well as the systems, procedures and routines by which people work. Structure, in turn, both influences and is influenced by HRD practice and its outcomes.

Most larger organisations will have a differentiated structure, with elements of bureaucracy in the routinised areas of activity, but with a task-centred, matrix structure in areas requiring flexibility and innovative activity. Type of structure is a significant influence on choice of HRD goals and strategy.

One very important structural issue is the place and operation of the personnel function in the organisation. As Mumford (1971) pointed out, 'the historical development of the personnel function ... may or may not have included training'. He observed that a similar and critical factor will be 'the number of other specialists such as work study, O. & M., medical services, already reporting to a manager'. This leads us into the next contextual factor: that of employee resourcing (ER).

- *The ER context*. The size, behavioural patterns, performance, occupational structure and learning needs of the workforce employed or utilised by the organisation will all influence the training and development roles and the tasks to be performed. However, it is the nature of the ER system that is the critical factor here, because it is ER strategy and practice that define the ways in which the organisation's workforce is planned, deployed and managed.

  - *HR planning* determines how many people should be employed, how, when and where, and how they will be utilised. The framework established here is the critical one within which HRD policy, strategy and plans must be formulated.

  - *Recruitment and selection* are the processes through which people move into the organisation: this human material, if well chosen, will prove to have the abilities and wish to respond positively and fruitfully to developmental initiatives. Ineffective recruitment and selection will almost always defeat all attempts to instil skills and knowledge and unlock potential.

  - *Leadership* provides the vision and values that drive HRD in an organisation.

  - *Teamwork*, like leadership, will either provide continuing developmental opportunities that maximise the organisation's investment in people, or will erect barriers that may lead to rapid depreciation in that most expensive of its resources.

  - *Appraisal* is the process at the heart of development, but attempts to use it also as a major method of control may defeat its developmental objectives, as will be seen in Chapter 13.

  - *Learning activities and opportunities* appropriate to the needs of individuals, groups and the organisation as a whole can be in part formally structured, but should also permeate daily operations in the workplace so that a process of continuous development and improvement can take place. Continuous development, principally through the integration of learning and work, has as its major objective the achievement of operational goals and the steady growth in the ability to learn and reinforce or generate new knowledge at every organisational level. Whereas the main concern in training is to help people to acquire skills related to a particular task or tasks, continuous development is primarily concerned with uncovering and utilising potential, and in developing those core skills to which the Introduction to this book refers: observation and reflection, analysis, creativity, decision-making/problem-solving and evaluation.

  - *Incentive and reward systems* will either help to encourage people to develop or will be so irrelevant to the HRD process that individual and team motivation to develop will be low.

  - *Measures to protect people* against discrimination, and in matters of health, safety and welfare, will again either remove barriers to individual and organisational growth or put major obstacles in their path.

• *Disengagement policies and practices* should ensure that when people leave the organisation positive steps are taken to facilitate their continued development after that exit point is reached, rather than leaving them with little hope or positive expectations.

These, then, are the major ER processes which constitute the 'umbrella' for the development of people in an organisation.

• *Technology.* This refers to the way in which work and work processes are organised, the type of technology used and the technology available for training and development. As we shall see in Chapter 16, there are many important changes taking place in training technology, and these too affect training and development roles and tasks.

To produce this list, I have made use of the model of the organisation as a system shown in Figure 4. This demonstrates in simple form how environment, goal and tasks, structure and culture, technology and employment system interact and influence the roles, both formally ascribed and informally developed, of those responsible for HRD in the business. The passive provider or inept training manager has little chance of improving the role of HRD in the organisation and may indeed find that, as a consequence of repeated failure to seize opportunities and to prove the value of training and development, the role becomes further reduced. The influential line manager who shows colleagues and team how little he or she values training and development will foster a climate of scepticism that will be hard to change. These conclusions are supported by evidence gathered by Pettigrew and his team, who wrote that:

> The change agents, role in transition, and managers were more aware of the issue of boundary management, had formulated a strategy which more often than not involved at least articulating a mission and sets of operational objectives, and were attempting to implement a broader range of transactions, through a wider set of relationships, than either the providers or passive providers.

Pettigrew et al (1982: 14)

They went on to discuss an issue raised in Chapter 8: the importance for those with HRD responsibilities of identifying their own power resources and power-bases, and then deciding what strategies to follow in order to influence others in the organisation to support them in the

Figure 4 The organisation as a system

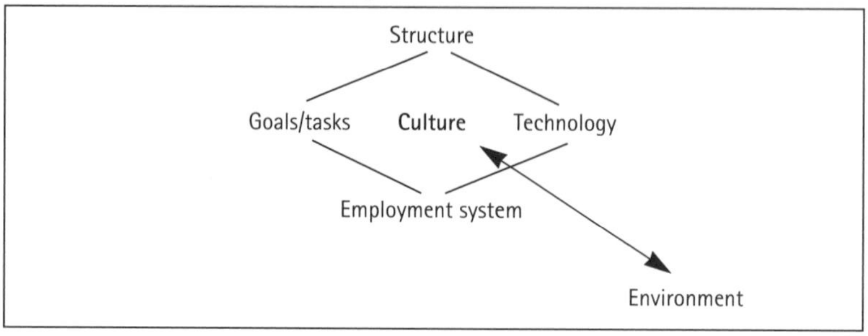

role they sought to occupy and the area and level of operations they saw to be essential. Skills related to boundary and network management are crucial to these tasks, as we shall be seeing in Chapter 10.

IMPROVING THE STATUS AND CONTRIBUTION OF HRD IN THE ORGANISATION

What can be done to ensure that training and development responsibilities at all levels are accepted and carried out, and that proactive training roles are widespread rather than rare in organisations?

We shall look separately at the concept of marketing HRD in the organisation in Chapter 11, but what follows is a part of that notion of HRD professionals needing to continually demonstrate the relevance of what they do for the performance and growth of the organisation.

> Changing the status of HRD in the organisation requires technically and politically expert practitioners who speak the language of the business and fully understand the organisation in which they have to operate; line managers who recognise their key role in employee development and are helped and encouraged to take it seriously; and top management who demonstrate the values and commitment needed to promote an organisational culture conducive to HRD, continuous learning and the development of strategically relevant knowledge.

The responsibilities and expertise involved in managing HRD at the three main levels of the business will be discussed more fully in Chapter 10, but an outline is relevant at this point.

Corporate level

Top management carries the responsibility for communicating a clear vision about what HRD means in the organisation and the part it is to play in organisational performance and growth. Without positive values about people coming from the top of the organisation, accompanied by a commitment to invest significant resources in HRD, the function can never become fully integrated into the business.

Since the organisational environment in which people live is created and sustained above all by top management, the primary responsibility for HRD must lie at that level. Let us look at an example.

Case-study: Kwik-Fit, 1990

Webster discussed the philosophy and systems for continuous development and improvement of its workforce at Kwik-Fit, a company distinguished both by its high standards of quality and customer service and by its policy of integrated and continuous development of the whole workforce. He described the ways in which, as human values spread through an organisation, they can produce an environment in which 'the vision takes root and flourishes'. He commented that this needs to be a purposive, not an accidental, process, since it is values and vision that give the organisation direction.

He saw in Tom Farmer, then CEO at Kwik-Fit, an awareness of the impact of every action he took as CEO in either producing healthy growth in the workforce or inhibiting it. It is at the top of the organisation that action must be taken to 'review the systems, the organisation structure, the physical layout and the human resource policies ... with the specific purpose of creating through them the environment in which people may thrive'.

Source: Webster, 1990: 44–7.

For senior managers and HR professionals operating at corporate level the vital qualities are political skills, broad business orientation, an understanding of wider ER issues, a strong belief in the value of investing in people for the long term and a proactive stance. Pressures of business changes will tend to lead to an increasing awareness of the need for HRD. Provided that they are accompanied by sufficient commitment at the top of an organisation, they can trigger off a more strategic approach to the function and a willingness to increase the level of investment in it. However, this will happen only if there is a conviction that HRD will have a real pay-off.

The role of the spokesperson for HRD (who at this level will probably be the personnel director or equivalent) is to ensure that there is this conviction. He or she must be knowledgeable about the implications of alternative proposed corporate strategies for employee resourcing and development, and give a persuasive assessment as to where the balance of advantage lies between one strategy and another. Tactics like being able to quote examples of other, similar companies who have a higher level of investment and whose business strategy is clearly successful will be persuasive. So also will obtaining external funding to support certain HRD initiatives: it will give greater internal credibility to the initiatives being proposed and will be particularly powerful if it can significantly offset the cost of those initiatives to the organisation.

Strategies for the business that fail to take fully into account ER issues, including those relating to HRD, are likely to prove impossible or damagingly expensive to implement. On the other hand, an informed understanding of employees' performance and potential can make possible a wider range of strategic options for the business.

Recommendations to the board (or equivalent) for a higher level of investment will not be convincing unless they rest on up-to-date, comprehensive data which have been obtained in collaboration with key parties in the organisation and been rigorously analysed (see the case of Barratt the builders in Harrison, 1992). It will be important to seek the active support of unit managers as well as that of senior executives who can influence their peers in this activity.

Unit/divisional level
Line managers carry the fundamental responsibility for ensuring that

people are enabled to perform their jobs effectively and efficiently, and to enjoy continuous learning opportunities through which their abilities and potential can be developed. This responsibility means that managers, whether alone or with the help of specialist staff, must:

- create a work environment, policy and systems at their management level that encourage and support the acquisition of the skills, knowledge and attitudes people need in order to perform well in their jobs

- regularly review work targets, appraise performance and assess potential in order to help people to improve in their jobs and develop in ways that will be beneficial to the organisation, as well as motivating to themselves

- regularly monitor and evaluate the results of formal and informal learning in the workplace.

At this level professional HRD staff should have a managerial orientation, working closely with line managers to help in the production of HRD policies and plans that will boost the performance of units. They will be helped in this by mastering the functional competencies related to the tasks they have to perform, but it is their mastery of the human processes involved in their work that will enable them to make their best contribution to the business and to individuals' learning and growth. In Chapter 10 a case-study will illustrate how line managers can effectively perform their HRD role, and in Chapter 14 guidelines will be given for developing a climate conducive to continuous learning and development in the workplace.

Operational level
HRD managers and professionals at this level need in essence the same skills as at business-unit level. They have a particular responsibility here for providing a climate within which HRD can take root in the workplace.

As a member of the operational team, each individual has a responsibility to consider what their own learning needs are in relation to their daily work, forthcoming changes and their career aspirations. Self-directed learning and self-development are increasingly important for everyone – not just to improve performance but to enhance employability security (see page 10). Furthermore if the organisation does not take the initiative in offering opportunities for individual development, then these may be the only ways whereby people can realise their potential.

The argument that individuals must take an active role in articulating their needs and in making a positive contribution to the decisions on how needs may be met is familiar enough: only in this way can planning, execution and evaluation of their development become a genuinely two-way process. Only thus can individuals hope to influence those who carry developmental roles (especially, of course, their own managers at whatever level), and so put pressure on managers to aim for a marriage rather than a divorce of individual and organisational training and development goals.

Unfortunately, there are often no incentives for individuals to press for training, since the rewards, material or otherwise, in most organisations, whether the individual is in or out of work, are so few (see pages 25–6). Furthermore, as Paul Victor, personnel manager of Rolls Royce observed, references to 'empowered individuals' often mask a very different reality, where true power remains at the higher levels, and an invitation to 'take the initiative in your development' is no more than 'an abrogation of responsibility' by management (Victor, 1995: 23). He believed that vague mission statements about achieving world-class status are meaningless as a guide to developmental action for the individual. What is needed is 'a clear picture of the business, its mission, strategy and objectives ... translated into meaningful terms for different departments, groups and individuals' (Victor, 1995: 23).

At every level of the organisation, HRD roles and responsibilities should be shared and should have a strong professional and ethical framework. Without that framework the practice of HRD lacks true professionalism, since it will not be imbued with those enduring values that link HRD in the particular organisation with HRD in the wider professional world.

Improving the status of HRD in the organisation

Take an organisation (or part of it) with which you are familiar, where training and development have low status and credibility. Produce an analysis of the reasons for this situation, and outline a strategy whereby the role and status of the function could be significantly improved.

Feedback notes
- The exercise will generate many different responses. Analysis should take account of our checklist of factors influencing training and development roles and tasks: the organisational environment, its business goals and strategy, its structure and culture, its workforce and ER system, and its technology.

- Reading Pettigrew *et al*, 1982: 13 to 15 will help you to analyse issues related to boundary management – an important theme to cover in relation to HRD roles. You should look at the particular demands made upon HRD at each organisational level and the extent to which in your organisation those demands are not being adequately met.

- Your analysis should lead to two or three key objectives that will result in significant improvement in the role and status of HRD in your organisation, and your strategy should be carefully chosen to enable those objectives to be achieved over a given timespan.

CONCLUSION

In order to achieve the learning objectives of this chapter a six-fold typology of training and development roles has been provided; national occupational standards and professional standards have also been described and compared. A five-dimensional framework has been used to understand factors influencing HRD roles and their development in the organisation, and within that framework the critical factor of the employee-resourcing system, with its nine major processes, has been stressed. Ways of improving the status and contribution of HRD at corporate, unit and operational/individual levels have been identified.

USEFUL READING

GILLEY, J.W. *and* EGGLAND, S.A. (1989) *Principles of Human Resource Development*. New York, Addison Wesley: Chapter 5.

HAMLIN, B. *and* DAVIES, G. (1996) The trainer as change agent: issues for practice', in J. Stewart, and J. McGoldrick (eds), *Human Resource Development: Perspectives, strategies and practice*. London, Pitman. pp. 199–219.

REID, M.A. *and* BARRINGTON, H. (1997) *Training Interventions: Managing employee development*. Chapter 6. 5th ed. London, Institute of Personnel and Development.

10 Organising, managing and developing capable practitioners

LEARNING OBJECTIVES

After reading this chapter you will:

- understand the scope of the human resource development (HRD) manager's role

- understand different ways in which the HRD function can be organised

- be able to draw up an action plan to organise HRD staff and develop their abilities and potential both as individuals and as members of a professional team.

THE MANAGERIAL ROLE AND ITS SCOPE

A conventional definition of a training manager role would be one that relates this to a specialist training section or department. Thus Gilley and Eggland (1989: 97) defined the role as 'focused on the administration and management of the learning system within the organisation through the planning, organizing, staffing, controlling and marketing of the Human Resource Development department. This role is better known as the "manager of HRD" '. This is an interesting definition for three reasons: it refers to the 'HRD manager' – the same terminology that now appears in the Lead Body Standards; it acknowledges the importance of auditing learning in the organisation as well as focusing on managing the organisation as a learning system (aspects to which we shall return in Part 4); and it stresses the need to market the function.

The definition is, however, limited in two ways:

- it envisages the specialist department as the locus of developmental activity in the organisation

- it sees employees as the sole focus of that activity.

The trend for HRD responsibilities to be located with line managers means that the specialist function must be managed as a resource base and enabler, a collaborator in all stages of the developmental process. With the growth of part-time and temporary work in an organisation there is also a need for the HRD manager to identify and respond to the learning needs of those more 'flexible' workers without whom the operations of many organisations could not be carried out.

The trends to outsource training and development operations and to extend the organisational learning network across the boundary of the organisation to encompass key stakeholders such as suppliers, customers and purchasers also carry important implications for HRD managers. They present a need to manage a learning system related to many who are not the direct employees of the organisation. This theme was introduced in Chapter 2 (page 19) and is elaborated here.

Walton (1996: 121) rightly remarked on the failure of most texts (including my own) to focus on the learning needs of what he called 'non-employees'. His chapter in Stewart and McGoldrick's book is recommended for the framework it provides relating to this group (Stewart and McGoldrick, 1996). He points first to the need expressed by Rothwell and Kazanas (1989) to educate external stakeholders in order to widen the influence of the organisation over its widen environment. He then produces a 'stakeholder wheel' encompassing:

- end users

- distributors

- suppliers

- volunteers

- franchisees

- self-employed subcontractors.

The organisation's learning network, then, can extend significantly beyond its own boundaries.

Putting training and development operations in context

Following on from the points made in the previous section, use of the term 'HRD manager' rather than 'training manager' better conforms with national occupational standards and points more clearly to the

---

The new HRD manager

You have been appointed as an organisation's first HRD manager (any organisation of your choice). You have the responsibility for advising on developmental policy and planning for the organisation (you may assume that your manager is a member of the top management team, and you may decide whether he or she is personnel director, managing director, or other). You will also have to draw up training and development plans for various sectors of the organisation. Finally, you will have to establish and hold responsibility for a central training budget (you may decide whether or not, in this exercise, there are also training budgets at divisional/unit levels of the organisation).

It is your first day, a Monday morning, and you are sitting in your small office, empty of everything except a desk, a chair, a telephone and a filing cabinet. Tomorrow you will meet with your manager to discuss how to plan and organise training and development in the organisation. What sorts of issues and questions will you raise with him or her at that meeting?

responsibility to meet the learning needs of certain 'non-employed' personnel as well as of the directly employed. When deciding how best to manage training and developmental operations for the business, the HRD manager must not only take careful account of the culture, structure and technology of the organisation, but must also identify those stakeholders inside and outside the system who have a potentially important part to play in the organisation's learning network.

Feedback notes

There are innumerable issues and questions that you could list. They include the following:

- *Organisational environment.*
  What are the current and projected future positions of the business in relation to its competitive environment?
  What are the forces for change inside and outside the business? Where are the main pressure points and what, if any, responses are being planned in relation to these?
  Is there an organisational policy and strategy for HRD? If so, what are the priorities? If not, why not?
  What education and training links already exist with people and institutions outside the organisation?
  If there are such links, what use is made of them, why, and with what results?

- *Business goals and strategy.*
  What are the current business goals and longer-term strategic objectives that HRD is meant to serve?
  At what levels does HRD operate in the business? Is there:

  - *no systematic training or longer-term development?* If so, why, and what impact has this failure had on the skills base of the organisation and its human potential for the future?

  - *isolated tactical training at operational level?* If so, does this produce adequate pay-backs for the organisation? What evidence is there here?

  - *focused HRD at the business unit level?* Is HRD making a direct contribution to the achievement of business targets at this level? Is it helping to meet present and future skills needs? What kind of relationship exists between training staff and business unit managers?

  - *strategic HRD at the corporate level?* Is HRD linked to key business drivers? Is there a coherent and durable strategy focused on clear HRD goals that underpin corporate goals? Who is the spokesperson for HRD at this level, and does he or she take a reactive or proactive stance in relation to HRD strategy? What are perceived to be the priorities for HRD and learning? Why?

- *Organisational structure, routines and culture.*
  What is the primary structure of the organisation – power, role, network or person structure?

Is the organisation decentralised/multi-site/part of a conglomerate/
large, medium-sized or small?

What is intended to be the precise nature of the organisational links
between HRD and other business functions in the organisation?

How is the employee resource (ER) function currently organised? Is
there internal consistency and coherency between ER processes?
Where does HRD 'fit' in relation to the wider ER function?

What is your own intended formal role, and what are your
prescribed responsibilities?

Are you to be given a free hand in planning and managing HRD?
What is the nature of your authority and discretion here?

Are you able to recruit any staff to help you?

What formal or informal procedures related to training and
development tasks and learning activities and experiences
currently exist in the organisation?

How is training and development activity costed and budgeted for
in the organisation?

To what extent will you be able to change current systems and
procedures?

When staff are sent on training programmes or other external
learning events, what is the nature and extent of your
responsibility for those staff?

What is the general climate of opinion – the dominating values and
beliefs – about HRD and learning in the organisation?

Which managers and other key personnel in the organisation
support and understand the language of HRD? Who have no
interest in HRD, or are likely to oppose various initiatives and
have the power to thwart them?

Is HRD generally perceived as a crucial function in the
organisation? What criteria are used to judge its contribution?

Are the concepts of 'organisational learning' and 'knowledge
development' discussed or understood? If so, what practical
meanings do they have?

Will there be any problems in involving line managers in discussions
about individual, team and organisational learning needs and how
best to respond to them?

• *The employment system.*
What is the size of the workforce, its pattern and its occupational
structure?

Is there any attempt to build a cohesive internal labour market (see
page 104 for our definition here). If so, which occupational/
professional groups are encompassed?

What are perceived to be the main current and future training and
development needs of different sectors of the workforce?

What are the incentives and rewards for people in relation to
training and development?

How, generally, is the function of HRD perceived in different
sectors of the workforce and by other key stakeholders? Positively
or negatively? Reasons?

Does training and development respond to the learning needs of all
stakeholder groups, or only to those of the direct employees of the
business?

If only the needs of direct employees are considered, what other groups should come under the umbrella of HRD in the business?

- *Technology.*
  What are the main systems and processes of work organisation in the workplace? What are their implications for training and longer-term development?
  Is new technology to be introduced into the workplace? Again, what are its managerial and skills-based implications?
  What kind of training and learning technology exists, or is available?
  What are the main media and methods of training and development that you could use, on and off the job? Are there facilitites for open learning, computer-assisted learning etc?

The list is long but becomes manageable if the questions are grouped under major headings, leading to reflection and analysis of their implications. The headings relate to the simple model initiated through concepts of structure and culture in Chapter 8 (page 132) and developed further in Chapter 9 (page 160). Now we can incorporate issues to do with the nature of the non-employed as well as of the employed workforce. Notice in this list the reference to the need for good fit between HRD systems and other ER systems and practices. Notice also the repeated references to the climate relating to learning.

Politics will go far to determine the support given to the HRD manager as he or she explores what needs really exist, and how they can best be met. One critical factor in this case-study will be the personality, attitudes and values of the new manager's own manager and his or her reactions to the new recruit. In their first meeting the training manager must not only try to establish the facts about training needs. He or she must also begin to build up a mental picture of the organisation, getting the 'feel' of it and identifying constraints and opportunities.

ORGANISING THE HRD FUNCTION

Stredl and Rothwell (1987: 291) list four questions relevant to the task of organising a training function:

- How much authority will be delegated, and to whom and about what?

- How many positions will report to the training manager?

- How will jobs be grouped?

- How will tasks, duties and responsibilities be divided?

Sloman (1994) lists three more of equal importance – although where he refers to 'training' I have substituted 'HRD':

- How can HRD activity be firmly embedded in the organisation, permitting it to operate strategically?

- How can the function develop a role involving the articulation of HRD needs rather than merely the response to them?

- What is the level of HRD sophistication in the organisation and what approach is best suited to it?

Let us look at three scenarios placing different kinds of demands on the HRD manager: the decentralised function, the line-managed function and the outsourced function.

The decentralised function

In organisations where there is a generalised push to decentralisation, HRD may be particularly vulnerable and, ultimately, could be stripped of its strategic influence.

In the UK there is evidence to show that a trend towards decentralising businesses to field levels has been accompanied by a decentralisation of personnel responsibilities, including those relating to HRD (British Institute of Management and Aston University, 1989). Decentralisation is a feature of public-sector organisations as well as of those in the private sector. One example is the hiving-off of many Civil Service and local authority functions to agencies of outside contractors. By the early 1990s local government decentralisation had already resulted in between 60 and 80 authorities' delayering management at the expense of the personnel function, pushing personnel off the top management team and 'absorbing' it lower down – for example, at Wandsworth, into the new corporate services division, together with public relations and the policy and education committee units (*Personnel Management*, 1992: 12). The financial problems of authorities could make HR functions increasingly vulnerable, to the point that they become marginalised. That will have a direct impact on the organisation and influence of HRD, which usually operates under the wider ER umbrella in local authorities (see also Kessler, 1990).

The British Institute of Management survey showed that while on the one hand decentralisation was increasing, so on the other hand was centralisation – of the policy, strategy and control function. The key question, however, is 'Who now holds the strategic facilitator role?'

Case-study: London Underground's plans to decentralise the personnel function

In January 1992 it was announced that London Underground intended to keep a small central personnel department, retaining responsibility for questions of corporate policy and standards, employee relations and management development. Thereafter most of the function would be devolved to the nine underground lines run as business units and having their own personnel managers and support staff. Those personnel staff were to be given wider responsibilities 'to enable them to act more like factory personnel managers'.

At the same time there was to be 'a massive increase in training linked to the introduction of multi-skilling and flexible rostering'. In the past there had been a high frequency of last-minute withdrawals from training programmes for operational reasons, with adverse effects on the cost and impact of training. Personnel Director Roger Straker expected that, when the new proposals had been carried out, training would be better organised and given a higher priority.

Source: Personnel Management (1992b: 1–5)

Such optimism about the retention of a strategic role for ER may be misplaced. The trend towards this kind of decentralisation poses strategic and organisational challenges for HRM generally and for HRD as a key HR process: those of 'tight–loose fit', discussed in Legge (1995: 132–5).

Basically those challenges are about how to strike a balance between a strong and unifying corporate business strategy and culture, and the special needs of divisions and units. If ER strategy has to be differentiated from unit to unit to meet the needs of the units' different business strategies, then the result may be that every unit will pursue its own personnel policies at the expense of any overall integrative ER strategy. This, indeed, is exactly what appears to have happened at Shell UK, which 'has had to rethink its approach to decentralisation after finding it led to worsening performance' (Pickard, 1992: 1). It found that pushing decision-making down to business units diluted the traditional corporate culture, and resulted in the units being 'given more independence, [becoming] too cut off from each other and from the expertise at the centre' (Pickard, 1992: 1). Shell's decision was to make business units more accountable to each other and more guided by a primary company culture while also retaining the basic decentralised structure.

The decision about whether or not to decentralise HRD will usually be out of the hands of the HRD manager. It is still important, however, for HRD managers to understand the context in which they have to function and its implications for them as managers. Typical approaches to decentralisation include:

* organising most of the specialist staff to work permanently in or with the units, retaining only a small core staff at headquarters to make and co-ordinate HRD policy and strategy (as at London Underground)

* setting up a minimal specialist function operating on a 'walk and talk the job' basis, as at Barratt the construction company in 1990 (Harrison, 1992)

* having a small specialist function working collaboratively with line managers who themselves have been trained and developed to carry an increasing range of employee development functions – a model examined closely in the next section

* contracting the function out (discussed below).

Good boundary management skills must be developed in HRD staff working in a decentralised organisation who are either permanently seconded to business units or who need to work collaboratively with those units from the base of a central training function. They will need to have:

* a wide-ranging knowledge of 'the business' to give them credibility in the units, and to enable them to fully understand units' training and development needs

* skills, motivation and professional commitment to ensure that they neither identify so closely with business units as to 'view the central

function as an influence to be kept at bay' (Fowler, 1992); nor identify so closely with the central function as to lose credibility at unit level and become inflexible in their approach.

The line-managed function

Here we are looking at a situation typical in a decentralised organisation: responsibility for HRD held substantially by line managers. There is still likely to be a specialist HRD function. However, its role will usually be one of ensuring overall strategic direction and of oversight and monitoring of implementation. Let us look at a practical example. It draws on the ways in which training and development are organised in benchmarking companies like ICI, Cummins Engine and Rover (now part of BMW).

> ### Case-study: Company X, Part 1: handing over HRD to the line
>
> *Vision and mission*
> Company X is a UK-owned company which operates across the world. It has a long history of investment in a skilled and committed workforce, and a creative capability that has led over the years to a stream of innovative products.
>
> *HRD purpose and strategy*
> There is a core of common training across the company, and small teams of expert specialists work within each strategic business unit in order to help managers implement that training and also to identify and respond to local needs. There is a specific training and development policy built into corporate business strategy, and this sets the strategic goals and directions for HRD in the company.
>
> *Organisational and policy integration of HRD at different levels of the business*
> At corporate level there is a coherent HR strategy owned by the board. A small headquarters HR team is responsible for maintaining the strategic direction of HR across the organisation. At this level an HRD director advises on the scope, overall policy and long-term strategic goals for HRD in the company. A corporate HRD budget is focused on meeting company-wide needs. In these ways there is what Mabey and Salaman (1995: 169) called 'organisational integration' of HRD into the business.
>
> Each strategic operating unit is responsible for its training policy and arrangements in line with group policy, but also responsive to its own business needs and local environment. At this level specialist training and development staff provide an efficient administrative HRD system, and training and development expertise and resource. They work within business units, helping line managers to produce and implement a coherent set of policies at unit level that will help to ensure a high-quality, committed workforce. Each unit has its own training and development budget to meet the needs of the business plan and any contingency activity that has to be carried out subsequently.
>
> Support is given to the training policy through other ER policies. For example, there is a world-wide framework for performance management which includes performance development as a key component. In such ways there is 'policy integration' of HRD into the business and a coherency with wider ER strategy (Mabey and Salaman, 1995).

Line management responsibility for HRD
Individual employees are responsible for their own development throughout their careers by:

- learning and applying the knowledge, understanding and skills necessary for the performance of their jobs

- working with their managers to identify current and future learning, training and development needs and opportunities.

It is upon the success of the line managers' HRD role that the effective implementation of training strategy across the business primarily depends. HRD responsibilities are clarified in a *Group Training Manual* which is issued throughout the world-wide group as:

- ensuring that employees are equipped with the necessary knowledge, understanding and skills to do their current jobs competently

- determining training and development needs, both present and future, setting priorities, allocating resources and reviewing results

- ensuring that training activity is reinforced as an aspect of the process of managing performance

- providing a work environment in which individuals can take responsibility for their own training and development.

Each unit and each manager must have documented plans, reviews, reports, records and performance evaluations as evidence that the principles of HRD and the company-wide performance management system are actively implemented at this level.

HRD leadership and commitment
At Company X, leadership must be in deed as well as in word. There are high-priority in-house training programmes for the most senior staff which reinforce the cultural, strategic and organisational developments needed. Strong leadership and commitment are expected from the chief executive of each business unit in and to the following areas of the company's training policy:

- a focus on customer-led quality, on understanding and responding to customer needs

- effective development of the company's people at all levels of the organisation – corporate, business unit and operational

- a competency-based approach to training for excellent performance, and equality of access to this training by every employee

- rewards for those employees who achieve relevant vocational qualifications

- a substantial investment in familiarising every employee with the company's and the units' strategic objectives, and in ensuring that each individual has performance targets and longer-term development to enable them to help those objectives to be achieved

- planned change will include a provision for appropriate and timely training of the staff involved.

HRD at Company X carries the hallmarks of a well-managed function:

- a clear vision and strategy that is in line with overall business goals and strategy

- strategic objectives that are carried through into detailed, practical plans for implementation of the policies that serve those objectives

- a form of organisational structure and company-wide procedures that ensure that the policies are carried out with the commitment and expertise of all who have been assigned training and development roles and responsiblities

- a system of training, guidance, monitoring, appraisal and rewards related to performance in those roles

- good management and utilisation of training and development resources.

The outsourced function

For the new HRD manager there are three points to consider in relation to outsourcing:

- Should any training and development activities be outsourced?

- Is there a danger that the whole function might in future be outsourced?

- Would the HRD function and its staff benefit from outsourcing?

In relation to the first point, the key issues are to do with cost-efficiency, added value and retention of control. Often an external party can provide training and development operations at a lower cost than is possible internally. Provided that the HRD manager can be assured that the organisation will retain control over targets and standards, and has good evidence that value will accrue to the organisation by outsourcing – whether on an occasional or permanent basis – then there can be many benefits. Three noted by Hardingham (1996a: 45–6) arise from an effective partnership between internal and external practitioners:

- 'The combination of internal clout and external credibility is a winning card to play in designing and delivering the most challenging types of training' – that is, training of major importance to the organisation, but which also involves major tensions, difficulties or fundamental behavioural changes.

- External training designers and deliverers can represent a source of best practice for internal HRD practitioners.

- The internal practitioners' own approach and values can be transformed through partnership with external agents. This, in turn, can help to change values within the organisation.

In relation to the second point, the training manager must continually keep in mind the fact that there are now a number of question marks around the role of the traditional training and development practitioner (Roy Harrison, 1996). Curnow (1995) argued powerfully that HR professionals and management consultants need to develop strengths in each other's mainstream competencies as the former increasingly carry an internal consultancy role, and the latter are having to behave more like personnel directors in their formulation of policy changes and proposals as part of corporate change programmes.

The issue of rediscovering a significant role for training staff was one of the most important to emerge at the 1996 Conference of the American Society of Training and Development. There was an awareness of the implications for directive trainers of the learner-centred approaches necessitated by the drive to develop 'learning organisations'; of the tendency to hand over HRD to line managers, especially in downsized and delayered organisations; of the powerful and efficient learning routes now available with the advance of information that need little support from a specialist function; and of the dissatisfaction expressed by many chief executives in the USA about the returns being offered to them by their training professionals – a recent study had indicated that 70 per cent of the $300b. annual investment in training in the USA was failing to produce any measurable improvement in job performance.

The kinds of question that the HRD manager needs to confront objectively include the following:

• What if there were no HRD function in this organisation? Where and how does it add value?

• If it is essential to the business, does it need to be carried out internally or could it be outsourced – in whole or in part?

• Should it be market-tested (a process involving tendering of certain operations to external agencies)?

• Is it sufficiently large to be made into an agency and floated out of the organisation?

Nuclear Electric Management Development Manager Paul Rann's creative use of a network of associate tutors to address management training needs at a time of cost reduction and closure of the company's management training centre demonstrates the value that can be achieved by unusual, creative forms of partial outsourcing (Poulteney, 1997). Contracting out or conversion into an agency can in reality offer opportunities rather than threats for HRD staff. Another example is that of Northumbria Water (NW), the privatised water company located in the North-East of England, where training and development operations were reorganised on an agency basis in the late 1980s, around the time of privatisation. HRD specialists were able to choose either to work in the agency or to stay in the parent organisation, where they would be developed for any new roles it might be more appropriate for them to take on. In its early years the agency was assured of a full workload from NW, but thereafter was expected to achieve commercial viability in its own right. The agency, CPCR, rapidly became a successful business and now has full autonomy, with NW only one of its many clients. Meanwhile, HRD remains a core function of NW's business, but is mainly in the hands of line managers. The HR department provides an umbrella of company goals and policy, and supporting administrative and personnel systems. It also provides training of managers for their HRD roles and monitors HRD across the company.

The possibility of most, if not all, of an organisation's learning delivery being outsourced in the future is one that the HRD manager should keep clearly in mind. Leigh (1996) argued that most organisations would benefit from handing their entire training function over to external suppliers and predicted that in many cases full outsourcing is now inevitable. Roy Harrison (1996) speculated that in order to survive 'the training designer will become a performance technologist and the training manager will be a performance improvement manager, separate from the HR function'.

What is essential is that a core strategic developmental role should remain at the heart of the business; if that too is contracted out, HRD will cease to be an organisational player.

Outsourcing training and development operations

Consider your own organisation, or one with which you are familiar. Are any training and development operations outsourced currently? What benefits or deficits do you think this has brought for the organisation? In your view, should any, or further, outsourcing take place?

MANAGING SPECIALIST HRD STAFF

Unless specialist staff are supported in the organisation, are committed and expert in their jobs, and are flexible in skills and outlook the whole function can soon decline into the role of 'passive provider'. There are seven key aspects to the management of such staff:

* employee resource planning

* job analysis

* recruitment and selection

* induction and basic training

* staff appraisal

* continuous development

* career development.

Employee resource (ER) planning

There must be an ER plan for the function, no matter how small in size it may be. It is essential for the training manager to work out the kind, number and level of staff currently required; and to identify what is likely to be needed through time in the light of the organisation's predicted needs for training and development. An informed assessment of the current staffing situation can then be carried out; new work and responsibilities can be allocated; and job and career development plans for training staff can be formulated.

Job analysis

There must be analysis of training and development roles and tasks in the organisation, and identification of the skills, knowledge and attitudes they require. These tasks need to be informed by:

* *national occupational standards in training and development.* These standards provide the basis for vocational qualifications for those with training and development responsibility, whether they are line managers or specialists. They also play an important part in providing a wider framework for those personnel than that provided simply by the context of the particular organisation in which they work at any one point in time. Furthermore, since those personnel will, increasingly, be encouraging other employees to acquire National Vocational Qualifications (NVQs), it is essential that they take the lead in this by themselves going through the whole process and achieving occupational and verification qualifications.

* *IPD professional standards related to employee development.* It is important that HRD practitioners see and present themselves as members of a professional community, working to recognised professional standards. We have seen in Chapter 9 the importance of those standards and the mindset about employee development in the business that they aim to develop.

* *analysis of the roles and responsibilities to be carried by HRD staff in the particular organisation, and of their organisational context.* Again, we have looked at these issues in Chapters 8 and 9. Ensuring that those staff fully understand the rationale for their roles, how those roles may be developed as their expertise in them grows, and how they can manage their roles in the particular organisation in which they work are all tasks for the HRD manager to perform as he or she builds and develops the HRD team.

Recruitment and selection

Job descriptions and personnel specifications will aid the recruitment and selection processes. They will also provide valuable information to help in the planning of training and development and allocation of work to staff. It should be remembered that with some appointments it will be more important for the person to make the job rather than the reverse, and this will determine how tight or loose the job description and personnel specification should be.

Attention needs to be given to who carries out recruitment, short-listing and selection. Many poor-quality training appointments are made because of lack of skill at this stage, or because those who have had the major say in selection have understood little about training jobs and the kinds of competency and motivation they require. It is as important to recruit staff with the disposition to operate in the culture of the particular workplace as those with the functional skills to do so. Ability means nothing if there is not the will to exercise it.

Induction and basic training

There must be proper induction of all new staff in order to explain the different contexts in which they will have to operate, and the work and organisation of the training function. Basic training may also need to be provided.

For many positions it will be advisable to have a probationary period, during which new staff can be regularly appraised and receive coaching, guidance and other forms of support and development. Mentors for new members of staff can be invaluable counsellors, friends and facilitators of learning during this important period. It is as important for the job-holder to be given this period to learn what the job and the organisation is really like, as it is for the organisation to be sure that the selection decision was a wise one.

Appraisal

Appraisal should lead to three outcomes:

- *feedback on performance*. Remember that the training manager will not be aware of all the detail of how staff perform in their jobs, and the appraisal interview is therefore an important source of feedback for the manager as well as for appraisees.

- *work-planning*. This should focus on taking stock of work over a period of time and drawing up work objectives and plans for the forthcoming period.

- *diagnosis of training and development needs and action related to them*. This will lead to the implementation of plans to respond to training and development needs and expectations of staff.

These appraisal sessions must be genuine developmental and motivating experiences, otherwise none of the outcomes can be achieved (see Chapter 13). Again, occupational and professional standards can provide guidelines for appraisal discussions and assessments.

Retraining and continuous development

Retraining is an important aspect of the development of HRD personnel when the management and orientation of the function are changing often quite dramatically. A focus on the 'learning organisation', for example, creates a need in many training staff to learn how to take on a more strategic role in the development of their organisation: a 'strategic facilitator' role (Chapter 9) will frequently call for quite new and complex skills, as well as different ways of looking at the world. In a stimulating article, Alan Phillips (1995) described how he took groups of National Health Service (NHS) trainers through a programme called 'Trainers as Leaders' to give them the confidence and basic competence needed to cope effectively with a changing scenario in the NHS, where development was fast emerging as a strategic activity. Instead of their 'conventional role, where they were often at the organisational margin' these trainers were increasingly being drawn 'into the organisational mainstream', and many needed help in adjusting quickly to its demands and making the most of the opportunities it offered (Phillips, 1995: 32). Such stories are useful examples not only of the importance of regular checks on HRD staff's retraining needs (which in this case emerged at annual appraisal, but which ideally should not be left so long to become evident), but also on the ways in which external consultants can provide valued expertise and experience in unfamiliar territory.

All personnel, including the HRD manager, should be actively committed to self-development on a continuous basis. There may be little time, money or opportunity for the formalised training and development of training staff, and self-development will therefore be the only way to ensure regular diagnosis of their learning needs and updating or changing of skills, knowledge and attitudes through time. Self-development is also important because staff, through becoming committed to the process, will gain valuable insights into the relationship between the understanding and practice of learning styles and skills and the developmental process. Finally, in face of the current trend to downsize and outsource HR functions, continuous learning and self-development are essential to improving the employability security of HR professionals. These themes will be returned to in Chapter 13, but it should be noted here that the IPD's Continuous Professional Development pack is an essential tool for the HRD practitioner.

Career development

There must be a strong focus on career-planning and development for staff. Attention must be given not only to those who are likely to be moving up but also to those who may not be able to move from their present job or organisational level. Williams made an observation in 1984 that remains relevant today. He noted that the 'upward and onward' view of careers:

> does not square with what organisations are able to offer today; promotion is for a still smaller minority than in the past. There needs, therefore, to be a shift away from the advancement orientated view of careers, and an increased emphasis on career development at the same organisational level or within the present job.
>
> Williams, 1984: 32

Davies and Deighan (1986) argued that it is as important to be concerned for the development of the 'solid citizens' and apparent 'dead wood' in a department as it is to have plans for the 'learners' and the 'high fliers' – more so, perhaps, since the solid citizens and the dead wood may be the people who constitute the majority, and in any event will have a strong influence on newcomers to the department. Unless ways are found to stimulate and regenerate these personnel, they may increasingly pull down the whole department. The requirement that every member of the department should have personal development plans will aid the processes of self-development and career development, and will give impetus to 'growing' a learning culture in the training and development department.

Since achieving vocational qualifications will become an increasingly important part of the career development of training staff, their manager must consider the kind of workplace experience and formal education and training that will help them to progress towards those qualifications.

ORGANISING AND DEVELOPING LINE MANAGERS WITH HRD RESPONSIBILITIES

In relation to the organisation and development of line managers who have specific training and development roles to perform, the same basic principles apply as we have already noted for specialist staff. The nature of their roles, and of the tasks, competencies, personal skills, knowledge and attitudes that they require, must be identified to establish necessary guidelines. Let us return to Company X.

Case-study: Company X, Part 2: Developing managers as trainers and developers

At Company X, HRD is a key area of every manager's job; managers are appraised and rewarded for their performance in this as in other key areas of responsibility. Appraisal and rewards are essential, because busy managers will not take their HRD roles seriously unless they perceive that these are regarded by the company as a key area of business activity.

Corporate HRD policy has four objectives to ensure that line managers are well equipped to carry out their HRD roles:

- to raise line managers' awareness of their responsibility for staff training and development

- to enable line managers to own training and development

- to develop line managers' skills in leading and managing people for performance

- to enable line managers to respond flexibly and effectively to an ever-changing business environment.

At Company X managers have proved to be excellent trainers, hundreds becoming certified trainers with NVQs at Level 3. A wide range of procedures, initiatives and formal programmes has been established in order to ensure that they take their training and development roles seriously and are equipped to perform them to a high standard. Some of the approaches used are:

- appointing line managers in key functions or departments to overview training and development

- running workshops about current major business topics with line managers and encouraging advocates among them for training and development implications of emerging plans

- selecting influential middle managers and training and developing them to achieve NVQs in training and development at Levels 3 and 4

- encouraging committed managers to raise the profile of training and development as part of the core responsibilities of line management through the agenda of management meetings

- establishing a mentoring system and training managers as mentors

- creating more flexible and accessible methods for delivering training and learning

- requiring all managers to have personal development plans, and ensuring that their staff have such plans also.

Continuous learning and improvement

All managers in the company must ensure that the focus of planned learning is on the job, where it can directly feed into the individual's development, the achievement of business targets and the longer-term growth of the organisation. They must record what they do in that respect, linking the components of:

* strategic business objectives

* the individual's business role

* performance-planning

* performance development

* personal assessment

* performance-related recognition and reward.

Managers are encouraged to achieve NVQs at Level 4 related to 'learning development' as a way of achieving added personal value in the work they do to develop a culture of continuous learning and development in the workplace.

Measures like these ensure that at Company X managers have the skills and the attitudes needed to promote effective development of people. Managers who are well trained themselves are the ones most likely to take training seriously and ensure their own staff are also trained and continuously developed in their work performance.

LEADERSHIP AND TEAMWORK

Unless training and development staff have skilled leadership and can act as an effective team both within the department and in the wider organisation, their basic abilities and commitment, and their impact on the organisation, will suffer. The training manager has two issues to consider:

* *leadership style*. What should be his or her leadership style – tight or loose, authoritarian or participative, task-centred or person-centred?

* *teamwork*. How should HRD staff be organised? As a close-knit team or a loosely-knit collection of individuals, or somewhere between the two?

If there is a devolved structure for the training department, with central staff transferred out to or already working in units, then there is a danger of professional isolation for those personnel. There is also a possibility that they will become so closely involved with the units in which they are working that they will lose their identity as members of the HRD team. Fowler (1992: 23) observed that the leader in that situation must act as 'head of profession', retaining functional responsibility for staff's professional and career development, and holding regular meetings with them.

Careful thought must be given to the leader's own preferred style and characteristics. It is pointless trying to be 'authoritarian' if this runs quite counter to your personality and to others' fixed perceptions of the kind of person you are. This has to be balanced against the preferred leadership style of the group, and their own personal, occupational and professional characteristics, which may call strongly for one style rather than another. The matter of 'fit' is so important as to be a critical factor at selection stage. However, 'fit' must be seen in a wider perspective: adapting to the preferences and expectations of a group is not productive if the group's behaviour and performance is at odds with what is needed in the organisation, or if currently they are prejudicing the effectiveness and credibility of HRD in the organisation.

Now here is a task based on a real-life case.

Vitex Ltd

After reading this case-study, please answer the following questions on the role of HRD manager:

1 How will you decide what kind of leadership style to use in your department?

2 Do you see individualised work or 'teamwork' as relevant to your new department? Give reasons for your reply.

3 What is the first action you will take in relation to establishing leadership and work processes in the department?

(A variant on this would be to organise this task as a group role-playing exercise instead, using the questions as the starting-point for a meeting between the new HRD manager and his or her staff.)

Vitex is a well-known engineering firm in south-east England. Ten years ago it had a workforce of 2,000 and was extremely successful, operating in many home and overseas markets. Its training department consisted of a training manager, three specialist training officers, two instructors responsible for apprentice and commercial training, a clerk and a secretary. Training tasks tended to be predictable and repetitive, and members of the 'team' operated mainly as individuals. Training policy and the annual company training plan were established by the training manager working in partnership with the personnel director; thereafter work was allocated to the appropriate people, with monitoring to ensure the training budget was not exceeded. There was little real evaluation of training and no in-depth diagnosis of needs. It was assumed that the future would be very like the past and present, and so training itself was mainly a matter of sending people on external courses, or doing some internal, job-related training if this seemed necessary. Training staff tended to work on an individualised basis, the three training officers working within different business units.

Vitex, up against very severe competition in its markets, is now a much smaller firm, with a workforce of around 800 working on three sites all within five or so miles of each other. It makes maximum use of new technology and has established a reputation for innovation and high-quality products. As part of the general move towards 'slimming down' and rationalisation, the size of the training department has been reduced to a training manager, a training officer, and a secretary/administrative assistant. There is no apprentice or Youth Training programme, and the previous training manager was moved three months ago into production management (where he had earlier experience). The training officer, a man in his forties without any professional qualifications but a good record as a training administrator and instructor, is one of the original three training officers. His colleagues have been redeployed in other service departments. There is a new secretary, a pleasant and efficient woman of 30, who was moved from the sales department to training a year ago.

You have just been recruited as the new HRD manager, with a brief to make the function much more business-led. Your role is a mix of HRD manager, internal consultant and role in transition (moving to change agent). Top management fully supports training but has made it clear that from now on the function must provide tailor-made answers to real organisational needs that have been expertly diagnosed. External resources can be used where the expense can be justified by the results likely to be achieved. Each business unit now holds its own training and development budget, with managers responsible for deciding on training needs in their units. The now-styled HRD department has only a small central budget to meet organisation-wide needs and special contingencies.

Feedback notes

The HRD manager can use our simple systems framework developed in Chapter 9 (page 160) in order to decide on the most appropriate kind of leadership style:

- *environment*. The organisational environment of the leader, the group and the task is organic, team-based and operating in an uncertain, highly competitive external environment. This should push the HRD department towards a flexible structure, with values that relate to helping achieve the 'mission' of Vitex, and provide expertise that will meet organisational needs. Effective teamwork will be essential, and the function must become business-led if it is to establish and maintain credibility and serve the needs of its 'clients' in the business units.

- *structure and culture*. Although the training department may have had a bureaucratic structure and culture in the past, these are no longer appropriate. Leadership that will develop a non-hierarchical, creative, 'change agent' department is clearly needed, and there must be a collaborative relationship with line managers as well as with the personnel function (about which no details were given in the case-study).

- *goals, strategy and tasks*. At Vitex, the goal is for HRD to provide tailor-made services to meet key organisational needs, so training and development tasks may change rapidly through time, and are unlikely to be routine or highly specialised. This emphasises the need for effective teamwork rather than a one-to-one pattern of organising and managing people in the HRD department.

- *people*. The leader's own preferred style and characteristics have to be considered, as do the preferred leadership style of the group, and their own personal and professional characteristics, which may make one style more obviously appropriate than any other. A problem may arise with the 40-year-old training officer, who has worked in a quite different kind of training situation, where the norm was administrative tasks rather than creative and diagnostic work. He is used to working as an individual in a hierarchical structure, not to operating as a member of a close-knit professional team. Particular attention must be paid to his training and development. The secretary, too, has worked in that situation for a year, and her expectations and perceptions of the new situation need to be explored.

- *technology.* It seems likely that the HRD manager could use new technology, eg computer-based training and learning, open learning projects, as well as more conventional media and methods. There must of course be clear justification and cost-benefit analysis, but the HRD function must become knowledgeable about innovative approaches to learning, and may be well advised to use and learn from external consultants to design and pilot certain learning systems. Those consultants, too, will have to be carefully selected, managed and monitored, and drawn into a partnership with internal training staff.

Conclusions from the above analysis

All the evidence points to the need for the leader to build a cohesive, flexible team, whose members can contribute to the overall goal of the training department, pooling knowledge and skills instead of working on an individualised and specialist basis. In this context, the contribution of the secretary, and the image she gives of the department, is crucial. If she proves capable and willing, her role and type of work could themselves change through time from being purely secretarial to incorporating other types of responsibility. A number of personnel and training officers start off as secretaries, and her routes for development (like NVQs, or gaining part or full membership of the IPD) should be integrated into a career plan. The training officer, too, has valuable experience and skills to offer: giving him an early assignment of collecting information from external sources on new learning systems and on funding sources to pilot new training technology initiatives would test his skills, explore his potential, give him the chance to work on something of real importance and expand his knowledge as well as his network of external contacts.

In initial team meetings with staff, the HRD manager will need to strike a delicate but firm balance between on the one hand pursuing a collaborative approach and on the other demonstrating leadership that has a clear, appropriate and powerful vision for the department, as well as a strategy to ensure that that vision can be realised at the practical level. The extent to which inputs from staff can or should influence the determination of organisational training and development policy and/or strategy is something that only the leader can determine.

CONCLUSION

In order to achieve the learning objectives of this chapter, we have looked at the importance of including in the scope of the HRD manager's role not only those who are employees of the organisation but also those outside the organisation who could be involved in its HRD activities and drawn into its learning network to the organisation's advantage. We have looked at the implications for HRD and HR professionals of the decentralised, the line-managed and the outsourced functions, and have discussed the advantages and challenges involved in the increasing trend to outsource training and development operations.

Seven aspects of the management and development of HRD specialists have been discussed, and guidelines for practice have been provided in relation to the organisation and development of line managers with HRD responsibilities. Key principles of leadership and teamwork for all with major roles to play in HRD have been identified.

USEFUL READING

FOWLER, A. (1997) 'How to outsource personnel'. *People Management.* Vol. 3, 4: 40–43.

GILLEY, J.W. *and* EGGLAND, S.A. (1989) *Principles of Human Resource Development.* Chapters 5 and 8. Maidenhead, Addison Wesley.

REID, M.A. *and* BARRINGTON, H. (1997) *Training Interventions: Managing employee development.* Chapter 6. 5th ed. London, Institute of Personnel and Development.

WALTON, J. (1996) 'The provision of learning support for non-employees', in J. Stewart and J. McGoldrick (eds). *Human Resource Development: Perspectives, strategies and practice.* London, Pitman. pp. 120–37.

WRIGHT, P.L. *and* TAYLOR, D.S. (1994) *Improving Leadership Performance: Interpersonal skills for effective leadership.* 2nd ed. London, Prentice Hall International. (Full of practical exercises, check-lists and diagnostic activities.)

11 Managing finance and marketing the function

LEARNING OBJECTIVES

After reading this chapter you will:

- be able to establish and manage a training budget

- understand what is involved in establishing a training record system

- understand the main issues related to marketing the HRD function.

MANAGING TRAINING AND DEVELOPMENT RESOURCES

The human resource development (HRD) manager's resource base will need skilful management if it is to be cost-efficient, add value and remain continuously relevant to a changing business situation and to the emergent needs of the workforce.

There are two main categories of training and development resources: the tangible and the intangible.

Tangible resources
- *Personnel* available within and outside the organisation.

- *Physical resources* – accommodation, equipment, training materials etc – available within the organisation and through external sources.

- *Finance* available within the organisation for the training and development of the workforce, whether allocated to a central training budget or to departmental training budgets; and also available from external sources.

Intangible resources
One of the most important intangible resources is time. The time available to carry out any activities in training, including the management and development of training resources, will have a crucial effect on training policy and strategy, on managerial strategy and effectiveness, and on day-to-day training and management.

Other intangible resources include assets such as the past image and reputation of training within the organisation; the learning capability and disposition of the workforce; external learning networks that can offer a potential source of knowledge and expertise to improve learning in the organisation; and natural learning opportunities available in the organisation in the normal course of work. These intangible learning resources should be identified and used to the benefit of job performance and the development of human potential in the business. We shall discuss them further in Part 4; in Chapter 20 (Part 5) they become a major focus of attention.

In order to be able to manage these resources effectively, the HRD manager must:

- *observe and reflect on the present situation.* He or she must look at the current training budget (or, if none is available, some equivalent figures that show the costs of running the training function and carrying out training activities) to establish what is done and what it costs; and must identify the other tangible and intangible training resources available – materials, equipment, accommodation, personnel – and consider how they are currently being used.

- *analyse this information by reference to key contextual factors* in order to establish whether the department's resources are being used rationally to meet key HRD needs.

- *be creative* and think of alternative, more efficient or effective, ways of using resources.

- *make decisions*, choosing the most feasible, cost-efficient and cost-effective action.

- *monitor and evaluate*, choosing those methods that are both simple and effective enough for the purpose, and agreeing well in advance who is to carry out these processes, and when.

Good resource management thus requires the use of those core learning skills defined by Kolb, Rubin and McIntyre (1974) in their learning cycle: observation and reflection; analysis; creativity; decison-making and problem-solving; evaluation.

The management of resources requires the development of measures of activity, and at this point material presented in my two previous IPD texts will be reproduced with few changes. What was relevant then, after all, remains so now: a straightforward approach that will provide the basic information needed and can be rapidly mastered and applied to a wide variety of situations. There are, of course, many financial management techniques that can be applied to the training investment, and in that regard consultancy-oriented texts like those of Moorby (1991: 68–93) and Bentley (1990: 32–42) are helpful for both the student and the practitioner.

MANAGING THE BUDGET

The first place where one expects to find a categorisation of training and development activities and their costs is in the budget. Budgeting can take three main forms: there may be a budget for the HRD department; money for training and development may be held in unit/departmental budgets for which line managers are responsible; or, as in our Company X case-study, there may be both a corporate training budget and unit budgets.

Whoever has budgetary responsibility, it is essential that resources and activities should be costed and managed in such a way that full value for money is obtained. It is also important that where, at first sight, priority needs cannot be met within current budgets, a sound case is put forward for obtaining more money or for meeting needs by the use of changed approaches.

Presentation of the budget
The type of format to be used in the presentation of financial information about training depends on four factors:

- *why the information is needed.* This will determine what information is to be collected, and what focus to give the costings.

- *for whom the information is needed.* This will determine the way the information is expressed and the specific format to be used. If financial information is needed by the accounts department, this should follow the format and language used in their accounting system. If data on costs and benefits of one training solution compared to another are needed by busy line managers to help them decide which solution to choose, then the data must be expressed in language that is immediately comprehensible to the managers.

- *when the information is needed and what is available.* If a request comes in today for information needed tomorrow, then it may prove impossible to obtain all the data theoretically desirable. The format must be tailored to match whatever data can be produced in time so that the overall presentation makes its proper impact even if it cannot fully cover the ground.

- *availability of time and expertise.* Extending the previous point, budgeting is a time-consuming activity involving a variety of skills. It is essential to put the task into perspective, calculating how much time and expertise should be devoted to it given its importance relative to other HRD tasks.

A basic approach to costing
Three pieces of information are essential when costing training and development operations:

- the overall annual running cost of training operations

- how to recover that cost

- how to identify and compare costs involved in training and development alternatives.

In relation to these, two terms are fundamental:

- *trainer day costs.* This refers to the daily costs involved in the basic running of a training function.

- *training day costs.* This refers to the total costs involved in running a training function and in carrying out its specific training activities.

Finally, there are three areas of tangible costs; they relate to personnel, overheads and administration.

Calculating annual running costs of training operations

Table 8 deals with basic costs of running a specialist training department. It does not include capital expenditure or costs of providing training services (except in relation to administration costs where, in order to get an acceptable figure, we have to consider the sort of demands likely to be made, given the training envisaged). In our next examples the provision costs will be calculated separately.

Personnel and overhead costs are fixed (that is to say, the organisation must pay them, whether or not training activities are carried out), but administration costs are variable, because they depend on what kind of training activities take place or are envisaged. If a forecasting exercise is being carried out, then administration costs can be estimated in one of three ways:

• If there is no annual training plan, but the pattern of past activity has been quite similar to that of proposed activity, then a reliable enough figure can be reached by taking an average of total administration costs incurred during, say, the last two years' training activities and adding on an amount for inflation.

• If there is an annual training plan then the training manager can look at the administration costs actually incurred by the activities involved in last year's plan and, knowing the kind of activities planned for the forthcoming year, assess how much more or less the related administration costs are likely to be. Again, an inflation cost will have to be built in.

• If there is no specialist training department, or any training overheads, and there is no relationship between past and planned provision, then the basic annual running costs of the training role and function can be calculated by reference to two areas of tangible costs:

  • *personnel costs*: the number of days each manager is likely to be

Table 8 Basic annual running costs of a training department (with acknowledgements to Alan Rutter, University of Northumbria Business School)

	Cost (£)
Personnel (two training officers and a secretary)	
Training staff salaries plus, say, 25 per cent for employment costs (pension, NI and other payments)	40,000
Support staff (administrative and clerical) plus 25 per cent	12,000
Overheads	
Annual rent and rates (or some approximate calculation of these) related to training accommodation (one training room; two offices); to heating, lighting and cleaning; and to other maintenance costs of training accommodation	6,000
Administration	
Estimate/actual:	
telephone and postal costs	
printing, photocopying etc costs	
computer costs (eg cost of computer time, software)	4,000
Total basic annual running costs	£62,000

Table 9 Cost of a trainer day (with acknowledgements to Alan Rutter)

	Cost £
Days actually worked by the two training staff (ie once holidays etc have been taken) = 240 each = total of *480 days*	
Annual running cost of the training dept (see Table 8)	62,000
So cost of each day the training staff are actually working	62,000 ÷ 480
Cost of one trainer day (to nearest £)	£129.00

spending in carrying out training and training-related activities for others, expressed as a proportion of their annual salary and employment costs. (A more sophisticated calculation would include lost opportunity costs – the estimated cost to the organisation of deploying line managers on training work when they could have been doing something else. However, that is a very speculative approach and politically sensitive, so better avoided when all that is wanted is a straightforward assessment of the most obvious costs.)

- *administration costs*: identifiable administration costs that will be incurred by work on training and training-related activities, expressed in annual terms.

Recovering running costs

First, we need to find out the cost of a trainer day in the organisation. Table 9 continues with the example we have just used, adding further information. (This same approach can, of course, be used to calculate the 'trainer day' costs of anyone who carries out training/development activities, whether or not they are training staff.)

This simple calculation of the trainer day cost tells us that, if required to recover the annual cost of running its training department (£62,000), this particular organisation would need to provide training for 480 days a year (ie 240 days by each of the two training staff) and charge £129 a day for that training.

We can now see how the basic running costs of a training department or function can be expressed as a trainer day cost, calculated as follows:

$$\frac{\text{Annual running cost of the training function}}{\text{Number of days each staff involved in training work}}$$

$$= \text{trainer day cost}$$

But if it is necessary for a training department to recover its identifiable costs on a rigorous financial basis, how can this be done? A case-study can provide a helpful illustration at this point.

Case-study: Mintech Ltd: Part 1 (In collaboration with Alan Rutter, University of Northumbria Business School)

Mintech Ltd has a training department employing two training officers (Mike and John) and a secretary.

The basic annual running cost of the department = £62,000

Number of days worked by the two officers:
  Mike: 250 + John: 250   = 500
  Trainer day cost   = *£124*

The department is involved in two sorts of training activity, the direct costs of which are shown below:

Training people	*Assisting people to attend external training*
The trainers keep a record of the number of days they spend on face-to-face training of people:	The trainers keep a record of the number of days they spend on work connected with external courses, ranging from analysis of needs through to evaluation of results:
Mike: 30 days John: 20 days *Total: 50 trainer days* *Cost: 50 × £124 = £6,200*	Mike: 220 days John: 230 days *Total: 450 trainer days* *Cost: 450 × £124 = £55,800*
The trainers add up the number of days that staff spend participating in these courses = 300	The trainers add up the number of days that staff spend participating in these courses = 3,000
Amount to be recovered for internal training activities: £6,200 for 300 training days *Total cost of internal training day = £21*	Amount to be recovered for external training activities: £55,800 for 3,000 training days *Total cost of external training day = £19*

But:

Additional costs (fees, travel, subsistence, accommodation, course materials, per person) per day = *£5*	*Additional costs* (fees, travel, subsistence, accommodation, course materials, per person) per day = *£200*

To recover its costs of £21 per person for everyone who undergoes internal training, and £19 per person for everyone who attends external training, as well as covering the additional costs involved, Mintech's training department can do one of two things:

If it has its own budget, then it must include in the budget estimate enough to cover a cost of £21 per day for every member of the organisation who will be attending internal training courses; and a cost of £19 per day for every member of the organisation who will be attending external training courses. It must then add to the estimate the additional costs of fees, travel, subsistence, accommodation and course materials involved in the training events concerned

or

If there is no central training budget, but each department has its own budget from which training costs must be met, then it must 'charge' departments £21 per day for every member of staff who will be attending internal training courses, and £19 per day for every member of staff who will be attending external training courses and add on the additional costs of fees, travel, subsistence, accommodation and course materials involved in the training events concerned.

The Mintech case study shows us that in order to calculate how to recover the costs involved in running a training department and in carrying out its training activities, the *training day cost* must be calculated, as follows:

$$\frac{\text{Trainer day cost}}{\text{Number of training days}} = \text{Training day cost}$$

Note that the number of training days is simply arrived at by adding up all the days it has taken to train people throughout the organisation, in one case internally, in the other case externally. So if 100 people each went on three days' external training in a year, then the total number of external training days would come to 300. We can conclude by saying that:

> The *trainer day cost* can be used to calculate the basic cost of running the training function, and the *training day cost* can be used to calculate the charge to be made by the function for training, if its running costs are to be recovered on a strict financial basis.

We have now seen how to provide two of the three crucial pieces of information that every manager of an HRD function should possess: the overall costs of running the function, and how to recover that cost.

Identifying and comparing costs involved in training alternatives

Using the same Mintech case-study, we can look at a typical situation facing many personnel and training officers: staff requests to go on education or training courses. We shall see how, by comparing the costs of internal and external supervisory training, a sound decision can be reached by someone who is concerned to achieve both relevant training and good management of resources.

Summary

Case-study: Mintech Ltd: Part 2

Three supervisors from different departments have applied to the training department to go on a day-release supervisory studies course at the local college. It lasts for a year, involves absence of half a day plus an evening (same day) over three terms, and ends with an examination leading to a national supervisory skills qualification. Mike, one of the two training officers, first identifies the costs involved in sending the three supervisors away on the day release course. To help him do this calculation, he uses the 'training day cost' identified in the Mintech case-study, Part 1.

Option A

Sending supervisors on external training course leading to national supervisory qualification:

	Cost (£)
Fees (£1,000 per person per year) £1,000 × 3	3,000
Travel and subsistence (£5 per person per day at college): £5× 3 × 30 days	450
Materials (books and other items used by trainees on the course) £60 × 3	180
Administrative overhead cost External training day cost × number of days × number of trainees (£19, already calculated, × 30 × 3)	1,710
Total cost of sending three people on course	**£5,340**

Mike could have made out a more complicated list which would have included indirect as well as direct costs. The indirect costs incurred by attending the external course would include: lost opportunity costs, reduction in output or quality of service of their staff due to less effective staff management during the periods of their absence, lost salary and related employment cost, due to the supervisors' reduction in hours worked 'on the job' during the period of the course, and so on. In practice such costs are rarely taken into account unless direct costs are occasioned by the supervisors' absence (for example, overtime payments due to their work having to be done by others). Of course, if Mike had needed to make a particularly powerful case against sending people away on an external course, he would have done well to draw attention to these 'hidden' costs!

The next step is for Mike to think carefully about the external course. His calculations show that sending three supervisors on the course will be an expensive undertaking, and it may not be possible to offer the same opportunity, in the current year, to any further supervisory applicants. So what are the other options? (At this point you may like to take over and do some creative thinking to generate a list of alternatives. For the purposes of this exercise I am developing only one other option, but in fact several are possible.)

One such option is for job-related training needs of all Mintech's 16 supervisors to be identified through appraisal interviews and other methods, and for the training department to organise internal courses to meet common needs, leaving needs specific to each individual to be met in some other way.

Mike discusses this idea with his colleagues and they agree that three one-week courses run by the training department in its conference room would cover the necessary material well, and would be a real benefit to at least 12, instead of only three, supervisors. The department has a good reputation within the company for running tailor-made programmes, and so it is unlikely that this would be viewed as inferior by the supervisors. Admittedly it would not lead to National Vocational Qualifications (NVQs), because the company is not yet tied into the NVQ system; but should that become an important consideration in the future, then this particular option can be reconsidered then. What will the option cost at this point?

Option B
Internal supervisory training course run by training staff

There would be three one-week courses, each led by one tutor and involving a total membership of 12 supervisors, four attending each course.

	Cost (£)
Fees	N/A
Subsistence Mid-morning and mid-afternoon refreshments for 4 participants and one trainer, @ £1.50 per head per day	112.50
Materials (£50 per trainee plus 3 trainers' copies)	750.00
Administrative overhead cost, Internal training day cost (£21, previously calculated, × 5 × 12) =	1,260.00
Total cost of training 12 supervisors internally =	£2,112.50

Mike was interested to note the cost per trainee involved in each of the options: £1,780 for Option A, but only £176.88 for Option B. He realised that in Option B he had not included the cost of identifying training needs of the supervisors, designing the one-week programmes for them and producing the necessary training materials. This was because he was confident that they could be substantially offset by repeat runs of the programmes for further groups of supervisors.

Through the various examples so far examined we have discovered how to extract three crucial pieces of information noted at the start of this chapter:

• the basic annual cost of running training operations

• how to recover the running cost on a strict financial basis

• how to identify and compare costs involved in training alternatives.

There is one more activity that needs to be carried out in order to ensure that cost-effective decisions are made in relation to the use of training resources: cost–benefit analysis. We will look at that in Chapter 12 when we examine a variety of ways whereby the value of training and development to the business can be assessed.

Running costs of a training department

Take a training department in your own organisation or some other with which you are familiar. Using the methods described thus far, produce a calculation of the approximate annual running costs of that department, and then identify how far those costs are recovered by the department's training operations. Produce any recommendations for action that you may feel necessary on completion of the exercise.

A STRATEGY FOR MANAGING TRAINING RESOURCES

What have we learnt about the management of resources thus far?

That planned learning events, especially training events, can be managed efficiently and effectively by ensuring:

- *accurate and meaningful costing.* The costs of learning activities must be estimated as accurately as possible, and expressed in a way that is meaningful to the managers of the organisation concerned.

- *relevance to organisational training policy and needs.* Decisions about expenditure on training activities must be consistent with decisions about the overall HRD policy and strategy of the organisation, and must meet real training needs and priorities.

- *consistency with other employee resource (ER) policies and processes.* Decisions about learning activities must also be consistent with other ER policies and processes, for example employee resource planning and utilisation, staff appraisal, promotion and career development planning, and financial and other reward strategies.

- *considered options.* Alternative ways of using resources and of achieving learning objectives must always be considered and costed before final decisions are made.

- *cost-efficient and cost-effective decisions.* Compare costs and benefits of the options (including that of doing nothing). Make a decision which strikes the best balance between being cost-beneficial, generally feasible and politically sensitive.

- *monitoring and evaluation.* All learning events must be carefully controlled, and their value as well as their validity must be assessed. This point will be covered in detail in Chapter 16.

ESTABLISHING AND MAINTAINING A RECORD SYSTEM

There is one other crucial activity involved in the management of resources that needs to be covered in this chapter: establishing and maintaining a record system.

In this section I am not attempting to explain in any detail how to set up a record system or design training records, since there are specialist texts to give that help. My concern is simply to outline the aims for such a system and key points for the manager to consider.

What the record system must ensure or show is that:

- *activities can be identified and monitored.* It should be possible at any time to check on how far, in what ways, at what cost, and with what results training and planned development activities are being carried out in every part of the organisation. The more collaborative the approach to training is, the easier it will be to obtain and record that information. Records must also be comprehensive, up to date and accurate.

- *training and development of individuals is recorded.* Personal records need to be kept showing the numbers and kinds of people who have been trained and developed. They must also facilitate monitoring to ensure non-discrimination.

- *the law relating to employment is being observed*. It must be possible at any time to identify how far, and in what ways, the law relating to employment is being observed. In the context of HRD this means that records must pay particular attention to areas of training activity related to dismissal, redundancy, discrimination, health and safety, and data protection, since in all of these areas failure to ensure that employees have the right knowledge and skills can mean that employers as well as employees become liable for breaches of the relevant legislation.

  Discrimination issues are receiving increasing publicity at present, and the importance of records in that connection cannot be over-stressed. I have made the point elsewhere that up-to-date information should always be available to show exactly what steps have been taken to prevent discrimination in the workplace, and to prove how people have been treated at work (Harrison, 1986). It must be clear from examining training records that all employees have equal opportunity for access to training and development relevant to their jobs and their future employment prospects in the organisation. We shall examine some of the implications of this in Chapter 17, when we look at ways in which such access can be facilitated for minority groups and disadvantaged individuals.

- *the record system itself adheres to the law*. The record system must adhere to legal requirements. For training and development activity, the relevant legislation is contained not only in the Data Protection Act 1984 but also in the much less widely known European Union Data Protection Directive 1995.

  The latter, as Aiken (1996) explained, has many implications for personnel departments, since from 24 October 1998 employees will be able to access all their files. Employers must also have instructions listing the purposes for which information is collected, clarifying access and security arrangements and guaranteeing that no additional use will be made of the information without first obtaining the consent of the person in overall charge of employee records. It is this Directive that, by withdrawing the advantages hitherto attached to manual record systems (the immunity from right of access), raises the issue of the point at which a fully computerised record system should be introduced. The implications of that issue for an HRD department which may not be an integral part of a wider ER function in the organisation are considerable.

- *the record system is cost-beneficial*. The record system must be cost-efficient and cost-effective. It should be as simple as possible, using sophisticated methods and processes only when the ensuing benefits can be shown fully to justify the human, physical and financial resources and costs. Particular attention must be paid to such questions as how detailed particular records should be; how long records should be kept; who should keep records; and how often records should be updated.

- *HRD records are consistent with other ER records*. Training and development records should have a positive relationship with records maintained in any other areas of ER in the organisation. Therefore, they should whenever possible be drawn up using a format and technology that complement rather than confuse other ER record-keeping and data analysis. Their content should also avoid unnecessary overlap with the content of other ER records.

• *confidentiality is observed*. Particular attention must be paid to confidentiality and therefore to what information goes on record; to who should have access to various records; and to how access can be protected.

These, then, are the seven key factors to be taken into account when establishing a record system. A record system is, together with the budget, an invaluable aid to the control of resources. However, like the budget, the criteria for determining what goes into records depends on four factors:

• why the information is needed

• for whom it is needed

• when it is needed and what information is available

• what time and expertise can be devoted to this task, given other demands on the HRD function.

MARKETING HRD

The HRD manager has another important area of activity: the marketing of HRD in the organisation. In Chapter 9 (page 147) we saw the current significance of the concept of HRD practitioners as 'internal consultants' – and the increasing threat of outsourcing that faces many training and development departments unable to convince their organisations that they are worth continued investment in the services they offer. Such considerations underline the need for ensuring that the HRD function offers real value to the business, and for effective marketing of that function.

Marketing in this sense means 'that HRD practitioners will aim all their efforts at satisfying their clients' (Gilley and Eggland, 1989: 242). It is not to do with glossy brochures or expensive selling efforts. It is to do with finding out the kind of service or product that best meets the needs of internal customers as well as of those outside the organisation for whom planned learning events provided or initiated by the company also have important value – those other stakeholders referred to in Chapter 10 (page 167) as 'non-employees'.

As Price (1966) argued, marketing does not assume that there is one way to strategic success. It enables the development of the right kind of products for a particular organisation. Marketing is therefore an integral part of the collaborative relationship that must exist between HRD professionals and their organisation if the function is to be taken seriously. To quote again from Gilley and Eggland's illuminating chapter (1989: 243), it is a matter of those professionals becoming 'skilled at understanding, planning and managing exchanges', so that value is offered to and received by the parties.

Little attention has been paid in the past in British academic texts to the concept of marketing as part of developing a strategic approach to HRD. Now, however, it has become commonplace to talk of the firm's value chain, of functional departments needing to serve internal as well as external customers, of the need for vision and goals to drive every area of business activity. Now, it is easier to see the meaning of 'marketing' in relation to HRD. In Chapter 15 we shall see how to formulate and agree on purpose and strategy for learning events and how to involve stakeholders actively in the design, delivery and evaluation of those events. The subject is raised here to ensure that marketing the HRD function overall is understood by the HRD manager and team to be one of their central tasks. Using rather different language, we are reiterating what was emphasised in Chapters 2, 3 and 9: that once its true value is understood and it achieves strategic integration at various levels of the organisation, HRD can realise its potential to be a key business function and a fundamental process to stimulate change, innovation and growth.

Marketing HRD in the business

What are the eight processes to develop a collaborative and committed approach to HRD across an organisation?

Feedback notes
- The processes are to be found in Chapter 3 (page 45). From them it was concluded that the strongest commitment to training and development in the organisation will arise from a shared awareness among stakeholders that strategic HRD is a logical outcome of the kind of business goals that drive the organisation, and that it is central to the achievement of sustained competitive advantage.

Expending effort on developing that awareness is more productive and meaningful than lengthy, complicated and time-consuming attempts to 'prove that HRD was worth it'. That defensive stance is likely to be relevant only when HRD as a function is not accepted in the organisation because it has never become a shared activity with a common language, something owned by managers rather than by specialists. Since all attempts to measure outcomes are fallible, no matter how rigorous and detailed they may be, any attempt to 'prove the value' of HRD in a hostile climate can be pulled apart because the will is not there to interpret the evidence objectively.

This is not to deny that training and development resources and activities should always be costed and managed in such a way that full value is obtained for the money available. HRD personnel must be able to speak as convincingly about the costs and benefits of what they do as any other manager in the business, and must be prepared to show at any time that resources are being efficiently as well as effectively expended on relevant learning processes and initiatives. It is simply a reminder that there should also be a continuing effort to develop an HRD process that will actively involve stakeholders and create a climate of awareness of the centrality of HRD to the business.

In the next chapter we shall examine ways in which a collaborative approach to HRD can be extended to include the setting of standards, the monitoring of progress and the assessment of HRD's value for the organisation and its people.

CONCLUSION

In order to achieve the learning objectives of this chapter we have identified tangible and intangible HRD resources. We have examined how to manage the budget using a three-stage approach to costing and covering the three main areas of tangible costs, related to personnel, overheads and administration. A six-point guide to the strategic management of resources has been developed, and seven basic principles involved in establishing a training record system have been identified. The chapter has concluded with a discussion of the meaning and importance of marketing in order for HRD to make a fully strategic contribution to the business.

USEFUL READING

GILLEY, J.W. and EGGLAND, S.A. (1989) *Principles of Human Resource Development*. Wokingham, Addison Wesley and University Associates Inc.

HACKETT, P. (1997) *Introduction to Training*. London, Institute of Personnel and Development.

MOORBY, E. (1991) *How to Succeed in Employee Development: Moving from vision to results*. Maidenhead, McGraw-Hill.

12 Establishing outcomes and assessing the investment

LEARNING OBJECTIVES

After reading this chapter you will:

- understand key principles associated with the setting, monitoring and measurement of human resource development (HRD) outcomes

- understand uses of and approaches to benchmarking and setting standards

- have an insight into a range of approaches and tools to assess the value for the organisation of its investment in HRD

- understand how to plan and carry out an HRD audit.

SETTING STANDARDS AND ACHIEVING OUTCOMES FOR HRD

Focusing HRD activity

Let us recall four crucial questions relating to the contribution made by HRD to the business. They were raised in Chapter 3 (page 44):

- Is there a good fit between the vision and strategy of HRD and wider organisational vision and policy?

- Will the expected outcomes of HRD prove relevant to key business needs?

- Does the way in which the HRD function is organised enhance its ability to implement its strategy?

- Are the HRD professionals expert in their roles and tasks?

These four questions highlight the extent to which HRD is strategic, business-led and guided by experts. Hendry (1995) advised human resource (HR) staff not to waste their efforts trying to achieve a tight fit between business and HR strategies; in his well-argued view, the variables involved in their interaction are so many and so constantly changing as to frustrate any attempt, no matter how frequent the fine-tuning. Instead he recommended what he called a loose coupling of the two. This means aiming simply for a generalised alignment where strategies for the business and those for its people both move forward in the same overall direction, with the latter flexible enough to respond effectively to any major changes in the former. He saw the key tasks of HR staff (including those involved in the HRD field) as:

- ensuring a continuous process of questioning and awareness by themselves about the business, and pushing this process across the organisation
- focusing HR activity on developing the values, culture and managerial style needed in the business if its long-term goals and policies are to be achieved
- improving the quality of management, and of problem-solving and decision-making behaviour, through HRD processes
- developing HRD practitioners who are sensitive to the changing needs, stage of growth and strategic orientation of the business.

Such advice is clearly needed at a time when – as noted in Chapter 2 (page 21) – there is little evidence of a durable or coherent alignment between HRM and the strategy of the business, and when HR practitioners are often under fire. To illustrate: in 1995 the Boston Consulting Group carried out a survey of personnel and HR directors in 61 of the top 250 British companies listed by turnover. A *Financial Times* commentary (Duffy, 1995) on the survey noted that over half the respondents perceived themselves to be more involved in strategic planning than a few years before (not surprisingly, since all were in large organisations operating in dynamic environments), but found that long-term forecasts of skills needs were rarely being incorporated into corporate strategy. The survey also revealed that the role of HR specialists was still ambiguous in many companies.

The same survey was critical about the impact of HRD, finding that while companies were spending more on training than in the late 1980s, four-fifths did not do effective cost-benefit analysis, and there was little creativity or sophistication in attempts to measure training: end-of-course trainee reaction sheets appeared to be the most typical approach. What companies wanted from their training departments remained unclear, as did the outcomes being achieved by those departments.

This echoed a key finding in an international HRM survey reported in 1990. The authors found that many personnel specialists at board level appeared to be little involved in developing corporate strategy, and seemed 'not to have created human resource strategies for their organisations; nor have they developed work programmes or targets against which the personnel department can be measured' (Brewster and Smith, 1990).

The vital tasks of establishing and measuring HRD outcomes, and of setting and maintaining standards related to those outcomes, appear therefore to be neglected in the majority of UK-based organisations. If this is so, it helps to explain both the failure of HRD to achieve widespread credibility as a strategic, business-led function, and the vulnerability of training departments in the face of those trends to downsize and outsource, as discussed in Chapter 10.

Setting and maintaining standards
Key stages in establishing and achieving HRD outcomes are:

- allocating responsibilities for delivery of strategy

- drawing up action plans in order to implement strategy

- setting targets and standards, the means for measuring them, and the timing and levels of responsibility for implementing the plans

- continued oversight, monitoring and adaptability to ensure that there is minimal drift between strategy and its implementation across the organisation

- continuous communication of interim progress and problems, and shared decisions about any amendments to plans needed to meet unexpected contingencies.

In the following review, try to assess how well informed your own training and development function and its practitioners are about the business and its environment, and how well-equipped they are to deal with the strategic imperatives facing HRD.

Assessing the quality of HRD service in my organisation

(With acknowledgements to Fonda and Rowland, 1995)

Does your training and development function collaborate
   in joint ventures with employee development (ED)
   functions in other organisations to develop and offer
   value-added services?   _____

Does your training and development function have its
   own business plans for developing its capability and
   performance, and are these plans related to the
   challenges facing your client businesses?   _____

Does your training and development function use regular
   structured feedback and benchmarking in order to assess
   its performance?   _____

Does it work to an explicit set of ethics and values that
   have been agreed at the highest level?   _____

As an HR professional, are you clear about who your
   customers, suppliers and business partners are, and do
   you understand the people and organisational
   implications of the challenges they are facing?   _____

Are you clear about the purpose of your job and the
   processes that you are responsible for managing?   _____

Do you create and pursue your own development plan?   _____

Do your assess your own performance with regard to:
   • meeting standards   _____
   • satisfying your customers   _____
   • your contribution to your customers' performance   _____
   • finding more cost-effective ways to improve your
     contribution?   _____

Use of such methods should lead to the setting of standards that are both relevant to the needs of the business and informed by external and internal best practice. They offer ways of regularly checking on the operations and value of the service provided by HRD to the organisation.

Let us look more closely at benchmarking and best practice.

Benchmarking, best practice and milestones

These are techniques associated with quality management, and can be defined in general terms as a continuous search for and implementation of best practices which lead to superior performance.

Benchmarking involves finding a particular standard, whether internal or external, and using that as a continuous marker for a particular strategy, process or initiative. There are three major types of benchmarking:

- *Internal:* looks at and compares similar processes within an organisation to achieve internal best practice. For HR, an example could be the selection, induction or appraisal process. The exercise of finding out how this is carried out in different parts of the organisation offers two benefits: the highlighting of inconsistencies and the identification of internal best practice that can then be used as a marker across the organisation.

- *Competitive*: where organisations in the same sector – for example, a hospital trust and a community healthcare trust – agree to work together to compare best practice in key areas. For example, two areas could be privacy and dignity matters, and publication and distribution of patient information.

- *Functional*: where a particular process is identified and then compared to best practice outside the organisation. Thus, an organisation wishing to improve its measurements of customer satisfaction may take two or three external organisations of different types as comparitors, and finally select one to use for benchmarking.

Benchmarking as a process is divided into four stages:

- preliminary planning

- analysis, when the gap between current and desired performance is identified as a result of benchmarking research

- action, in which changes are implemented and measured

- review and recycling stages in order to achieve continuous improvement.

In the UK there is a reluctance in many companies to use benchmarking to improve their processes, despite the fact that this can help them to become significantly more competitive. Benchmarking is not merely copying, or picking up handy hints. It is about carefully planning comparisons in order to decide how to enhance performance. Organisations (for example, Rank Xerox) agree to being benchmarked because they acquire insight and information from the process, too, and because it gives them a higher profile in the competitive environment.

Best practice involves gathering information across the academic and practitioner field to formulate general principles that will help to determine how best to carry out a particular process or initiative. Although internal and competitive benchmarking are likely to produce improvement, it is the search for best practice and new ideas that is most likely to change an organisation's collective mindset, and so lead to transformation. This is illustrated in the following case-study.

Case-study: English Nature's use of benchmarking and best practice

English Nature, the Government's adviser on nature and conservation, aspires to be a learning organisation, and so decided to benchmark approaches to training with a wide range of companies in order to achieve that transformation. The account produced by Dolan, its training manager, illustrates the many ways in which examining practice in other organisations can help an HRD department to set standards, decide on particular practical approaches and monitor progress.

Twelve companies across all sectors were visited because they had adopted innovative approaches to learning and business development. Their beliefs, strategies and a range of key features were analysed and compared with those noted in the 'learning organisation' literature that had already been studied at English Nature. Common traits soon became evident, and it emerged that in a number of respects English Nature already had the elements needed. The company introduced many initiatives to develop the rest, at the heart of which was a range of programmes to strengthen the links between learning and action across the organisation. Company personnel also continued to develop external learning networks with other organisations in conservation and business.

(*Source*: Dolan, 1995)

Milestones should be set to enable progress towards the achievement of planned outcomes to be monitored and discussed at crucial points.

Case-study: HRM strategic milestones in a British investment bank

During 1990–91 County NatWest, an investment bank, asked all its business units, including its personnel department, to establish strategic milestones for a five-year period, against which, by specified target dates, their performance would be measured. This forced the personnel department into considering its contribution to the organisation at the strategic level in the context of the bank's overall five-year business plan.

The requirement to produce strategic milestones as an input to the business plan 'marked an important watershed in defining the contribution of personnel to the business at a strategic level. It forced the department to reflect on the nature of that contribution.' Eighteen separate strategic milestones were duly authorised by the senior management of the Bank. The milestones were consistent one with the other, and overall addressed issues that consultation within business units and across the three personnel teams had shown to be critical to business success.

Each milestone was then assigned to a designated individual and was incorporated into their own targets of performance. Quarterly reviews on progress, involving the whole department, were subsequently held to ensure that the milestones were on target.

(*Source*: Riley and Sloman, 1991)

Integration between HRD initiatives and the employee resource system

Where HRD's value to the business is accepted, it will be one of a number of processes expected to contribute directly to corporate goals and also to support other functions in their similar endeavour. HRD strategy in such an organisation will be focused on those goals, aiming for outcomes that will result in the right skills being continuously in the right place at the right time, supporting corporate and unit-level strategy.

Leading HRM organisations, whether in the private or public sector, focus on achieving integration between methods to set relevant standards and achieve continuously improving performance, and an employment system that releases the effort and commitment needed to make those methods work. Some of the most widely used methods and supporting systems include the following:

Methods to set standards and continuously improve performance

- Regular team briefings.

- Shop-floor-located continuous improvement teams.

- Accessible training rooms which also act as informal break-away areas for discussing quality issues and continuous improvement projects.

- HRD initiatives expressed as a series of projects incorporating milestones, each with a senior management champion, and facilitated by HRD staff.

- Emphasis on targets throughout the organisation, deriving from business needs.

- Performance indicators and benchmarks used as business measures, relating to unit and company targets appropriate to the nature of the business.

- Value analysis teams drawn from across the organisation, to improve quality, reduce costs and ensure that products and services remain competitive.

- Learning networks with customers, suppliers, producers and other key stakeholders.

Typical ER systems that support the setting and achievement of standards

- Flat organisational structures and emphasis on flexibility of work and skills, rather than on detailed individual job descriptions.

- Regular, voluntary appraisal of training needs of teams and individuals, from which development plans ensue.

- High quality job-related training and personal development.

- Commitment to developing employability security.

- Facilities for open learning and encouragement and support for individuals to take the initiative in their development.

- Good basic pay and harmonised terms and conditions of work.

- No financial incentives or reward schemes except those tied to the acquisition of qualifications and additional relevant skills – the aim is to develop people whose motivation drives the success of the company and whose skills and experience will benefit from working in a successful business.

- High standards of health, safety and counselling services (usually off site and always confidential and optional for the individual).

- Accessibility of all company information to all company employees – contributing to the business means understanding the business, and employees are trusted to use access with discretion.

There must be regular monitoring of the workplace environment and culture to test whether integration is occurring. Thorn Lighting (Co. Durham – a world-class manufacturer of lighting systems) use a 'health of the business' survey for this purpose. It is an internal questionnaire that examines four areas to do with sharing the vision, integrating the effort, sustaining a healthy community and making intelligent decisions. Each area is broken down into a series of descriptive statements, with ratings awarded against each statement. (A similar approach is used in the initial diagnostic Investors in People climate survey.) At Thorn, the survey is carried out every year and the results then compared with previous norms in the company, external norms in comparable businesses (Cranfield holds manufacturing norms that offer competitive benchmarks) and UK norms. The results are communicated quickly to the workforce for discussion and action-planning.

Case-study: Standards and indicators at Cummins Engine Ltd, Darlington, UK (With acknowledgements to the company)

In Chapter 2 we looked at an historical case-study about HR strategy in the 1980s at Cummins Engine, Darlington, a US-owned manufacturing company with locations across the world. To bring that case up to date, 'customer-led quality' is the vision that now drives Cummins' new Production System, providing the focus for goals, standards, performance and recognition.

At the Darlington plant Human Resource Management and Development (HRMD) is identified as one of seven 'Functional Excellence' functions. HRMD is regarded as a core function in the business, because the company believes that it is only by a continuous and focused investment in attracting, developing and retaining high-calibre people that it can be guaranteed the human capability it needs to face up to a fast-moving environment and maintain its world-class competitive edge.

The HRMD function operates in relation to 11 policy areas where standards of performance are set and maintained:

- leadership
- environment
- health, safety and security
- administration
- staffing
- performance management
- training and development
- organisational design
- compensation and benefits
- employee relations
- community.

Standards to be achieved in each of these policy areas are expressed in terms of performance indicators with points allocated to each. Every year the HRMD function is rated by its internal and external customers against those indicators. A score is achieved in this way for the department's performance in each of the 11 policy areas. To take an example: ' Performance Management' has seven performance indicators, which together carry a total possible score of 10.

The plant has five business goals to do with customer-led quality, and HR staff must make a contribution each year to those goals. They also take lead responsibility for the goal related to developing 'Outstanding People'. Contribution is achieved through projects managed by HR staff which also form the basis for their appraisal as individuals. In 1996, for example, the training and development manager had a number of projects, each with its targets, time-scale and methods of measurement, which together constituted her personal responsibility for helping to develop 'Outstanding People'.

At companies like Cummins Engine, benchmarking, best practice, standards, performance indicators, targets and milestones are all used to establish outcomes and measure performance of an HR/HRD function in relation to its key policy areas and to assess its overall contribution to the business (see, for example, a very similar account of the development of the HR department at Raytheon Corporate Jets in Proctor, 1995).

Common across all such companies, too, is the process used. It is one whereby HR staff and their business partners regularly agree together on which HR outcomes to target. Thereafter the presumption in the company is that if those outcomes are clearly materialising, and if – as at Cummins – the function and its staff have the confidence and respect of management and workforce, then HRD is justifying its investment. It is only a failure of outcomes to materialise, or poor ratings on the annual customer survey of the HRMD function, that would lead to a special exercise to assess the value of that investment.

THE REALITIES OF HRD AND ITS OUTCOMES

Problems of measurement

In determining what outcomes HRD should produce for the business, and whether that contribution has been achieved, it is worth recalling some of the realities of organisational change:

- *Many organisations are in the process of radical and continuous change.* These changes are frequently perceived to be driven purposively by HRM strategy. HRM in this sense is taken to mean an approach that seeks to align an organisation's systems, structures and skills with business strategies in order to improve organisational effectiveness.

- *These changes are usually associated with changes in organisations' environments.* Research indicates that such claims made for the impact of HRM strategy are in reality often misplaced. The changes in question are more often the unexpected results of a trial-and-error reaction to environmental pressures than the planned outcome of any rational analysis of that environment and the formulation of HRM strategy to deal with it.

- *The changes occur on a number of levels*: structural, cultural, job design, pay systems, competencies, and the composition and deployment of the workforce. Tracking their start and finish is difficult, as is the estimation of how far and in exactly what ways the introduction of change in one part of the HR system has affected other areas. Again, then, the extent to which HR strategy has produced the changes, and exactly how or at what level it may have done this, is often quite unclear.

- *These changes occur at a variety of points through time.* Agreeing on where to start and at what point to finish the measurement of HR outcomes is therefore a critical decision. Too soon, and measurement may be vulnerable to the argument that the outcomes have had no chance to become established. Too late, and so many other variables could have been responsible for producing those outcomes that there can now be no certainty as to their true cause.

- *These changes are perceived in different ways by the actors.* We can remind ourselves at this point of John Storey's comments, quoted towards the end of Chapter 1 (see page 15). What may at the time have been intended as a radical HR initiative, and subsequently be genuinely perceived as such by senior management or HR staff, can be viewed quite differently by others in the organisation – and indeed may have gone virtually unnoticed by some.

- *There is often a significant difference between espoused and actual HR goals and strategy.* As has been observed at various points in this book, the so-called 'flexible workforce' can in reality mean the low-cost, easily manipulated, vulnerable workforce. 'Empowerment' can conceal the fact that the locus of decision-making remains essentially unchanged, that management style is still authoritarian and that resource control remains centralised at the top.

It is therefore often hard, if not impossible, to be certain about the specific outcomes of HR or HRD strategy. As the last point makes

Table 10 Establishing the outcomes of HRM strategy

Collective bargaining has not been replaced by new-style HRM practices. (Workplace Industrial Relations surveys, 1980, 1984 and 1990)
HRM does not improve industrial relations in the workplace. (London School of Economics survey, Fernie and Metcalf, 1994)
Firms with clear and innovative HRM policies and practices perform better in quality, productivity, absenteeism levels and labour turnover – and have good employee relations. (London School of Economics survey, Guest and Hoque, 1994)
There are positive linkages between measures of HRM and financial performance. (Lancaster and Wales Universities Report, Fox, Tanton and McLeay, 1992)

clear, there can also be doubt about the nature of the outcomes actually sought by management. Such uncertainties are increased by the diverse ways in which outcomes can be measured and by the matter of who does the measurement. Let us look at the examples in Table 10.

How can four major surveys produce such apparently different judgements about the outcomes of HR strategy? There are a number of explanations, but some of the most significant are these:

Definitions of HRM itself were different

- Workplace Industrial Relations (WIR) surveys initially defined HRM as changes in methods of communication to get greater commitment, participation and harmonisation of conditions of employment; they did not define it in terms of productivity levels. Fernie and Metcalf (1994) did not therefore set out to analyse HRM by reference to its contribution to productivity levels.

- In their report on the 1991 WIR data, Fernie and Metcalf were not looking specifically at types of 'HRM' and 'non-HRM' firms. Guest and Hoque (1994), on the other hand, *were* doing so.

- Fox, Tanton and McLeay (1992) were concerned with examining HRM practice on the ground, regardless of how it was theoretically defined. Their interest was in looking for any evidence they could find of internal cohesion between its core practices and of integration between HRM and corporate or business strategy.

Locations studied were different

- Guest and Hoque (1994) were looking at greenfield sites.

- Fernie and Metcalf (1994) were looking at small and medium-sized firms.

- Fox *et al* (1992) were looking mainly at engineering and electronic companies.

Time-scales were different

- The earlier WIR surveys were in 1980, 1984 and 1990.

- Fernie and Metcalf (1994) were looking at a later 1991 WIR survey.

- Guest and Hoque (1994) were measuring in 1993–4.

- Fox *et al* (1992) studied a sample of firms over the long term between 1978 and 1988.

Underlying values in each case were different

- Fernie and Metcalf (1994) came from a group of academics with considerable reservations about the value of HRM in the workplace and a particular concern about its impact on collective rights and bargaining.

- Guest was a well-known proponent of 'new-style' HRM with its aspirations to improve productivity, commitment, flexibility and creativity.

- Fox *et al* (1992) were not concerned with HRM values as such; they were simply curious to discover whether any relationship could be discovered between aspects of HR strategy and the financial performance of the firm and, if so, how it might be objectively measured.

On the issue of the values of those who measure, of course in the ideal world these should not influence findings. However, in reality they can do so, if only by focusing attention – often unconsciously – on the selection of some data rather than others to study in the first place. However rigorous the researchers, the influence of underlying values on mindsets and decision-making can never be discounted.

So although it is important to set standards and targets, to monitor progress and to attempt to assess the outcomes of HRD strategy and initiatives, it has to be realised that this process will always be inexact. It will also be time-consuming and therefore expensive. Pragmatically, a key issue is the nature of the true driving forces behind HRD strategy, and the kinds of outcomes that are actually hoped for by management. It is those driving forces and those outcomes that will override any formally espoused aims of HR strategy if they conflict with them. Ultimately, they will exercise the strongest single influence on whether or not formal HR aims are achieved.

Therefore it is the *process* of HRD in the business rather than the formally prescribed *strategy* for HRD that becomes crucial. That process must aim to uncover at the start the real outcomes that management wants to secure from HRD strategy. It must ensure that those outcomes, whatever their nature, are openly and fully discussed until all their practical implications are clear. It must then secure agreement on what to do if a gap is revealed between the formally espoused and the actual intentions of management; or between what is intended and what can feasibly be achieved; or between the kind of outcomes sought and the extent to which they can be meaningfully measured. In that latter connection, the process used must lead to a willingness of HRD staff and management to take shared responsibility in monitoring, measuring and action in relation to outcomes.

Clearly, where the gap between espoused and actual intent is very wide there are likely to be relatively few HR practitioners who carry the credibility and political influence to pursue the matter to its conclusion and resolve the inherent conflict. However, to place this issue in perspective, the main problems to do with setting outcomes for HRD are usually more straightforward. They are more likely to arise from a simple lack of certainty about how to proceed. In the Cummins case-study we see a helpful example of how, working together, HR specialists and managers share the responsibility for setting clear and feasible outcomes, establishing how best those can be measured and jointly monitoring and evaluating HR action in the workplace.

Assessing 'value for money'

'Value for money' is usually interpreted as a pay-back approach: an attempt to measure in financial or analogous terms a return on training investment (Lee, 1996). A typical 'value for money' exercise would involve measuring the impact of training outcomes on variables like turnover, profit, increases in sales, conversion of leads to sales – what accountants call the 'direct return' achieved. One example, provided by practice in the insurance company Frizzell Financial Services, was described by Lee in his article. Another was recounted by Armstrong (1987: 33–4) describing practice at Book Club Associates in the late 1980s. There, all training and development programmes aimed to improve output and minimise costs, and were designed to support productivity drives. Their specific objectives were easy to define because the company's performance management programmes included the specification of clear performance standards against which people's performance was formally appraised. That kind of approach to establishing payback involves building on the techniques and skills explained in Chapter 11:

- *measuring identifiable costs (outflows) of training, direct and indirect.* This means identifying the basic annual cost of running the training function and the costs of running particular training activities.

- *measuring identifiable benefits (inflows) to the firm in financial terms* (or those that can easily be equated with money). Performance measures can be categorised, starting with the most easily quantifiable and going on to more difficult qualitative indicators (Robinson and Robinson, 1989).

- *comparing costs and benefits to give a cost-benefit ratio or rate of return for capital employed.* This involves assessing whether other types of HRD intervention would be more cost-beneficial than the one currently being considered – on-the-job learning rather than a formal course, for example. Cost-benefit analysis is concerned with establishing the costs of an activity and then comparing these with the benefits it is likely to confer. It should take into account efficiency as well as effectiveness in establishing the benefits. To illustrate, let us return to Mintech, the case-study introduced in Chapter 11.

Mintech Ltd Part 3 (see Parts 1 and 2 in Chapter 11, pages 191–3, 193–5)

When Mike has finished his calculations, it becomes obvious that running an internal supervisory training programme using Mintech's own training staff would be the most cost-efficient option. But will it be the most cost-beneficial? On what issues should Mike seek information in order to make a final decision?

Feedback notes

There are important issues raised by the two alternatives, not least the potential clash between individuals' wish to improve their career prospects by obtaining a recognised qualification, and the organisation's need to cut costs. The following list shows at least six major issues that should be considered when weighing up training alternatives, together with a sample of the kind of questions to be raised under each heading.

- *budgeting.* Would each option be affordable in terms of training budgets?

- *training policy and strategy.* Which of the options would be most consistent with Mintech's overall and departmental training and development strategies?

- *training needs.* Have supervisory training needs been carefully analysed? Is there any conflict here between individual and departmental or organisational needs? Which alternative would best meet the balance of needs?

- *training benefits and evaluation.* Which of the options is most likely to help job performance, motivation and commitment of the supervisors, and carry other benefits for the organisation? What information can be obtained about the value of each option, both by reference to past initiatives at Mintech and to external best practice?

- *transfer of learning.* How will transfer of learning be ensured if the supervisors attend the external course? Would there be better transfer if they attended an internal course?

- *other options.* Are there any other ways in which the same kind and level of results offered could be achieved, but at less cost? What about team-briefings, quality circles, project groups? What would be the costs of doing nothing? Would that lead to reduced motivation of the supervisors; to lack of development of their ability and potential; to longer learning time for new techniques; or to poorer-quality work, and higher rates of absenteeism or sickness?

In reality, after he had looked at these six questions Mike discussed options A and B with his colleagues and with the managers not only of the three supervisors who had come to him originally, but also those of other Mintech supervisors. It emerged from this process of reflection and discussion that the company's supervisors needed two different kinds of development:

- *a programme of development for new supervisors, or those shortly to be promoted* to that level, and for others whose inclusion would bring clear benefits to the company and to themselves. This would include opportunities for up to four people each year to attend the external course, or for a greater number to do the course by a special distance learning package; and for such supervisors also to have planned work experience and guidance.

- *an internal training programme for all Mintech supervisors.* This would not only meet areas of common need, but would also help the supervisors to develop a common language and team identity through a shared and work-related learning experience. It would also maximise the value of the design activity involved in producing the first course.

The exercise of establishing the costs of each of the options and comparing each option with the benefits likely to occur enabled the true value of each option to be confidently assessed. In consequence the desired outcomes of HRD were clarified and a cost-beneficial, as well as cost-efficient, route to achieve them was found.

It is essential to be able to identify clearly the main costs – however they are expressed – of HRD to the organisation; the past, current and expected future outcomes that justify those costs; and, where additional pressure on management to invest is needed, the estimated costs of failure to train and develop. Without this information it is impossible to make valid decisions about whether to increase or reduce expenditure and the allocation of other resources, or to alter strategy in order to achieve a better balance of costs and benefits, or to put effort into trying to change existing managerial attitudes towards HRD where this is evidently essential.

Cost-benefit analysis will involve financial calculations, but not exclusively. It will involve discussion of not only quantitative data but also of qualitative outcomes and methods of measurement. It should encompass a consideration of strategies to do with 'growing people' as much as of strategies to do with 'training for competency'. The crucial issue is to assess what kind and level of investment is needed in order to produce the kind of outcomes that will be seen as valuable, and be valued by, the key parties.

Focusing on the future
As the case-study and subsequent discussion have shown, value for money has a wider meaning than simply financial measurement of past initiatives. It is also about what Lee (1996: 31) called 'pay forward': the idea that investment in training must primarily be future-oriented, to do with enhancing the capability of the whole organisation to learn and change: 'Hence the notion that the benefits are projected into the future and cannot be identified separately from the outcomes of the wider change process.'

The longer-term organisational outcomes sought may be to do with culture change, increased strategic awareness and identification with business objectives across the organisation, improved teamwork and adaptability, or other relatively long-term changes. By their nature, such outcomes cannot be produced by HRD interventions alone. Wider and reinforcing ER policies and initiatives will be needed, and these in turn will have to move forward alongside other business initiatives. HR personnel and line managers must therefore be partners in developing and implementing a strategy to achieve changes across the business in which HRD will play its due part. The focus must be on jointly agreeing HRD standards and targets, projects to realise those aims, resources to support them, and milestones along the route when progress reports will be shared and ongoing plans either confirmed or amended in consequence.

Such a focus requires an emphasis not on the payback of HRD but on forward investment in HRD. The key issues become these:

• What, given our business goals and strategy, did we initially agree that we should do about training and developing our people and facilitating continuous learning and improvement in the workplace?

• Has it been done?

• Are we now achieving what we agreed we needed to achieve with our people in order to make our business strategy work?

This approach to assessing the value of HRD does not, of course, discount the need to evaluate the design and delivery of specific learning events (see Chapter 16). That kind of activity should be initiated by HRD staff as a necessary part of their professional concern to check on the quality of the work they do and the services they provide to their clients.

THE HRD AUDIT

Auditing is a way of assessing the nature and impact of HRD activity at particular points in time. It has been described as 'A process that produces an official accounting and verification, most often conducted by third party evaluators. Auditing typically relies on samples of information that are critical to the organisation and its decision makers' (Murphy and Swanson, 1988).

The aim of an audit is to supply a snapshot of what is going on across the organisation in order to compare what is happening with what should be happening, and to identify any action needed. We have seen how the level of excellence of the HRMD function is internally audited each year at Cummins Engine. We have also seen how Thorn Lighting audits its 'health of the community' with an annual survey. Audits enable trends to be identified and therefore form part of a strategy to ensure continuous improvement of a function or of an area of operations in an organisation.

What will the focus be, and who will do the audit?
The first questions to ask are 'What should be audited?' and 'Who should do the auditing?' Choices of focus could include the:

• effectiveness and efficiency of HRD staff as a service to the business

• effectiveness and efficiency of line managers as HRD managers

• contribution of HRD to specific business goals, such as those to do with quality and performance

• contribution of particular HRD activities or programmes

• skills, flexibility and culture of the workforce.

Auditors could come from within or outside the organisation, or from both.

What kind of questions should be asked?
This depends on the focus of the audit. If it is going to look at the effectiveness of HRD staff in providing an internal consultancy, then key questions would be these:

- Does the organisation of HRD staff in the business enhance the ability of the HRD function to work with management on analysing and responding to key HRD needs?

- Are the HRD staff good choices, given their tasks?

- Do they provide timely, efficient and expert services to the business?

- Do they compare favourably with any external consultants who could be used?

If, on the other hand, the audit is more concerned to look at the fit between the goals and strategy of the HRD function and those of the business, then an approach akin to that applied during the Investors in People initial diagnostic stage would be more appropriate. The outcomes of such an audit, however structured, would be to ensure better strategic fit between HRD and the business, with a particular view to improving links at the three levels of the business discussed towards the end of Chapter 9:

- *corporate level*, where there should be integration of HRD considerations into corporate strategic decision-making and the development of a business-linked HRD strategy for the organisation

- *business unit/managerial level*, where there should be a collaboratively produced HRD system for training, appraising and developing people to achieve effective performance, adaptability, and capability related to organisational change and growth

- *operational level*, where routines and processes should be in place to ensure competency and self-initiated development in the workplace, with managers who build a supportive learning environment.

If an audit is concerned with examining the way in which the HRD function is organised in the business, its remit will include:

- identifying tasks involved at strategic, managerial and operational level for training and developing people, and also identifying those who perform the tasks

- assessing how far the roles and deployment of HRD staff reflect the strategic, managerial and operational needs of the business

- assessing the extent to which HRD staff are competent at:

  - *corporate level*, where the need is for people with political skills, broad business orientation, a wide-ranging HR background and a proactive strategic stance

  - *managerial level*, where the need is for people with a more general managerial orientation and background

  - *operational/functional level*, where there is a need for technically focused professional staff

- exploring the 'fit' between the HRD function and the umbrella ER function.

If an audit is assessing the contribution of HRD to the achievement of the organisation's quality and performance goals, it will look at parameters appropriate to that focus. The US-based Malcolm Baldridge National Quality Award includes HRM as one of its key areas relating to quality in the business, and requires organisations to examine HRM in the workplace by reference to five areas or standards, each of which is defined and to each of which performance indicators are attached. One of these areas is 'employee development'. The others are:

- HRM strategy and the implementation process

- employee involvement

- employee performance and recognition

- employee well-being and morale.

Carrying out the audit

When the focus of the audit and the categories of its questions have been determined, plans must be made to carry it out. Murphy and Swanson (1988: 15) suggest six steps:

- Establish objectives for each category of audit.

- Describe what the evaluator expects to find (this is essential in order to determine how to avoid bias in the auditing methodology and ensure that the most objective approach to auditing will be carried out).

- Determine data collection procedures.

- Collect data samples.

- Report what was found, and compare findings with the initial expectations of the evaluator; too close a match will obviously raise questions about the audit process, although enquiry may reveal that full confidence can be placed in that process.

- Report on conclusions.

Fombrun, Devanna and Tichy (1984), in their discussion of auditing, showed how the focus of questions needs to change depending on which data sources are being used (see Table 11).

Table 11 Auditing HRM (Based on Fombrun *et al*, 1984: 238–239)

Primary data sources	Focus of questions
Senior management (interviews)	Strategy. Definitions of present state of the organisation and desired future state.
Line management (interviews; questionnaires)	Interactions with HR function. HR problems; role they envisage for the HR function.
HR staff (in-depth questionnaires)	Jobs, activities, conflicts, internal strengths and weaknesses of the function.
Archival information and documents	Describe job histories, past evaluations, formal structures and general background on the organisation and on the HR function in particular.

The outcomes of auditing

Auditing can lead to valuable outcomes that go beyond those that formed its initial frame of reference. The following are typical:

- identification of HR areas needing further research

- as a result of the audit process, development of a relevant language and of concepts across the organisation for discussing HR problems and opportunities

- reorganisation of HR roles and functions

- during the audit process, development of a greater awareness of the scarcity of human resources and problems of developing and conserving them which then begins to inform the 'political debate' about HR and business strategy

- awareness by the HR team of a need for more strategic evaluation of HR overall in the business

- a more strategically aware HR function

- promotion of choice of business options likely to have more beneficial outcomes for employees and thereby to improve their commitment and performance.

Carrying out an audit of training and of instrumental learning

Produce a simple plan for an audit of training and instrumental learning in an organisation. 'Training' here means the planned and systematic process whereby people learn the skills needed to perform their jobs to standard. 'Instrumental learning' means the 'on-the-job training of an informal nature' (Gilley and Eggland, 1989: 33) whereby people learn to do their jobs better and reach high standards. You will find feedback notes for this exercise in Appendix 6.

Let us end this section with a case-study. It shows a variety of purposes and outcomes for audits and the value of using them in a consistent way through time.

Case-study: The HR audit process at British Airways (BA), 1981–91

The vision and corporate strategy: 1981
In 1981, when British Airways was effectively bankrupt for a combination of reasons, but notably because of a disastrous and continuous loss of customers, the new chief executive, Colin Marshall, assessed the situation and determined on a new mission for the company: it was to become 'The Harrods of the airways of the world'. The corporate strategy to achieve this mission was complex, but an immediate priority was to win back customers by changing the attitudes, behaviour and performance of customer-contact staff.

The first audit
Having identified that the existing bureaucratic, inward-looking, rigid

and complacent culture that prevailed in British Airways was particularly strong at the top of the hierarchy, Marshall recruited a new top management team whose values matched his own and would underpin the new customer-oriented culture. A two-way audit was carried out by an external consultancy firm. It covered the perceptions of customers about the service provided by BA, and the perceptions of customer contact staff about their jobs, their roles and their relationships with customers and with BA's management.

The audit highlighted many weaknesses in the company's customer service, primarily due to poor HRM in BA and to major behavioural and performance problems amongst the contact staff. An organisation-wide training and teamwork programme was mounted which, over the following three years, and running alongside wider HR, structural and technological interventions, played a key part in radically changing the culture of the company.

The second audit: three years on
At this point another two-way audit was carried out. This time it explored in depth the mutual perceptions of contact staff and their managers, in order to build on that aspect of the first audit. It revealed a mirror image of the same kind of tensions between staff and their managers as had already been shown to exist between customers and contact staff. In response to these problems of management style and behaviour, a series of short 'Managing People First' courses were then designed for the whole management sector of BA. These courses were key components of a comprehensive training and development programme that stretched across the world, managed increasingly, as time went on and internal HR skills developed, by BA's own training personnel.

Review of progress led to longer courses for managers, professional and technical staff. These focused on teambuilding and teamwork, objective-setting and other areas in order to build a more target-centred, efficient and productive organisation.

The third audit: 1989–90
The impact of these changes, together with continuing innovation in appraisal, financial rewards systems, organisational structure and business strategies and technology, led to striking improvements in customer service and all-round quality. Customer numbers, profits and productivity all soared, and the success was sustained.

Late in 1989 a new personnel director was appointed, who audited the HR function to assess its effectiveness throughout BA. The information from the audit led, early in 1990, to a radical downsizing and reorganisation of that function. The top HRM team was cut from 11 to 6, and those senior people were redeployed, each taking key responsibilities in different parts of the business at unit level as well as general strategic and co-ordinating roles. Many HR responsibilities were reallocated to line managers, and some line managers were brought in to replace specialist staff.

At BA, regular use of the audit technique enabled identification of ongoing learning needs and HR standards in the company, and the facilitation and reinforcement of sustained organisational change.

KEY ISSUES IN ESTABLISHING, MONITORING AND MEASURING HRD'S VALUE FOR THE BUSINESS

We can conclude not only from information in this chapter but from recalling many issues that have emerged throughout the book thus far that, in order to set and achieve outcomes for HRD that are of value for the organisation and its people, it is essential to:

• agree on the key business goals that HRD strategy must support

• agree on the particular HRD initiatives that will most efficiently and effectively give such support – and agree on an HRD budget

• agree on ways of measuring the outcomes of those initiatives

• have a clear strategy and plans in place for the implementation and monitoring of those initiatives

• make good use of targets, performance indicators, surveys and milestones in order to establish clear outcomes and monitor progress towards achieving them

• be able to make a convincing presentation to key parties at any time about progress towards outcomes

• confirm or jointly agree to amend plans in the light of any critical changes in the business or its environment or of unforeseen problems in the implementation of the plans themselves.

The following basic principles need to be observed when assessing the value of HRD in the business:

• Evaluation of HRD strategy and activity should be related to outcomes originally agreed for them.

• Measurement will not of itself achieve credibility for HRD. It is measurement of a kind already agreed between the key parties that is essential.

• Seek broad and flexible indicators and measures that will capture the essence of HRD activity without interfering overmuch in operations by imposing excessive and time-consuming checks and balances.

• For hard objectives, use quantitative measures. For softer objectives, use a range of techniques such as behaviourally anchored rating scales, surveys and benchmarking to ensure cross-checks on value and outcomes.

• Measurement and evaluation should be simple, focused on the future rather than the past, and efficient. 'Measure everything that matters' is not a natural law: it is a dangerous obsession.

Evaluation is much more a matter of process than of procedure. HRD professionals need to ensure that the human processes they use in key areas of their work will elicit management's active involvement from the earliest stage. In this way HRD has every chance of becoming taken for granted as an essential part of business activity instead of being required to prove its worth at every step and responding by 'drowning in a sea of quantitative and qualititive measures' (Lorenz, 1994).

CONCLUSION

In order to achieve the learning objectives of this chapter we have examined how to focus HRD activity on key strategic outcomes. We have identified five stages in setting HRD standards, and explored the use of benchmarking, best practice, strategic milestones and performance indicators. The importance of achieving integration of HRD initiatives within the wider ER system has been stressed, and methods and systems common in 'best HRM practice' organisations have been noted.

Attention has been drawn to the difficulty of establishing the outcomes of HRD policy in an organisation, and problems of measurement have been illustrated by reference to four national HR surveys. It has been emphasised that there must be a focus not only on value for money achieved by past strategies but also on what added value the organisation's investment in HRD is likely to achieve for the business in the future. Three key issues related to assessing future value have been explained. The chapter has concluded with five principles that should underpin the assessment of HRD's value for the business.

USEFUL READING

APPLEGARTH, M. (1991) *How to Take a Training Audit*. London, Kogan Page.

FOMBRUN, C.J., DEVANNA, M.A. and TICHY, N. M. (1984) 'The human resource management audit,' in C.J. FOMBRUN., N.M. TICHY and M.A. DEVANNA (eds), *Strategic Human Resource Management*. New York, Wiley.

FONDA, N. and BUCKTON, K. (1995) *Reviewing the Personnel Function: A toolkit for development*. London, Institute of Personnel and Development. (Contains specially designed assessment tools to address key personnel and HRD issues, and builds on the frameworks of the Personnel Standards Lead Body and Management Charter Initiative.)

LEE, R. (1996) 'The 'pay-forward' view of training'. *People Management*. Vol. 2, 3: 30–32.

PEARSON, R. (1991) *The Human Resource: Managing people and work in the 1990s*. London, McGraw-Hill. pp. 234–50. (Discusses how to research HRM in order to produce practical action and make a strategic contribution.)

ROBINSON, D.G. and ROBINSON, J.C. (1989) *Training for Impact*. San Francisco, Calif., Jossey Bass.

Part 4

THE PERFORMANCE MANAGEMENT AND DEVELOPMENT SYSTEM

13 Learning needs of individuals

LEARNING OBJECTIVES

After reading this chapter you will:

* have a framework for identifying and understanding people's learning needs at work and the relationship of those needs to the demands of the organisation's performance management system (PMS)

* understand the importance of an effective balance between learning needs generated by the PMS and those related to the organisation's future capability

* know how to produce an integrated organisational programme for induction and basic skills training, appraisal and improvement of performance, and continuous learning and development.

Please note that throughout this chapter the term 'individual needs' may be taken to refer also to group/team needs.

PERFORMANCE MANAGEMENT AND THE OVERALL EMPLOYEE DEVELOPMENT PROGRAMME

Performance management

Managing performance has been defined as a continuous process in which 'organisations clarify the level of performance required to meet their strategic objectives, convert them into unit and individual objectives and manage them continually ... (so) that they remain relevant and consistent with overall strategic objectives' (Lockett, 1992: 14).

Performance management is driven by the vision, corporate goals and business strategies of the organisation. The first essential, therefore, is that top management produces and communicates a powerful and cohering vision of the organisation, and ensures that goals and strategies to achieve it are relevant and understood by all employees.

Lockett (1992: 37–46) described the performance management cycle as involving seven stages: establishing the performance contract, clarifying performance requirements, agreeing on support requirements, reviewing performance, and taking actions related to meeting, exceeding or failing to meet the performance contract. Reflecting on this cycle and looking back to Chapter 3 at Table 2 (page 41), we can see that in the context of employee development the key elements of a PMS are those to do with:

• setting targets and establishing desired performance levels

• appraising and improving performance

• ensuring continuous learning and development

• giving recognition and rewards.

All organisations need to manage people's current performance and develop potential for the future if the organisation is to achieve its current targets and also prosper in its environment over the longer term. Unfortunately, the balance between performance management and longer-term development is rarely satisfactory. Formal PMSs frequently fail and, in their preoccupation with controlling performance, managers often forget the need to establish a workplace climate that makes possible blame-free discussion of learning needs, so that the long-term development of people so essential to the future of the organisation can occur.

Interaction between the management of performance and longer-term employee development
Throughout this fourth part of the book the focus is on the interaction needed between the organisation's PMS and its overall planned employee development (ED) programme. 'Planned programme' in this sense means not so much a detailed master plan – since that implies something so comprehensive, so systematised, so in need of constant fine-tuning in order to keep pace with change, that in the end it may become inoperable – but rather the overall pattern of ED activity whereby that organisation seeks to ensure both the effective operation of its current PMS and the continuous development needed for the future.

Learning needs in this context derive from:

• the overall vision of the business, its long- and short-term goals, and the planned and emergent strategies related to them – as discussed in Chapters 2 and 3

• the characteristics of specific jobs – to be discussed in Chapter 14

• the performance of people in their jobs and their intended developmental path in the organisation over the longer term – the focus of this chapter.

In this chapter the main task is to produce a conceptual framework and practical guidelines to relate employees' learning needs to the PMS of the organisation and to its longer-term goals and direction. For those wishing to obtain detailed guidance on organisational and individual training needs analysis, specialist texts such as Boydell and

Leary (1996), Hardingham (1996) and the Bees (1994) are recommended. Approaches to job training analysis will be discussed in Chapter 14.

This chapter falls into two parts. In the first, a framework for understanding and action is presented. It has four dimensions: the learning process; approaches and types of learning; individual job performance; and tensions between control and development in PMSs. In the second, the framework is used to identify how to establish and improve performance levels, and to achieve continuous learning and development.

A FRAMEWORK FOR UNDERSTANDING

The learning process

> Learning is a relatively permanent change in behaviour that occurs as a result of practice or experience.
>
> > (Bass and Vaughan, 1967: 8).

This well-known working definition treats 'learning' as a noun – as a state to be achieved. It emphasises the importance of experience and reinforcement in achieving 'relatively permanent change in behaviour'. Interestingly it does not refer to changed ways of perceiving, thinking and knowing (in the sense of understanding, making sense of the world). Later in their book, of course, the authors did have much to say about those outcomes. I am drawing attention to them here in order to emphasise the need to see learning not just as behavioural change but also as knowledge. Management must foster that kind of individual and collective learning that not only produces changed behaviour but also adds to the store of valuable knowledge that the organisation possesses and on which its long-term future depends. This theme will be developed fully in Chapter 20, when the concept of the knowledge-productive organisation is discussed.

The word 'learning' can of course also be used as a verb, indicating a dynamic process. HRD practitioners must understand this process if they are to help their organisations regularly to achieve those 'relatively permanent change[s] in behaviour' necessary to business survival and growth. There are many theories about the learning process (see Marchington and Wilkinson, 1996: 161–8 for a helpful summary). I have chosen only two to discuss here because, taken together, they have much of value to tell us about how learning can be managed in an organisational context.

The experiential cycle

Learning can be viewed as a circular process, as in Figure 5 – itself the underpinning of the cycle illustrated in Appendix 4. The circle has no start or finish, and often people move through it almost instinctively, sometimes so skilfully that they soon produce more effective behaviour in situations that initially cause them problems. Often, however, they make mistakes at one or more points, so that behavioural change is slow or fails to occur.

Figure 5 The experiential cycle of learning (based on Kolb, Rubin and McIntyre, 1974)

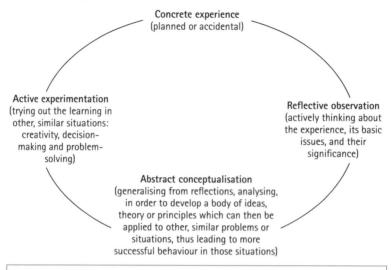

Concrete experience
(planned or accidental)

Active experimentation
(trying out the learning in
other, similar situations:
creativity, decision-
making and problem-
solving)

Reflective observation
(actively thinking about
the experience, its basic
issues, and their
significance)

Abstract conceptualisation
(generalising from reflections, analysing,
in order to develop a body of ideas,
theory or principles which can then be
applied to other, similar problems or
situations, thus leading to more
successful behaviour in those situations)

Learning from my own experience

When was the last time you felt that you really learnt something? Take yourself back to that occasion, reflect on it, and try relating it stage by stage to the experiential learning process.

As your response to the question will probably show, the learning process is not as easily explained as this particular theory of learning implies, but it does give helpful insights. Applied to an organisational situation, it can enable us to see where learning is being inhibited because people are struggling with experiences, tasks or demands that are simply too difficult for them at this stage; or perhaps – if provided in simulated form in a training programme – the experiences are felt to be artificial or irrelevant. Perhaps the learners lack time, encouragement or ability to reflect on and therefore learn from experience (whether it is a work project, part of a structured training or educational programme, or an unexpected event). Perhaps they lack the skills that would produce accurate diagnoses of situations or the generation and testing of new responses. Whoever is responsible for the learning process, be it the individual directing his or her own learning or the manager of a learning event, he or she must therefore ensure the right kind of stimulation, practice and feedback at crucial stages of learning.

If those with responsibility for the development of people in the organisation can 'manage' a variety of everyday work situations in ways that will foster the key skills involved in the learning cycle, then those skills can be continuously applied to an ever-widening range of organisational issues. Not only individual but organisational performance will thus be enhanced.

Stimulus-response theory

Our second theory about learning explains the mastery of the learning process in terms of four key factors (see Bass and Vaughan, 1967, Stammers and Patrick, 1975 and Gagne, 1977 for an extension of this simple framework): Drive, Stimulus, Response and Reinforcement.

- *Drive.* For learning to occur there must be a basic need that makes someone want to learn, and that acts as the continued spur to that activity: in other words, there must be a drive, or motivation, to learn.

- *Stimulus.* A stimulus means a message that makes an impact on our senses because it relates to one or more of our primary or secondary drives. For learning to be effective, people must become actively involved in the learning situation. Methods of learning must, by stimulating various senses, make a sufficient impact to ensure that people learn in that situation.

- *Response and reinforcement.* In every learning situation the learner must acquire appropriate responses – ie skills, knowledge, attitudes – which will lead to improved performance or to some other kind of needed development. These responses must be reinforced by practice, experience and feedback until they are fully learnt. Unproductive responses must be highlighted before they become habitual.

Again this may seem an over-simplified and mechanistic explanation of human learning. It recalls the so-called 'law of effect' in classical conditioning theory, and pictures come to mind of the dog, cat or pigeon being 'trained' to perform in desired ways by a process of instruction, reward and punishment. It seems at odds with Kolb's naturalistic concept. In reality, however, both learning theories discussed thus far point to the importance of five factors when making decisions about organisational and individual learning needs, and how best to respond to them:

- *Stimulation.* The learning process can only be activated by some state of arousal in the individual or the organisation. This will happen naturally if a particular situation makes a direct impact on already strongly felt needs. On the other hand, arousal may have to be stimulated deliberately in order for desired learning to take place.

Take the example of training that management is convinced is essential for a group of employees, but for which they themselves see no need. How can the group become convinced of the importance of that training? Exhortations or commands will not be enough: people can be driven into a training room, but once there they cannot be forced to learn. Management must communicate a clear purpose for the training, and demonstrate that the specific outcomes it promises will bring mutual benefits. If that communication fails to be convincing, and the group comes unwillingly to training, then (and this should in any event be the case) the learning experience itself must be so designed as to make clear from the start how the needs of the organisation and of the individual are equally involved here. It must by its own nature and momentum quickly arouse and sustain the learners' attention so that they soon come to see for themselves the importance of learning whatever new knowledge, skills or attitudes are at issue. Individuals cannot be made to learn, but learning will occur once they can identify with its purpose, undergo a relevant learning experience and are in the hands of skilled trainers or facilitators.

- *Purpose and planning.* Being clear about the purpose of learning, and planning for it to occur, are essential components of the organisational learning process. Kolb, Rubin and McIntyre (1974) believed that learning should be an explicit organisational objective, 'pursued as consciously and deliberately as profit or productivity'. They stressed that there must be 'a climate seeing the value of such an approach ... developed in the organisation'.

  The definition of the purpose of a learning event, and the setting of objectives to achieve it, may be the responsibility of the individual learner, the manager of a group at work or a human resource (HR) specialist. The purpose may be generalised or specific; it may be corporate and long-term – as, for example, a purpose of developing a 'learning organisation'; or it may be to do with an individual or team achieving immediate targets. Establishing purpose and planning for learning to occur will not necessarily lead to formal training or developmental events, nor will there be an inevitable need for 'trainers' or 'tutors'. The importance of agreeing at corporate level on purpose and then of planning key organisational strategies for learning is that top management is thereby required to reflect and think through what it is trying to achieve in its overall ED programme.

- *Learning processes and strategies.* Learning processes must help employees to move through the key stages of their organisational life – entry, familiarisation with and mastery of the job, continuous improvement and development, and preparation for exit. Learning strategies must be those best suited to a particular purpose. Often, integrating learning with work – the 'experiential' approach – will be appropriate and cost-effective. However, there will also be times when it is relevant to provide a more formalised learning approach or route.

- *Reinforcement of learning.* There must be regular practice and feedback if learners are to acquire new learning quickly and confidently and test it out in their practical situations. Kolb's theory emphasises this when it shows the stage of experimentation leading into further experience, which then generates the possibility of review, analysis and modification or repetition of the new learning.

- *Review at organisational and individual levels.* Learning should be reviewed at organisational as well as at individual levels so that only the most relevant learning strategies are developed and subsequently reinforced across the organisation as well as in the particular workplace. Appraisal is an important, although of course not sufficient, way of ensuring feedback and review of experience.

Developing motivation to learn in the workplace

Consider your own organisation, or one with which you are familiar. Identify an area where there is *either* a clear need for guided learning to occur but where nothing positive seems to be happening *or* real enthusiasm for learning by managers and their staff. Use our five-factor framework to analyse reasons for the situation you have identified. If there is lack of enthusiasm for learning, what action would you recommend to ensure a higher level of motivation?

Learning approaches and types

Types of learning

Having looked at factors that can inhibit as well as stimulate the learning process, let us now consider three different types of learning (Mezirow, 1985) that are essential components of any overall ED programme: the instrumental, dialogic and self-reflective.

- *Instrumental learning.* This means learning how to do the job better once the basic standard of performance has been attained. A key strategy to achieve instrumental learning, once initial formal training has been given (and quite often in place of that formal training), is learning on the job. This can involve an interaction of formal and informal processes and can be highly effective, provided that there is someone to encourage learners in the course of their daily tasks to identify problems, formulate appropriate action, try it out, observe the effects and learn from them. That 'someone' may be a trained member of the workteam. For example, at McDonald's, new entrants go through a three-hour induction and are then partnered with a 'buddy' who comes from a 'training squad' of specially trained employees belonging to their work team. 'In a typical restaurant employing a crew of 50, about five will be members of the training squad' (Cannell, 1997). The on-the-job learning for which 'buddies' are responsible is rigorously organised and very effective. On the other hand, the 'someone' may be a high-performing member of a workgroup who has proven training skills and the disposition to foster job-related learning in others.

  Managers need to be good at helping – or training and encouraging others to help – new recruits to learn from their mistakes as well as successes, and to focus on continuous improvement of work processes rather than simply on the achievement of task targets. They also need to set the recruits new challenges from time to time in order to stretch their abilities. Such managers should be recognised for their achievement in developing powerful on-the-job learning systems in the workplace. Those systems are of unique importance to the organisation when they ensure that tacit as well as explicit knowledge and skills (see page 56) are transferred from the experienced to the inexperienced, from the highly skilled to those building up their understanding and ability to do a job or task.

- *Dialogic learning.* Dialogic learning involves interacting with others in ways that will produce a growing knowledge and understanding of the culture of the organisation, and of how it typically achieves its goals. The value of dialogic learning is that it can help to acclimatise the individual so that they can more quickly make sense of the organisational world they have entered and develop the confidence to operate competently in the workplace.

Dialogic learning is therefore important at the stage when newcomers enter the organisation, or when people are promoted into parts of the organisation with which they are unfamiliar. Mentoring is one of the most powerful ways of ensuring dialogic learning, as we shall see shortly (page 236).

• *Self-reflective learning.* This is the kind of learning that leads individuals to redefine their current perspective in order to develop new patterns of understanding, thinking and behaving. It is needed when people have to operate in roles or situations that are very different from those to which they have become accustomed in the past. Because self-reflective learning involves challenging, and breaking out of, old mindsets it requires unlearning as well as new learning. As Argyris (1982) pointed out, that is possible only in an environment that 'enables and empowers individuals to be responsible, productive and creative' and to see error as a positive learning vehicle, as well as 'acknowledging uncertainty and spanning information boundaries'.

Educational and training programmes have an obvious part to play in generating self-reflective learning. So too have work-based learning processes like quality circles, briefing groups, benchmarking and best-practice exercises, secondments, new project work and action-learning sets, because such processes all expose people to new ways of thinking and new situations, making them question familiar prescriptions, operations and routines.

Single- and double-loop learning

It will have become apparent that instrumental and dialogic learning involve a different approach from that required by self-reflective learning. The difference is to do with the stance of the learner – in the first two cases seeking continuously to improve skills, behaviour or attitudes so that they fall in line with existing standards and norms, and in the third case taking a questioning, proactive approach in a situation where standards and norms themselves may need to be challenged.

This introduces one of the best-known – yet quite often poorly understood – ways of classifying approaches to learning: the concept of single- and double-loop learning. Chris Argyris first formulated the concept (1977) and developed it with Donald Schon in 1978. In essence it distinguishes the approach that simply tackles 'surface symptoms of a problem' (single-loop learning) from the approach that is concerned to 'question why the problem arose in the first place and. . .tackle its root causes' (double-loop learning) (Pickard, 1997: 34).

Not all researchers in the field of individual and organisational learning believe that the concept of single- and double-loop learning adequately explains the different types of learning outcome in question. Some see it as too simplistic, ignoring the possibility of discontinuous, non-linear learning to explain the sudden leaps in understanding that result in people breaking out of customary ways of thinking and perceiving. However, the concept is undeniably powerful, well researched and has influenced generations of scholars and practitioners. It will receive further comment later in this book, notably in Chapters 17 and 20.

Individual job performance

'Performance' can be explained as the outcome of the interaction between an individual's needs, perception of the results required and rewards being offered, and the amount of effort, energy and expertise that the individual has or wishes to apply to the task in hand. Handy (1985) called the outcome of this process the 'motivation calculus'. He explained that performance can be understood by reference to four parameters, which revolve around the learner, their manager and their workplace: needs, results, rewards and 'E' factors. We can see links here with the learning theory discussed earlier in this chapter.

- *Needs*. How far, in their minds, do individuals' jobs or tasks relate in any positive way to needs that they bring to work? What we should try to discover is not all their needs, but those which influence them at work. If a particular task or job relates to those needs only in a minor way, then clearly we cannot expect more than minimal performance from the job-holder.

  We must be careful about the labels we attach to people. A particular individual may be regarded as 'ambitious' – but ambition can take many forms. Trying to motivate such an individual to take on extra work by dangling the carrot of 'enhanced chances of promotion' will be ineffective if in fact he or she is driven by the need not for the increased responsibilities or high level of skill that promotion would involve but for some form of professional or work group status. Taking on another task when already expending maximum effort on an existing workload could mean a reduction in that individual's overall effectiveness and a consequent loss of status. Or perhaps he or she has a need for personal power which is already being satisfied through influence exercised over members of the workgroup.

- *Results*. How far do individuals appreciate what is wanted from them? Do they fully understand what their jobs involve, the results they are supposed to achieve, and the opportunities, constraints and challenges that surround those jobs? Have they had any opportunity to set work targets jointly with their managers, rather than simply have these imposed on them? There is much evidence to show that joint formulation of work plans and targets leads manager and job-holder to share a common view of the job, and to increased motivation and commitment in the job-holder. Do individuals know when they are achieving good results, and why? Do managers help them by acting as good role models, reinforcing effective performance and discouraging poor performance?

- *Rewards*. Does the task or job offer valued rewards to the individual? Rewards can take many different forms: not just money and position (which may have less impact than managers believe, and/or may not be within their power to offer) but status and praise – non-financial recognition. It is essential to talk and listen to employees about all the rewards that they value, instead of simply acting on assumptions.

It is important also to understand how people view the promise of rewards. Often promises are treated with scepticism because they have been made before but, for whatever reason, not been fulfilled.

• *'E' factors.* How far do individuals see it as worthwhile to expend effort, energy, excitement and expertise in the task, given the results that are required, the rewards it appears to offer them, and the workloads they already carry? And what level of those 'E' factors do those individuals actually possess? Are assessments about this accurate, or is either less or more expected of job-holders than they are actually able to give?

It is the interaction that takes place between needs, results, rewards, and 'E' factors that explains the performance of individuals, but for every individual that interaction is unique. Over time, the records of a poorly performing member of staff may show high levels of absenteeism, sickness and notes of continued refusals to take on new tasks. These records may cause unfavourable judgements to be made about him or her, so that training or development is considered inappropriate. In such cases the individual has been written off. Yet with more insights into the factors that lie behind performance quite a different picture may emerge. That picture may lead to an awareness that changes need to be made in the ways in which staff recruitment, work allocation, leadership functions or appraisal are carried out in a department. Once again, as so often before in this book, we see the importance of the organisation's total employee resourcing system in framing the particular activities related to the management and development of people in the workplace.

To summarise: when we are trying to understand people's performance at work we must try to find out the meanings that govern their actions instead of simply making assumptions about those meanings, or interpreting others' behaviour by reference to the meanings that govern our own.

> To identify the nature and causes of poor performance accurately and know how best to respond to it, it is necessary to understand the relationship between the individuals concerned, their managers, their workplace environment and the ER system of the organisation.

Tensions between control and development in PMSs

Case-study: Performance management at British Rail, 1988

An impressive account of the new appraisal system introduced for the entire management sector in British Rail in 1988 was given by Crabb in 1990. It seemed from his article that all the appropriate actions had been taken to ensure effective management of performance, and also relevant training and development of individuals. The actions included:

- simplification of the grading structure

- performance-related appraisal and rewards

- around five objectives for all managers, one of which has to be staff development

- annual appraisal, with a mid-year review, to ensure a check on work performance and on the implementation of agreed action plans

- an opportunity to discuss training and development needs at six months' remove from the date of pay awards.

A survey taken after the installation and initial operation of the system showed 'generally encouraging' results (Crabb, 1990: 15), with most managers clear about their jobs and objectives.

Yet the survey also revealed that 'many managers were going through the motions and not following through on the results of the reviews'. Why should this be? Perhaps there was no training for the scheme – none was mentioned. A second reading of the article, however, suggests that there was probably too great a tension between those objectives of the appraisal scheme that were to do with controlling performance against targets and those to do with developing people.

Source: Crabb, 1990

Central to performance management is a drive to control: to control the targets that are set for people; to control their performance by rewarding the achievement of targets; and to control their training by focusing it on closing gaps between standards sought and standards achieved. The increasing popularity of competency-based frameworks in PMSs must be treated with caution in this context. An obsessive preoccupation with competencies and an inexpert approach to competency-based analysis can be costly and counter-productive (Healy, 1995; Sparrow, 1996), narrowing the focus of performance management to exclude the development of more generalised abilities needed to survive in an unpredictable future.

On the other hand, a robust competency framework can productively focus attention on key areas for performance in the organisation and on what is needed to ensure adequate or superior performance levels in those areas. We have already seen (Chapters 5 and 9) that national occupational standards are grounded in the concept of competency. In Chapter 14 we shall look at ways of analysing competencies, and Chapter 18 will show their importance in management education and development. Competency-based analysis, when well constructed and implemented, can be a cost-effective process which brings many benefits. It must, however, be integrated into a balanced PMS, where the need for control does not override the need for development.

Controlling behaviour is a significant aspect of many PMSs, and it starts at the selection stage – a major thrust of assessment-centre methodology is to measure personality variables related to the kind of behavioural style sought by the organisation. One way of understanding the appraisal process is as a strategy to enforce the values and styles of behaviour that top management have decided are desirable in employees. Many reports now appear on schemes that measure behaviour as well as task performance.

There is nothing inherently threatening to the individual in working for an organisation that seeks or demands compliance to certain norms of behaviour – such, after all, is human life in social institutions. What matters is that there should be clarity and acceptance between the parties about what constitutes desirable norms, and about how they will be measured and recognised. The Birmingham Midshires appraisal scheme described by Mumford and Buley (1988), for example, succeeded because it gained the acceptance of its employees – it was an open and shared acknowledgement of a business need to develop a new kind of culture, and a way of helping employees to operate effectively in that culture. The success of that building society in subsequent years must owe something to the success of its well-balanced PMS.

What is threatening, however, is an excessive focus on control, and abuse of the power to control. Appraisal, for example, can easily be manipulated by appraisers to reinforce their power over their staff (see Townley, 1989: 98–108). Again, when an organisation is delayering and decentralising, appraisal can offer a way of retaining considerable corporate power and control: 'Organizations...can move the organization on the centralized–decentralized continuum by redistributing the power to appraise the performance of key staff personnel' (Devanna, 1984: 109).

Bevan and Thompson (1991: 39) in their large-scale research into performance management in UK organisations, noted with concern the increasing impact of the reward-driven approach which 'emphasises the role of performance payment systems on changing organisational behaviour and tends to undervalue the part played by other human resource development activities'. They predicted that the tension between the two approaches would cause both to malfunction, and found that the reward-driven strategy was already tending to dominate.

Of course, there are organisations that are well aware of the tensions and work hard to avoid them. The training manager of Haringey Council's Housing Services described how the Services decided to introduce a Performance and Development Review system which would not be linked to pay or incorporate competencies (Harris, 1995). The article is an important commentary on most of the points discussed thus far. It describes a PMS with all the appearance of having achieved a strong integration of the drives for control and for development. It also demonstrates the role that the training professional can and should play in promoting that integration. A recent study on PMSs in the National Health Service (Fowler, 1995) indicated that staff not only understand more about their work when a comprehensive PMS is in operation – they also feel good when the system achieves a balance between hard elements of work-targeting and soft elements of employee communication, consultation and development.

> **Integrating performance management and development of people in your organisation**
>
> Describe the main elements of the PMS in your own organisation. Assess how far – if at all – there is effective integration between the reward-driven and development-driven integration strategies, and what explains the situation you have identified. You will find it helpful to read some of the articles mentioned in this section of the chapter.

In the next and final part of this chapter we shall place individual learning needs within the framework of learning processes, types of learning, human performance and PMSs that we have developed thus far. We shall take as our reference points three of the four developmental elements of a PMS and their associated organisational learning strategies (see page 224):

Developmental elements of PMSs	Organisational learning strategies
Setting targets and establishing desired performance levels	Induction and basic skills training
Appraising and improving performance	Review and appraisal
Developing for the future	Continuous learning and self-development

The fourth developmental element – giving recognition and rewards – is of course crucial because as we have already noted, without a clear reason and reward for learning, employees cannot be expected to take that learning seriously. However, detailed comment on the many types of reward system that can be used to support a PMS and can encourage longer-term development is not within the scope of this book. Readers are therefore recommended to refer to specialist texts, especially Armstrong (1993, 1996).

A FRAMEWORK FOR ACTION

Establishing performance levels
Induction
Although the HRD manager may be involved in aspects of the selection process, we shall take as our practical starting-point the entry of a newcomer into an organisation (or the movement of an employee into a new job in some part of the organisation hitherto unfamiliar to him or her).

The purpose of induction should be not only to introduce newcomers to their job and workplace, to its main systems and procedures, and to the business goals and environment; it should also help them to understand and adapt to the vision of the organisation and its implicit values and norms. In other words, induction should facilitate dialogic learning.

Induction also needs to promote self-reflective learning. It is through self-reflection that individuals learn more about their own values and belief systems (and where those may need to change), achieve greater self-assurance and self-esteem, and are helped to function confidently and in new ways in the organisation they have just joined (or in the organisational unit or role to which they have just moved internally). Such learning should continue through the formative stages of the newcomer's job/role occupancy.

Many organisations arrange induction programmes for groups of new recruits rather than on an individualised basis. They include a carefully balanced range of activities and experiences through which dialogic and self-reflective learning can be promoted. Outdoor development courses are often used in this context, focusing on acclimatisation to company culture, and also on fostering skills relating to teamworking, problem-solving, creativity and holistic personal development. Many induction programmes culminate in individuals being helped to produce personal development objectives and plans which will contribute to their work performance and personal growth.

Mentors can be chosen to act as wise guides and counsellors during the induction process and thereafter. They can facilitate not only dialogic and self-reflective but also instrumental learning, because, in the atmosphere of trust and friendship that effective mentoring creates the new recruit feels able to admit openly to any performance problems, to reflect on and learn from them, and steadily to improve. To summarise:

> Induction should be concerned with providing essential organisational and job-related knowledge, and with the promotion of dialogic and self-reflective learning. It should lead to an effective process of instrumental learning and continuous development.

Producing an induction programme

Take a particular group of new recruits in your own organisation (or one with which you are familiar) and produce a programme for their induction. You will need to give a rationale for the programme and an indication of its structure, content, objectives and time-scale. You will also need to record the sources of information you have had to explore in producing your programme.

Feedback notes
- First, there has to be an overall purpose for induction. Fowler (1996) suggested that induction should aim to reduce low-quality work, high error rates and overlong learning periods. The purpose for your induction programme could perhaps be along lines proposed by Fowler: to enable new employees quickly to become fully integrated members of their working groups and to prevent a high incidence of early leavers by helping the newcomers to adjust to their new jobs and organisational environments.

- Consideration must be given to the kinds of learning to be achieved – dialogic, instrumental and self-reflective – and how they are to be ensured; also to the likely learning styles and skills of the new recruits (we shall look in detail at learning styles in Chapter 16) and how best to respond to these. Decisions must be made on how to achieve a balance between individual and group training, on what information to impart over what time-scales, on the duration, content and learning methods to be used, and on the roles to be taken during induction by line managers, HR staff and other personnel.

- Important sources of information will include:

  - *exit interview records* or other data indicating reasons for early departure from the organisation. Do these hold any implications for induction?

  - *views of recent recruits*. If they went through an induction programme, what did they get out of it, both positive and negative, and have they any views on whether or not it should now have different aims, design, content or operation? If they did not have any kind of planned induction, what do they think should be offered to newcomers?

  - *views of managers* for whom the recruits will be working, or who may need to be involved in the induction process for other reasons. What do they think induction should achieve, and what programme would they find meaningful?

  - *internal and external best practice*. There may be approaches to induction in different parts of the organisation that are innovative, successful and could be adapted to suit the needs of this programme. Likewise contacts with external organisations and reading the literature to find best practice will help to ensure quality.

  - *any up-to-date job descriptions and personnel specifications* for new recruits. These will offer important information about the recruits' main areas of work, about the organisational environment and culture that they will enter, and about the kinds of personal profile required by different jobs and roles. This information will also be important when planning basic training for new recruits.

Basic training

Objectives and programmes for basic training should be set out in an organisation's employee development policy. However, if that policy has only just been established, or if no such policy has yet been agreed, how can needs of potential learners be identified?

- *Define the objectives of basic training*. Objectives might be to attract and retain the calibre of people needed by the organisation; to provide training that is standards-based and related to National Vocational Qualifications (NVQs); to establish a cost-effective way of reinforcing company culture as well as ensuring good standards of job performance; and to build a base for flexibility of skills.

- *Audit existing learning and performance.* In looking at the ways in which employees currently acquire basic skills, be aware that sensitive political issues may be involved in proposing new training approaches related to the acquisition of new skills. Therefore the *process* of audit as well as its operational design and implementation is important if outcomes are to be achieved to which all parties will be committed. A short case-study is useful at this point.

Case-study: Basic training at SmithKline Beecham

At SmithKline Beecham in 1995 the company sought to achieve all four of the basic training objectives noted above through achieving multi-skilling of operators and craftsmen on a site where there were still strong traditional demarcation lines. The divide was particularly marked between these two groups, and working practices were deeply entrenched.

Given the importance of a partnership approach, working parties made up of white- and blue-collar workers set about identifying situations where it would be sensible for an operator to carry out basic engineering tasks. Outsiders, including a senior union official, were brought in to talk about multi-skilling elsewhere in order to give insights into best practice and to show the positive outcomes of the process.

There were inevitable difficulties as current ways of learning were examined in order to identify how best to organise the training for new skills. However, helped especially by winning a substantial grant from the European Commission under the Force programme (later superseded by the Leonardo programme) which required employers to forge links with transnational partners, mindsets began to change. The internal and external partnership approach helped to build trust, and eventually a powerful basic skills training programme using a mix of national occupational standards and internal standards was developed.

Source: Arkin, 1995

- *Produce proposals and plans.* Draw up and achieve agreement on integrated plans for induction, basic training and education, and continuous development for all learners.

Basic training needs to be available not only to enable new recruits to move confidently and competently into their new posts but also to support them throughout the early stages of job occupancy. It is at these stages that performance problems are most likely to occur, but providing newcomers have the ability to achieve good job performance (ie that there has not been a selection error), such problems are not likely to endure and indeed can become valuable learning vehicles.

This emphasises the need for regular monitoring and support during probationary periods. It is essential to identify any problems as they arise in order to ensure that they are corrected before becoming ingrained and habitual. Monitoring and support are also important because where new recruits are left to learn by trial and error on their own and neither they nor the organisation can judge their real capabilities low morale and lack of confidence can develop, leading to the kind of negative outcomes described in one of our first case-studies (page 22).

Newcomers to a job or role should also be helped to formulate personal development plans at an early stage, and should have the active support of their managers and mentors (the two should usually be different) to pursue the plans through time. Clear, measurable targets for job performance also need to be agreed between the individual and the manager, giving an objective and reliable basis for the regular discussion, feedback and planning of work.

Approaches that can enhance the quality of basic training and probationary periods include – again – mentors to provide support and guidance; short training events; special assignments and projects; coaching by managers or other relevant parties in the organisation; access to flexible learning packages; and visits to other organisations or departments and educational events to achieve a higher level of professional knowledge or a broadening of business awareness.

Much of the information needed to enable a good basic skills training programme to be drawn up cannot be obtained until details about the individual recruit are known. It is important that, whatever strategy for learning is chosen, it should be adaptable to individual learning styles as well as being capable of developing skills, knowledge and attitudes that the personnel specification shows are unlikely to be present in new recruits, and yet are vital to effective performance in the job or role.

Basic training in your organisation

Use the three-point check-list we have just developed to assess basic training in an area of your own organisation and to produce any recommendations needed to improve that training. You may find it helpful before starting this Activity to read relevant articles such as Arkin, 1995 and Cannell, 1997.

Appraising and improving current performance
Here we will look at three issues: types of improvement need, the appraisal of performance, and the development discussion.

Types of improvement need
Learning difficulties in current work can arise in relation to:

- *task performance*, where they are connected with difficulty in carrying out one or more specific tasks related to the job

- *task management*, where they are connected with difficulty in general planning, problem-solving and decision-making in the job

- *boundary management*, where they are connected with difficulty in operating confidently and effectively in the role and job by reference to the social and political environment in which the job-holder must operate

- *motivation*, connected typically with mistaken expectations about the job, or its level and content, or with unsatisfactory training, support and rewards, or with poor supervision and feedback on performance.

There are four major influences on performance:

• *the learner*, who needs the right level of competence, motivation, understanding, support and incentives in order to perform effectively

• *the learner's workgroup*, whose members will exercise a strong positive or negative influence on the attitudes, behaviour and performance of each new recruit

• *the learner's manager*, who needs to act as an effective role model, coach, stimulus and communicator related to performance

• *the organisation*, which may produce barriers to effective performance if there is no powerful, cohering vision; ineffective structure, culture, or work systems; unsupportive ER policy and systems; or inappropriate leadership and management style.

The HRD manager should build up close informal as well as formal interactions with managers and other personnel in the organisation, so that he or she can develop valid insights about the issues that lie behind performance instead of being over-influenced by the views of others. He or she will need to ask probing questions to determine whether performance should be improved by training, development or some other process. We shall return to this point later in the chapter.

The appraisal of performance

Three issues have a particular influence on the nature and outcomes of appraisal: the wider ER and organisational context; the relationship between the parties; the nature of the appraisal scheme.

• *The wider ER and organisational context.* We have already seen in Chapter 8 how pervasive the influence of organisational context is on the employee development process. Appraisal should always be planned as an integral part of wider employee resourcing and development strategy and policies, since without their reinforcement it can achieve no lasting outcomes, and indeed is more likely to lead to disappointed expectations and reduction in morale and commitment. It is equally fruitless to try to introduce a developmental appraisal system into an organisation that has a rigid, divisive role structure and a culture and management style that discourages openness, the use of initiative and a long-term developmental perspective. Finally, as we have already noted, unless the organisation's approach to performance management achieves an integration between reward-driven and developmental thrusts, then appraisal itself can achieve little in terms of developmental outcomes.

• *The relationship between the parties.* The relationship between the parties is the single most powerful influence on the conduct and outcomes of an appraisal discussion, and constitutes one of the major areas of difficulty related to it. If the appraiser–appraisee relationship is not open and supportive it is most unlikely that a formalised appraisal system can make it so. In short:

> It is a dilemma in appraisal that the relationship that produces information about learning needs may be so poor that the validity of that information becomes suspect, and any chance of effective development of the individual in the workplace thereafter may be stifled.

- Three hundred and sixty degree appraisal is growing in popularity and reduces reliance on the limited number of sources otherwise involved in reviewing the individual's performance. Rhone Poulenc Agriculture, for example, have incorporated it into their manager development programme (Jacobs and Floyd, 1995). A similar approach is that of the 'balanced scorecard' method, which takes account of external as well as internal feedback. One organisation introducing this as a major lever in radical restructuring and the development of a new business culture is the Halifax Building Society (Littlefield, 1996). HR professionals need to be well informed on such innovative developments which, however, are not without pitfalls (Ward, 1995). Although the views of peers, customers, functional bosses and other parties will all carry weight, those of the line manager are still likely to be the most powerful in determining the outcomes of appraisal in most organisations and for most individuals.

- *The nature of the appraisal scheme.* Much has been written elsewhere about the characteristics of effective appraisal schemes. Suffice it to say here that for a scheme to be developmental it must have objectives and an approach to appraisal that reflect that aim; the full commitment of management and staff and a consistency with the basic management structure of the organisation; the opportunity for mutual learning and understanding; and a process that emphasises review, diagnosis and action planning.

In choosing a case-study to illustrate these themes it was tempting to opt for one in the larger organisation setting. However, I decided to take a different context, both in order to present a scheme as it is developing through time (earlier versions of this study appeared in my previous 1988 and 1992 Institute of Personnel Management texts) and to show the ways in which fundamental principles of appraisal hold true whatever the setting and however formalised or informal the process. The education sector has seen impressive advances in appraisal in recent years (for a useful example see Fox, 1995), but at Newlands School appraisal was introduced at a time when schemes were still controversial, especially in the hothouse world of the independent preparatory school.

Case-study: Appraisal at Newlands School

Newlands, a day preparatory school for boys in Gosforth on the outskirts of Newcastle upon Tyne, introduced formal appraisal into the school in 1987 after full discussion between the head, governors and staff. The objectives are to aid work-planning and performance, to identify and respond to training and development needs, and to contribute to individual and organisational growth.

The culture and structure of the organisation

Since 1977, when it was under threat of closure and a new head, Nicholas Barton, was appointed, the school (capacity, 245 boys, 4 to 13 years old, with a nursery department for 24 3- to 4-year-olds) moved rapidly to becoming one of the most highly regarded in the North East. Although non-selective in its recruitment, with a pupil population spanning a wide socio-economic and ethnic spectrum and fees lower than most competitor schools in the locality, it achieves consistently outstanding academic and sporting results, has a full waiting-list, and attracts and retains talented staff.

The school has a network structure. The governors are mainly local professional and business people, including some ex-Newlands parents, and work with the head at several levels. The teaching staff are involved in a wide range of curricular and extra-curricular activities: the school day extends to include supervised prep. and optional games and leisure pursuits every evening, while adventure holidays and trips abroad for the children occupy much staff time during vacations. The boys, too, have important team roles to play, with the head boy and the many monitors carrying responsibilities that keep them in close everyday contact with the staff and the head. The culture of the school rests on values of the family, and parents are involved in many enterprises which further energise school life. The school operates in a very competitive, dynamic local environment. For over 17 years now, however, it has steadily maintained a leading position without compromising its vision of optimising the development and attainments of boys of all educational levels and backgrounds.

The appraisal scheme

The appraisal process is two way (the head's own performance is appraised by the governors in the context of a report that he presents twice termly to the full governing board). After distributing self-appraisal forms in the spring term, the head carries out about 20 appraisals in the summer term, each lasting two hours on average. Although he is closely involved every day with staff, that contact revolves around ongoing operational activities; appraisal offers a unique opportunity to take time out with each individual to discuss work progress and plans, and training and development for the coming period. It also gives staff the chance to suggest any changes that they feel could advantageously be made to the management of the school in relation to their areas of work and concern.

Relationship between appraisal and rewards

Bonuses at the school (as distinct from allowances for special educational responsibilities) were introduced in 1990. They do not reward performance but recognise commitment, initiative and self-development by staff. The philosophy here is that high standards of performance will be secured by attracting high-calibre recruits who receive in return above-average pay and conditions. Bonuses, on the other hand, acknowledge staff's ongoing contribution to the overall advancement of the school by diverting to them some of the financial rewards that the school gains from their commitment. Valued effort can be of many kinds, in recognition of the different contributions that can be made by staff. Bonus awards are determined just before the annual appraisal interview, not as a result of it, and can be discussed at that interview if the individual wishes. Not all staff achieve bonuses; nor are bonuses of equal value. However, the system is accepted as fair, and disagreements, which are rare, are dealt with promptly and openly.

Outcomes of appraisal

The first round of appraisals in 1987 led to significant timetabling and wider organisational changes. Three years later, the scheme was evaluated by asking staff to respond to a questionnaire on its perceived aims, design and outcomes. This resulted in improvements to some of the paperwork and procedures involved in operating the scheme. Its principles, however, remained unchanged, since staff support for these was evident from the survey.

Management development and succession

Early in 1996 a management team was established at Newlands, consisting of the head, the deputy head, the director of studies and the head of juniors. The purpose was to provide, as part of the evolving management structure of the school, a united and experienced team to support the head both in operational and more strategic tasks. The team meets each week to discuss all school matters. It, rather than the head and governors alone, now carries out selection interviews, and it will play a key part in guiding the longer-term future of the school by ultimately helping to select the present head's successor. Inevitably members of the team will become involved in running appraisals.

(By permission of Newlands Preparatory School, Gosforth, Tyne and Wear)

In this study we can see a productive interaction between the appraisal process and the wider employee resource, business and organisational context. At Newlands School, as in larger organisations, appraisal can make a strategic contribution by:

- demonstrating the importance of individual and team development, as well as of performance management

- reinforcing the wider team-based culture of the organisation

- helping to secure the long-term growth of the organisation.

The development discussion

The discussion of development needs, whether or not within the context of formal appraisal, makes many demands on managers anxious both to ensure high standards of performance in their units and to help individuals develop over the longer term – and on the training analyst who needs to understand performance problems in order to produce relevant training and development initiatives. Some common problems are disagreement on learning needs, failure to agree priorities and claims of discriminatory treatment.

Disagreement on learning needs

- Some may not admit to failings in their performance, and become hostile and defensive at any attempt to discuss them. Some, lacking self-confidence, may have too low an opinion of their performance and potential.

- Some may have too high an opinion of their performance and potential and be overconfident and resentful, seeing no need for training or development.

- Some managers may not be skilled or confident enough to deal with these forms of behaviour.

- Some may not know enough about the detail of what the individual actually does in their job, or about technical aspects of it, to feel able to give a view on the performance of the individual or to identify development needs accurately.

Failure to agree priorities
- A manager, for example, may think that an individual needs interpersonal skills development, whereas the individual may think that this relates to only a very minor problem, and see other training or development as much more important. A manager may want to focus all effort on training to reduce current gaps in performance, whereas the individual may be trying to achieve some discusion also of how their longer-term development in the company can be enhanced and where they are likely to be going in the company, ultimately.

Claims of discriminatory treatment
- The individual may not be able to appreciate why he or she is being denied opportunities for development that someone else enjoys. If the manager cannot give convincing reasons, then clearly the individual has a justifiable grievance. This could lead to a case for discrimination being taken to an industrial tribunal (on grounds of failure to be given certain kinds of training or development that would give access to job or career opportunities in the organisation).

What can be done about such problems? It would be foolish to pretend that they can always be resolved, but useful aids are:

- training to tackle common problems and to build up those task and process skills essential for productive discussion of performance and development needs. Haringey Council's Housing Services, for example, trained all its housing managers over four years from 1990 in the skills of performance managers, with a particular emphasis on developing skills related to correcting poor performance constructively (Harris, 1995)

- special emphasis on training appraisers in the avoidance of discrimination in appraisal and its outcomes. Records must be maintained to show patterns of training and development across a workforce, procedures used to identify needs and provide related learning opportunities, and outcomes of such action

- the availability of ongoing guidance and counselling to help appraisers and others involved in the monitoring and improvement of individuals' performance try out their new skills and improve with practice

- the avoidance of an appraisal scheme design incorporating ratings or rankings when the aim of the appraisal scheme is simply to improve current performance and develop individuals over the longer term

- the use of individual performance objectives which help individuals to understand their priorities and how their work fits in with the objectives of the organisation (according to Fraser (1996), around 90 per cent of organisations still use objectives for this reason)

- the appropriate use of competencies within an appraisal scheme. Despite criticisms made of excessive use of competencies (referred to earlier in the chapter) it must to be accepted that around 60 per cent of organisations appear now to be using them as part of their appraisal system (Fraser, 1996). Approached with a sense of proportion, discussion of competencies needed in the job can help individuals to better understand their performance, and to identify areas of strength even in a generally weak performance.

It may also be advisable to establish an appeals procedure related to an organisation's appraisal scheme. Some organisations prefer not to do so because of the fear that such a procedure will make appraisal appear a potentially divisive process instead of a vehicle for joint problem-solving, planning and learning. The idea of a 'grandparent' figure in appraisal – a counterbalance to the immediate appraiser – is another used in a number of schemes; however, the most powerful influence on outcomes remains likely to be the individual's manager.

In any discussion of performance, a strategy of self-appraisal can be valuable in reducing interpersonal tensions, because it gives the early initiative in the discussion to the job-holder, enabling their viewpoint on their performance and needs to be clearly expressed and to be the main driving force behind the opening up of the discussion. The manager/job training analyst must focus on listening, since the need is to learn and understand, not to judge. Once immediate needs have been agreed, there should be a discussion as to what kind of longer-term perspective the job-holder has on his or her work and career, and the kind of developmental actions that might bring the best advantage to individual and organisation in the coming period. An emphasis on mutuality of interest means that the job-holder should be able to secure important gains in employability security, while the organisation gets the assurance of increased commitment from the individual to the tasks and projects in which he or she is to be involved. Focusing on commitment to the work rather than on the less meaningful concept, in these days of downsizing, of 'loyalty to the organisation' is likely to be beneficial in such discussions.

When in formal appraisal meetings the discussion of needs is concluded, action agreed should be recorded, noting:

- a clear distinction between job-related training and development, and learning experiences to support the individual's longer-term personal development plan (an aspect of career planning which will be covered in detail in Chapter 18)

- the recommended training and development plan for the individual for the coming period

- timings for key elements of the plan

- resources needed for the plan
- the first date for appraiser and appraisee to meet in order to discuss progress with the plan.

Tackling the improvement of formal appraisal in an organisation

Appendix 7 presents a seven-step approach to appraisal which you may find helpful to apply in your own organisation or in one with which you are familiar, if formal appraisal there is in need of some improvement. I devised the approach during a consultancy assignment for a unit of a large organisation with a heavily documented appraisal scheme which, however, allowed its units flexibility in applying the scheme to suit their own type of work and staff. Caution, however, should be exercised, as the following narrative explains.

Formal appraisal in the unit concerned had an unhappy history of failure to achieve meaningful improvements in the management of performance or development of its people. Its operational weaknesses had been compounded over recent years by lack of any clear, effective HR strategy or systems to support developmental appraisal, and by the backcloth of a business strategy for the unit that, although convincing at design stage, repeatedly ran into problems of implementation. The unit had for many years had an uneasy relationship with the wider organisation, which regarded it as something of a maverick: performing strongly in relation to some targets but poorly in relation to others, with a generally capable and committed workforce but unreliable in its direction and management.

The approach to appraisal was welcomed by staff during a series of workshops attended by mixed appraiser/appraisee groups across the unit. In conjunction with the workshops it was seen by most to lend clarity to a confused process, and to identify ways in which appraisees could gain more control and exercise more initiative in relation to the annual formal appraisal process.

In the event, although the appraisal discussions themselves appeared to proceed more effectively and to receive more commitment from staff, and although top management resourced the whole training and appraisal process generously and was actively involved in it, the outcomes of the process proved little different from those in the past. This was unsurprising, since the original barriers to the success of appraisal in the unit, although identified and discussed with management on this occasion and apparently taken seriously at the time, subsequently remained. The expectations created by the significant level of investment in improving the appraisal process were frustrated, and led to a further decline in staff morale. During the following year organisational and strategic changes occurred in the unit that increased rather than reduced those barriers.

Retrospectively the consultancy assignment can be seen, perhaps, as a wasted exercise. Sadly, appraisal, like the HRD process of which it is simply one element, cannot resolve deep-rooted problems of business strategy, organisational effectiveness and HRM – at best it can expose them, but at worst it will be destroyed by them.

Ensuring continuous learning and development

In organisational life everyday experience is the most fundamental influence on people's learning. This experience consists not simply of the work that people do, but of the way they interact with others in the organisation, and the behaviour, attitudes and values of those others. It consists, therefore, of people's entire work environment. If people are to learn continuously and to take advantage of the rich resources offered by the organisation as a learning system, they must be able to cope with the demands that change places on them, and must have a mastery of the learning process. How can this learning ability be fostered? How, for example, can those responsible for employee development in a large organisation, with several thousand people in its workforce, hope to ensure continuous development in the workplace?

Continuous learning and development at Company X

Go back to Chapter 10 and read through the two-part case-study about Company X again (pages 173–4 and 181–2). Then identify the ways in which a climate conducive to continuous learning and development has been achieved and how the commitment of line managers to supporting such learning is ensured in that company.

Feedback notes

The case-study produces a store of relevant information, which we can summarise by recalling that, at Company X, development of people is viewed by management as a fundamental business process, enabled and encouraged by:

- a clear HRD vision and strategy that is in line with overall business goals and strategy

- strategic HRD objectives that are carried through into detailed, practical plans for implementation of the policies that serve those objectives

- a form of organisational structure and company-wide procedures that ensure the policies are carried out with the commitment and expertise of all who have been assigned training and development roles and responsibilities

- a system of training, guidance, monitoring, appraisal and rewards related to performance in those roles

- good management and utilisation of training and development resources.

The role of the HR professional in promoting self-development

It is easy to produce a list of 'what to do about self-development' guidelines. I am about to do so myself! However, not all HR professionals practise self-development even though the professional body (the Institute of Personnel and Development) has produced an excellent code, a Continuous Professional Development pack, and has built into its professional qualification the need for continuous updating. As long as chief executives like Kuijpers (1995) can continue to berate HR practitioners for their inability to earn the credibility needed if the profession is to achieve strategic status, it is clear that progress in continuous development by those practitioners is unsatisfactory.

We noted earlier in this chapter that no new learning will occur unless there is a stimulus to activate the learning process. Many professionals' very livelihood depends on keeping up to date, on looking ahead, on constantly sharpening their learning skills. In the open, less integrated, less easily defined 'profession' of personnel/human resource management, such urgent spurs to continuous learning and development are rarely present. This, however, creates a dangerous illusion of security.

In today's organisational world, the urge to downsize, delayer and outsource seems as yet undiminished, oblivious often to rational argument (since research does not demonstrate the expected benefits, and has identified many inherent dangers). In that world, simply continuing to do what has been done for so long – no matter how expertly – will not suffice, certainly not in an area (HRM) that is often struggling for credibility and advancement. Those who are valued, survive and flourish – whether as full-time employees or self-employed – will be those who have a convincing vision of HRM and who can provide clear, practical processes and policies to meet unfolding needs. They will not only have an up-to-date understanding of trends and best practice in their field, they will also be profoundly well informed about the business environment, and have an evident ability to operate in it and to cope effectively with the tensions that surround HRM and development in changing organisations. Without continuous learning and self-development, these kinds of capability cannot be achieved, leaving HR professionals unlikely to progress, make a meaningful impact in the world, or improve their employability security.

Research reported in 1997 (Littlefield, 1997) supports that conclusion. In a three-year study by Roffey Park Management Institute (1997) of 200 employees who had gone through delayering exercises, HR professionals emerged as among the hardest hit. For around 60 per cent of the 163 people who responded to a follow-up survey at the end of the period, promotion opportunities had become rare, especially for those not holding senior positions. Even for the 21 per cent – mostly senior HR managers – who had recently been promoted, board representation was often being experienced as a 'bear garden', and many were considering a move. However, around two-thirds of respondents welcomed the extra responsibilities and opportunities to broaden their skills that accompanied delayering, and many (especially the more junior HR staff) were using their increased employability to look elsewhere to promote their careers. For those unable or unwilling to continuously develop themselves and take more control over their future, the outcome tended to be low morale, frustration and stalemate.

If we think in this way about the dangers inherent in neglecting our own professional self-development and the importance of responding in time to warning signs to which we should pay heed, then it is easier to produce meaningful guidelines about how best to stimulate others in a similar quest:

- *Become an effective learner.* HR practitioners who are trying to help people become effective learners must themselves have an adequate mastery of each of the major learning styles and skills. They can rate themselves by using Honey and Mumford's learning inventory (1992), or Kolb *et al* (1974), which offers an interesting alternative. Illuminating comparisons can be drawn from the two sets of scores. It is then essential to develop a plan of action for self-improvement.

- *Promote self-directed learning.* In many organisations individuals now have to draw up personal development plans and review these with their managers formally at appraisal and regularly during the year. In training appraisers and appraisees, the HRD manager has the opportunity to explain why self-directed learning matters and how it can be achieved.

  As we have just noted, simply urging people to develop themselves is not likely to have much success. Honey and Mumford have produced a 'Learning Environment Questionnaire' (1996) which can encourage managers to look at their own behaviour and practise and diagnose which of the four roles needed to create a learning climate in the workplace they possess or should develop: the Role Model, the Provider, the System Builder or the Champion.

- *Promote awareness about continuous learning and development.* HR staff can have informal discussions with managers and other key personnel in the organisation – over coffee or lunch, after meetings, during talks about people's learning needs. In a variety of informal, as well as more formal, ways they can build up an awareness in the organisation about what continuous development means, and about its relationship to flexibility and to enhancing people's motivation through improving their employability security.

- *Design events to develop learning styles and skills.* If training and other planned learning events are to be fully accessible to all who need them, they should be designed in such a way as not only to avoid the discriminatory barriers forbidden by law, but also to accommodate whenever necessary a range of learning styles, rather than appealing to only one type of learner – the activist, or the reflector, for example.

  On the other hand, such events must also help learners to acquire or develop those styles most suited to the tasks they have to carry out. A training managers' course, for example, should promote all four types of learning style, in order to produce at the end of the day people who are not (for example) predominately activists but who have a balance of skills across the four categories, thus enabling them to function effectively in the different situations in which training experts have to operate.

- *Seek to identify and reduce organisational barriers to the development of appropriate learning styles and skills.* HR professionals should likewise promote an awareness of the value the organisation can derive from recognising and encouraging a diversity of learning approaches.

For example, the preferred mode of learning in a particular organisation may be by initial basic skills training and then simply by unsupervised trial and error through time. This may be because there is no understanding of other ways in which people could develop their performance. Trial and error may appear a cheap way of learning to perform to adequate levels. In reality, however, it is likely to involve significant indirect costs caused, typically, by high turnover of new recruits, high rates of wastage, poor quality, lost production time during the extended learning period, and many demotivated, underperforming workers. Indirect costs over the longer term are likely to accrue through lack of innovative skills and flexible attitudes, and a tendency for closed mindsets. Approached with the right degree of social and political sensitivity, it should be possible to help key parties to view the organisation's or unit's preferred mode of learning more critically, and to see the value of trying to vary customary approaches to learning and development.

- *Influence assessors and appraisers to consider learning styles when examining performance, and in the selection process.* Finally, HR practitioners should seek to influence those involved in all forms of assessment and appraisal processes including selection, transfer, promotion, and disengagement from employment (an easier task if there is a call for appraisal training in the organisation, and/or if personnel and training are closely integrated functions). Criteria should be developed that relate to the learning, problem-solving and decision-making styles and skills needed, and these criteria should help to guide judgements. In this way not only should assessments and decisions become more valid but, in the process of discussing this extra dimension, there should be an improvement in managers' understanding of how central a part learning style and skills play in people's behaviour and performance at work.

CONCLUSION

In order to achieve the learning objectives for this chapter we have explored the relationship between an organisation's overall employee development (ED) programme and its performance management system (PMS) by first producing a four-dimensional framework for understanding people's learning needs. Two major theories about the learning process have been described, and five factors related to understanding the practical implications of that process for the overall ED programme have been identified. Three types of learning – instrumental, dialogic and self-reflective – have been outlined as essential components of that programme, and the concept of single- and double-loop learning has been explained.

Four aspects of an individual's performance at work have been discussed, and the PMS of an organisation has been described through reference to developmental elements. Tensions to do with drives for control and development in PMS have been explored.

Explanations have been given of three dimensions of a framework to integrate performance management and employee development: establishing performance levels, appraising and improving performance, and stimulating continuous learning and development. The importance of continuous development for HR professionals themselves has been stressed, and six ways in which those professionals can promote the process in their organisations have been outlined.

USEFUL READING

ARMSTRONG, M. (1993) *Managing Reward Systems*. Buckingham, Open University.

BASS, B. M. *and* VAUGHAN, J. A. (1967) *Training in Industry: The management of learning*. London, Tavistock Publications.

FOWLER, A. (1995) 'Objectives and appraisal boost staff morale'. *People Management*. Vol. 1, 2: 12.

FOWLER, A. (1996) *Employee Induction: A good start*. 3rd ed. London, Institute of Personnel and Development.

HARDINGHAM, A. (1996) *Designing Training*. London, Institute of Personnel and Development.

HONEY, P. *and* MUMFORD, A. (1992) *A Manual of Learning Styles*. 3rd ed. Maidenhead, Honey.

HONEY, P. *and* MUMFORD, A. (1996) *Managing Your Learning Environment*. Maidenhead, Honey.

MARCHINGTON, M. *and* WILKINSON, A. (1996) *Core Personnel and Development*. London, Institute of Personnel and Development.

14 Learning needs in the job

LEARNING OBJECTIVES

After reading this chapter you will:

- have been introduced to an eight-stage approach to the planning, design and delivery of learning events

- in relation to the first stage, be able to use an appropriate strategy when analysing jobs for training purposes

- have a framework for understanding the main approaches and techniques used in job training analysis and their applicability to different situations

- be able to produce a job training specification and a job training proposal.

AN EIGHT-STAGE APPROACH TO PLANNING AND DELIVERING LEARNING EVENTS

In Chapter 13 we saw that it is not necessary to have formalised training or planned learning events for valuable learning to be achieved. Using ongoing work as a vehicle for continuous learning can develop individuals, groups and the organisation as a whole, both for the shorter and the longer term. We saw how the organisation can be managed in order to promote such work-based learning, and how to generate attitudes and practice conducive to continuous development in the workplace.

However, planned learning events usually form a core component of an organisation's overall employee development programme (page 224). It is with such events that this and the next three chapters are concerned. In these chapters the term 'learning event' will be used to indicate any learning activity that is formally designed in order to achieve specified learning objectives.

Table 12 shows the eight stages involved in the inception, design and delivery of a learning event. The first stage is covered in Chapters 13 and 14; in Chapter 15 we shall examine stages 2 to 4; and in Chapter 16 stages 5 to 8.

Table 12 Eight stages in the inception, design and delivery of planned learning events

1	Identify/confirm needs.
2	Agree on the overall purpose and objectives for the learning event.
3	Identify the profile of the intended learning population.
4	Select strategy, and agree on direction and management of the learning event.
5	Select learners and produce detailed specification for the learning event.
6	Confirm strategy and design event.
7	Deliver event.
8	Monitor and evaluate event.

Stage 1: Identifying/confirming needs
Identifying needs in individuals and in jobs
In Chapter 3 we looked at the analysis of organisational learning needs within the strategic, business-led framework of human resource development (HRD) established in Chapter 2. In Chapter 13 we examined the analysis of employees' learning needs, in relation both to the performance management system (PMS) and the longer-term goals of organisation and individual. More detailed information and guidance on the analysis of organisational, group and individual needs can be found in the specialist texts noted in that chapter and in its reading list.

However, it is also necessary to identify any important learning needs embedded in jobs: that is to say, the demands made by a job in terms of type and level of skills, knowledge and attitudes. This information can be obtained through a process called job training analysis, itself summarised as:

> The process of identifying the purpose of a job and its component parts, and specifying what must be learnt in order for there to be effective work performance. A key outcome of job training analysis is usually a job training specification which enables learning objectives to be established and appropriate training to be designed.

A crucial part of the process is to identify the performance standards and methods of measurement required in a job in order that objectives for a learning event can be set and evaluation subsequently be carried out. Analysis should also identify aspects of a job that make it difficult to learn, so that special attention can be given to them during the learning event.

All jobs comprise three broad components: skills, knowledge and attitudes.

- *Skills*. Skills may be, for example, manual, diagnostic, interpersonal or decision-making. They include any component of the job that involves 'doing' something.

- *Knowledge*. Knowledge may be, for example, technical, procedural or concerned with company organisation. In the context of this chapter it relates to that which enables sense to be made of a job in order to ensure its competent performance. It is knowledge that endows meaning. It has been defined as 'a person's range of information' or sum of what he or she knows and understands (Allen, 1990). We shall be returning to the full organisational implications of that definition in the final chapter of this book.

- *Attitudes*. It may be important in a job that certain attitudes are demonstrated at all times, for example courtesy and sensitivity in dealing with customers or clients; flexibility and co-operation when working in a close-knit team; or calmness and patience in coping with various tensions. The training analyst must note any attitudes that are critical to job performance.

Each of these components has implications for learning design and methods. A programme focused on the development of skills will be very different in its design and operation from a programme where the central focus is the promotion of certain attitudes, or on areas of complex theory or concepts which the job-holder may need to acquire. With different combinations of these components occurring from one job to the next, it is essential to choose an appropriate analytical approach and techniques.

In this chapter we shall cover four aspects of identifying and responding to learning needs inherent in the job:

- a strategy for carrying out job training analysis

- job training analysis approaches

- job training analysis techniques

- producing a training and development proposal.

A SIX-STEP STRATEGY FOR CARRYING OUT JOB TRAINING ANALYSIS

In this section I have drawn on a framework developed in a rather different form by Reid and Barrington (1997: 297–301).

1 Initial investigation
Any request for training should always be met first with investigatory questions like the following:

Is training really the answer?
For example, poor performance may be due to ineffective supervision, lack of financial or other incentives, or lack of innate ability. If any of these is the primary cause, then training is not going to improve performance, and job training analysis is pointless.

Is training the most cost-beneficial answer?
There may be other ways in which knowledge, skills or attitudes may be developed without involving the expense of formal training. Would careful integration of work and learning be more cost-beneficial? Or would buying in the skills, or some other non-training solution be more appropriate?

Are there sufficient incentives for individuals if training is given for this task?

Fairbairn (1991) pointed out that training will not be effective unless people want it; and they will only want it if they see that the skills, knowledge and attitudes it is promoting are in reality important in their job, and recognised, encouraged and rewarded in their workplace. There must therefore be an analysis of how far the task or job is valued in the organisation, and how far effective performance in it will be supported and rewarded in some way that is meaningful to the individual.

This is particularly relevant when organisations are attempting to achieve multi-skilling. For example, at Cummins Engine, Darlington (the company used as a case-study in Chapters 3 and 12) in the late 1980s and early 1990s employees were offered financial rewards for going through a series of modular skills training courses related to different areas of skill. That rebounded to some extent, because the message it appeared to convey was that training, rather than the outcomes resulting from it, was what was valued: training had become an end in itself. As a result, Cummins had to find ways of shifting the emphasis from rewarding people for undergoing training to rewarding them for the more skilled performance that was the outcome of training (see Harrison, 1996a for a full account of how HRD helped to ensure productivity and lay the foundations for long-term growth at Cummins during the 1980s).

Is analysis really necessary?

Perhaps reliable and up-to-date information already exists about the job? Perhaps there is already a job training specification, either internally or externally produced?

Is the job likely to change?

If so, a new analysis will be needed when the change takes place, and that consideration has a bearing on the analytical approach to be chosen now. If change is likely, then why, how often, and over what period of time? Or is this a routine and stable job, which will not alter much through time and will therefore repay the expense of detailed analysis now? Is it a job that many people do, or is it fairly unique?

Should the person be adapted to the job, or the job to the person?

With certain jobs – for example, those at the top level of the organisation, those that are very specialised or those involving a high degree of innovative talent – it may be more important for the person to make the job than the job make the person. The job-holder's vision of how the role should be translated into reality, and the identity they give to the job, may matter far more than any pre-determined specification. In such a situation selection, not training, is the critical process.

2 Select the analyst

In most organisations it is specialist staff, whether internal or external, who carry out job training analysis. However, it is the line manager and the person who actually does the job who know most about the job, so whoever carries out the analysis must be acceptable to those parties. A related point is that much of a sensitive nature can be uncovered during the process of job training analysis: motivation, discipline and supervision problems; misunderstandings caused by ill-defined responsibilities; and conflict and inefficiency arising from inappropriate organisation structures or cultures. The training analyst, having identified these issues, must know how to draw them to the attention of those who can deal with them, and must influence those parties to take action. Until that happens training cannot be effective.

3 Gain co-operation

Before the job training analysis process starts, everyone involved in and likely to be significantly affected by the activity must be given a clear explanation of its purpose, how it will be carried out, by whom, over what period of time, and with what probable outcomes. If the analysis is likely to have outcomes tied to pay awards and/or gradings, then there must be an appeals procedure. Willing co-operation of all the parties is essential to the success of job training analysis.

4 Select the analytical approach and techniques

Information obtained in steps one to three will enable the analyst to decide which approach and techniques to choose (these will be explained in the next section).

5 Carry out the analysis

Here the analyst needs to consider two factors: the sources of information to use and the depth of analysis required.

Sources of information

Written sources are liable to be produced on differing bases, and may be out of date, or not comprehensive. Care must therefore be taken when referring to technical manuals or to records of various kinds. Records will hopefully reveal essential information such as whether the job is one where there have been many problems in performance; where the norm is that good standards of performance are achieved relatively easily; and whether there are any trends in labour turnover, absenteeism, sickness or lateness that could relate to difficulties experienced in the job. Job descriptions will be particularly useful, but will need careful checking to ensure they are up to date, accurate and comprehensive.

Oral sources of information – eg the job-holder, the job-holder's manager, co-workers – are all liable to be biased, and may sometimes contradict one another in their perception both of the content and characteristics of the job and – very important – in its order of priorities. Such sources may be deliberately or unintentionally misleading. Handling them will require considerable interpersonal and political skill.

Depth of analysis

In job training analysis, no matter which analytical approach is chosen, the important question is how much detail is needed about a task and the skills, knowledge and attitudes required to do it. Annett, Duncan, Stammers and Gray (1979) suggested that every task in a job should continue to be broken down and described until the point is reached where the remainder of the task can be readily learnt without training and does not in any case require flawless performance. As we shall see when looking at the different approaches, this principle will not always apply.

The analyst must also look for any problems in the workplace – either social or work-related – that could make it difficult for the trainee to apply learning acquired in a training programme. If the training given is to result in effective performance in the job, it must prepare trainees for the kind of job environment in which they will have to carry out that job.

6 Produce the job training specification

When the process of analysing the job is finished and the information has been carefully checked, the analyst will in most cases have to produce a job training specification, ensuring that it is agreed as accurate by the key parties. Such a specification can be summarised thus:

> The job training specification describes in overall terms the job for which training is to be given, or the key problem areas in a job which training will enable learners to tackle; it then specifies the kinds and levels of knowledge, skill and, where relevant, attitudes needed for effective performance, together with the standards that will operate in the job and the criteria for measuring achievement of standards.

To understand how to produce a job training specification we need to look more closely at job training analysis approaches, since each approach tends to call for a particular format of job training specification.

JOB TRAINING ANALYSIS APPROACHES

There are many approaches to job training analysis. Important sources of information include the relevant section in Reid and Barrington (1997: 284–7), Boydell and Leary's full and illuminating treatment of approaches (1996) and Hackett's clear practical guidelines (1997). Outstanding in the field, as are so many US texts on HRD, is Mills, Pace and Peterson (1988).

For this section I have simply selected four of the commonest job training analysis approaches:

* comprehensive analysis
* key task analysis
* problem-centred analysis
* competency-based analysis.

Comprehensive analysis
This involves a very detailed examination of every aspect of the job until each task has been fully described in terms of its knowledge, skills and (if relevant) attitudes. The task must also be described by

reference to its objectives, its frequency of performance, its standards of performance and ways of measuring that performance.

Clearly this is an extremely time-consuming analytical approach and requires much skill. The first question to ask, therefore, is 'In which circumstances is it to be recommended?'

Here are some criteria to apply:

* when tasks are unfamiliar to learners, difficult, all more or less equally important to be performed well, and must be learnt quickly and to standard. In such a situation there is a need for a thorough approach that will cover the full scope of the job

* when change is unlikely and new recruits are fairly frequent. If these conditions apply, the expense involved in comprehensive analysis will soon be offset by the number of times training resulting from it can be carried out before it is necessary to do any fresh analysis. New recruits may be frequent because this is a category of job held by large numbers of people in the workplace, or perhaps because there are unavoidably high levels of turnover

* when the job is closely prescribed. If little or nothing can be left to the initiative of the job-holders, then it is essential that they learn the correct ways of performing virtually all tasks in the job

* when resources are adequate. There must be the resources available (time, skill, numbers of staff) to carry out this detailed, complex and time-consuming approach.

What is involved in comprehensive analysis? Two key tasks:

Producing a job description
This is a broad statement of the purpose, scope, responsibilities and tasks that constitute a particular job. The job description should contain:

* the title of the job

* its overall purpose, preferably expressed in a sentence summarising the purpose as far as the organisation is concerned

* the name of the department in which the job-holder works

* the title of the person/s to whom the job-holder is responsible directly and (if different) ultimately

* brief details of any other key relationships, for example with staff in another department/division/unit, and/or with people or institutions outside the organisation

* an indication of any major resources for which the job-holder is accountable (finance, physical resources, personnel)

* an indication as to whether the job-holder works mainly on his or her own, is part of a fixed team, or is expected to move through various teams according to task needs

* a list of major tasks and priorities

- brief details of any difficulties commonly experienced in the job which need attention in training.

Producing a job training specification

For every task of the job, divided as necessary into sub-tasks or elements, the job training specification should show the skill, knowledge and (if relevant) attitudes required; the standards of performance to be reached; and how performance will be measured. The way the specification is laid out and the kind of information it contains will depend on the analytical techniques used. However, the specification is a guide to action (because it leads to the design of a training programme) and must therefore have a simple, easily understood format and be clearly expressed.

Key task analysis

This approach takes only the crucial tasks within a job – ie those tasks in which performance of a certain kind is critical to competency in the job overall. Comprehensive analysis is used most commonly for jobs consisting of simple, usually manual, repetitive and unchanging tasks. On the other hand those jobs involving more complex skills such as observation and reflection, analysis, creativity, decision-making and problem-solving, and evaluation need a clear overview of the job, together with a focus on what is most essential for successful performance. For such jobs the key task approach is often the most appropriate.

Once again, a brief job description needs to be produced in exactly the same format as in comprehensive analysis. However, the job training specification must this time be selective, covering only those tasks crucial to competent job performance.

Key task analysis is appropriate for any type of job where the following conditions apply:

- *Tasks are varied, and not all are critical.* The job should consist of a large number of different tasks, not all of which are critical for competent performance. It is assumed that the job-holder requires training only in those tasks that are crucial (key) to effective performance in the job.

- *Changes are likely.* The job is changing in emphasis or in content, so that priority tasks, standards and identification of skills and knowledge may have to be identified and analysed regularly.

Problem-centred analysis

This approach focuses on defining problem/s that require a training solution. The analysis seems to identify the nature and causes of each problem and the skills, knowledge, and attitudes (if relevant) needed to cope successfully with it. The analytical process actively involves job-holders in considering what kind of training they would find most effective.

Warr and Bird (1968) did pioneering work on this approach with their 'training by exception' technique, developed when their attempts to use, first, comprehensive and then key task analysis to identify supervisory training needs failed because of the diversity of supervisory tasks and the amount of time needed to analyse them contrasted with the usefulness of the information obtained.

The problem-centred approach is most appropriately used when:

- training is urgent, but analytical resources limited

- the job-holder's work is satisfactory except in one or two 'problem' areas

- involvement of learners in analysis is important.

It is a relevant approach to use in conjunction with key task analysis when designing training for people new to jobs for which they already have most of the skills and knowledge required, but where they must get to grips quickly with any problematic areas. The two approaches also work well together when it is important to ensure that the job-holders have a clear understanding of key tasks and difficulties commonly associated with them.

With the problem-centred approach there is no one way of gathering and collating the information. Whichever methods are used must ensure that the perspectives on the problems of job-holder/s, their supervisors, managers and any other key parties are obtained. This approach does not involve drawing up a job description or a job training specification because its outcome is simply a description of the problems and how they can be tackled in training. Problem-centred analysis will reveal:

- *common training needs*. Needs will emerge that are common to all or most of the group. These can form the basis of a core training programme or other kind of learning event.

- *individualised training needs*. There will also be needs specific to individuals that will have to be met using personal learning plans.

- *training/learning strategies suggested by job-holders*. These will be the learning approaches and methods that job-holders are confident will best help them to overcome identified problems.

- *learners' commitment*. Because of the methodology it involves, the approach is likely to obtain the commitment of those who will be participants in the ensuing planned learning events. They have to take a leading role in the diagnosis and analysis of their problems and needs and in suggesting training solutions, and so the objectives and relevance of the learning events do not need to be explained to them. From the start of the analytical process they begin to 'own' those events, and the drive to learn is a natural outcome.

Competency-based analysis

This approach involves identifying what is needed to produce effective performance in a role, job or function. Like the problem-centred approach, it is both job- and person-related, and tends to be used in an organisation when:

- *there is a need to develop clearly defined standards of performance relating to one or more occupational groups*. This is usually because lack of such standards is impeding attempts to measure and improve performance and to establish clear guidelines for selection, training, development, rewards, and succession and career-planning.

and/or when

• *there is a need to relate training within the organisation to national vocational training standards and qualifications.* Competencies identified in a particular organisation as necessary to performance of jobs at different levels can be related to lists of competencies required at each of four or five levels in order to achieve National Vocational Qualifications (NVQs) across different occupations (see Chapter 5). Appropriate schemes of training, development and assessment in the workplace can then enable individuals to acquire NVQs at the necessary level.

and/or when

• *the main concern is to identify the core behavioural attributes needed in order to perform effectively across a job sector (usually, but not necessarily, management) and the extent to which those attributes are, or are not, possessed by all job-holders in that sector.*

Woodruffe (1991) observed that the word 'competency' carries two different meanings:

• Used in a job-related sense, it refers to areas of work at which a person is competent. Here, he recommended use of an alternative term: *areas of competence.*

• Used in a person-related sense, it refers to dimensions of behaviour that lie behind competent performance. Here, he recommended use of the term *competency.*

We have already outlined the concept and practical applicability of a competency framework (Chapter 9, page 151 and Chapter 13, pages 233, 245). Here, we can recall that many organisations now base training and development programmes on definitions of 'competencies' relating to a particular group or sector in the organisation. An illuminating discussion of the competency route and its organisational and political implications is contained in Weightman (1994), and a useful assessment of pros and cons can be found by reading the three articles by Martin (1995), Healy (1995) and Sparrow (1996).

Competency-based analysis results in the production of:

• a statement of the role or purpose of the general category of job being studied (ie managerial jobs, or managerial jobs at a particular level) in the organisation

---

Job training analysis

Outline four job training analysis approaches and identify the kinds of situation most appropriate for the use of each. Then take one type of job in your organisation where a different approach to job training analysis would lead to more effective training; explain why.

- a breakdown of that role into its discrete areas of competence

- statements of the competencies needed to perform satisfactorily in each of those areas

- criteria for measuring competency in each area.

In this section we have looked at four job training analysis approaches: comprehensive, key task, problem-centred, and competency-based analysis. Now let us examine some of the techniques with which they are associated.

JOB TRAINING ANALYSIS TECHNIQUES

Again, this section simply outlines a range of techniques described in more detail in specialist texts such as those mentioned below. Widely known techniques that need no repetition here include:

- activity analysis (Miller, 1962)

- manual skills analysis (Seymour, 1966 and Gentles, 1969). This is one of the best known techniques. However, it is very time-consuming and requires a high degree of specialist skill. The obvious danger with such a costly technique is that one change to an operating method may well lead to the whole analytical process having to be repeated

- critical incidents analysis (Flanagan, 1954)

- faults analysis, and stages and key points analysis (Reid and Barrington, 1997).

There are three sets of techniques that, because they are particularly valuable in relation to complex jobs/roles, will be discussed at this point. They are those involved in role analysis, interpersonal and interactive skills analysis, and competency-based analysis.

Role analysis
In managerial jobs especially, it is vital to be clear about the role, or roles, that the job holder must carry. As was demonstrated at the start of Chapter 9, training for anyone who is moving into a training manager's job will benefit from being based on role analysis, because of the importance of role issues in training management.

The technique involved derives from the behavioural sciences, notably from the work of the industrial psychologist Macgregor (1960), who emphasised how important it was to build up a shared perception of the manager's role among members of that manager's role set. French and Bell (1978) summarised the various procedures to be carried out. Basically they require job-holder, manager and (usually) one or more other members of the role set (ie those people with whom the role-holder regularly interacts) each to produce a list of the duties and behaviour that they perceive necessary if the job-holder is to be effective. A role description is then produced from joint discussion of the different lists. It contains the key features of the job.

Machin (1981) showed how an 'Expectations' approach can highlight any disagreements within the role set about the role being analysed and how it is designed to generate open discussion in order to produce full understanding of the role, the resolution of most disagreement and a job description which has the assent of the parties. If, despite this, conflicting perceptions and expectations remain, then the analyst must bring these to the attention of management. If the conflict is not tackled it will impede job performance, create wider organisational problems and produce situations for which training is not an effective remedy.

Interpersonal and interactive skills analysis

A wide range of jobs, especially supervisory, managerial, professional and technical, make heavy demands on the job-holder in terms of their requirements for skill in dealing with face-to-face situations and in achieving the effective interaction of people and tasks in a work cycle. Such skills are difficult to analyse, but there are a number of well-established techniques available. These include Rackham, Honey and Colbert's (1971) techniques for analysing interactive skills; transactional analysis, described fully by Carby and Thakur (1977); and diagnostic techniques and instruments related to developing leadership and teamwork skills produced by researchers and trainers like Belbin (1981), Leigh and Maynard (1996), and Wright and Taylor (1994).

Competency-based analysis

There are many techniques that can be used here, including behavioural event interviewing (Boyatzis, 1982), a complex technique for which special training is required. To give a flavour of what is involved in this kind of analysis, let us carry out a task based on analysing two case-studies. They are repeated from my 1992 text and, in the sense of management development's having moved on since then in both organisations, they are out of date. However, both remain valid when used to illustrate in a quite striking way two different approaches to competency-based analysis.

Competency-based management development

What strategy lay behind the use by BP and Manchester Airport plc of a competency-based approach to management development? What is the main difference between the approaches they used?

British Petroleum (Source: *Greatrex and Phillips, 1989*)

In the late 1980s BP carried out much work on management competencies in order to ensure effective management performance, and training and development to cope with the major changes that were then taking place in the company. Because of new directions in its business strategy, its culture had to become more market-oriented and client-centred, and its managers had to be more entrepreneurial in their approach to the business. There was also a need for a less hierarchical management structure, devolved accountability, and a more open and flexible management style throughout BP.

There was a concern to avoid reliance on any universal list of competencies. Instead, analysis was organisation-specific, identifying those competences needed in order to manage effectively in the BP environment.

By 1989 a rigorous process of analysis had produced a list of 11 core areas of competency, grouped into four clusters of behaviours that differentiated high-performers from the rest. BP had always placed a high value on assessment centres as a way of diagnosing training and development needs and highlighting potential. It now incorporated competency assessment into its assessment boards, and individual managers were assessed and ranked in relation to the 11 competency areas using a five-point behaviourally defined scale to identify the extent to which they possessed each individual attribute. From this process of analysis and diagnosis, development programmes for individuals were in due course drawn up.

BP derived its competencies from its vision and values and then used them in many of its personnel initiatives and in its culture change. The approach proved particularly valuable as an aid for training, personal and career development, and for the self-development of managers.

Manchester Airport plc (Source: *Jackson, 1989*)

A competency-based approach to management development was also used by Manchester Airport in the late 1980s in order to achieve a systematic approach to the selection, training and development of senior managers at a time of fast growth and major changes when the Airport had just (1986) become a public limited company (plc).

The first stage in the design of a programme was to develop a template for superior performance at senior management level. In 1988 the directors met to agree the attributes that the company expected from its managers at this level. They were based on 15 of the defined (US) McBer list of managerial competencies, which have been found quite widely to predict success in performing managerial jobs. The role of the group had to be examined, since it was clear that in assessing what was needed for future performance reliance could not be placed on past types of competency.

The profile that emerged identified clusters of behaviours associated with the three core competencies needed by all senior managers at Manchester Airport plc, whatever their specific jobs:

- *understanding what needs to be done* – critical reasoning; strategic visioning; business know-how

- *getting the job done* – achievement drive; proactivity; confidence; control; flexibility; concern for effectiveness; direction

- *taking people with you* – motivation; interpersonal skills; concern for impact; persuasion; influence.

This profile was checked against job analysis information already in existence at the airport to ensure its validity. It was also agreed that the new criteria for successful performance of the job would be used for subsequent selection and promotion decisions within the group. Performance review and reward decisions would be based on the criteria agreed as underpinning superior performance (Jackson, 1989: 4).

All managers then had to go through a two-day assessment centre; they were assessed by the directors (who had received special training) and the consultants, who had helped internal personnel staff design the whole project. Each manager was rated against every attribute. Attributes associated with core competencies were defined in behavioural terms at four levels, from 'Low' to 'Outstanding'. Thus, for example:

Attribute involved in 'Getting the job done': Direction.

Definition: being able to tell others what they must do and confront performance problems; to plan, organise, schedule, delegate and follow up.

Low: unable to confront others about performance problems, to enforce rules, or to insist that subordinates comply with directives. No experience or is unwilling to delegate to subordinates the responsibility for doing anything other than less significant tasks.

Outstanding: confronts staff when they fail to meet standards. Has contingency plans for all objectives. Sets demanding objectives for staff. Demonstrates the ability to organise large numbers of people.

After the assessment process individual profiles were drawn up, summarising the assessed level for each competence. Written reports were produced, and each manager had feedback sessions first with a consultant, then with personnel and top management staff. Personal Improvement Plans were produced by each individual and were incorporated in annual targets for the forthcoming year.

Jackson detailed the positive results of the project, and concluded that the model for superior performance was confirmed by the evidence.

Feedback notes
• In both examples the strategy was the same: to define the core competencies needed by all managers in the specific organisational context in which they have to operate (whether or not they break them down into different levels within the management sector, as was done at Manchester Airport); and to use those competencies both as criteria for assessment of individuals in order to define training and development needs and as aids to improving work performance.

• The difference lies in the ways competencies were identified. At BP, analysis of the performance of the company's managers led to identification of clusters of attributes associated with the core competencies perceived to underpin effective work performance. Analysis thus started with examining prevailing patterns of behaviour and led ultimately to the identification of core competencies needed by all BP managers.

• We are not told here what technique was used to identify core competencies, but it could well have been Boyatzis' (1982) Behavioural Event Interviewing. This technique involves taking a range of job-holders currently working in the organisation. Usually they are chosen by senior managers, although sometimes the views of peers and subordinates may also inform that choice. The aim is to select a mix of those agreed to be excellent in their performance and those who are rated as adequate but no more than that.

• The next stage is to interview the job-holders, using interviewers specially trained for this purpose who have no knowledge of the performance ratings of the job-holders. Each individual is asked to describe a number of events in which they played a key part, and is then probed to establish exactly what he or she did in each event; why; the thought processes that shaped behaviour at the time; and the outcome of the event.

• There is then a complex and lengthy process of analysing the data from these interviews, with a number of cross-checks used to ensure uniformity of standards and techniques and objectivity of analysis. The analysis leads to the production of a 'competency profile' of each individual which is then compared with previously obtained rankings of their job performance (see above). In this way, the characteristics and behaviour patterns unique to those who are high-achievers emerge, and core competences required for excellent performance can thus be identified and described in appropriate behavioural terms.

• A similar process, but aimed at identifying the characteristics of effective (rather than, or as well as, excellent) performance, can be devised by widening the sample group to include some who are generally agreed to be less than satisfactory in their job performance.

• At Manchester, that BP process was reversed. Core competences were defined first, using a universal model (McBer's). They were then checked against definitions of management jobs in the company and felt to be valid. Next, analysis was carried out to define the clusters of attributes needed to reach a satisfactory standard in each of those core competences. Finally, individuals were assessed to find how much or little of each attribute they possessed, and development plans were produced after discussing and agreeing with managers that these were indeed attributes they recognised as necessary to effective performance in their jobs. Checks were made to ensure that the universal model had been used in a way that fully met the particular needs of the airport's senior managers.

Performance analysis
Analysing a job-holder's performance can be classed as a technique in the sense that it should reveal any problems being experienced or likely to be experienced in reaching required performance standards; typical faults encountered in the work and how to deal with them; and other valuable information.

Where performance analysis is not an intrinsic part of an analytical technique it should always be carried out in addition. There has already been discussion about how to tackle the analysis of performance in Chapter 13. More detailed discussion can be found in the usual specialist texts.

PRODUCING A TRAINING PROPOSAL

In this chapter we have so far surveyed four approaches to job training analysis and a variety of analytical techniques that can be used singly or in various combinations, given the particular job training analysis approach chosen and the situation to which it is to be applied. Now it is important to understand how to incorporate key information from analysis into a training proposal for submission to management.

As was noted at the start of the chapter, a key outcome of job training analysis is usually a job training specification with the following components:

- a description in overall terms of the job for which training is to be given, or the key problem areas in a job which training will enable learners to tackle

- a specification and prioritisation of the kinds and levels of knowledge, skill and, where relevant, attitudes needed for effective performance

- a statement of the standards that will operate in the job and the criteria for measuring achievement of standards.

Job training specifications supply crucial information needed in order to produce a training proposal for a planned training programme. In Chapters 15 to 17 we shall be examining in detail how to plan, design and deliver learning events. At this point it is relevant simply to note that in addition to a job training specification, the following information will be relevant to training design and must be considered when drawing up a training proposal:

Previous programmes
Have programmes been run for this job before? If so, are there any evaluations, formal or informal?

Job changes
Have there been any changes in the job – its purpose, key tasks etc – since the job training specification and personnel specification (if any) were drawn up? If so, do those changes have training or development implications?

Training standards to be attained and type of learners
What type of learners will be involved in this training event, and what are the standards to be achieved? For example, if this is to be a basic skills training course for new recruits, then will it need to take those new recruits up to an above-average or only to an essential level of performance?

A good personnel specification should list qualities/competencies needed to perform a job at two levels, not one: 'desirable' and 'essential'. This will enable differentiation at selection stage between applicants likely to perform the job to a high standard immediately, and those likely to be able to perform to only an adequate level. The basic skills training course must take those different performance levels of new recruits into account.

Timing of the training programme
When and for how long is the event to run? How does its timing relate to work schedules of the departments concerned, and to the time-scale for achieving the performance goals with which the event is concerned?

All of this information must be available as basic reference material when producing training and development proposals for submission to senior management and any other parties whose approval is needed for a planned learning event. A proposal should be as brief as possible (see an example in Gilley and Eggland, 1989: 211–12), expressed in language to which its audience can readily relate. A proposal should cover the following:

- *the aim of the training/development event* – why it is needed, what it will cost, the outcomes it should achieve, and their value to the organisation

- *the learners*, by reference to number, types and levels of jobs in the information, and any other relevant information

- *its time-scale, and how it will be monitored and evaluated*

- *a brief outline of the training/development* proposed, showing design, main content areas, learning strategy, and key personnel who will be involved in its delivery

- *any training of those personnel that may be needed* (for example, any competency assessment for NVQ purposes to be done will require expertise for which training will be essential).

Here is an exercise that requires you to integrate learning and knowledge from both this and the previous chapter in order to feel confident you understand the first stage of our eight-stage approach to the planning and delivery of learning events. In the next chapter we shall move on to stages two and three.

Producing a training and development proposal

Using the six headings just noted, produce a training and development proposal for a learning event that will meet needs related to a job in your own organisation or one with which you are familiar. The job should be one for which either a job training specification is available, or for which you yourself, as part of this activity, can produce one.

CONCLUSION

In order to achieve the learning objectives of this chapter, an eight-stage approach to the inception, design and delivery of a learning event has been introduced. It will be completed in the next two chapters.

In the context of the first stage, a six-step strategy for carrying out job training analysis has been explained and illustrated. Four methods of carrying out job training analysis have been discussed, and eight types of widely used analytical techniques identified. Three of these have been covered in some detail: role analysis, interpersonal and interactive skills analysis, and competency-based analysis. A summary of approaches to performance analysis has also been provided. Guidelines have been established for the production of a job training specification and a training proposal.

USEFUL READING

ALBAN METCALF, B.M. *and* WRIGHT, P.L. (1986) 'Social skills training for managers', in C. HOLLIN *and* P. THROWER (eds), *Handbook of Social Skills Training, Vol. 1: Applications across the lifespan*. London, Pergamon.

BOYDELL, T. *and* LEARY, M. (1996) *Identifying Training Needs*. London, Institute of Personnel and Development.

COOPER, C.L. (ed.) (1981) *Improving Interpersonal Relations: Some approaches to interpersonal skills training*. Aldershot, Gower.

HACKETT, P. (1997) *Introduction to Training*. London, Institute of Personnel and Development.

MILLS, G.E., WAYNE PACE, R., *and* PETERSON, B.D. (1988) *Analysis in Human Resource Training and Organization Development*. Wokingham, Addison Wesley.

REID, M.A. *and* BARRINGTON, H. (1997) *Training Interventions: Managing employee development*. 5th ed. London, Institute of Personnel and Development.

THOMAS, K. *and* MELLON, T. (1995) *Planning for Training and Development: A guide to analysing needs*. London, Save the Children. (Aims to assist those working in the voluntary sector responsible for identifying training needs, establishing development plans and budgets, and evaluating programmes.)

15 Purpose, objectives and strategy for learning events

LEARNING OBJECTIVES

After reading this chapter you will:

• understand the importance of clear and appropriate overall purpose and objectives for a learning event

• know how to produce a profile of a learning population and relate this to a choice of learning strategies

• understand the practical issues affecting the choice of learning strategies

• be able to draw up an overall purpose, behavioural objectives and strategy for a learning event.

THE EIGHT-STAGE APPROACH TO PLANNING AND DELIVERING LEARNING EVENTS (CONT.)

Let us look again (Table 12) at the eight-stage approach introduced in Chapter 14. We shall summarise the first stage and then examine stages two to four.

As we have already seen, learning needs can in the first stage be identified in a number of ways, relating both to a current situation and to future contingencies. Once needs have been agreed and prioritised, there must be confirmation that some form of learning event is required to meet those needs. The next stage is to clarify the purpose and overall objectives of learning.

Table 12 **Eight stages in the inception, design and delivery of planned learning events**

1	Identify/confirm needs.
2	Agree on the overall purpose and objectives for the learning event.
3	Identify the profile of the intended learning population.
4	Select strategy, and agree on direction and management of the learning event.
5	Select learners and produce detailed specification for the learning event.
6	Confirm strategy and design event.
7	Deliver event.
8	Monitor and evaluate event.

STAGE TWO: ESTABLISHING OVERALL PURPOSE AND OBJECTIVES

It is essential to define the overall purpose and objectives of a planned learning event clearly, since these provide the context of the event. If there are errors at this stage, expensive resources are going to be wasted in carrying out irrelevant activities. To summarise:

> The overall purpose of a learning event answers the question *why* the event is taking place, whereas its objectives define *what* attitudinal, behavioural or performance outcomes are to be achieved.

The interrelationship between purpose and objectives

Ideally, the designer of the learning event should have been involved in formulating the learning objectives, in line with an overall purpose that has already been agreed with a 'client' in the organisation. In reality, the designer may have to work to objectives that have already been established by someone else. This can pose many problems if, even when it seems clear that objectives should be changed or modified in some way, such change seems impossible. Here is a case-study based on a real-life situation. Certain specifics have been changed in order to ensure the anonymity of the institution which, needless to say, is not my own!

Case-study: 'X' University and the course review

The business school of X University had just gone through the external teaching review process, and one of its programmes – a two-year part-time post-experience management course – had been singled out for critical comment. The programme has been running for many years, but in the last five has undergone a significant change of emphasis. Key points made were:

1 The programme had in the past carried a clear educational purpose which had been reflected in its formalised and theoretically focused methods of assessment. Five years ago, however, the business school decided that, in order to reflect national trends, there had to be a change in focus to the development of managerial competencies (although it decided not to deliver a competency-based programme tied to national occupational standards – the focus was on competencies in the more generalised sense).

2 Consistent with this overall purpose, the learning objectives had become skills-oriented. However, the dominating method of assessment remained the formal examination. All subjects were assessed in that way, and the format of each paper remained what it had long been: a three-hour, closed-book paper, with a choice of four out of ten or twelve questions.

3 Students who did well in the examinations, and in the programme overall, were consistently those with a proven record of high academic attainment, whether accompanied by practical competence or not. Those without such a record, however competent they were known to

be in the workplace and however well they did in the practical activities and assignments on the course, achieved notably less well. Such students in fact made up the bulk of those who failed the programme - usually about 15 per cent.

4 The skills-oriented objectives of the programme called for a resource level that the course leader, struggling with the large classes that she was obliged to recruit and with inadequate staffing ratios, could rarely obtain. Access to film, closed-circuit television, video, computers and library facilities was difficult because of the heavy demand on those resources made by other programmes. Technical support was also patchy and unreliable.

5 Students recruited onto the programme were very heterogeneous in their skills and knowledge related to the course content. This was unsurprising in such a large part-time programme, where the selection process was not very discriminating. They also entered the programme with widely varying levels and types of learning skills and styles. Several had no ongoing experience of one or more of the core modules, and practical activities during class time provided the only medium through which they could be helped to 'acquire' such experience. Visits to external organisations were rare because of the large numbers of students and timetabling problems. Good outside speakers were highly valued, but those charging fees were little used because of their cost; the performance of voluntary speakers, on the other hand, was variable.

The review concluded that the examination failure rate was understandable in the circumstances but unacceptable, and noted the declining rate of recruitment onto the course, coupled with decline in the quality of recruits. The business school was advised to reconsider the overall purpose of the programme, its learning objectives and its assessment methods; and to revise the cost and activity base of the programme in order to generate more resources if it could find no other way to resolve its resource problems.

The business school responded to the review by confirming the purpose and most of the overall objectives of the course, and by altering the structure and methods of assessment accordingly. A new emphasis was placed on assessing competencies at final as well as interim stages mainly through the vehicle of work-based projects. Resourcing, however, remained a taxing problem not only in relation to this programme but more generally in the business school and the university.

In this case-study, note the influence exercised by the overall purpose and the learning objectives of the management programme. Discrepancies there started off a chain of difficulties which led, in the end, to unsatisfactory outcomes of the whole complex learning event. If, five years ago, the course leader and her colleagues had looked more critically at the educational and practical implications of running the kind of revised programme the business school wanted them to deliver – in other words, if at the start of the change process they had queried the programme's overall purpose and objectives – then some at least of the problems would have been avoided and the resource issue would have been highlighted at a time when it could have been properly considered.

Note, too, how little is said in the study about contextual factors that would, in real life, be important to examine in order to decide whether or not the programme itself should be continued. Perhaps it has outlived its purpose, and consideration needs to be given to other ways of improving the business school's ability to achieve its business goals. What is the nature of those goals, and the business and human resource (HR) strategies to achieve them? What role does the school play in the wider university? What is the position of the university itself in what will undoubtedly have become a dynamic competitive environment?

We can conclude our examination of this case-study by stating that:

> The designer of the learning event should always challenge its purpose or overall objectives if they seem inappropriate in some important way, given the nature of the event, its planned outcomes, the context in which it must operate and the place it occupies in the organisation's overall employee development programme.

Levels of objectives

Except in very simple learning situations, it is helpful to formulate learning objectives at two levels: final and intermediate.

Final behavioural objectives

Sometimes known as 'ultimate' or 'criterion' or 'overall' objectives, these, however they are titled, explain the kind of outcomes that the learner should have achieved once the learning event is completed.

Intermediate behavioural objectives

Sometimes known as 'interim' or 'specific' objectives, these, however they are titled, explain the kind of outcomes that the learner should have achieved at key stages of the learning process.

You may have noted the use of the phrase 'behavioural objectives' in the above definitions; also the reference to 'outcomes'. This is because the clearest guide to design can be obtained not so much by stating what the learning event aims to do in general terms but in closely specifying what the learner should be capable of by the end of parts or the whole of the event.

To illustrate this point, consider the difference between two ways of defining one of the objectives of this chapter:

> *Example 1*
>
> One of the aims of this chapter is to explain the term 'learning objectives'.
>
> *Example 2*
>
> After reading this chapter and completing the various checks it contains, you should be able to understand what is meant by 'learning objectives' in order to be able to draw up objectives related to a learning event.

From the reader's point of view, Example 1 says what the chapter aims to do, but only in a very generalised way, with no explanation of intended outcomes. On the other hand, Example 2 gives concise information on 'what'. It should therefore act as a stimulus to readers by explaining what they will be able to do by the end of the chapter (provided, of course, that the learning outcome is something they want to achieve).

From my own point of view, if I had been given the kind of generalised brief set out in Example 1 it would have been hard to decide what to put into the chapter. However, with Example 2 it is clear that providing a simple explanation of 'learning objectives' will not be enough. I realise that I shall have to help the reader to understand the meaning of the term 'learning objectives', and then to make practical use of the concept. So I shall have to build in a variety of practical illustrations (like this one), exercises, and review activities, as well as theory.

Expressing objectives in behavioural terms identifies not only what the learning event aims to do, but what sort of skills, knowledge or attitudes the learner should acquire and the kind of content and methods of learning that will be appropriate. Objectives should also indicate the conditions in which learners will ultimately carry out the learning, and the standards they will need to reach

We can therefore conclude this section on the purpose and objectives of a planned learning event by stating that:

> Behavioural objectives give a clear focus to the learning event and to its design by explaining the outcomes they will help the learners to achieve. The most helpful objectives are those that describe not only the kinds of behaviour to be achieved at the end of the learning event but also the conditions under which that behaviour is expected to occur and the standards to be reached in that behaviour.

STAGE THREE: IDENTIFYING THE PROFILE OF THE LEARNERS

Once needs, overall purpose and ultimate objectives of the learning event have been agreed, the type of learners to be involved should be identified. At this stage, little may be known about individuals – selection for the learning event will probably come at a later stage. What will be known is the sort of numbers likely to be involved, the levels of the organisation from which they will be drawn (some, of course, may come from outside the organisation, perhaps from suppliers or purchasers) and the kinds of learning strategies likely to be most relevant for them.

Information should at this stage be sought on four aspects of the learning population. Subsequently, when individuals have been selected for the learning event, this information will need to be expanded and the design of the event adjusted as necessary:

- numbers and location
- jobs and competencies
- learning styles and skills
- attitudes and motivation

Numbers and location of learners

Small numbers should enable quite individualised learning. However, the location of the learners will be important: a small number spread over different, and widely dispersed, physical locations indicates at first sight a need for some form of distance learning, with occasional workshops to bring the group together (see, for example, the sales training programme proposed by Hugman in Harrison, 1992). On the other hand, it may be important that, although widely dispersed in a physical sense, these learners form a cohesive group and establish a strong team identity through the vehicle of the learning event. That suggests a different approach to learning design. If it is a small group from a single workplace, the best strategy may be to arrange the event around their work location, or in proximity to it. Alternatively, it may be desirable to take them away from the work environment and focus their attention on wider issues. That could argue for one or more external residential events.

Numbers and location of the learners must, therefore, be viewed in the context of the purpose and objectives of the learning event in order to help decide on an appropriate learning strategy.

Jobs and competencies of the learners

At this early stage, it is important to acquire as much information as possible on the kind of jobs held by the learners and their general level of competence in them. Once individual learners have been selected, a more detailed analysis will need to be carried out.

Learning styles and skills

We have already looked at learning styles in Chapter 13. We noted Honey and Mumford's (1992) four-fold categorisation system, but it should be remembered that people can usually develop learning skills in more than one mode, and that some learners can move easily between the four modes, able to learn equally well in any of them.

While little may be known at this stage about specific individuals, none the less the type of jobs held by the proposed learning population, together with their overall age and ability range, their length and type of experience, and other similar information will give useful insights into the type of learning styles and skills they may possess. This information will indicate those learning situations and methods most likely to promote stimulating and effective learning for them.

In selecting a learning strategy – and later in designing the detail of learning events – it is important to consider not only how the event can build on the learners' primary learning styles and learning skills, but also to what extent the event should itself seek to change those styles and skills. Honey and Mumford's work, for example, has indicated that trainers as a profession tend to be activists rather than reflectors or theorists. If this is the case (and getting a particular learning group to complete the LSI questionnaire and send it to the designer some time before the learning event begins should give some helpful indicators), then any event seeking to train trainers should aim to redress that imbalance by involving learning experiences that promote styles and skills in all four modes, rather than simply encourage continued dependence on and preference for only the activist approach to learning.

When a learning event calls for learning styles and skills of quite a high order, and the type of learners envisaged are unlikely to have reached the required level, then a 'study skills' input can serve a useful purpose before the main event begins. Useful too are 'access' or 'foundation' courses which introduce the main topics at a lower level than will be experienced in the main learning event, thus building a grounding of skills that will make entry to that event easier and progress more effective.

Attitudes and motivation
Even at this early stage enough will probably be known about key behavioural aspects of the intended learning population (rates of absenteeism and turnover, performance levels, reactions to earlier learning events and any conflict patterns) to assess their likely motivation related to proposed learning events being organised for them. Little useful learning can occur if the individual does not want to learn, so it is important to assess the probable needs and expectations learners will bring to the learning event and to take these consciously into account when choosing an overall learning strategy.

Motivation can be considered under two headings (Gagne, 1977): social motivation and motivation related to task mastery.

Social motivation
This relates to the social situation in which the learners are placed: their social needs, characteristics, problems and types of relationship with each other and with the training staff. All these factors will affect their motivation during the learning event. Take as an example the design of a course in a new and difficult area of skills for a group of people who may come from different departments, levels or even organisations. If they are brought together into a cohesive group from the start, sharing expectations and concerns, this will help to build up an atmosphere of social supportiveness that will stand them in good stead as they try to master the various learning tasks.

Many organisations, including educational institutions, hold outdoor development periods towards the start of training or educational programmes. The aim is to bind participants into a close-knit group, motivated to tackle a long-term learning experience as a team rather than as a heterogeneous collection of individuals; and to develop appropriate learning styles and skills. Outdoor development periods can also be used at key stages during a long learning event as a way of consolidating and progressing learning in major areas. In a sense they can act as strategic milestones in an extended developmental programme.

Another approach, often used in conjunction with outdoor development work, is to help individuals to develop personal learning goals and plans that relate to the learning event as well as to outcomes that they value at a personal level. Skilfully done, such an exercise improves the individual's motivation to learn because relevance of the learning to their needs is clearly established.

Motivation related to task mastery

Here the issue is raised of what drives different learners to succeed. Some may seem spurred on by a need to 'win', achieving most in a competitive learning situation; others may be stimulated by any opportunity to learn something new – a 'curiosity' motive. While classifying learners in such ways may prove to have considerable practical value in some design situations (see, for example, Otto and Glaser, 1972) generalised assumptions must be avoided. As we saw in Chapter 13 (pages 231–2) performance is the final outcome of a complex interaction between needs, results, rewards and 'E' factors. Design of any learning event must pay careful attention to that concept of the motivation calculus.

In Chapter 16, where there is another look at motivation at the more individualised level, you will find a practical check-list to help the designer and trainer in the task of achieving and sustaining learner motivation, and of stimulating learners to master their tasks.

When selecting a learning strategy, three points about motivation should be considered. Depending on their relevance to the particular case there may have to be considerable flexibility built into the learning system, so that adjustments to planned content, delivery and focus of certain components can be made just before, or even during, the learning event.

• *unpredictability*. Motivation will vary, often significantly, from one group of learners to the next, even with types of learning events that have often been run before.

• *individual differences*. There can be significant individual differences in motivation and expectations within a group of learners.

• *dynamism*. Motivation is dynamic, often changing during the course of a learning event.

There must be careful monitoring of learning events. Time must be spent before, at the start of, during and at the end of key events in diagnosing the needs and expectations of the learners and in responding to them. This requires close collaboration between designer and trainer (if the two processes are carried out by different parties) from the outset and during monitoring stages so that any motivational problems that do arise can be carefully analysed, and the style, pace or content of the learning event adjusted accordingly.

Let us end this section by tackling a real-life consultancy assignment (although minor details have been changed to ensure anonymity of the client organisation). The main purpose of this task is to reinforce the learning we have covered in this section. However, because the assignment itself is about appraisal, you should read Chapter 13 again before starting, and refer to its contents to help you in the exercise.

The retail store's appraisal project: Part 1

You are a management consultant, and you have just been invited to visit the local branch of a national retail store in order to discuss the possibility of carrying out training in appraisal skills for about 15 managers and supervisors. The work is to be done in the next two months.

You arrive at 9.00 am and are met by the personnel officer (PO), an IPD-qualified woman of about 55, well liked by employees, and a long-serving member of the store. She tells you that the managing director (MD) with whom you are both going to spend the morning is new to the job, having been appointed six months ago from a senior management position in another chain of stores. He is 38, a high-flier with an impressive record of success behind him. He is already establishing himself as a man of action: open, committed to increasing the store's turnover and full of ideas about how that can be done. Once he makes a decision he puts it into practice at once. He needs to make a major impact on the store, with results in 18 months at the latest.

Throughout the subsequent discussion the PO says very little, since the aim of that discussion is for the MD and yourself to analyse the proposed assignment and arrive at some shared conclusions.

You start off by asking the MD to explain what the assignment is about. He replies that he wants you to 'train all the managers and supervisors (about 15) in appraisal so that I can find out what their performance really is, get a few standardised disciplinary procedures sorted out, diagnose training and development needs, assess potential, and get the managers working together as a team'. He wants the training done within the next two months.

He explains that the store, a long-established one, is profitable but that its turnover has declined in the last five years, and competition is increasingly severe. It has had a paternalistic role culture for some years, which has stifled the drive and initiative of its managers and supervisors, most of them long-serving employees in their forties and fifties. A few have become complacent because profits (due to cost increases and customer loyalty) are still good.

At the time the new MD arrived there were some redundancies (approved although not initiated by him) at all levels of the store, and a makeshift appraisal scheme was used to determine who should go. This caused quite a lot of trouble and has led to a belief in some quarters that the MD himself is a hatchet-man, with a list of those he intends to get rid of in the next year or so. This is, in fact, a mistaken belief. The MD is genuinely determined to build up a high-calibre, committed and enthusiastic team of people who will regain the store's hold on the market. He has already reduced the management hierarchy from five to three levels and, having given early retirement on advantageous terms to three directors, has reorganised their jobs and brought in two new directors in their early thirties who work closely with him, and are fully committed to his way of doing things. His style is open and positive. He sets high standards and rewards those who achieve, while seeking to understand reasons for poor performance before passing any judgements. His views on appraisal can be summed up in the phrase: 'I may not know much about the detail of appraisal, but I know what I want it to achieve for me.'

He says that he wants to start off with closed appraisals, because he thinks anything else at this stage would be 'too threatening'. By closed appraisals he means that each appraiser should produce a written report on his or her staff. Those reports may or may not be followed up by an appraisal discussion with the staff concerned, but in any event, staff will not be able to see them. The reports will then 'be pushed through the system', to enable him to see what sort of skills and potential exist in his workforce and what kind of performance is being achieved, as well as examining needs for training and development. The MD adds that he does not want a complicated ranking system on the reports, just something simple and understandable.

The MD wants to be involved in the training. He himself is appraised by the chief executive of the chain of stores, and appraises his two directors. He intends the appraisal system to stop at supervisory level, with supervisors appraised but not, at this stage, appraising levels below them.

You have broken off the discussion for lunch, and are due to resume in a couple of hours time. What issues will you then raise with the MD, and what will you try to achieve during your discussion with him, in order to reach agreement on the task that you will help the organisation to carry out?

Feedback notes

The initial discussion between the consultant (myself), the MD and, later on, the PO took in reality almost a day. However, at the end of that time the crucial issues had been straightened out, leaving the way clear for agreed action to take place. Obviously you will have all sorts of ideas about how to tackle the discussion, and all I can usefully do, therefore, is to tell you the major issues that any similar discussion needs to confront, and how they were actually dealt with in this case.

The overall purpose of the learning

The first issue to clarify is the true reasons for the consultancy assignment. At present there is no clear overall purpose, and there is also an inconsistency in objectives. Many questions relating to the initial need for training must therefore be asked. There is also a confusion in terms: the MD refers at one point to 'appraisal' and at another to 'assessment' as if they are the same activity, whereas to the consultant they are quite different activities, the former related to examining current work performance, the latter to diagnosis of potential. Terms must be defined at the outset and a common language developed if any lasting agreement is to be reached between the parties.

• What is the MD really after? He mentions the need to find out people's abilities and performance, but also a need to develop fair disciplinary procedures. He refers to a need to discover people's potential, but also wants to find out their training and development requirements. He talks about a major need for teamwork, but then refers to closed appraisals. These are mutually contradictory needs.

Too many of the results he wants from appraisal will appear threatening to his managers and supervisors, and will almost certainly result in their opposition to appraisal and any training related to it.

- Discussion of this issue did, in fact, lead to agreement that what he most wanted was to introduce appraisal as an aid to reviewing work performance, helping work-planning, and diagnosing training and development needs. If this could be achieved as a first step, then establishing effective disciplinary procedures, sorting out how to perform assessments of potential, and so on could be tackled at a later date. By that time there should be more confidence in appraisal related to current work and to training and development, and the appraisal scheme will have had the chance to get over any teething problems and be working well. This part of the discussion also looked at what was meant by the terms 'appraisal' and 'assessment'. The MD realised he had been using the terms indiscriminately. Once the distinction between them had been clarified and agreed, many other things became clearer, and a shared frame of reference and language began to develop between us.

The learning objectives

The next issue is the behavioural learning objectives. The MD has referred to 'appraisal skills training', but what, specifically, are to be the outcomes of any training that takes place? Initially his one answer, that his managers should be able to operate a closed system of appraisal, presupposes three things: that there is an appraisal scheme already in existence, to which training can be related; that it has the support of his managers and supervisors, so that they will welcome training; and that closed appraisal is consistent with his overall purpose of using appraisal as an aid to reviewing work performance, helping work-planning, and diagnosing training and development needs.

Discussion of this issue took a long time, but in the end significant progress was made. It emerged that:

- there was no appraisal scheme worthy of note; the one used for selection for redundancies was agreed to be unsuitable from every point of view

- before skills training could take place, an appraisal scheme would have to be designed

- closed appraisal, especially at this particular time, would be viewed with great suspicion. It would be wiser to involve the managers and supervisors in the design of an appraisal scheme, opening up the entire design as well as the operational process from the start. Such an approach would also be consistent with the MD's other major need – to bind his managers and supervisors together into a close-knit managerial working team: the design task could start to build up that relationship

- if the objectives of the appraisal scheme were simply to do with work review and planning and the diagnosis of training and development needs, then no rating or ranking system related to performance was needed. Furthermore, dispensing with it would further reduce fears of the managers and supervisors that there was some ulterior motive behind the exercise.

Profile of the learning population

The third issue is the learners. What are their characteristics and situations in relation to the consultancy assignment? It is vital to get as much information about them at this early stage as possible, in order that the whole of the learning task facing the consultant is clearly understood.

- Discussions on this issue confirmed that the managers and supervisors were mainly in the 40-50 age range. Most had been with the store since their youth. In terms of learning styles and skills, they had no management training or education, although they had whatever technical and professional qualifications were needed. They would tend to be activists in the learning situation, distrustful of theories and simulated situations unless very clearly relevant to their work situation.

- As to motivation, over the last 10 years, with a rather old-fashioned, complacent and authoritarian leadership of the store some managers had become disillusioned and pessimistic about their futures. Others felt that they had received little support from senior management in their attempts to perform well, and this had bred a lack of confidence as well as confusion and some stagnation. Overall, energy and excitement were at quite a low ebb, and although the MD had a high opinion of the managers' real levels of ability and potential, it was essential to restore their original enthusiasm. Also, one or two seemed to see no need to work harder or differently from the way in which they worked at present: what therefore would be the incentive for them to do any of the things desired by the MD?

- The MD believed that motivation would improve as they began to realise the possibilities that lay before them: a market which they could start to win back; and the opportunity to become a small, high-calibre and high-achieving professional team, with rewards for those who proved their worth in meeting challenging standards. It was also evident as he spoke that he was quite determined that appraisal would be introduced: he was totally committed to both the concept and the reality of appraisal. Furthermore, his two directors would be positive in their support for the initiative. This would do much to convert any apathy, suspicion or apprehension into willingness to experiment. It would engender a commitment to make appraisal work, once there was a belief that this was not just one more 'flavour of the month' technique but a strategy offering real benefits.

- In terms of relevant skills and knowledge, few of the managers (including, said the MD, himself) knew anything much about appraisal.

The agreement reached with the MD

The final issue was to establish, after all this discussion, what the learning strategy should actually be and how it should be implemented. The following agreement was reached:

- The consultancy assignment would proceed in stages, with both consultant and client able to withdraw at the end of any stage if that seemed necessary or desirable.

- Stage 1 would consist of initial information-gathering by the consultant to determine whether the kind of diagnoses made in this initial discussion were valid, or whether other needs and problems existed which called for a review of the tentative conclusions reached at this stage.

- If the diagnoses did prove to be valid, the consultant would run a workshop for all 15 managers and supervisors, with the aim of working with them to design a simple appraisal scheme for the store. Initially it would be a pilot scheme, covering only managers and supervisors. If subsequent evaluation proved positive, it would then be extended to the rest of the store. Recommendations for a scheme would be presented to the MD at the conclusion of the workshop, in order that he could present a report on them to the board of directors.

- Stage 2 would consist of appraisal skills training, to develop those skills needed to introduce and operate the pilot scheme. The details of that stage (which again would fall into the two components of initial information-gathering and a workshop) would be determined once a decision had been made on whether the consultant was to go ahead and carry out that stage.

- Stage 3 would take place once a pilot scheme had been introduced and was under way. It would consist of a review day on which consultant, management team (which included those titled 'supervisors'), MD and personnel officer would come together to review the scheme's operation and agree on any further action needed.

Thus agreement between consultant (myself) and client (the MD) was reached by a process of jointly identifying the real learning needs and agreeing on:

- the overall purpose and objectives of learning

- the profile of the learning population

- a learning strategy.

Note how important it was for me to do what was advised early on in this chapter: challenge learning objectives I was asked by the client to achieve when those objectives seemed inappropriate or ambiguous.

STAGE FOUR: ESTABLISHING STRATEGY, DIRECTION AND MANAGEMENT

Choosing a learning strategy

As we saw in Part 1, strategy is the route to be followed in order to realise vision and overall purpose. In the case of a learning event, strategy must therefore relate to its overall purpose and general objectives. Learning strategy involves looking at alternative ways in which purpose and objectives for learning can best be achieved and then choosing the kind of events and delivery pattern which seem most likely to achieve the purpose.

In the case-study the agreed learning strategy was to help the learners to design their own appraisal scheme, using the consultant as a facilitator; and then to provide skills training to ensure effective operation of the scheme. In order to enhance teamwork and develop the learners as managers, the strategy included taking the whole management group away on two residential workshops, rather than organising learning events for some or all of them within the workplace itself.

A good fit must be achieved between learning strategy and the resources available for learning together with the organisational climate in the workplace. Let us look briefly at those two factors.

Resources
We have already dealt with learning resources in Chapter 10. They involve internal and external, tangible and intangible resources. Particular attention must be given to deciding whether to use external providers and how such provision should be managed (see Hackett, 1997). Alternative learning strategies must be analysed in relation to their likely cost, the time they will involve, and the extent to which they will utilise and relate to learning in the workplace.

Organisational culture and climate
It is important to reflect on the climate of the organisation, and especially of that part of it from which learners will be drawn, in relation to different options for learning strategy. As we have seen in Chapter 13, there must be a conducive workplace culture, as well as policies, procedures, roles and skills, if continuous development through the integration of learning and ongoing work is to be an effective learning strategy. An organisation planning to move into the delivery of learning through computerised learning systems and distance learning packages will not only have to set up the administrative machinery to make that strategy possible, but will have to prepare people – both learners and their managers – who have thought of learning only in terms of conventional training or educational programmes to see the benefit of these approaches, and how they can best be organised and the learning from them effectively transferred to the workplace.

The climate in the workplace, too, needs to be one that will support learners who come from a learning event with new knowledge, skills and, perhaps, changed attitudes. Cultures are slow to change, and those who have 'been away' on a learning event may find invisible and possibly impenetrable barriers awaiting them on their return. New learning must be fertilised if it is to take root, but too often that process does not occur because no one in the organisation has seen the need to prepare the ground.

Direction and management of the learning event
Different strategies will make different demands on expertise, so careful thought must be given to how the learning strategy and event will be directed and managed. Who and how many will be needed to carry out the work involved in design, direction and control, administration, delivery and evaluation? If the learning strategy to be pursued is one of training courses, then internal or external specialists

will have to provide these, and will need careful selection, briefing and management. If the strategy includes an educational programme using day or block release, there will have to be effective liaison with the educational institution concerned. Any requirement to assess workplace competencies and then use those for accreditation purposes will need extensive preparation, including training of workplace assessors. If there are to be elements of work-related learning, or a strategy of continuous development, then relevant experiences and how best to organise them must be agreed with the managers concerned, and it will probably be advisable to establish mentor roles. Agreement must also be reached on how, at what stages, and by whom monitoring and evaluation of the learning event will be carried out (see Chapter 16).

What matters most is that design and content are agreed between the key parties to be fully relevant to the purpose and objectives of the programme and to the type of learners concerned; that they are feasible and cost-efficient; and that ways of transferring learning to the workplace are agreed and put in place before the programme begins.

To demonstrate the importance of these issues of learning strategy, and the direction and management of the learning event, we can conclude our case-study.

Case-study: The retail store's appraisal project: Part 2

Once the overall purpose and learning objectives had been agreed in outline, the MD, PO and consultant (myself) spent considerable time together deciding how to carry out the first stage of the project. Here, the discussion revolved around resources. The following points emerged:

Direction and management of the project

The management of the project was agreed without difficulty: the MD would approve the overall parameters of each stage of the project, leaving the PO and myself to work on the detail relating to staffing, materials and physical accommodation.

I would determine the detailed behavioural objectives, both final and intermediate, of each workshop, and would be responsible for its design and delivery. I would return six or so months later to carry out a one-day review (Stage Three of the Project) with the workshop members, and the PO would arrange pre-workshop and post-workshop briefing/debriefing sessions for all workshop members and their managers, with special reference to following up action agreed in the workshop. The PO would also organise longer-term evaluation a year after the entire project had ended.

Staffing posed problems. It needed more than one person to run a workshop, whether the Stage One workshop (designing an appraisal scheme) or the Stage Two workshop (developing appraisal skills). The Stage One workshop required one more tutor, while the Stage Two workshop, if carried out, would require four. It was decided that the PO would act as co-tutor on the first workshop, thus reducing costs and increasing internal training expertise. It was agreed to leave the matter of staffing of Stage Two until a decision had been made about whether or not that stage would, in fact, go ahead.

Another resourcing problem was that for the Stage One workshop (on the assumption that one would be needed), there would have to be *either*

Option 1: one workshop for all the course members, with consultant and PO there throughout the two or three days;

or

Option 2: two workshops, with half the membership attending one, half attending the other, staffed by consultant and PO throughout on both occasions.

The direct cost of running the first option was less than the cost of running the second, because the first involved only one set of consultancy fees and only one sustained period of absence for the PO instead of two. However, difficulties of releasing all 15 store staff at the same time, together with obvious indirect costs incurred if these key people were all to be away from their departments for three days during a week, might make the second option necessary. Checking of dates when consultant and course members would all be available at one time also made it clear that Option 1 could not take place within the two-month period initially desired by the MD.

On the other hand, Option 2 would take longer to carry out than Option 1, and this again brought us up against the time factor. It would also split up the learning group, when keeping them together in order to build them up as a work team was an important objective. Finally, if Option 1 could be carried out over a Sunday plus Bank Holiday period when the store was closed, all managers could attend.

Physical resources

Materials and equipment needed for the workshops were available, and these constituted a relatively cheap part of the programme. Accommodation proved more difficult: the store had conference accommodation, although of limited size, and at first the MD felt that, to reduce costs, all workshops should be held there. We then discussed the psychological advantages of taking the whole management and supervisory team of 15 away from the store to a local hotel for the duration of the workshops. The relationship between consultant and course members, so important to cement quickly given the demanding task they jointly faced, should benefit greatly from such a location, and the social, as well as task mastery, motivation of the course members should receive a strong and continued boost. Equally important, managers and supervisors would be together as a team for a sustained period, away from their usual work situation, and this would be a very positive way of starting to develop the managerial team identity that the MD saw as so crucial. This strategy was subsequently agreed by the MD.

Finance

A maximum budget for the entire three-stage consultancy project was agreed, based on tentative costings I had produced. The budget was tight but not inflexible: it did, for example, allow for the possibility of some increase in initial costings over the period of the three stages. However, financial considerations posed problems related to staffing the workshops, as already explained.

Organisational climate

After discussion, it was agreed that it would be sensible to proceed more slowly than originally hoped in order to give time for a positive climate about appraisal to be developed in the store. The MD also decided that the objective of building up a strong managerial team from the start was more important than his wish for the whole project to be concluded quickly. It was therefore decided that Option 1 would be followed (one workshop, involving all 15 people, at a Bank Holiday weekend), with a relaxation of his initial time-scale, so that Stages One and Two would be spread over a five-month instead of a two-month period. This time-scale would have the final and important advantage of allowing time for a considered decision to be reached after the end of Stage One on whether to proceed to Stage Two, rather than a rushed and possibly invalid decision.

I hope that this case-study has helped to reinforce understanding of how to produce, implement and manage learning strategy and the event to which it relates. Here is a final task to test out learning from this chapter.

Planning a learning event

Produce a handout for distribution to either training practitioners attending a course on distance learning methods or line managers attending a course on 'on-the-job coaching'.

The handout should summarise the overall purpose of the course, its learning objectives and strategy, and how it will be directed and managed.

CONCLUSION

In order to achieve the learning objectives of this chapter our eight-stage approach has been continued by examining Stages Two to Four. In revisiting Stage One briefly it has been stressed that once performance and development needs have been identified, there must be confirmation that a particular type of learning event is indeed the appropriate response to those needs. In Stage Two, the importance of establishing relevant and feasible purpose for learning events has been emphasised and two levels of learning objective have been identified – final and interim. In Stage Three, attention has been drawn to the need for four kinds of information about learners and to two main types of motivation to learn: social and task mastery.

In Stage Four three practical considerations have been identified that should inform the choice of strategy for planned learning events, and key issues related to the effective direction and management of those events have been identified. A major two-part case-study has been used to integrate learning and understanding in this chapter.

In Chapter 16 the four remaining stages of the eight-stage approach will be covered.

USEFUL READING

BASS, B. M. *and* VAUGHAN, J. A. (1967) *Training in Industry: The management of learning*. London, Tavistock Publications.

BLOOM, B. S. (1956) *Taxonomy of Educational Objectives – Cognitive domain*. Essex, Longman.

GILLEY, J. W. *and* EGGLAND, S. A. (1989) *Principles of Human Resource Development*. Maidenhead, Addison Wesley.

HACKETT, P. (1997) *Introduction to Training*. London, Institute of Personnel and Development.

HARDINGHAM, A. (1996) *Designing Training*. London, Institute of Personnel and Development.

KRATHWOHL, D. R. (1964) *Taxonomy of Educational Objectives – Affective domain*. Essex, Longman.

NADLER, L. And NADLER, Z. (1989) *Developing Human Resources*. London, Jossey Bass.

ROBINSON, D. G. *and* ROBINSON, J. C. (1989) *Training for Impact*. London, Jossey Bass.

ROMISKOWSKI, A. J. (1981) *Designing Instructional Systems*. New York, Kogan Page.

16 Design, delivery and evaluation of learning events

LEARNING OBJECTIVES

After reading this chapter you will:

- understand the issues involved in the selection of learners
- be able to apply practical guidelines related to principles of learning to the design and delivery of a learning event
- understand the practical implications of five key questions related to evaluating a learning event, and know how to evaluate events effectively and efficiently.

THE EIGHT-STAGE APPROACH, STAGE FIVE: SELECTING LEARNERS AND PRODUCING THE LEARNING SPECIFICATION

In this chapter we conclude our analysis of the eight stages involved in the design of learning events by looking at stages five to eight. These involve the selection of learners and the design, delivery and evaluation of learning events.

At selection stage, the choice of whom to take into a learning event will often be out of the hands of those planning and designing that event. However, if criteria for selection are within their control, then they should focus attention on the overall purpose and objectives of the event, identifying the people for whom the learning outcomes will clearly be of most benefit and who have appropriate competencies, attitudes and learner characteristics.

Mistakes in selection are frequently made. The danger is probably greatest with externally provided courses, because when places are hard to fill the temptation is strong for the provider to accept people whose needs or abilities do not match the course profile. A menu-driven approach to the provision of learning events will tend to lead to an insufficiently discriminating selection process. Organisations quickly become wary of internal as well as external providers who try to 'sell' off-the-shelf products rather than respond flexibly and appropriately to specific learning needs.

Trainability tests
Useful information about the extent to which potential learners are in fact 'trainable' can be obtained from trainability tests – originally

pioneered for manual workers by Sylvia Downs at the Industrial Training Research Unit at Cambridge.

The trainability test comprises the detailed instruction of a job applicant in a piece of work which is part of the job being applied for. The applicant then has to perform the task without further assistance, while under scrutiny from the instructor. He or she is rated according to the number and type of errors made while performing the operation. Such tests:

- are designed to include parts of the training that trainees find difficult, as well as elements of the job itself

- involve a structured learning period

- include the use of detailed error check-lists written in behavioural terms (Downs, 1984).

Thus the focus is on how the individual learns the task, and a key criterion for selection becomes trainability. There are four factors that need to be considered before a decision is made to use such tests:

- *cost*. A trainability test is a specialised instrument. Each job has to have its own test, so the expense can be high.

- *design and validation*. Tests need to be carefully designed and validated, so those who administer them must be fully trained – another high-cost element.

- *time*. Trainability testing is very time-consuming and therefore, again, expensive.

- *insurance*. There must be special attention to insurance against accidents for non-employees who take the tests.

Trainability tests have proved to be a major aid to selection and training in a wide range of manual jobs, especially in the clothing industry. As to their applicability to non-manual jobs, work has been done in developing trainability tests for supervisory and managerial positions, and in this connection Task Observation, while not amounting to full trainability testing, can provide useful information about existing levels of ability in certain key tasks. The individual is asked to perform a typical activity which is an important part of the total job, and their existing level of competence is then assessed. Work-sampling of this kind, taken to its logical conclusion, leads to the comprehensive and structured methodology of assessment and development centres. Such centres (see Chapter 18) can provide another useful, if expensive, method of selecting for entry to learning events.

Specifying the learning required
This takes us back to Chapters 13 to 15. The knowledge, skills and attitudes required in the job and needed by the learners must be identified and analysed so that a specification can be produced of the gaps that the learning event should fill. Learning purpose, objectives and strategy can then be formulated.

Here is an example of the planning of a lengthy learning event, to demonstrate key points made in the previous chapter and in this one so far. It was used in my 1992 text but contains updated material, since the programme did not finish until 1994 and further research based on the data it generated has subsequently taken place.

Case-study: Planning and designing a management development programme for clinical directors

(See also Harrison and Miller, 1993; Harrison, Miller and Gibson, 1993, and Harrison, 1996).

Throughout the first eight months of 1991 the then Northern Regional Health Authority (NRHA) and Durham University Business School (DUBS) worked together to plan, design and jointly manage a three-year management development programme for 24 clinical directors (CDs) in the region. The programme was funded by the National Health Service's Management Executive (ME), so decisions about overall purpose, ultimate objectives, learning strategy and the outline structure of the programme had to be made at the stage when funding was being sought – in the event, a year before the programme itself began.

Overall Purpose

The purpose of the programme, which was evaluated by two external bodies as well as by the NRHA and DUBS, was to help senior clinicians in, or preparing to take on, CD roles to effectively fulfil the managerial demands of that role in order, ultimately, to ensure high standards of patient care. There were 24 participants, split into three cohorts of eight over the 1991–94 period to enable an individualised learning system to drive the cycle of three staggered repeat programmes. Figure 6 shows the configuration of learning events characterising each programme and their time scale, using the first run of the programme as the reference point.

Analysis of learning needs

Once funding had been obtained to run the programme (early in 1991), eight months were spent by NRHA and DUBS programme designers expanding a base of initial information on learner- and job-related needs in order to produce a sound specification for the programme. The CD role was a new one within the radically changed NHS structure introduced in April 1991. It was sparsely documented at any level, and proved to be different in its interpretation and operation across virtually every organisation where it existed. The first eight participants, too (selected in mid-1991 for entry that September to the first of the series of three programmes) were very heterogeneous in their professional, managerial and personal characteristics. Lengthy interviews were held by NRHA and DUBS staff with each of them and with their managers during that summer, to identify needs and expectations of these key parties in relation to the programme. This exercise was repeated with each cohort, and adjustments to their programmes made accordingly.

A problem-centred approach and role analysis proved the best methods to identify and analyse learning needs, but the needs identified during this period were so diverse that it proved difficult to agree on how to interpret findings and to classify and prioritise the needs. There were three sets to reconcile:

Figure 6 The Clinical Directors' Programme – first cohort

NRHA–DUBS Clinical Directors' Programme: Intake 1 (1991–93)

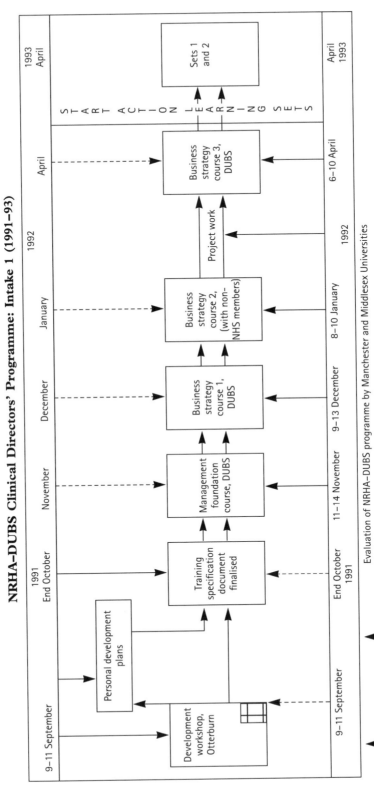

Evaluation of NRHA–DUBS programme by Manchester and Middlesex Universities

Key = Collaborated with = Controlled by

Organisational needs derived from the overriding concern of the ME to improve the quality of patient care by ensuring effective management in the reorganised NHS. They also derived from needs expressed by the NRHA client and the participants' organisations – the NHS units who nominated them for the programme and gave them the time and other support to attend. These needs set the focus and direction of the programme, and helped to generate its overall purpose and objectives.

Group needs were derived from those areas of skill, knowledge and competency that all programme participants – and their organisations – saw as essential in a programme to enable them to learn quickly how to become not only managers but, in most cases, managers who had a significant strategic role at business-unit level in their local organisations.

Individual needs were identified both in the interviews and in the diagnostic workshop held as the first stage of the learning event (see below). They were expressed in personal development plans (PDPs) that were followed up by NRHA and NHS mentors throughout the programme. These helped to drive the programme and achieve objectives related to the provision of a tailor-made sequence of learning events that would help each individual to understand fully the new role and perform confidently and competently. They thus helped to ensure instrumental, dialogic and self-reflective learning (see pages 229–30).

The core NRHA/DUBS team identifying and analysing these needs was initially composed of four. In mid-1991 it expanded to include two external management consultants recruited by DUBS for their particular NHS-related expertise, to help in the initial design process and to lead the delivery of the programme. During this period the school's programme staff therefore had to guide both design work and a complex process of human interactions, ensuring an effective two-way flow of information and ideas. They acted as a bridge between the NRHA and the DUBS group as all strove to make sense of a mass of often incomplete data and to develop shared perceptions and language about the programme.

There were tensions during the period, relating to matters of interpretation and focus and to the relative roles to be played by the NRHA and DUBS in selection of learners, organisation of the diagnostic workshop, and monitoring and evaluation of the ongoing programme. However, the agreement to take the overall purpose and objectives of the programme as the base reference point in all discussions enabled differing views eventually to be reconciled and workable compromises to be reached. By August 1991 a draft job training specification had been produced, and an agreed plan for the first programme was almost ready for delivery in September.

Programme design and delivery

At this point flexibility was crucial, since a three-day personal development diagnostic workshop organised for the first cohort of CDs by the NRHA staff was to take place a few weeks before the formal programme started. It incorporated teambuilding through an outdoor development period; analysis of a previously completed computerised assessment questionnaire about the CDs' managerial competencies and needs as identified by themselves and a sample of their managers, subordinates and peers; and work on personal learning goals and plans. The insights obtained from this exercise had to be incorporated into the final programme plan.

Every programme component had its own stated purpose and three or four clearly defined final learning objectives. Within each formal module, interim objectives were established for each session. These interim and final objectives became the criteria against which the learners were asked by the programme planners to evaluate the modules. From start to end of each programme continuous fine-tuning took place in order to adapt the programme to emerging needs. The growing cohesiveness of the core team facilitated this process: working increasingly closely together, its members developed over the first year a shared language and philosophy about the programme that facilitated joint action on any problems in delivery.

At the conclusion of the formal components, each programme moved for a six- to eight-month period into action learning (AL, see Figure 6) sets, each comprising four clinicians with an experienced set adviser. To design this component, the planning team had once more been expanded to incorporate two international AL experts contracted by DUBS. Again, the planning process was initially hampered by differences in views between the experts and both groups in the core team about how best to integrate the formal and action-learning components of the programme. Again, however, it was the overall purpose and ultimate objectives of the programme, together with the shared commitment of the parties to achieving them, that helped to resolve differences and drove that essential period forward (Harrison, 1996).

In this study the focus has been not only on the overall purpose, objectives, learner population and learning strategy chosen for a complex learning event, but also on its planning, management and design process. Further comment on the latter follows under the next heading.

STAGE SIX: CONFIRMING STRATEGY AND DESIGNING THE LEARNING EVENT

Confirming strategy

Once the participants in a learning event have been selected, it is essential to confirm or modify the learning strategy and design initially proposed. Although in most cases confirmation will be all that is required, from time to time the more detailed information gained when examining the needs of the participants may indicate the need to change strategy or design, sometimes radically. Occasionally the information may even indicate that the objectives or purpose set for the learning event are misconceived. Ignoring such indicators may put at risk the viability of the whole event.

Designing the learning event

Designing the learning event requires first that each component carries clear behavioural objectives aligned with its overall purpose and final objectives. This approach, linking needs, purpose, objectives and outcomes exemplifies the operation of what is known as the systematic training cycle. An explanation of that cycle was given in Chapter 9 (Appendix 4) when describing the work of the national Lead Bodies in producing occupational standards.

Achieving external and internal consistency

However, linking key design elements to achieve 'internal consistency' (Kessels, 1993) is not of itself sufficient to achieve the confidence of key parties in a programme's outcomes and assure its success. Our case-study has demonstrated the importance of involving key actors from the earliest stages in programme planning and delivery so that their perceptions about the event become and remain mutually compatible. Kessels described this as a process that generates 'external consistency' – shared expectations and orientation of the key parties involved in a learning event so that an increasingly close fit is achieved between the event itself and the external environment in which its learning must take root.

Research carried out by Kessels in the Netherlands and first reported in 1993 has provided strong evidence to indicate that although internal consistency is important in determining the success of planned learning events, external consistency has the most decisive impact. Even in programmes shown in his study to have achieved a high degree of internal consistency, lack of strong involvement of stakeholders led to reduction in desired impact – and sometimes to failure of the event.

As will be seen later in this chapter, there is little doubting the impact achieved by the NRHA/DUBS clinical directors' programme; but it was the process of involving the parties from the start, as much as the systematic approach to the tasks of programme design, that appears to explain the unanimity with which the different parties judged it to have been successful once completed. Throughout this book the importance of process as well as of tasks in HRD has been stressed – especially in Chapters 3 and 12. Here, again, it is process that is being emphasised as crucial to effective performance in roles related to training and the facilitation of learning.

Choosing content, media and methods

We can distinguish between media and methods thus:

* Media of learning are the routes, or channels, through which learning is transmitted to the learner.

* Methods of learning are the ways in which that learning is transmitted.

'Training technology' refers to the technical aids available to promote the acquisition of skills in a learning event. 'Learning technology', on the other hand, has a broader meaning: it refers to the way in which learning media and methods are incorporated into the design and delivery of a learning event. It can often leave much to be desired. Events can be expensively produced and persuasively designed, yet be delivered using such inappropriate media and methods that they are ineffective. The more HRD staff become skilled in the technology of learning, the less their organisations will have to bear the consequences of such expensive mistakes.

The opposite danger, of course, is to become so immersed in the pursuit of new training technology that the fundamentals which make for a successful learning event are forgotten, as Nick Rushby, head of

Table 13 Some media and methods of learning

Media	Methods
Oral (spoken word)	Talk, lecture, discussion, seminar
Printed (written word)	Handouts, books, distance learning texts
Radio, TV, computers	Wide variety of methods, didactic and interactive
On the job	Learning from a supervisor or co-worker Learning by trial and error Using a training manual or a self-administered training package Coaching; job rotation
Off the job	Any learning event organised away from the workplace
Vestibule	Simulated work situation, in a training room or centre, or other premises near the workplace.

the Training Technologies Unit at Sundridge Park Management Centre, remarked:

> I have an uneasy feeling that training technologists become too concerned for the glamorous technology – to the detriment of the training, and of the necessary process of innovation which involves much more than providing alternative ways of training'.

(Rushby, 1988)

Table 13 shows some major media together with examples of the kind of methods most frequently associated with them. Clearly one learning event may use several media as well as a number of different methods.

For a full discussion of media and methods, there are regular articles in personnel and training journals (see, for example, Fowler, 1995) and specialist texts such as Gough (1996). One of the clearest and most practical discussions I have read remains that in Gagne's book (1977), which not only offers excellent practical advice about the design of learning events but illuminates it at the scholarly level, with his discussion of the psychology of learning. In what follows I draw significantly on his ideas.

It is important to be clear that there is no single best medium or method, whether in relation to a particular kind of learning objective, learner or learning event. Certain media and methods may enjoy current popularity. For example, interactive computer-based learning methods are in vogue because of their increasing availability, diminishing cost, the stimulation they offer the learner and the fact that they are adaptable to the learner's needs in terms of time, place, pace and feedback. They operate well particularly within the generalised medium of flexible learning, to which maximum publicity was initially given in the 1980s by the wide variety of Manpower Services Commission-sponsored Open Tech projects and by the Open College initiative. Flexible learning can also incorporate the use of television, radio, cassettes, printed texts and other methods.

Yet whatever their popularity at a particular point in time, there is no evidence to support a generalised superiority of any one medium or method, so other criteria for choice in the specific learning situation must be found. A simple three-point check-list can act as an adequate guide to the designer. We shall illustrate its use in a task that I have retained from my 1992 IPM text because the popularity of time management courses remains undimmed!

Designing a one-day workshop on time management

The workshop will have up to 20 members. It is to be held in a company's training centre; and the learning objective is that course members should, by the end of the day, know and be able to apply about six methods of time management in the organisation of their daily workload. What considerations will guide your choice of media and methods?

Feedback notes

Here is a three-point check-list to use when choosing media and methods:

1) *Consider the purpose and objectives of the learning event and the characteristics of the learners.* Clear learning objectives will indicate to the designer the typical situations to which the learner will have to respond after completing the learning event, and the behavioural outcomes that the event must help the learner to achieve. Types of situations and outcomes will help to suggest relevant media and methods.

   Factors like the biographical and occupational characteristics of the learners, the geographical location and the size of the learning group need to be analysed when choosing media and methods. Learning styles and skills will have a particularly strong influence on the ways in which learners are likely to adapt to different approaches because, being usually formed at an early age, it is unlikely that they can quickly change. Initially, therefore, the choice of media and methods should be capable of adaptation to existing styles and skills. For example, many learners may find distance learning hard to cope with, but can learn quite effectively in a face-to-face learning medium. Those who do not learn well when lectures predominate may respond better to group and practical work of various kinds. Those who cannot review their own learning processes can be helped to do so by using a learning styles inventory, and by reflective discussion with a trainer or mentor.

2) *Consider the principles of learning and their practical application.* Which approaches are likely to achieve most stimulation and retention of learning? In a one-day workshop there will be a need for a judicious mix of tutor-led talk, printed materials that can reinforce key points and act as a permanent record, and interactive events. When considering whether to use methods such as case-studies or an in-tray exercise, prior information from the learners or with previous participants in a similar event can aid choice. For example, a pre-workshop check may reveal that, for certain tasks,

in-tray exercises may be more productive than case-studies because the latter are likely to be viewed by these learners as too artificial and difficult to absorb. An in-tray exercise may offer more readily transferable learning, more stimulation, and quicker mastery.

So at this second stage we have narrowed the field of choice further by considering how best to respond to key principles of learning.

3) *Consider practical issues*

We must look at what is most feasible by reference to our total budget and to the learning environment. Remember here the importance of the organisational climate. For example, some senior managers may not see the value of external courses as a way of developing their line managers, while others may see such courses as an essential part of the developmental process, and fully support them as a learning route for their staff. Information on past effectiveness of certain media and methods in organisational learning events should also be checked, as should best practice in similar learning events elsewhere.

As this check-list shows, most learning events need a combination of different media and methods, and must be flexible enough to enable changes to be made if learning problems develop. In today's world, training and development professionals need to be highly knowledgeable about the wide choice of media and methods, and creative as well as cost-conscious in selecting those best suited to the purpose and most likely to bring additional value to the learning situation.

Case-study: Thames Valley University: the 'whole organisation' approach to learning technology

Cost-cutting and changing attitudes and expectations in students, together with rapid technological advance, have all had an explosive effect on most educational institutions. The development of multimedia products is becoming widespread, and the implications of the global Internet network in particular cannot sensibly be ignored. As Lymer pointed out, the World Wide Web is 'not just a tool to provide access to existing data in more flexible, user-friendly, timely ways' but is changing the way new information is generated by offering users 'a new medium through which to exchange ideas, formulate proposals and generate solutions in ways not previously possible' (Lymer, 1996: 9–10).

Thames Valley University (TVU), chosen in 1997 by the Institute of Personnel and Development as a key provider of learning materials for its professional qualification flexible learning scheme, is in the forefront of innovation both in educational and in learning technology. TVU has not just expanded its open learning operations, using the term to mean 'any scheme of education or training that seeks systematically to remove barriers to learning whether [of] time, place or space' (Nicholls, 1997a). It has transformed itself into a 'flexible learning environment'(Nicholls, 1997) which enables its 27,000 students – 65 per cent of whom are part-time and therefore not eligible for State subsidies – to have an affordable, fully accessible and self-paced education.

Transformation is the appropriate term. The whole university has been radically reorganised, with 40 per cent of its campuses turned into technologically sophisticated learning resource centres. At the Ealing centre, for example, each of its 12 floors houses books, videos and CD–ROMS relating to a different subject group, and each contains study and seminar areas, and teaching and learning support facilities, including a shop where computers can be purchased or hired.

The most significant change at TVU has been its 'strategic approach to printed resources', comprising free course folders and books for all students, made possible by economies of scale and by a reduction of course modules from eight to six. 'Everything at TVU is a heavily managed process designed to give the student as much support as possible while encouraging self-directed learning' (Nicholls, 1997).

TVU offers a powerful example of how self-development – whether in an educational institution or any other workplace – can flourish when there is a supportive, well-managed and creatively resourced environment conducive to meeting a wide variety of individual needs and providing encouragement and stimulation to learn. It demonstrates the added value to be achieved when there is close alignment of a creative approach to learning with the overall vision and strategy of the organisation: that which benefits the learners also represents a unique source of competitive capability for the business.

Source: Nicholls, 1997, 1997a

Applying principles of learning to the design and delivery of learning events

We have just discussed the importance of considering basic principles of learning when choosing media and methods. We can now expand that discussion by examining how principles of learning themselves should inform the design and delivery of a learning event.

In providing a set of eight guidelines, I am again drawing significantly on Gagne's (1977) ideas.

Design an appropriate structure and culture

In this context, 'structure' means the framework of a learning event – the way it is shaped and the type of interactions planned to occur within it. 'Structure' also refers to how tightly or loosely controlled the event should be. For example, where active participation is particularly desirable in a programme, how structured or unstructured should that programme be?

'Culture' is about the learning climate established for the event – about the style and pattern of relationships between the parties and the values they will be encouraged to share in the learning situation.

Stimulate the learners

This involves ensuring that the purpose and objectives of the event are perceived by the learners to relate directly to their needs. To ensure continued stimulation throughout the learning event, choose media and methods that will actively involve them (using the three-point check-list we have just developed). Key points in learning must stand out and become memorable – in other words, they must achieve 'perceptual distinctiveness'. It is the beginning and end of a learning event that make most impact, so it is important that the essence of what is to be learnt is outlined at the start, and that at the end learning is summarised in a way that takes the learners back to that starting-point. This closes the learning loop.

Help understanding
Choose content that strikes a chord with the learners, and regularly check on their understanding of it as the event unfolds. Be ready to go back to difficult points and to vary the learning pace and approach in order to ensure a better grasp of the material and concepts.

Incorporate appropriate learning activities
Activities in which the learners are involved during the event must involve situations or the use of skills and knowledge that are relevant to their real-life environment and roles, that carry the learning process forward, and that build expertise and confidence. Remember three aspects of motivation noted in Chapter 15: unpredictability, individual differences and dynamism (page 277). Be ready to adapt the learning situation to emergent learning needs.

Build on existing learning
Initially (until a strong positive relationship has been established between learners and those guiding the learning event) it is helpful not to fight against what learners think, feel or are sure they know. Instead, aim to make past learning and current mindsets an aid to the learning process. If brought to the surface in a non-judgemental way they can be tested naturally by problems and activities built into the learning event. Unlearning and relearning are complex processes and can be painful, yet they are essential to the acquisition of much new learning. The skill lies in creating an atmosphere where entrenched learning and views can become clear and then be treated in such a way as, in time, to become integrated with new learning or – where irrelevant – gradually fall away. Sometimes the tensions between old and new learning are too great to resolve. Such a breakdown in the learning process indicates possible faults in the original diagnosis of needs, or in the purpose set for the event, or in the choice of learners.

Guide the learners
There must be regular feedback and guidance on learning progress. The instructor or facilitator will need technical competence to carry out instructional functions, and also interpersonal skills to ensure a supportive relationship with the learners as they struggle with areas of difficulty.

Ensure that learning is retained
There are two major issues to consider here: practice and rewards.

Practice reinforces learning until the point is reached when the behavioural patterns become habitual. But how much and what distribution of practice? The concept of learning curves is useful here. A learning curve means the average amount of time it takes to achieve mastery of what is to be learnt. Curves vary greatly from task to task and person to person, being related to the difficulty of the task, the characteristics of the learners, and the duration and spacing of practice.

We can rarely provide the ideal amount and spacing of practice that each learner requires. We must therefore select the most critical and/or the most difficult learning tasks and give those priority. Thus, for example, throughout this book I have built in tasks and examples around issues that are critical to the mastery of human resource development (HRD) theory and practice, and also around those which usually cause significant difficulty. The tasks and examples are also designed and spaced to stimulate and maintain interest in what would otherwise soon become a mass of indigestible material!

Training designers should record learning curves in relation to typical learning events in which they will be involved. However, careful monitoring of the learning process will always remain necessary since learning curves can at best only be generalised predictors.

Quite simple *rewards* such as a smile or a word of praise may be enough to reinforce effective behaviour in the learning situation. It is also important to explore with the learner why learning has proved successful, since sometimes correct responses are achieved only by chance.

Punishment of incorrect responses is less predictable in its consequences. A critical comment, a harsh word, a misplaced joke may frighten or shame the learner into renewed effort, but equally may inhibit further learning. In the extreme case the learner may simply give up. Usually, failure is in itself punishment enough. To correct it, careful demonstration by the trainer, followed by repeated practice by the learner, may be effective; or a repetition of the initial instruction session, using slightly different methods; or a supportive discussion of precisely what the learner has found to be an obstacle, and how he or she may be helped to overcome that obstacle. There are many ways in which initial failures can be overcome providing always that the basic ability to learn is there.

Where the ability or motivation to learn is lacking, there has probably been a selection error which may prove impossible to resolve. Always, therefore, ensure provision for the counselling and guidance of learners. Exit points and processes from a learning event when it is clear that effective learning is not going to be possible also need to be established.

Ensure transfer of learning
There are two points at which transfer of learning needs to be effective: transfer of learning into a learning event, and from it upon its completion. Past learning will transfer positively into the event if that learning can be used in the new situation. It will transfer negatively if it seems to the learner impossible to apply or if it contradicts what is being taught in the new situation (we have already noted some ways of dealing with negative learning).

The same principles hold true for the transfer of learning from the learning event into the workplace situation. Successful transfer at that point will depend on how far:

- the event has been appropriate to the learners' needs in their work situation

- its learning tasks have been within the capability of the learners and been mastered by them

- it has achieved stimulation and relevancy of learning throughout its duration

- participants will be enabled and encouraged to use their new learning in the workplace.

The process of achieving external consistency (page 294) is one that leads to the achievement of these aims. It does so by committing the external parties so powerfully to the learning event that their support for the transference of its outcomes is thereby ensured. (Illuminating case-studies on transfer of learning are contained in Marchington and Wilkinson, 1996, Chapter 10.)

Preparing a talk

You have been asked to speak for an hour and a half to a local meeting of your IPD branch on 'How to decide on training methods'. Prepare an outline of the talk, including its purpose and main objectives, and explain how its design incorporates key principles of learning (for advice, see Fowler, 1995).

STAGE SEVEN: DELIVERING THE EVENT

Delivery should pose few problems if the event itself is an appropriate response to needs; if learning strategy, learners and those delivering the learning event have been well chosen; if the event has been effectively designed; and if the planning and managerial processes are of good quality. Flexibility will remain crucial in this as in earlier stages. Going back to our case-study, fine-tuning of focus and delivery had to continue throughout the clinical directors' programme. Subsequent evaluations confirmed that this adaptability to emergent needs had been central to the programme's ability to achieve its desired outcomes. To summarise:

In delivering as well as in designing a learning event, the political, interactive and managerial processes involved will be as critical as technical expertise in ensuring the achievement of desired outcomes.

For a full discussion of the planning, design, management and delivery of learning events, see Gilley and Eggland (1989: 213–40). Helpful guidelines are also given in specialist texts such as Hardingham (1996) and Siddons (1997).

STAGE EIGHT: MONITORING AND EVALUATING THE EVENT

Monitoring and evaluation are essential to the success of any learning event. They ensure control during its delivery, validation of its outcomes by comparing actual against intended results, and information needed in the planning of future events. Since this stage can be particularly resource-hungry, the main principle is to achieve a sensible balance between on the one hand the need to check what is happening at various stages of a learning event, and on the other hand doing what is feasible and cost-efficient.

Evaluation of a learning event is about validation – that is to say about checking whether learning objectives have been achieved. However it must go wider than that and question whether all that has been done is worthwhile, given the overall purpose of the event and the investment made in it. To summarise:

> Evaluation looks at the total value of a learning event, not just at whether and how far it has achieved its learning objectives. It thereby puts the event in its wider context and provides information essential to future planning.

Six general points need to be made about evaluation:

- The more the learning event is concerned with 'soft' (ie behavioural) skills and issues rather than 'hard' (ie quantifiable and simple) skills, the less easy it is to measure.

- The higher up the organisation the learning event, the less easy it is to measure its impact, because of the complexity of the jobs and the great variety of factors affecting behaviour and performance in them.

- The further in time that measurement occurs from the learning event, the less easy it is – again because of the multiplicity of intervening variables.

- In order to achieve any meaningful measurement, there should be an analysis of the 'before/after' situation. Measurement of changes achieved once the learning event is over should be done at more than one point in time in order to measure retention of learning in the work situation.

- Measurement must be apt, systematic, objective and feasible. It must focus not on all outcomes but on those agreed by the key parties to be the most important.

- Measurement must be a collaborative process, with strategy, focus and methods approved at the highest level.

Providing that the key parties agree on what is to be measured, how and to what purpose, there should be no insurmountable problems in agreeing on the outcomes and value of the learning event – unless, of course, there are wider organisational problems that the learning event cannot resolve, yet which directly affect the function and its initiatives.

We have now examined all stages of the eight-stage approach to the planning and delivery of learning events introduced in Chapter 14. Before concluding this chapter, the evaluation of learning events will be examined in more detail, since it is often thought more difficult than in reality it needs to be.

EVALUATION: FIVE KEY QUESTIONS

In Chapter 12 evaluation was discussed at a macro level: in relation to the organisation's total investment in HRD. In this section the purpose is to move to the micro level and provide a simple, practical approach to the evaluation of planned learning events.

The section does not encompass a review of key literature on evaluation or cover techniques in any detail. For that kind of discussion, the reader is referred to specialist texts, particularly Kearns and Miller (1996) and Bramley (1996). Both offer stimulating advice and illustration of methods of evaluating past learning events. Kearns and Miller, however, provide particular value because they also show the importance of assessing the future impact of investing in planned learning activities, and explain how this can be done.

Faced with an evaluation task, there are five crucial questions to answer:

- *Why* evaluate?
- *What* to evaluate?
- *Who* should evaluate?
- *When* to evaluate?
- *How* to evaluate?

1 Why evaluate?
There are many reasons why evaluation may be required in the specific situation. Perhaps cost has to be justified, or effects on learners, or impact on job performance, or outcomes relevant to the profitability, performance, flexibility or survival of the organisation as a whole. Each kind of aim involves the evaluator in a different set of activities, and will provide the frame of reference for the four remaining questions.

2 What to evaluate?
A fourfold framework is helpful here, drawn from models provided by Warr, Bird and Rackham (1970) and Hamblin (1974), whose texts give practical guidance on evaluation techniques and procedures. The dimensions to be evaluated are those of the so-called CIRO approach, namely the:

- *Context* within which the learning event has taken place: organisational, analytical and diagnostic
- *Inputs* to the learning event: tangible and intangible, internal and

external resources; the learning system designed for the event; and the recruitment to the event

- *Reactions* to the learning event: those of the learners and other relevant parties

- *Outcomes* of the learning event, both at its end and over the longer term.

Under question five we shall look at how to evaluate each of these four dimensions.

3 Who should evaluate?

Depending on the answers to the first two questions, there will be a range of possibilities here. Trainers, line managers, the personnel function, top management, external consultants, all will have particular skills to offer. However, because each will bring their own viewpoints and aims to the task, none can be relied upon to be free of bias. It is here that it becomes so important to understand the evaluation task and its purpose: failure to ensure a good choice of evaluator will make the organisation very vulnerable to manipulation. Evaluation is a sensitive and technically difficult matter whose outcomes can be only as reliable and valid as the process that produces them.

The choice of evaluators should be determined by five criteria:

- *objectivity.* What, if any, connection have potential evaluators had with the design, running and outcomes of the learning event? Are they likely to cover up any weaknesses or strengths in the event – or to exaggerate them?

- *expertise.* Have they carried out evaluation before? For whom? With what results? Does their explanation of how they will approach the task convince you of their knowledge, skill and professionalism?

- *interpersonal skills.* What sort of relationship do they have, or can they be expected to form, with those whose views they need to obtain? Are they likely to receive trust and co-operation? What sort of relationship have they established with you, and what does that tell you about their interpersonal skills?

- *credibility.* This will depend partly on the factors already examined above but also, and crucially, on the understanding they demonstrate of the organisation and its environment.

- *cost.* If you are considering using consultants, will the fee be worth the result? What will happen when they leave? Will they have trained your staff to take over from them, especially in implementing any further stages of a lengthy project? Could anyone else do the job more cheaply but as well? Could your own staff do the job – and could they be spared to do it?

4 When to evaluate?

There are several choices possible here:

- If the purpose of evaluation is to find out how valid the learning event was in helping the learners to reach identified standards by its end, then monitoring standards reached *before* and *at the end* of the learning event may be sufficient. However, it would be advisable to evaluate at least once again, at a later date, in order to assess how far learning has been retained and its ultimate impact.

• If the cost-efficiency of the inputs is to be evaluated, evaluation using reactions of the learners *during* and *at the end* of the event, and pre- and post-tests of the learning they have acquired in relation to the objectives of the learning event will probably prove sufficient.

• If the cost-effectiveness of a programme needs to be evaluated in order to decide whether the organisation should invest again in such a programme, it may prove necessary to evaluate by reference to job performance *in the short-term,* and *the longer-term* impact on both job performance and overall organisational trends in, perhaps, profitability, morale and flexibility.

Timing must also take practical considerations into account. To evaluate in depth using sophisticated methods at five different points in time, for example, would be very costly. This may not be possible or justifiable given the benefits likely to accrue from the exercise. On the other hand, a simple form of monitoring carried out at fairly regular intervals will be cheap. Given all the advantages of information, control and good planning that it offers it will usually repay the repetitive effort it requires.

5 How to evaluate?

This depends on what is being evaluated and when evaluation is needed. The CIRO approach already explained in this section offers a basic framework for evaluation.

Evaluate the *Context* of the learning event

This involves examining how accurately needs were initially diagnosed, why this particular kind of learning event was decided on as a solution, and whether the right kind of learning objectives were set.

Look, therefore, at how and by whom the information that gave rise to the diagnosis of the need for the learning event was collected, and at what process they used. Then examine how that information was analysed, what learning needs emerged from it and what measure of agreement there was between key parties on the kinds of skills, knowledge and attitudes to be acquired.

Next examine how learning objectives were set; how well they related to the overall purpose of the event and the needs it was intended to serve; how far they took into account the organisational context within which the learning would have to take place and any constraints or advantages offered by the organisational culture and structure in relation to the learning event; what standards were established; and how the achievement of standards was to be measured.

Evaluate the *Inputs* to the learning event

Here the concern is to discover how well the learning event was planned, managed, designed and delivered by establishing how cost-efficient, cost-effective and feasible and well chosen its major inputs were.

It is necessary to identify and, within reasonable limits, cost the resources used to meet learning needs (time, money, staff and expertise, physical accommodation, materials, and the natural learning resources in the organisation); to assess the cost and appropriateness of the chosen learning system, media, methods and content; and to establish how far selection choices for entry to the event were appropriate, so that the right learners were chosen for the event.

Evaluate key *R*eactions to the learning event

This involves discovering the learners' feelings – their immediate reactions – about the event. Establishing what people feel as distinct (often) from what outcomes have actually been achieved is important because those views and feelings will influence others, including future potential participants, as well as explaining any motivational problems or successes during the event. It also involves discovering the reactions of other parties directly involved in or with the learning event, and comparing them with the reactions it was hoped the event would achieve.

For example, in the British Airways 'Putting People First' and 'Managing People First' programmes in the late 1980s and early 1990s membership of the courses was voluntary. However, the hope was that those who went on the first programmes would be so enthusiastic in their reactions that this would influence their peers to opt for the training. This hope was fulfilled, and final numbers wishing to be trained comprised virtually the entire workforce in the sectors concerned.

If the main concern is with assessing perceptions and feelings about what learning has been achieved, then reactions should be sought mainly from participants and from their tutors. If, on the other hand, there is a particular concern to find out how people felt about course content, methods and delivery then the views of the learners, deliverers and any observers will be the most significant.

It may be important to test reactions after every session of an event, or after every key element, or – in a modular programme – at the end of every module. Evaluation of reactions must suit the needs of the exercise. Hamblin (1974) recommended the use of session assessments on training courses, where each session can be looked at in terms of any aspects in which the evaluator is interested: enjoyment, length of time given to discussion, level of presentation, informational content, relevance, length of the session; or to monitor the progress of a practical activity, perhaps with a view to establishing typical learning curves of different types of learners.

Evaluate key *O*utcomes of the learning event

This involves attempting to establish what actually happened as a result of a learning event – its outcomes, which should be measured at any or all of the following levels, depending again on the object of the evaluation exercise:

* *the learner level.* This involves recalling not only the reactions of the learners to the learning event, since they themselves are a type of outcome (as described above), but also establishing changes in the

learners' knowledge, skills, and attitudes at the completion of the training that can be objectively ascertained (for example by tests) and comparing them with levels of knowledge, skills and attitudes identified at the start of the programme (by techniques such as appraisal, tests, repertory grids, etc).

- *the workplace level.* This involves identifying changes that subsequently take place in the learner's job behaviour. These can be measured by appraisal, observation, discussion with the learners' managers/peers/customers/clients, and performance records, as well as by the reactions (see above) of the learners themselves, and how far these are in line with the views of others about that performance (research quoted by Warr *et al*, 1970 indicated that there is usually quite a close correlation between those two sets of views).

- *the team/department/unit level.* This involves identifying changes that take place in part or all of a team, department or unit as a result of a learning event, using the kind of techniques described in relation to evaluating outcomes at the workplace level.

- *the organisational level.* This involves identifying changes that take place in the organisation as a whole after the completion of the training programme and that appear strongly related to that programme.

These last two kinds of outcome are the most difficult to evaluate yet, with careful thought, meaningful evaluation even here should be possible. It will, however, depend on the setting of clear objectives for the learning event, and on prior agreement on how achievement of those objectives will be measured. At departmental level the sort of changes that could be involved include alterations in departmental output, costs, scrap rates, absenteeism, turnover, or accident frequency; improvement in productivity rates, labour costs, absenteeism and turnover rates: or the effectiveness in some other way of the total organisation. At organisational level they could be about change in the culture of the organisation, more flexibility and reduced levels of conflict in relation to the introduction of change (see Harrison, 1996a), and enhanced ability to attract and retain valued workers.

Depending on when evaluation is to be carried out, the methods used could include one or more of the following:

- *pre-course, interim and post-course assessment.* Put the participants through an assessment process before the learning event in order to establish their present standards of performance and typical attitudes and work behaviour. Put them through a similar process during and after the programme in order to measure changes.

- *pre-course, interim and post-course opinions* (semi-structured or unstructured) about performance. Obtain general views about their behaviour and performance from various parties, including external people (as relevant), both before the learning event and when they are back in the workplace. Ask for *specific* examples of changed performance, behaviour and attitudes rather than unsubstantiated views.

- *pre-course and post-course ratings of performance*. Obtain the views of peers and colleagues in deciding how far the learning event has achieved its objectives with the managers concerned, using behavioural rating scales and other structured evidence of specific behaviour and performance.

Case-study: The clinical directors' programme, Part 2

Because of its strategic importance in the region, the programme was subjected to evaluation by two universities outside the region on behalf of the Northern Regional Health Authority (NRHA) and the Management Executive (ME). It was also monitored continuously by the programme staff at the NRHA and at Durham University Business School (DUBS). The latter used daily reaction sheets for the critical first module – the Management Foundation Course – (Table 13) to test perceptions of and reactions to the achievement of module objectives, and the modules' delivery and content seemed effective. Subsequently, they distributed questionnaires only at the end of each module, testing reactions to each main component. This elicited essential information while avoiding what otherwise could have been an excess of questioning in view of evaluation exercises also being conducted at regional and national level.

Finally, DUBS organised a detailed evaluation exercise near the end of the programme in September 1993 and a longer-term evaluation in February 1995, both linked to review seminars. On each of these occasions evaluative data were obtained not only in the form of opinions from the key parties but also in the form of specific examples provided by the clinical director participants (CDs) and their managers of changes in knowledge, attitudes, behaviour and performance.

The information obtained demonstrated clearly that the stakeholders had a shared perception of the purpose and objectives set for the programme, and that for the overwhelming majority both purpose and objectives were valuable and had been satisfactorily achieved. Caution must, of course, be exercised at this point. Distortions can be caused by biases of evaluators, by timing, by the design of and items within questionnaires, and by concerns over who would see the evaluations and to what use they would put the data. That said, however, evidence of the programme's perceived effectiveness was wide-ranging and came from multiple sources through time.

Of particular significance was the impact of the longer-term evaluation exercise in relation to assessing the value of the action learning (AL) component (Harrison, 1996). In longer-term evaluation questionnaires, four CDs cited AL as one of the most valuable elements of the programme. The strategic role of these clinicians had steadily expanded since the conclusion of the programme. For three of them it had been fully supported by their organisational context where they received encouragement, support and, often, further training and development to fully practise that role in line with their new learning. For the fourth, the organisational context had been less favourable but by February 1995 it was at last changing in a positive way.

Of the eight other CDs who by then were also in markedly more strategic roles, but who had made no comment on AL, four rated the programme's formal modules highly, although their learning had *not* subsequently been supported by their organisational contexts; and one saw the programme's unique value in its 'focused, small-group, safe environment to explore and experience issues away from work'. Three had been critical of AL in their earlier evaluations. Both of the clinicians who were *not* by then in more strategic roles failed to mention AL in their long-term evaluations.

This information indicates the critical importance of a supportive and developmental organisational context in ensuring the long-term positive impact of an AL period. It demonstrates the unique value of obtaining evaluations at some stage after the completion of a learning event. Had the evaluation process stopped on completion of the CD programme, perceptions of the value and impact of the AL component would have been quite different, and the planners would have been reluctant to use AL again in a similar programme, given its high cost in relation to the benefits evident at that point.

Finally, here is a task to integrate learning from this section.

Evaluating a management development programme

You are a training manager, planning a six-month management development programme involving a mix of off-the-job formal modules and work-related projects, visits to external organisations and other experiential learning approaches. What are the five or six activities that you must carry out in order to evaluate the programme for purposes both of validation and future planning?

Feedback notes

Here is a six-point guide to evaluating a learning event effectively and efficiently:

- *Plan the evaluation in advance of the programme.* As you plan it you are likely to realise that adjustments need to be made to aspects of programme-planning in order to ensure that effective evaluation can be carried out.

- *Ensure external consistency* by involving the learners' managers and other stakeholders in deciding on an evaluation process, and in monitoring and evaluating the programme. This will help to create the shared perceptions about the programme that will generate commitment to transfer its learning to the workplace and provide full support for the learners to practise their new learning over the long-term. Identify time-scale, resources and arrangements for managing the exercise when agreeing on who should evaluate.

- *Identify strategic milestones for the programme*, working backwards from the timing of its completion – when its final objectives should have been achieved – to its inception. (If you need to check on the meaning of 'strategic milestones', see Chapter 12.) Carrying out a check on progress at each milestone will enable information to be shared with key parties. They can then become involved in decisions about any adjustments that may be needed to the programme or its organisational context in order that the next milestone can be met.

- *Identify targets and performance indicators* within the programme in order to decide how the achievement of outcomes related to each milestone is to be measured. If they do not enable meaningful evaluation to be done, change them.

- *Monitor the development of learning*, ideally from a point before the learning event begins to some point subsequent to completion. Job training analysis and personal development diagnosis and planning as carried out in our case study (Part 1) will supply useful reference points as, of course, will the specified learning objectives.

- *Ensure feedback of results to the key parties in order to influence the planning of future events.* The results of effective evaluation can go far beyond validation of a particular programme. Bee and Farmer (1995) described how a study that started life as a simple training evaluation task became an exercise in helping the management of change at London Underground.

CONCLUSION

In order to achieve the learning objectives of this chapter we have examined the last four stages of our eight-stage approach to the design, delivery and evaluation of learning events.

Stage Five involved summarising points covered in Chapters 13 and 14 relating to selecting learners and specifying learning requirements. In Stage Six there was a discussion of the confirmation of learning strategy, design of a learning event, a three-step approach to choosing content, media and methods, and an eight-point guide to applying principles of learning to the design of an event. In Stage Seven a case-study was used to illustrate key points to do with delivering a learning event.

The study continued in Stage Eight – monitoring and evaluation – where six major evaluation issues were noted and and five key questions were discussed: what, why (involving the use of the CIRO approach), who, when and how to evaluate.

The chapter concluded with an activity to draw together and test key learning-points, and with a six-point guide to evaluating learning events.

USEFUL READING

BRAMLEY, P. (1996) *Evaluating Training.* London, Institute of Personnel and Development.

DUNCAN, K.D. and KELLEY, C.J. (1983) *Task Analysis, Learning and the Nature of Transfer.* Sheffield, Manpower Services Commission, Dept of Employment.

FRENCH, W. (1987) 'Training and retraining in skills' and

'Management and employee development' in W. French, *The Personnel Management Process*, 6th ed. Boston, Houghton Mifflin. pp. 361–99.

GAGNE, R.M. (1977) *The Conditions of Learning*. New York, Holt Saunders.

GILLEY, J.W. *and* EGGLAND, S.A. (1989) *Principles of Human Resource Development*. Maidenhead, Addison Wesley.

GOUGH, J. (1996) *Developing Learning Materials*. London, Institute of Personnel and Development.

HARDINGHAM, A. (1996) *Designing Training*. London, Institute of Personnel and Development.

HARRISON, R. (1996) 'Developing human resources for productivity', in J. Prokopenko and K. North (eds), *Productivity and Quality Management: A modular programme: Module 13*. Geneva, International Labour Office and Tokyo, Asian Productivity Association. Part II: 1–53. (Gives a detailed account of Cummins' Engine, Darlington's drive during the 1980s to harness HRD to key business goals, and of the ways in which HRD strategy was implemented, monitored and evaluated through time.)

PATRICK, J. *and* STAMMERS, R.B. (1977) 'Computer assisted learning and occupational training'. *British Journal of Educational Technology*. Vol. 3, No. 8: 253–67.

PISCIOTTO, M., ROBERTSON, I. *and* COLLEY, R. (1989) *Interactivity: Designing and using interactive video*. London, Kogan Page.

SIDDONS, S. (1997) *Delivering Training*. London, Institute of Personnel and Development.

17 Learning needs related to special groups and contingencies

LEARNING OBJECTIVES

After reading this chapter you will:

* understand why the basic steps involved in the inception, design, and delivery of training and development related to special groups and contingencies are the same as those for any planned learning event

* have achieved an increased understanding of widely encountered areas of special need through analysis of practical examples, and be able to generalise from that analysis to produce a set of underlying principles

* be able to apply a check-list of practical questions to the planning of training and development for special groups and contingencies.

INTRODUCTION

This chapter covers human resource development (HRD) related to special groups and contingencies. The main principles to be observed are the same from one case to the next, and take us back to our eight-stage approach to the inception, design and delivery of learning events introduced in Chapter 14:

1) Confirm needs

2) Agree on the overall purpose and objectives.

3) Identify the learning population profile.

4) Select the learning strategy, and agree on its direction and management.

5) Select the learners, and specify the learning.

6) Confirm the strategy and design or choose the event.

7) Manage the delivery of the event.

8) Monitor and evaluate.

Responding to the demands of business strategy and of change in the workplace

Whether as a planned response to the needs of business strategy or on a contingency basis, from time to time new HRD policies and initiatives will have to be introduced. Typical triggers would be a drive for customer care or total quality; new company policies or concerns relating to equality in the workplace; standards of health and safety at work; new legislation; preparation for a downsizing or delayering programme; the introduction of new tasks, patterns of work organisation or new technology; or changes in organisational culture and structure.

To analyse learning needs related to such imperatives, it is necessary first to establish the kind of competencies and attitudes required, together with standards to be achieved and methods of measuring performance in relation to those standards. Then, turning to the learning population that has been identified – which in some cases may be the entire workforce, in others a section or sector of it – a profile of that population has to be established. Information will have to be obtained on:

- the number of learners to be involved, and the time-scale for training, or other developmental initiatives to be designed and delivered

- the current levels and kind of competencies and attitudes that typify the learning population

- the kind of programme or other initiative most likely to bridge the gap between what is needed and the current situation, and provide the most effective and cost-beneficial type of learning

- any barriers or facilitators for the development of new learning in the workplace

- priorities for action – initiatives that are most likely to ensure advantage for the organisation and adequate recognition and rewards for the learners

- the analytical methods to be used (see Chapters 13 and 14).

Practical guidelines for HRD related to special groups and contingencies

The main principles to be observed in relation to the inception, planning, design and delivery of such learning events are the same from one case to the next, and go back to the basic theory covered in Chapters 14 and 16. However, particularly important questions to ask in the planning and design processes are these:

At which levels and across which sectors in the organisation do the needs exist?

Needs may exist at one or all of the following levels: corporate, business unit or operational. They may be specific to one group (for example, team leaders) or may relate to many or all employees (for example, initiatives to do with equal opportunities, health and safety, total quality or customer care).

At what stages of the performance management cycle should the learning events related to these needs be provided (see Chapter 13)?

Should they be provided in relation to:

- induction and basic training (and therefore be aimed at newcomers or those newly promoted)

- improving current performance (and therefore be aimed at existing job-holders)

- continuous development and career planning (and therefore be aimed at all employees)?

How should the needs be analysed?

A variety of approaches and techniques has been outlined in Chapters 13 and 14. However, with a special contingency, auditing is particularly useful (see Chapter 12). It will identify perceptions of key parties about learning needs, reveal learning outcomes required and generate valuable ideas about learning design, content and methods.

Are knowledge, skills and attitudes needed in relation to:
- task performance?

- task management?

- boundary management?

- motivation?

(See page 239)

What kind of learning should be involved:
- instrumental?

- dialogic?

- self-reflective?

(See pages 229–30)

Could the learning events lead to National Vocational Qualifications (NVQs)?

If so, this will enhance employability security for the learners and should provide an additional stimulus for the event.

In this chapter you will find areas of special need that are widely encountered in organisations: teamwork, equality in the workplace, and the learning and development of non-employees. Examples of good practice help to demonstrate general principles of planning and design.

TEAM DEVELOPMENT

Teamworking is one of the most familiar outcomes of downsizing, delayering and decentralisation. There are many examples available to illustrate ways in which training can be organised, but not all of them focus equally on the needs of leaders and of members.

Team leaders as first-line managers are critical to organisational and team success. They carry the responsibility for organising and managing people, ensuring the quality and profitability of products or services, improving safety, cost control, and other functions which require them to possess a considerable knowledge of the commercial, economic and customer-care aspects of a business. They also need mastery of many interpersonal skills and processes. Research has made it clear that the competencies and attitudes needed to perform well in team leader roles are specific to the particular organisational context (Warr and Bird, 1968). Careful analysis is therefore required to ensure the relevance of the purpose, design and outcomes of initiatives to develop team leaders.

Many team training programmes ignore the needs of those who come to team leader roles with experience of supervising sections or individuals but who have no understanding of the processes involved in managing flexible and autonomous teams and no awareness of how different the roles of team leader and of the traditional hierarchical supervisor are. In the following case-study, this mistake appears to have been avoided.

Case-study: Developing teamworking at Yardley Cosmetics

Yardley's manufacturing site in Basildon employs around 650 people, mainly women. Yardley was taken over by the US group Wasserstein Perella in 1990, and a radical programme of strategic change and organisational restructuring then commenced. The need was to improve customer service in a company that had been a traditional functional hierarchy, with poor communication across the business and little control over sourcing and supply of materials for its large range of products.

Steve Reddington, the new business director, came from Unilever to Yardley in 1990 with experience in co-ordinating a total quality programme. Initial changes were to do with breaking down functional barriers by setting up cross-functional management teams. The concept of internal customers and suppliers was developed, and clear and interrelated targets were set for all managers in the supply chain.

A 'common-sense' approach to teamworking was a natural consequence of the new order, but some formalisation rapidly became necessary. As production controllers were replaced by production managers, so supervisors were replaced by team leaders 'whose role was to help people achieve their goals and work as members of their own team' (Arkin, 1995a: 31). Triggered by the need to focus on customer service and quality in order to improve competitive edge, it was decided to invest in employee development, particularly via a new training centre with a training co-ordinator. A major need was team development – an area that had received little attention in the years before the take-over. The context for this training was that of the three production units: cosmetics, fragrances and body-care. A carefully integrated plan to select, train and develop teams and their leaders was established:

- A project team was set up to identify the skills and attributes needed by team leaders and members in their new work environment.

- Training consultants then designed a programme to improve team communication and problem-solving skills while also focusing on understanding the teamworking concept so that people would be thinking, as well as working, together.

- As the first stage of the programme, current supervisors and other employees went through an assessment centre in order to identify those to be given team leader positions. Not all supervisors made the transition, while some employees who had previously held only operator positions were found to have the necessary potential.

- Presentations were held on site to explain the team training programme, and then four half-day modules were organised first for workers in the cosmetics production unit. They were also attended by the training co-ordinator and a training adviser who would later deliver the same programme to those working in the two other production units.

- In parallel, modules were delivered that focused on 'helping team leaders think of themselves as coaches rather than supervisors' (Arkin, 1995a: 31).

Meanwhile the company was moving into another key stage of restructuring: the creation of integrated business units. Purchasing and planning departments were disbanded and those working in them were brought into the manufacturing units which, in turn, took responsibility for all aspects of production. Each unit was given clear goals and had to operate as a competitive unit benchmarked against other companies. At this point it became clear that team leaders would need further training, especially in running team briefings, in order to give the teamworking initiative sustained impetus within the new business-unit context.

Source: Arkin, 1995a

Analysis of this case-study reveals that:

- *External factors can trigger off a more strategic approach to employee development throughout an organisation.* In this case, the initial triggers were to do with a more competitive environment and consequent changes in business strategy. The investment in employee development, especially by setting up a training centre, was a mark of the company's determination to ensure that over the long term, as well as immediately, training would be a major lever to the achievement of the new business goals.

The speed with which the first stage of training was organised in response to those triggers clearly owed much to the working partnership between external and internal training consultants. As we saw in Chapter 9, external consultants can bring benefit to the organisation in many ways, especially when changes in mindsets as well as in skills are needed, and when internal HRD staff must acquire new skills quickly.

- *New initiatives in training and development must be aligned with business strategy.* In this case, changes in business strategy led to organisational restructuring as well as new customer service and quality goals. Training became essential in order to achieve the goals and to ensure that employees operated effectively in the new structure. Alignment of HRD with business goals gave the necessary commitment at all levels to that learning process.

- *Planning, design and evaluation of learning events should be done on a continuous basis.* It is easy to see how the eight stages involved in planning, designing and delivering a learning event were followed in this case-study. What should also be noted is the way in which the company ensured that, as business and organisational changes continued, the focus of training changed to take account of these.

• *The identification of the key skills, knowledge and attitudes of the learning group involved is crucial in determining what they need to learn.* Identification of the level of competence and motivation already possessed by the learners in relation to that which they need to reach in their new work environment should be a starting-point in the design process. It enables a clear focus to be established and standards of performance and behaviour to be put in place. In this case-study, the identification and analysis of learning needs in the roles and jobs concerned (by the project team) was paralleled by assessment of those selected to occupy those roles and carry out those jobs (through the medium of the assessment centre).

It is in that combination of leader and members that the power of the team as a group lies. In this case-study there was a focus both on developing team skills within a team and on helping team leaders to function effectively in their new roles.

For purposes of comparison, another study of team training should be read. Proctor's (1995) account of teamworking at Raytheon Corporate Jets discussed a wide-ranging approach to the development of team skills and motivation. The account described the training events that were designed to meet new business needs, and gave insightful detail about the assessment centre process whereby new team leaders were selected. Most importantly it showed how team training was integrated within a wider and consistently developed performance management system, employee resource context and changing organisational structure. That whole change process was driven by new business, organisational and human resource (HR) goals, and one of its major unexpected consequences was a more strategic, business-led HR department.

DEVELOPMENT RELATED TO ACHIEVING EQUALITY IN THE WORKPLACE

The legal context
Inequality at work occurs when a person or group is treated in an unjustifiably less favourable way than another is, or would be, treated in the same sort of situation. It is essential to ensure that every effort is made to prevent discrimination occuring in the organisation and to achieve full equality of treatment and opportunity for all employees.

At present the law offers protection for people against discrimination on grounds of sex, marriage, race, disability, and ethnic or national origins (for a fuller account, see Marchington and Wilkinson, 1996: 76–85). However, there are other forms of discrimination, particularly those related to age, religion (it is only in Northern Ireland that discrimination on grounds of religion is forbidden by law) and sexual orientation.

Discrimination related to age is particularly widespread in Britain yet ageism cannot be afforded in a country that, in the grip of demographic change, has a significantly ageing workforce. Discrimination related to disability is also widespread. Long-standing legislation had no teeth, since there were no civil remedies for its breach (Marchington and Wilkinson, 1996: 77). The Disability Discrimination Act 1995 encourages supported employment across a wider range of occupations and locations than hitherto by allowing profit-making firms as well as voluntary bodies to operate schemes to support people with learning disabilities in employment (see especially the 'Next Step Project' described by Arkin, 1995b). As an aside in the context of this section, but worth noting none the less, few disabled people are likely to join the employed workforce despite the radical improvement in the confidence and employability that such schemes can produce. This is because, as Arkin pointed out, most of the disabled are still victims of the benefits trap.

The role of HRD in achieving equality in the workplace

So what are the implications of all this for HRD? First, to ensure that the employer operates within the law. Next, to ensure the kind of good practice that will help the organisation to attract, retain and develop a fully effective workforce. To achieve equality in the workplace the employer must:

- ensure that there is no unlawful discrimination

- develop good employment practices for all employees equally

- identify groups who are underrepresented in certain jobs and take any necessary action to remedy this

- have, by effective monitoring, a defence against complaints of racial discrimination by individuals

- eliminate overt discrimination and employment practices that are discriminatory in the ways they operate

- provide special training for employees who would otherwise be unable to enjoy the full benefits of an equal opportunities policy (CRE, 1983).

This indicates that HRD should focus on three general areas of need related to: the raising of awareness and development of good practice, avoidance of unlawful discrimination, and positive action across the organisation.

General awareness and practice in the organisation

Training and guidance should be available for everyone who makes policies and procedures, administers, or is in any way actively involved in the key employee resourcing (ER) processes in the workplace, in order to ensure that all practical steps are taken to avoid discrimination. Such personnel include supervisory and managerial staff, HR specialists and reception staff. The key processes are those to do with:

- ER-planning

- recruitment and selection

- basic pay, terms and conditions of work

- appraisal, training and development

- career development, promotion and transfers

- benefits and rewards

- health, safety and welfare

- termination of employment.

Such training and guidance must ensure that managers and others understand what direct and indirect discrimination means, and know how to identify any discriminatory attitudes that may affect decision-making. They must understand the importance of recording ways in which applications for positions, training and rewards are handled, as well as the decisions made in those cases. Without such records to demonstrate that all reasonable practical steps have been taken to avoid discrimination occurring, it will be difficult to disprove claims of unlawful treatment.

There must also be knowledge of the law related to providing access to opportunities for training, promotion and other forms of reward or development. For example, if it is a condition of a management development programme that all participants must spend six months on a course in another area or region, and there is no convincing justification for this (because there is a good course run locally or the learning could be achieved by some other medium), then the condition could be held to be unlawful because it discriminates against married women with children who would always find such a condition more difficult to comply with than other types of employee would.

Problems of communication and understanding often cause or increase discriminatory attitudes and behaviour at work. Training to raise awareness of how these problems can arise and of the special needs of minority groups in the workplace, can make a significant contribution to reducing these problems.

All organisations should have an equal opportunities policy. Guidance must be given so that it is fully understood at every level and so that the roles and responsibilities it involves are clear and are carried out competently.

Avoiding unlawful discrimination in HRD
Information about training, educational and other developmental opportunities, and how to apply for them, must be made known to all eligible employees. They must not be communicated in ways that could exclude or disproportionately reduce the numbers of applicants from a particular minority or racial group or sex.

There must be no direct or indirect discrimination in selecting people for training and development, and checks must be made regularly to see whether people from a particular group or sex do not apply for employment or promotion; are not recruited or promoted at all; or are appointed, but in significantly lower proportions than their rate of application. If any of these problems are occurring then the training manager must find out whether a major cause lies in a lack of appropriate training or qualifications among these individuals. If it does, and if the reason is that training or other forms of development were not as accessible for them as for other employees, or that the design or 'language' of the learning methods involved posed particular problems for them, then changes must be made.

Positive action in training

Although it is not lawful to discriminate against some groups in order to improve the position of others previously disadvantaged, this does not preclude positive action to help those in the latter category. For example, where in the previous 12-month period there have been no or proportionately few employees of a particular sex or racial group in certain jobs, areas, or level of work, then:

* employers may provide access to training facilities that will help to fit them for such work or responsibilities

* employers may encourage them to apply for training or education, whether it is provided internally or externally

* the training manager may design training schemes for school-leavers designed to reach members of such groups; and may arrange training for promotion or skills training for those who lack particular expertise but show potential (supervisory training may include language training).

It is also lawful to give access to relevant training when minority groups have special needs in respect of education or training. For example, if the workforce includes employees whose English is limited, then the training manager should ensure that communications are helped by training in English and communication skills, training for managers and team leaders in the background and culture of ethnic minority groups, and even by providing, where possible, interpretation and translation facilities for grievance and other procedures and terms of employment.

> Discrimination in employment will not be solved by one or two major actions ... Solutions will be found by avoiding complacency and paying attention to the several areas where discrimination can manifest itself or where the needs of ethnic minority employees require sensitive examination ... Good human resource management involves making the best use of all available talent; it requires effective, ie bias free, systems of selection, training and motivation.
>
> (Roots, 1982)

Women's management training regularly attracts interest as more evidence is uncovered to reveal continuing bias against women striving for promotion in male-dominated sectors or organisations. However, women in non-managerial jobs have career development needs too, and Arkin (1991) described an award-winning personal and career development programme for such women, Springboard, pioneered at the BBC. Because Springboard remains a widely used initiative, I am repeating here the case-study included in my 1992 IPM text, *Employee Development*.

The Springboard programme

What does the case-study emphasise, related to the planning, design and delivery of programmes catering for special groups and needs?

Springboard evolved from a 'Women's development programme' launched by the BBC in 1989 that won the Lady Platt Award for the best equal opportunities training initiative.

That programme arose out of a perceived need that, while the BBC had done much to open up opportunities for women managers, it was essential to widen these initiatives, extending personal and career development opportunities to women (between 8,000 and 9,000) employed in non-managerial positions at the BBC. Better utilisation and motivation of such a huge organisational resource was clearly in the interests of the business as well as being of benefit to those individuals.

Consideration of the kinds of learning media and methods to be used indicated at first sight that distance learning would be the most appropriate medium, given the extremely large size of the learning population. However, analysis of the profile of that population highlighted the importance to the learners of support and encouragement from other women, and this led to the decision to design a programme which involved much face-to-face learning. Its components were:

• three one-day workshops held over three months

• a workbook involving about three hours' work a week for participants, and involving a range of self-assessment and personal learning plan activities

• the formation of formal and informal networks

• a mentoring system in the workplace

• the involvement of senior women in the organisation.

The programme, designed by the BBC's management training unit working with Biographic Management consultancy, became so highly regarded that it was renamed Springboard and tailored for the use of other organisations, including Grand Metropolitan Foods, Europe, who incorporated it within a much larger initiative called the 'Learning Edge', designed to create a learning environment in which all employees could develop their full potential.

Source: Arkin, 1991

Feedback notes

Analysis of the study shows how carefully the programme was tailored to the needs of the organisation as well as of the individuals concerned. Particular points to note here are that:

• *learning media and methods must be appropriate, efficient and flexible, given the needs and situation of the learners.* Choice was determined by an analysis of the purpose and objectives of the programme and of the profile of the large learning population involved, of the need to encourage, motivate and stimulate the wide variety of learners, and of the practicalities of the situation. This resulted in a programme that offered a well-integrated range of media and methods that were relatively cheap and highly effective. The costs of designing and reproducing the workbook would have very quickly been offset by the numbers of people using it. It provided an ideal way of helping learners to prepare for practical sessions, reflect on learning, and transfer it continuously to their own individual situations. Thus the choice of media and methods echoes the principles discussed in Chapter 16 (pages 294–6).

* *external recognition of a new programme can lead to its extension to similar groups in other organisations.* We can see the value that external recognition (the Lady Platt award) can bring to a programme. The extension of Springboard has helped many more women than the BBC group for which it was originally intended.

* *new HRD initiatives must be integrated into wider HRD strategy and plans.* This is the significance of Grand Metropolitan's reaction – a new programme designed to meet the needs of a special group became an integral part of overall HRD strategy in the organisation. Unless this happens new initiatives can lose their impact and die once the needs of a particular set of individuals have been met.

Training and development initiatives that facilitate re-entry after periods of absence from employment can also make a significant contribution to the business, as well as meeting individual needs. Without such schemes, for example, many women who take maternity leave do not or cannot return to their organisations. Particular organisational benefits of such initiatives include:

* improved returns on the training of staff, and the retention of skills and talents that might otherwise be lost

* saving in recruitment and relocation costs

* a pool of trained, committed ex-employees available to cover peaks in workload, holidays, long-term absence and maternity leave

* increased employability security for individuals.

LEARNING AND DEVELOPMENT OF 'NON-EMPLOYEES'

Part-time and temporary workers

We saw in Chapter 10 (page 167) the short-sightedness of focusing all of an organisation's HRD investment on full-time employees. The contribution of part-time and temporary workers can be crucial to the success and growth of the business, and certain non-employees too can have an important part to play in extending the organisation's influence over its environment and enhancing its long-term profitability.

In Chapters 1 and 7 there was much discussion of the meaning of the term 'flexible workforce' and the trends that had produced this concept. Research by the Policy Studies Institute (1993) indicated that flexible workers are an underperforming resource, and failure to integrate part-time and temporary workers into the organisation's HRD system is now giving rise to concern at government level (White,

1996). Here is a case-study showing how innnovative HRD policies can achieve significant improvements in building up a genuinely flexible workforce in which temporary workers play a leading role.

Case-study: Developing a flexible workforce at Beeton Rumford

The Earl's Court Olympia catering company, Beeton Rumford, employed around 200 temporary workers. It was unusual in the catering trade in its promise of a good benefits package and equal commitment to the development of all its workers, not only those occupying full-time positions. The determination of the managing director, Richard Tate, to have an integrated workforce was so great that he banned the term 'casual'. He first developed his philosophy in an earlier career with Trust House Forte.

At Beeton Rumford the role of temporary employees was crucial but had in the past been undervalued. After 1991 the aim had been to ensure that through focused recruitment aimed at attracting and retaining high-calibre staff, and through eradicating from the company the casual ethos, temporary staff would be recognised by themselves and others as the backbone of the organisation, supported by rather than supporting full-time staff. After 1991 the company had been restructured from a functional to a customer-focused business, and a separate staff department had been established to recruit, train and manage temporary personnel.

At first, much relatively unproductive effort went into improving the status and training of temporary staff. Operational managers found it hard to support such a change in focus, given the stop-start nature of the business: despite their efforts the large pool of expensively recruited and trained temporary talent would disappear at the end of every catering event.

Further ER policy change took place, and this brought the improvements sought. Now, temporary staff were no longer laid off at 24 hours' notice but were treated as full-time in terms of the focus of their jobs, being given information about events scheduled over the coming year in order to aid their own planning activity. At the heart of the development strategy was a six-tier career structure based on its own competencies, with appraisals carried out during each exhibition.

Source: Pickard, 1995

Beeton Rumford offers a model of best practice in how to respond to changing business needs and labour market patterns by placing skills training in a wider and integrating human resource management (HRM) and organisational context. The survey (Gallie and White, 1993) that underpinned the Policy Studies Institute report already noted revealed that it is this wider context that tends to be unsatisfactory for so-called 'flexible workers'. Most have less access than permanent full-time workers to four key areas of HRD practice:

- upskilling through training, growth in the job and increased responsibility

- performance management systems (PMSs) which combine appraisal reviews, target-setting, performance feedback and merit pay

• increasing personal discretion in tasks

• decentralised decision-making.

Commenting on the research, White (1996) noted that although the lowest skill categories of part-time and temporary workers fared worst, part-timers in management were particularly excluded from PMSs, and temporary workers (expecting less than one year's employment) suffered disproportionately in every area except that of initial training. Contract workers, on the other hand, did well: 'the healthier picture for this group indicates that it is possible to adapt development systems to meet the needs of flexible workers'.

Crossing organisational boundaries
Extending the scope of HRD beyond an organisation's boundaries is important for two reasons. First, it ensures that those on whom the organisation depends for the ultimate quality of its products and services are trained to the same standards as its own employees and understand its business processes and systems – the training rationale. Second, external stakeholders have skills, knowledge, networks and ways of perceiving and understanding the business environment and the organisation that can enhance organisational learning and knowledge. Developing learning networks across organisational boundaries can therefore improve an organisation's strategic capability (page 6) – the learning rationale. To achieve this, however, the process of learning involved must be 'focused, continuous and systematic ... aligned with satisfying the needs of the organisation and its stakeholders' (Batchelor, Donnelly and Morris, 1995: 1).

The customer–supplier relationship is a case in point. Supplier development programmes tend to be driven by the training rationale. Most focus on issues of task, process and skill development. However, a few, driven by a different rationale, seek to achieve a proactive learning partnership where people from inside and outside the organisation work together to improve their strategic thinking and creativity. The aim is a relationship where the organisation responds to the learning needs of the stakeholder in ways that produce double-loop learning – an approach already explained in Chapter 13 (pages 230–31) and involving a questioning of why certain problems occur in the first place and an identification of underlying causes instead of only their surface symptoms. This contrasts with single-loop learning, where the aim is simply to reduce or eliminate a problem by training to improve performance (the training rationale). It is when double-loop learning occurs that things begin to change and new, more appropriate, ways of thinking and behaving develop.

Argyris (1996) explained the value of double-loop learning by reference to what he called 'skilled incompetency': the way in which skilful actions of individuals and groups can become counterproductive if they lead to defensive routines which, spreading across a workplace or entire organisation, produce a culture that avoids confrontation. In such a culture basic assumptions that people hold about work, organisational goals, and the business vision and environment cannot be tested. Fundamentally important issues can thus become undiscussable.

Nothing will then change until 'something occurs that blows things open' (Argyris, 1996: 87).

Research shows, however, that in order to overturn what has now become embedded in the culture of an organisation nothing less than trauma is usually required – a threat to the organisation's survival, and/or the bringing in of new blood at the top. Argyris himself used the example of ultimate catastrophe: the 1986 Space Shuttle disaster. Only then 'were the mixed messages and defensive routines used during the decision to launch exposed. The disaster made it legitimate for outsiders to require insiders to discuss the undiscussable.'

Here is an example of an innovative approach to inter-organisational learning (learning between organisations rather than learning within a single organisation) that aims to achieve double-loop learning without resorting to or being overtaken by traumatic interventions.

Case-study: Rover's supplier networks

In 1994 Rover Group was acquired by BMW AG and became an independent subsidiary. Rover remained firm in its commitment to place all aspects of learning at the heart of the business (see Harrison: 1993, 315–20), and included within the scope of the learning process not only its own employees (called 'associates') but also the extended enterprise, including suppliers. The Just in Time Distribution Efficiency Programme (JIT/DEP) and the learning initiatives to support it represented a unique manifestation of this commitment.

JIT/DEP set a target of 14 days from the placement of a customer order to delivery to the customer. To support this target Supplier Networks were established across the UK – by 1994 there were four, with a total of 40 companies ranging from multi-nationals to small businesses. The networks were not focused upon geographical area and involved non-competing Rover suppliers who wished to participate for mutual benefit.

The aim of the network groups went much further than supplier training. It was to achieve mutual learning between Rover and the network organisations by establishing a sounding board for developments introduced under JIT/DEP which affected suppliers. In this role suppliers were to enable the sharing of confidential information so that their recommendations could influence final policy decisions at Rover. The groups would make it possible for network members to form a genuinely open, challenging learning partnership with Rover personnel, identifying fundamental causes and proposing what might be quite radical ways of eliminating problems that suppliers were experiencing or envisaged having through the operation of JIT/DEP.

> The Network Groups define the problem, research it and recommend courses of action in a presentation to Rover at director level ... [They] carry out research with other suppliers and they have access to all of those key factholders within Rover who can clarify issues of systems, policy and future strategy.
>
> (Batchelor *et al*, 1995: 10)

Source: Batchelor, Donnelly and Morris, 1995

In such a strategy the learning needs of suppliers are aligned with the learning needs of the organisation: in the resolution of the former lie, increasingly through time, the resolution of the latter because both organisation and stakeholder are working together to anticipate and generate solutions to challenges that affect them both. Another, in the long-term even more important, outcome is that in this learning relationship the parties are developing a far greater understanding of the organisation, its systems and environment than either could do alone. In that process both are learning how to improve their position in their environment by adapting to it and shaping it with continuously improving levels of capability.

In Chapters 1 and 2 the importance of 'strategic capability' was explained. (If you have forgotten this concept, you may find it helpful to check the explanations on pages 6 and 31–2). This kind of response to the learning needs of stakeholders is essential to the development of the strategic capability of organisations like Rover that have to deal with turbulent organisational as well as external environments. In its reliance on trust, collaboration and recognition of mutuality of interest between organisation and stakeholder it transcends the limitations of conventional, internally focused approaches to the 'learning organisation'. In its focus on the development of strategically valuable knowledge and ways of thinking and understanding, it demonstrates how to build not so much a learning organisation but a knowledge-productive organisation that can regularly develop the strategic assets on which its future profitability depends. We shall return to this concept of knowledge creation in the final chapter.

Finally, it is appropriate at this point to mention one category of non-employee rarely given prominence either in research or the generalist literature of HRD: the voluntary worker. Increasingly these personnel offer knowledge, skills, commitment and a network of contacts that are of unique value to the business. Think, for example, of the reliance that the National Health Service places on volunteers in areas of hospital and community care work. The management committees of housing association trusts too rely heavily on voluntary members who work with chief executives in developing and maintaining the strategic direction of those associations. In charitable bodies likewise, voluntary staff carry a heavy burden of responsibility.

While the personal orientation of volunteers is by definition different from that of other non-employees, their loyalty to the cause of the organisation is as great or greater, and their contribution is essential. Competition for volunteers is intensifying as, for a variety of reasons, their supply diminishes (Welch, 1997a) and essential services are scaled down when recruitment efforts fail. Adapting an organisation's HRD policies to meet volunteers' special learning needs can therefore now be seen not as an optional but as a necessary element in recruitment and retention strategy.

PRINCIPLES TO OBSERVE IN RESPONDING TO THE LEARNING NEEDS OF SPECIAL GROUPS AND CONTINGENCIES

The case-studies contained in this chapter have been chosen as examples of best practice in areas of special learning need that are common across many organisations. Studying them for their wider implications, we can identify a number of key principles to observe in responding to such needs:

* Particular learning events should be analysed in the context of the needs of the business and its strategic goals. This should secure management's commitment to such events and ensure that the investment made in them produces due value for the business.

* Each new HRD initiative should be fully integrated within and be supported by the framework of wider HRD and ER policy and systems.

* The success of learning initiatives to meet special needs can produce an ever-widening impact on the ER function and on ER policy-making in the organisation. It can also lead to the identification of other important learning needs within the organisation. External recognition can trigger the extension of the initiatives both within and beyond the organisation.

* The identification of key competencies needed in the job and the person is central to the planning and effective outcomes of such learning events, and their evaluation should influence any subsequent planning and design.

* Learning media and methods must be appropriate, efficient and flexible, adaptable to the needs of the particular learners.

* Where possible, training should lead to vocational qualifications, in order to enhance employability security and the motivation of learners.

* The scope of special learning and development initiatives should cover 'flexible' workers and extend across organisational boundaries to respond to the needs and interests of key stakeholders who, although not employed by the organisation, have a vital contribution to make to its success.

CONCLUSION

In order to achieve the learning objectives of this chapter, the needs of special groups and contingencies have been placed in the overall context of adaptation to emergent demands of business strategy and of change in the workplace. Key information to obtain when special needs become evident has been outlined, and practical guidelines to observe when responding to such needs have been identified.

Certain widely encountered areas of special need have been used as the focus for the case-studies and discussion in the chapter – teamwork, equality in the workplace, the development of 'flexible workers' and inter-organisational learning networks. The importance of the latter has been emphasised in relation to achieving double-loop learning, which can enhance strategic thinking and capability, and influence the direction of the organisation through time. From the practical examples certain key principles have emerged, and these have been summarised at the end of the chapter.

USEFUL READING

BELBIN, R.M. (1964) *Training the Adult Worker*. London, HMSO.

INSTITUTE OF PERSONNEL AND DEVELOPMENT. The IPD publishes a range of Guides and Key Facts on employment issues. For details, call the Publishing Department on 0181-263 3387

KATZENBACH, J. *and* SMITH, D. (1992) *The Wisdom of Teams*. London, McGraw-Hill.

LEWIS, J. *and* McLAVERTY, C. (1991) 'Facing up to the needs of the older manager'. *Personnel Management*. Vol. 23, 1: 32–5.

MUNYARD, T. (1988) 'Homophobia at work and how to manage it'. *Personnel Management*. Vol. 20, 6: 46–50.

THOMAS, K. *and* MELLON, T. (1995) *Planning for Training and Development: A guide to analysing needs*. London, Save the Children. (Aims to assist those working in the voluntary sector who are responsible for identifying training needs, establishing development plans and budgets, and evaluating programmes.)

Part 5

THE LANDSCAPE OF CORPORATE LEARNING AND KNOWLEDGE PRODUCTIVITY

18 Developing careers for individual and organisational growth

LEARNING OBJECTIVES

After reading this chapter you will:

- understand the importance of a strategic approach to career development in the organisation and the typical triggers for such an approach

- be able to identify the ways in which career management can be integrated into the organisation within a career development process based on mutuality and the concept of the psychological contract

- understand the meaning of the career life cyle, career anchors and career transition points, and their implications for career management systems

- understand key methods of assessing the needs and potential of individuals in relation to career development.

THE LANDSCAPE OF CORPORATE LEARNING AND KNOWLEDGE PRODUCTIVITY

Throughout this book a central theme has been the importance of integrating learning and work in order to achieve operational goals and 'the steady growth in the ability to learn or generate new knowledge at every organisational level' (page 159). In Part 5 discussion of human resource development (HRD) broadens to encompass the kind of role that HRD can play in enabling an organisation to become knowledge-productive – capable of producing, developing and regenerating the knowledge to meet current challenges and to advance over the longer term. To do this we shall explore in these last three chapters some dominating features of what Kessels (1996: 172) has called 'the rich landscape [of organisational learning and development] where personnel and teams find their way and construct knowledge'.

The focus in this chapter is on the value of the effective management of careers in the promotion of sustained organisational, as well as individual, growth. In Chapter 19 we shall see how management development can help to ensure the strategic knowledge and capability it needs for the future. Concepts of innovation, growth and strategic direction will lead us into Chapter 20, where themes of strategic HRM, organisational learning and knowledge productivity that have occurred throughout the book finally merge as they reach their culmination.

CAREER DEVELOPMENT

Career development has been defined as 'an organised, planned effort comprised of structured activities or processes that result in a mutual career plotting effort between employees and the organisation' (Gilley and Eggland, 1989: 48).

Traditionally, the concept of 'career' was one of upward movement involving, therefore, as Sparrow and Hiltrop (1994: 427) observed:

• entry criteria linked to educational attainment or vocational training

• a planned structure of job experiences and promotional steps

• progressive status and/or salary

• membership of an external professional or occupational body with its own codes and culture.

Although, as we shall see later in this chapter, the traditional concept of 'career' has not changed as radically as is commonly assumed, it has none the less begun to shift in its emphasis. Fewer organisations are now able to guarantee lifetime job security and, in many waves of delayering, have produced flatter structures. These two trends have led to a greater emphasis on 'career' in the sense of job occupancy carrying with it coherent induction, training and development, increased employability security by the accrual of experience and qualifications valued in the external labour market, and more challenge, problem-solving and decision-making responsibilities at every organisational level.

The concept of 'career' is also now more focused on mutuality of interest and need rather than on planned upward movement. This, of course, should always have been the case. As Schein (1978: vii) observed nearly two decades ago career development marks the point at which the shifting needs of an organisation's people confront the shifting nature of its work, going to the heart of the psychological contract joining the two parties, employer and employee. The challenge it embodies is one of matching the needs of the organisation with those of the people who work for it, and to do so from entry into the organisation, through each career transition point thereafter, until exit, in order to achieve a mutually beneficial relationship over time.

The double reference to 'mutuality' in the above paragraph is deliberate. Unless mutuality is embedded in career development systems, the commitment of the individual to any career planning process will be lost: there will be a crisis of credibility and a negative impact on organisational as well as individual learning and growth. Let us look at this issue more closely.

If the individual's career aspirations are to be brought into productive alignment with the organisation's need for the achievement of business targets and for business growth, the individual must be understood, and treated not as the 'servant' of the organisation but as an organisational stakeholder with the power either to expend or withdraw energy, expertise and commitment. The relationship that binds individual and organisation is twofold. There is a legal contract that specifies duties, terms and conditions, and material rewards; it clarifies the legal obligations of the parties. There is also a psychological contract consisting of felt and perceived expectations, wants and rights. It is this contract that provides the framework for the continuing relationship between the parties. If the organisation wishes to change the legal contract of employment, it can do so only on the basis of renegotiation and a new agreement between the parties. In the same way, if the basis of the psychological contract changes during the individual's career with the organisation, then that too should be acknowledged as cause for the parties jointly to identify the key issues raised by the changed situation, what each party wants in that new situation, and a renegotiation of what each will offer to the other.

Career development is a major part of the psychological contract, and if negotiated and managed effectively it offers a unique opportunity to achieve organisational as well as individual growth.

Triggers for a more planned approach to career development

Taking your own organisation, or one with which you are familiar, identify any major change that has triggered a need for a more planned approach to the management and development of careers there. You may focus on particular occupational or professional groups, or on the whole workforce.

Feedback notes
In your response you will probably have listed one or more of the following triggers, since these are the most typical across organisations today:

• *a policy of continuous internal promotion and growth* in order to attract and retain scarce skills and ensure continuity of supply. The concept of lifetime employment is now under threat even in its country of origin, Japan, and the rigours as well as the organisational benefits of the strategy of recruiting high-calibre employees and then investing heavily in their internal development and promotion have been well documented (see, for example, White and Trevor, 1983 and Wickens, 1987). However, where external supply is weak or unreliable, and the need to obtain and retain scarce skills is high, 'growing our own' may be the only feasible policy for the organisation and will, in turn, require a planned approach to career development for those individuals or groups of employees concerned.

• *affirmative action programmes*, such as the Civil Service's and National Health Service's in relation to female employees. Their implications mean that long-term career progression patterns have to be identified and career paths clearly established in the organisation.

• *a need to improve levels of motivation and job satisfaction, commitment to the organisation and productivity*. Where employee satisfaction surveys reveal a high level of discontent with internal careers, the organisation is well advised to take action to change the situation. A well-known example is the Rover Tomorrow agreement in September 1991 (known as the New Deal), when the company effectively offered its employees jobs for life by giving a pledge of no compulsory redundancies in return for the adoption of Japanese-style flexible working practices. Before that time, only managers had problem-solving responsibilities; afterwards, the days of 'one man one job' disappeared. All employees became known as 'associates' with the production line reorganised around 100-strong cells in which everyone had a say in the best way to achieve improvements. Employees' perspectives on their careers in the company changed dramatically for the better (Harrison, 1993a: 60, 303–04, 315–20).

• *a radical shift in the organisation's developmental path, involving a change of culture that needs to be combined with a career development programme*. A typical example would be the need, following downsizing, to develop remaining employees into a flexible workforce and therefore to negotiate a new psychological contract focused on a career development system that can gain their commitment to the changed situation.

The common factor linking all such triggers is an imbalance – due to external or internal changes – that has developed in the psychological contract between the individual and the organisation, and a consequent need to review and renegotiate that relationship. The following study provides a case in point.

Case-study: SCO's approach to career development

SCO, a computer software company founded in the USA, is typical of many young, fast-growing firms whose rapid rise has depended on a judicious mix of acquisition strategy and restructuring in order to develop new skills and products. Career development in such firms is inevitably an uncertain process. Yet the type of employees needed – with rare and high-level technical skills – have to be attracted and then motivated to stay long enough to make an impact on the firm's growth that repays the investment in recruiting them.

Macaulay and Harding's (1996) account of SCO's approach to employee development identified the starting-point as the recognition by the company of the need to change traditional employee expectations about career development to one more consistent with what it was possible and appropriate for the company to offer. Internal surveys and focus groups revealed widespread employee discontent with the gap between expectations and reality: 'loyalty no longer guaranteed security or promotion' (Macaulay and Harding, 1996: 34). Employees were also critical of the HR department which, they felt, did not offer the expected level of support or expertise in relation to personal development.

A 'best practice' review of other world-class organisations showed the need for a career development system that was closely aligned with the company's vision and direction, that attracted, motivated and rewarded high-performing people, and that communicated well. This led SCO to develop a plan of action focusing on four parameters:

• building a learning culture through emphasising self-development and career management driven by the individual

• improved feedback and communication

• a more effective performance management system (PMS)

• increasing the ability of individuals to bring about change.

The authors explained the kind of practical interventions involved in this plan: the production and distribution to all employees of a self-development guide containing a variety of inventories and activities, and stressing the joint nature of development in the company; career management workshops; project teams for specific business issues, incorporating technical problem-solving workshops; lunchtime training sessions on key company issues; a move towards total quality and continuous improvement; workshops on managing transition; and a review of the PMS.

The account made it clear that these interventions have not been trouble-free, and that the company is only at the start of a complex process requiring management's sustained commitment to invest heavily in time and effort over the long term if the desired rewards are to be achieved. The company, however, sees no alternative if it is to survive and grow in its turbulent and highly competitive market environment.

Source: Macaulay and Harding, 1996

How far is the traditional concept of 'a career' obsolete?
The final paragraph of our case-study is arguably its most important. Schein (1978) differentiated between the concept of the 'internal career' – meaning the individual's pursuit of an occupational path during his or her lifetime – and that of the 'external career' – meaning the developmental path established by the organisation for employees during their time with that organisation. There is also another kind of differentiation: between those types of career paths that involve repeated movement for the individual between the external and the internal labour market, whether primary or secondary (see pages 103–4) and those that offer meaningful progression within a single organisation for most of an individual's employed life.

The career development issues facing organisations today have no easy solutions. Few firms may now feel able to offer long-term internal career paths to their employees. Some cannot offer any meaningful career paths at all; others may still be able to offer them for certain employees, but not all. For those whose career paths involve the need for, or inevitability of, regular movement between external and internal labour markets, the consistent pursuit of self-development and opportunities for continuous learning is essential in order to ensure high employability security.

However, despite the strong advocacy of self-development and continuous learning in the HR literature (including this book – see, for example, Chapters 10 and 13), taking responsibility for one's own development and career is not an easy or straightforward matter. It requires an informed and objective assessment of the kind of skills and experience that will be relevant for the individual for the future, together with access to opportunities to develop those skills and acquire that experience. Where the future is impossible to predict, it will be difficult for the individual to find a focus for self-development and continuous learning activities in which he or she can feel confidence, even supposing that such activities are accessible and affordable.

As was made clear in a report of research by the Institute for Employment Studies (Hirsch, Jackson and Jackson, 1995) people do need help in managing their careers. Such help is not always available or of the necessary quality. We have already seen (Chapter 7) the inadequacies of the UK's national vocational education and training system in terms of its provision of education and training for flexibility, continuous development and due focus on the long term. Within organisations, it is not enough for companies to allocate major resources to self-development – as many are doing. There must be a strategy for careers that tackles career management in an integrative and holistic way. It is also essential that line managers ensure the effective implementation of that strategy. However, we have observed elsewhere what exceptional effort and commitment are needed on the part of top management in an organisation to ensure that line managers take full responsibility for building and maintaining an environment in which it becomes possible for employees to take responsibility for their own development and to make fully informed choices in so doing (for example, pages 163–3, 173–7, 181–2). To quote Kessels (1996: 172), elaborating on the significance of the 'rich landscape' of learning opportunities in an organisation: 'Given the vital importance of the learning processes involved, leaving the necessary learning to random opportunity would be imprudent.' He therefore argued for 'self-regulation, which entails facilitating and stimulating development and organizing supportive feedback'.

If it were indeed to be the case that the old concept of 'lifetime careers' is redundant – whether that means a career mainly with one organisation or one achieved through a planned series of moves through a small number of organisations – then, left to themselves, the career paths of many individuals would founder. It was noted on page 13 that:

> In those organisations which have to survive in increasingly turbulent environments and can no longer offer long-term job security, open recognition of mutuality of interest seems more likely to generate high performance and adaptability than appeals to loyalty and commitment.

And on page 14 it was noted that an integrated strategy was essential:

> to produce a strategy for building up and retaining valuable skills and experience for the organisation while at the same time giving support to individuals at critical transition points in their working lives. In this context a planned approach to career development both in the internal and external labour market is essential.

Without such a purposive approach by organisations to career development, 'employability security' could prove to be just one more fashionable term disguising a very different situation for many in the internal and external labour markets; and the organisations themselves would not reap the benefit of individuals' learning that, better supported and stimulated, should bring organisational benefits.

To put the issue into perspective, however, it is essential to look at the evidence. What there is does not support the view that the traditional concept of 'a career' has radically changed in recent years, or needs to do so. Average job tenure in Britain, at five and a half years by 1997, had hardly changed from 20 years before, when it was six years (Smith, 1997). White-collar insecurity in particular, whether measured by employees' expectations of their future or by actual unemployment rates, is by the mid- to late 1990s a fallacy: there is insecurity, but it preponderantly affects unskilled, low-paid workers, the young and the over-fifties. They are the groups in most need of attention and help.

In 1996 Guest and Davey reported on research undertaken by the Department of Organisational Psychology at Birkbeck College for the Career Research Forum, established in London in 1994. Disappointingly, for those wanting more employability security and the organisational support that would help to achieve it, there was a failure of most organisations studied to get fully to grips even with the problems that have traditionally beset internal career management systems – succession planning, the evaluation of existing policy and practice, and the encouragement and support of line managers for the self-development of their staff (Guest and Davey, 1996: 24).

On the other hand, the research provided no evidence for the widescale development of the long-heralded 'new', flatter, more flexible, boundary-less organisation, or for a concomitant fundamental break with traditional approaches to career development. The bureaucratic, hierarchic organisation with its largely internal career development system did not seem to have given way on any notable scale to the flexible, flat, project-based 'learning organisation'.

Although the organisations studied had experienced some form of downsizing, delayering and/or restructuring, the patterns were random rather than coherent, partial rather than complete. Some displayed elements of the new organisational form but none had achieved full transformation. The authors concluded that: 'Our findings echo those of other researchers in indicating that this is an opportunistic rather than a strategic development. We are a long way away from the extensive use of new forms of contract' (Guest and Davey, 1996: 23).

Similar findings emerged from research carried out at the Institute for Employment Studies (IES) and also reported in 1996. It revealed that many of the interventions reported in the late 1980s and early 1990s by firms attempting to get employees to manage their own careers proved subsequently to have a short life. Personal development plans, career development workshops, and assessment and learning resource centres too often proved to be forms of 'tinkering with the career development process' (Hirsh and Jackson, 1996: 20). They lacked coherency, durability or consistency with wider employee resource (ER) processes and practices.

What did emerge as critical to the business was the ability of the workforce as a whole to adapt to continuous change. A strong emphasis on quality and customer service had brought HRD to the fore as a business issue, and in that context the importance of career development lay less in guaranteeing upward progression to the few than in ensuring more role adaptation, project teamworking and lateral job movement across the workforce.

Case-study: Career development at BP; an update

In Employee Development (1992, IPM) I reported on career development at BP, using information provided to me at that time by the company. The study is summarised here and then updated:

When Robert Horton became Chairman of BP in 1990 he published the following statement about BP's mission:

BP vision, values and themes

> BP is a family of businesses principally in oil and gas exploration and production, refining and marketing, chemicals and nutrition. In everything we do we are committed to creating wealth, always with integrity, to reward the stakeholders in BP – our shareholders, our employees, our customers and suppliers and the community.
>
> We believe in continually developing a style and climate which liberates the talents, enthusiasm and commitment of all our people. We can then respond positively to the increasing pace of change in a rapid and flexible way to achieve real competitive advantage. With our bold, innovative strategic agenda BP will be the world's most successful oil company in the 1990s and beyond.
>
> (Harrison, 1992: 452)

As part of the process of developing a new culture and structure at BP, Horton promised vigorous promotion of career development and the recognition of both individual contribution and collective teamwork. Employees would be encouraged to strike a balance between their responsibilities to BP and to their home life. There was to be a particular focus on personal development, with the hope that every employee would agree a personal development plan with their manager.

The issuing of his statement coincided with the unveiling of Project 1990, announcing the radical restructuring of the Group, with delayering and decentralisation of authority. Job cutbacks were followed swiftly by programmes right across the group aimed directly at changing attitudes and behaviour (Butler, 1990).

In 1996 Hirsh and Jackson provided further information about career development at BP. It gave an illuminating insight into the problems that so often occur as companies attempt to implement and sustain career development strategies at times of complex business and organisational change.

Their article showed that the change process at BP did not go smoothly. There were tensions between the old corporately managed hierarchic career and the newer concepts of teamworking and empowerment, and fears for job security made it harder for those newer concepts to take root. By 1996 the focus in career development had moved from highlighting the need for self-management of careers to emphasising the need for partnership: a joint approach by individuals and the company to managing careers. Personal development planning remained a central concept, but initially it tended to founder for lack of sufficient assistance to individuals – sometimes because of failure in some parts of the devolved structure to put appropriate systems in place, sometimes because of a tendency to try *ad hoc* initiatives which were not sustained.

As is so often the case, the main focus of attention tended to be with the high-potential, fast-track managers, linking in to corporate succession planning. The needs and expectations of others in the workforce were felt by some employees to have been relatively neglected in that process.

Despite these setbacks, the authors saw positive signs for the future lying in three factors: the 'clear and honest communication about what has been happening to the business' that had 'helped staff to adjust their ideas about careers' (Hirsh and Jackson, 1996: 25); the realisation by the company that career management is a long-term process and must be tackled as such; and the company's determination to ensure that changes were handled at local more than at corporate level, and that business unit managers understood, accepted and carried out the responsibilities they held for the career development of all their staff.

Source: Hirsch and Jackson, 1996

Such case-studies show how difficult it can be for companies to ensure that their intentions related to career development are implemented and sustained. They also demonstrate the importance of longitudinal research in order to establish 'what is really going on here' and the ultimate outcomes of various HRD initiatives. The need for such research has already been emphasised in Chapters 1 and 16 of this book.

The IES research into career development already mentioned (page 334) identified three major areas where reality of organisational practice falls far short of espoused intent. Organisations repeatedly fail to achieve:

* an appropriate and honest message
* workable career development processes
* a real intention to deliver.

Looking at these gaps and applying the concept of mutuality discussed at the start of this chapter to the management and development of the individual's organisational career, we can see the importance of four processes in any organisation's approach to career management (Herriot and Pemberton, 1995).

Informing

The provision of information should be a continuous process, starting at recruitment. Its aim is to keep organisation and individual informed about what each expects of the other now and in the future. Vehicles for such information-sharing include the induction process, mentoring, appraisal discussions, employee satisfaction surveys and personal development plans.

Negotiating

This process should occur whenever employees' wants and needs significantly alter. Such a change may occur because of some altered personal circumstance on the individual's side, or on the organisation's side because of necessary changes in business goals and strategy, workplace environment or ER policies.

Monitoring

There is a need for continuous checking to ensure that new skills and knowledge are being developed to meet emergent organisational, team and individual needs. We saw in Chapter 2, for example, how at Wesdale Acute Hospitals NHS Trust line management carries primary responsibility for identifying the ongoing training needs of staff through annual appraisal, personal development plans, monitoring of staff performance, and development and evaluation of training events. Together, these processes are intended to ensure that a 'bottom-up' as well as 'top-down' approach is taken to developing HRD strategy in the Trust. In 1995–97 many changes unanticipated by management and workforce took place within the Trust. These were triggered by the need – arbitrarily imposed by Government policy – to move away from public-sector funding towards a private-sector financial initiative in order to enable the building of the new district general hospital in 1999 to proceed; and by the exposure of acute financial problems caused in part by pressures similar in kind to those being experienced at that time in a growing number of NHS Trusts in the UK. As cost reductions intensified, the timetable for planned organisational restructuring had to be shortened, and this in turn had a strong negative impact on employees' perceptions relating to their job security and their changing duties and responsibilities. The process of renegotiation at all levels became continuous, not only to take into account issues related to contracts of employment but also to ensure that the Trust responded in practical and convincing ways to the changed wants and expectations of a workforce, and to its reduced ability to offer employment security to all its personnel.

Renegotiating and/or exiting

There should be planned exit routes at each career transition point for the different occupational groups in the organisation, so that organisation and individuals are enabled to adjust the psychological as well as the legal contract in the least damaging way to the parties when the situation requires. Disengagement of individuals, whether at the planned retirement date or before it, whether because of poor organisational or individual performance or disappointed career expectations, whether arising from the wish of the employee or the need of the business, should be achieved with fairness, with mutual respect, and be aided by supportive and consistent HR processes.

For the organisation, the concern must be to retain for as long as possible those who embody the organisation's strategic and competitive capability: that is to say, those whose skills, knowledge and disposition makes them of crucial value to the future plans of the organisation. The concern must also be to maintain a reputation and image in the labour market of being a fair employer, with a genuine concern for employees, even when job security can no longer be promised.

Such a balanced and realistic approach to career management is shown at Nestlé UK. Analysing its career management system and the needs and expectations of company and employees, the firm identified not a need for innovatory practice but rather a need to simplify, integrate and strengthen the focus of its traditional approach (Prentice, 1996).

We can conclude this section by noting the following points:

- There is little sign of widespread job insecurity or of a need to jettison the traditional concept of career management. There is insecurity, but it is experienced most by those groups who are – as seen in Chapter 5 – always the least advantaged in the employment market.

- There are organisations moving away from the traditional bureaucratic model, but few have made the full transition to a quite different, flatter and more flexible organisational form.

- What is needed in most career development systems is less an attempt at radical innovation, more a recognition of certain enduring critical success factors.

BUILDING AN EFFECTIVE CAREER MANAGEMENT SYSTEM

Six critical success factors

It is commonly in the area of succession planning that organisations tend to focus most of their career development effort. However, a career management system should be wider in its scope, recognising six critical success factors:

- a transparent process owned by line managers

- a process that can evolve through time and is integrated with existing HR systems, ensuring fair operation of the internal labour market

- a system, based on full information about people's career expectations and about the needs of the organisation, that ensures that the business has committed people in the right roles at the right time, with their capability for the future identified, developed and safeguarded

- measurement of standards to show whether the system works

- clear communication about development processes and responsibilities to all employees and provision for all employees of relevant and full information about career paths

- support for employees in planning their development.

Such a system need not involve radical change, although it is essential to ensure that it takes fully into account structural and cultural factors. In this connection, Mayo (1994) observed that career management is made more difficult when an organisation has to operate in a rapidly changing and unpredictable world and in situations where there are structural trends such as flatter organisations, decentralised profit centres and elimination of central overheads. None the less, as his many examples powerfully demonstrated, given strong direction from the top and integration of career development policy with business and HR policy more widely, much can be achieved (see also Hall, 1984: 173–80).

The importance of integration

The career management system must be integrated in a number of ways and at three organisational levels:

Strategic integration

For career management to be a strategic activity rather than simply responding in *ad hoc* ways to each changing situation, it needs to be pursued at corporate, unit and operational levels of the organisation (Hall, 1984: 176–81). The process of career development will secure the full commitment of the organisation only when it is seen by line managers as well as top management as a business-led activity. It must, therefore, also be a jointly managed process to ensure its wider organisational integration.

- *At corporate level* it must be part of business strategy and planning, where it should be the direct responsibility of senior management, not of personnel specialists. Only in this way can there be full commitment to developing objectives and a policy for career development throughout the organisation, and means to ensure that policy is implemented. At this level the framework for career development is set by the decisions made about work to be done, the structure required for the organisation, the roles needed within the structure and the goals to be achieved across the organisation.

- *At unit level* managers must be stimulated to take responsibility for managing the career development of their people. This responsibility needs to be made into a key result area, on which they are appraised, trained and rewarded. The skills they need to acquire are those related to job design, career coaching and counselling, mentoring, succession planning, the giving of feedback and the assessment of potential. They, working in partnership with the HR function (if there is one), can enhance career development by arranging job movements, including inter-unit co-operative arrangements such as transfers, secondments, special projects and other assignments.

• *At operational level* there should be a process of joint career planning that involves individual and manager (or some other person or body responsible for career development in the organisation) in exchanging information about wants and expectations and in negotiating ways in which the individual's career can be progressed in ways that will also meet organisational needs.

HR integration
In his classic text on career development Schein (1978: 191) showed how the HR system can act as the repository of those key processes whereby the aims and interests of organisation and individual are matched.

Some central integrative body (often a career or personnel development committee) needs to develop company-wide policy, systems and procedures for career development. Evaluation of career development activity can then reveal whether the system is achieving its success criteria, and whether chosen development programmes and other activities are providing the most mutually beneficial growth paths for individuals and for the organisation.

This is particularly important when the organisation is undergoing fundamental restructuring leading to new pay systems and the identification of new competencies. In April 1996, for example, each department and agency in the Civil Service took control of its own pay and grading structures, with the certainty of profound effects on Civil Service careers and culture (Murlis, 1996).

Organisational integration
Some of the most intractable problems in developing career paths in an organisation lie in the need to achieve consistency and coherency in career management systems from one occupational or professional group to the next (see, for example, Herriot, 1992). In organisations like the NHS and the Civil Service the complexity of the occupational structure makes internal integration in this sense very difficult. Each group has its own historical patterns of recruitment, training, pay, and terms and conditions of service; often it has its own negotiating rights.

There are also important issues about the need to ensure full access to career paths for minority groups in the organisation, whether these be employees in full-time or part-time positions; and about how to manage career breaks not only for women wishing to leave temporarily to have children (Hirsh, 1985) but, of increasing relevance given today's demographics, for those who have responsibility for the care of elderly family members. Few European companies have thought much about eldercare policies (Goodhart, 1994a), in this respect comparing poorly with large US companies. Goodhart noted exceptions: Ford and Daimler-Benz, offering up to 12 months and flexible working time to carers; the BBC, with a support group for employees caring for older relatives; and a growing number of the big clearing banks. However, in general, Continental European companies are significantly more progressive in career break policies, seeing more clearly the stress factors related to attempting to combine a full-time career with childbearing or eldercare, and the adverse affects on productivity and performance likely to result from them.

Finally, how to integrate international career development into a company's career management system is a field of study in its own right. The literature is growing (see especially Sparrow and Hiltrop, 1994) as penetration of international markets increases. In leading European organisations career development has become the major challenge in human resource management (HRM) (Evans, 1992), international careers becoming a common feature of so many senior, and even middle, managers.

In this chapter there is no space to consider such issues in more detail. The reader is instead referred to specialist texts such as those noted within and at the end of this chapter in order to obtain relevant knowledge and to be able to relate theory to practice in their own organisations.

Without carefully planned integration all that will result from joint action planning at unit or individual levels of the organisation is a proliferation of initiatives without any overall coherency or purpose, bringing frustrated expectations as action fails to materialise. Schein (1978: 198) quoted the example of a manager and employee agreeing that a functional move would be to the individual's benefit – but lacking any process or resource to evaluate the wider benefits such a move might bring, or to ensure that it could be implemented, monitored and evaluated. The HR system or its equivalent must carry out those wider, integrating roles.

The management of careers in the organisation
From discussion thus far it can be seen that five different kinds of planning are needed for a career management system to achieve its aims in an organisation:

• planning for staffing

• planning for performance management and development

• planning for change

• planning for levelling off and disengagement

• planning for replacement and restaffing.

Table 14 builds on a framework first established in Chapter 3 (page 41) and discussed further in Chapter 13 (page 224). It makes clear that the HR planners, HRD staff, management and the individual all have roles to play in ensuring that a process of mutual benefit links the needs and aspirations of the individual to those of the organisation in a continuous cycle of activity. For the process to be effective it needs to be simple, visible and well communicated. It needs to ensure that

Table 14 Integrating organisational and career development (developed from an original framework suggested in Schein, 1978: 201)

HR planning	HR activity	Learning strategies	Career transition points
For staffing	Job analysis, job design. Audit of skills. Deploying personnel to build up a cohesive internal labour market.	Induction and basic skills training.	Entry to organisation.
For performance management and development	Establishing desired performance levels. Improving performance. Facilitating continuous development. Establishing reward systems. Assessment of potential. Planned approach to career development.	Coaching, mentoring and continuous feedback. Performance review and appraisal. Continuous learning and self-development. Promotions, job movement and access to continuing education and training opportunities.	Progress within particular areas of work. Mid-career with the organisation.
For change	New internal skills audit. Re-analysis of patterns of skill supply in external labour market. New balancing of skills and capabilities to adapt to changed internal and external situation. Achievement of consistency with wider HR policies and systems to facilitate and support change.	Retraining of individuals, teams, management sectors. Organisation development programmes to achieve cultural change and the development of new organisational and individual capabilities.	Changes in psychological contract with the organisation.
For levelling off and dis-engagement	Career counselling, joint planning, job redesign, disengagement counselling and planning.	Using experience and wisdom of those nearing final stages of their career with the organisation.	Later career with the organisation.
For replacement and restaffing	Policies to ensure retention of strategic capability of the organisation at corporate, unit and individual levels. Integrative approach to disengagement and new recruitment.	Supportive disengagement strategies and timely phasing in of new internal and external recruits.	End of career with the organisation. Retirement or return to the external labour market.

career planning leads to strong organisational performance and growth, all employees having some kind of meaningful career path during their time with the organisation. That path may or may not involve upward movement, but it will be meaningful it if offers employees work that is consistent with their abilities, potential and feasible aspirations, and if it also offers rewards that recognise the value of that work to the organisation.

> **Career paths in your own organisation**
>
> Identify the career paths open to different occupational groups in your own organisation. Analyse how far those paths are integrated into an overall planned career management system, and assess the extent to which that system meets the six critical success factors noted earlier in this chapter. What are the main actions needed to improve the planning and/or operation of the system?
>
> Before answering this question you may find it helpful to read Schein, 1978, Chapter 14, and the account of Xenova biopharmaceutical company's development of a dual career path system that recognised both the scientific and managerial skills of its employees (Garmonsway and Wellin, 1995).

The career life cycle

Let us now consider the practical implications of Hall's (1984) concept of career development across the life cycle of employees. The concept encompasses the stages shown in the right-hand column of Table 14.

Entry to the organisation

At this point individuals need information about themselves and their career opportunities. They should be involved in self-assessment activities, in drawing up personal development plans to initiate a long-term process of self-directed career planning, and have opportunities for a variety of developmental experiences. (We have already discussed this stage in Chapter 13 under *induction and basic training*.)

Progress within particular areas of work

This stage too has been discussed in Chapter 13. Established employees who are steadily progressing in particular jobs or areas of work need interesting, challenging tasks and supervision that gives autonomy and support while making clear its high expectations of what the individual can achieve. There should be skilled career coaching, counselling and planning, mentoring, job design, appraisal, feedback and development planning in order to manage employees' career paths effectively at this stage. Training in such skills will therefore need to be provided at unit level, together with the kinds of monitoring, incentives and rewards to help develop positive attitudes in managers at this level. Linking individual career plans to work objectives is another way of ensuring that those plans are aligned with the needs of the business as well as of the individual.

Mid-career and change

These are particularly difficult stages to manage (see Lewis and McLaverty, 1991). It is essential not only to facilitate the continued development of the high-fliers, but also to help those unable to move up, on or out to see that they still have 'careers' in the sense of meaningful work, challenges, and opportunities for stimulation and achievement. The 'menopausal manager' is a particular problem here (Sofer, 1970; Davies and Deighan, 1986). The stimulation and growth of those who have reached their job ceiling can be enhanced by such developmental strategies as job rotation, cross-functional moves, job redesign, recognition and rewards for job peformance, and temporary assignments outside of the company, including eg consultancy opportunities. It is also important to keep more mobile employees informed about corporate career opportunities and high-level technical or professional positions available elsewhere in the company, since these openings are often not adequately publicised.

Later career

As employees move towards the end of their career with the company, either as a natural process or as a result of downsizing or delayering, their careers still need careful management. It is particularly important that the effects of low morale and stress caused by preoccupation with the forthcoming termination of employment do not quickly spread through a workforce. Advance warning of downsizing and redundancy decisions, counselling for those who have to leave and also for the survivors, help with job searches and pre-retirement programmes, and a phased approach to disengagement (including the opportunity for secondments and for a protracted period of part-time work before, and possibly after, departure) – these are some of the many ways in which disengagement can become a more positive, even developmental, process than is too often the case.

The organisation needs to identify key transition points in people's careers – 'moments of opportunity' where it is important to develop a set of shared values and renegotiate, if necessary, the psychological contract between organisation and individual in order to promote mutually beneficial career planning. At each key point there must be the provision of accurate and up-to-date information to help that planning process. There must also be a framework that provides guidelines on blending on-the-job development and other developmental tools with more formal development experiences at each career phase. The tools to be used for different developmental purposes must be identified.

End of career with the organisation

It is the final stage of employment in the organisation that is often the most difficult to manage. In the past in the UK, Inland Revenue rules have discouraged gradual retirement, even though such a strategy can mitigate most of the negative aspects of early retirement for the organisation and the individual. By 1997, however, changes were in hand opening up a range of possibilites for phased, partial or part-time retirement in the UK as in so many EU member countries (Reday-Mulvey and Taylor, 1996). Imaginative planning, such as that demonstrated in relation to part-time early retirement in the French-owned pharmaceuticals and chemicals group, Rhone Poulenc, can minimise organisational and personal disruption, help individuals to manage disengagement effectively, and ensure that those vital to the organisation's continued strategic capability are retained and remain committed to their work and roles (Reday-Mulvey and Taylor, 1996).

However, the issue of retirement is more complex than this. By the year 2030 in the 18 Western European member states of the Organisation for Economic Co-operation and Development (OECD) the size of the over-65 age group will have risen to 70 million, compared with 50 million in 1990 (Willman, 1994). Over the same period the number of people of working age will have fallen to fewer than three for every person aged 65, compared with five in 1994. These trends are similar across all leading world economies, but are much less marked in newly industrialised countries. The economic impact will be radical, but so complex as to be impossible to predict with any accuracy. The most likely outcome, however, will be a marked shift in competitive advantage from the old to the newly industrialised countries.

As Willman (1994) observed, once the flow of young people into organisations begins to diminish so will there be an increasing need to hold on to older workers and to attract back into employment those currently not in the labour market. Consumers too will be ageing, and so products and services will have to meet their distinctive needs. Retirement policies, once relatively simple and attracting little of management's attention (except in those organisations that advertised their status as benevolent employers sensitive to all employees' needs) will have to carry a heavier burden of bottom-line responsibility. They will have the potential to make a direct negative or positive impact on a company's ability to remain competitive.

Positive policies for disengagement, as for retention, should aim to help individuals to understand that the most important focus for them is that of their long-term career path, rather than simply their career within a particular organisation. They must also help the survivors of reorganisation to retain their morale and career orientation at a time when both will be weakened yet when the organisation must continue to function effectively. The need for such help should not be underestimated, as was made clear by a number of surveys reported by Doherty and Horsted (1995). Finally, they can be beneficial to the external image of the organisation, thus improving its chances of continuing to attract high-calibre recruits and of sustaining proactive links with local communities.

ASSESSMENT RELATED TO CAREER DEVELOPMENT

At the heart of any career management system there must be a process of assessment in order to establish the needs and identify the potential of individuals.

Such assessment can be done in a variety of ways – through systems established by the organisation and/or by processes initiated by the individual. In the former category, appraisal systems have an important role to play in identifying the career development objectives and proposed plans of an individual and in offering a vehicle for manager and individual to agree on appropriate action. (This has already been discussed in Chapter 13.) However, the formal appraisal discussion is not an adequate or appropriate occasion for comprehensive assessment of potential. Of the processes that are relevant we shall look at one used widely in private- and public-sector organisations: assessment and development centre methodologies.

Assessment and development centre methodologies
In an informative article Stevens (1985) wrote:

An assessment centre is a systematic approach to identifying precisely what is required for success in a particular job and then labelling these requirements in terms of a short list of tightly defined criteria. Leadership, integrity, tenacity and team-building skill are typical criteria which might be included for a management position.

An assessment centre typically combines a series of exercises. As they tackle these, participants are observed by a trained team – usually, but not always of company managers – who subsequently pool and discuss their information in order to reach as objective an assessment as possible of each individual. The aim is to ensure the identification of those who most closely fit the requirements of the job, and to build up a list of individuals' training and development needs.

Dulewicz (1991) noted many problems commonly associated with this methodology: poor design of exercises, inexpert assessors, lack of commitment of managers to ensuring transfer of learning to the workplace and lack of long-term monitoring. He recommended the appointment of a mentor for each participant and concluded that the critical factor was always the commitment of the individual, and how much the participant does to develop him- or herself.

Such accounts, while demonstrating some of the difficulties involved in the use of assessment centre techology, also provide evidence of their advantages, which typically include:

- *improved decision-making.* Decisions relating to the selection, tranfer, promotion, and to training needs of staff are based on substantially more 'facts' than in the past.

- *improved feedback.* Assessment centre methodology offers an increased opportunity for meaningful feedback related to performance and potential, and this is especially valuable in relation to career and other counselling services.

You may have noticed that although our heading for this section included reference to development centre methodology, we have so far only discussed the use of assessment centres. What, if any, is the difference between the two approaches? Well, to many writers there is no difference. Stevens (1985) saw centres not only as a way of assessing potential but also as a way of helping to diagnose people's training, and 'centre' makes it worthwhile differentiating it from an 'assessment centre'.

In both types of centre, groups of participants take part in a variety of job simulations, tests and exercises with observers who assess their performance against a number of pre-determined, job-related dimensions. If the collected data are used to diagnose individual training needs, facilitate self-development or provide part of an organisational development audit, then the most appropriate description would be 'development centre' (Rodger and Mabey, 1987). If, however, the data are used primarily to feed into decisions about promotion or some other form of employee redeployment, then the term 'assessment centre' is more relevant.

It is essential that employees understand the purpose of a centre in their case, and do not confuse the two. Bower (1991: 53) told how Rover's assessment centres, used primarily for selection during the 1980s, brought only mixed success. Their decision to shift from assessment to development centres using competence-based criteria proved more successful because it gave 'greater visibility and credibility to the process, and ... spin-off benefits in performance appraisal, training objectives and for succession and development planning purposes'.

Development centres can offer a particularly valuable opportunity for the individual to clarify career anchors, notably by bringing personal values and motivation to the surface. Schein (1978: 127) used the concept of career anchors to highlight the importance of the individual's self-perceived talents, motives and values in determining career choice path. He identified five types of anchor: technical functional competence, managerial competence, security, autonomy, and creativity. Each reflects a different type of underlying motive, need, values and perceived as well as discovered talents in the individual. Each is determined in part by experience and opportunity, and in part by latent talents and motives. A career anchor is thus significantly affected by those four processes to which attention has been drawn earlier in this chapter: informing, negotiating, monitoring and renegotiation. It may change or be reinforced at each of the main transition points through which the individual's career in the organisation passes between entry and exit.

A useful case-study exploring the demoralising effects on employee motivation of the downsizing trend and recounting the value of an assessment centre in helping individuals clarify personal values and its career implications for them appeared in *People Management* in 1995 (Holbeche, 1995). Here is another, demonstrating ways in which career anchors can be identified and evaluated through well-planned career development workshops.

Case-study: Helping to achieve career insights at Allied Domecq Spirits and Wine

John Refausse, HR director (customer services and development) at Allied Domecq Spirits and Wine, described a career planning workshop introduced in 1995 as part of a much wider programme of organisational change following some years of re-engineering and far-reaching strategic change in an international company formed by the acquisition of Allied Lyons – the mainly UK-based firm – and the Domecq group. Flatter management structures, significant job changes and movement into new markets all meant that there was a mismatch between organisational needs and expectations and those of individuals. In a climate of uncertainty for the business as well as for its workforce it was seen in the mid-1990s to be essential to help people adjust to the changes and become less focused on job security, more capable of planning their own future careers.

The workshop was piloted in 1995 for senior middle managers who confronted such uncertainties. Its aims were to help them 'take stock of their own achievements, identify the factors that had contributed to their past successes and understand how they matched up against the core competencies of the business' (Refausse, 1996: 34).

Development centre methodology enabled participants to generate and handle a wealth of information that clarified their career anchors and helped them to assess these, and produce development plans and statements of their career aspirations. The workshop enabled individuals to gain insights into their fundamental motivation and talents, and into the past career choices they had made. This in turn 'helped them to look at their current roles and consider how these might be made to fit their aspirations and needs more closely' (Refausse, 1996: 35).

The article described motivational outcomes for the eight participants. Two negotiated major career moves shortly afterwards: one, managing director of a wine subsidiary, achieved greater autonomy from her line manager; another applied successfully for promotion from a specialist to a general managerial post, having discovered during the workshop a 'creative professional' career anchor that he had never previously identified or considered.

Source: Refausse, 1996

Accounts of innovative and apparently successful development centres abound (see, for example, a description of Novotel's assessment centres for management development in Littlefield, 1995, Worts' account of career development at Skipton Building Society, 1996 and Woodruffe and Wylie, 1994 on development centres at NatWest). To assess their true value, however, they need to be followed up through time, and the views of participants as well as of observers and organisation must be obtained. Iles and Mabey (1993), commenting on a range of empirical studies, found that some career development practices tended to be much better regarded by recipients than others, and that development centres, psychometric tests with feedback and career review with superiors were particularly well viewed. The reasons were revealing:

- focus on the future as much as on the past and present

- promotion of reflection and insight as well as measurement of skills or competencies

- two-way, collaborative processes

- overt, with participants able to see clear evidence for assessments

- realistic, not only on account of the methodology used but also because managers were involved as assessors and because of the focus on the actual career criteria and activities used in the organisation.

Again what we see here is the concept of mutuality embedded in the career development process. There has been an achievement of those three essentials identified on page 338:

- an appropriate and honest message

- workable career development processes

- a real intention to deliver.

However, many of the 'third generation' centres set up purely to develop people and therefore avoid any focus on asssessment for other purposes have run into difficulty in the late 1990s (Woodruffe, 1997) on grounds of affordability. As Woodruffe (1997: 32) observed, there is a concern now by some organisations to move away from that sole focus on development and to use the information generated by a centre also to 'influence their decisions about participants' careers and to decide on the further development that an individual will be offered'. This hybrid approach, which for participants raises fears of assessment and selection for promotion and therefore of a divisive element, is the more likely in organisations whose approach to performance management tends towards the control rather than development end of the spectrum – as we saw in Chapter 13. Woodruffe's article provided helpful advice on how to mitigate the most demotivating effects of such hybrids when they are unavoidable.

It can be concluded from this discussion that six principles should underpin assessment and development centre methodologies:

*   *The methodology must be placed in context.* The use of development centres must be placed in a firm context of major training and development programmes, so that they are seen to be a positive aid, not a threat, to all who go through them.

*   *Involvement of management.* Line management must be involved from the start in the development and operation of assessment/ development centre methodology.

*   *Expertise.* There must be a high level of skill in the design and operation of assessment and development centres and in the handling of feedback to participants. Dulewicz's article (1991) shows the damage that can be caused if this expertise is lacking.

*   *Openness, honesty and confidentiality.* Trust and commitment of the parties can only be assured if there is clarity and agreement about the true purpose – or purposes – of a centre, about who will have access to the information produced by the assessment processes, and about how that information will be used.

*   *Action.* The methodology must lead to action although, as Rodger and Mabey (1987) observed, 'for a whole host of reasons development activities may not happen immediately'.

*   *Evaluation.* The results achieved by the use of such methodology must be evaluated, including analysis of the effects its introduction has had on personnel at various levels in the organisation.

Self-assessment and self-development

Assessment of learning needs can also be carried out by individuals alone, using self-assessment in order to determine their strengths and weaknesses, formulate appropriate ways of meeting the needs thereby revealed, and plan for on-going monitoring and evaluation of their performance. Pedler, Burgoyne and Boydell (1978) recommended four stages in the process:

- *Self-assessment.* This must be preceded by careful analysis on the part of individuals of their work and life situation.

- *Diagnosis.* Analysis must lead to the identification of individuals' learning needs, and to their prioritisation.

- *Action-planning.* This must cover the identification of objectives, and of aids and hindrances to action; the determination of resources (including people) needed to carry out the action plan; and an agreed time-scale.

- *Monitoring and review.* Monitoring and review procedures must be determined, and a time-scale established for those processes to take place.

Self-assessment involves individuals in rating themselves in each area of skill in their job, and/or in each area of occupational competence. Questionnaires to facilitate the process can be completed by individuals working alone or with someone else. Tackling self-assessment with the help of another has the secondary advantage of developing diagnostic and counselling skills in that partner who, in the process of questioning, also has to practise and learn more about those skills of observation, listening, discussion and appraisal that are vital to the good coach. Mutual learning and benefit can thus emerge from the exercise.

In self-assessment it is essential to identify organisational barriers as well as aids to learning and development, and to plan how best to circumvent or overcome those barriers. We should also remember that development can take place not only at but away from work, and not only through formalised activities but in a wide range of informal ways. Belonging to activity and interest groups outside work can help to develop skills, knowledge and attitudes highly relevant to individuals' career aspirations and can expand their CVs.

An increasing number of organisations now provide resources and facilities to aid self-development. These include personal and career development workshops and seminars to encourage individuals to take responsibility for their careers, and resource centres, as at Fujitsu (Co. Durham) where there is access to a variety of opportunities for self-directed and self-paced learning at the company's expense, although in the employee's time. Such centres can offer occupational guides, educational references, computerised self-assessment questionnaires or other diagnostic instruments to help people consider their career interests, values and competence, together with computerised educational and training programmes. Some organisations provide access to career and counselling services of local colleges and universities and to their vocational and non-vocational courses.

CONCLUSION

At the start of the chapter the concept was introduced of an organisation's corporate learning and development system as a landscape wherein strategically valuable knowledge can grow and be utilised. The theme of the role that HRD can play in enabling an organisation to become knowledge-productive has been highlighted as a central preoccupation of this fifth and final part of the book.

In order to achieve the learning objectives of this chapter, career development has been examined as a dynamic process involving a psychological contract that recognises the mutuality of organisations' and individuals' wants and needs. Typical triggers for a planned approach to career development by the organisation have been identified, and it has been concluded that despite common assumptions, the traditional concept of 'a career', involving significant periods of employment in a single organisation, still has widespread validity. What is of particular importance for many organisations now, however, is not so much to guarantee upward progression to the few but more to ensure role adaptation, project teamworking and lateral job movement across the whole workforce.

Four key processes for any organisation's approach to career management have been identified, and six factors have emerged as critical to the success of career management systems. A framework to integrate career management with human resource and business planning systems has been provided, and five different kinds of planning have been noted as essential for a career management system to achieve its dual purpose of stimulating and enhancing individual and organisational growth. The concept of the career life cycle has been examined in order to demonstrate the relationship between planning processes, learning strategies and career transition points as the individual moves through the internal career system of the organisation.

Discussion of methods of assessing potential for purposes of career development has focused on the use of assessment and development centre methodologies and on self-development processes and techniques.

USEFUL READING

GILLEY, J.W. and EGGLAND, S.A. (1989) *Principles of Human Resource Development*. Maidenhead, Addison Wesley. pp. 47–73.

HALL, D. (1984) 'Human resource development and organizational effectiveness', in C.J. Fombrun, N.M. Tichy, and A. Devanna, (eds), *Strategic Human Resource Management*. New York, Wiley. pp. 159–81.

HERRIOT, P. (1992) *The Career Management Challenge: Balancing individual and organizational needs*. London, Sage.

HIRSH, W., JACKSON, C. and JACKSON, C. (1995) *Careers in Organisations – Issues for the future*. Institute for Employment Studies Report. London, Institute for Employment Studies.

ILES, P. and MABEY, C. (1993) 'Managerial career development programmes: effectiveness, availability and acceptability'. *British Journal of Management*. Vol. 4, 3: 103–11.

INSTITUTE OF MANPOWER STUDIES. (1990) *You and your graduates:*

The first few years. IMS Report 191. London, Institute of Manpower Studies.

INSTITUTE FOR EMPLOYMENT STUDIES. (1996) *Strategies for Career Development: Promise, practice and pretence.* IES Report, No 305. London, Institute of Manpower Studies.

KESSELS, J.W.M. (1996) 'Knowledge productivity and the corporate curriculum', in J.F. Schreinemakers (ed.), *Knowledge Management: Organization, competence and methodology: Proceedings of the Fourth International ISMICK Symposium,* 21–22 October, Rotterdam, the Netherlands. Würzburg: ERGON-Verlag: 168–74.

MAYO, A. (1994) *Managing Careers.* London, Institute of Personnel and Development.

MEGGINSON, D. *and* WHITAKER, V. (1996) *Cultivating Self-Development.* London, Institute of Personnel and Development.

SPARROW, P. *and* HILTROP, J-M. (1994*) European Human Resource Management in Transition.* London, Prentice Hall.

WOODRUFFE, C. (1994) *Assessment Centres: Identifying and developing competence.* London, Institute of Personnel and Development.

19 Enhancing managerial and strategic capability

LEARNING OBJECTIVES

After reading this chapter you will:

* understand what management training and long-term development – termed in this chapter MD – involves and how it should ensure a strong link between the human resource development (HRD) and employee resourcing functions, the business strategy of the organisation, and longer-term organisational performance and advancement

* know what the basic components of a MD system are and how that system can best be managed

* understand the debate about the competency framework as a basis for an MD system and be able to evaluate those issues in the context of the particular organisation

* appreciate the relationship between the MD process and the development and transformation of knowledge in the organisation, and be able to assess the implications of that relationship for the organisation's strategic capability and performance.

INTRODUCTION

Managers are the key decision-makers of the organisation. Therefore MD must be a priority for any company seeking to enhance its competitive advantage. MD's overall purpose is 'to increase the organization's present and future capability in attaining its goals' (French, 1987: 379). In recognition of the implications of the MD system for all those who manage and are managed, and for the survival and advancement of the organisation this chapter also embraces issues of knowledge development, strategic change and organisational transformation. It is therefore lengthy, but this length is – hopefully – balanced by the number of checks and case-studies introduced in order to illuminate what could otherwise appear to be rather dense areas of text, and to aid learning at each key stage.

There is a wide variety of methods and techniques that can be used in the development of managers. This chapter does not attempt to explore these, since its primary concern is with MD as a strategic process and as a powerful way of linking HRD, performance management and the long-term future of the organisation. However, for students and practitioners needing to extend their technical knowledge, specialist books and articles such as French (1987), Sadler (1989) and Mumford (1997) are recommended.

MANAGERS AND THE MD PROCESS

Using the International Labour Office's classification, Brewster and Tyson (1991: 218) defined managerial and professional staff as those who:

- are salaried members of an organisation

- have achieved a higher level of education and training or recognised experience in a scientific, technical or administrative field

- perform functions of a primarily intellectual character involving a high degree of judgement and initiative

- may hold delegated authority to plan, manage, control and co-ordinate the work of other organisational members

- do not occupy positions as first-line supervisors, foremen or top-level executives.

In many organisations today that classification system is losing validity. Brewster and Tyson pointed to the blurring effects of technology on the lines of distinction between managerial tasks and the work of other occupations. There are also the effects of delayering and decentralisation. Even though (as seen in Chapter 18) the results of delayering may not be as radical as some suppose, none the less they do involve devolution of responsibility for problem-solving and decision-making. Decentralisation often results in 'supervisors' having to take on team management roles, while an increasing number of those occupying traditional middle management positions may find themselves in charge of semi-autonomous business units. Professionals, too, are frequently having to assume more managerial responsibilities (as seen in the case of those clinical directors in the National Health Service described in Chapter 16).

The meaning and parameters of 'management' are therefore expanding, and in view of this MD can be described as:

> the planned process of ensuring through appropriate human resource (HR) processes and learning environment the continuous supply and retention of effective managers at all levels to meet the requirements of an organisation and enhance its strategic capability

The process comprises three essential components:

- analysis of present and future management needs

- assessment of existing and potential capability of managers against those needs

• producing and implementing policy, strategy and plans to meet those needs.

It should focus on manager development and management development. *Manager development* is to do with building on the performance and potential of individuals and teams, and avoiding obsolescence in order to provide a continuous supply of competent, committed and adaptable managers. *Management development*, meanwhile, concerns building a shared culture and enhanced capability across the whole management group in order to improve the organisation's ability and capacity to survive, innovate and advance in its environment. Management development in this latter sense forms part of the overall development of the organisation. 'Organisational performance and managerial effectiveness are inevitably intertwined ... managerial effectiveness can only be considered in its organisational context' (Brodie and Bennett, 1979).

MD can have many agendas. Mabey and Salaman (1995: 147–8), drawing on work by Lees (1992: 89–105), showed how varied they can be and how each carries its own characteristics, assumptions and problems. They identified four common agendas:

• functional performance, typified by the Lead Body Standards framework

• political reinforcement, focusing on sustaining the current political order in the organisation

• compensation, where MD is offered as a reward to secure 'loyalty' and commitment to the organisation

• psychic defence, where MD provides a safe haven for the release of anxieties arising from competitive career drives.

The focus of MD in your organisation

What is the policy on MD in your own organisation? Identify the key plans and programmes intended to implement that policy, and analyse which focus on 'manager development' and which – if any – on 'MD'. Finally, assess how far MD in your organisation is built around the three essential activities we have just noted, and which agenda it primarily serves.

Major themes in MD
A number of interrelated themes lie at the heart of MD. They are introduced here and will reappear subsequently.

Multiplicity of meanings
For the actors themselves, MD can have many meanings. As Lees (1992: 91) pointed out, it can be construed as the intersection of three variables: individual career, organisational succession and organisational performance. Seen in that way, much of its ambiguity arises from the difficulty of achieving fit between those variables, especially when each can be so differently interpreted by the key

parties. Those parties in their turn bring their own belief systems and political and social ambitions to bear on the MD system. Achieving external consistency is therefore of great importance in the MD process (see page 294).

Tensions between systematism and organisational reality

There is frequently a tension between the push for a systematic approach to MD, common in textbooks and typified by the Lead Body Standards framework, and the pull of organisational reality. Regarded as a rationally ordered set of activities, MD is about ensuring that there are the competencies to run the business at corporate, unit and operational levels, both now and in the future. Figure 7 shows the kind of cycle typifying such a viewpoint. Such a rational and linear approach to MD, however, runs the risk of failing to recognise the inherent confusion, unpredictability and political tensions involved in the work that managers do.

As we shall shortly see, many insights into managers' often hectic and fragmented roles have been provided by research. It is clear that MD systems must help managers and those identified for managerial roles to cope with the messy flux of organisational life. Managers have to operate at the heart of complex webs of social interaction, continuously adapt to changing internal and external pressures and opportunities, and think and operate across many boundaries. Learning to deal with such demands involves non-linear as well as linear processes and the exercise of intuitive and tacit skills as much as explicit and systematically acquired knowledge and competencies.

Forms and frameworks

Although, as we shall see later this chapter, there is a significant move towards competency-based management training and education, many

Figure 7 **A systematic approach to management development**

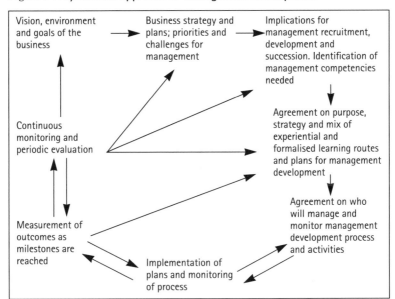

argue that since the tasks of managers are hard, if not impossible, to define at any but the most generalised level, a framework of functionally derived competencies is unlikely to prove a reliable guide to the capability needed to manage in a particular organisation or situation. French (1987: 379), analysing a number of surveys of US corporations, found that a recurring theme was the need to anticipate changing organisational and managerial circumstances and to adapt the form of MD to meet those circumstances.

Few would disagree that MD must focus on organisational values and attitudinal change. Lippitt (1983: 37–8) warned that dogmatic attitudes rendering management incapable of keeping abreast of a changing world could negate the value of any manager development strategy. MD must involve self-reflective as well as instrumental and dialogic learning (see page 229). Implicit here is the need to strike a balance between internal MD and external management recruitment, and between carefully structured programmes and work-based experiential learning. The MD system must be supported by other HR systems in order to enable and reinforce necessary changes in managerial values and attitudes, as well as in competencies.

The importance of educational standards
High-level managerial skills and capability will not come easily – if at all – to the poorly educated. As we have seen in Part 2 of this book, there is much evidence to show that Britain is slow to produce people with the required levels of intellectual development and attainment. France, Germany, Japan and the USA are all ahead in this respect, and emerging industrial countries invest heavily in their education systems in order to produce capable leaders and workforces for the future. With the predicted rise of knowledge workers and the demands they will make on managers, the problems caused by a deficient basic education will accelerate.

By this measure, British firms have cause for concern. They may now possess some of the leanest, most efficient, low-cost workforces in Europe – but they also have some of the most poorly educated, poorly trained and poorly developed managers. The lost opportunities that this represents in terms of ability to cope with new technologies, to manage and develop people, and to think and act strategically in order to achieve high organisational performance are formidable. It is reassuring to have some signs (Storey, 1991) that attitudes seem at last to be changing and that there is experimentation with an ever-widening range of approaches and methods in MD, even though these may only exceptionally be incorporated into any long-term, coherent strategy.

NATIONAL PERSPECTIVES

Key reports on management training and education
During the first six or seven decades of this century, as we saw in Chapter 1, management techniques came under intense scrutiny in the USA and the UK as industrial society, realising the importance of a planned approach to the management of the enterprise, struggled to apply 'science' to the organisation of workers and the workplace. In

the UK during the 1970s and 1980s management came under critical fire, this time by reference to the training and development of those with the responsibility for the strategic direction of the business in a climate of intensifying competitiveness. A stream of reports emerged, all pointing to the urgent need for improvement. Of these, four are particularly relevant at this point:

- *Competence and Competition* (Institute of Manpower Studies, 1984) focused on vocational education and training in Britain, comparing it unfavourably with key competitors West Germany, the USA and Japan. The link between education and training on the one hand and the ability to achieve and sustain competitive edge on the other was made clear, and the inadequacy of that link in Britain was powerfully expressed.

- *A Challenge to Complacency* (Coopers and Lybrand, 1985) expanded on the message of the above report, showing in particular a disturbing mixture of ignorance and apathy amongst British senior managers in relation to the development of their human resources. Attitudes emerged as a vital focus in any attempts to improve the development of managers and their people.

- *The Making of Managers* (the so called 'Handy Report', National Economic and Development Office, 1987) compared management training and education in the USA, West Germany, France, Japan and Britain. Again the comparison proved unfavourable to Britain, where the processes emerged as haphazard, lacking the commitment of top management, and dominated by short-termism and chronic underinvestment. The Report estimated that 36 per cent of middle managers had received no management training since starting work and concluded that 'management training in Britain is too little, too late, for too few' (ibid: 10–11)

- This judgement was confirmed in *The Making of British Managers* (Constable and McCormick, 1987), which argued that lack of opportunity was now the main deterrent to effective MD.

One message emerging from all these reports was that those who are uneducated, untrained and undeveloped themselves are not likely to be committed to the education, training and development of others – so the widespread apathy and ignorance of British management about MD, identified in some of these reports, seemed likely to continue. The same was true of the ignorance often displayed about how best to organise learning and the lack of importance and expertise attached to its systematic planning and evaluation. During the late 1980s this ignorance was displaying itself with particularly damaging effects in relation to youth training (Keep, 1989).

Mid 1990s: the state of play

By the mid-1990s the situation had changed in one significant respect. Managers had become better qualified and more likely to link their training to strategic business needs than they had been 10 years before. An Institute of Employment Studies report was quoted in *People Management* (1995a) as showing a 12 per cent increase in the number of UK managers qualified to degree level – although male qualified managers were in the significant majority. However, in the same year the Institute of Management (IOM, 1995) published a report indicating problems in another direction: too few independent non-executive directors in small and medium-sized businesses were being effectively selected and trained, and less than a quarter had any formal training at all. Management training and qualifications, then, were only partial in their scope, leaving question marks against the state of development of those in whose hands the final direction of the business lies.

In terms of quality, Mabey and Salaman (1995) quoted evidence of a significant recent improvement in management training, although with signs that much of this had come at managers' own initiative and some at their expense. Also by 1993, 1,000 employers representing 25 per cent of the UK workforce had signed up to the Management Charter (Wills, 1993). That could have a far-reaching impact on management and business performance provided that 'the good practice and infrastructural support proclaimed by the Charter are translated into action' (Mabey and Salaman, 1995: 137). However, it is unclear how far the examples of best practice published by the Council for Management Education and Development typify a critical mass of organisations, and how far they reflect reality in any case. We can recall here the story of Lucas in Chapter 1 and the discussion on the difference between the espoused, the apparent and the real.

Accredited education and training does not, of course, necessarily equate with managerial effectiveness; its impact therefore needs to be evaluated. Chambers (1990) contended that most of the national reports and surveys, while promoting a healthy debate on management education, had led to a preoccupation with the provision of more management qualifications instead of a search to find the answer to the fundamental question: do qualifications produce more effective managers? Mumford, Robinson and Stradling's 1987 report on the development of directors had concluded that the possession of a management qualification is of little relevance: what promotes the most effective learning is experience and role models. Most of the directors studied had not attributed their success to any formal development processes, which explained the emphasis of the report on the value of self-development in a greatly diversified range of roles over a wide variety of organisational settings.

Such an emphasis is in line with Japanese practice in larger organisations. The Japanese and the Germans virtually ignore the Master of Business Administration (MBA) route to MD, yet as a sector their managers, judging by business performance standards, are highly effective. The focus in the larger firms is on recruiting people with a high standard of all-round educational achievement and then giving them a rigorous, coherent, continuing discipline of experience, supplemented by on- and off-the-job training when relevant. Self-development is crucial. These processes usually continue for 10 or more years before promotion to management becomes a possibility. However, it should not be forgotten that in both Japan and Germany recruits have a high standard of educational attainment when they enter employment – not a characteristic of the average British manager. The case for the educated employee therefore seems clear, but the case for the management-educated manager less so.

Mabey and Salaman (1995: 140) distinguished between training and learning. Most of the reports on MD focus on the former, yet it is the process and outcomes of learning rather than the specific thrust of training that will make the most fundamental impact on managerial capability. As we saw in Chapter 4 in our discussion of small enterprises, even though in many such organisations there may be few signs of a systematic, formalised approach to training, learning processes are often likely to be operating there that are bringing about a profound and beneficial effect on individual growth and on organisational capability. We shall return to the links between individual and organisational learning, and MD and organisational performance in the final section of this chapter.

COMPETENCY FRAMEWORKS FOR MANAGEMENT DEVELOPMENT

The Management Charter Initiative

The immediate outcome of such reports, especially Handy's, was the Management Charter Initiative (MCI) supported by the Confederation of British Industry, the British Institute of Management and the Foundation of Management Education. A Council for Management Education and Development was established which, in 1988, broadened in scope to become the National Forum for Management Education and Development, a policy-making, standard-setting and accrediting body. The MCI, run by and for employers, is the non-profit-making operating and marketing arm of the Forum. It is supported by the Department for Education and Employment and works closely with Training and Enterprise Councils (TECs) and Local Enterprise Companies (LECs) at local levels in order that gradually 'the MCI as a mass movement will become a "bottom up" rather than "top down" organisation' (Blake, 1990). It aims to improve the performance of UK organisations by increasing the standard and accessibility of management education and development.

The MCI has promoted the establishment of national professional management qualifications with three levels: certificate, diploma and degree/masters' level, existing qualification courses such as the Diploma of Management Studies and MBA being integrated into a national, hierarchical structure. This ladder of qualifications is envisaged as complementing the continuous development of managers in the workplace. After a widespread consultative process and the issuing of many models of best practice, first-level and middle management standards were launched in 1990. The Council for National Academic Awards pioneered a set of courses to test the concept of and market for a national certificate in management. National Management Standards were due to be finalised in July 1997, the Institute of Personnel and Development (IPD) then reviewing its own professional Management Standards to achieve broad consistency. By the end of 1997, therefore, both national occupational standards and professional standards for managers were to be in place in the UK.

The work of managers

The MCI has used functional analysis to derive management competencies (see Chapter 9 for an explanation of this method). Fears continue that this will lead to a skills training approach in management education and development. However, the national standards and the competencies they embody are proving popular with many companies, which see their value in staff recruitment and appraisal as well as in training and development, and in enabling first-level management trainees to get a national certificate qualification.

Opponents of the use of competencies as the basis for MD and the assessment of performance argue that the complexity, diversity and contextualised nature of managerial work makes the concept of measurable units of competence leading to national qualifications both suspect and dangerous (Syrett, 1988; Dixon, 1988; Sadler, 1989). There is research evidence to support these views, as the following summaries indicate.

The tasks of managers are hard to define at any but the most generalised level

As we saw in Chapter 1, schools of thought from Scientific Management through to Human Relations, and early Organisational Psychology to Systems Theories have emphasised the rational, controlling nature of managerial work. It is this thinking that dominates the functional analysis approach to national management standards. However, research into what managers actually do consistently shows a different picture:

> Managerial work across all levels ... is characterized by pace, brevity, variety and fragmentation ... It is hectic and fragmented requiring the ability to shift continuously from relationship to relationship, from topic to topic, from problem to problem.
>
> Partridge, 1989: 205)

Mintzberg (1973) listed 10 key management activities or roles, in three general categories: interpersonal, informational and decisional. He showed managerial roles to be highly variable, involving the often simultaneous pursuit of a variety of objectives in changing ways according to the judgement of the individual manager in the particular situation. This explains why managers are usually allowed very wide discretion, enabling the individual to choose how best to operate, what tasks to tackle and how, at any one point in time. In this view, 'competence' is a matter of wide-ranging, ever-changing and fragmented activity across many organisational, job, task, time and resource boundaries, not of the orderly execution of discrete units of activity in unchanging ways through time.

There is also the point that the 'competence' of managers depends on others' efforts and behaviour as well as upon their own. While managers 'may well be responsible for the performance of their units ... it is almost impossible to determine the individual contribution of the manager' (Partridge, 1989: 207).

Management is a political and pressurised activity

Research shows that management is not an objective and consistently rational activity. Instead, it involves constantly trying to find 'a way through contradictory demands in a world of uncertainty' (Edwards, 1990). Political skills and creative ability are crucial in enabling managers to cut through these complexities in order to produce the results for which they are responsible.

Managers' roles and jobs are changing, often rapidly

Research carried out by Ashridge Management College has indicated that the managerial role is moving 'from an old order based on efficiency, production, optimisation, conformity and authority, to a new order emphasising enterprise, marketing, management of change, initiative and leadership' (Sadler and Barham, 1988: 51). Sadler (1989: 243) predicted that by the turn of the century typical managers would be in charge of service, not production, activities, and economic activity would be knowledge-intensive rather than labour- or capital-intensive, the skills needed being those related to managing change, information technology, innovation and the development of the individual.

Internal contextual factors, with the organisation's stage of growth and its environment, powerfully affect managers' work

This argues for MD to be – to use a clumsy phrase but one that tends to appear frequently in the literature – 'contextualised', ie 'related closely to its particular organisational context'. It takes us back to one of those themes raised at the start of the chapter about the importance of managers' learning from their ongoing organisational experience rather than from prescriptive educational or training programmes.

The functional approach to the analysis of competencies is, of course, not the only one. The competency movement goes wider than the work of the MCI, with Boyatzis (1991) in the USA one of its dominating figures. At a time when the whole question of management effectiveness is under scrutiny, and when many traditional selection and assessment techniques are attracting criticism, the appeal of a competency framework for MD is powerful. If valid, it enables the MD system from recruitment to disengagement to be linked to defined behaviours that in turn are linked to improved performance (Cascio, 1982). Sparrow and Hiltrop (1994: 401–23) provided an evaluation of competency frameworks both in the national and international context; it is essential reading for any student or practitioner who wishes to become informed on the subject. It is also valuable as an introduction to international MD – a topic of importance but not within the scope of this chapter.

Understanding competency frameworks

After reading about competency-driven MD systems (for example, in Boyatzis, 1991; Wills, 1993; Weightman, 1994; Woodruffe, 1994; Cockerill, 1994; Sparrow and Bognanno, 1994) explain and illustrate what is meant by 'a competency framework' and what, in essence, it comprises.

Feedback notes

- A competency framework provides a template against which teams as well as individuals should be developed, since no individual will have more than a few of the competencies needed for superior organisational performance. It provides a clear set of performance criteria both at organisational and at individual levels, and identifies the expected outcomes of achieving those criteria.

- Management competencies are the set of character features, knowledge and skills, attitudes, motives and traits that comprise the profile of a manager and enable him or her to perform effectively in the managerial role.

- Boyatzis (1991) distinguished between threshold and superior management competencies, in order to differentiate between what is needed for adequate and for superior performance.

- He also distinguished between surface and core elements of competency in the individual. Core motives and traits that influence competency are the least amenable to development, being embedded in the individual's personality. Surface, or explicit, skills and knowledge are the most amenable, and so can form a basis for developmental activity.

- Organisational competencies are to do with those holistic capabilities that enable an organisation to survive, innovate and advance. A unique feature of the current interest in competency frameworks is the attempt to formalise and link both individual and organisational competencies to strategic priorities and to HR systems (Alvarez, 1996). One striking example is BP's competency framework described by Sparrow and Hiltrop (1994: 417–19). It embodied 67 essential behaviours related to four organisational culture dimensions, and involved a lengthy and apparently successful process of cross-national, cross-cultural implementation. It was part of a strategy to radically change the structure, culture and strategic performance of the organisation world-wide, as has already been described in Chapter 18 (pages 336–7) and was supported by extensive changes to BP's HR policies and systems.

The strategy-making dimension

Despite the attractiveness of a concept that so strongly links HRD, performance management and organisational performance, doubts remain about competency models framing MD systems. One final and fundamental question can be posed here: is a competency framework likely to reinforce *any given* strategy and approach to the business, regardless of the appropriateness of that approach?

In a powerful article, Alvarez (1996) expressed the fear that the current preoccupation with competencies could dangerously narrow managerial perspectives, developing 'disempowered' managers and endangering the proactivity and intellectual independence needed to question given strategy in the light of an ever-changing environment. Certainly a competency framework is likely to develop from and become part of the dominant logic of an organisation, defined as 'the way in which managers conceptualise the business and make critical allocation decisions' (Prahalad and Bettis, 1986: 490). It is important to realise that:

> The dominant managerial logic in an organisation puts constraints on the ability of that organisation to learn. A competency framework reinforcing the way in which top management typically sees the business and the behaviours that will lead to successful performance could therefore, should that logic become inappropriate, actually endanger the business.

In any event, strategy-making involves far more than merely functional competencies, and so a reliance on simple lists of attributes or competencies when planning the development of strategic managers is indeed likely to mean that 'the integrated work of managing still gets lost in the process of describing it' (Mintzberg, 1994a: 11).

Of course it will be important to develop some functional competencies. For example, for many managers at unit level, formal planning and the specific techniques and skills it requires are still central to their work. However, any higher-level capacities underpinning effective strategic management are much less easy to define, and there is continuing debate about how far abilities such as those to do with judgement, intuition, mental elasticity, abstract thinking, tolerance of risk and ambiguity are discrete skills or interrelated synergistic capacities – and about how to generate the mindsets and disposition to use them in the manager's strategic context (Sisson and Storey, 1988; Cave and McKeown, 1993; Bates and Dillard, 1993; McMillen, Boyatzis and Swartz, 1994; Marsick, 1994; Mintzberg, 1994 and 1994a).

None the less, a pragmatic rather than prescriptive approach to MD can produce creative systems that do improve the performance of those managers who have a strategic role to occupy. At this point, let us carry out a task related to a case-study first used in my 1992 IPM text. The approach to MD described here is relevant to our discussion, and the lessons to be gained from reflecting on the study remain important.

Management development at British Rail in the late 1980s

How was MD made into a more effective process at British Rail (BR) during the late 1980s?

In 1990 BR faced severe problems of current managerial competence, coupled with needs for longer-term career development and succession planning.

Changed managerial roles, tasks and competencies

BR was one of those organisations, increasingly common in the public and private sectors today, whose structure had to change completely in line with the demands of product diversification or the need to provide local services more efficiently and effectively. During the 1980s and early 1990s it became a decentralised business, with 125,000 employees across the country in what were effectively separate businesses, further subdivided into profit-accountable units. Managerial jobs in the new structure were radically different. They were also bigger, requiring highly able business managers who had to develop their businesses, build revenues, reduce costs, and seek and penetrate new markets. They were expected to possess an entrepreneurial outlook and skills:

> Commercial judgement, financial competence, strategic planning, marketing, customer-orientation and the ability to sell ideas persuasively are topics which now matter just as much as the traditional focuses of leadership, motivation, of staff, problem-solving and time management.
>
> (Colloff and Goodge, 1990: 50)

Succession planning for an unpredictable future

By the late 1980s BR faced the additional problem of a gap in supply: there were not enough managers of the kind now needed. Succession planning in the past had been of the conventional long-term kind, developing graduates over a 20-year time-span, with courses and assessment processes geared to identifying those who could fill particular posts in the following five or ten years. Now, the time-scale was much shorter, and the nature of the business – and therefore of the kind of managers needed to run it – was subject to such a fast rate of change that the competencies needed for the effective manager today or tomorrow might change dramatically over a longer period, and be impossible to predict in terms of even five years, let alone longer.

A business-led MD system

The new system had several components, including a systematic performance and development review programme for the top managers, involving two reviews a year and time for improvement between reviews. This process was intended to enable identification of high-fliers and their needs in the context of business objectives. A data-bank was established, high-fliers attending a special MBA programme run with three business schools.

The development centre

This lay at the heart of the new system. It consisted of three days of intensive management assessment and development planning, focusing on needs created by smaller business units, rising expectations of customers, and market changes. The centre was described by the authors as being 'exceptionally clear [in its] purpose, an elitist centre, a business-oriented centre, and a centre committed to concerted action through line management' (Colloff and Goodge, 1990: 51).

Its openly espoused aim was to create able entrepreneurs who could quickly occupy senior management positions. It was a development programme for high-fliers, created to improve personal career decisions, succession planning and senior appointments.

Selection was stringent, involving assessment of seven competencies agreed by the centre, relevant line managers and nominees as crucial to success for business unit managers at BR. An enterprise project had to be completed, which involved taking a new business opportunity, costing it, and projecting figures that would show a likely profit. Selection did not depend on management level, experience, qualifications or age. The centre as the authors described it was élitist, but not closed.

Key competencies initially had to be entrepreneurial in their bias, since the priority was to get business units up and running. It was expected that they would be redefined when the units reached maturity and needed more of the kind of skills to do with running a mature business efficiently.

Developing the key competencies

Every participant emerged with a development programme identifying present competency levels, appropriate developmental priorities, learning targets, and a timetable of training and development methods. Most programmes involved six months of intensive work, usually a mix of in-company experience, projects and guidance, and senior-level training courses. Participants' managers were fully involved in the planning and implementation of the programme.

Monitoring and evaluating the outcomes of MD

Evaluation by reference to reactions of the learners and their managers revealed a high level of perceived value attached to the MD system and its outcomes. Evaluation by reference to outcomes in the job and departmental situation showed that most development programmes had been fully carried out, and none had been ignored.

By 1990 the centre had identified senior management potential in about 80 per cent of its participants, and had uncovered much previously unknown management potential. In addition, reports and plans were being fed into BR's new process for auditing and managing talent, and details of the abilities of participants were being made known to business units, with further information for appointment or succession planning purposes available on request.

Costs

Although setting up costs were high, the ongoing MD programme was found to be low cost: no direct expenditure was involved and it contributed to the participants' current job performance.

Source: Colloff and Goodge, 1990

Feedback notes

The main ways in which the MD process was improved at BR in the late 1980s included the following:

• The aims of MD were clearly defined and directly aligned to business strategy.

• The new MD system was designed carefully, with the full commitment of top management to achieve those aims.

• Its objectives were clearly communicated.

• Personal development programmes ensured that individuals were developed systematically and relevantly, with the commitment of themselves and of their managers.

• Succession planning in the light of an unpredictable future was tackled, focusing on general areas of competency rather than rigidly defined units of competence; on reviewing those competencies for their relevance through time; on actively involving business units in the nomination and development of high-fliers; and on operating an assessment centre that was open to anyone with the required indicators of potential.

- There was careful monitoring and evaluation of outcomes.

- Costs were minimal, as learning arose mainly from guided experience.

Pulling together the issues

Thinking back over the information contained in this chapter so far, what conclusions can be drawn about the appropriateness of applying a competency framework to an organisation's MD system? To simplify, perhaps the following:

- In the short term, and in the more stable organisations, a competency-based approach to MD can produce excellent results, enabling the linking of performance criteria, development activity and performance outcomes at individual and organisational levels.

- However, competencies should always be analysed in the context of the particular organisation and agreed as meaningful and relevant by the key parties involved in and affected by the MD programme.

- There is evidence to show that a competency-based approach can also be of value when the business is moving into changed conditions, provided that there is a high degree of certainty and agreement on the kind of future-oriented qualities and skills needed by those who will have to cope with those conditions.

- Where it is clear that tomorrow's environment will be radically different from today's, with complex, unfamiliar problems and no certainty as to the exact nature and interrelationship of the competencies needed to deal with it – in other words, when that environment is *turbulent* rather than simply *dynamic* (continuously changing) – then an alternative framework to the MD system should be considered.

SUCCESSION PLANNING AND MANAGEMENT DEVELOPMENT

The BR case-study was also a valuable illustration of how to integrate succession planning and MD – an issue dealt with in detail by Gratton and Syrett (1990) in their survey of different approaches to succession planning in a range of UK organisations. They emphasised that systems for succession planning should vary according to the needs of business strategy in the organisation, and should take account of rapidly changing organisational structures. They also noted that despite the importance of building the needs of the individual into succession programmes if key personnel are to be retained and committed, many companies still focus succession planning on career structures imposed on participants.

The traditional model of succession planning

Conventionally, succession planning has been based on a model of identifying needs related to the business plan, identifying high-fliers at an early stage and grooming them over an extended time-scale for positions at the top of the organisation. Development has usually been a matter of initial formal training followed by specialisation until a late stage, when those still left in the race have been rotated through various functions in order to become 'generalists'. Assessments, often using incomplete, unreliable and subjective information, result in a diminishing number of the original cohort continuing to climb steadily up the ladder, others falling from it at various points into permanent positions in the structure. Wastage, in this model, can come arbitrarily, and may mean that some of the most valued people leave the organisation unpredictably, with consequent gaps at stages where they may prove difficult or impossible to fill.

This traditional model assumes that there is a long-term business plan, that it is accessible to those responsible for HRD, that it is sufficiently detailed for succession planning needs to be identified from it, and that the longer-term future of the organisation can be forecast and is not likely to be radically different from the past. The model also presupposes a stable, hierarchical structure of positions through which people are developed and progress along specified career pathways that remain in place through time. Finally, it assumes the exercise of centralised rather than localised control over the whole process, with ownership of career development by the centre rather than by individuals.

Succession planning in turbulent environments

The traditional model may cope with dynamism, but it is not relevant for an organisation operating in a turbulent environment whose threats and opportunities are likely to be complex, unfamiliar and unpredictable. Furthermore, in decentralised organisations, as we saw in the BR case, the kind of managers and competencies needed will change. Managing strategic business units requires a profound knowledge and understanding of the business and its environment, as well as entrepreneurial skills that can come only from multi-functional experience and adaptability to rapidly changing situations. In such an organisation, succession planning and MD policy based on competencies defined by reference to the current roles and tasks of those in senior positions cannot be a valid approach to succession planning. An attempt to identify and put in place a specific successor to every key position will also be unrealistic and unjustifiably costly.

Here is a case-study that first appeared in my 1992 IPM text. It is only of historical interest now – events and people described here will have moved on. However, it represents a model of good practice that still has validity, and demonstrates important principles about how to organise an MD system in a large, divisionalised business.

Case-study: Organising the MD system at United Biscuits (UB) in the early 1990s

By the early 1990s UB had moved rapidly from being a small centralised organisation dominated by a paternalistic leader (Sir Hector Laing) to a large, divisionalised organisation where managing directors had a high level of autonomy.

The central personnel group carried out at that time a review of perceptions related to MD across the company, and from this it was clear that there was widespread agreement on the need for management succession to be achieved through a continued strategy of cross-divisional or cross-functional moves. The group therefore decided to involve the divisional managing directors actively in responsibility for MD.

A management executive was set up consisting of the managing directors (one of whom was selected to be the chairman and also became the next chief executive of UB), and the personnel director and management development director. The executive produced a business-led mission for employee development (including MD) and a strategy focused on ensuring that the best people were available, and on high individual performance levels.

Mission

To generate and drive training and development activities enabling all individuals to achieve the standards of performance demanded by the business.

Strategy

All employees were to receive the necessary training and development to do their job and prepare them for their next roles. Management development would be achieved through a UB development programme, with three components: management essentials; experienced manager development, and high potential managers' development.

The respective roles of centre and divisions in MD were then identified: the centre was to have responsibility for all MD policy and practice, and would have to agree all senior appointments. Divisions were to implement company-wide practices.

Components of the MD system

Management essentials targeted direct entry graduates, other external recruits and managers promoted from within (typically aged under 30). The aim was to give them job knowledge and skills, ensure they were knowledgeable about all the key business functions of UB and achieved required standards of performance, and equip them with skills and knowledge related to managing people. This component lasted about two years, ending with a diagnostic career development workshop leading to the identification of ongoing development needs and planning related to their subsequent careers.

Manager development targeted all other established managers (about 98 per cent of the sector). It focused on needs tightly related to the individual's job performance and on self-development activities that had to be recorded by the individual as they occurred. Because of their developmental responsibilities, all UB managers were trained and developed in how to appraise, identify training needs, coach and develop, and use work-related experiences to help people learn.

High potential manager development was managed through appraisal, audit, and divisional reviews, co-ordinated and driven by the Management Development Executive. All individuals were evaluated annually using a dossier of their learning and development activities. All had to attend three centrally organised programmes: in business management, managing change, and strategy.

Results after two years

There were quite severe initial tensions caused by the apparent loss of autonomy by personnel directors working in the divisions. However, the relationship between them and the new executive soon became more effective and the executive, meeting every two months, had after two years demonstrated a strong commitment to the MD system. It introduced a new and more business-focused appraisal scheme, changed the remuneration system and identified strengths, weaknesses and future needs of functions in the business. HR-planning and succession planning were now reviewed annually. Assessments and career development movements of individuals were continuously monitored and divisional priorities and plans for MD were agreed at executive level.

Working to a common purpose with shared responsibility for auditing and agreed standards for training and development activity gradually produced a system the management of which was carried out by a strong team of divisional MD and training managers.

Source: Doyle and Norman, 1991

Managing succession planning and MD

Note in the UB case-study not only the flexible, non-traditional approach to management succession, but also the way in which the MD system itself was managed. Two points are important here. First, the development of managers, one of the most powerful sectors in any organisation, is a political process, needing effective collaboration between the key parties if it is to succeed. As we saw in the case of the clinical directors' programme in Chapter 16, external consistency is crucial to the success of formal MD initiatives. Second, if longer-term outcomes are to be achieved, MD must be integrated with wider HR systems in order to achieve consistency across the processes of planning, recruitment, selection, appraisal, rewards and development. This argues for the HR function to play a key role in managing the MD system. However, that system must also have the full commitment of management at every level, so its management must not be dominated by specialists.

Further considerations arise when the organisation is decentralised. It is essential to actively involve the units as well as the centre in planning, operating and evaluating the system, but the UB study illustrates the need to ensure that while the MD is 'owned' by units it is also well integrated across the whole organisation. The danger of loosening central control is that divisions/units will take too much power into their own hands, and end by doing things their own way according to their own cultures. The danger of putting central control into the hands of a personnel function is that they may hold insufficient power, and be seen as 'outside' the real management system.

From these case-studies three requirements emerge for the successful management of MD systems:

- *Management development must be owned by managers and achieve strong external consistency.* Managers, HR practitioners and other key stakeholders should work in partnership, and be clear as to their respective roles and responsibilities.

- *Management development requires skill.* Managers must be trained in the processes involved in training and developing others, and must have a shared commitment to implementing the MD system across the organisation. HR staff need a thorough knowledge of the business, its goals and strategy in order to advise on the design, delivery and evaluation of the MD system.

- *Management development needs a vision and strategy understood and supported by the managers involved in its control.* The system must be driven by business needs as well as respond to individual needs. It must enable the continuous identification, assessment and development of potential and be grounded in an agreement between managers and HR specialists as to its purpose and management.

LINKING MANAGEMENT DEVELOPMENT AND STRATEGIC CAPABILITY

> By and large in most organisations ... MTD is bolted on and not actually integrated into the business strategy. It raises all sorts of difficulties'.
>   (Quoted in Brown, Peccei, Sandberg and Welchman, 1989: 75).

We started this chapter by noting the need to consider managerial effectiveness in its organisational context. When MD is integrated with corporate strategy it will help to ensure that there is the capability needed to achieve effective direction and control of the business. However, for that to occur management planning and development must be recognised as essential components of corporate strategy and must be consistent with the goals and perspective of that strategy. This is rarely achieved (Sisson and Storey, 1988; Brown, *et al.* 1989; Cave and McKeown, 1993).

Developing strategic capability

At this point it is relevant to look more closely at the concept of strategic capability introduced in Chapter 1 (page 6). It is necessary now to expand on that initial definition in order to see clearly the links between MD, corporate strategy and the direction and performance of the firm. My own concept of what I call 'strategic capability', derived both from literature reviews and work in the field, is:

> A capability that is based on a profound understanding of the competitive environment, the resource base and potential of the organisation, and the values that engender commitment from stakeholders to corporate goals. It provides the strategic vision, the rich and sustained knowledge development, the integrity of common purpose and the durable, coherent direction and scope to the activities of the firm that are needed to secure long-term survival and advancement.

In this view, it is strategic capability that significantly determines the extent to which the organisation achieves the best possible fit between the unique tangible and intangible assets that it possesses and the competitive position it occupies in its environment. It involves selecting resources, and combinations of resources, most likely to generate the new strategic assets of the business. It also involves producing and ensuring the implementation of strategies that will ensure those assets lead to the enhanced business performance of the organisation (Chandler, 1962; Grant, 1991: 17, Barney, 1991). Strategic capability is also to do with building a quality of life in the organisation that will generate the sustained commitment of internal and external stakeholders to the organisation's corporate goals.

Differences in the quality of strategic capability can help to explain differences in the behaviour and performance of organisations. Let us take an example in order to explain how strategic capability can operate to an organisation's advantage. It is fictional, since I have developed it in order to illustrate this particular concept of strategic capability. However, it has emerged from observation of both good and poor practice across many types and sizes of organisations and, as we shall see in a real-life case-study in Chapter 20, in terms of good practice it is realistic.

Case-study: Stratcap Ltd, the strategically capable firm

Stratcap Ltd is a pharmaceutical firm that always manages to be one step ahead of its rivals in the market. Its strong business performance has always, over 30 years, rested on clear vision, well-chosen business and financial strategies, and a powerful performance management system. It invests continuously in research and innovation, and in training and developing its people both in the skills needed now and in the flexibility required for the future. It aims always to have a flow of new products in the pipeline, so that when patents expire, new strategic assets can be brought onstream to enable profitability to be maintained. Although more than once the company has had to radically change direction in the market, it has not only survived but advanced. Its route to growth has been more by expanding market share, diversification and product development than by acquisitions and mergers. When it moves down the latter route it chooses its partners carefully, with major programmes of organisational development to facilitate the necessary culture and structure change that will bring the workforces and work systems into true integration.

At corporate level much attention has been given to selecting and developing a high-quality strategic management team, able to make the right kind of investment decisions in relation to the firm's financial and human assets. Board members, both executive and non-executive, are chosen particularly because of their profound understanding of the competitive environment and of the firm's capacity to respond to it. They must convince by their record that they have a long-term sense of direction to guide the firm along the most appropriate paths and select those products and services that will sell best in the market. They must be able to generate vision, goals and strategies that will achieve stakeholder satisfaction, corporate vitality, adequate short-term profitability and the competitive positioning that will sustain profitability.

At business unit level there is recognition that the quality of unit directors and managers will determine the success with which each business in this world-wide organisation decides to compete and seek competitive advantage. Long-term development of managers in the organisation focuses on building up business skills, and the ability to accurately determine product-market scope, marketing approach and major investments. It is also about developing an effective management style and organisational culture.

At operational level much care is given to those HR policies and operating and information systems that will increase strategic thinking and strategic awareness across the workforce. A strong vision of the business must drive the performance management and development system which it is the responsibility of business unit managers to direct and control.

In Stratcap Ltd competitiveness is considered as the result of continuous change as the organisation anticipates and responds to the challenges of its dynamic business environment and searches for new answers to the crucial question, 'How can we be different?' One of the most important functions of HRD – and especially of the MD system – in the company is to ensure that throughout the organisation and at every level there is a steadily improving ability to craft unique, flexible and adaptive strategy through both forward planning and continuous informal learning.

In MD a vital thrust is to find ways of helping current and potential strategic managers at all levels to achieve:

• clearer strategic vision in order to improve their strategic decision-making

• strategic thinking both in themselves and in the teams that they manage

• a sharper focus on what is strategically important

• improved understanding of the rapidly changing business environment

• improved linking of strategy to operational implementation.

There is particular investment in those methods that will improve the accuracy of the assessment and selection of strategic decision-makers at middle management and corporate management levels, and that will achieve continuing competence and adaptability of managers through time.

Organisational stucture and top management styles promote informal learning and lateral thinking. Across all functions at Stratcap Ltd there is much use of such tools and processes as benchmarking, business performance measures and reviews, environmental scanning, organisational climate surveys and the techniques of quality management. The focus is on teams rather than individuals, and on training and educating employees in the teamwork and interpersonal skills and attitudes that will continuously improve current performance and generate ideas for new products and services.

Connecting and transferring knowledge

MD must encompass a critical mass of managers who give the firm its strategic capability. Without this there will be insufficient *knowledge connectivity*. By knowledge connectivity – a crucial term to which we shall return in Chapter 20 – we mean those processes, routines and systems that ensure transfer of information and knowledge from individuals and small groups to the organisation as a whole in order to achieve collective learning (von Krogh, Roos and Slocum, 1994). Ways of transferring knowledge into and across the organisation so that it influences strategic decisions must be planned, because neither individual nor group learning have *of themselves* a counterpart in organisational learning (Adler and Cole, 1993). Again, we shall develop this theme in Chapter 20.

So who should be developed in order to provide this 'critical mass'? A growing body of research suggests that across most of today's more decentralised organisations it is the management team, broadly defined, rather than the chief executive, that most affects the quality and outcomes of strategy-making (Ghoshal and Bartlett, 1994; Hedlund, 1994). Therefore MD systems in such organisations need to focus on the development of middle as well as senior managers. Their strategic role can have a direct impact on the performance of the organisation especially in those delayered structures where innovation and market-sensitivity are essential to innovation and the advancement of the business in its competitive environment (Floyd and Wooldridge, 1994). This includes those working in quasi-market sectors such as the National Health Service, and thus reminds us of the importance of new strategic managers, such as clinical directors (see Chapter 16).

A number of commentators believe that the scope of MD should widen to take in every employee and to focus on the total process of learning, continuous improvement and change in the organisation (Wille, 1990). Such a learning environment – the rich landscape of corporate learning to which we referred in Chapter 18 (page 330) – should ensure a broadening of mindsets and a continuous supply of leaders and managers who best 'fit' the organisation and its environment, vision and strategy through time.

Management development and the knowledge base of the organisation
The relationship between managerial learning and the organisation's culture, dominant logic and collective learning ability is a crucial one when planning an MD system. It will be explored more fully in Chapter 20, but at this stage some initial points need to be made.

Collective, organisational learning has been defined thus: 'Co-ordinated systems change, with mechanisms built in for individuals and groups to access, build and use organizational memory, structure and culture to develop long-term organizational capacity' (Marsick, 1994: 28). Imagine the organisation as a continuous 'stream of knowledge' (von Krogh, Roos and Slocum, 1994: 54) both implicit and explicit. Imagine then the ways in which different approaches to the development of managers in the organisation can affect that stream of knowledge. They can replenish it, change its shape and course, give it new outlets, or increase its force so that it can refresh and revitalise the sometimes barren territory of strategic decision-making. Finally, imagine knowledge as the firm's powerhouse, within which are stored the cognitions, the mental maps and mindsets, and the values and ideas that generate in organisational members, and especially managers, a shared way of looking at and making sense of their organisational worlds and the environment around it, and a collective ability – or inability – to innovate.

By using our imagination in these ways we can begin to grasp the vital connections that have to exist between the MD system of an organisation, the knowledge base of that organisation, collective learning and strategy-making. Of course we are simplifying here, because despite a wealth of literature and research there is still no consensus on the ways in which those connections actually occur or can be made to do so. However, an important step is to become aware that there *is* an interactive process, and that MD does have a powerful influence on managers' values, knowledge and decision-making, for better or worse. Whether the potential is realised depends not only on the validity of MD strategy and methods, and on the motivation and learning ability of participants. It also depends on the extent to which – as Marsick observed in our quotation – the organisation is structured and managed in ways that encourage, absorb and make full use of new learning and knowledge. In the final chapter of this book we shall return to this theme.

One area of research that does offer valuable insights relates to the organisation's dominant logic. We have already referred to this concept, which Prahalad and Bettis (1986: 491) described as a mind-set or a world view of the business and the administrative tools to accomplish goals and make decisions in that business that is 'stored as a shared cognitive map among the dominant coalition'. There is much evidence to suggest that although managerial training and development can be a powerful stimulus to the short-term business performance, it can threaten long-term advancement if it reinforces a rigid and inappropriate dominant logic (Miller, 1993; Levinthal and March, 1993; Nevis, DiBella and Gould, 1995).

If, therefore, MD is to enhance strategic capability and thereby improve the overall longer-term performance of the organisation, it must not just disseminate new information, stimulate the development of new knowledge and ensure new learning; it must help managers *unlearn* ways of thinking and behaving that are no longer appropriate given the organisation's changed or changing environment; and it must enable them to reorganise and apply in different ways – '*relearn*' – much of the learning they already possess. We can understand these concepts better if we recall the clinical directors' programme in Chapter 16. There, new information had to be absorbed; old ways of thinking and behaving that were inconsistent with becoming a strategic manager had to be challenged so that they could be unlearnt; yet at the same time, in order to be able to occupy both the professional role they still held and the new managerial role they now occupied, the clinical directors had to reorganise old knowledge, skills and values so that they could cope adequately with the demands of both roles – relearning as well as learning had to be achieved.

The role of formal programmes in MD

As was outlined at the start of this chapter, it is often argued that the only effective form of development for strategic managers is organisation-based and grounded in their ongoing tasks, and that formal interventions have a very limited role to play (Mumford, Robinson and Stradling, 1987). There is doubt too about the validity of the old scientific management model in which so many formal MD programmes are grounded, based as it is on a rational, systematic and primarily functional approach to the tasks of management (Taylor, 1991). Finally, there is concern about the limited ability of formal programmes to achieve the fundamental shifts in mindsets needed by strategic managers who are new to their role or who are moving to a higher level. This concern remains even when organisationally oriented approaches like action learning are incorporated in such programmes, given the grounding of action learning itself in the rational, linear concept of the management process (Harrison, 1996).

Yet if we recall the success of the clinical directors' programme described in Chapter 16 – and there are many such success stories – it is perhaps wiser to conclude that MD strategy can usefully incorporate both formalised and experiential learning, both job-related and future-oriented development, and a judicious mix of learning routes and methods. What is essential – as we saw in Chapters 16 and 17 – is to achieve external as well as internal consistency, and to be continually aware of the impact an MD system can have on the importing, development, transformation and practical use of knowledge in an organisation. Only with the ability to generate new knowledge can innovations come that will provide new strategic assets. Only with a reliable source of such assets can organisations in today's uncertain and increasingly complex environments remain secure and advance.

Using MD to improve business performance and strategic capability

You are the MD manager for one of the country's leading companies supplying a diverse range of electronic, analytical and computational products and services. It has always been characterised by high innovation and quality and by its positive values related to managing its people. Read through the following account and then outline the kind of MD programme that you think will be appropriate for the situation it describes.

The company's business environment

A combination of external pressures has meant that by the mid-1990s the company's managers have had to become more strategic in their culture and abilities, capable of responding to the macro issues the company is facing, both as individuals and as members of a company-wide management community. The managers come mainly from a technical background, fewer than 40 per cent having any formal business education. Most have worked for years in an extremely successful company where costs received little emphasis. They are also used to the autonomy and local cultures of the company's functional matrix management system. With key markets on the decline, new technology needing heavy investment, major competition from small companies and low-cost foreign companies, and costs rising rapidly within the company, these managers now have to quickly learn new attitudes and become much more entrepreneurial in their abilities and outlook.

The MD programme

Working with a national business school whose reputation for high-quality, effective business programmes is excellent, you now have to design a company-wide MD programme aimed at senior middle managers, aged 30 to 40, with 10 years' or more service in the company, a technical background and education, and responsibility for 20 to 50 people. Promotion is increasingly unavailable, so it is important that this programme is seen not as a promotion ticket but as a way of improving managerial competence in current roles. Key criteria for the programme are that:

- It must be business-focused, cost-efficient, have the involvement of senior management and reflect corporate issues.

- It must have a national focus.

- It must be capable of being delivered by each of the company's regional training teams, and within their resource.

- It must emphasise managers' responsibility for self-development and stimulate them to a real commitment in this respect.

- Teamwork must be a key feature, so that participants learn from and support each other in the learning processes.

- The programme must focus on making the target population more effective in their current roles.

Feedback notes

- The programme must focus on strategic business issues that the company faces. One measure of the success of the programme will be how far it enhances managers' ability to understand and deal effectively with those issues.

- Methods must involve learning from and through experience, in order to increase competence and test it on real issues. Methods can include live project work, practical assignments, the use of benchmarking and best practice to suggest improvements to business strategy at corporate and unit levels, SWOT analysis and business planning, and the development of a wide variety of strategic options in order to enhance the quality of strategic choice.

- A well-known example of the latter method occurred in Shell in 1984 when, as part of a strategic development programme, Shell's international planners were given a scenario that talked about $15 a barrel of oil, when the current price was $28. The aim of forcing these senior managers throughout the company to consider such an apparently absurd scenario was that they should begin to think about their world in a different way - as a world of $15 oil. In response, the managers asked to be told when the price would fall, how far it would go on falling, and how long the fall would last. The reply was that the future was unknowable, and that they must take one sample scenario – price fall at the end of 1985; it is April 1986 and the price is $16. They must respond to three questions: What do you think your

Government will do? What do you think your competition will do? And what will you do? Although the case was 'only a game', it started off serious work throughout Shell in exploring the question 'What will we do if it happens?' In early January 1986 the price of oil was $27. By April it had fallen to the unprecedented level of $10. The game had become reality, and broadening the scope of scenario-planning then proved its value: it had significantly accelerated collective learning, with advantage (de Geus, 1996).

• Knowledge and techniques needed to tackle strategic issues whether already identified or emergent over time can be provided in part by theoretical inputs, in part by help from skilled senior managers, and in part by external educationalists. Teamwork can be achieved by group-based projects supported by informal networking systems extending beyond the programme back into the various workplaces of the participants. However, this approach can be slow. In order to accelerate institutional learning Shell changed its planning rules in the mid-1980s: the announcement came without warning - strategic planning from now on must be carried out in the first half of the calendar year (there was already a business planning cycle that dealt with capital budgets in the second half). In the first year of the changed planning cycle the results were mostly just a rehash of the previous year's business plans, but in the second year the plans were fresher and in each subsequent year their quality continued to improve (de Geus, 1996). So intervention in the planning systems of the firm may also be needed to produce a step change in strategy-making ability.

• There must be the active involvement of regional training staff during the programme. This can be achieved through a rotation of such staff in the delivery of the programme, as well as through their involvement in programme design.

• The business school must work collaboratively with the company, not impose ivory-tower attitudes or content on the programme. Faculty members will therefore need to form part of the core planning team (say, two, together with the MD manager and a rotating regional training manager). They can then partner senior managers on the programme and respond to participants' need for 'a blend of internal knowledge and external wisdom which participants can exploit, particularly in developing their projects' (Carter and Lumsdon, 1988).

Such a programme was in fact organised at Hewlett Packard, although operating in the wider context of developing the company's European managers. Carter and Lumsdon's (1988) article described the challenges and successes involved in an initiative that produced major results for Hewlett Packard while also gaining the commitment of top management and the European middle managers who were programme members. The whole programme centred on groups of managers carrying out project work related to the 10 most important strategic issues facing Hewlett Packard Europe. Top management took a leading role in identifying and explaining the issues, agreeing the projects, evaluating them, and being committed to their implementation. Relationships with the business schools involved in the programme proved very effective because of the many ways in which they responded positively to the perspectives and needs of the managers.

The task at Hewlett Packard was to change the attitudes and improve the current effectiveness and strategic capability of their middle managers. This was done through a programme that not only helped to provide the necessary training in skills, but also broadened the knowledge and began to influence the culture of the management group concerned: in other words it focused on both manager and management development, and took account of attitudinal factors and organisational values (Lippitt, 1983).

As was the case in the Shell example, the Hewlett Packard programme also made the vital link between MD and competitive advantage. Developing managers, and especially senior managers, to improve their abilities related to strategic choice, decision-making and implementation has a direct impact on the strategic capability of the organisation and so ultimately should enhance the ability of the business to compete in its environment (Fonda, 1989).

In many companies, such aims are overlaid by a long-term need: to provide a continuing supply of high-calibre managers who are in key respects different from those who have dominated the system in the past, and who can therefore break the dominant managerial logic that may now threaten the survival and advance of the business in its changed environment.

The Hewlett Packard and Shell stories show how the knowledge base of an organisation and its strategy-making process can change as new insights, skills and ideas are applied to the analysis of strategic issues and to decisions about how best to respond to them, and also how these things can change as these new approaches are reinforced – and sometimes activated – by new business systems and processes. Old ways of understanding the organisation's world can be expected to change with the emergence of new ways of thinking and new values. But unlearning and relearning can take root only if after a formal programme there is full transference of the learning and competencies that have begun to develop there. Workplace systems and processes must support new learning.

CONCLUSION

In order to achieve the learning objectives for this chapter we have looked briefly at the changing nature of management and noted the three essentials of the MD process. Major themes in MD have been outlined before national perspectives and the current state of play of MD in the UK have been examined.

Competency frameworks for MD have been examined, by reference both to the MCI's work on national management standards and to wider perspectives. The advantages and concerns involved in using competencies to link HRD, performance management, the strategic capability of the firm and organisational performance have been evaluated.

The need to integrate MD and management succession planning has been discussed, and both traditional and more flexible approaches for organisations operating in turbulent environments have been described. Approaches to managing succession planning and MD in order to achieve a productive partnership between the parties have been explored.

In the final section the meaning and contribution of strategic capability to the survival and advancement of the organisation have been detailed. Links between MD, individual and organisational learning and the strategic capability of the organisation have been examined in order to understand better the ultimate relationship between the MD system of the organisation and the performance of the business over the longer term. Themes of the development and transformation of knowledge and the impact on strategic capability have been raised in this section, and will be taken further in the final chapter.

USEFUL READING

ADLER, P.S. *and* COLE, R.E. (1993) 'Designed for learning: a tale of two auto plants'. *Sloan Management Review.* Vol. 34, 3: 85–94.

BARNEY, J. (1991) 'Firm resources and sustained competitive advantage'. *Journal of Management.* Vol. 17: 99–120.

BATES, D.L. *and* DILLARD, JR, J.E. (1993) 'Generating strategic thinking through multi-level teams'. *Long Range Planning.* Vol. 26, 5: 103–10.

DE GEUS, A.P. (1996) 'Planning as learning', in K. Starkey (ed.), *How Organizations Learn*, London, International Thomson Business Press. pp. 92–9.

FLOYD, S.W. *and* WOOLDRIDGE, B. (1994) 'Dinosaurs or dynamos? Recognizing middle management's strategic role'. *Academy of Management Executive.* Vol. 8, 4: 47–57.

FONDA, N. (1989) 'Management development: the missing link in sustained business performance'. *Personnel Management.* Vol. 21, 12: 50–53.

LEVINTHAL, D.A. *and* MARCH, J.G. (1993) 'The myopia of learning'. *Strategic Management Journal.* Vol. 14: 95–112.

MABEY, C. *and* SALAMAN, G. (1995) *Strategic Human Resource Management.* Oxford, Blackwell.

MARSICK, V.J. (1994) 'Trends in managerial reinvention: creating a learning map'. *Management Learning.* Vol. 25, 1: 11–33.

MINTZBERG, H. (1994a) 'Rounding out the manager's job'. *Sloane Management Review.* Vol. 36, 1: 11–26.

MUMFORD, A. (1997) *Management Development: Strategies for action.* 3rd ed. London, Institute of Personnel and Development.

PRAHALAD, C.K. *and* BETTIS, R.A. (1986) 'The dominant logic: a new linkage between diversity and performance'. *Strategic Management Journal.* Vol. 7: 485–501.

SAYLES, L.R. (1964) *Managerial Behaviour.* New York, McGrawHill.

SPARROW, P.R. *and* BOGNANNO, M. (1994) 'Competency requirement forecasting: issues for international selection and assessment', in C. Mabey and P. Iles (eds), *Managing Learning*, London, Routledge in association with the Open University. pp. 57–69.

SPARROW, P. *and* HILTROP, J-M. (1994) *European Human Resource Management in Transition.* London, Prentice Hall.

STEWART, R. (1984) 'The nature of management? A problem for management education'. *Journal of Management Studies.* Vol. 21, 3: 323–30.

20 Managing the knowledge-productive organisation: themes of survival and advancement

LEARNING OBJECTIVES

After reading this chapter you will:

- understand the difference between organisational survival and advancement

- be able to identify the contribution that HRD can make to the key internal capabilities of an organisation, and be aware of its links with organisational learning and the development of knowledge

- understand important practical implications of principles related to the enhancement of individual and collective learning and development, the expansion of knowledge, and the organisation's capacity and capability to survive and advance over the longer term.

INTRODUCTION

The first chapter of this book took as its twofold purpose the setting of human resource development (HRD) in organisations in a historical context and the exploration of tensions inherent in attempts to make the HRD process serve both organisational and individual interests.

Throughout the book themes of challenge, uncertainty and the need for integration and consistency have been pursued. Theories, concepts and prescriptions have jostled for place in an attempt to express both the intellectual rigour involved in the study of HRD and the imperative for it to achieve outcomes that will substantiate its claim as a powerful strategic lever for the business.

In this last chapter the focus moves to the most vital issue to confront an enterprise: how to develop the ability not only to survive but also to advance in order to remain profitable. 'Profitability' in this wide sense involves the generation of a rate of economic return sufficient to satisfy current stakeholders and to enable investment that will secure the future of the organisation over the long term.

If HRD policies and activity cannot contribute to this 'profitability' then they will carry no credibility in the eyes of those who look to the continued existence of the business to meet their varied wants and needs.

One case-study links the main themes of the chapter: that of strategic and organisational change at Hydro Polymers, Aycliffe, UK. Although it is supplemented by a small number of tasks to reinforce learning, in this chapter as in the first the concern is primarily to express a viewpoint and encourage reflection, debate and creativity in fields where it would be naïve to pretend that any secure prescriptions can yet – or perhaps ever – be offered.

THE DISTINCTION BETWEEN ORGANISATIONAL SURVIVAL AND ADVANCEMENT

Many companies do not survive for long, and some – as we saw in Chapter 4 – may not wish to do so. A third of the Fortune 500 industrials listed in 1970 had vanished by 1983. On the other hand, a small group lasted for more than 70 years, some 'sticking to their knitting' but doing it increasingly well, others from time to time completely changing direction in order to remain profitable. The latter type have somehow developed the human and organisational capacity for sustained profitability. They consistently achieve the confidence of shareholders even when, from time to time, short-term results may flag. They also manage to innovate radically at key stages in their existence in order to leapfrog over their rivals and secure durable advantage. They survive, but they also advance (a distinction explained particularly clearly in von Krogh, Roos and Slocum, 1994: 64).

What enables an organisation both to survive and advance?
Let us look first, then, at the qualities that appear to be needed if an organisation is to be able not just to survive, but also at certain stages to transform itself and advance in its environment.

It requires an ability and capacity for change as well as stability
There must be enough stability in the organisation to ensure that current operations can be performed consistently and well, and to ensure that it can alter its portfolio of products or services and its operational effectiveness in line with a need for improved achievement of its strategic goals.

However, there must also be the capacity to experiment, learn and innovate so that change of a kind that completely 'reinvents' corporate character, the behaviour and direction of the business and makes possible the generation of a quite different type of strategic asset is possible (Lorenz, 1992). Let us at this point define what is meant by 'strategic assets': 'Strategic assets are those unique, hard to copy, durable products, services or processes that are valued in the external market and so become the firm's source of competitive advantage' (Amit and Schoemaker, 1993).

This kind of 'transformational' change (to use a term that tends to be applied indiscriminately to much change that is in reality nothing of the kind) enables the organisation to expand in its environment. IBM achieved this after traumatic decline in the late 1980s in its customary markets. Shell's history is full of moves from survival mode to expansion and back again, and the information given about the company's approach to improving strategic planning in Chapter 19 helps to explain the way of thinking that has enabled it to do that, even if it does not reveal the answer to the real conundrum: where and how did that way of thinking itself emerge?

The *capability* to advance needs key decision-makers in the organisation who can think in lateral ways about the company, what it should be doing and where it should be going. *Capacity* to advance requires an organisational structure, material and financial resources, and a workforce with the skills and adaptability to be able to generate and absorb the necessary changes in direction and work with them. Only by having both capability *and* capacity can an organisation conceive and implement plans for new patterns of provision of services (as in a hospital trust), or a quite different type of product (as when Marks & Spencer and Virgin entered the personal pension field), or a radically new process. (I am grateful to Professor Andrew Gray, Durham University Business School, for first suggesting to me the need for a clear distinction between capability and capacity: not as easy as it looks!)

This requires adaptive but also generative learning

Surviving as an organisation through time without any major change of direction requires what is called adaptive learning (Senge, 1990). This is perhaps simply another way of describing the 'single-loop learning' approach explained in Chapter 13 (page 230). It means that individuals and groups, acting on feedback, adjust their behaviour continuously in relation to fixed goals, norms and assumptions so that the organisation becomes increasingly efficient and effective at achieving its current goals. Behaviour itself does not fundamentally change but steadily improves in relation to required performance standards.

Creativity and the innovation arising from it, however, require generative learning (Senge, 1990). Here, the very goals, norms and assumptions of the organisation itself must be open to questioning and the possibility of fundamental change. Whether generative learning arises out of adaptive learning, is a quite different process or involves a combination of several kinds of learning – single-loop, double-loop, even triple-loop (Swieringa and Wierdsma, 1992) – is immaterial at this point. What is important is that generative learning can produce – singly, in sequence or simultaneously – the three most common types of transformation in the true sense of that word. Each significantly alters the behaviour of most people in the organisation, as Blumenthal and Haspeslagh (1992) explained:

- *Radical operational improvement* is focused on the complete redesign of business processes and related changes to structure, skills and behaviour across the organisation. 'Business process re-engineering', now somewhat discredited, typifies attempts, often unsuccessful, to achieve this type of transformational change.

- *Strategic transformation* occurs when fundamental changes in strategy result in equally fundamental changes in structure, processes, people and culture. The 1991 reorganisation of the National Health Service (referred to in Chapter 16, where it formed the external context for the clinical directors' programme) was an attempt to achieve this kind of transformation by introducing management and organisational structures new to the NHS and by creating the artificial internal market.

• *Genetic re-engineering* is achieved when top executives apply a holistic management approach which results in the constant renewal of the organisation by anticipating and responding appropriately whenever major changes in the market occur. This kind of transformation was sought by Hydro Polymers, as the case-study in this chapter will show. It is achieved not by a sudden, one-off and usually traumatic change process. It is the result, continuing through the long term, of a series of systemic changes which achieve a 'mesh of the formal and the flexible' (Lorenz, 1992) by tackling formal and informal aspects of the organisation in an integrated and consistent way through time. It involves creating many new structures, processes and behaviours across the organisation which are so profound and wide-ranging in their nature and effects that they can be loosely termed 'genetic' to distinguish them from changes that are more narrowly focused and less durable.

OD: process and interventions

Organisation development (OD) can usefully be mentioned at this point, although it is of course a specialist subject to be studied in its own right (see especially Beckhard, 1969 and Cummings and Huse, 1989). OD is a process to improve organisational health and effectiveness, distinguished by its planned and system-wide application of behavioural science knowledge and practices to improve the organisation's ability to assess and solve its problems. Its focus is on the organisation's strategies, structures and processes and on the interpersonal and intergroup problems that inhibit problem-solving and threaten quality of life and productivity in the organisation.

OD can therefore help to facilitate any or all of the three kinds of transformational change that have been identified above – and indeed OD programmes and the appointment of specialist regional OD staff were a significant feature of the 1991 NHS reforms. However, its focus on personal and social needs rather than on technical and rational aspects of the organisation means that any OD intervention would need to be part of a wider strategy if such change is to be fully achieved and sustainable.

HRD AND THE KEY CAPABILITIES OF THE ORGANISATION

How can HRD enhance an organisation's capacity to survive and advance in its environment? Let us look now at the contribution that it can make to the profitability of the organisation by taking as our reference point the key capabilities of an organisation.

Capabilities refer to 'the capacity for a team of resources to perform some task or activity' (Grant, 1991). In the literature of business strategy and competitive performance, the so-called 'resource-based view of the firm' highlights organisational resources and capabilities as critical in explaining variations in the ability to become and remain profitable (Penrose, 1959; Wernerfelt, 1984; Barney, 1991; Rumelt, 1991; Peteraf, 1993; Schendel, 1994).

A capability must, of course, be 'valuable' if it is to be a differentiator of firm performance in the competitive environment. It must enable the firm to exploit opportunities and reduce threats in its business environment, and so must have a number of characteristics:

• It must meet or create a market need.

• It must have uniqueness (scarcity value).

• It must – therefore – be hard to copy (because difficult to understand in terms of its basic components and how they interact).

• It must be so deeply embedded in the organisation, and in such complex ways, that there is little possibility it can be transferred to any other organisation (therefore making it hard for competitors to poach).

Although there is no consensus in the literature on how to classify capabilities, a study of that literature suggests the existence of three generic types that, together, have a significant influence on the performance of the firm: resource-based, organisational and strategic. The impact they actually achieve will be mediated, as indicated in Figure 8, by the outcomes of policy decisions in the business and by the firm's strategic position in its industry at any given time – its 'positional capability', which, arising from the interaction of a range of external factors that produce a munificent or hostile environment for the organisation, broadly decide its potential for growth and profitability (Porter, 1980, 1985; Coyne, 1986; Hamel and Prahalad, 1993).

In this chapter the focus is not on the outcomes of policy decisions or on how the firm should deal with external factors in order to improve its competitive position; it is on how to develop those internal capabilities that are the source of the organisation's present and future strategic assets.

Figure 8 HRD, organisational learning and the key capabilities of the firm

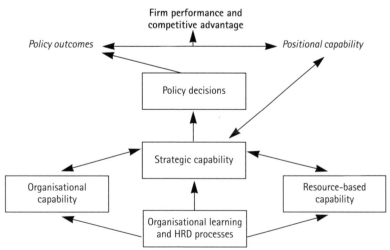

Resource-based capability

This capability can be described loosely as what the firm 'knows and can do', vested primarily in the legacy of knowledge, strategic assets, networks and reputation bestowed by its past human resources, and in the skills, values and performance of its current people. It is to do with the distinctive quality of everyone in the organisation, and with the firm's core and end products. It includes its base of competencies and knowledge, both tangible and intangible, tacit and articulated (Polanyi, 1958; Nonaka, 1991; Hall, 1993).

The task for HRD in relation to resource-based capability is one with which few managers or HR practitioners are not familiar. It is to help to build up the levels and kinds of educational and knowledge base, and the human competence, motivation and commitment that the business needs to achieve its goals.

Here is the first part of a case-study that will unfold throughout this chapter. It serves to explain and illustrate the relationship between HRD and the resource base of an organisation needing to improve its current performance and position itself better for a challenging future.

Case-study, Part 1: Hydro Polymers, Aycliffe, Co. Durham

The context: 1982–84

Between 1946 and 1963 Bakelite Ltd, a US company well established in the UK, carried out chemical processing at a site in Newton Aycliffe, Co. Durham. After various changes in corporate structure, Norsk Hydro, Norway's largest industrial company, purchased the PVC Resin and Compound Facility at Aycliffe in 1982, merging vinyl production with their existing loss-making Vinatex plants at three other sites in the UK to form Norsk Hydro Polymers Ltd (NHPL).

In 1982 the Aycliffe plant was characterised by traditional restrictive working practices and attitudes, and a low-morale workforce. It compared badly in terms of both productivity and product quality with competitors, many of whom were already using sophisticated microprocessor production control techniques. In 1983 new strategic aims were announced for NHPL in order to enable it to improve its position in an increasingly competitive market. Flexible working practices and a larger investment programme were seen as essential to prevent further decline in performance.

In 1984 the company, at that time 90 per cent unionised, was restructured following a negotiated agreement on radical changes in working practices and payment systems. A Statement of Intent was issued, with goals of harmonisation of terms and conditions (including sick pay), improved flexibility in the workforce, a regular weekly wage for all and the removal of bonus schemes. Job losses were unavoidable as the company faced 'an abyss' (Ennew and Ford, 1990: 11). Most, but not all, were achieved by natural wastage and voluntary redundancy.

1985–90: The drive for education, training and competency

In 1985 a drive started to improve the educational and competency base of the company in order to enhance its capacity, as well as capability, for learning and change. A £6m investment programme enabled its employees to commence training courses to broaden their skills and raise their level of educational attainment. The aim was training to standards and for competence.

To start the process it was important to find role models. Sixteen operators on the process plant, handpicked because the company believed they would succeed, were chosen to go on occupational qualification courses. At that time the average age of people on the site was 44. Despite having left school with only low levels of educational attainment, all were successful; one of the first to get a competency qualification was 57. This success proved to be a milestone in beginning to change the climate on the shop floor to one of learning and attainment. It marked the start of a remarkable and sustained improvement in the plant's educational base as more and more employees took up opportunities to study for qualifications.

At the same time the drive for harmonisation broadened to encompass pension schemes. A permanent insurance scheme and an Employee Share Ownership Programme were introduced. In 1986 the parent company sanctioned further capital expenditure and production areas became microprocessor controlled. Between 1982 and 1984 £10m was invested in the Aycliffe site.

The move to a philosophy of total quality

In 1986 all PVC production was moved to Aycliffe from two of the other UK sites, one of which was then closed down. It was a noteworthy achievement for a site that only four years before had been on the brink of closure. Resin capacity was increased at the plant there.

Between 1986 and 1990 further developments occurred. There were new job evaluation schemes and further restructuring that led to the need for increased training. In 1987 a single bargaining unit was introduced and 1988–89 saw the final stage of the harmonisation programme. In 1988, too, senior management at NHPL, influenced by the total quality philosophies of Deming (1988) and Juran (1988), authorised a structured educational and training programme to achieve continuous improvement across the company. At the end of that year the second stage of fundamental change at the Aycliffe site began, with the aim of achieving a company-wide quality culture. In 1990 a move to annualised hours completed the harmonisation programme agreed in 1984.

1990: the outcomes

Between 1986 and 1990 productivity, quality, industrial relations, management style and organisational structure had all improved dramatically as a result of the three-fold push for modernisation, workforce flexibility and retraining. In shop-floor interviews carried out at the time Ennew and Ford (1990) found that training in the operation of new technological equipment had resulted in more satisfying jobs, while regular communication between supervisors and operators was breaking down the previous 'us–them' culture. Employees appeared to be motivated not simply, as in the past, by financial rewards, but by the intrinsically more satisfying nature of their work. Absenteeism had been reduced to 2 per cent and turnover to 1 per cent, comparing favourably with industry and regional figures. The new framework for jobs and grades which underpinned the new payment systems had been accepted by the workforce and compared favourably with the widely unpopular payment systems used before 1984.

The most significant change in work organisation had occurred in the production areas and maintenance function, with operators well trained in the operation of the new microprocessor-based equipment. Cross-training meant that they were now able to perform routine maintenance functions, encouraging a more flexible and basic service. Maintenance craftsmen were freed to concentrate on the more complex tasks.

It is clear from the company's records and from the ACAS research that the resource-based capability and capacity of the Aycliffe plant had by 1990 been genuinely transformed. HRD policies worked in parallel with new employee resource (ER) policies and systems to produce flexibility, and a major investment in plant modernisation made a fundamental contribution to the company's sustained rate of progress between 1984 and 1990.

Source: Information from the company and Ennew and Ford, 1990

Organisational capability
'Organisational capability' involves building the structure, the business systems and processes, and the routines and procedures that will enable an enterprise to deploy, combine and recombine its distinctive resources in ways that generate a flow of strategic assets. It is about having networks of stable contacts between internal and external parties that form the firm's 'strategic architecture' (Baud and Scanlan, 1995: 112–13). It also involves developing an organisational culture that can be a unique source of competitive advantage because it enables rapid learning, unlearning and relearning throughout the organisation. If resource-based capability is about 'can do', organisational capability is about enabling powerful resources to become fully productive not only to meet current performance requirements but also in relation to whatever future the firm may face or seek to achieve.

The task for HRD in relation to organisational capability is, again, not an unfamiliar one, even if often less coherently or effectively pursued than the task of building up human performance to satisfactory level. It is about developing skills, awareness, knowledge and understanding to ensure that:

• the organisation is driven by a strong sense of shared purpose and is focused on a handful of goals that drive the performance of everyone in the business

• there is skilful design and use of management systems and business processes that enable decision-making to be pushed down to the levels where quick responses can be made to competitive forces

• at all levels of the organisation there is good teamwork, continuous learning ability, and willingness to change – and the necessary conducive environment and systems

• there are roles and networks to ensure effective operational and learning relationships with internal and external customers, clients and suppliers

• there is knowledge connectivity (see page 374) and development.

HRD processes can help to ensure that new knowledge enters the organisation, is reflected on, learnt and then – if the context is favourable – transferred across the organisation in ways that enhance the knowledge base of the firm and its collective decision-making ability.

Consider how organisational capability was developed at Hydro Polymers up to 1994 in the second part of our case-study.

Case-study: Part 2: Hydro Polymers, Aycliffe, Co. Durham

1990: the organisational structure and culture

By 1990 it was not only the company's human resources and productivity and quality levels that had undergone profound change. The style of management had become 'much more team orientated and this ... encouraged a move away from the conventional hierarchical organisation structure whose vertical functions were perceived to create interdepartmental barriers' (Ennew and Ford, 1990: 12). In interviews with personnel at the Aycliffe plant at the time, Ennew and Ford concluded that seven years of a 'consistent and participative management style' had helped to achieve this much improved organisational capability.

New challenges

However, the plant now once again faced major threats to its survival, not this time from within but externally. Throughout the 1980s competitive pressures had been fierce as markets reduced. Now there was new global competition and a world recession. Resin prices fell, compound margins were shrinking, and the parent company was unlikely to invest further capital for the foreseeable future. Despite the achievements of the five previous years, the prediction being made in 1989–90 was that unless further major changes were introduced, profits at Aycliffe were going to diminish by two-thirds over the following five years.

New vision and strategy

Total quality management (TQM) became the new vision of the company, whose espoused mission was now that the company should be the leading supplier of vinyl resins and compounds to the UK market. There were five new strategic goals:

- anticipating and exceeding customer needs and expectations

- growing scale and profitability through capacity expansion, product and technology innovation

- continuous improvement to reduce costs and enhance performance

- progressive and business-linked development, training and involvement of all employees

- responsible care towards employees, the local community and broader environment.

Knowledge development, teamwork and improved decision-making and performance management system

The combined effects of traumatic threat to survival, new vision and goals which were clear, relevant, and to which all could relate produced a powerful, cohering focus on harnessing knowledge, expertise and experience from within a total quality environment and on accelerated learning. Continuous improvement was no longer enough. What was essential was dramatic and regular leaps forward in productivity, innovation and profitability in order not only to keep up with but to outpace the competition. Training and education remained key drivers but they now had to support the achievement of different goals. Increased recruitment of graduates was the main measure to boost innovation, importing new knowledge and values quickly into the company in order to accelerate the development of new ideas and leading to new products and processes.

During 1990 training expanded in scope to incorporate in-house management training for supervisors – all of whom achieved a Level 4 qualification – and advanced training in Total Quality Management for senior and middle managers. In the workplace there was the same 'twin peak' approach, focusing on achieving competency through training linked to National Vocational Qualifications (NVQs).

A seven-step training plan was now adopted, to be implemented flexibly. It is still the fundamental framework in the company for training, education, competency and the sustaining of a culture of accelerated learning and of innovation. It aims to continuously improve the resource-based capability of Hydro Polymers and to integrate this improvement with full organisational capability – my terms, admittedly, not theirs, but precise descriptions none the less of the thrust of policy and action across the company.

Organisational capability has been achieved in significant part by the new team-based structure, project management and networks of communication that enabled people to work together in changing patterns as new work flows in and through the organisation and as suggestions derived from new knowledge and a shared understanding of the company's goals become translated into fresh projects. The training framework now comprises eight modules:

1) Total quality awareness

This one-day module was repeated each week in 1991 to cover the whole workforce. All new recruits now go through it as soon after recruitment as possible; by February 1997 only 40 employees were still waiting to do so. The rationale is to use the module to help to build and reinforce a shared vision of the company and an understanding of what to do in order to ensure that it is realised.

2) Team building

In this module, the focus is on the skills and understanding needed to build effective teams and reach consensus in decision-making. Everyone on the site is expected to be involved in continuous improvement, and so new projects are always being suggested and introduced. Initially, as with all the other modules, this was repeated regularly with the aim of preparing employees quickly to learn how to work in teams. By 1997 training had covered about 75 per cent of the workforce. It is now given whenever someone moves into teamwork for the first time.

The same philosophy – an initial drive to cover all relevant parts of the workforce, and subsequently each module being offered to people as and when they need it, given the stage of work that they have reached – has been applied to the remaining modules:

3) *Meeting skills*

4) *TQM tools and techniques*

5) *Presentation skills*

6) *Facilitator training* for shop-floor volunteers, who then facilitate the company's structure for total quality (see below) and teach other improvement tools and techniques, and quality awareness

7) *Project management* (incorporating a special routine called 'Hydro's 6 Project Steps')b

8) *Quality Planning.*

By the end of 1990, 83 staff had been through Modules 1 and 4, 12 part-time facilitators had been trained, and 10 improvement projects had been launched. A Steering Organisation had been set up, consisting in outline of a Quality Council, Improvement Teams covering the three areas of the business – Resin, Compound and Support – and Local Steering Groups and process owners reporting to each of those Teams. From 1991 a stream of new projects, almost all arising from local ideas, had been launched, and more full-time and part-time quality facilitators had been appointed.

By 1993, total quality was no longer promoted as a special activity, but had become an integral part of everyone's work. Teamwork was the norm and project management was seen as a natural feature of life, as new projects continued to be launched, based on opportunities identified by people across the organisation and at all levels, local and cross-functional, board level, managerial level and process level. The company won the Barclays Bank Northern Business of the Year Training award for its outstanding training and education programme related to the management of change. Such awards are now a regular feature of life at Hydro Polymers.

1994: outcomes

By early 1994, all the measures of organisational effectiveness and profitability showed an acceleration in the positive outcomes for which 10 years of steady investment in technology, education, training and flexibility had been a preparation:

- An increasingly educated and competent workforce with an average length of service of 20–25 years, whose turnover had fallen below 1 per cent, whose safety record had improved yearly and whose sickness levels had diminished from a high point of nearly 5 to just under 2 per cent.

- A relatively painless reduction in headcount from 703 in 1984 to 492 in 1993, with more specialists introduced, some from within, some from outside. Employees were aware that downsizing would continue because greater human resource (HR) and technological effectiveness made that inevitable. However, they also appreciated that their own greatly improved levels of educational attainment had led to more flexibility of skills and more internal promotions. This in turn was giving them marketable qualifications and access to a wider range of experience and expertise.

- Increasing market share, customer complaints down by 50 per cent, and production up from 344 tonnes/man in 1990 to 408 tonnes/man in 1993 despite the fall in headcount.

- Major cost savings from certain new projects introduced at Aycliffe, and £3m taken out of costs in the first three years. The company had made profits when its major competitors were losing money, and investors were now seeing it as Norsk's most valuable asset.

- Greater flexibility: the number of craftsmen had dropped from 150 to 50, none working on the resin plant shifts. Despite this, and although the production shifts involved thousands of operations and 20 different units, operators were now doing all the routine maintenance and only one or two of them were craftsmen. In 1984 the company had been 90 per cent unionised; now it was less than 50 per cent.

The combination of greatly improved resource-based and organisational capability and concomitant capacity had helped to place the company ahead of the competition and enabled it to remain profitable despite the negative prediction made in 1989–90.

Source: Information from the company and Ennew and Ford, 1990

Strategic capability

As we saw in Chapter 19, this capability crucially involves:

- choosing the most appropriate vision, long-run goals and objectives for an enterprise

- determining and managing the courses of action and the allocation of resources necessary for achieving those goals

- selecting and ensuring the development of strategic assets that ensure continued profitability of the business.

I believe that strategic capability is the essential link between organisational and resource-based capability and positional capability. A well-developed, high-performing, adaptive and creative workforce, working within an effective organisational system and culture and with flexible routines and procedures cannot, surely, be productive until there is a focus for action, a route to follow, goals to act as stimuli and to give purpose. There must be leadership as well as management, a choice of goals and assets, conscious choices made about direction and purpose.

Stalk, Evans and Schulman (1992: 58) attributed the US retail firm Wal-Mart's extraordinary success in the 1980s to a strategic vision and a set of business decisions and a competitive capability that in a short space of time took the company from nowhere to a dominating position not only in the USA but throughout the world. They concluded that the strategic choices that managers make will increasingly determine organisations' fates.

Cannella and Hambrick (1993) found that when established leaders in an organisation left, or were forced out, after a firm was acquired by another there was usually a significant and, sometimes, catastrophic decline in subsequent firm performance. This was because they took with them a unique knowledge of the particular firm and also because the high internal status they had possessed there was lost, leaving a vacuum in leadership and vision.

Such examples do not of themselves prove a point, but their logic carries a strong conviction. They also demonstrate that strategic capability is multi-faceted and complex, and therefore brings challenges to those who seek to develop it in an organisation. Furthermore, its essence can be seen to derive not from the ability to produce formal, planned strategy, but from certain attributes at various levels of the organisation, notably:

- a sense of direction founded upon long-term objectives

- a profound understanding of the competitive environment and of strategic industry factors

- an ability to select and develop strategic assets that will produce long-term profitability

- an ability to ensure the development of strategically valuable knowledge in the organisation, and its effective management and use.

The task for HRD in relation to strategic capability is the least familiar and least understood, yet it is surely the most challenging and rewarding of those tasks it needs to perform. Here, it has to strive to promote across the organisation the kinds of learning experiences that will help to ensure:

- improved understanding of rapidly changing business environments

- clearer strategic vision, senior managers and other leaders producing a continuous stream of actions that induce clarity, consensus and commitment regarding the organisation's basic purpose (Nonaka, 1991)

- improved understanding and use of strategic decision-making informational tools and processes. These include benchmarking, business performance measures and reviews, environmental scanning, organisational climate surveys and competency development (Fonda, 1993)

- improved understanding of strategy-making modes, and the skills and disposition needed for their operation

- improved assessment and selection of strategic decision-makers and of appraisal, assessment and development processes underpinning management succession

- improved linking of strategy to operational implementation

- strategic thinking and learning throughout the organisation

- effective management and development of the knowledge base and the learning systems of the firm.

The point has been made earlier that for strategic capability to be enhanced it needs to be developed not only in current and potential leaders and managers but also in those other organisational members and external parties who have information and knowledge to offer with a bearing on key strategic issues facing the firm. In companies like Hydro Polymers this means everyone who works in the organisation and an increasing number of external stakeholders. It is no longer possible for the chief executive to 'learn for the organisation'. There must be an integration of strategic thinking at all levels for this kind of company, operating as it has to do in a turbulent environment: that is to say, one that is constantly and in unpredictable ways producing major, complex and unfamiliar problems and challenges.

Another task must be to develop the skills related to managing individuals working in innovative organisations – those with a need to generate quite new assets and strategies. There are tensions here. Flexible organisations that innovate operate in a pressured world; they are more complex and demanding, more uncertain in their work patterns and routines than the traditional, hierarchical type of organisation. As more people learn – as they have done at Hydro Polymers – how to initiate ideas, activities and projects that create work for still others, and are encouraged by the organisation to do so, there is a danger of losing the balance between operational and creative activity to the point that neither is satisfactorily being achieved.

'Empowerment' requires a high degree of managerial skill and commitment that must be consciously developed, and an integrity of purpose to ensure that it is pursued consistently and with commitment. Too often 'empowered workers' have become disillusioned and cynical as fear of losing authority and control causes management to retrench, as once effective teams become split by rivalries, and as strategic coherence breaks down. Creating awareness of such possible consequences is important; it is the first step towards ensuring that they will not be inevitable.

Finally, there will be reduced employment security in delayered, lean organisations, and increased stress levels in project-driven systems where not all can pursue the ideas and assignments that bring the most attractive rewards. Such systems need careful management if they are to yield strategic value and maintain the quality of resource base needed by the organisation.

Case-study: Part 3: Hydro Polymers, Aycliffe, Co. Durham. (With acknowledgements to the company)

1994–97: The thinking organisation

At Hydro Polymers the aim since 1984 has consistently been to educate, not just train, the workforce in order to create a thinking culture – one where everyone thinks strategically, looking out into the environment for new challenges and ideas, and thinking for the future as well as for immediate improvements. In this kind of organisation people continually generate ideas, reflect on processes going on around them, think about what they are doing and question everything all the time. People at Hydro Polymers are not paid to learn – there are no bonuses or special payments for attaining qualifications – but they are encouraged to do so both in the nature of the work that they do and in the opportunities offered for self-learning. Open learning is a major part of the culture, and there is access to the Open College, Open University (OU) and MBA courses (there are on-site tutorials for OU students). There is an important focus on mentoring, everyone having a self-development plan. The level of vocational qualification attainment is high and increasing.

The conscious aim at Hydro Polymers has never been to become a 'learning organisation' (a phrase which is becoming clichéd and hard to express in any practical way) but rather to develop a 'thinking organisation'. This quite simply means a workplace where, stimulated and focused in their learning by the vision and long-term aspirations of the business, people are encouraged to import new information, and are enabled by the structure, business processes, routines and culture of the firm to disseminate it widely in order to create new insights and knowledge, and influence strategic as well as operational decision-making. It is, in our terminology, a company that seeks to create and sustain a richly productive landscape of corporate learning. In this thinking organisation it is essential to achieve a style of relationships that produces trust, partnership and involvement. The style at Hydro Polymers has fundamentally changed over the past 13 years: it is now one of participative dialogue, and not of the confrontational behaviour that in the early 1980s so divided management from the rest of the workforce. Close relationships are built too with suppliers and local firms, involving them in various training and team events.

The team structure and project-based organisation facilitates and also reinforces this style, so that strategic capability is clearly encouraged through organisational effectiveness. Figure 9 shows the structure of the continuous improvement process at Hydro Polymers, designed to achieve integration between training, steering of projects, project management, strategic planning, benchmarking and customer-surveying.

Collective learning

The company relies on continuous improvement, accelerated learning, and the innovative skills and capacity that bring lasting profitability. There is no suggestion scheme in the company because of the focus on building up teams and on engendering collective learning and shared commitment to new ideas. Financial rewards for new ideas were tried out for teams, and there is a small element of this still (mainly in the form of three annual prizes for teams who have produced the most outstanding projects, families also sharing in the awards) but it makes far less impact than other forms of recognition now given regularly to successful projects. These include:

• features in the company newsletter

• presentation of projects to top management by those responsible for running them

• Xmas hampers and gifts from Norway (more valued than the former annual bonus of, on average, £300, even though the cost is much less)

• celebratory events in which the community is involved. The site has its own golf club and fitness centre, most of the employees are local

Figure 9 Current continuous improvement process at Hydro Polymers, 1997. (With acknowledgements to Steve Cleary, Total Quality Co-ordinator)

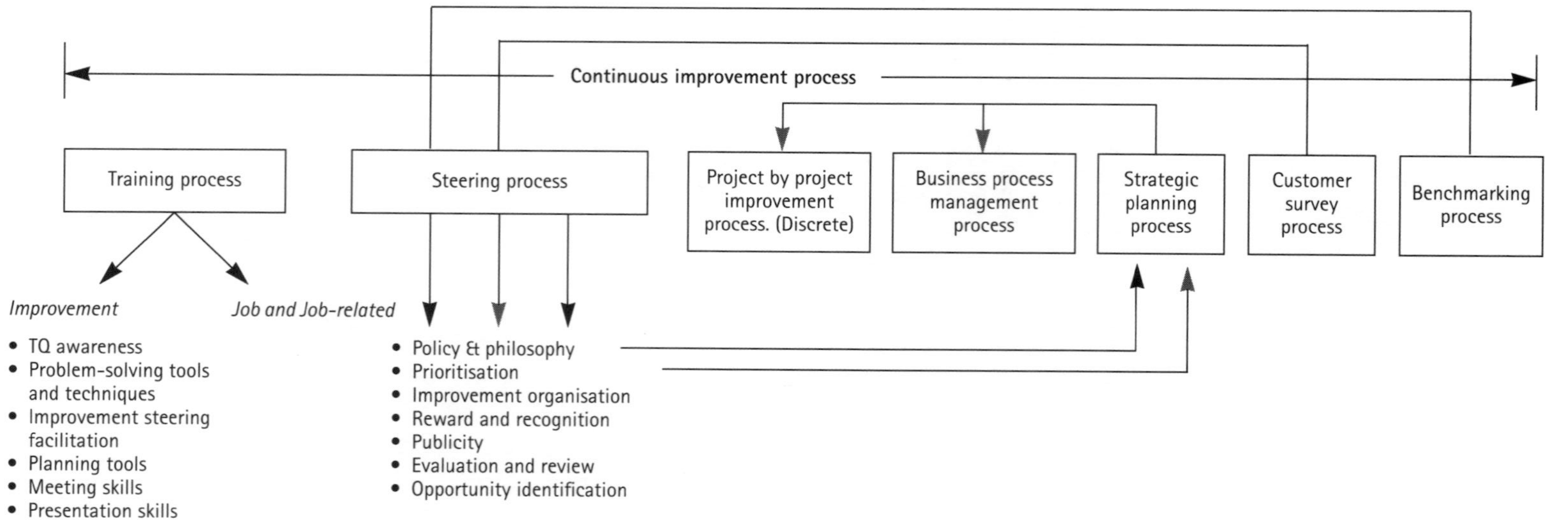

people, and families and partners are all included in celebrations of major success stories. This helps to achieve one of the company's strategic objectives, and reduces the boundaries between 'organisation' and 'community' by fostering the feeling of partnership and shared investment in the company and its achievements.

The new strategic role of middle management

Once a structure is flattened, there cannot be a 'ladder of success', so there have to be other motivators. At Hydro Polymers money is not used by management as a motivator: as at Newlands School in Chapter 13, basic pay is good, as a recognition of the high calibre of those who enter and work for the company. The motivation lies, the company intends, in the workplace environment that has been created there. It is one in which people feel that they are fulfilling a valued role and that they are a crucial part of the company's outstanding success in continuous introduction of change and in sustaining accelerated learning that has placed it ahead of the competition.

It is the supervisors who are seen to be the key to the company's success. They drive the quality programme and they are the team leaders. Competent people at any level have the opportunity to take on new roles and as a result of this many managers are now more involved in strategic planning for the two or three years ahead. Strategic planning at Hydro Polymers has a very specific meaning: it is about obtaining information from a wide variety of sources and generating a wide range of options, systematically analysing them, and doing all this with a longer- rather than shorter-term perspective.

Current outcomes (1997)

It is very clear, tracking the company's history over so many years, that there is a new climate of training, learning and involvement at Hydro Polymers. It is now accepted that the person doing the job is the one with most knowledge about it; all employees are enabled by the workplace system to be involved in what happens to their plant, the processes and the business; they all hold responsibility for change and are trained to be aware of the need for quality throughout all their work.

By a wide range of quantifiable measures, striking improvements have continued to be made through the projects introduced across the business, saving more than £5m in five years, helping the company to remain profitable and building security for employees. In 1995–96 alone, 57 new projects were introduced and 55 completed, with savings of £712,407 achieved. One of the major projects in 1996, involving a team of five, eliminated all incoming raw material testing and minimised pass-off times. Savings were calculated at £47,000 in that year, rising to £119,000 in 1997. Business processes were understood and were being steadily improved by the workforce. Hydro Polymers, like Cummins Engine at Darlington, is a company that is 'in it for the long haul'; thus far it has not only survived but has advanced. It is a case worthy of much reflection.

Table 15 Building HRD into the business

Strategic level	HRD's strategic focus is on:	HRD must:	Crucial processes for HRD:	HRD specialist/manager needs to:
1 Corporate	• formulating HRD mission, goals and strategy to achieve corporate goals • influencing and developing strategic and organisational capability	• 'fit' with wider HR strategy • be aligned with corporate strategy • help to secure appropriate balance between corporate goals for survival and for advancement • produce HRD strategy that is capable of implementation at Level 2	• collaboratively developing mission and goals for HRD • strategic planning and thinking • influencing key stakeholders	• have board-level position/access and skills • be pro-active as well as reactive • have deep knowledge of competitive environment • fully understand the value chain and strategic assets of the business • speak the language and logic of the business
2 Business unit/ managerial	• developing HRD policies and systems in line with strategic needs of the business unit • ensuring achievement of business targets • influencing and developing strategic, organisational and resource-based capability	• 'fit' with wider HR policies and systems • be aligned with business unit policy • have a clear plan within the overall business plan, with agreed evaluation measures • ensure feedback on policies to Level 1	• working with HR and business unit managers to produce policies and plans for acquisition, retention, growth/downsizing of workforce • developing key performance indicators • strategic thinking and business planning	• have strategic alliances with line managers and others • have collaborative relationships with other HR specialists • have deep knowledge of competitive environment of company and of business unit • fully understand how strategic assets can be developed • speak the language and logic of the business unit
3 Operational	• ensuring individual and team performance targets are met • improving acquisition, quality and motivation of people for the business.	• 'fit' between needs of the business and needs and aspirations of people • ensure HRD activities are expertly carried out and appropriately evaluated • ensure feedback of outcomes to Level 2.	• working with teams and individuals to implement business plans for training, appraisal, personal development planning to achieve targets and improve core competences and capabilities.	• have effective working relations with internal and external stake holders • have effective and efficient systems and procedures • have deep knowledge of culture of the workforce • be expert and continuously self-developing.

The third part of our case-study illustrates some key points about strategic capability and life in innovative and delayered organisations.

Survival and advancement: the focus for HRD

Table 15 shows how HRD can be built into the business by focusing on the development of the organisation's key capabilities. To pull a number of themes together at this point: in order to ensure an effective partnership between HRD specialists – whether internal or external – and to ensure an organisation seeking not just survival but transformational capacity and capability there need to be three things:

1 Focus on improving the key capabilities of the organisation

HRD staff can help the organisation to select, train and develop individuals and teams in order to improve the resource-based and organisational capabilities of the firm. They should also work with the organisation to generate the collective, organisational learning – and learning abilities – that will continuously improve the firm's strategic capability. They should develop a climate of awareness and a shared language in the organisation to describe strategic capability and to stimulate ideas about the ways in which it can be improved.

2 Focus on developing the kinds of learning and development that aid flexibility and innovation

This will require a strong base of education and training, together with appropriate employee resource policies and systems related to selection, deployment, conditions and rewards, flexibility and disengagement. The Hydro Polymers study provides an example of this: the company is adamant that the accelerated achievement since 1990 has been made possible only by the new educational, competency and attitudinal base produced by the previous six years of steady investment and development described in the first part of our study.

Strategic learning occurs when existing goals and processes are modified to match perceived changes in the external environment. Relying on natural learning processes in the organisation is not enough to ensure this will happen, since those processes tend to be myopic, concentrating on existing strategic goals and on tasks in hand. As we have already seen, they are also influenced by the dominant managerial logic in the organisation. It is rare for that logic to be questioned, let alone changed, without some traumatic event or intervention taking place, and any change must be backed up by the structure, systems and HR policies that ensure it stays in place and is maintained through time.

Again, our case-study provides an illustration of these points. It has shown how the new ownership of Hydro Polymers in 1982 led to a change in strategic direction – the 'traumatic event' that enabled the previous dominant managerial logic to be overturned; how a threefold thrust of education and training, flexibility and technological innovation had to be established and then sustained in order to ensure the durability of that change in direction; and how further 'traumatic events' around 1990 in the external environment led to a dramatic acceleration in learning, capability and performance of the company.

3 The stimulation of new knowledge leading to new sources of unique and valuable assets for the organisation

This involves working in innovative ways over the long term, with the support of a structure differentiated enough to enable both operating and innovative activities to be pursued without the one unduly dominating the other. A system of project management where there is an allowance for some projects to be dropped if, after initial work and experimentation, they do not prove as useful or relevant as expected can be part of the innovative structure of the organisation; it must, however, run in parallel or be effectively linked with an operating structure that ensures that the daily work of the organisation is also performed effectively.

The final part of the Hydro Polymers study contains useful information on such issues of structure, culture, operating efficiency and an expanded capacity for innovation. It can of course be argued that project management of the kind it describes may in fact tend only to produce 'autonomous' innovation that results in continuous improvement and accelerated learning rather than 'systemic' or radical innovation that generates discontinuous change – that is to say, change of a quite different kind from any experienced in the past (Chesbrough and Teece, 1996: 67).

There are two responses to this argument. First, the case-study does not contain information about Hydro Polymers' wider research and development activity, or the structure that supports it, so no judgement can be made about the company's overall innovative capability on the basis of that study. Second, it can be argued (as indeed I did at the start of this chapter) that the fundamental, sustained and wide-ranging changes that have taken place at Hydro Polymers for 13 years now fall into the category of 'genetic re-engineering' – change of the fundamental kind most likely to develop capacity for systemic innovation. The landscape of corporate learning in the company is now so rich and its key internal capabilities are so well developed that the company's capacity to advance now seems as strong as its ability to survive.

At this point it is relevant to consider at a more theoretical level the kinds of learning and knowledge that are likely to expand an organisation's capacity for discontinuous change and therefore for radical transformation, when that is needed.

THE 'LEARNING ORGANISATION'

Although the field of organisational learning is not new – indeed one at least of its major academics, Chris Argyris, was famous in management circles as far back as the 1950s – in the past decade it has attracted a resurgence of interest. There are two main triggers here: the high profile achieved by Japanese companies and management techniques and a consequent desire by competitors to understand the source of their ability to learn fast and effectively in the pursuit of innovation; and a growing preoccupation in the strategic management literature with the 'central evolutionary and transformational processes' through which organisations can renew themselves and with the kind of learning that can produce the knowledge that generates new strategic assets (Chakravarthy and Doz, 1992).

This interest has consistently focused itself on the 'learning organisation' – a well-developed subject in some senses, yet in others a curiously unsatisfactory one. It is well developed in terms of the sheer size of its academic and practitioner literature. It is unsatisfactory in terms of the failure thus far of that literature to achieve entirely convincing outcomes either at intellectual or practical levels. Let us look at some of the areas of uncertainty.

Conceptual ambiguities
One of the most widely quoted definitions of the learning organisation is that of Pedler, Burgoyne and Boydell (1991): 'an organisation which facilitates the learning of all its members and continuously transforms itself'.

As Coopey (1995) observed, this is not a definition that lends itself easily to practical implementation or measurement. It typifies the difference in stance between what Argyris and Schon in their masterly text (1996: 180) described as the 'practice-oriented, prescriptive literature of the "learning organization"... and the predominantly skeptical scholarly literature of "organizational learning"'. Pedler, Boydell and Burgoyne (1988), an influential group of writers and consultants on learning organisations (or learning companies, a term they often prefer to use) have themselves admitted to a wide gap between the concept of the learning organisation and its reality. This is unsurprising, given not only the looseness of the concept but also the uncertainty surrounding processes involved in organisational and individual learning, unlearning and relearning revealed in a stream of academic papers over the past two decades (and already mentioned in this chapter). Too often, for example, it is assumed that the terms 'the learning organisation' and 'organisational learning' are synonymous. They are not. Another false asumption is that organisational learning is the sum of the learning of individuals and groups across the organisation. It is not: studies such as those by Argyris and Schon (1996) and Adler and Cole (1993) have confirmed that without effective processes and systems linking individual and organisational learning the one has no necessary counterpart in the other.

A further area of concern is the philosophical base of the learning organisation concept. Coopey (1995) argued convincingly that the notion of a learning organisation tends largely to ignore issues of who controls that organisation and the uses to which new learning will be put. In his view, the extent to which the 'learning organisation' offers a genuinely new approach to management and the organisation of people and their work is questionable. To indicate why, he asked the question, 'Who decides that this will become a learning organisation?' He added the supplementary questions, 'Why? And who then is most likely to control and gain increased power from the new learning that such an organisation will presumably achieve?' Too often, he proposed, the answers are likely to be 'management' rather than all organisational members collectively. For him, the traditional scientific management approach still dominates in Western organisations. At this point we may recall the quotation from Bratton and Gold given in Chapter 1 (page 8): 'Even where organisations espouse an ED approach, all too often sufficient amounts of the machine ideal remain in place, and hidden from view, to present an effective and powerful barrier to organisational learning' (Bratton and Gold, 1994: 228).

A sense of proportion must be retained here, of course. In organisations like Hydro Polymers one sees not an attempt to become 'a learning organisation' (an aim that is expressly *not* sought by the management of that company, such is their suspicion of the prescriptive approaches it would seem to involve), or any signs of calculated exploitation of people's improved learning ability. What becomes evident both from personal discussions with personnel in the company and from a variety of historical records is a genuine determination to develop a culture and system where people are encouraged to think as widely as they can in order to stimulate individual growth and ensure the company's long-term survival.

Still, the possession of knowledge does bring issues of power into play, and we can perhaps see the real nub of the matter here by considering the approach of 'action learning'. It has been hailed as 'a model of the learning organisation' (Morris, 1991). Whatever doubts there may be about that comparison (see Harrison, 1996), certainly action learning is widely believed to lead to a radical questioning process that develops an openness to new experiences – 'shaking the cage' of entrenched attitudes and mindsets. However, on the evidence it is questionable how far that cage can actually be shaken beyond limits guarded by the organisation's senior levels. One commentator foresaw difficulties for members or facilitators of action learning sets when the questioning and proposed action began to challenge corporate norms and the dominating managerial logic: 'As action learning is by definition on-line there may be a limit to how much experimentation one is willing to undertake when real risks are at stake' (Raelin, 1994: 305). In a similar way there are unresolved issues about the uses to which a 'learning organisation' can be put by those who retain their old power base in that organisation.

However, like the concept of action learning so too the notion of the 'learning organisation' remains persuasive because of its rationality, human attractiveness and presumed potential to aid organisational effectiveness and advancement (see, for example, Senge, 1990; Mills and Friesen, 1992). The emphasis is on openness, support, a climate of trust and challenge, learning from reflection and experience and a focus on a commitment to the learning that can resolve hitherto intractable organisational problems. It is the resolution of those problems and the enhanced organisational learning capability that has thereby been developed that promise to regenerate the organisation over the longer term.

Practical ambiguities
Here again, though, the operational reality of the 'learning organisation', like action learning (Harrison, 1996) is more complex. That reality at the formal level must be about developing the learning

systems, mechanisms and structures that will ensure the 'coordinated systems change' (Marsick, 1994) to which we first referred in Chapter 19 (page 365). Yet at the more informal level it must also be about creating that rich landscape of learning and development possibilities to which we have repeatedly made reference. In such a landscape people must be able to wander relatively free of managerial constraint, so that intuitions and spontaneous insights as well as more rationally based learning can, with reflection, debate and experimentation, produce a wealth of knowledge, much of which will prove to be strategically valuable for the organisation. Such a skilful balance between formal systems and informal features presupposes an approach to the knowledge development and human relationships in an organisation that does not fit easily with the lack of expertise and awareness about HRD and learning that organisational research repeatedly shows to prevail.

There is a dissonance, too, between the rational and prescriptive framework of guidelines, questionnaire surveys and self-checks that typify the practitioner-oriented literature of the 'learning organisation' and the uncertainties that actually surround the processes of individual and collective learning. A rational model of the 'learning organisation' will undoubtedly encourage adaptive learning, but it is questionable whether the generative learning that leads to radical innovation and change is of the same order and therefore is equally likely to emerge. This point has been made earlier and it is a complex one (see Swieringa and Wierdsma, 1992; Argyris and Schon, 1996). Suffice it to observe here that commentators such as Tosey (1993: 188), influenced by the seminal work of Bateson (1973, 1979), see radical change in mindsets 'emerging spontaneously rather than by being caused in a direct, linear way' and as being embedded in the workings of emotions and personality as much, if not more, than in reasoning.

It is limiting, then, to view strategic change as an entirely rationally based activity, yet well-known UK exponents of the learning organisation such as Morris (1991) and Pedler and Boutall (1992) do appear to regard such change as essentially to do with rational and purposive activity. Reg Revans (1971), himself another influential name in the field not just of 'Action Learning' but also of learning organisations, when stressing the importance of companies being committed to learning put his emphasis on the finding of better ways of tackling existing problems and of rationally reorganising work.

It may well be, therefore, that the kind of 'learning organisation' most typically encountered in the practitioner-oriented literature would in reality be more likely to reinforce than challenge dominant managerial logics. That would matter little where what is needed is continuous learning of a kind that will lead to an improved ability in 'doing the knitting'. It would be a dangerous weakness if what is needed is the discontinuous learning that produces transformational change.

Conclusion

In summary, much is written on 'learning organisations' but there are inconsistencies and areas of ambiguity and uncertainty. It has yet to become clear quite how such organisations come into existence, whether in fact they do so, what is or could be their specific impact on organisational capabilities and how they can be managed. It is unclear too if they are intended to represent an ideal state to which all should aspire – a highly-developed organisational type – or if they are conceived primarily as an image of continuous learning which can inspire and stimulate.

None of these points should be taken as decrying the importance of the current preoccupation with learning organisations. It valuably focuses attention on crucial tasks for organisations: to develop knowledge, to unlearn and relearn as well as learn, to distinguish between the capability needed to survive in the short term and the capacity and skills required to innovate for long-term profitability. That attention can stimulate practical responses that benefit individuals and organisations. What has been expressed is simply a cautionary note.

Obtaining information to develop your knowledge about 'learning organisations'

You are recommended at this point to obtain the kind of information that will challenge and, hopefully, expand your existing knowledge about the 'learning organisation' and the debate surrounding it. This task therefore has two purposes: to aid your understanding; and to engage you yourself in a process of knowledge development upon which you can then reflect. Particularly helpful sources of information to act as starting-points are:

- Mabey and Salaman's (1995) comprehensive and well-illustrated chapter on learning organisations in their 1995 textbook

- a series of articles appearing in 1995 in *People Management*: Garratt's identification of the learning organisation's intellectual roots and possible future; Burgoyne's scene-setting analysis of the potential role for human resource management (HRM) in nurturing a new kind of company that both teaches and learns from itself; Heracleous' account of Hay Consultants' approach to applying the principles of the learning organisation to the facilitation of strategic change; and Mayo and Lank's description of ICL's attempts to develop a learning culture. (See Garratt, 1995; Burgoyne, 1995; Heracleous, 1995; Mayo and Luck, 1995.)

ORGANISATIONAL LEARNING AND KNOWLEDGE DEVELOPMENT

The debate about the learning organisation is particularly inconclusive on the important practical issue of how learning itself can be managed. At this point, therefore, we shall change the focus to one which may be more relevant for that purpose: how knowledge – a primary outcome of learning – can be developed in an organisation, and the implications for organisational learning and knowledge productivity.

The development of knowledge is repeatedly claimed to be an essential determinant of organisational profitability (Senge, 1990; Huber, 1991; Nonaka, 1994; McGrath, MacMillan and Venkataraman, 1995: 264).

It is, however, less easy to determine how that can be done, since knowledge develops in different ways in individuals and in organisations according to processes and variables that are only imperfectly understood.

It is helpful first to gain some simple insights into the knowledge-development process by distinguishing between data, information and knowledge itself.

Knowledge, as we saw in Chapter 14, has been defined as 'a person's range of information' or sum of what they know and understand (Allen, 1990). This draws attention to knowledge as the end result of some process to do with collecting or unconsciously absorbing pieces of information, and processing them internally in ways unique to each individual – because of the intervention in that process of factors such as intellectual capacity, previous knowledge, experience and values, customary ways of perceiving and treating information, and a range of social and emotional variables. Ultimately either old knowledge is confirmed or new knowledge emerges.

Information has indeed been defined as 'items of knowledge' (Allen, 1990). The possession of new information therefore can lead to challenging the existing knowledge that others possess and (as already described) adding to or changing the knowledge we ourselves hold. Yet the availability of new information does not inevitably change people's current knowledge. First, information may be disregarded, discounted, or simply not noticed. Second, the way in which various pieces of information are put together and construed will make a difference to the kind of knowledge people actually gain. Three committees – as an example – will almost certainly arrive at rather different conclusions on any matter put before them (a form of 'knowledge'), even though they may be given identical information on which to base their decision. This is partly because their membership profiles are significantly different by reference to their values, levels and kinds of intelligence, perspectives, existing knowledge and customary ways of making sense of the kind of information now before them. If each committee has to make a decision on an issue about which its members feel strongly, the powerful emotions that will also then come into play will tend to result in even wider differences in conclusions and decisions.

Data have been defined as 'known facts or things used as the basis for inference or reckoning' (Allen, 1990). Information is formed as the result of a process of selecting and assembling *data* in a particular pattern. Two researchers, each using the same database, can come to very different conclusions – as we saw in Chapter 12 – depending on which data they select or reject, and on their own mindsets, perceptions, expectations and wants related to that data.

In providing these definitions I have of course greatly simplified – and therefore inevitably distorted – what are profoundly complicated and little-understood processes. The development and management of knowledge in an organisation is a subject which has for decades exercised minds in a number of fields – organisation theory, systems thinking, human resource management and development, the psychology of learning and anthropology to name only the most obvious. No consensus has been reached on how knowledge does in fact form, grow and change; or on the exact nature of the process linking data, information and knowledge; or on the relationship between individual, group and collective learning and how it can or does effect the knowledge base of an organisation, its competitive capability, its performance or its advancement.

It is important to stress how imperfect is our own knowledge base here. If we appreciate its limitations we are more likely to resist the lure of simplistic prescriptions and recognise instead that we live in an imperfect world where failure can teach as much as success and where any progress has to be pragmatic. Reflecting on what has *not* been learnt, on the kind of knowledge that is *not* yet possessed, and then identifying reasons for this, is an essential part of that pragmatism.

A useful illustration of this last point can be found by returning to the Hydro Polymers case-study.

Development of knowledge at Hydro Polymers, 1982–94

Reading through Part 1 of the case-study on Hydro Polymers, explain how strategically relevant knowledge was developed in the company between 1982 and 1994, and what the main results of that development were, both for the firm and for individuals.

Feedback notes
- In 1982 the company just taken over by Norsk was a poorly performing business, characterised at the human level by backward-looking, conflictual styles of behaviour and an ignorance of how to improve productivity and market position. There were no signs in the system of attempts to develop the knowledge base of the firm or its individuals, or even of an awareness that such development was important for the future of the company. The weak educational and competency base of the workforce and the many human and material barriers to flexible working and the sharing of skills, knowledge and ideas meant that there was little capacity, motivation, or ability to do so in any case. It is therefore unsurprising that the company was barely surviving and could not advance.

- The new vision, strategic goals and drivers for change that were established by the new management in the company between 1982 and 1984 ensured – among much else – that it became essential for everyone in the organisation to become more informed about the business and its performance and growth. New knowledge was imported and disseminated through processes of selection, training, improved production technology and structural change.

- Developing the intellectual potential and the competency levels of employees while at the same time giving them clear goals, a compelling vision, full information about the business and its competitive position and systems and procedures for the generation and application of new ideas – all this, taken together, resulted in an upheaval and transformation in the firm's knowledge base from 1984 onwards.

• The main outcomes of that transformation in the short term were improvements across a wide range of performance indicators and a significant change in the culture of the workplace and in the style of behaviour and interactions at every level. Individuals acquired more marketable skills, experience and qualifications and became more motivated as their work and roles became more stimulating and responsible.

• In the longer term the changed knowledge base of the organisation, interacting with other changes, enabled the greatly accelerated pace of learning and improvement that followed the new challenges emerging in 1989–90. Those challenges themselves were responded to with confidence by the workforce, rather than with the introverted and negative forms of behaviour that had been prevalent in the company up to 1982.

• If top management begins to create the kind of changed climate and sense of purpose that was achieved at Hydro Polymers through its new strategic direction and threefold thrust from 1994 onwards, it will become increasingly inevitable that people will start to seek and use new knowledge in order to drive the business forward. This is because the development of knowledge has been signposted, facilitated and rewarded as an essential organisational task, resulting in the new ways of understanding business issues, new ideas, and new solutions that will enable the organisation and its people to find a new and more hopeful future.

• An organisation whose climate and systems encourage and facilitate the development of knowledge that is strategically valuable has been called a 'knowledge-productive' organisation (Kessels, 1996: 10). The term focuses not so much on learning as a process, but on the development by whatever means of knowledge that enables an organisation to survive and to advance as necessary in its environment.

The management of tacit and explicit knowledge
It is essential at this stage, when we are considering how to develop strategically valuable knowledge, to consider also how that knowledge should be managed. To do so requires a distinction to be made between explicit knowledge and that which is tacit – personal and uncodified. In Chapter 4 (page 56) we discussed the importance of tacit skills in relation to competitive capability. Here, we return to that discussion and widen its scope.

Explicit knowledge is that which has been articulated and 'codified', for example in procedures, protocols, guidelines, check-lists, reports, memoranda, files and training courses; or, as we shall see below, expressed in patents and other legally protected formulae. Because it is or can be articulated, it can easily be observed, learnt, copied or poached. When strategically valuable knowledge is explicit, it is therefore vulnerable.

Tacit knowledge has the highest potential value for an organisation seeking competitive advantage, because it is embedded deep in the individual or collective subconscious, expressing itself in habitual or intuitive ways of doing things that are exercised without conscious thought or effort (Nonaka, 1991: 102). This kind of knowledge is hard to understand, to copy or to poach, and is therefore more likely than explicit knowledge to be the source of the organisation's most distinctive competencies.

When tacit and new explicit knowledge interact or are made to do so, tacit knowledge can expand. Innovation occurs as expanded tacit knowledge becomes embodied in new products, services and strategies. There are many examples to illustrate the role of tacit knowledge in developing an innovative organisation. These are better read directly in the text or articles in which they first appeared than reproduced in edited form here. Although the theory of tacit knowledge is often thought to derive from the work of Nonaka and therefore to be Japanese in origin, in fact it stems mainly from the writings of the Hungarian-born social philosopher, Michael Polanyi (1958, 1966), who spent much of his working life in England. However of all the academics now writing in the field it is Nonaka who has become the leading exponent, producing some of the most compelling illustrative case-studies (1991, 1994; Nonaka and Takeuchi, 1995) in order to explore the ways in which 'knowledge-creating companies' develop.

The management of knowledge is a complex area of research and in this section only generalised guidelines can be suggested. What should by now be clear, however, is that the way in which knowledge is managed in an organisation should largely be determined by its type and uniqueness. As Hall (1996) pointed out, some codified, explicit knowledge is of such value to the organisation that it has to be managed as a legal entity, often with property rights (for example, patents, copyright and licences). Other codified knowledge may be so sensitive that access to it has to be restricted. Other again may be related to particular jobs, positions, tasks or functions, and so may call for training in order that it can result in improved efficiency or effectiveness.

Tacit, implicit knowledge, on the other hand 'will be enhanced most effectively by a process of socialisation' (Hall, 1996: 6) – and this is where the culture of an organisation has particular significance. If the climate in the workplace encourages and facilitates teamwork, informal meetings and discussions, exchanges of views and observations of internal 'best practice' then, as Nonaka's (1991) account so memorably illustrates, it is likely to result in tacit knowledge being shared widely among organisational members without that knowledge having to be made explicit. Explicit knowledge is mobile and therefore vulnerable. When uniquely valuable tacit knowledge is embedded in a number of people rather than a few, it is less likely to become explicit or vulnerable to poaching.

MANAGING THE KNOWLEDGE-PRODUCTIVE ORGANISATION

Five principles can now be suggested. They underpin the management and development of learning and knowledge in an organisation needing to survive and to have the capability and capacity to advance. They therefore bring together the key themes of this final chapter:

- There is a need for a powerful and cohering vision of the organisation to be communicated and maintained across the workforce in order to promote awareness of the need for strategic thinking at all levels. We call such a vision 'cohering' because it brings people, their knowledge and ideas together in a common search for whatever will drive the organisation forward. Such a vision, provided that it is supported by appropriate resource-based, organisational and strategic capability, will direct attention to the need to obtain from all sources information relevant to the advancement of the business and to import, disseminate and organise that information in ways that will ensure its ultimate impact on the profitability of that business.

- 'Innovation is experiencing a renaissance', with at least two major research projects underway in the UK, a Green Paper published by the European Commission in 1995, and novel experiments in private and public sectors (Pickard, 1996a: 29). Organisations seeking to be innovative will need to develop strategy in the context of a vision of the business that is not only powerful and cohering but also open-ended and ambiguous. This will encourage a search for a wide rather than narrow range of strategic options, will promote lateral thinking and will orient the knowledge-creating activities of employees. 'Ambiguity can prove extremely useful as a source of alternative meanings...new knowledge is born in chaos' (Nonaka, 1991: 103). They will also need to differentiate their structures to support both operating and innovatory activity.

- Within the framework of vision and goals, frequent dialogue, communication and conversations are major facilitators of organisational learning (Argyris, 1977: 115–24). In Shell, for example, de Geus (1996: 94) explained how planning is a crucial learning process 'because people change their own mental models and build up a joint model as they talk'. Talking, in formal and informal contexts, can help to create common ways of thinking and perceiving among employees and to develop a shared language and understanding – knowledge – about a range of major organisational issues and business processes.

Networks, routines and processes within and between organisations are therefore needed that will encourage and enable organisational members to discuss their observations, make distinctions and causal associations, and exchange insights relating to information about and views on their organisation and its business environment. Such knowledge structures and connectors are essential to transfer tacit as well as explicit knowledge and to promote the development of new knowledge through time (Bohn, 1994: 62; von Krogh *et al*, 1994: 61–4).

- For new knowledge both tacit and explicit to be developed it is essential to continuously challenge people to re-examine what they take for granted and to encourage the reflection that 'is always necessary in the knowledge-creating company, but ... is especially essential during times of crisis or breakdown when a company's traditional categories of knowledge no longer work' (Nonaka, 1991: 103). Such challenging behaviour requires a positive social climate of openness, support and trust, and time for experimentation, dynamism and humour (Nonaka, 1991; Nevis, diBella and Gould, 1995: 80–81; Boisot, Griffiths and Moles, 1995).

• Any more prescriptive approach to learning and its outcomes may be counter-productive. What is essential is a conducive learning and innovation climate, and a 'rich landscape' of educational and developmental opportunity available for organisational members, together with the organisational framework and business processes to ensure that information can flow into and through the organisation in ways that encourage the emergence of strategically valuable knowledge. Although there must be a sufficiently differentiated structure to support experimentation and innovation as well as operational activity, the emphasis should not be on management systems to control learning itself. Rather there should be a search for 'new ways to encourage people to think creatively and feed their thoughts back into the organisation' (Russell and Parsons, 1996: 32) and help to ensure the skills needed to manage the projects that arise from that creativity.

With the right kinds of information and infrastructure, as the Hydro Polymers case-study has shown, people will organise themselves – given also, of course, a powerful and shared vision of the business and its need to maintain profitability through time. With the right approach to the management of knowledge, their learning will have beneficial outcomes for the business as well as for themselves.

Is your organisation knowledge-productive?

Take your own organisation, or one with which you are familiar. First, identify any ways in which you see it importing, developing and using knowledge in ways that promise to enhance its ability to survive over the longer term. Then analyse your organisation by reference to each of the five points listed above and identify your most important findings.

CONCLUSION

In order to achieve the learning objectives of this chapter, the difference between organisational survival and advancement has been explained in the context of profitability – the ability of an enterprise to achieve a rate of economic return sufficient to satisfy key stakeholders and to enable investment for the long-term future. HRD's potential contribution to profitability has been identified by reference to the key capabilities of an organisation, and illustrated in a major real-life case-study.

Theories of the learning organisation, organisational learning and the growth of knowledge have been outlined and evaluated, and their practical implications discussed. Finally, principles have been suggested to underpin the management and development of learning and knowledge. They focus on the meaning and importance of knowledge productivity for organisations seeking to advance in their environment, and they bring together the key themes of this final chapter.

This book has involved a long journey across the corporate landscape of learning, development and knowledge. Sometimes that landscape has seemed barren, sometimes rich, and often the way ahead has seemed uncertain. Those harmonies so hopefully sought at the start remain not quite as nebulous, yet still they have not fully emerged. If that is a disappointment, it should also be a stimulus.

It is timely, then, to recall the quotation from Franklin Bobbitt that opened this book. It must not become an epitaph for HRD practitioners and managers for, if it does, HRD itself has no likelihood of attaining strategic status, nor will it deserve to do so. It will have no useful or uniquely valuable outcomes either for the organisation or for those dependent on its survival and advancement for their own:

> We have aimed at a vague culture, an ill-defined discipline ... an unparticularized social efficiency...

To read one's epitaph may prove a doubtful privilege, but it can stimulate transformational change, so the last message should after all be one of hope, like Vaughan the alchemist with whom this journey also started out, 'looking towards the west wind and hearing secret harmonies'...

USEFUL READING

ADLER, P.S. and COLE, R.E. (1993) 'Designed for learning: a tale of two auto plants', *Sloan Management Review*. Vol. 34, 3: 85–94.

ARGYRIS, C. and SCHON, D.A. (1996) *Organizational Learning II: Theory, Method and Practice*. New York, Addison Wesley.

BARNEY, J. (1991) 'Firm resources and sustained competitive advantage'. *Journal of Management*. Vol. 17: 99–120.

HAMEL, G. and PRAHALAD, C.K. (1993) 'Strategy as stretch and leverage'. *Harvard Business Review*. Vol. 71, 2: 75–84.

HUBER, G. (1991) 'Organizational learning: the contributing processes and literatures'. *Organization Science*. Vol. 2: 85–113.

KESSELS, J.W.M. (1996) 'Knowledge productivity and the corporate curriculum', in J.F. Schreinemakers (ed), *Knowledge Management: Organization, competence and methodology*. Proceedings of the Fourth International ISMICK Symposium, 21–22 October, Rotterdam, the Netherlands. Wurzburg, ERGON-Verlag. pp. 168–74.

LEVINTHAL, D.A. and MARCH, J.G. (1993) 'The myopia of learning'. *Strategic Management Journal*. Vol. 14: 95–112.

NONAKA, I. and TAKEUCHI, H. (1995) *The Knowledge-Creating Company*. Oxford, Oxford University Press.

PETERAF, M.A. (1993) 'The cornerstones of competitive advantage: a resource-based view'. *Strategic Management Journal*, Vol. 14: 179–91.

STALK, G., EVANS, P. *and* SHULMAN, L.E. (1992) 'Competing on capabilities: the new rules of corporate strategy'. *Harvard Business Review*. March–April: 57–69.

STARKEY, K. (ed) *How Organizations Learn*. London, International Thomson Business Press. pp. 92–9.

VON KROGH, G., ROOS, J. *and* SLOCUM, K. (1994) 'An essay on corporate epistemology'. *Strategic Management Journal, Summer Special Issue*. Vol. 15: 53–71

APPENDICES

APPENDIX 1

THE COMPREHENSIVE AND THE PROBLEM-CENTRED APPROACHES TO ANALYSING ORGANISATIONAL HRD NEEDS

These two approaches are based on the same general principles, but in their detailed operation they cater for different kinds of situation.

The *total*, or *comprehensive*, *approach* involves a systematic, full-scale analysis of all the organisation's training and development needs, identified by discussions with managers (and unions as relevant), by analysis of the corporate business plan, and by examination of any other sources of likely change affecting people in the organisation. Its product is an organisation-wide training plan containing unit and individual plans for the forthcoming year (a year is usually the planning period for this kind of approach). It can be relevant for organisations where the environment is relatively stable, and where longer-term training plans can feasibly be produced and pursued, although it is unlikely to be used unless there is a specialist personnel/training function. If you are following this approach you must ensure that you have the necessary time and other resources, and that it will justify such expenditure.

For organisations operating in an unpredictable environment, facing severe pressures, and/or (like many small to medium-sized firms) lacking the resources or expertise for the 'total' strategy, something more selective and immediate in its payback is needed. For them, the 'problem-centred' analytical approach may be the most appropriate.

The *'problem-centred' approach* focuses on urgent problems facing the organisation and requiring a training/development response. It places minimum reliance on paperwork. The assumption here is that the planning of training must be ongoing and focused on immediate needs, with long-term strategy at a minimum; there may be no formalised training plan other than papers that from time to time have to be drawn up for budgetary or external purposes. Training must respond quickly to any urgent needs, and so flexibility in the function and its operations is essential.

Both approaches are systematic; it is the time-scale and scope of assessment and planning that are the major differentiating factors. Here is a step-by-step guide to their implementation.

THE TOTAL, OR COMPREHENSIVE, APPROACH

Step 1: Identify major needs

The first step is to study the organisation's business strategy and plan. Training/personnel staff should then discuss with every manager the training and development needs for their units. At this stage they need to discuss the implications of any impending organisational changes, new technology initiatives, new plant and machinery or new staff coming into the organisation. In establishing training needs they should be influenced by managers' interpretation of events as well as by areas of need identified in corporate strategy.

Step 2: Agree possible solutions

During this phase of the discussion the degree to which training can contribute to meeting departmental needs must be assessed. Performance targets and outputs of the department must be examined, together with any other data that give substance and objectivity to the discussion. Information about many training needs may come from the results of appraisal interviews. Where an appraisal system is not yet operative, information will come from such sources as managers' views and the views of any other key parties, performance records, career plans and potential reviews.

Problems initially perceived by managers to have a training and development solution may prove on analysis to need some other solution, or vice versa. It is therefore essential to be clear as to the real nature of a problem. If performance is poor, for example, it may be because of inadequate or non-existent training, but it could as easily be because of poor motivation, ineffective management or faulty equipment.

Thus in this second step the training manager (with help as needed) has detailed talks with line management to ensure that the departmental and individual needs they raise will be best and most cost-effectively tackled by some form of training or development. They will also need jointly to define and agree those needs, and apply a prioritisation system that reflects overall objectives established in the organisation's corporate training policy.

Step 3: Select training options

At this point it is important to discuss options for training, with a view to the process being as cost-efficient as possible. Initially the possibility of on-the-job events to achieve the required learning should be discussed rather than looking at external courses of action as a priority. Such discussion can lead to a significant shift from a reliance on external courses to an emphasis on in-house training, much of it delivered by consultants. It can also lead line managers, supervisors and other non-specialist training personnel in the organisation to take significant responsibility for design and delivery of training once they have acquired the necessary level of competence. Such a shift must obviously be accompanied by the appropriate training and development of such external and internal personnel and by careful monitoring of processes and outcomes.

Step 4: Create training plan
Next, the training manager constructs the first draft of the annual training plan, which identifies each department's and each individual's training needs and the relevant courses of action agreed with the managers of those departments and individuals.

Step 5: Prioritise learning events
The budgeting process conducted by the training manager starts at this point when, within the training plan, he or she classifies training needs and events on a scale (which could simply be an 'A to E' rating system, A being 'essential training/development', E 'desirable but not necessarily this year'), according to priorities established in corporate training policy. This means that each training event is prioritised in accordance with corporate business needs so that, when finalised, the training plan is geared to make an optimum contribution to the achievement of business objectives as well as to individual needs.

Step 6: Apply budgetary constraints
After training has been categorised, the training manager should then estimate the costs involved in the initial draft of the training plan, including the options that were discussed with managers. Costing should be done using current costs (an inflationary factor can be added later), examining both direct and indirect costs as in Chapter 10.

In an organisation where managers are required to submit departmental budgets for the coming financial year in, say, late January, total budget figures need to be allocated before the beginning of the financial year. This will enable managers to allocate resources appropriately according to their budget allocation, based on their January submissions. Once the training manager receives his or her budget allocation, adjustments to the plan are quite straightforward if it has been built up on a prioritised pyramid of costs (descending from 'essential' to 'can be deferred if necessary'). Reappraisal of the options available may result, for example, in the use of more internal 'training, or in dropping some training in the category that lists training agreed to carry lowest priority'. In the latter event, subsequent reassessment of the original need should be carried out, to see whether or not training is still appropriate and needs to be done in the next budget year.

Step 7: Communicate results
Once the training plan has been fully costed and agreed by the board, a copy of the relevant sections should be given to each manager as an *aide-mémoire* and plan for each department. This then becomes an essential tool of reference for the review meetings that the training manager holds with managers throughout the forthcoming year.

Step 8: Monitor and evaluate implementation

A continuous appraisal of progress and budgetary control should be maintained by the training department, using information supplied by management and those who go on training and development programmes. The task is not a difficult one when the training plan has been costed in relation to specific learning events and departments, with clear categories covering course fees, travel and related expenses, and fees paid to external consultants and trainers. Monitoring is vital for two reasons:

- It enables tight control to be exercised over ongoing training, so that if at any point costs are exceeded appropriate action can be taken. If, on the other hand, it should happen that costs fall below estimate, there is flexibility either to include any hitherto-deferred training or to carry out training to meet some unexpected contingency.

- It enables the training manager to build up a 'value for money' statement which can be included in the annual report on the training plan. This can include statements related to key parameters like:

  - outcomes of training, in relation to key needs it was intended to serve (using quantifiable and also qualitative measures)

  - expenditure overall on training, compared with previous year

  - number and cost of person days of training, compared with previous year

  - number and cost of person days of training carried out externally and in-house, compared with previous year.

THE PROBLEM-CENTRED APPROACH

Here is how the eight steps can be applied using the problem-centred approach. (Throughout, reference is made to 'the training manager', but this should be taken to mean anyone who carries the responsibility for formulating training policy and a training plan for the organisation.)

Step 1: Identify major needs

The training manager should identify with managers on a continuing basis the most urgent problems or challenges they face for which it is felt some form of training or development would be the best solution. Analysis itself is carried out in a similar way to that outlined in the comprehensive approach. At regular intervals (determined by the length of the business planning cycle) the training manager must check on any information available about business plans and likely future changes in order to see if training is needed to feed into those.

Step 2: Agree possible solutions

Here, as with the 'total' approach, the training manager must analyse whether particular problems are not only relevant for training to tackle, but are problems to which training would be the most cost-effective and cost-efficient response. In making a decision consideration must be given, within the constraints of corporate policy and employee resource systems, to alternative options such as changing equipment, jobs, people or organisational structure.

With the problem-centred approach, priorities are determined by the extent to which one problem, if resolved, would make a greater impact on immediate business performance than another. Areas of weakness which are currently impeding the achievement of results crucial to the company's survival must therefore be tackled first. Longer-term issues, such as succession planning needs, must also be tackled on an on-going basis in the light of their importance in ensuring the continuity and calibre of uniquely valuable personnel.

Step 3: Select training options

Here, agreement must be reached on which people are to be trained, how many, when and where they will need training, and how they will be trained. Training can be done in any cost-effective, feasible and agreed way, but must take place in or near the work environment wherever possible, both to reduce costs and to ensure immediate relevance and transferability of learning. Events selected under the problem-centred approach must be mainly concerned with achieving results in the shortest possible time and in the most efficient manner.

Step 4: Create training plan

Training to meet certain major needs will usually be planned and agreed some time in advance (for example, health and safety training, retraining to cope with redundancies or redeployment of workers, or training to enable key workers to operate new technology). That apart, the training plan will be informal rather than heavily documented. A record should, however, be kept of the number and names of the learners, training objectives, the type, location and timing of the training, and its timing, cost and outcomes related to objectives.

Step 5: Prioritise learning events

Although training, with the problem-centred approach, is done on a rolling basis rather than on the basis of an annual plan, attention must still be paid to prioritising events. Planning no more, probably, than a few weeks or months ahead, the training manager must still ensure that the training effort is put into those problem areas across the company where there will be the most significant return in terms of impact on the business. So, as with the prioritisation of departmental or divisional training needs, attention must be given first to areas that have a critical impact on the firm's survival and are crucial to its future stability and growth.

Step 6: Apply budgetary constraints

The training manager may not have a budget (or may only hold a small central budget for core training and development needs), but be paid from the budgets held by line managers. It is therefore particularly important that he or she has a clear idea of what the business overall, and particular departments within it, can afford for the training they are requesting. All training must be carefully costed. When line managers hold budgetary control, particularly close attention should be given to 'hidden' costs like lost opportunity and lost production, replacement or other costs involved in covering for people away from their jobs for a period of time. The training manager must be able to convince others that training can offer the value needed to offset costs.

Step 7: Communicate results

With the problem-centred approach, initial requests for training must be acted upon quickly, and information about training and development activities that will be going ahead must be communicated to the managers concerned as soon as possible.

In situations where the problem-centred approach is used, certainty can rarely be built into any stage of the cycle. Even at the last minute, action plans may have to be cancelled or postponed because of some contingency. Communications at that point must work particularly well in order to ensure that everyone is informed about the reasons for the changes and that, wherever possible, alternative ways of responding to the initial request (assuming it is still valid) can be agreed.

Step 8: Monitor and evaluate implementation

Evaluation is essential in order to ensure that scarce resources (including time) are being used effectively. The initial clear specification of the nature of the problem and the exact outcomes training is intended to produce, together with agreement between training manager and line managers about how those outcomes will be measured, should ease the task of evaluation. Identifiable improvements in competencies, and measurable impact on the indicators chosen beforehand – for example, material wastage rates, levels of employee absenteeism, turnover, learning times, indices of customer satisfaction, speed and quality of service provided – should all be used in order to assess the extent to which training has had an impact on the problems it was intended to resolve or reduce.

REFERENCES

HARRISON, R. (1992) 'Employee development at Barratt', in D. Woodall and D. Winstanley (eds), *Case Studies in Personnel*. London, Institute of Personnel and Development. pp. 103–15.

APPENDIX 2

NATIONAL VOCATIONAL QUALIFICATIONS (NVQs)

NVQs must, by definition, meet the needs of an occupational sector as a whole, not just those of an individual organisation. They must also prepare people for changing demands on occupations. Each qualification approved by the National Council for Vocational Qualifications (NCVQ) is assigned to one of five levels within the NVQ framework, from Level 1 (semi-skilled) to Level 5 (higher professionals). This framework provides comparability between different occupations and between vocational and academic qualifications. Some qualifications are easier to integrate into the NVQ system than others, because many professions have a highly structured system for gaining qualifications, some including competencies but some being more educationally based.

Credit accumulation and transfer (CAT)

CAT is a system that enables people to achieve a level of competence and associated NVQs through various methods of training and work experience, at various centres, and over varying periods of time. The aim is that all qualifications should be designed in such a way that they can be offered on a modular basis and be tested by judging someone's competence in the job. This is similar to the highly successful French vocational training and education schemes.

To this end, every NVQ is made up of a number of units comprising groups of elements which state precisely in outcome terms what people are expected to do, together with the performance criteria that define the key characteristics of competent performance for each element. Credits are then given for the acquisition of units. Using the CAT system a workplace supervisor with training responsibilities could gain one or perhaps two units of a training and development NVQ mainly through having his or her workplace performance assessed as meeting the standards laid down in those elements. Having been assessed as competent in those specific areas of activity, the supervisor could add to them subsequently as he or she chooses.

Each unit therefore builds up the credit balance of an individual's 'competence account'. Ways are being explored to express all existing qualifications in terms of units. Units certificated by different awarding bodies can then be accumulated, and it should prove possible for units common to two or more qualifications to be transferred in order to avoid repetition in training and assessment.

Accreditation of prior learning (APL)

Since APL and performance in the workplace, or a realistic simulation of it, are central to the process of achieving an NVQ, assessment of workplace competence and of prior learning require close collaboration between colleges, training organisations and employers. The award of an NVQ depends upon a competent assessor being satisfied that a candidate has provided enough evidence of competence across all the elements/outcomes with their performance criteria and range, which make up the units in a particular qualification. This has clear implications for appraisal schemes, and also for the identification of training needs and the design of training and development experiences that can both meet job-related needs and help in achieving NVQs.

APPENDIX 3

NATIONAL EDUCATION AND TRAINING TARGETS FOR THE YEAR 2000 (1995)

Foundation learning

By age 19:
85 per cent of young people to reach NVQ Level 2 or equivalent
75 per cent to achieve NVQ Level 2 in core skills of communication, numeracy and information technology.

By age 21:
35 per cent to achieve NVQ Level 3 in these core skills
60 per cent to reach NVQ Level 3 or equivalent.

Lifetime learning

60 per cent of workforce to reach NVQ Level 3 or equivalent
30 per cent of workforce to reach NVQ Level 4 or equivalent
70 per cent of 200-employee organisations and 35 per cent of those with more than 50 staff to gain Investors in People status.

(*Source*: *People Management*, 31 May 1995, page 8)

APPENDIX 4

TDLB STANDARDS: 'STANDARDS AND QUALIFICATIONS FOR TRAINING AND DEVELOPMENT'

Key Purpose

The key purpose for training and development has been defined as:

'Develop human potential to assist organisations and individuals to achieve their objectives.'

This statement reflects training and development's dual role to assist both organisations and individuals.

To achieve this Key Purpose the Lead Body adopted the Systematic Training Cycle to define areas of competence.

The Systematic Training Cycle

The cycle was chosen because:

* it describes systematically and comprehensively the whole training and development process

* it is familiar in all sectors and to all parts of the training community

* most training and development roles can be located within it.

The Systematic Training Cycle still forms the basis of the revised functional map, which attempts to describe the functions carried out by trainers.

The Key Purpose is split into five AREAS OF COMPETENCE which, when taken together, constitute the achievement of the Key Purpose. You will see that Areas A, B, C and E correspond to distinct stages of the Systematic Training Cycle. Area D corresponds to the assessment and progress of individuals only. It comprises the assessment and verification units, which are the cornerstones of the NVQ Quality Assurance System.

Some training and development occupations also require competence in occupational areas other than training. For roles such as Training Manager, Training Administrator and Training Centre Manager, standards from other Lead Bodies are appropriate and might be combined with relevant units from the Training and Development framework to define the requirements of these roles.

FUNCTIONAL MAP: KEY PURPOSE AND MAIN AREAS

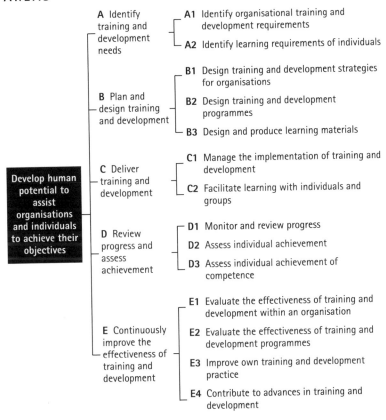

'Standards and Qualifications for Training and Development' extracted from EMPLOYMENT STANDARDS OCCUPATIONAL STANDARDS COUNCIL (1996) *A Briefing Note.* Sheffield, Department for Education and Employment. p. 5.

'Functional Map' extracted from EMPLOYMENT STANDARDS OCCUPATIONAL STANDARDS COUNCIL (1996) *Functional Map – National Standards for Training and Development.* Sheffield, Department for Education and Employment. p. 1.

Both © Crown Copyright, by permission of the DfEE.

APPENDIX 5

THE IPD CODE OF PROFESSIONAL CONDUCT AND PROFESSIONAL CONDUCT REGULATIONS

(A revised Code is available from the IPD from May 1997.)

The Institute of Personnel and Development is the professional human resource association for the United Kingdom and the Republic of Ireland. All IPD members, therefore, should be concerned with the maintenance of good practice within the profession and must commit themselves to this code of professional conduct. They must also have regard to any further codes of practice, guidance notes and statements which may be issued from time to time by the Institute.

Human resource practitioners must not act in a way which could encourage or assist unlawful conduct by either employers or employees. Although they often have a professional responsibility for personnel at the place of work, their ultimate responsibility is to their employer. Where such responsibilities conflict, they may seek the advice of the Institute and, having considered the options available, may sometimes wish to make their feelings known. Action might range from recording their reservations about an employer's decision they have to implement through to resignation from their job.

Mission
The mission of the Institute of Personnel and Development is:

- to lead in the development and promotion of good practice in the field of the management and development of people, for application both by professional members and by their organisational colleagues

- to serve the professional interests of members

- to uphold the highest ideals in the management and development of people.

Objectives
The charitable objectives of the Institute are:

- to promote and develop the science and practice of the management and development of people (including the promotion of research and the publication of the useful results of such research) for the public benefit

- to establish, promote and monitor standards of competence, good practice, conduct and ethics for those engaged (or about to engage) in the practice of the management and development of people, for the public benefit.

The Institute will seek to fulfil its objectives in the following ways:

- by establishing, monitoring and promoting standards and ethics for the profession

- by seeking opportunities and pursuing activities, using the specialised experience of professional members supported by staff and other resources, to advance the practice of management and development of people, including the development of the learning organisation

- by influencing developments and issues relating to the management and development of people through effective representation of the views of the profession

- by disseminating and exchanging information, experience and the results of research and development for the public benefit and the continuing professional development of members

- by establishing programmes of education and training and continuing professional development with recognised standards of achievement, to support the systematic development and accrediting of members

- by providing a wide range of member services at local, national and international levels to support the professional needs of members

- by developing and maintaining appropriate links with other bodies and organisations at local, national and international levels in order to influence positively decisions and thinking affecting the management and development of people

- by providing relevant commercial activities which support the professionalism of the Institute and its members and which earn commercial returns for re-investment into its main purposes.

Purpose of this code
The rest of this code sets out, for employers and others, the areas of activity in which IPD members operate and the standards of professional conduct to which they must adhere.

Activities
Human resource practitioners who are members of IPD can be expected to have acquired a body of knowledge and skills and, depending on whether they are specialists or generalists, to have attained a level of professional competence in one or more of the following areas:

- employee resourcing – managing and rewarding performance

- maintaining sound relations between employer and employees

- training and development

- health and safety.

Standards of professional conduct

Although managing and developing people forms an important part of every manager's job, IPD members can provide specialist professional knowledge, advice and support on the most effective use of human resources. Along with a total commitment to the overall goals of the organisation, they need a detailed understanding of economic, financial, political and social factors so they can play a full role in decision making.

In carrying out these responsibilities, IPD members must respect the following standards of conduct:

Accuracy

They must maintain high standards of accuracy in the information and advice they provide to employers and employees.

Confidentiality

They must respect their employer's legitimate needs for confidentiality and ensure that all personnel information (including information about current, past and prospective employees) remains private.

Counselling

With the relevant skills they must be prepared to act as counsellors to individual employees, pensioners and dependants or to refer them, where appropriate, to other professionals or helping agencies.

Developing others

They must encourage self-development and seek to achieve the fullest possible development of employees in the service of present and future organisation needs.

Equal opportunities

They must promote fair, non-discriminatory employment practices.

Fair dealing

They must maintain fair and reasonable standards in their treatment of individuals.

Self-development

They must seek continuously to improve their performance and update their skills and knowledge.

They will at all times endeavour to enhance the standing and good name of the profession; adherence to this code of professional conduct is an essential aspect of this. They should also be aware of the other codes, statements and guidance notes which are available from IPD headquarters. Complaints that members have not followed the principles laid down here may be made under the professional conduct regulations.

Extracted from INSTITUTE OF PERSONNEL AND DEVELOPMENT (1995) *The IPD, IPM and ITD Codes of Practice: The IPD code of professional conduct and professional conduct regulations.* London, Institute of Personnel and Development. pp. 5–6. By permission of the IPD.

APPENDIX 6

CARRYING OUT AN AUDIT OF TRAINING AND OF INSTRUMENTAL LEARNING

You will need to explain briefly the kind of organisation in which the audit is to be carried out, and its overall perceived levels of productivity and performance. You should also explain why it is important at this point in time to carry out an audit of training and instrumental learning.

Using Murphy and Swanson's six-step approach, you could produce a plan that looks something like this:

1 Objectives for the audit
- To assess in each sector of the workforce how far formal on- and off-the-job training activities result in learners' reaching required standards of performance, and what kind of activities leads to the steady improvement of their job performance thereafter.

- To identify any other ways by which people learn to achieve effective standards and to improve their performance.

- To identify any barriers to effective training and instrumental learning.

2 What the evaluator expects to find
- That people are helped to achieve effective standards of performance by most of the planned training activities that occur.

- That their management and organisation in the workplace are aimed at the improvement of job performance.

- That there is widespread use of briefing groups, quality circles, and other approaches whereby they are encouraged themselves to identify problems, formulate courses of action to resolve them, experiment with these, and assess how far they actually improve their job performance.

3 Data-collection procedures
Data will be gathered over a three-month period by means of a questionnaire going out to samples across the whole workforce, and by means of follow-up interviews on a selective basis. The procedures will ensure that the views and expectations of trainers, managers and learners about training and instrumental learning are identified, and that their suggestions for change are also gathered.

You should elaborate in this section on the samples you will use and your rationale for that choice; on the design of the questionnaire/s; and on the check-lists to be used for interviews.

You will also need to explain who is to collect the data, and how he or she will be selected and organised (if it is not yourself). It may be that external consultants are used; or that the task could be done by a student on secondment who is able to use it as a project; or that it is done by someone within the organisation. Great care must be taken with the selection of those who carry out the various parts of the audit exercise.

4 Collection of data samples
You will need to produce a carefully worked out time-schedule for this stage.

5 Report of what was found in relation to expectations
The findings must be clearly and logically set out. In this audit, if the evaluator's expectations are realised, then the findings will be largely positive, showing, for example, that most formal courses do result in a perceived improvement in people's ability to perform their jobs, as seen by job-holders and their managers; and that although certain changes are needed in terms of content and delivery, the broad thrust of training activities is considered by most of the key parties – trainers, learners, their managers and top management – to be satisfactory and worth the general cost of the provision, with tangible evidence available to suppport those perceptions.

However, if the evaluator finds what he or she expected to find, then a particularly careful check needs to be made of the evidence and of how it was collected. Research that confirms previous expectations is naturally suspect, which is why a rigorous approach to the whole auditing process is essential.

Negative findings should be recorded. The following weak aspects are typical of this kind of audit:

- *Concerns about the impact and costs of training activities.* In terms of impact on job performance, certain training activities may be found to be unsuccessful, and decisions will have to be made about whether to amend or discontinue them. In terms of costs, certain training activities may be considered reasonably successful but not to warrant the general kind of costs they incurred (this is often the case with external courses which, after such an audit, may be discontinued in favour of a piloting of the same training executed in-house, with the agreement to extend that latter strategy if the pilot proves successful).

- *Inadequate incentives for good job performance and for a steady pattern of improvement in standards reached.* The audit may reveal that formal training activities are not having their desired results because those who go through them do not feel they are being adequately rewarded, and so have no motivation to apply new skills and knowledge – so reward systems, whether of finance, career development, or levels and kinds of responsibility and status would need to be examined (see Fairbairn, 1991).

• *Lack of managerial support for risk-taking and learning from failure.* Instrumental learning involves people trying out different ways of improving their performance in a given job. If the emphasis of managers is on the avoidance of mistakes, and/or on 'one best way' of performing tasks, and if failure is heavily penalised rather than being used as a vehicle for questioning and helping people to learn and improve, then effective instrumental learning cannot occur. Instead, learners will tend to reach a particular level of performance and remain there. If this is all that is required of them, the result may be seen as satisfactory; if, however, learners are expected to make steady improvements in their performance, changes will need to be made in the learning environment.

6 Write and report conclusions

The final report must be clear, concise, as brief as possible and express findings in language meaningful to those to whom the audit is to be made available. Conclusions in this kind of audit might include some or all of the following types of recommendation, depending on findings, and assessed cost and feasibility of actions proposed against needs defined:

• To continue to run most of the training activities, with a specified range of changes, and with more careful attention to the selection of trainees and to arrangements for transfer of learning after the acitivies, and continued monitoring of performance.

• To discontinue a minority of activities, piloting other forms of learning, or different kinds of training course, if desirable, while carefully monitoring the costs and outcomes of any pilot events and comparing them with costs and outcomes of those they have replaced, and those anticipated.

• To carry out training and development of certain managers in order to improve their ability to diagnose learning needs and transfer the learning of their trainees to the job; and to help learners steadily improve their performance thereafter.

APPENDIX 7

A SEVEN-STEP APPROACH TO THE APPRAISAL PROCESS

This approach can be used regardless of the particular type of appraisal scheme in an organisation, providing that the appraisal process:

- is based on self-appraisal (see Guidelines for the Seven-Step Approach below)

- has at its heart a formal appraisal discussion that takes place either annually or more frequently between managers and individual members of each manager's team

- is developmental in purpose, focusing on work review, forward work-planning, and support and development of individuals for their current job performance and for their future in the organisation.

OUTLINE

1 Agenda-setting meeting
Up to 15 (working) days before appraisal discussion – allow 30 minutes.

2 Producing the self-appraisal
Up to 10 (working) days before appraisal discussion.

3 Transmitting the self-appraisal
Up to five days before appraisal discussion.

4 The appraisal discussion
Allow at least two hours.

5 Meeting to finalise appraisal form
Up to five days later – allow 20 minutes.

6 Transmitting copy of the form
By (insert date).

7 First review of progress of action plan
Within three months of Appraisal Discussion.

GUIDELINES FOR SEVEN-STEP APPROACH TO THE APPRAISAL PROCESS

1 Agenda-setting meeting

Appraiser and appraisee go together through the organisation's written guidelines on the appraisal scheme and the appraisal form to be completed. They agree on dates for Steps 2 and 3, and on how the appraisal discussion itself will be structured. They check that they each have a copy of the appraisee's appraisal form and action plan from the previous appraisal discussion. They get spare copies of a new appraisal form to use in Step 2.

2 Producing the self-appraisal

Appraisee fills in the self-appraisal parts of the appraisal form for the coming period (using a spare copy). The *appraiser* does the same, trying to 'second guess' the likely responses of the appraisee in order to test his or her own understanding.

3 Transmitting the self-appraisal

The *appraisee* sends the appraiser a copy of the 'self-appraisal' produced in Step 2. *Appraiser* compares the appraisee's actual responses with those expected by the appraiser and reflects on any gaps here. He or she also identifies any further information needed from the appraisee or elsewhere before the appraisal discussion takes place.

4 The appraisal discussion

Performance review and work planning

This part of the discussion should be initiated by the appraisee, using the self-appraisal already completed. It should focus on reviewing the appraisee's job performance during the previous period, relating this to his or her key targets of performance set at the start of that period. Areas of achievement and any underachievement should be identified and discussed, together with aids and barriers to fully effective performance. This stage should lead to work targets' being set for the coming period and agreement on necessary resources related to those targets.

Job-related and career-related support and development

This part of the discussion should focus on how best to support and enhance in the coming year not only *job performance* but also *personal growth as part of long-term career development*. The latter requires a discussion of the career path that the appraisee hopes to follow during his or her time with the organisation, and the generation of creative ideas on what might be done in the coming year to support him or her in moving along that path.

The action plan for support and development

A plan should be agreed outlining the *actions of any kind* that appraisee and appraiser agree as being the most feasible, most cost-beneficial and most likely to make a positive impact on the appraisee's (a) job-related performance and (b) longer-term development and personal growth.

Summarising the discussion and agreeing next steps[1]

The appraisee summarises his or her understanding of what has occurred and been agreed during the meeting; *the appraiser* agrees or explains any disagreement. *Appraisee or appraiser* confirms that he or she will write up the appraisal form accordingly, omitting a section for 'Final Comments' by appraiser and appraisee until Step 5. The *appraiser* confirms, where necessary, that he or she will confer with other parties whose approval may be needed in order to finalise the proposed action plan. The date is set for Step 5.

5 Meeting to finalise appraisal form

Appraisee and appraiser agree on the write-up of the form, or note in a 'Final Comments' sections any disagreement. Their 'Final Comments' should also draw attention to any wider organisational issues that have emerged from the appraisal discussion. The *appraisee* asks the appraiser for confirmation of the action plan and for the date of the first check on its implementation.

6 Transmitting copy of the form

The *appraisee* keeps the original form, duly completed and signed by all the parties. The *appraisee* sends copy of the form to whoever is designated to receive it.

7 First review of progress of Action Plan

Appraisee and appraiser meet as agreed to review progress in implementing the action plan and take any action needed at that stage.

[1]Although the form can be written up by the appraiser at this stage, experience suggests that the appraisal process will be enhanced if the writing up is done later, and by the appraisee, with a further short meeting held to finalise the form, as suggested in Step 5.

REFERENCES

ABBOTT, B. (1994) 'Training strategies in small service sector firms: employer and employee perspectives'. *Human Resource Management Journal.* Vol. 4, 2: 70–87.

ADLER, P.S. *and* COLE, R.E. (1993) 'Designed for learning: a tale of two auto plants'. *Sloan Management Review.* Vol. 34, 3: 85–94.

AIKEN, O. (1996) 'Be prepared for a data remember'. *People Management.* Vol. 2, 11: 38–40.

ALLEN, R.E. (1990) *The Concise Oxford Dictionary of Current English.* 8th ed. Oxford, Clarendon Press.

ALVAREZ, J.L. (1996) 'Are we asking too much of managers?'. *Financial Times.* 12 July: 13.

AMIT, R. *and* SCHOEMAKER, J.H. (1993) 'Strategic assets and organizational rent'. *Strategic Management Journal.* Vol. 14, 1: 33–46.

ANNETT, J., DUNCAN, K.D., STAMMERS, R.B. *and* GRAY, M.J. (1979) *Task Analysis: Department of Employment and Productivity training information paper, No. 6.* London, HMSO; reprinted Sheffield, Department of Employment.

ARGYRIS, C. (1957) *Personality and Organization.* New York, Harper and Row.

ARGYRIS, C. (1977) 'Double loop learning in organizations'. *Harvard Business Review.* September–October: 115–24

ARGYRIS, C. (1982) *Reasoning, Learning and Action.* San Franciso, Calif., Jossey-Bass.

ARGYRIS, C. (1996) 'Skilled incompetence' in K. Starkey (ed.), *How Organizations Learn.* London, International Thomson Business Press. pp. 82–91.

ARGYRIS, C. *and* SCHON, D.A. (1978) *Organizational Learning: A theory of action perspective.* Reading, Mass., Addison Wesley.

ARGYRIS, C. *and* SCHON, D.A. (1996) *Organizational Learning II: Theory, method and practice.* Wokingham, Addison Wesley.

ARKIN, A. (1991) 'A springboard to equal opportunities'. *Personnel Management.* Vol. 23, 2: 57–8.

ARKIN, A. (1995) 'Breaking down skills barriers'. *People Management.* Vol. 1, 3: 34–5.

ARKIN, A. (1995a) 'More than just a cosmetic change'. *People Management.* Vol. 1, 8: 30–31.

ARKIN, A. (1995b) 'Training caters for special needs'. *People Management.* Vol. 1, 16, 32–3.

ARMSTRONG, M. (1987) 'Human Resource Management: a case of the emperor's new clothes?'. *Personnel Management.* Vol. 19, 8: 30–35.

ARMSTRONG, M. (1993) *Managing Reward Systems.* Buckingham, Open University.

ARMSTRONG, M. (1996) *Employee Reward.* London, Institute of Personnel and Development.

AUTHERS, J. (1994) 'Hard test at end of a crash course'. *Financial Times.* 24 August.

AUTHERS, J. *and* WOOD, L. (1993) 'Little knowledge is a dangerous thing'. *Financial Times.* 15 December.

BALLS, E. *and* GOODHART, D. (1994) 'Can Europe compete? The high price of social cohesion'. *Financial Times.* 28 February: 11.

BARNEY, J. (1991) 'Firm resources and sustained competitive advantage'. *Journal of Management.* Vol. 17: 99–120.

BASS, B.M. *and* VAUGHAN, J.A. (1967) *Training in Industry: The management of learning.* London, Tavistock Publications.

BASSETT, P. (1996) 'Price of workplace flexibility may be rising job insecurity'. *Times 'Analysis' section,* 11 June: 31.

BATCHELOR, C. (1992) 'Management: the growing business'. *Financial Times.* 8 December: 9.

BATCHELOR, J., DONNELLY, R. *and* MORRIS, D. (1995) 'Learning networks within supply chains'. *Working paper, Coventry Business School.* Coventry, Coventry University.

BATES, D.L. *and* DILLARD, JR, J.E. (1993) 'Generating strategic thinking through multi-level teams'. *Long Range Planning.* Vol. 26, 5: 103–10.

BATESON, G. (1973) *Steps to an Ecology of Mind.* London/Paladin, Granada.

BATESON, G. (1979) *Mind and Nature.* Glasgow, Fontana/Collins.

BAUD, D.C. *and* SCANLAN, G. (1995) 'Strategic control through core competencies'. *Long Range Planning.* Vol. 28, 2: 102–14.

BEAUMONT, G. (1996) 'Review of 100 NVQs and SVQs'. *A Report Submitted to the Department for Education and Employment.* 25 Albion Road, Chesterfield, S40 IBR (Freepost SF10305), Beaumont.

BECKET, M. (1996) 'Small business packs statistical punch'. *Daily Telegraph, Business Monitor section.* 12 August: 27.

BECKHARD, R. (1969) *Organization Development: Strategies and models.* Reading, Mass., Addison Wesley.

BEE, F. *and* BEE, R. (1994) *Training Needs Analysis and Evaluation.* London, Institute of Personnel and Development.

BEE, F. *and* FARMER, P. (1995) 'HR projects on the right track'. *People Management.* Vol. 1, 16: 28–30.

BELBIN, R.M. (1981) *Management Teams: Why they succeed or fail.* London, Heinemann.

BENTLEY, T. (1990) *The Business of Training: Achieving success in changing world markets.* Maidenhead, McGraw-Hill.

BEVAN, S. *and* THOMPSON, M. (1991) 'Performance management at the crossroads'. *Personnel Management.* Vol. 23, 11: 36–9.

BICHARD, M. (1996) 'Shake-up inspires new state of mind'. *People Management.* Vol. 2, 3: 22–7.

BILLOT, H. (1996) 'Business alloys'. *People Management.* Vol. 2, 20: 38–41.

BLAKE, N. (1990) 'Local levels', *Times Higher Education Supplement.* 6 April.

BLUMENTHAL, B. *and* HASPESLAGH, P. (1992) 'Corporate transformation: amalgams and distinctions'. Working Paper. France, INSEAD.

BOBBITT, F. (1918) *The Curriculum.* Cambridge, Mass., The Riverside Press. Reprinted, 1971, Boston, Houghton Mifflin.

BOHN, R.E. (1994) 'Measuring and managing technological knowledge'. *Sloan Management Review.* Vol. 36, 1: 61–73.

BOISOT, M., GRIFFITHS, D. *and* MOLES, V. (1995) 'The dilemma of competence: differentiation versus integration in the pursuit of learning'. *Paper prepared for the Third International Workshop on Competence-based Competition.* Ghent, November 16–18.

BOWER, D. (1991) 'Case study: Rover', in V. Dulewicz, 'Improving assessment centres', *Personnel Management*, Vol. 23, 6: 52–3.

BOYATZIS, R. (1991) 'Building on competence: the effective use of managerial talent', in G. Salaman (ed.) *Human Resource Strategies,* London, Sage.

BOYATZIS, R.E. (1982) *The Competent Manager: A model for effective performance.* New York, Wiley.

BOYDELL, T. *and* LEARY, M. (1996) *Identifying Training Needs.* London, Institute of Personnel and Development.

BRAMLEY, P. (1996) *Evaluating Training.* London, Institute of Personnel and Development.

BRATTON, J. *and* GOLD, J (1994) *Human Resource Management: Theory and practice.* London, Macmillan.

BREWSTER, C. *and* SMITH, C. (1990) 'Corporate strategy – a no-go area for personnel?'. *Personnel Management.* Vol. 22, 7: 36–40.

BREWSTER, C. *and* TYSON, S. (eds) (1991) *International Comparisons in Human Resource Management.* London, Pitman.

BRITISH INSTITUTE OF MANAGEMENT (BIM) AND ASTON UNIVERSITY. (1989) *The Responsive Organization.* London, British Institute of Management.

BRODIE, M. *and* BENNETT, R. (1979) 'Effective management and the audit of performance'. *Journal of General Management.* Vol. 4 (spring).

BROWN, H., PECCEI, R., SANDBERG, S. *and* WELCHMAN, R. (1989) 'Management training and development: in search of an integrated approach'. *Journal of General Management.* Vol. 15, 1, autumn: 69–82.

BURGOYNE, J. (1995) 'Feeding minds to grow the business'. *People Management.* Vol. 1, 19: 22–5.

BUTLER, G.V. (1986) *Organization and Management: Theory and practice*. London, Prentice Hall International in association with the Institute of Personnel Management.

BUTLER, S. (1990) 'Cutting down and reshaping the core'. *Financial Times*, 20 March.

CAMBRIDGE UNIVERSITY SMALL BUSINESS RESEARCH CENTRE. (1992) *The State of British Enterprise: Growth, Innovation and Competitive Advantage in Small and Medium-sized Firms*. Cambridge, Small Business Research Centre.

CANNELL, M. (1997) 'Practice makes perfect'. *People Management*. Vol. 3, 5: 26–33.

CANNELLA, A.A. JR, and HAMBRICK, D.C. (1993) 'Executive departure and acquisition performance'. *Strategic Management Journal*. Vol. 14: 167–79.

CARBY, K. and THAKUR, M. (1977) *Transactional Analysis at Work. Information Report No. 23*. London, Institute of Personnel Management.

CARTER, P and LUMSDON, C. (1988) 'How management development can improve business performance'. *Personnel Management*. Vol. 20, 10: 49–52.

CASCIO, W.F. (1992) *Applied Psychology in Personnel Management*. Reston, Va. Reston Publishing Co.

CATALANELLO, R. and REDDING, J. (1989) 'Three Strategic Training Roles'. *Training and Development Journal*. Vol. 43, 12: 51–5.

CAVE, E. and McKEOWN, P. (1993) 'Managerial effectiveness: the identification of need'. *Management Education and Development*. Vol. 24, part 2: 122–37.

CHAKRAVARTHY, B.S. and DOZ, Y. (1992) 'Strategy process research: focusing on corporate self-renewal'. *Strategic Management Journal, Summer Special Issue*. Vol. 13: 5–14.

CHAMBERS, C. (1990) 'Self reliant'. *Times Higher Education Supplement*. 6 April: 26.

CHANDLER, A. (1962) *Strategy and Structure*. Cambridge, Mass., Massachusetts Institute of Technology Press.

CHESBROUGH, H.W. and TEECE, D.J. (1996) 'When is virtual virtuous? Organizing for innovation'. *Harvard Business Review*. January–February: 65–73.

CHILD, J. (1984) *Organization: a Guide to Problems and Practice*. 2nd ed. London, Harper and Row.

CLARE, J. (1994) 'Employers sceptical about GCSE alternative'. *The Daily Telegraph*. 1 November: 4.

CLARE, J. (1995) '"Blue Peter" teaching that betrays pupils'. *Daily Telegraph*. 7 September: 6.

CLARE, J. (1996) 'Dearing seeks to cut examination gap between schools and work'. *Daily Telegraph*. 28 March: 4.

CLARE, J. (1996a) 'NVQs branded waste of £100m by watchdog'. *Daily Telegraph*. 5 October: 5.

COCKERILL, T. (1994) 'The kind of competence for rapid change', in C. Mabey and P. Iles (eds), *Managing Learning*, London, Routledge in association with the Open University. pp. 70–76.

COLLOFF, S. and GOODGE, P. (1990) 'The open track to elite status'. *Personnel Management*. Vol. 22, 11: 50–53.

COMMISSION FOR RACIAL EQUALITY (CRE). (1983) *Equal Opportunity in Employment: A guide for employers*. London, Commission for Racial Equality.

COMMISSION OF THE EC. (1989) *Education, Training, Youth*. Brussels, Task Force for Human Resources, Education, Training and Youth.

CONSTABLE, J. *and* McCORMICK, R. (1987) *The Making of British Managers: A Report for the British Institute of Management and Confederation of British Industry into Management Training, Education and Development*. London, British Institute of Management.

COOPERS AND LYBRAND AND INVESTORS IN PEOPLE UK. (1996) *Making people Your Business: A joint report*. London, Coopers and Lybrand and Investors in People UK.

COOPERS AND LYBRAND ASSOCIATES. (1985) 'A challenge to complacency: changing attitudes to training'. *A Report to the Manpower Services Commission and the National Economic Development Office*. Sheffield, Manpower Services Commission.

COOPEY, J. (1995) 'The learning organization, power, politics and ideology'. *Management Learning*. Vol. 26, 2: 193–213.

COYNE, K.P. (1986) 'Sustainable competitive advantage – what it is and what it isn't'. *Business Horizons*. January–February: 54–61.

CRABB, S. (1990) 'On the right track to high performance'. *Personnel Management Plus*. August: 14–15.

CUMMINGS, T.G. *and* HUSE, E.F. (1989) *Organization Development and Change*. 4th ed. New York, West Publishing Co.

CURNOW, B. (1995) 'Two worlds that need each other's expertise'. *People Management*. Vol. 1, 14: 25.

DAILY TELEGRAPH. (1996) 'Training can cost jobs'. 21 September: 19.

DAILY TELEGRAPH. (1997) 'Blue Circle mixes new trade unionism with old danger'. Editorial, 7 January: 23.

DAVIES, H. (1995) 'Don't downsize the soul of the organisation too'. *People Management*. Vol. 1, 21: 29.

DAVIES, J. *and* DEIGHAN, Y. (1986) 'The managerial menopause'. *Personnel Management*. Vol. 18, 3: 28–33.

DAWKINS, W. (1994) 'Lifetime jobs may hurt company competitiveness'. *Financial Times*. 22 November: 5.

DE GEUS, A.P. (1996) 'Planning as learning', in K. Starkey (ed.), *How Organizations Learn*, London, International Thomson Business Press. pp. 92–9.

DEAL, T.E. *and* KENNEDY, A.A. (1982) *Corporate Cultures: The rites and rituals of organizational life*. Reading, Mass., Addison Wesley.

DEMING, W.E. (1988) *Out of the Crisis*. Cambridge, Cambridge University Press.

DEVANNA, M.A. (1984) 'The executive appraisal', in C. Fombrun, N. Tichy, N. and M.A. Devanna (eds), *Strategic Human Resource Management*. New York, Wiley. pp. 101–09.

DIXON, M. (1988) 'How best to find out what managers need'. *Financial Times*, 6 April.

DOHERTY, N. *and* HORSTED, J. (1995) 'Helping survivors to stay on board'. *People Management*. Vol. 1, 1: 26–31.

DOLAN, S. (1995) 'A different use of natural resources'. *People Management*. Vol. 1, 20: 36–40.

DORE, R. (1987) *Taking Japan Seriously: A Confucian perspective on leading economic issues*. London, The Athlone Press.

DOWNS, S. (1984) 'Trainability testing'. *Personnel Management*. Vol. 26, 10: 79.

DOYLE, M. *and* NORMAN, R. (1991) 'Ensuring contining commitment to management training and development by winning senior management support', in *Proceedings of the Institute of International Research in association with Sundridge Park Management Centre: Third Annual Forum on Developing Effective Business-led Management Training*, London, 28 February–1 March. London, Institute of International Research Ltd.

DRUCKER, P. (1988) 'The coming of the new organisation'. *Harvard Business Review*. January–February: 45–53.

DRUCKER, P. (1993) *Post Capitalist Society*. Boston, Butterworth-Heinemann.

DUFFY, H. (1995) 'Testing times for training'. *Financial Times*. 15 March: 19.

DULEWICZ, V. (1991) 'Improving assessment centres'. *Personnel Management*. Vol. 23, 6: 50–55.

EDWARDS, P. (1990) 'Uncertain worlds'. *Times Higher Education Supplement*. 6 April.

EMPLOYMENT DEPARTMENT GROUP. (1991) *A Strategy for Skills. Guidance from the Secretary of State for Employment on training, vocational education and enterprise*. Moorfoot, Sheffield, Employment Department. November.

EMPLOYMENT OCCUPATIONAL STANDARDS COUNCIL (EOSC). (1996) *A Briefing Note*. Rotherham, Cambertown Ltd.

ENNEW, E. *and* FORD, C. (1990) *The Management of change: Reflections of change at Norsk Hydro Polymers Ltd, Newton Aycliffe, County Durham, 1984–1990*. London, Advisory, Conciliation, and Arbitration Service Work Research Unit.

EQUAL OPPORTUNITIES COMMISSION. (1993) *The Publicly-Funded Vocational Training System in England and Wales*. Manchester, Equal Opportunities Commission.

EVANS, J. (1993) 'An unqualified success story'. *Personnel Management*. Vol. 23, 9: 22–3.

EVANS, J. (1993a) 'Taking account of experience'. *Personnel Management*. Vol. 23, 12: 56–7.

EVANS, P. (1992) 'Developing leaders and management development'. *European Management Journal*. Vol. 10, 1: 1–9.

FAIRBAIRN, J. (1991) 'Plugging the gap in training needs analysis'. *Personnel Management*. Vol. 23, 2: 43–5.

FERNIE, S. *and* METCALF, D. (1994) *What Has HRM Achieved in the Workplace?* London, Employment Policy Institute.

FINANCE SECTOR LEAD BODIES GROUP (1995) *Rediscovering Job Security: Evolving employer–employee relationships in the finance sector*. Create, 2 Holly Hill, Vauxhall Lane, Southborough, Tunbridge Wells, TN4 OXD.

FLANAGAN, J.C. (1954) 'The critical incident technique'. *Psychological Bulletin*.Vol. 51: 327–58.

FLOYD, S.W. *and* WOOLDRIDGE, B. (1994) 'Dinosaurs or dynamos? Recognizing middle management's strategic role'. *Academy of Management Executive*. Vol. 8, 4: 47–57.

FOMBRUN, C.J., DEVANNA, M.A. *and* TICHY, N.M. (1984) 'The human resource management audit', in C.J. Fombrun, N.M. Tichy and M.A. Devanna (eds), *Strategic Human Resource Management*. New York, Wiley.

FONDA, N. (1989) 'Management development: the missing link in sustained business performance'. *Personnel Management*. Vol. 21,12: 50–3.

FONDA, N. (1993) 'Competing through capability: making the links with business strategy', in *Speakers' Papers, Durham University Human Resource Development Unit Conference – Achieving A Leading Edge Through Developing People*, Ramside Hall Hotel, Durham, 24.9.1993. Durham University Business School Library, Mill Hill Lane, Durham DH1 3LB.

FONDA, N. *and* ROWLAND, H. (1995) 'Take me to your (personnel) leader'. *People Management*. Vol. 1, 25: 18–23.

FOWLER, A. (1992) 'How to: structure a personnel department'. *Personnel Management Plus*. January: 22–3.

FOWLER, A. (1995) 'How to: decide on training methods'. *People Management*. Vol. 1, 25: 36–7.

FOWLER, A. (1996) *Employee Induction: A good start*. 3rd ed. London, Institute of Personnel and Development.

FOWLER, A. (1997) 'How to: outsource personnel'. *People Management*. Vol. 3, 4: 40–43.

FOX, K. (1995) 'Learning lessons about motivation'. *People Management*. Vol. 1, 25: 32–5.

FOX, S., TANTON, M. *and* MCLEAY, S. (1992) 'Human resource management, corporate strategy and financial performance', *Executive Summary of Research Project Undertaken for HM Government's Economic and Social Research Council's 'Competitiveness and Regeneration of British Industry' Initiative*. Lancaster University and University of Wales.

FRASER, C. (1996) 'Performance appraisal: what is best practice?'. *Croner Human Resource Briefing: Management and strategy*. Issue No. 67, 10 April: 6–8.

FRENCH, J.R.P. *and* RAVEN, B.H. (1959) 'The bases of social power', in D. Cartwright (ed.), *Studies in Social Power*. Michigan, University of Michigan Press, Ann Arbor.

FRENCH, W.L. (1987) *The Personnel Management Process: Human resources administration and development*. 6th ed. Boston, Houghton Mifflin.

FRENCH, W.L. *and* BELL, C.H. (1978) *Organisation Development: Behavioural science interventions for organisation improvement*. 2nd ed. London, Prentice Hall International.

GAGNE, R.M. (1977) *The Conditions of Learning*. New York, Holt Saunders.

GAILLIE, D. *and* WHITE, M. (1993) *Employee Commitment and the Skills Revolution*. London, Policy Studies Institute Publishing.

GARMONSWAY, A. *and* WELLIN, M. (1995) 'Creating the right natural chemistry'. *People Management*. Vol. 1, 19: 36–9.

GARNETT, J. (1992) 'My biggest mistake'. *Independent on Sunday*. 8 March.

GARRATT, B. (1995) 'An old idea that has come of age'. *People Management*. Vol. 1, 19: 25–8.

GENILLARD, A. (1993) 'Students' salad days are over'. *Financial Times*. Germany 8. 25 October: VIII.

GENTLES, E.M. (1969) *Training the Operator*. London, Institute of Personnel Management.

GHOSHAL, S. *and* BARTLETT, C.A. (1994) 'Linking organizational context and managerial action: the dimension of quality of management'. *Strategic Management Journal*. Special Summer Issue. Vol. 15: 91–112.

GILLEY, J.W. *and* EGGLAND, S.A. (1989) *Principles of Human Resource Development*. Wokingham, Addison Wesley and University Associates Inc.

GOLDSTEIN, I.L. *and* GOLDSTEIN, H.W. (1990) 'Training as an approach for organisations to the challenges of human resource issues in the year 2000'. *Journal of Organizational Change Management*. Vol. 3, 2: 30–43.

GOODHART, D. (1994) 'Can Europe compete? Convergence in the workforce'. *Financial Times*. 28 February: 11.

GOODHART, D. (1994a) 'Fresh thinking needed on old labour problem'. *Financial Times*. 8 March: 14.

GOODHART, D. (1994b) 'US and Europe reach rare consensus'. *Financial Times*. 14 March: 4.

GOODHART, D. *and* WOOD, L. (1994) 'Staying on can mean missing out'. *Financial Times*. 20 July: 21.

GOUGH, J. (1996) *Developing Learning Materials*. London, Institute of Personnel and Development.

GRAHAM, G. (1994) 'Lack of training shuts out poor'. *Financial Times*, 14 March: 4.

GRANT, R.M. (1991) *Contemporary Strategy Analysis: Concepts, techniques, applications*. Oxford, Blackwell.

GRATTON, L. *and* SYRETT, M. (1990) 'Heirs apparent: succession strategies for the future'. *Personnel Management*. Vol. 22, 1: 34–8.

GREATREX, J. *and* PHILLIPS, P. (1989) 'Oiling the wheels of competence'. *Personnel Management*, Vol. 21, 8: 36–9.

GRIBBEN, R. (1996) 'A pressing need to learn from a chequered past'. *Daily Telegraph Special Report: Training and Enterprise Councils 1*. 3 July: 33.

GRIBBEN, R. (1997) 'Workers agree pay curbs to protect jobs'. *Daily Telegraph*. 7 January: 2.

GUEST, D. *and* DAVEY, K.M. (1996) 'Don't write off the traditional career'. *People Management*, Vol. 2, 4: 22–5.

GUEST, D. *and* HOQUE, K. (1994) 'The good, the bad and the ugly: employment relations in new non-union workplaces'. *Human Resource Management Journal*. Vol. 5, 1: 1–15.

GURDON, G. (1994) 'Toyota U-turn to end "jobs for life"'. *Daily Telegraph*. 22 January: B7.

HACKETT, P. (1997) *Introduction to Training*. London, Institute of Personnel and Development.

HALL, D. (1984) 'Human resource development and organizational effectiveness', in C.J. Fombrun, N.M. Tichy and A. Devanna (eds), *Strategic Human Resource Management*. New York, Wiley. pp. 159–81.

HALL, D.T. (1986) 'Dilemmas in linking succession planning to individual executive learning'. *Human Resource Management*. Vol. 25, 2: 235–65.

HALL, R. (1993) 'A framework linking intangible resources and capabilities to sustainable competitive advantage'. *Strategic Management Journal*. Vol. 14: 607–18.

HALL, R. (1996) 'Supply chain management – the challenges for the 21st century'. *Paper presented to the CIPS Conference at Durham University Business School*, 9 May. Durham University Business School, Mill Hill Lane, Durham City, DH1 3AY.

HAMBLIN, A.C. (1974) *Evaluation and Control of Training*. Maidenhead, McGraw-Hill.

HAMEL, G. and PRAHALAD, C.K. (1993) 'Strategy as stretch and leverage'. *Harvard Business Review*. Vol. 71, 2: 75–84.

HANDY, C. (1987) 'The making of managers'. *A Report for the National Economic Development Council, the Manpower Services Commission, and the British Institute of Management on Management Education, Training and Development in the USA, West Germany, France, Japan and the UK*. London, National Economic Development Office.

HANDY, C.B. (1985) *Understanding Organizations*. 3rd ed. Harmondsworth, Penguin.

HANDY, C.B. (1989) *The Age of Unreason*. London, Business Books.

HANSON, P. and VOSS, C. (1994) *Made in Europe: A four nations best practice study*. UK: IBM.

HARDINGHAM, A. (1996) *Designing Training*. London, Institute of Personnel and Development.

HARDINGHAM, A. (1996a) 'Improve an inside job with an outside edge'. *People Management*. Vol. 2, 12: 45–6.

HARRIS, V. (1995) 'Moving ahead on cultural change'. *People Management*. Vol. 1, 6: 30–33.

HARRISON, J. and LORD, P. (1992) 'Investors in People and the accreditation of training in SMEs', in *Proceedings of the 15th National Small Firms Policy and Research Conference*, Southampton, November. Northern Ireland Small Business Institute: United Kingdom Enterprise Management Research Association.

HARRISON, R. (1986) *Equality at Work*. Oxford, Pergamon Press. Super Series No. 506.

HARRISON, R. (1992) 'Employee development at Barratt', in D. Woodall and D. Winstanley (eds), *Case Studies in Personnel*. London, Institute of Personnel and Development. 103–15.

HARRISON, R. (1993) 'Developing people – for whose bottom line?', in R. Harrison (ed.), *Human Resource Management: Issues and strategies*. Wokingham, Addison Wesley. pp. 299–329.

HARRISON, R. (1993a) *Human resource management: Issues and strategies*. Wokingham, Addison Wesley.

HARRISON, R. (1993b) 'Strategic human resource management at HMH Sheetmetal Fabrications Ltd., 1993', in R. Harrison (ed.),

Human Resource Management: Issues and strategies. Wokingham, Addison Wesley. pp. 335–39.

HARRISON, ROY. (1995) 'Carrots are better levers than sticks'. *People Management*, Vol. 1, 21: 38–40.

HARRISON, R. (1996) 'Action learning: route or barrier to the learning organization?'. *Employee Counselling Today*. Vol. 8, 6: 27–38.

HARRISON, R. (1996a) 'Developing human resources for productivity', Module 13 in J. Prokopenko and K. North, *Productivity and Quality Management: A modular programme: Part II*. Geneva, International Labour Office and Tokyo, Asian Productivity Association. pp. 1–53.

HARRISON, R. *and* MILLER, S. (1993) 'Doctors in management: two into one won't go – or will it?'. *Journal of Executive Development*. Vol. 6, No. 2: 9–13.

HARRISON, R., MILLER, S. *and* GIBSON, A. (1993) 'Doctors in management, Part II: getting into action'. *Journal of Executive Development*,.Vol. 6, No. 4: 3–7.

HARRISON, ROGER (1972) 'How to describe your organization'. *Harvard Business Review*'. September–October.

HARRISON, ROY (1996) 'A role-over week for training as we know it'. *People Management*. Vol. 2, 11: 47–8.

HEALY, M. (1995) 'Innovators beware!'. *People Management*. Vol. 1, 6: 24–5.

HECKSCHER, C. (1995) *White Collar Blues: Management loyalties in an age of corporate restructuring*. New York, HarperCollins.

HEDLUND, G. (1994) 'A model of knowledge management and the N-Form corporation'. *Strategic Management Journal. Special Summer Issue*. Vol. 15: 73–90.

HENDRY, C. (1994) 'The Single European Market and the HRM response', in P.A. Kirkbride (ed.), *Human Resource Management in Europe: Perspectives for the 1990s*. London, Routledge. pp. 93–113.

HENDRY, C. (1995) *Human Resource Management: A strategic approach to employment*. London, Butterworth Heinemann.

HENDRY, C. *and* PETTIGREW, A. (1986) 'The practice of strategic human resource management'. *Personnel Review*. Vol. 15, 5: 3–8.

HENDRY, C., JONES, A., ARTHUR, M. *and* PETTIGREW, A. (1991) *Human Resource Development in Small to Medium Sized Enterprises: ED Research Paper No. 88*. Sheffield, Employment Department.

HERACLEOUS, L. (1995) 'Spinning a brand new cultural web'. *People Management*. Vol. 1, 22: 24–7.

HERRIOT, P. (1992) *The Career Management Challenge: Balancing individual and organizational needs*. London, Sage.

HERRIOT, P. *and* PEMBERTON, C. (1995) 'A new deal for middle managers'. *People Management*. Vol. 1, 12: 32–4.

HERZBERG, F. (1968) 'One more time: how do you motivate employees?'. *Harvard Business Review*. Vol. 46, January–February: 53–62.

HIRSH, W. (1985) *Women, Career Breaks and Re-Entry*. London, Institute of Manpower Studies.

HIRSH, W. *and* JACKSON, C. (1996) 'Ticket to ride or no place to go?'. *People Management*. Vol. 2, 13: 20–25.

HIRSH, W., JACKSON, C. *and* JACKSON, C. (1995) *Careers in*

Organisations – Issues for the Future. Report. London, Institute of Employment Studies.

HOFSTEDE, G. (1980, 1984) *Culture's Consequences: International differences in work-related values.* Vol. 5. London, Sage.

HOLBECHE, L. (1995) 'Peering into the future of careers'. *People Management.* Vol. 1, 11: 26–7.

HOLDEN, L. (1991) 'European trends in training and development'. *International Journal of Human Resource Management.* Vol. 2, 2: 113–31.

HOLLAND, G. (1995) 'A summer holiday action plan for Mrs Shephard'. *People Management.* Vol. 1, 15: 21.

HONEY, P. *and* MUMFORD, A. (1992) *A Manual of Learning Styles.* 3rd ed. Maidenhead, Honey.

HONEY, P. *and* MUMFORD, A. (1996) *Managing Your Learning Environment.* Maidenhead, Honey.

HUBER, G. (1991) 'Organizational learning: the contributing processes and literatures'. *Organization Science.* Vol. 2: 85–113.

ILES, P. *and* MABEY, C. (1993) 'Managerial career development programmes: effectiveness, availability and acceptability'. *British Journal of Management.* Vol. 4, 3: 103–11.

INCOMES DATA SERVICES. (1993) *Training and Development.* London, Institute of Personnel and Development.

INCOMES DATA SERVICES. (1997) *Recruitment, Training and Development.* London, Institute of Personnel and Development.

INDUSTRIAL RELATIONS SERVICES. (1994) *Using TECS and LECS for Personnel Issues: An IRS survey of employers' experience.* London, Industrial Relations Services.

INSTITUTE FOR EMPLOYMENT STUDIES. (1996) *Strategies for Career Development: Promise, practice and pretence IES Report, No 305.* London, Institute for Employment Studies.

INSTITUTE OF MANAGEMENT (IOM). (1995) *Coming on Board.* London, Institute of Management.

INSTITUTE OF MANPOWER STUDIES. (1984) *Competence and Competition: Training and education in the Federal Republic of Germany, the United States and Japan.* London, Manpower Services Commission/National Economic Development Office.

INSTITUTE OF PERSONNEL AND DEVELOPMENT (IPD). (1996) 'IPD Code of Professional Conduct and Professional Conduct Regulations, in Institute of Personnel and Development, *The IPD, IPM and ITD codes of practice.* London, Institute of Personnel and Development. pp. 5–10.

INSTITUTE OF PERSONNEL AND DEVELOPMENT (IPD). (1996a) *IPD Professional Standards.* London, Institute of Personnel and Development.

INSTITUTE OF PERSONNEL AND DEVELOPMENT (IPD). (1996b) 'The lean organisation: managing the people dimension'. Consultative document. London, Institute of Personnel and Development.

JACKSON, L. (1989) 'Transforming managerial performance – a competency approach', in *Proceedings of the Institute of Personnel Management National Conference,* Harrogate, October. London, Institute of Personal Management.

JACOBS, R. *and* FLOYD, M. (1995) 'A bumper crop of insights'. *People Management*. Vol. 1, 3: 23–5.

JENNINGS, P.L., RICHARDSON, B. *and* BEAVER, G. (1992) 'Improving the role of accreditation in the training and development of small business owner/managers' in *Proceedings of the 15th National Small Firms Policy and Research Conference*, Southampton, November. Northern Ireland Small Business Institute: United Kingdom Enterprise Management Research Association.

JENNINGS, R. (1991) 'Contributing to business strategy and operating performance by ensuring that ED is an essential investment not an expendable cost', in *Proceedings of the Institute of International Research in Association with Sundridge Park Management Centre: Third annual forum on developing effective business-led management training*. London, 28 February–1 March. London, Institute of International Research.

JOHNSON, R. (1984) 'Adult training in Europe'. *Personnel Management*. Vol. 16, 8: 24–7.

JOHNSON, R. (1984a) 'Youth training in Europe'. *Personnel Management*. Vol. 16, 7: 24–6.

JOHNSON, R. (1990) 'Wanted: your input on training'. *Personnel Management Plus*. June: 30.

JOHNSON, R. (1994) 'From flip charts to virtual reality'. *Personnel Management*. Vol. 26, 13: 31–3.

JONES, R.A. *and* GOSS, D. M. (1991) 'The role of training strategy in reducing skills shortages: some evidence from a survey of small firms'. *Personnel Review*, Vol. 20, 2: 24–30.

JURAN, J.M. (1988) *Managerial Breakthrough*. New York, McGraw-Hill.

KEARNS, P. *and* MILLER, T. (1996) *Measuring the Impact of Training and Development on the Bottom Line*. Technical Communications.

KEASEY, K. *and* WATSON, R. (1993*) Small Firm Management: Ownership, Finance and performance*. Oxford, Blackwell.

KEEP, E. (1986) 'Can Britain build a coherent vocational training system?'. *Personnel Management*. Vol. 18, 8: 28–31.

KEEP, E. (1989) 'Corporate training policies: the vital component', in J. Storey (ed.), *New Perspectives in Human Resource Management*. London, Routledge. pp. 109–25.

KEEP, E. (1989a). 'A training scandal?', in K. Sisson (ed.), *Personnel Management in Britain*. Oxford, Blackwell. pp. 177–202.

KEEP, E. *and* MAYHEW, K. (1994) Scoping Paper for the 'What Makes Training Pay' *Project*. London, Institute of Personnel and Development.

KELMAR, J. (1990) 'Measurement of success and failure in small business – a dichotomous anachronism' in *Proceedings of the 13th National Small Firms' Policy and Research Conference*, Harrogate, November. Northern Ireland Small Business Institute: United Kingdom Enterprise Management Research Association.

KESSELS, J. (1993) 'Towards design standards for curriculum consistency in corporate education' (dissertation, Twente University). Hulshorst, Netherlands, Foundation for Corporate Education.

KESSELS, J.W.M. (1996) 'Knowledge productivity and the corporate curriculum', in J.F. Schreinemakers (ed.), *Knowledge Management: Organization, competence and methodology: Proceedings of the Fourth international ISMICK Symposium.* 21–22 October, Rotterdam, the Netherlands. Würzburg, ERGON-Verlag. pp. 168–74.

KESSLER, I. (1990) 'Personnel management in local government: the new agenda'. *Personnel Management.* Vol. 22, 11: 40–44.

KIRBY, D.A. (1990) 'Management education and small business development: an explanatory study of small firms'. *UK Journal of Small Business Management.* Vol. 28, 4: 78–87.

KOIKE, K. (1988) *Industrial Relations in Modern Japan.* London, Macmillan.

KOLB, D.A., RUBIN, I.M. and McINTYRE, J.M. (1974) *Organizational Psychology: An experiential approach.* Englewood Cliffs, New Jersey, Prentice Hall.

KUIJPERS, R. (1995) 'Why time is running out for HR, unless....'. *People Management.* Vol. 1, 10: 19

LEAHY, M. (1996) 'Tempered steel'. *People Management.* Vol. 2, 22: 29–30.

LEE, R. (1996) 'The "pay-forward" view of training'. *People Management.* Vol. 2, 3: 30–32.

LEES, S. (1992) 'Ten faces of management development'. *Management Education and Development'.* Vol. 23, 2: 89–105.

LEGGE, K. (1995) *Human Resource Management: Rhetorics and realities.* London, Macmillan.

LEIGH, A. (1996) 'Why you should learn to rely on the experts'. *People Management.* Vol. 2, 20: 49.

LEIGH, A. and MAYNARD, M. (1996) *The Perfect Leader.* London, Arrow.

LEVINTHAL, D.A. and MARCH, J.G. (1993) 'The myopia of learning'. *Strategic Management Journal.* Vol. 14: 95–112.

LEWIS, J. and McLAVERTY, C. (1991) 'Facing up to the needs of the older manager'. *Personnel Management.* Vol. 23, 1: 32–5.

LIKERT, R. (1961) *New Patterns of Management.* New York, McGraw-Hill.

LINKLATER, J. and ATKINS, H. (1995) 'Discovering what makes others tick'. *People Management.* Vol. 1, 18: 35–6.

LIPPITT, G. (1983) 'Management development as the key to organisational renewal'. *Journal of Management Development.* Vol. 1, 2: 36–9.

LITTLEFIELD, D. (1995) 'Menu for change at Novotel'. *People Management.* Vol. 1, 2: 34–6.

LITTLEFIELD, D. (1995a) 'New campaign to raise profile of IIP standard'. *People Management.* Vol. 1, 19: 13.

LITTLEFIELD, D. (1995b) 'Trouble free training'. *People Management.* Vol. 1, 24: 10.

LITTLEFIELD, D. (1996) 'Halifax employees to assess management'. *People Management.* Vol. 2, 3: 5.

LITTLEFIELD, D. (1997) 'Demoralised HR staff quit delayered firms'. *People Management.* Vol. 3, 5: 8–9.

LITTLEFIELD, D. and WELCH, J. (1996) 'Training policy steals the political limelight'. *People Management.* Vol. 2, 7: 5.

LOCKETT, J. (1992) *Effective Performance Management: A strategic guide to getting the best from people*. London, Kogan Page.

LORENZ, A. (1996) 'British parts suppliers face productivity challenge'. *Sunday Times, Business Section*. 2.6: 10.

LORENZ, C. (1992) 'Different routes through the minefield of change'. *Financial Times*. 20 November: 14.

LORENZ, C. (1994) 'Dissent in the measurement ranks'. *Financial Times*. 25 March: 16.

LYMER, A. (1996) 'Educational impacts of the World Wide Web'. *Account*. Vol. 8, 1: 9–10.

MABEY, C. and SALAMAN, G. (1995) *Strategic Human Resource Management*. Oxford, Blackwell.

MACAULAY, S. and HARDING, N. (1996) 'Drawing up a new careers contract'. *People Management*. Vol. 2, 7: 34–5.

MACGREGOR, D. (1960) *The Human Side of Enterprise*. Maidenhead, McGraw-Hill.

MACHIN, J. (1981) 'Inter-manager communication: matching up to expectations?'. *Personnel Management*. January, Vol. 13, 1: 26–9.

MACKINNON, I. (1995) 'How to approach your TEC for financial help and more'. *People Management*. Vol. 1, 1: 51.

MANGHAM, I.L. and SILVER, M.S. (1986) *Management Training: Context and practice*. London, Economic and Social Research Council and Department of Trade and Industry.

MANWARING, T. and WOOD, S. (1985) 'The ghost in the labour process: job redesign' in D. Knight (ed.), *Critical Perspectives on the Labour Process*. Aldershot, Gower.

MARCHINGTON, M. and WILKINSON, A. (1996) *Core Personnel and Development*. London, Institute of Personnel and Development.

MARLOW, S. and PATTON, D. (1992) 'Employment relations, human resource management strategies and the smaller firm', in *Proceedings of the 15th National Small Firm's Policy and Research Conference*, Southampton, November. Northern Ireland Small Business Institute: United Kingdom Enterprise Management Research Association.

MARRIS, R. (1995) 'Worrying fortunes of the Anglo-Saxon underclass'. *Times*. 28 September: 29.

MARSICK, V.J. (1994) 'Trends in managerial reinvention: creating a learning map'. *Management Learning*. Vol. 25, 1: 11–33.

MARTIN, S. (1995) 'A futures market for competencies'. *People Management*. Vol. 1, 6: 20–24.

MAYO, A. (1994) *Managing Careers*. London, Institute of Personnel and Development.

MAYO, A. and LANK, E. (1995) 'Changing the soil spurs new growth'. *People Management*. Vol. 1, 23: 26–8.

MAYO, E. (1933) *The Human Problems of an Industrial Civilisation*. New York, Macmillan.

MCGRATH, R.G., MACMILLAN, I.C. and VENKATARAMAN, S. (1995) 'Defining and developing competence: a strategic process paradigm'. *Strategic Management Journal*. Vol. 16: 251–75.

MCMILLEN, M.C., BOYATZIS, R.E. and SWARTZ, L. (1994) 'Contextual integration of knowledge, experience and action learning for management education'. *Management Learning*. Vol. 25, 2: 215–29.

MEZIROW, J.A. (1985) 'A critical theory of self-directed learning', in S. Brookfield (ed), *Self-Directed Learning: From theory to practice*. San Francisco, Calif., Jossey Bass.

MILES, R. *and* SNOW, C. (1995) 'The new network firm: a spherical structure built on a human investment philosophy'. *Organizational Dynamics*. Vol. 23, 4: 5–18.

MILLER, D. (1993) 'The architecture of simplicity'. *Academy of Management Review*. Vol. 18: 116–38.

MILLER, R.B. (1962) 'Task description and analysis' in R.M. Gagne (ed.), *Psychological Principles of System Development*. Eastbourne, Holt, Rhinehart and Winston.

MILLS, D.Q. *and* FRIESEN, B. (1992) 'The learning organisation'. *European Management Journal*. Vol. 10, 2: 146–56.

MILLS, G.E., PACE, R. *and* PETERSON, B.D. (1988) *Analysis in Human Resource Training and Organization Development*. Wokingham, Addison Wesley.

MILROY, D. (1992) 'A cry from the heart of a professional with a true vocation'. *Guardian, Education section*. 17 November: 2, 3.

MINTZBERG, H. (1973) *The Nature of Managerial Work*. New York, Harper and Row.

MINTZBERG, H. (1983) *Structure in Fives: Designing effective organizations*. Englewood Cliffs, New Jersey, Prentice Hall.

MINTZBERG, H. (1994) 'The fall and rise of strategic planning'. *Harvard Business Review*. January–February: 107–14.

MINTZBERG, H. (1994a) 'Rounding out the manager's job'. *Sloan Management Review*. Vol. 36, 1: 11–26.

MOODY'S INVESTMENT SERVICE. (1994) *Lifetime Employment and its Credit Implications for Japanese Corporations*. Tokyo, Moody's Investment Service.

MOORBY, E. (1991) *How to Succeed in Employee Development: Moving from vision to results*. Maidenhead, McGraw-Hill.

MORGAN, G. (1986) *Images of Organization*. London, Sage.

MORRIS, J. (1991) 'Action Learning: the long haul', in J. Prior (ed.), *Handbook of Training and Development*. Aldershot, Gower. pp. 611–28.

MUMFORD, A. (1971) *The Manager and Training*. London, Times Management Library.

MUMFORD, A. (1997) *Management Development: Strategies for action*. 3rd ed. London, Institute of Personnel and Development.

MUMFORD, A., ROBINSON, G. *and* STRADLING, D. (1987) *Developing Directors: The learning processes*. Sheffield, Manpower Services Commission.

MUMFORD, J. *and* BULEY, T. (1988) 'Rewarding behavioural skills as part of performance'. *Personnel Management*. Vol. 20, 12: 33–7.

MURLIS, H. (1996) 'Can unity be preserved in the midst of diversity?'. *People Management*. Vol. 2, 4: 21.

MURPHY, B.P. *and* SWANSON, R.A. (1988) 'Auditing training and development'. *Journal of European Industrial Training*. Vol. 12, 2: 13–16.

NADLER, L. (1980) *Corporate Human Resources Development: A management tool.* New York, Van Nostrand Reinhold.

NAKAMOTO, M. (1995) 'Signs of ebbing strength at home'. *Financial Times.* 1 March: 21.

NATIONAL COMMISSION ON EDUCATION. (1993) *Learning to Succeed – A radical look at education today and a strategy for the future.* London, Heinemann.

NATIONAL ECONOMIC DEVELOPMENT OFFICE. (1987) *The Making of Managers: A report for NEDC, MSC and BIM on management education, training and development in the USA, West Germany, France, Japan and the UK.* London, National Economic Development Office.

NEVIS, E.C., DIBELLA, A.J. and GOULD, J.M. (1995) 'Understanding organizations as learning systems'. *Sloan Management Review.* Vol. 36, 2: 73–85.

NICHOLLS, A. (1997) 'Towards new horizons'. *Guardian Higher.* 21 January: ii.

NICHOLLS, A. (1997a) 'Thames Valley: A new line on learning'. *Guardian Higher.* 21 January: iii.

NOEL, L., JAMES, N. L. and DENNEHY, R. F. (1991) 'Making HRD a force in strategic organisational change'. *Industrial and Commercial Training.* Vol. 23, 2: 17–19.

NONAKA, I. (1991) 'The knowledge-creating company'. *Harvard Business Review.* November–December: 96–104.

NONAKA, I. (1994) 'A dynamic theory of organizational knowledge creation'. *Organization Science.* Vol. 5, 1: 14–37.

NONAKA, I. and TAKEUCHI, H. (1995) *The Knowledge-Creating Company.* Oxford, Oxford University Press.

O'HEAR, A. (1993) 'The new schools chef could start by slimming the menu'. *Daily Telegraph.* 3 March: 18.

OLDFIELD, C. (1996) 'Quarter of small firms say they want to sell up'. *Sunday Times, Business Section 2.* 15 December: 2.

OTTO, C.P. and GLASER, R.O. (1972) *The Management of Training.* London, Addison Wesley.

PARTRIDGE, B. (1989) 'The problem of supervision', in K. Sisson (ed.), *Personnel Management in Britain,* Oxford, Blackwell. pp. 203–21.

PAYNE, R. (1991) 'Taking stock of corporate culture'. *Personnel Management.* Vol. 23, 7: 26–9.

PEDLER, M. and BOUTALL, J. (1992) *Action Learning for Change: A resource book for managers and other professionals.* Eastwood Park, Avon, NHS Training Directorate.

PEDLER, M., BOYDELL, T. and BURGOYNE, J. (1988) *Learning Company Project: A report on work undertaken, October, 1987 to April, 1988.* Sheffield, Training Agency.

PEDLER, M., BURGOYNE, J. and BOYDELL, T. (1978). *Manager's Guide to Self-Development.* Maidenhead, McGraw-Hill.

PEDLER, M., BURGOYNE, J. and BOYDELL, T. (1991) *The Learning Company: A strategy for sustainable development.* Maidenhead, McGraw-Hill.

PENROSE, E.T. (1959) *The Theory of the Growth of the Firm.* Oxford, Blackwell.

PEOPLE MANAGEMENT. (1995) 'Investors scheme proves a success'. *People Management 'Training Policy' section.* Vol. 1, 16: 9.

PEOPLE MANAGEMENT. (1995a) 'News & analysis, employee development: more managers have degrees'. *People Management.* Vol. 1, 13: 9.

PEOPLE MANAGEMENT. (1995b) 'Pubs use NVQs to attract employees'. *People Management.* Vol. 1, 14: 9.

PEOPLE MANAGEMENT. (1996) 'IIP used to help change', *People Management 'Training' section.* Vol. 2, 7: 8.

PEOPLE MANAGEMENT. (1996a) 'Pressure on for local control over training'. *People Management.* Vol. 2, 3: 8.

PERSONNEL MANAGEMENT PLUS. (1994) 'TECs' role and accountability likely to be reviewed under Labour'. *PM Plus.* August: 9.

PERSONNEL MANAGEMENT. (1991) 'German apprenticeship scheme introduced for sixth-formers by Hoechst'. *Personnel Management.* Vol. 23, 5: 9.

PERSONNEL MANAGEMENT. (1992) 'London borough council abolishes top personnel post in reorganisation'. *Personnel Management.* Vol. 24, 3: 12.

PERSONNEL MANAGEMENT. (1992a) 'London Underground to decentralise personnel function in wake of job cuts'. *Personnel Management.* Vol. 24, 1: 5.

PERSONNEL MANAGEMENT. (1992b) 'Low financial rewards discourage young people from skills training'. *Personnel Management.* Vol. 22, 11: 14.

PERSONNEL MANAGEMENT. (1993) 'Need for national training framework'. *Personnel Management.* Vol. 25, 10: 23.

PERSONNEL MANAGEMENT. (1994) 'BHS opts for in-house alternative to NVQs'. *Personnel Management.* Vol. 26, 5: 17.

PETERAF, M.A. (1993) 'The cornerstones of competitive advantage: a resource-based view'. *Strategic Management Journal.* Vol. 14: 179–91.

PETERS, T.J. *and* WATERMAN, R.H. (1982) *In Search of Excellence.* New York, Harper and Row.

PETTIGREW, A. M., ARTHUR, M. B. *and* HENDRY, C. (1990) 'Training and human resource management in small to medium sized enterprises: a critical review of the literature and a model for future research'. *Research Paper No. 56.* Sheffield, Employment Department.

PETTIGREW, A.M., JONES, G.R. *and* REASON, P.W. (1982) *Training and Development Roles in their Organisational Setting.* Sheffield, Manpower Services Commission.

PETTIGREW, A.M., SWALLOW, P. *and* HENDRY, C. (1988) 'The forces that trigger training'. *Personnel Management.* Vol. 20, 12: 28–32.

PFEFFER, J. (1981) *Power in Organizations.* Marshfield, Mass., Pitman.

PHILLIPS, A. (1995) 'Learning how to take the initiative'. *People Management.* Vol. 1, 17: 32–5.

PICKARD, J. (1992) 'Shell UK pulls responsibility back to centre'. *Personnel Mananagement Plus.* April: 1.

PICKARD, J. (1995) 'Food for thought'. *People Management.* Vol. 1, 20: 30–31.

PICKARD, J. (1995a) 'Prepare to make a moral judgement'. *People Management*. Vol. 1, 9: 22–5.

PICKARD, J. (1996) 'Barrier ahead to a single currency'. *People Management*. Vol. 2, 6: 22–7.

PICKARD, J. (1996a) 'A fertile grounding'. *People Management*. Vol. 2, 21: 28–37.

PICKARD, J. (1997) 'A yearning for learning'. *People Management*. Vol. 3, 5: 34–5.

POLANYI, M. (1958) *Personal Knowledge*. Chicago, Ill. University of Chicago Press.

POLANYI, M. (1966) *The Tacit Dimension*. New York, Anchor Day Books.

POLICY STUDIES INSTITUTE. (1993) *Employment in Britain Survey*. London, Policy Studies Institute Publishing.

PORTER, M.E. (1980) *Competitive Strategy*. New York, Free Press.

PORTER, M.E. (1985) *Competitive Advantage*. New York, Free Press.

POTTINGER, J. (1989) 'Engineering change through pay'. *Personnel Management*. Vol. 21, 10: 73–4.

POULTENEY, J. (1997) 'Rapid reaction'. *People Management*. Vol. 3, 2: 38–40.

PRAHALAD, C.K. *and* BETTIS, R.A. (1986) 'The dominant logic: a new linkage between diversity and performance'. *Strategic Management Journal*. Vol. 7: 485–501.

PRAIS, S.J. (1985) 'What can we learn from the German system of education and vocational training?', in G.D.N. Worswick (ed.), *Education and Economic Performance*. London, Gower. pp. 40–51.

PRAIS, S.J. *and* NATIONAL INSTITUTE OF ECONOMIC AND SOCIAL RESEARCH TEAM. (1990) 'Productivity, education and training: Britain and other countries compared'. *National Institute Economic Review*. London, National Institute of Economic and Social Research.

PRAIS, S.J. *and* WAGNER, K. (1981) 'Some practical aspects of human capital investment: training standards in five occupations in Britain and Germany'. *International Institute of Economic and Social Research Review*. November: 46–65.

PRENTICE, G. (1996) 'Getting the basics right'. *People Management*. Vol. 2, 4: 24–5.

PRICE, D. (1996) 'How marketing can sell your personnel product'. *People Management*. Vol. 2, 12: 21.

PROCTOR, J.D. (1995) 'Getting teams off the ground'. *People Management*, Vol. 1, 9: 28–31.

RACKHAM, N., HONEY, P. *and* COLBERT, M. (1971) *Developing Interactive Skills*. Northampton, Wellens Publishing.

RAELIN, J.A. (1994) 'Whither management education? Professional education, action learning and beyond'. *Management Learning*. Vol. 25, 2: 305.

RAINBIRD, H. (1993) 'Vocational education and training', in M. Gold (ed.), *The Social Dimension: employment policy in the European community*. London, Macmillan. pp. 184–202.

RAINBIRD, H. (1994) 'The changing role of the training function: a test for the integration of human resource and business strategies'. *Human Resource Management*. Vol. 5, 1: 72–90.

READY, D.A., VICERE, A.A. and WHITE, A.F. (1994) 'Linking executive education to strategic imperatives'. *Management Learning.* Vol. 25, 4: 563–78.

REDAY-MULVEY, G. and TAYLOR, P. (1996) 'Why working lives must be extended'. *People Management.* Vol. 2, 10: 24–9.

REFAUSSE, J. (1996) 'Self-knowledge to lift career spirits'. *People Management.* Vol. 2, 10: 34–5.

REID, M.A. and BARRINGTON, H. (1997) *Training Interventions: Managing employee development.* 5th ed. London, Institute of Personnel and Development.

REVANS, R.W. (1971) *Developing Effective Managers.* London, Longman.

RILEY, K. and SLOMAN, M. (1991) 'Milestones for the personnel department'. *Personnel Management.* Vol. 23, 8: 34–7.

RITCHIE, J. (1993) 'Strategies for human resource management: challenges in smaller and entrepreneurial organisations', in R. Harrison (ed) *Human Resource Management: Issues and strategies.* Wokingham, Addison Wesley. pp. 111–35.

ROBINSON, D.G. and ROBINSON, J.C. (1989) *Training for Impact.* London, Jossey Bass.

RODGER, D. and MABEY, C. (1987) 'BT's leap forward from assessment centres'. *Personnel Management.* Vol. 19, 7: 32–5.

ROFFEY PARK MANAGEMENT INSTITUTE. (1997) *Career Development: The impact of flatter structures on careers.* London, Butterworth Heinemann.

ROOTS, P. (1982). 'Special provision for ethnic minorities'. *Personnel Management.* Vol. 14, 11: 24–7.

ROTHWELL, W. and KAZANAS, H.C. (1989) *Strategic Human Resource Development.* London, Prentice Hall.

RUMELT, R.P. (1991) 'How much does industry matter?'. *Strategic Management Journal.* Vol. 12, 3: 167–85.

RUSHBY, N. (1988) 'How many psychotherapists are needed to change a light bulb?'. *Personnel Management.* Vol. 22, 1: 57.

RUSSELL, C. and PARSONS, E. (1996) 'Putting theory to the test at the OU'. *People Management.* Vol. 2, 1: 30–32.

SADLER, P. (1989) 'Management development', in K. Sisson (ed.), *Personnel Management in Britain,* Oxford, Blackwell. pp. 222–43.

SADLER, P. and BARHAM, K. (1988) 'From Franks to the future: 25 years of management training prescriptions'. *Personnel Management.* Vol. 20: 48–51.

SCHEIN, E.H. (1978) *Career Dynamics: Matching individual and organizational needs.* Reading, Mass., Addison Wesley.

SCHENDEL, D. (1994) 'Introduction to "Competitive organizational behaviour: toward an organizationally-based theory of competitive advantage"'. *Strategic Management Journal, Winter Special Issue.* Vol. 15: 1–4.

SCOTT-CLARK, C. and RAYMENT, T. (1995) 'Scandal of our dummy degrees'. *Sunday Times.* 3 September: 12–13.

SEGALL, A. (1996) 'OECD praises example of British jobs market'. *Daily Telegraph.* 22 May: 28.

SENGE, P.M. (1990) *The Fifth Discipline: The art and practice of the learning organization.* New York, Doubleday.

SEYMOUR, W.D. (1966) *Skills Analysis Training*. London, Pitman.

SHONFIELD, D. (1995) *The Jobs Mythology: IDS Focus 74*. London, Incomes Data Services.

SIDDONS, S. (1997) *Delivering Training*. London, Institute of Personnel and Development.

SILVERMAN, D. (1970) *The Theory of Organizations*. London, Heinemann Educational Books.

SISSON, K. *and* STOREY, J. (1988) 'Developing effective managers: a review of the issues and an agenda for research'. *Personnel Review*, Vol. 17, 4: 3–8.

SKIDELSKY, R. (1994) Profile in *The Observer Magazine*, 27 March: 34–6.

SKINNER, D. *and* MABEY, C. (1995) 'How do organisations conceive, design and implement human resource strategies?'. Working Paper, April. Milton Keynes, Open University Business School, Centre for Human Resource and Change Management.

SLOMAN, M. (1994) 'Coming in from the cold: a new role for trainers'. *Personnel Management*. Vol. 26, 1: 24–7.

SMITH, A.D. (1995) 'Europe has a multitude of systems and certificates'. *Guardian*. 30 May.

SMITH, D. (1996) 'Auf wiedersehen, single currency'. *Sunday Times News Review*. 14 January: 3,4.

SMITH, D. (1996a) 'The training that just isn't working'. *Sunday Times*. 28 April: 8.

SMITH, D. (1997) *Job Insecurity vs Labour Market Flexibility*. London, Social Market Foundation.

SMITH, D. (1997a) 'Lost in the myths of insecurity'. *Sunday Times, News Review*. 9 February: 5, 9.

SOFER, C. (1970) *Men in Mid-Career: a Study of British managers and technical specialists*. Cambridge, Cambridge University Press.

SPARROW, P. (1996) 'Too good to be true'. *People Management*. Vol. 2, 24: 22–7.

SPARROW, P. *and* HILTROP, J.-M. (1994) *European Human Resource Management in Transition*. Hemel Hempstead, Prentice Hall.

SPARROW, P. *and* PETTIGREW, A. (1988) 'How Halfords put its HRM into top gear'. *Personnel Management*. Vol. 20, 6: 30–34.

SPARROW, P.R. *and* BOGNANNO, M. (1994) 'Competency requirement forecasting: issues for international selection and assessment', in C. Mabey and P. Iles (eds), *Managing Learning*, London, Routledge in association with the Open University. pp. 57–69.

ST AUGUSTINE. (1964) *Confessions*. Transl. by R. S. Pine-Coffin. London, Penguin.

STALK, G., EVANS, P. *and* SHULMAN, L.E. (1992) 'Competing on capabilities: the new rules of corporate strategy'. *Harvard Business Review*. March–April: 57–69.

STAMMERS, R. *and* PATRICK, J. (1977) *The Psychology of Training*. London, Methuen.

STEEDMAN, H. (1987) 'Vocational Training in France and Britain: Office Work', *Discussion Paper No. 14, National Institute of Economic and Social Research*. London, National Institute of Economic and Social Research.

STEEDMAN, H. (1990) 'Speaking practically, the French have it'. *Independent*. 5 September.

STEVENS, C. (1985) 'Assessment centres: the British experience'. *Personnel Management*. Vol. 17, 7: 28–31.

STEWART, B. (1996) 'Firms do better when EVA keeps the score. *Sunday Times, Business Focus*. 8 December: 2.5.

STEWART, J. and MCGOLDRICK, J. (eds) (1996) *Human Resource Development: Perspectives, strategies and practice*. London, Pitman, pp. 120–37.

STOREY, D.J. and JOHNSON, S. (1987) *Job Generation and Labour Market Change*. London, Macmillan.

STOREY, D.J., WATSON, R. and WYNARCZYK, P. (1990) 'Fast growth small businesses: case studies of 40 small firms in north-east England'. *Research Paper No. 67*. Sheffield, Department of Employment.

STOREY, J. (1991) 'Do the Japanese make better managers?'. *Personnel Management*. Vol. 23, 8: 24–8.

STOREY, J. (1992) *Developments in the Management of Human Resources*. Oxford, Blackwell.

STOREY, J. (1994) 'How new-style management is taking hold'. *Personnel Management*. Vol. 26, 1: 32–5.

STOREY, J. (ed) (1994a) *New Wave Manufacturing Strategies: Organizational and human resource management dimensions*. London, Paul Chapman.

STOREY, J. and SISSON, K. (1990) 'Limits to transformation: human resource management in the British context'. *Industrial Relations Journal*. Vol. 21, 1: 60–65.

STREDL, H.J. and ROTHWELL, W.J. (1987) *The ASTD Reference Guide to Professional Training Roles and Competencies*. Amsherst, Mass., HRD Press Inc.

SWIERINGA, J. and WIERDSMA, A. (1992) *Becoming a Learning Organisation: Beyond the learning curve*. Wokingham, Addison Wesley.

SYRETT, M. (1988) 'Taking licence with the future of management'. *Sunday Times*. 10 April.

TATE, R. (1995) 'Food for thought'. *People Management*. Vol. 1, 20: 30.

TAYLOR, F.W. (1947) *Scientific Management*. New York, Harper and Row.

TAYLOR, H. (1991) 'The systematic training model: corn circles in search of a spaceship?'. *Management Education and Development*. Vol. 22, part 4: 258–78.

TAYLOR, R. (1994) 'Reconciling commitment and flexibility'. *Financial Times*. 1 June: 15.

TAYLOR, R. (1994a) 'TUC tackles a "slippery" idea'. *Financial Times*. 31 August:11.

TEECE, D.J., PISANO, G. and SHUEN, A. (1994) 'Dynamic capabilities and strategic management'. *Working Paper*. Cambridge, Mass., Harvard Business School.

TERAZONO, E. (1994) 'Education system criticised'. *Financial Times*. 6 December: XVIII.

THATCHER, M. (1995) 'TECS highlight "crisis" in jobless training scheme'. *People Management*. Vol. 1, 20: 12.

THATCHER, M. (1996) 'The big challenge facing small firms'. *People Management*, Vol. 2, 15: 20–25.

THE DAILY TELEGRAPH. (1996) 'Way off the mark'. *Daily Telegraph Editorial*. 28 March: 15.

THOMAS, M. and ELBEIK, S. (1996) *Supercharge Your Management Role*. London, Butterworth-Heinemann.

TORRINGTON, D. and WEIGHTMAN, J. (1985) *The Business of Management*. London, Prentice Hall.

TORRINGTON, D., HALL, L., HAYLOR, I. and MYERS, J. (1991) *Employee Resourcing*. London, Institute of Personnel and Development.

TOSEY, P. (1993) 'Interfering with the interference: a systemic approach to change in organisations'. *Management Education and Development*. Vol. 24, Part 3.

TOWNLEY, B. (1989) 'Selection and appraisal: reconstituting "social relations"?', in J. Storey (ed.), *New Perspectives on Human Resource Management*. London, Routledge. pp. 92–108.

TRIST, E. and BAMFORTH, K. (1951) 'Some social and psychological consequences of the longwall method of coal-getting'. *Human Relations*, Vol. 4: 3–38.

ULRICH, D. (1987) 'Organizational capability as a competitive advantage: human resource professionals as strategic partners'. *Human Resource Planning*. Part 4: 169–84.

UNEMPLOYMENT UNIT AND YOUTHAID. (1996) *Working Brief No. 52*. 409 Brixton Road, London, SW9 7DG.

VAN DER KLINK, M. and MULDER, M. (1995) 'Human resource development and staff flow policy in Europe', in A-W. Harzing and J. van Ruysseveldt (eds), *International Human Resource Management*. London, Sage. pp. 157–78.

VICTOR, P. (1995) 'Companies cannot pass the buck on training'. *People Management*, Vol. 1, 18: 23.

VON KROGH, G., ROOS, J. and SLOCUM, K. (1994) 'An essay on corporate epistemology'. *Strategic Management Journal*. Summer Special Issue. Vol. 15: 53–71.

WALTON, J. (1996) 'The provision of learning support for non-employees', in J. Stewart and J. McGoldrick (eds), *Human Resources Development: Perspectives, strategies and practice*. London, Pitman. pp. 120–37.

WARD, P. (1995) 'A 360-degree turn for the better'. *People Management*. Vol. 1, 3: 20–22.

WARR, P., BIRD, M. and RACKHAM, N. (1970) *Evaluation of Management Training*. Aldershot, Gower.

WARR, P.B. and BIRD, M.W. (1968) 'Identifying supervisory training needs'. *Training Information Paper No. 2*. London, HMSO.

WEBSTER, B. (1990) 'Beyond the mechanics of HRD'. *Personnel Management*. Vol. 22, 3: 44–7.

WEIGHTMAN, J. (1994) *Competencies in Action*. London, Institute of Personnel and Development.

WELCH, J. (1996) 'TECS grasp chance to be strategic masters'. *People Management*. Vol. 2, 15: 13.

WELCH, J. (1997) 'Bank trainers take on "troubleshooter" role'. *People Management*. Vol. 3, 2: 7.

WELCH, J. (1997a) 'Charities face battle to recruit volunteers'. People Management. Vol. 3, 5: 12.

WERNERFELT, B. (1984) 'A resource-based view of the firm'. *Strategic Management Journal*. Vol. 10: 17–32.

WHITE PAPER. (1972) *Training for the Future*. London, HMSO.

WHITE, M. (1996) 'Flexible response'. *People Management*. Vol. 2, 6: 33.

WHITE, M. *and* TREVOR, M. (1983) *Under Japanese Management*. London, Heinemann.

WHITFIELD, M. (1995) 'High-flyer hazards'. *People Management*. Vol. 1, 24: 9.

WICKENS, P. (1987) *The Road to Nissan*. London, Macmillan.

WILLE, E. (1990) 'Should management development be just for managers?'. *Personnel Management*. Vol. 22, 8: 34–7.

WILLIAMS, R. (1984) 'What's new in career development'. *Personnel Management*. Vol. 16, 3: 32–3.

WILLMAN, J. (1994) 'With a greyer picture of the future in mind'. *Financial Times*. 8 March: 14.

WILLS, S. (1993) 'MCI and the competency movement: the case so far'. *Journal of European Industrial Training*. Vol. 17, 1: 9–11.

WOLF, M. (1994) 'Can Europe Compete? A relapse into Euroscelerosis'. *Financial Times*. 24 February: 21.

WOOD, A. (1994) *North South Trade and Income Inequality*. Brighton, Institute for Development Studies.

WOOD, L. (1992) 'Change starts at the top'. *Financial Times*. 25 August: 8.

WOOD, L. (1993) 'CBI urges wide reform of TECs'. *Financial Times*. 10 November

WOOD, L. (1993a) 'TEC chiefs call for wider action'. *Financial Times*. 10 May: 9.

WOOD, L. (1994) 'Scepticism over "apprenticeship" ', *Financial Times*. 13 July: 10.

WOOD, L. (1994a) 'TEC directors face a period of re-training'. *Financial Times*. 12 April: 10.

WOOD, L. (1994b) 'TECs "more keen" to merge with chambers'. *Financial Times*. 13 July: 10.

WOOD, L. (1995) 'Training funds reform attacked'. *Financial Times (News: UK)*. 29 March: 9.

WOODRUFFE, C. (1991) 'Competent by any other name'. *Personnel Management*. Vol. 23, 9: 30–33.

WOODRUFFE, C. (1994) *Assessment Centres: Identifying and developing competence*. London, Institute of Personnel and Development.

WOODRUFFE, C. (1997) 'Going back a generation'. *People Management*. Vol. 3, 4: 32–4.

WOODRUFFE, C. *and* WYLIE, R. (1994) 'Going the whole hog: the design of development centres at NatWest'. *Competency*. Vol. 2, 1.

WORTS, C. (1996) 'Building a society with special skills'. *People Management*. Vol. 2, 2: 36–9.

WRIGHT, P.L. *and* TAYLOR, D.S. (1994) *Improving Leadership*

Performance: Interpersonal skills for effective leadership. 2nd ed. London, Prentice Hall.

YATES, I.R. (1990) 'Gaining competitive advantage through human resources leadership', in *Proceedings Conference Board European Human Resources Conference, London, 28–29 November.* London, Conference Board.

INDEX

added value 19, 21, 45, 116, 176, 187

advancement of an organisation *see* Organisational advancement

appraisal of performance *see* Performance, appraisal of

assessment centres for career development 346–50

audit *see* Human resource development (HRD), audit

Belgium, comparisons with 106, 113, 114, 117

benchmarking 204, 208, 395

British Institute of Management, the 74, 361

Business Bridge scheme 63

business goals *see* Organisational goals

Business Link network, the 48, 62, 77

business needs xii, xiv, 18, 37, 40, 41, 63, 156, 206, 323, 417
  and anticipated HRD outcomes 44, 206
  and ER planning/learning strategies 41, 63, 158, 292, 417

business plan(ning) *see* Business strategy

business strategy xi, xiv, xvi, 4, 5, 6, 18, 21, 24–5, 26, 28, 31, 38, 130, 156, 158, 168, 202, 223, 224, 316, 369, 372, 375, 415–16
  failure to link with HRD 25
  five steps for employee development within 23
  in smaller organisations 50
  linked with HRD 28–32, 44, 130, 202, 312, 316
  see also HRD strategy

capabilities of a business/organisation *see* Core capabilities

career development 330–42, 344
  assessment of 346–51
  concept of mutuality in 330–31, 349

career management/planning system(s) xiii, 9, 14, 180, 330, 339–51
  levels of integration within 340–42
  monitoring/evaluation of 338–9, 341

case-studies
  Allied Domecq: career development insights 348–9
  Barclays Bank: changing training roles 148
  Beeton Rumford: workforce flexibility 323
  Blue Circle Social Partnership deal 106–7
  BP: career development 336–7
  BP: competency-based management development 263–4, 265–6
  British Airways: HR audit process 218–19
  British Rail: management development 365–8
  British Rail: performance management 232–3
  clinical directors' management development programme 290–93, 308–9
  Company X: HRD and line management 173–4
  Company X: managers as trainers/developers 181–2
  CoSteel 16
  'County NatWest' bank: strategic milestones 205–6
  Cummins Engine Ltd: HR goals and strategy 35–6
  Cummins Engine Ltd: standards and indicators 207–8

English Nature:
benchmarking/best practice
205
'Ensdale County Council' 22–3
Hoechst UK 121
Hydro Polymers: dual system of
education and training
388–90, 391–4, 396–400
'Jones' small manufacturing firm
57–8
Kwik-Fit (1990) 161–2
London Underground:
decentralisation of HR function
171
Lucas 15
Manchester Airport: competency-
based management
development 264–6
'Mintech Ltd': cost-benefit
analysis 212–13
'Mintech Ltd': training course
costs 193–5
'Mintech Ltd': training recovery
costs 191–3
Newlands School appraisal 241–3
'Notown College' 95–7
NVQs in a pub chain 84
quality retail business 43–4
retail store appraisal project
278–82, 284–6
Rover: learning networks 325
SCO: career development 332–3
'Sentex Engineering Company
Ltd' 110–11
SmithKline Beecham: basic
training 238
Springboard (BBC): women's
career development 321–2
'Stratcap Ltd': strategic capability
373–4
Thames Valley University
approach to learning
technology 297–8
United Biscuits: management
development reorganisation
369–71
Vitex Ltd 183–4
'Wesdale Acute Hospitals NHS
Trust' 29
'X University' and management
course review 271–3
Yardley Cosmetics: developing
teamwork 315–16
commitment of employees 2–4, 9,
11, 12–13, 14, 28
commitment of management 5, 21,
162

competency-based (framework for)
performance analysis 233, 245,
260–62, 263–6, 348
competency development xi, 6, 9, 31,
261
competitive advantage 5–6, 14–15,
27, 31, 380, 390
competitive capability 4–6, 9, 27,
339, 386–400
national 14, 70
Confederation of British Industry
(CBI), the 61, 74, 76, 79, 95,
361
consistency
external 14, 294, 301, 309
internal 21, 28, 31, 36, 155, 223,
241, 294
in HRD see human resource
development (HRD)
continuous (learning and)
development 9, 115, 159–60,
179–80, 235, 247–50, 252,
314, 390
core capabilities xiii, xv, 4–5, 7,
386–402, 411
gap within 26–7
organisational 390–94, 411
resource-based 388–90, 394, 411
strategic 394–400, 411
corporate learning see Organisational
learning
cost-benefit analysis/ratio 212, 214
culture(s) of/in an organisation see
Organisational culture

decentralisation xi, 171–3, 234, 314,
324, 355
decision-making xii, 49, 134, 159,
172, 188, 202, 211, 250, 324,
390, 395
delayering xi, 5, 8, 10, 11, 27, 28,
171, 176, 234, 248, 313, 314,
345
development centres 347–50
discrimination 244, 317–22
disengagement of personnel 14,
159–60, 339
downsizing xi, 5, 7, 8, 10, 11, 28,
176, 248, 313, 314, 345

Economic Value Added (EVA) see
Added value
educational policy of the European
Commission 111–12 see also
VET, policy in Europe
employability security 7, 10–13, 207,
330, 335

employee development *see* Human
  resource development (HRD)
employee resourcing policy/strategy/
  system xi, xiv, 4, 10, 15, 21,
  41, 159–61, 169, 172, 177,
  206–7, 214, 232
  in smaller organisations 51
  integrated with HRD 206–8, 214,
  318
empowerment xi, 9, 79, 164, 209,
  396
equality in the workplace 317–22
  role of HRD in achieving 318–22
ethics in the HR function 155, 156,
  164
Europe, comparisons of Britain with
  10, 11, 14, 103–22, 125, 341,
  342, 345, 358

flexibility 10, 11, 106
  of the labour market 10, 105–7
  of the organisation i, xi, 396
  of the workforce 27, 28, 209,
  322–4, 332
  within the organisation xi, 10,
  27
  see also Retirement, flexible
France, comparisons with 91, 106,
  113, 114, 115, 116, 117, 125,
  358, 359

Germany, comparisons with 25–6,
  69, 76, 91, 95, 104, 108, 112,
  113, 114, 115, 116, 117,
  118–22, 123, 125, 359, 360
  company training 120–21, 360
  education system 119–20, 358
goals of an organisation *see*
  Organisational goals
Greece, comparisons with 104, 113,
  114

harmony between personal and
  organisational development
  2–4, 7–8, 27
human resource development (HRD)
  anticipated outcomes 44, 201,
  214
  audit 215–19, 429–31
  auditing outcomes 218–19
  business-led xiv, 18, 33, 37–9, 40,
  45, 156, 201
  business unit planning 41–4, 172
  concepts/theories of 2–7, 300
  consistency in xiii–xiv, 23, 28,
  39–41, 204, 209–15, 220,
  278–82, 294

costs, direct and indirect 42, 212
  evaluation/assessment of 44–5,
  212, 220
  extended across organisational
  boundaries 324–6
  failure to link with business
  strategy 25, 26
  goals/objectives, development of
  33–46, 130, 208
  history of xii, xvi, 1–8
  identification of needs 130
  improving the status/contribution
  of 161–4
  in an international context
  102–26
  in relation to policy-making xi,
  19, 24–5
  in relation to special groups and
  contingencies 75, 312–27,
  341–2
  integrated with the ER system
  206–8
  linked with business strategy
  28–32, 44, 130, 202, 312,
  316
  management of 166–86
  marketing within the organisation
  198–200
  measurement/establishment of
  outcomes 31, 202–6, 208,
  209–14, 220
  organisational context of 24–5,
  400–402
  plans per area/sector 41–2
  politics of, the 129–44, 158
  problem-centred approach to
  39–40, 415–16, 418–20
  process xiii, 4, 10, 13, 45, 211
  role in organisations 1, 7, 9,
  10–14, 21–3, 34, 158, 178,
  208
  setting and maintaining standards
  in 201, 202–6
  strategic framework for 18–32
  strategy/strategic management of
  xii–xvi, 5, 7, 18–19, 22, 24–32,
  33–46, 130, 158, 159, 168,
  201, 202, 206, 209–11, 220,
  322
  see also Personal development; and
  all entries beginning with the
  words Learning or Training
human resource development
  function, decentralised 171–3
  line-managed 173–5
  organisation of 170–77
  outsourced 172, 175–7, 198

specialist staff, management of
177–80
human resource development
manager 166–70, 199
of the line 181–2
role of 166–86
human resource management (HRM)
xi, xvi, 4, 19, 24–5, 34–5,
48–9, 52–3, 63, 147, 202, 206,
217, 323
different perceptions of 4, 15,
210, 248
different values in 211–12
in smaller organisations 50–51,
54
major issues within 52–3
methods to improve performance
206–8
strategic approach to 4, 5, 24–5,
38, 209
human resource planning xi–xii, 4,
40, 159, 163
human resource professionals xiii,
xiv, xvi, 21–3, 44, 155, 161,
162, 198, 201, 247, 248
credibility of 26, 198

induction 235–7
Industry Training Organisations
(ITOs) 72, 158
Institute of Personnel and
Development (IPD) xii, xiv,
10, 16, 74, 153–7, 247, 361,
426–8
Code of Professional Conduct
155, 426–8
Continuous Professional
Development pack 180, 247
Professional Standards in
Employee Development xii,
xiv, 18, 110, 145, 153–7, 178
internal consultant on training
provision 147–9, 151,
198–200
Investors in People (IIP) 51, 61,
63, 72, 73, 76, 78, 79, 84, 99,
158
Ireland (Republic of), comparisons
with 113, 114

Japan, comparisons with 9, 91, 106,
116, 117, 122–4, 359, 360,
402
company training 123–4, 360
education system 123, 358
job analysis 178, 262–3, 266
job description(s) 258–9, 261

job training analysis 253–66, 310
different approaches to 256,
257–62
key task approach 259
personnel involved 255–6
problem-centred/comprehensive
approaches 39–40, 257–60,
415–20
six-step strategy towards 254–7
techniques 262–6
see also Competency-based
performance analysis
job training specification 257, 259

knowledge connectivity 374–5, 390
knowledge development/productivity
xv, 169, 329–30, 391–2,
406–12
and organisational learning
406–10
management (principles) of
409–12
process, definitions of the 406–7,
409–10

law and legal considerations 11–12,
197, 318–20
Lead Body Standards for Training
and Development 39, 424–5
leadership in relation to HRD 159,
182–5, 315, 394
learners, profile of 274–82, 284, 296,
312, 313, 317
selection of 288–9
trainability of 288–9
learning approaches/methodologies/
process xii, 8–9, 62, 225–31,
248
action learning 404, 405
choice of 294–8
computerised 283
experiential cycle/approach, the
225–6, 228, 358
reinforcement 228, 299, 300
review/appraisal of 228
single- and double-loop 230–31,
324–5, 385
stimulus-response theory 227–8
types of learning 229–31, 237,
249, 275, 298, 385–6, 404
learning curve(s) 299–300
learning difficulties 239–40
learning event(s)/activities/
opportunities 159, 252–4,
270, 286, 290–93, 302, 312,
313, 417, 419
consistency in/between 294, 309

definition of xii, 228
design and delivery of xiii, xiv, 7,
    199, 215, 249, 252–68,
    270–86, 290–94, 298–301,
    312, 316
direction and management of
    283–6, 312, 417
eight-stage approach to 252–4,
    270, 288, 312
for special groups and
    contingencies 312–27
monitoring/evaluation of 277,
    284, 302–10, 312, 316–17
purpose/objectives of 271–4,
    279–82, 284, 289, 296, 312,
    417
learning needs 252–68, 326
identification of 37–40, 146, 224,
    243–4, 253–4, 289–93, 312,
    313–14, 317
of special groups and
    contingencies 313–14,
    320–23, 326, 327
problem-centred/comprehensive
    approaches 39–40, 290,
    415–20
see also Job training analysis
learning organisation, the 2, 6–8, 9,
    32, 37, 64, 176, 179, 228, 326,
    336, 402–6
learning strategies/styles 40, 41, 228,
    229–31, 237, 249, 273–4,
    275–7, 282–6, 289, 293, 300
choice of 282–3, 289, 293, 312,
    314
Local Enterprise Councils (LECs)
    73, 86, 125, 361
see also Training Education
    Councils (TECs)

Management Charter Initiative
    (MCI), the 60, 360, 361–2,
    363
management (training and long-term)
    development (MD) 6, 44,
    354–80
competency-based frameworks for
    361–8
definitions and themes of 355–8,
    372
in strategic planning 6, 364–8,
    372–80
programmes for 377–80
qualifications 361
succession planning 368–71, 395
systematic approach to 357
mentoring 14, 62, 63, 179, 236, 239,

321, 344 see also Business
    Bridge scheme
mission see Organisational mission
Modern Apprenticeship scheme 73,
    76–7, 115, 116, 117
motivation of employees 2–3, 9, 25,
    163, 276–9, 332, 416

National Advisory Council on
    Education and Training
    Targets (NACETT) 72, 79,
    81
national education policy 87–101,
    421
goals, achievement of 98–101
history 1985 to 1996 88–90
national occupational training and
    development standards see
    Training and development,
    national occupational
    standards national training
    policy 67–86
aims, the seven 68
framework for implementation of
    72–80
incentives for investment in
    69–70, 71
strategy 71–2
National Vocational Education and
    Training (NVET) 67, 70, 72,
    73, 74, 78, 80, 87, 93, 98–101,
    102–3, 105, 107, 112–13,
    124–6, 129, 421 see also
    Vocational Education and
    Training (VET)
national vocational standards 72,
    80–85
Netherlands, comparisons with the
    106, 108, 113, 114, 117
networking, internal and external 13,
    135, 379, 411
NVQs see Vocational qualifications

organisational advancement/
    development/growth xv, 6, 7,
    14, 25, 37, 40, 59, 74, 383–6
organisational culture(s) 8, 24,
    132–8, 143, 158, 167, 168–9,
    170, 202, 283, 375, 390, 410
change in 27, 28, 214, 332
human investment culture 135–6
person culture 136–7, 168
power culture 134, 168
role culture 143–5, 168
organisational development strategy
    xii, xiv, 1, 252, 386
see also Business strategy

organisational environment 157–8,
168, 184, 395
organisational goals xi, xiii, xiv, xv,
4, 7, 14, 15, 16, 18, 19, 27,
31, 158, 159, 168, 202, 220,
223, 224, 273, 316, 354, 385,
394
conflict between 50
in smaller organisations 50
organisational learning xi, xv, xvi,
6–7, 32, 146, 167, 169,
329–30, 375–6, 379, 387, 397,
402, 403, 405, 406–10
ability/capacity 375, 387
and HRD 147, 167, 387
and knowledge development
406–10
barrier(s) to 8
strategy xii, 6, 40
organisational mission 19, 24–5
statement 27, 33
organisational needs see Business
needs
organisational restructuring 10, 27,
341
organisational strategy see Business
strategy
organisational structure(s) 132–8,
143, 158, 159, 167, 168–9,
170, 336, 385
galaxy structure 136–7
network structure 135–6, 168
pyramid structure 143–5
web structure 134
organisational survival xv, 6, 8, 49,
383–6
organisational values 33–4, 44, 130,
202, 358
organisational vision xiv, xv, xvi, 7–8,
19, 25, 31, 33–4, 223, 376,
385, 411
in relation to HRD 44, 130, 144,
201
organisation as a system, the 160
Organisation for Economic Co-
operation and Development
(OECD) 11, 14, 345

part-time working 10, 11, 12, 105,
322–6
people development see Personal
development
performance 25, 231–2
appraisal/analysis of 27, 163, 179,
224, 234, 235, 239–46, 266,
307, 416, 432–4
'E' factors 232

establishing levels of 235–9,
260–61, 307
financial 20
influences on 240
measures/measurement of 20–21,
63, 208, 212, 253, 307, 313,
395
results 231
rewards for 231–2, 235
targets 239, 416
see also HRD, measurement/
establishment of outcomes
performance management 223–5,
232–5
and longer-term HRD 224–5,
364
cycle of seven stages 224, 313
framework for action 235–50
framework for understanding
225–35
reward-driven approach to 234,
235
tensions in 232–5
performance management system
(PMS) xii, 224, 232–5, 323–4
personal development 14, 15, 16, 37,
207
five steps within strategic
framework for 23
in smaller organisations 48–50,
53–63
strategic framework for 18–32
see also Human resource
development (HRD)
power in an organisation 138–44,
404
types/definitions of 138–40
psychological contract, the 331, 332,
339, 345

qualifications, as reward for
commitment 9
see also Vocational qualifications
Qualifications and National
Curriculum Authority, the 98,
115
quality circles 4, 213
quality improvement 59

resources for training see Training and
development resources
retention of personnel xiv, 345–6
retirement, flexible 10, 345–6
retraining 14, 179–80
role analysis see Job analysis
roles, training and development
typology 145–9

school educational system in Britain 88–90, 117, 358
   National Curriculum, the 89, 90, 117
Scottish Vocational Education Council (SCOTVEC) 81–2
self-assessment/appraisal 351, 432–4
self-development 180, 247–50, 334, 347, 350–51
skill shortages 70, 75–6
skill supply strategy 55, 59
Skills Challenge scheme 62–3
small to medium-sized enterprises/organisations (SMEs) 47–64
   barriers to a coherent training approach 61–3
   characteristics of 49–50
   management within 48–50
   training issues within 53–65
   triggers for training in 58–60
Social Chapter, the EU 105
social contract, the 11
social environment within an organisation 2–3, 8, 9, 16, 38
Spain, comparisons with 104
stakeholders xiii, xv, 19, 21, 27, 125, 167, 199, 206, 309, 324, 326, 372, 396
standards see Training and development, Lead Body standards and qualifications, national occupational standards; Institute of Personnel and Development, professional standards in employee development
strategic capability of an organisation xiv–xv, 6, 8, 20, 31, 326, 339, 372–80, 385–6, 387, 394–400
strategic facilitator (of training) 148–9, 151, 157, 179
strategic framework of HRD in the organisation see HRD, strategic framework for
strategic management of HRD see HRD strategy/strategic management of
strategy implementation 19, 24–8, 203
subcontractors xiii, 19
suppliers xiii, 19, 167
survival of an organisation see Organisational survival
Sweden, comparisons with 113, 117
systematic training cycle 38–9, 293, 424–5

'tacit' skills 56–7, 409–10
teamwork and teamworking 4, 5, 9, 13, 27, 28, 136, 159, 182–5, 214, 283, 314–17, 379, 390, 410
technology, changes in 27, 38, 160
   introduction of 9, 59, 170, 358, 416
tertiary education system in Britain 94–8, 117
training
   basic 237–9, 250, 313
   definition/role of xii, 5–6
national policy 67–86
   organisational policy 157, 213
   perceived value of 255
   see also Industry Training Organisations (ITOs); National Training Policy; Youth Training Schemes
training and development xi, xv, 5–6, 21, 26–7, 39, 59, 63–4, 150, 319, 322
   as part of corporate strategy 130
   barriers to 61–3
   basic 237–9, 250, 313
   cost-effectiveness 56, 60, 62, 416, 417, 419, 429–31
   costing out 189–95, 213, 417
   evaluation/appraisal of 39, 159, 213, 418, 420
   events design and delivery 39
   external provision of 62, 131, 175, 283, 316
   finance and financial management 187, 304, 415–20
      see also Training and development resources, budget
   for flexible, adaptable workforce 9, 28
   for multiskilling 28
   for teambuilding 28
   for upskilling 323
   incentives for 25
   identification of needs see Training needs of an organisation
   informal 56
   job-related 207
   Lead Body standards and qualifications 39, 424–5
   management of xi, 6, 51, 140–44
   monitoring of 39, 418, 420
   national occupational standards 149–53, 155, 156–7, 178, 233, 361

outsourcing of 167
programmes/programs for 5–6,
    21, 260, 266–8, 276, 315, 415,
    419
proposal for, production of a
    266–8, 417, 419
provision in smaller organisations
    53–63
relationship between skill and pay
    60 role(s) of 145, 157–61, 178
roles typology xii, 145–9, 150–51
triggers for 130–32, 316
see also Learning events; Learning
    strategies
training and development resources,
    budget for 188–96
costing out 189–95, 199
intangible 187–8, 283
management of xii, 187–98
record system for 196–8
tangible 187, 283
Training and Enterprise Councils
    (TECs) 62, 72, 73–80, 84, 90,
    95, 114, 117, 125, 158, 361
four types of programme 73–4
strategic role of 78–9
Training for Work programme/
    scheme 73, 75
training manager, the 146, 166–7
see also Human resource
    development manager
training needs of an organisation 5,
    73, 159, 179, 213, 260, 416
identification of 39, 63, 130, 142,
    207, 314–15, 415, 416
see also Job training analysis
training provider, the 146, 157

unemployment, statistics and
    comparisons 11
United States, the, comparisons with

13, 14, 16, 95, 105, 106, 107,
    109, 117, 118, 148, 176, 217,
    341–2, 358, 359, 363, 394
university education in Britain 94–8
unskilled, the plight of the 107–8

value added see Added value
value analysis teams 206
vision see Organisational vision
vocational education and training
    (VET) 102–26, 261
in Germany 118–22
in Japan 122–4
in relation to labour market
    103–11
international differences 112–26
policy in Europe 103–22, 125
weaknesses in the UK system 112,
    334
vocational qualifications 60, 61, 72,
    73, 75, 76, 77, 80–85, 89,
    92–3, 113–15, 125, 154, 155,
    156, 178, 180, 237, 261, 314,
    327, 421–2
accreditation 81, 115, 422
and IPD professional standards
    153–4
Beaumont Report (1996), the
    82–3
benefits 85, 327
credit accumulation and transfer
    (CAT) 421–2
difficulties 84–5
rates/percentages by nation
    113–14
tax concessions/training credits to
    encourage 69, 76
voluntary workers 326

Youth Training Schemes 69, 73, 76,
    93, 114

The People and Organisations Series

PROFESSIONAL QUALIFICATIONS

This series has been commissioned specially for students setting out on a professional career in personnel and development.

The Institute of Personnel and Development's new professional qualification scheme came into effect in July 1996. It comprises three parts:

- core management
- core personnel and development
- any four from a range of more than 20 generalist and specialist electives.

The series starts by addressing core personnel and development and four generalist electives: employee reward, employee resourcing, employee relations, and employee development. Together, these cover the personnel and development knowledge requirements for graduateship of the IPD (or their N/SVQ Level 4 equivalents).

INFORMATIVE AND COMPETENCY-BASED

Each of these core texts follows the syllabus closely and should constitute students' main source of ideas, information, and guidance. The emphasis is as much on skills development as on theory, so students will gain a firm foundation for applying and using their knowledge in a variety of situations. The books include mini-cases and examples drawn from a wide spectrum of organisations and employment contexts.

AUTHORITATIVE

Each book is written by the chief examiner in the relevant area, follows the syllabus closely and provides essential reading not just for students taking the IPD Professional Qualification Scheme but for all those undertaking courses with a human resource management component.

SERIES EDITORS

Mick Marchington is professor of human resource management at the Manchester School of Management, UMIST, where he has worked since the mid-1980s. He is currently chief examiner for Core Personnel and Development and has played a major part in the redesign of the Professional Qualification Scheme. He has written widely elsewhere on employee relations and human resource management, specialising in the areas of employee involvement, workplace industrial relations, human resource management in retailing and, more recently, on the links between human resource management and total quality management. He wrote the chapter on employee relations in *Strategic Prospects for HRM* (1995, IPD) and also contributed to the IPD's research report on *Quality*.

Mike Oram is a human resource professional whose career has also spanned general management, information systems, legal affairs, and academia. He has for many years been at the forefront as group personnel manager and company secretary with the Prestcold Group and as director of personnel and corporate affairs with Toshiba (UK) Ltd. He is co-author of *Re-engineering's Missing Ingredient: The human factor* (1995, IPD) and is also a fellow of the IPD. As the IPD's vice-president for Membership and Education he has been closely involved in discussions leading up to the new qualification scheme.

EMPLOYEE RELATIONS

John Gennard and Graham Judge

To help prospective personnel managers develop the necessary skills, the authors have taken a wholly pragmatic managerial perspective. The book is written to the syllabus requirements and combines theory with practice to enable all students to apply their knowledge and understanding in unfamiliar or difficult situations.

Each chapter contains exercises, mini case-studies, and examples of real-life situations from all sectors of industry, commerce, and public authorities.

The book is divided into two parts and covers:

- employee relations organisations

- employee processes

- outcomes of employee relations

- employee relations management and the corporate environment

- negotiation skills – general overview

- handling grievances

- handling disciplinary matters

- bargaining

- devising, implementing and monitoring schedules

- evaluating new employee relations management.

John Gennard is professor of human resource management at Strathclyde Business School. He is also the IPD's chief examiner for employee relations.

June 1997 288 pages (approx.) Paperback ISBN 0 85292 654 5
£19.95

EMPLOYEE REWARD

Michael Armstrong

Reward is one of the central creative accountabilities for all personnel professionals. When used effectively as a strategic tool, it can play a key role in communicating values, promoting flexibility, and maximising individual contributions to organisational objectives. This book sets out the central competences that all practitioners need in their portfolio.

Decisions about pay are inevitably influenced by local labour markets, the wider national and international context, the state of the economy, and beliefs about whether money, fringe benefits, and less tangible forms of remuneration can genuinely motivate employees. Michael Armstrong demonstrates to students how employers:

- evaluate, price, and analyse jobs and roles while ensuring competitiveness and equal pay for work of equal value

- design graded structures, pay spines, and newer broadbanded systems

- integrate reward with performance management

- forge links with individual, team, and corporate results, skills-based pay, competence-based pay, and incentive schemes

- determine the right levels of benefits, allowances, and pensions

- reward directors, executives, expatriates, and sales staff.

Michael Armstrong is one of Britain's best-known authors and an acknowledged authority on reward. He has been closely involved in drafting the Employee Reward module of the new IPD professional standards and is now the chief examiner for this module.

... seems set to become the Wisden of UK employee reward matters ... this is the most definitive and up-to-date book [on reward issues] available. Buy.

Duncan Brown, Principal, Towers Perrin

1996 432 pages Paperback ISBN 0 85292 623 5 **£19.95**